*Major Problems
in the History of American
Families and Children*

D0023618

MAJOR PROBLEMS IN AMERICAN HISTORY SERIES

GENERAL EDITOR

THOMAS G. PATERSON

Major Problems
in the History of American
Families and Children

DOCUMENTS AND ESSAYS

EDITED BY
ANYA JABOUR
UNIVERSITY OF MONTANA

HOUGHTON MIFFLIN COMPANY
Boston   New York

For my students—
past, present, and future

Editor in Chief: Jean L. Woy
Senior Development Editor: Frances Gay
Associate Project Editor: Lindsay Frost
Editorial Assistant: Teresa Huang
Production/Design Assistant: Bethany Schlegel
Senior Manufacturing Coordinator: Marie Barnes
Senior Marketing Manager: Sandra McGuire

Cover image: *A Whoop and a Holler on Independence Day,* 1980, Jane Wooster Scott (20th c./American). Oil on canvas. Collection of Governor and Mrs. John Y. Brown (Phyllis George). © Collection of Governor and Mrs. John Y. Brown (Phyllis George)/ Jane Wooster Scott/SuperStock.

Copyright © 2005 by Houghton Mifflin Company. All rights reserved.

No part of this work may be reproduced or transmitted in any form or by any means, electronic or mechanical, including photocopying and recording, or by any information storage or retrieval system without the prior written permission of the copyright owner unless such copying is expressly permitted by federal copyright law. With the exception of nonprofit transcription in Braille, Houghton Mifflin is not authorized to grant permission for further uses of copyrighted selections reprinted in this text without the permission of their owners. Permission must be obtained from the individual copyright owners as identified herein. Address requests for permission to make copies of Houghton Mifflin material to College Permissions, Houghton Mifflin Company, 222 Berkeley Street, Boston, MA 02116-3764.

Printed in the U.S.A.

Library of Congress Catalog Card Number: 2002109483

ISBN: 0-618-21475-5

3456789-MP-07 06 05

Contents

CHAPTER 8

*Children and Child-Savers in Progressive-Era
America, 1880–1920*

Page 250

CHAPTER 9

*The Family and the State: Origins of the Modern
Welfare System in the Early Twentieth Century*

Page 290

C H A P T E R   1 0
The Homefront: American Families During World War II
Page 323

C H A P T E R   1 1
The 1950s: Family Life in Modern America
Page 370

CHAPTER 14
Families and Children in Contemporary America
Page 483

Preface

While still in graduate school at Rice University in the early 1990s, I had a unique opportunity: the chance to design and teach a course on a topic of my choice. I was then working on a dissertation based on extensive family correspondence and ideas about home, gender relations, and childrearing methods were at the forefront of my consciousness. So, too, were the echoes of then-Vice President Dan Quayle's 1992 public denunciation of television sit-com lead character Murphy Brown for bearing a child out of wedlock and the subsequent public discussions of "family values." My choice seemed clear: I would teach a class on the history of American families. Drawing on the wealth of scholarship produced from the 1960s through the 1980s, I would offer an historical overview of family life in the United States and, in the process, give my students a solid background against which to measure claims that "the American family" was in decline. The syllabus for my class, "American Families," stated, "Despite current concern about 'family values,' too little attention is paid to the history of the family, the varieties of functions performed and forms taken by the family, and how ideas about what a family should do—and what a family actually does—have varied over time and by region, ethnicity, class, and race, among other factors. . . . This course will highlight the diversity of American families for the past four centuries. . . ." Inspired by the growing and fascinating literature on family history, I also saw scholarship on "the family" in the past as a way to counter popular jeremiads about the loss of family values in my own time. Thus, from the beginning, my interest in this topic was both professional and personal.

Approximately a decade later, I was offered yet another opportunity: the chance to design a reader on the history of family and childhood in the United States. In the intervening years, I had turned my dissertation into a book about marriage, family life, and childrearing, and taken a position as the specialist in the history of women and families at the University of Montana. I was working on a second book, this one on girls' coming-of-age experiences. After several years of teaching classes in U.S. women's history, I was contemplating re-introducing the family history course. In the interim, the history of children and adolescents had developed into a significant field, warranting its own conferences and professional organizations. While the furor over "family values" had abated somewhat, it had been replaced by a new set of anxieties about the future of America's children, symbolized by the Columbine school shootings of April 1999. Once again my own professional interests, developments in scholarship, and political "hot spots" coincided. I decided to undertake the project and engage in a dialog with the best scholars in the field in order to produce a text on the history of families and children that would serve the needs of instructors and students of this growing field.

In designing this book, I have benefited from the suggestions of the many scholars who generously shared their syllabi, reading lists, and insights with me. Their comments helped me to choose specific pieces as well as to conceptualize the anthology as a whole. I also learned from a new class I taught on "American Families and Children" using a pilot version of this reader. My students cheerfully agreed to be test subjects as well as test-takers, and their interests and insights have shaped this volume in significant ways. Based on the input of both scholars and students, I established several goals for the project: complete chronological coverage (that is, spanning the entire period from before European settlement to the present); inclusiveness and diversity (finding ways to address the unique experiences of "minority" families without "ghetto-izing" them); and a framework that would allow instructors to omit, re-arrange, or add to chapter topics as they saw fit. Thus, for instance, *Major Problems in the History of American Families and Children* begins with Native American families in the seventeenth century and ends with a mother's comments on her toddler's toys, *circa* 2003; ethnic, racial, class, geographic, and religious diversity are reflected throughout the book and in specific chapters (such as Chapter 5, which addresses the experiences of enslaved African Americans, and Chapter 12, which deals with "new" immigrants); and the volume is organized both thematically and chronologically, so that instructors may choose to emphasize either themes (power, for instance, is a dominant theme in Chapters 2, 5, 8, and 12) or time periods (for example, Chapters 6, 10, and 13 deal with the Civil War, World War II, and the 1980s, respectively). Another goal has been to provide a balanced presentation of the many points of view and approaches to the field by including both seasoned and recent scholarship.

I have also tried to present history as a discussion of ideas rather than a set of accepted truths. As in other books in this series, *Major Problems in the History of American Families and Children* includes both scholarly essays that offer contrasting or complementary interpretations of important issues and primary documents that enable students to evaluate the evidence for themselves. After an opening chapter reviewing the field, each chapter begins with an introduction that identifies the topics under analysis, reviews the major interpretations, suggests important approaches and source material, and poses questions for readers to consider. Headnotes to the documents and essays explain how they relate to the subject(s) under consideration and offer historical context. Finally, each chapter concludes with a "Further Reading" section to guide interested readers to additional sources.

Many people contributed to this project. For sharing their syllabi, their reading lists, and their insights with me, thanks are due to Joseph Austin (Bowling Green State University); Jane Turner Censer (George Mason University); Crista DeLuzio (Southern Methodist University); Lloyd deMause (Institute for Psychohistory); Margaret Crocco (Columbia University); Sherman Dorn (University of South Florida); Anna Mae Duane (Fordham University); Jon Gjerde (University of California at Berkeley); Harvey J. Graff (University of Texas at San Antonio); Joseph Hawes (University of Memphis); Rodney Hessinger (Hiram College); Shawn Johansen (Frostburg State University); Albrecht Koschnik (Florida State University); David MacLeod (Central Michigan University); Emily Mieras (Stetson University); Julia Mickenberg (University of Texas at Austin); Edgar-Andre Montigny (University of Toronto); Gail S. Murray (Rhodes College); Mary Beth Norton

(Cornell University); Kathy Peiss (University of Pennsylvania); Elizabeth Pleck (University of Illinois at Urbana-Champaign); Maria Schmeeckle (Illinois State University); Marie Jenkins Schwartz (University of Rhode Island); Amanda Seligman (University of Wisconsin at Milwaukee); Sam Thomas (Michigan State University); Alex Urbiel (Ramapo College); Scott Walter (Indiana University); and Jessica Weiss (California State University at Hayward). Thanks are also due to the following reviewers who provided helpful comments on the table of contents: Paula S. Fass (University of California at Berkeley); Kriste Lindenmeyer (University of Maryland at Baltimore); James Marten (Marquette University); Patrick J. Ryan (University of Texas at Dallas); and Alexander Urbiel (Ramapo College of New Jersey). I also thank Harvey J. Graff for convening a session on "Teaching the History of Children and Adolescents" at the 2002 annual meeting of the Social Science History Association and inviting me to participate. Most of all, of course, I thank all of the people who have produced such a marvelous body of scholarship to choose from. Whether their work is included in this reader or not, this project could not have been conceptualized, much less completed, without their contributions to the field.

The staff at Houghton Mifflin also made this volume possible. Jean Woy, Editor in Chief, and Thomas G. Paterson, General Editor of the Major Problems series, convinced me to undertake the project and provided me with suggestions and support at key points in the process. Fran Gay, Senior Development Editor, and Lindsay Frost, Associate Project Editor, cheerfully and efficiently shepherded the project from manuscript to bound book, and Maria Leon Maimone, Permissions Editor, eased the process immeasurably.

A. J.

*Major Problems
in the History of American
Families and Children*

Studying Families
and Children in
Historical Perspective

Long before scholars took an interest in the study of families and children, people collected and preserved mementos of their family history: family bibles with records of births and deaths, photographs of weddings and christenings, love letters exchanged by courting couples—mere memorabilia of interest only to immediate family and friends, most thought. It was not until the 1960s that pioneers in the new field of social history—the history of "ordinary" people's lives—also began to blaze new paths into the history of families and children.

Early work on the history of families and children generally fell into two groups: work by antiquarians and work by demographers. Antiquarians delighted in the minutiae of everyday life. Delving into dusty attics and musty basements, they wrote detailed narratives of "the way things were" in times past. Meanwhile, demographers relished the academic rigor of solid facts and numbers. Borrowing from the social sciences, they produced quantitative analyses of census records, wills, inventories, birth and death records, and the like.

Both approaches had merit, but each was limited as well. While antiquarians conjured up the sense of "being there," demographers offered empirical evidence. Yet antiquarians were limited to those families who had left and preserved memorabilia—mostly the wealthy and powerful—while demographers' charts and tables could be dense and impenetrable. Both approaches also often slighted analysis, the first because its practitioners lacked academic training, the second because its adherents stuck close to "the facts." As the field gained momentum, however, these lines began to blur, and family and childhood historians began to make use of both anecdotal and statistical evidence. In addition, many historians of families and children borrowed from other disciplines—psychology, sociology, and anthropology, for instance—to yield insight into their research. By the 1970s and 1980s, historians were likely to use multiple approaches and a range of sources in their search for understanding families and children in the past. This allowed scholars not only to draw broader conclusions about their subjects, but also to widen the scope of the field to include a greater cross section of society.

Today, the history of families and children is an established and growing field. Most colleges and universities offer courses in these topics, and many re-spected scholars have adopted the study of families and children as their research specialty. What makes the study of families and children particularly attractive? Part of the answer is surely that scholars in the field typically utilize interdiscipli-nary methods and employ comparative (cross-cultural) analysis. But in addition, when it comes to families and children, in particular, studying the past is surely informed by reflections on the present. While they ask themselves historical ques-tions about families and children, then, scholars in the field must also grapple with other questions: What is the connection between studying the past and shap-ing the present? How can historians use their awareness of contemporary concerns to inform their research without falling into the pitfall of present-mindedness— that is, evaluating the actions of historical figures by our standards rather than by their own? Why, ultimately, is it important to study families and children in historical perspective?

 E S S A Y S

The essays included in this chapter reflect changing trends in the field and offer some (by no means definitive) answers to these questions. The first essay, originally presented at the 1982 annual meeting of the American Psychiatric Association and later pub-lished in John Demos's 1986 collection of essays, *Past, Present, and Personal*, offers a "report from the trenches" of family history. Demos, of Yale University, reviews the then-dominant approaches to family history—demography, structure, affect, and function—and suggests the promise and the problems with each approach. He also highlights the importance of cross-disciplinary insights (especially psychology) and of the connection between the past and the present.

The second essay, excerpted from Evergreen State College family history specialist Stephanie Coontz's 1992 book, *The Way We Never Were: American Families and the Nostalgia Trap*, reviews changes in American families—and observers' reactions to those changes—from the colonial era to the present to lend force to her argument that studying the history of the family helps us to avoid oversimplifying the past. Under-standing the complexity of family history, she argues, allows us to avoid "wild claims and phony forecasts" and makes it possible to assess the present state of the family more realistically.

Both of the first two essays move easily back and forth between the history of *families* and the history of *children*. Indeed, it is only in recent years that the history of childhood has emerged as a separate subdiscipline. The third essay, originally pre-sented at the "History of Childhood in America" conference held in Washington, D.C., in 2000, represents the coming of age of this field. Like the other authors included in this chapter, Joseph M. Hawes of the University of Memphis and N. Ray Hiner of the University of Kansas urge scholars to avoid simple answers to complex questions. They warn against the dangers of present-mindedness and antiquarianism, and they urge historians to make clear distinctions among childhood as a social construction, as an experience, and as a set of behaviors. Finally, they offer a set of questions to guide further research.

Digging Up Family History:
Myths, Realities, and Works-in-Progress

JOHN DEMOS

This essay is a "report from the trenches" in a field of research that was unexplored, not to say unimagined, as little as two generations ago. The field is (what has come to be called) "family history." The trenches are as yet only half-dug; hence they are shallow in many spots, ragged along most of their edges, and littered with loose dirt throughout. But rough and unfinished as every part of this seems, it is possible to discern the contours, the proportions, the design of the whole. And since the work is very much ongoing, it is reasonable to look for further progress just ahead. In fact, the field *and* the trenches are swarming with eager diggers, whose enthusiasm alone must count for something. The diggers, of course, are professional historians, drawn to the lure of new discoveries. They dig for themselves and for each other—but would be pleased to interest a wider audience.

I

For a territory so recently brought under investigation, no one "map" can be regarded as definitive. But the map to be presented here aims, nonetheless, for general coverage. And it does so by way of four principal sectors or subdivisions—each of which merits separate consideration.

The first sector one comes to—at least the first that family historians came to—is clearly marked as *demography*. Work in this area began some three decades ago and has continued without pause to the present day. The initial advance came from a pioneering band of French demographers associated with the so-called *Annales* school. Their lead was soon communicated to a group of English scholars—the Cambridge Group for the Study of Population and Social Structure—and then, as the news spread further west, across the Atlantic to the Americas. As a result we now know a great deal about the demographic contours of family life in virtually every part of modern history, and not a little about the *pre*-modern situation as well. We know, for example, all about "mean household size"—MHS in the argot of the Cambridge Group—through a full four centuries of English history. The gist, in that connection, is a remarkably stable mean of 5–6 persons per household until the onset of the Industrial Revolution, and a very gradual decline thereafter.

Actually, mean household size is not by itself a very interesting *datum*, except, perhaps, as it serves to confute a stubborn piece of historical mythology. It is still rather widely believed that "extended families" were the predominant form until just a century or so ago. But if by "extended" we mean three (or more) generations, including married siblings and their various children, all living under one roof—that has *not* been the shape of Western family life for as far back as the records allow us

John Demos, *Past, Present, and Personal: The Family and the Life Course in American History* (New York: Oxford University Press, 1986), pp. 4–19. Copyright © 1986 by John Putnam Demos. Used by permission of Oxford University Press, Inc.

to see. Instead, the simple "nuclear" unit (husband, wife, and their natural-born children) has always been with us—admitting only of limited add-ons (a servant, an apprentice, an aging grandparent or two) in particular times and places. To be sure, many pre-modern communities supported a density of kin-contacts unknown in our own day; for siblings and cousins and in-laws frequently did inhabit the same village or parish neighborhoods. But not the same *households*. Thus if co-residence is the defining factor, the concept of "extension" seems misapplied.

Mean household size is the net product of other demographic indices: age of marriage, frequency of *re*marriage, rates of fertility and mortality. And the latter hold much interest in their own right. They also hold some surprises for conventional wisdom in this area. The present writer can recall his own surprise, in a graduate seminar-project twenty years ago, upon discovering that most New England colonists of the seventeenth century married in their middle-to-late twenties. (That range has, in fact, been found typical for many other pre-modern populations as well.) He can also recall his astonishment at the sheer longevity of his "Puritan" study-sample: nearly seventy years, on the average, for those who survived the special health hazards of early childhood. (In this respect New England turns out to have been very remarkable; most contemporaneous settings supported a far lower standard.) Other results have been *un*surprising, though not unimportant: for example, high rates of fertility (eight to ten completed pregnancies per married couple), and thus (where mortality was not equally high) large complements of children.

These summary comments cannot possibly do justice to the richness and complexity of recent demographic research. For, in addition to establishing the quantitative boundaries of family life, demographic analysis has thrown light into some of its most private corners. For example, we can now discover, from evidence of birth-spacing and "age-specific maternal fertility," the point at which given populations first began to practice birth control. This development—a veritable sea-change in family history—is inaccessible to all other methods of study, since the people involved would not ordinarily document their practice in such intimate matters.

Much of the demographic work raises questions of comparative—that is, trans-historical—psychology. To wit: (1) What are the implications, for psychological life, of pre-contraceptive attitudes? (Perhaps a lessening of certain internal pressures and conflicts?) And (2) what is the impact, on personality development, of growing up in a very large family? (More, or less, or simply different "sibling rivalry"? A diluted experience of the "oedipus complex"?) And (3) how might "separation" issues be construed in settings where death is a common experience for people of all ages and every social station? (A distinctive range of "mourning reactions"? A certain degree of "psychic numbing"?)

These last are questions only, for which demography cannot by itself supply direct answers. There has been, in fact, a tendency among enthusiastic practitioners of the demographic art to leap from numerical *quantities* to psychological *qualities*. Thus, for example, high levels of early-life mortality have led some scholars to infer low levels of parental concern for infants and young children. The implicit—sometimes explicit—premise is that parents would not allow themselves to become much attached to offspring whose propects of survival were at all in doubt. Similarly, rates of illegitimacy and of what demographers call "bridal pregnancy" have been taken as a measure of power relations within the family. In certain communities of eighteenth-century America, 30 to 40 percent of all brides were going to the altar pregnant: that much one can demonstrate by comparing their wedding-dates with the birthdays of their eldest children. But can one then assume—as some scholars *have* assumed—an absence of "control" by the older generation, and a high degree of "autonomy" in the younger one? The factors involved here are too numerous, and the relationships between them are too complex, to permit such straightforward efforts of inference. And they suggest a larger point as well: demographic study is best seen as setting the stage—not writing the script—for the vital inner dramas of family history.

II

It is to the inner dramas that we turn next. The division of power, the demarcation of roles and responsibilities: thus the family in its "structural" aspects. Here, too, history unfolds a long and changeable story, which historians are only beginning to understand. The concept of "patriarchy" has served as an entering wedge. In pre-modern times—so the argument frequently goes—*fathers* ruled families with a more or less iron hand. Later (roughly the nineteenth century) their grip was progressively loosened by all the trends of economic and cultural modernization. Most scholars would be willing to accept this very rough model of historical change, but the particulars are so enormously variable that the model by itself does not mean a great deal. "Patriarchy" in relation to whom? and by what means? and to what specific ends? And how does one measure "power" and "responsibility" in the first place? Such questions suggest a need to disassemble the "family structure," the better to see its constituent parts. One can study the marital pair—husband and wife—as a structure of power in its own right. One can study parents and children as another kind of structure, with further refinements that distinguish fathers and mothers, daughters and sons. One can even bring grandparents and grandchildren into view, where there are long-term issues of "lineal descent."

But with the structural lines at least roughly drawn, it remains to identify the substantive contexts in which power relations are most fully expressed. Here, too, there is much room for historical flux and change. For example: in many pre-modern communities inheritance was a vital nexus of power in the family. Fathers might try to constrain the behavior of their maturing children by granting (or withholding) family properties. Unfortunately, it is not enough in these matters to study the set phrases of wills and other probate documents; a man who is left out of his father's will may be unusually rich or rebellious, or may simply be living far away. In order to "read" such materials aright, other evidence is needed—evidence on the particulars of that family's experience.

A second fulcrum of power between the generations is—or, at least, was—the issue of "mate selection." Typically, in pre-modern times, parents were much involved in the courtship and marital decisions of their grown children. But the picture is easily overdrawn. Few children anywhere were obliged to marry against their personal inclinations; indeed, positive inclination was seen as one of the requisites of a good marriage (but not the only one). In some pre-modern families parents would initiate a match and seek to bring it to fruition, while the young people involved might exercise a kind of veto; in others, the young initiated, and the parents vetoed. As time passed, the balance moved strongly in favor of the second pattern, and eventually parental influence might be circumvented altogether. Here, surely, was a "power-shift" of great historical consequence.

And yet any such change must be described with caution. The closer one gets to the details of power relations within the family, the more complicated—and the less amenable to summary formulas—they come to seem. This sounds obvious enough, when stated in such general terms, but it merits underscoring in a specific historical case. Consider, then, John Dane—born in England in the opening years of the seventeenth century, son of a tailor and himself trained as a tailor, an altogether ordinary specimen of pre-modern humankind. The only *extra*ordinary thing about him is a little autobiographical memoir, written near the end of his life and fortuitously preserved to our own time. Thus we have, in his own words, some revealing information on his relation to his parents.

> Being . . . about eight years old, I was given much to play and to run out without my father's consent and against his command. Once when my father saw me come home, he took me and basted [i.e. beat] me. . . . My father and mother . . . told me that God would bless me if I obeyed my parents, and what the contrary would issue in. I then thought in my heart—oh, that my father would beat me more when I did amiss!
>
> When I was grown to eighteen years of age or thereabouts, I went to a dancing school to learn to dance. My father, hearing of it . . . told me that if I went again he would baste me. I told him that if he did, he should never baste me again. With that my father took a stick and basted me. I took it patiently and said nothing for a day or two, but one morning betimes I rose and took two shirts on my back and the best suit I had, and put a Bible in my pocket, and set the doors open, and went to my father's chamber door, and said, "good-bye, father; good-bye, mother." "Why, whither are you going?" "To seek my fortune," I answered. Then said my mother, "go where you will, God will find you out." This word, the point of it, stuck in my breast; and afterward God struck it home to its head.
>
> I thought my father was too strict—I thought Solomon said "be not holy overmuch," and David was a man after God's own heart and he was a dancer. . . . [And so] I went on my journey and was away from him half a year before he heard where I was. *(There followed a period of some two years when John Dane practiced his trade, on his own, in several different English towns.)* . . . But at last I had some thoughts to go home to my father's house; but I thought he would not entertain me. But I went, and when I came home my father and mother entertained me very lovingly.
>
> *(In time he left again, and married—no mention of consulting his parents about this—and settled with his bride in still another part of the country. And then, in about 1635, he made the fateful decision to migrate to New England.)* When I was much bent to come, I went to my father to tell him. . . . My father and mother showed themselves unwilling. I sat close by a table where there lay a Bible. I hastily took up the Bible, and told my father that if where I opened the Bible, there I met with anything either to encourage or discourage, that should settle me. I opening of it . . . the first line I cast my eyes on was: "Come out from among them, touch no unclean thing, and I will be your God and you shall be people." My father and mother never more opposed me, but furthered me in the thing, and hastened after me as soon as they could.

How shall we evaluate this little *vignette* as an instance of the politics of family life long ago? On the side of "patriarchy" we may count (1) the father's readiness to "baste" his young son for misbehavior (and the son's acceptance of that procedure);

(2) the father's assumption that he can prevent his son (even as a youth of 18 years old) from learning to dance; and (3) the son's assumption (though by this time he was married and a fully independent tradesman) that he must obtain his parents' consent before moving to America. On the other side—against patriarchy—there is (1) the son's pursuit of his own aims and wishes from a very early age; (2) the son's declaration of independence when (again, at age 18) he leaves home to "seek his fortune"; (3) the clever way in which the son maneuvers around his parents' opposition to his plan of removal to New England. (To be sure, he does get timely assist from the Bible!) Where should the greatest emphasis be placed? This is a question on which reasonable scholars may well disagree.

In fact, power is an especially problematic issue, given the always imperfect record of centuries past. Role, by contrast, is much easier to study. Usually there are some prescriptive materials (such as sermons and advice books) to indicate the predominant values, and sufficient personal documents to exemplify behavior. Consider productive life, for example. Throughout the pre-modern world family-members (save only the youngest) produced for their common good, in visibly direct and meaningful ways. Of course, most pre-modern families were rooted to farms—a situation which even today promotes a good deal of work-sharing. In early America there was some division of labor: men in the "great fields," plowing and planting; women in the orchards and dairies, or indoors by the hearth; older children helping out as needed, mostly with their same-sex parent. But each could appreciate—could *see*—the contributions of the others; and all could feel the underlying framework of reciprocity. Moreover, in certain "crisis" periods, like the harvest, all worked side-by-side for days on end. With the advent of urbanization and modern commerce and industry, this framework broke apart. Men were now "providers," "breadwinners," producers *par excellence.* Women were literally domesticated; their role became that of "homemaker" in a newly exclusive sense.

These changes carried, in turn, important implications for child-rearing. In the colonial period the primary parent had been *father.* Books of child-rearing advice had been addressed to him; the law had preferred him (to mother) in the matter of child custody; and all parties affirmed his superior "wisdom" in understanding and nurturing the young. (Woman were considered too irrational and unsteady to take the lead here.) In the nineteenth century the pattern was rapidly, and radically, altered. Father's obligation to "provide" left him little time and energy to nurture (at least in personal ways). Mother's duties, meanwhile, became virtually all-encompassing. ("All that I am I owe to my angel-mother": thus a favorite period cliché.) The same sort of role-separation has, of course, continued largely intact to the present day. But with some new winds beginning just now to waft through American family life, it may be instructive to remember the earlier period.

The topic of family structure raises, inevitably, fundamental questions of gender. And gender itself makes a lively center of study. Indeed "women's history" (so called) has become one of the most lively of all research sub-fields in the past ten or fifteen years. The substance can be sampled in a plethora of books and articles; the spirit is evident in some of their titles: *A Heritage of Her Own, Clio's Consciousness Raised, The Majority Finds Its Past,* and so on. But although the spirit is broadly feminist, it is not, for the most part, overtly polemical. And the resultant gains for historical understanding are truly of the first importance.

The earliest forays in women's history—antedating the recent upsurge—expressed what now seems a rather narrow concern with politics. The origins of organized feminism; the struggle for the suffrage; the activity of women reformers more generally: such were the leading questions. But as one work led on to another, the boundaries widened—and the questions deepened. There emerged a rough outline of women's past experience—at least, American women's past experience—which went approximately as follows. In colonial America women were defined as being inferior to men ("He for God, and she for God in him"), but, practically speaking, they retained considerable scope for initiative and self-assertion. As previously noted, they made important contributions as farmers' wives and daughters; and some of them also worked as tradespeople, physicians, innkeepers, and the like. They could not vote or be otherwise active in public affairs; but their influence was exerted, was *felt,* in countless informal ways. Then came the nineteenth century, with its massively transformed human ecology—and, for women, a severe loss of status and function. "Homemaking" proved to be a form of domestic imprisonment; polite culture was sheer vapidity; public life remained (more than ever) off limits. And when, at mid-century, organized feminism was born, it expressed an anguished cry from the depths of oppression. The plot-line of women's history ever since has been a stop-and-go effort to escape from those depths—or, stated in less extreme terms, to push back the limits of constraint.

But this historiographic overview is now being reconsidered, and at least partially revised. Its advocates are charged with having fabricated a "golden age" of women's history (the colonial period), and, concurrently, with having ignored certain positive features of the succeeding period. Indeed, recent scholarship very nearly reverses the balance. Colonial women are still seen as active, to be sure, within the family and elsewhere—but always under the heavy dominance of men. Nineteenth-century women had, at least, a *place* that was primarily theirs (home), and a *vocation* that was theirs alone (child-rearing); hence, within some confines, they knew "autonomy"—and made the most of it.

The debate, thus briefly summarized, is as yet far short of resolution. However, it seems necessary to stress that "autonomy" has both a social and a psychological aspect. Historians, unfortunately, are not always clear about the distinction; too often we stress the former, while ignoring (or misunderstanding) the latter. Indeed, this whole territory quivers with subterranean resonance, some of which links women's history directly with psychiatric history. The first important cohort of psychiatric patients—including Freud's early patients—was composed of troubled women from the "comfortable classes" of the late Victorian era. "Hysteria," "neurasthenia," "breakdown": whatever the favored diagnostic category, their symptoms reflected strikingly on their life-situation. The prevalent cultural values declared that women should be submissive, selfless, ceaselessly effective on behalf of others ("ministering angels," in the idiom of the time). But these women, in their illness, managed to be *in*effective, self-absorbed, and tacitly dominant over friends and family members. The illness, in short, seemed to mock the cultural values, and may plausibly be viewed as a form of pretext.

Many of these patterns and tendencies can be organized around the concept of "identity." Simply put, women's identity and men's seemed to diverge so radically in the nineteenth century that all human communication across the gender-boundary was impaired. Experience differed, of course (again the work/family dichotomy); but feelings, intelligence, "sensibility," and "moral inclination" also differed in elemental ways. As a result, courtship was heavily burdened with anxiety and doubt, and women, in particular, underwent a characteristic "marriage trauma." There must have been redeeming, even rewarding, aspects of Victorian marriage in many individual cases, but they are not easily discovered from the vantage point of a century later. Sex was one part of the problem—cultural standards defined women as "passionless," and the standards were sometimes enforced by the surgical procedure of clitoridectomy—but it was not the only part. Women expected "understanding" and "sympathy" only from other women; together they created what one historian has called a "female world of love and ritual." Men did something similar in their own world (substituting "animal energy" for love); and social experience of all kinds seemed to divide on same sex principles.

These male/female questions lead on endlessly, and there is no need in the present context to follow their trail any further. Instead, we must turn to age and aging—a topic of equally large importance. For every family is (and was) both a system of gender relations *and* a system of age relations. Power, status, and responsibility within the family are defined by the second no less than the first.

But in order to put age relations in historical perspective one has to know how the people involved have defined and demarcated the aging process. The verdict of scholars in this area, while still very tentative, has at least an underlying coherence. In general, history has brought a greater and greater differentiation of the life course, and a sharper experience of its constituent parts. One of the earliest and most influential books in the entire literature of family history presented a remarkable picture of childhood over time. In pre-modern society childhood was barely recognized as such; young people appeared chiefly as "miniature adults." Only in the seventeenth and eighteenth centuries—and then only in elite groups—did children begin to receive special consideration for their distinctive needs, interest, and vulnerabilities. By some accounts adolescence is an even more recent invention. In fact, it was a famous American psychologist, Professor Granville Stanley Hall, who put adolescence on the map (so to speak) of modern popular culture. But these developmental categories themselves expressed fundamental changes of experience. And experience is what counted most of all. To some extent, modern adolescence expressed an altered balance of social circumstance—the decline of apprenticeship, the growth of mass public education, the development of new living-situations for young people exiting from their families of origin. But there was also an innerlife aspect—the growth of "identify diffusion" (in the psychoanalyst Erik Erikson's terms) in the face of ever-widening life-*choices*.

Historical studies of childhood have necessarily underscored the matter of child-*rearing*. We have already noticed, in another connection, the shifting balance of responsibility as between fathers and mothers. But what of the goals and methods of child-rearing; and, finally, what of its outcomes? Historians have been much intrigued by these questions, too—though somewhat frustrated by the limits of the written record. Often enough one finds abundant evidence of *prescription,* but precious little of *practice.* Nonetheless, certain broad trends do come clear. In early America child-rearing was framed by the doctrinal imperatives of evangelical religion. "Original sin" was associated with all of humankind, not least with its youngest specimens. Infants came into the world as carriers of a "diabolical" tendency, and right-thinking parents would react accordingly. The tendency was identified with "pride" and "self," and above all with "will." Thus the advice-literature urged the "breaking" and "beating down" of will—those were the favorite verbs—from the earliest possible age.

It took many generations for such advice to disappear altogether; but by the mid-nineteenth century the emphasis—and, most especially, the tone—had shifted. Children of that era were viewed as being morally neutral, even "innocent." "Nurture," not will-breaking, became the touchstone of the advice-literature; parents were urged to mold their young by the "gentle arts of persuasion"—and by their own good example. In fact, the ends of child-rearing had changed along with the means. There was a new and growing emphasis of qualities of independence, resourcefulness, initiative—a whole expressive mode. Only thus would a young person be prepared to seize the main chance and "go ahead" in the open society of modern America. At the same time, most authorities stressed the need for an inner "compass" that would hold behavior within morally acceptable bounds.

Translated into the language and concepts of our own time, the nineteenth century seems to have replaced an old child-rearing regime based on shame with a new one based on guilt. Parents in the colonial period had frequent recourse to scolding, humiliation, and edicts of temporary banishment. The famous Puritan preacher Cotton Mather wrote as follows about his own practice: "The first chastisement which I inflict for an ordinary fault is to let the child see and hear me in an astonishment, and hardly able to believe that the child could do so base a thing . . . [And] to be chased for a while out of my presence I . . . make to be looked upon as the sorest punishment in the family." Nineteenth-century parents, by contrast, stressed the hurt given to others—especially to themselves—by the child's misbehavior.

It is necessary to mention, if only in passing, scholarly interest in the later life-course. For example, recent years have brought a boomlet of studies on the history of old age. Much of this itself reflects a historical phenomenon—the emergence, in the twentieth century, of old age as a "social problem." Gerontology and geriatrics, two relatively new "sciences" with policy, clinical, and research dimensions all their own, have perforce turned some heads toward the past. If old age is a social problem now, what was it in former times? Surely, much has changed. The numbers have changed, for one thing: the numbers of the elderly within the total population, and the numbers within any given "birth cohort" who can expect one day to *be* elderly. Social factors have changed as well. Retirement—a more or less abrupt detachment from the world of productive work—is now the critical marker of the aging process; there was no precise pre-modern equivalent. Pensions, nursing homes, social insurance: these, too, in most respects are recent inventions.

The "problem" theme has served to tilt historical interpretation. If old age is difficult *now,* probably it was less so *then.* When the elderly were fewer, perhaps they were more valued—even "venerated." When they were not retired, they may have felt themselves to be more useful and capable. These hypotheses quickly add up to an historical *schema* paralleling the "golden age" view of women's history. Fortunately, they are empirically testable, at least in their main parts; and the tests to date suggest much need for caution. Pre-modern old people probably *were* better off than their present-day counterparts, as to social and economic position; but they seem to have paid a price for this, in various forms of psychological disadvantage. How one gauges the overall balance is more an intuitive than a scholarly judgement.

III

Moving right along, one arrives at a third major area of "trench-digging" within the larger field. It is not, to be sure, recognized as a separate area by some of the diggers themselves, and it does adjoin (or overlap) parts of the territory previously described. Yet it should be distinguished from the others as clearly as possible. And it should be identified, in bold letters, as "emotional experience"—or, more simply, as "affect."

Because of their failure to identify this area for what it is, historians have not studied it with much care—or effectiveness. Indeed, they have *assumed* and *inferred* more than they have studied. And what are their reigning assumptions? First, that affective experience was generally impoverished in the past: second, that families, in particular, knew only a fraction of the emotional rewards that *we* look for in our domestic life today; and, third, that individuals possessed little capacity for emotional sharing with others. Pre-modern marriage—so the argument goes—was a matter more of "convenience" and "instrumental advantage" than of loving care. And pre-modern child-rearing was full of indifference, callousness, and outright brutality. In this regard the reigning view is a "progressive" view: family life, over time, has (allegedly) been getting better and better.

And yet there are strong grounds for skepticism about this—about the parts, and about the whole. Admittedly, it is not difficult to find evidence that appears—by the light of our own values—to support the progressive view. But do notice the qualifier: "by the light of our own values." A modern-day American may well be surprised by the formal style of pre-modern marriage ("I am, as ever, your affectionate Husband, B. Franklin"). And the same observer will probably be shocked by certain elements of pre-modern parenting (the calculated use of fear and shame, and the regular resort to corporal punishment). But seen in the context of an entire cultural *Gestalt*—theirs, not ours—such behaviors made sense, and were not inconsistent with genuinely warm feeling. Perhaps the point becomes clearer if we reverse the roles of observer and observed. Some of our own practice might well look "unfeeling" to our pre-modern forebears: for instance, the way we consign infants to separate beds and cribs, hold them to "schedule feedings," and leave them sometimes to "cry through" a tantrum. A further objection to the progressive view is its reliance on behavioral fragments culled virtually at random from a motley array of records. Often such fragments are themselves anomalous by the standards of their time (hence their appearance in the records). Again, the counter-example of our own time may be instructive: Imagine a study of modern American family life based on "cases" covered in big-city newspapers.

The study of emotional experience remains, then, an important challenge to historians—important, but difficult, and largely unsatisfying in its results to date. A new start may well be necessary, if there is to be sustained progress in the long run. Context must, in the first place, be much more cleanly handled than has typically been the case so far. And there are other points to consider as well. A critical problem in "emotional history" is the complexity—the sheer untidiness—of the data; time and again, evidence of affect comes to us wildly entangled with other things (ideas, opinions, behavior, not to mention elements of the setting in which affect is expressed). In order to counter this problem, special steps must be taken to hold emotion itself clearly in focus. In addition, scholars may need to adopt careful principles for distinguishing between *different* emotions; perhaps they may even decide to adopt one or another theory of emotion (borrowed, presumably, from academic psychology). And they will be further obliged to separate what one scholar calls "emotionology"—attitudes, values, and ideas about emotion—from actual emotional experience. (Here is the old methodological bugaboo of prescription *versus* behavior, in a somewhat different guise.) None of this has happened yet; fortunately, however, there are signs of change just ahead.

IV

With demography, structure, and affect all noticed in their turn, one large territory yet remains. In a sense, all the issues discussed thus far have a point of reference internal to the family (its size and shape, its distribution of power and responsibility, its emotional qualities). And, in the same sense, what is left to discuss has an external reference: the family viewed from the standpoint of its individual members, on the one side, and of the larger community, on the other. How, in short, are we to construe the overall pattern of relations between the family and its constituency, as history moves along?

To ask this is to raise issues of "function," of "cost" and "benefit," and of "fit" between one unit of experience and all the others. The family not only *is*, the family also *does*: it has its own center of activity, at once unique and profoundly influenced from outside. Long before family historians appeared, family sociologists had developed a model of change-over-time, around precisely these questions. The family, they suggested, had experienced a long-term "erosion" of function. Where once it had served a broad range of plainly "instrumental" needs, in modern society it was reduced to two elements: the "socialization" of children and the provision of emotional support to its adult members. Historians, for their part, have measured this model against the evidence and used it to generally good effect. The family of premodern times was indeed a hive of instrumental activity: of production (e.g. the "family farm"), of schooling, of worship, of medical practice, and of care for all sorts of "dependents" (orphans, elderly people, the insane, even criminals). And the transition to modern times has, for certain, reduced this range dramatically. Public schools, hospitals, asylums, prisons now stand in *place* of the family at many points. To recognize this is not to belittle the importance of those family functions which yet remain. The heterogeneity of modern society at large, and the isolation of domestic space from other settings, has raised the stakes all around. Perhaps, then, child-rearing has become more vital and difficult than before, and emotional support within families has taken on an ever-greater urgency.

Yet even as family historians have (by and large) endorsed and applied this interpretive model, they have sought to refine it in several ways. The model exaggerates, or at least oversimplifies, change. Recent studies have, for example, discovered much interaction between the nineteenth-century family and the work-place. Some early manufacturing establishments built up their labor force by way of entire family units—husband, wife, and children hired together. In other cases, the interaction was more circuitous. The famous "mill girls" of Lowell, Massachusetts, and elsewhere, were, in effect, the center of a broad-gauge human exchange—between rural families with labor to spare, on the one hand, and the factory-system, on the other. Meanwhile, foreign labor was brought to America by a process known to scholars as "chain migration." Typically, a young man from Europe, the Far East, or Canada forged the first link in the chain by migrating and finding work; then he helped his relatives to join him in the same community—often as an employee of the same *company*. Thus, when studied from close up, the work force of particular factories seems a honeycomb of kin-based connections.

As with industrial work, so, too, with other sectors of social experience: the family was a presence in all. Account books kept by merchants and tradesmen reveal a pattern of regular reliance on kin; likewise the rosters of urban political "machines," and even lists of converts in religious revivals. The pattern should not be exaggerated, and the effects must not be construed as running entirely one way. The family was as much acted *upon* as it was an actor in its own right. Moreover, events in the long term surely worked to weaken most of these relationships, so that now only vestiges survive. Still, no adequate account of modern social history could leave them out altogether.

This, indeed, is a measure of the growing maturity of historical research on the family. In its first phase, such research was necessarily set apart from historical studies at large. The boundaries had to be surveyed, the benchmarks established, the basic internal topography understood, before any links to adjacent territories could be explored. But now the situation has changed. The links hold greater and greater interest, and not only for family historians but for scholars right across the board.

V

As noted at the outset, the enterprise of family history is very much ongoing. No single question can be considered as finally resolved, and new questions are popping into view all the time. Nonetheless the results so far have considerable shape and structure; and at several points they refute, or revise, well-known elements of conventional wisdom. Moreover, they set some limits around what all of us—whether historians, social scientists, or simply concerned citizens—may reasonably expect of our future. Is the family likely to transform itself into something radically new and different, or even to disappear entirely? No, *not* likely—given its impressive record of durability through many prior centuries. Might gender-roles so alter that parental and household responsibilities are no longer predominantly assumed by women? Quite possibly—given the variable patterns, in this matter, of the past. Will childhood itself wear a different aspect (e.g. more "hurried," as one recent prognosticator has put it) in times to come? Yes, insofar as childhood responds to cultural circumstance; but probably no, where inner-life development is concerned.

To raise these questions is to spotlight the unceasing traffic between our past, our present, and our future. And it is also to conjure up another kind of traffic, one that crosses the borders of academic disciplines and finally confronts personal experience. From such imaginative journeys we may all hope to profit.

Mythology and History in the
Study of the American Family

STEPHANIE COONTZ

When I begin teaching a course on family history, I often ask my students to write down ideas that spring to mind when they think of the "traditional family." Their lists always include several images. One is of extended families in which all members worked together, grandparents were an integral part of family life, children learned responsibility and the work ethic from their elders, and there were clear lines of authority based on respect for age. Another is of nuclear families in which nurturing mothers sheltered children from premature exposure to sex, financial worries, or other adult concerns, while fathers taught adolescents not to sacrifice their education by going to work too early. Still another image gives pride of place to the couple relationship. In traditional families, my students write—half derisively, half wistfully—men and women remained chaste until marriage, at which time they extricated themselves from competing obligations to kin and neighbors and committed themselves wholly to the marital relationship, experiencing an all-encompassing intimacy that our more crowded modern life seems to preclude. . . .

Like most visions of a "golden age," the "traditional family" my students describe evaporates on closer examination. It is an ahistorical amalgam of structures, values, and behaviors that never coexisted in the same time and place. The notion that traditional families fostered intense intimacy between husbands and wives while creating mothers who were totally available to their children, for example, is an idea that combines some characteristics of the white, middle-class family in the mid-nineteenth century and some of a rival family ideal first articulated in the 1920s. The first family revolved emotionally around the mother-child axis, leaving the husband-wife relationship stilted and formal. The second focused on an eroticized couple relationship, demanding that mothers curb emotional "overinvestment" in their children. The hybrid idea that a woman can be fully absorbed with her youngsters while simultaneously maintaining passionate sexual excitement with her husband was a 1950s invention that drove thousands of women to therapists, tranquilizers, or alcohol when they actually tried to live up to it.

Similarly, an extended family in which all members work together under the top-down authority of the household elder operates very differently from a nuclear family in which husband and wife are envisioned as friends who patiently devise ways to let the children learn by trial and error. Children who worked in family enterprises seldom had time for . . . extracurricular activities . . . ; often, they did not even go to school full-time. Mothers who did home production generally relegated child care to older children or servants; they did not suspend work to savor a baby's first steps or discuss with their husband how to facilitate a grade-schooler's "self-esteem." Such families emphasized formality, obedience to authority, and "the way it's always been" in their childrearing.

Stephanie Coontz, *The Way We Never Were: American Families and the Nostalgia Trap* (New York: Basic Books, 1992), pp. 8–22. Copyright 1992 by Perseus Books Group. Reproduced with permission of Perseus Books Group in the format textbook via Copyright Clearance Center.

Nuclear families, by contrast, have tended to pride themselves on the "modernity" of parent-child relations, diluting the authority of grandparents, denigrating "old-fashioned" ideas about childraising, and resisting the "interference" of relatives. . . .

The Elusive Traditional Family

Whenever people propose that we go back to the traditional family, I always suggest that they pick a ballpark date for the family they have in mind. Once pinned down, they are invariably unwilling to accept the package deal that comes with their chosen model. Some people, for example, admire the discipline of colonial families, which were certainly not much troubled by divorce or fragmenting individualism. But colonial families were hardly stable: High mortality rates meant that the average length of marriage was less than a dozen years. One-third to one-half of all children lost at least one parent before the age of twenty-one; in the South, more than half of all children aged thirteen or under had lost at least one parent.

While there are a few modern Americans who would like to return to the strict patriarchal authority of colonial days, in which disobedience by women and children was considered a small form of treason, these individuals would doubtless be horrified by other aspects of colonial families, such as their failure to protect children from knowledge of sexuality. Eighteenth-century spelling and grammar books routinely used *fornication* as an example of a four-syllable word, and preachers detailed sexual offenses in astonishingly explicit terms. Sexual conversations between men and women, even in front of children, were remarkably frank. It is worth contrasting this colonial candor to the climate in 1991, when the Department of Health and Human Services was forced to cancel a proposed survey of teenagers' sexual practices after some groups charged that such knowledge might "inadvertently" encourage more sex.

Other people searching for an ideal traditional family might pick the more sentimental and gentle Victorian family, which arose in the 1830s and 1840s as household production gave way to wage work and professional occupations outside the home. A new division of labor by age and sex emerged among the middle class. Women's roles were redefined in terms of domesticity rather than production, men were labeled "breadwinners" (a masculine identity unheard of in colonial days), children were said to need time to play, and gentle maternal guidance supplanted the patriarchal authoritarianism of the past.

But the middle-class Victorian family depended for its existence on the multiplication of other families who were too poor and powerless to retreat into their own little oases and who therefore had to provision the oases of others. Childhood was prolonged for the nineteenth-century middle class only because it was drastically foreshortened for other sectors of the population. The spread of textile mills, for example, freed middle-class women from the most time-consuming of their former chores, making cloth. But the raw materials for these mills were produced by slave labor. Slave children were not exempt from field labor unless they were infants, and even then their mothers were not allowed time off to nurture them. Frederick Douglass could not remember seeing his mother until he was seven.

Domesticity was also not an option for the white families who worked twelve hours a day in Northern factories and workshops transforming slave-picked cotton into ready-made clothing. By 1820, "half the workers in many factories were boys and girls who had not reached their eleventh birthday." Rhode Island investigators found "little half-clothed children" making their way to the textile mills before dawn. In 1845, shoemaking families and makers of artificial flowers worked fifteen to eighteen hours a day, according to the New York *Daily Tribune.*

Within the home, prior to the diffusion of household technology at the end of the century, house cleaning and food preparation remained mammoth tasks. Middle-class women were able to shift more time into childrearing in this period only by hiring domestic help. Between 1800 and 1850, the proportion of servants to white households doubled, to about one in nine. Some servants were poverty-stricken mothers who had to board or bind out their own children. Employers found such workers tended to be "distracted," however; they usually preferred young girls. In his study of Buffalo, New York, in the 1850s, historian Lawrence Glasco found that Irish and German girls often went into service at the age of eleven or twelve.

For every nineteenth-century middle-class family that protected its wife and child within the family circle, then, there was an Irish or a German girl scrubbing floors in that middle-class home, a Welsh boy mining coal to keep the home-baked goodies warm, a black girl doing the family laundry, a black mother and child picking cotton to be made into clothes for the family, and a Jewish or an Italian daughter in a sweatshop making "ladies" dresses or artificial flowers for the family to purchase.

Furthermore, people who lived in these periods were seldom as enamored of their family arrangements as modern nostalgia might suggest. Colonial Americans lamented "the great neglect in many parents and masters in training up their children" and expressed the "greatest trouble and grief about the rising generation." No sooner did Victorian middle-class families begin to withdraw their children from the work world than observers began to worry that children were becoming *too* sheltered. By 1851, the Reverend Horace Bushnell spoke for many in bemoaning the passing of the traditional days of household production, when the whole family was "harnessed, all together, into the producing process, young and old, male and female, from the boy who rode the plough-horse to the grandmother knitting under her spectacles."

The late nineteenth century saw a modest but significant growth of extended families and a substantial increase in the number of families who were "harnessed" together in household production. Extended families have never been the norm in America; the highest figure for extended-family households ever recorded in American history is 20 percent. Contrary to the popular myth that industrialization destroyed "traditional" extended families, this high point occurred between 1850 and 1885, during the most intensive period of early industrialization. Many of these extended families, and most "producing" families of the time, depended on the labor of children; they were held together by dire necessity and sometimes by brute force.

There was a significant increase in child labor during the last third of the nineteenth century. Some children worked at home in crowded tenement sweatshops that produced cigars or women's clothing. . . . Many producing households resembled the one described by Mary Van Kleeck of the Russell Sage Foundation in 1913:

In a tenement on MacDougal Street lives a family of seven—grandmother, father, mother and four children aged four years, three years, two years and one month respectively. All excepting the father and the two babies make violets. The three year old girl picks apart the petals; her sister, aged four years, separates the stems, dipping an end of each into paste spread on a piece of board on the kitchen table; and the mother and grandmother slip the petals up the stems. . . .

By the end of the nineteenth century, shocked by the conditions in urban tenements and by the sight of young children working full-time at home or earning money out on the streets, middle-class reformers put aside nostalgia for "harnessed" family production and elevated the antebellum model once more, blaming immigrants for introducing such "un-American" family values as child labor. Reformers advocated adoption of a "true American" family—a restricted. exclusive nuclear unit in which women and children were divorced from the world of work.

In the late 1920s and early 1930s, however, the wheel turned yet again, as social theorists noted the independence and isolation of the nuclear family with renewed anxiety. The influential Chicago School of sociology believed that immigration and urbanization had weakened the traditional family by destroying kinship and community networks. Although sociologists welcomed the increased democracy of "companionate marriage," they worried about the rootlessness of nuclear families and the breakdown of older solidarities. By the time of the Great Depression, some observers even saw a silver lining in economic hardship, since it revived the economic functions and social importance of kin and family ties. With housing starts down by more than 90 percent, approximately one-sixth of urban families had to "double up" in apartments. The incidence of three-generation households increased, while recreational interactions outside the home were cut back or confined to the kinship network. One newspaper opined: "Many a family that has lost its car has found its soul."

Depression families evoke nostalgia in some contemporary observers, because they tended to create "dependability and domestic inclination" among girls and "maturity in the management of money" among boys. But, in many cases, such responsibility was inseparable from "a corrosive and disabling poverty that shattered the hopes and dreams of . . . young parents and twisted the lives of those who were 'stuck together' in it." Men withdrew from family life or turned violent; women exhausted themselves trying to "take up the slack" both financially and emotionally, or they belittled their husbands as failures; and children gave up their dreams of education to work at dead-end jobs.

From the hardships of the Great Depression and the Second World War and the euphoria of the postwar economic recovery came a new kind of family ideal that still enters our homes in "Leave It to Beaver" and "Donna Reed" reruns. . . .[T]he 1950s were no more a "golden age" of the family than any other period in American history. . . . [O]ur recurring search for a traditional family model denies the diversity of family life, both past and present, and leads to false generalizations about the past as well as widely exaggerated claims about the present and the future.

The Complexities of Assessing Family Trends

If it is hard to find a satisfactory model of the traditional family, it is also hard to make global judgments about how families have changed and whether they are getting better or worse. Some generalizations about the past are pure myth. Whatever the merit of recurring complaints about the "rootlessness" of modern life, for instance, families are *not* more mobile and transient than they used to be. In most nineteenth-century cities, both large and small, more than 50 percent—and often up to 75 percent—of the residents in any given year were no longer there ten years later. People born in the twentieth century are much more likely to live near their birthplace than were people born in the nineteenth century.

This is not to say, of course, that mobility did not have different effects then than it does now. In the nineteenth century, claims historian Thomas Bender, people moved from community to community, taking advantage . . . of nonfamilial networks and institutions that integrated them into new work and social relations. In the late twentieth century, people move from job to job, following a career path that shuffles them from one single-family home to another and does not link them to neighborly networks beyond the family. But this change is in our community ties, not in our family ones.

A related myth is that modern Americans have lost touch with extended-kinship networks or have let parent-child bonds lapse. In fact, more Americans than ever before have grandparents alive, and there is good evidence that ties between grandparents and grandchildren have become stronger over the past fifty years. In the late 1970s, researchers returned to the "Middletown" studied by sociologists Robert and Helen Lynd in the 1920s and found that most people there maintained closer extended-family networks than in earlier times. There had been some decline in the family's control over the daily lives of youth, especially females, but "the expressive/emotional function of the family" was "more important for Middletown students of 1977 than it was in 1924." More recent research shows that visits with relatives did *not* decline between the 1950s and the late 1980s.

Today 54 percent of adults see a parent, and 68 percent talk on the phone with a parent, at least once a week. Fully 90 percent of Americans describe their relationship with their mother as close, and 78 percent say their relationship with their grandparents is close. And for all the family disruption of divorce, most modern children live with at least *one* parent. As late as 1940, 10 percent of American children did not live with either parent, compared to only one in twenty-five today.

What about the supposed eclipse of marriage? Neither the rising age of those who marry nor the frequency of divorce necessarily means that marriage is becoming a less prominent institution than it was in earlier days. Ninety percent of men and women eventually marry, more than 70 percent of divorced men and women remarry, and fewer people remain single for their entire lives today than at the turn of the century. One author even suggests that the availability of divorce in the second half of the twentieth century has allowed some women to try marriage who would formerly have remained single all their lives. Others argue that the rate of hidden marital separation in the late nineteenth century was not much less than the rate of visible separation today.

Studies of marital satisfaction reveal that more couples reported their marriages to be happy in the late 1970s than did so in 1957, while couples in their second marriages believe them to be much happier than their first ones. Some commentators conclude that marriage is becoming less permanent but more satisfying. Others wonder, however, whether there is a vicious circle in our country, where no one even tries to sustain a relationship. Between the late 1970s and late 1980s, moreover, reported marital happiness did decline slightly in the United States. Some authors see this as reflecting our decreasing appreciation of marriage, although others suggest that it reflects unrealistically high expectations of love in a culture that denies people safe, culturally approved ways of getting used to marriage or cultivating other relationships to meet some of the needs that we currently load onto the couple alone.

Part of the problem in making simple generalizations about what is happening to marriage is that there has been a polarization of experiences. Marriages are much more likely to be ended by divorce today, but marriages that do last are described by their participants as happier than those in the past and are far more likely to confer such happiness over many years. It is important to remember that the 50 percent divorce rate estimates are calculated in terms of a forty-year period and that many marriages in the past were terminated well before that date by the death of one partner. Historian Lawrence Stone suggests that divorce has become "a functional substitute for death" in the modern world. At the end of the 1970s, the rise in divorce rates seemed to overtake the fall in death rates, but the slight decline in divorce rates since then means that "a couple marrying today is more likely to celebrate a fortieth wedding anniversary than were couples around the turn of the century."

A similar polarization allows some observers to argue that fathers are deserting their children, while others celebrate the new commitment of fathers to childrearing. Both viewpoints are right. Sociologist Frank Furstenberg comments on the emergence of a "good dad–bad dad complex": Many fathers spend more time with their children than ever before and feel more free to be affectionate with them; others, however, feel more free simply to walk out on their families. According to 1981 statistics, 42 percent of the children whose father had left the marriage had not seen him in the past year. Yet studies show steadily increasing involvement of fathers with their children as long as they are in the home.

These kinds of ambiguities should make us leery of hard-and-fast pronouncements about what's happening to the American family. In many cases, we simply don't know precisely what our figures actually mean. For example, the proportion of youngsters receiving psychological assistance rose by 80 percent between 1981 and 1988. Does that mean they are getting more sick or receiving more help, or is it some complex combination of the two? Child abuse reports increased by 225 percent between 1976 and 1987. Does this represent an actual increase in rates of abuse or a heightened consciousness about the problem? During the same period, parents' self-reports about very severe violence toward their children declined 47 percent. Does this represent a real improvement in their behavior or a decreasing willingness to admit to such acts?

Assessing the direction of family change is further complicated because many contemporary trends represent a reversal of developments that were themselves rather recent. The expectation that the family should be the main source of personal fulfillment, for example, was not traditional in the eighteenth and nineteenth centuries. . . . Prior to the 1990s, the family festivities that now fill us with such nostalgia for "the good old days" (and cause such heartbreak when they go poorly) were "relatively undeveloped." Civic festivals and Fourth of July parades were more important occasions for celebration and strong emotion than family holidays, such as Thanksgiving. Christmas "seems to have been more a time for attending parties and dances than for celebrating family solidarity." Only in the twentieth century did the family come to be the center of festive attention and emotional intensity.

Today, such emotional investment in the family may be waning again. This could be interpreted as a reestablishment of balance between family life and other social ties; on the other hand, such a trend may have different results today than in earlier times, because in many cases the extrafamilial institutions and customs that used to socialize individuals and provide them with a range of emotional alternatives to family life no longer exist. . . .

Wild Claims and Phony Forecasts

Lack of perspective on where families have come from and how their evolution connects to other social trends tends to encourage contradictory claims and wild exaggerations about where families are going. One category of generalizations seems to be a product of wishful thinking. As of 1988, nearly half of all families with children had both parents in the work force. The two-parent family in which only the father worked for wages represented just 25 percent of all families with children, down from 44 percent in 1975. For people overwhelmed by the difficulties of adjusting work and schools to the realities of working moms, it has been tempting to discern a "return to tradition" and hope the problems will go away. Thus in 1991, we saw a flurry of media reports that the number of women in the work force was headed down: "More Choose to Stay Home with Children" proclaimed the headlines; "More Women Opting for Chance to Watch Their Children Grow."

The cause of all this commotion? The percentage of women aged twenty-five to thirty-four who were employed dropped from 74 percent to 72.8 percent between January 1990 and January 1991. However, there was an exactly equal decline in the percentage of men in the work force during the same period, and for both genders the explanation was the same. "The dip is the recession," explained Judy Waldrop, research editor at *American Demographics* magazine, to anyone who bothered to listen. In fact, the proportion of *mothers* who worked increased slightly during the same period.

This is not to say that parents, especially mothers, are happy with the pressures of balancing work and family life. Poll after poll reveals that both men and women feel starved for time. The percentage of women who say they would prefer to stay home with their children if they could afford to do so rose from 33 percent in 1986 to 56 percent in 1990. Other polls show that even larger majorities of women would trade a day's pay for an extra day off. But, above all, what these polls reveal is women's growing dissatisfaction with the failure of employers, schools, and government to pioneer arrangements that make it possible to combine work and family life. They do not suggest that women are actually going to stop working, or that this would be women's preferred solution to their stresses. The polls did not ask, for example, how *long* women would like to take off work, and failed to take account of the large majority of mothers who report that they would miss their work if they did manage to take time off. Working mothers are here to stay, and we will not meet the challenge this poses for family life by inventing an imaginary trend to define the problem out of existence.

At another extreme is the kind of generalization that taps into our worst fears. One example of this is found in the almost daily reporting of cases of child molestation or kidnapping by sexual predators. The highlighting of such cases, drawn from every corner of the country, helps disguise how rare these cases actually are when compared to crimes committed within the family.

A well-publicized instance of the cataclysmic predictions that get made when family trends are taken out of historical context is the famous *Newsweek* contention that a single woman of forty has a better chance of being killed by a terrorist than of finding a husband. It is true that the proportion of never-married women under age forty has increased substantially since the 1950s, but it is also true that the proportion has *decreased* dramatically among women over that age. A woman over thirty-five has a *better* chance to marry today than she did in the 1950s. In the past twelve years, first-time marriages have increased almost 40 percent for women aged thirty-five to thirty-nine. A single woman aged forty to forty-four still has a 24 percent probability of marriage, while 15 percent of woman in their late forties will marry. These figures would undoubtedly be higher if many women over forty did not simply pass up opportunities that a more desperate generation might have snatched.

Yet another example of the exaggeration that pervades many analyses of modern families is the widely quoted contention that "parents today spend 40 percent less time with their children than did parents in 1965." Again, of course, part of the problem is where researchers are measuring from. A comparative study of Muncie, Indiana, for example, found that parents spent much more time with their children in the mid-1970s than did parents in the mid-1920s. But another problem is keeping the categories consistent. Trying to track down the source of the 40 percent decline figure, I called demographer John P. Robinson, whose studies on time formed the basis of this claim. Robinson's data, however, show that parents today spend about the same amount of time caring for children as they did in 1965. If the total amount of time devoted to children is less, he suggested, I might want to check how many fewer children there are today. In 1970, the average family had 1.34 children under the age of eighteen; in 1990, the average family had only .96 children under age eighteen—a decrease of 28.4 percent. In other words, most of the decline in the total amount of time parents spend with children is because of the decline in the number of children they have to spend time with!

Now I am not trying to say that the residual amount of decrease is not serious, or that it may not become worse, given the trends in women's employment. Robinson's data show that working mothers spend substantially less time in primary child-care activities than do nonemployed mothers (though they also tend to have fewer children); more than 40 percent of working mothers report feeling "trapped" by their daily routines; many routinely sacrifice sleep in order to meet the demands of work and family. Even so, a majority believe they are *not* giving enough time to their children. It is also true that children may benefit merely from having their parents available, even though the parents may not be spending time with them.

But there is no reason to assume the worst. Americans have actually gained free time since 1965, despite an increase in work hours, largely as a result of a decline in housework and an increasing tendency to fit some personal requirements and errands into the work day. And according to a recent Gallup poll, most modern mothers think they are doing a better job of communicating with their children (though a worse job of house cleaning) than did their own mothers and that they put a higher value on spending time with their family than did their mothers.

Negotiating Through the Extremes

Most people react to these conflicting claims and contradictory trends with understandable confusion. They know that family ties remain central to their own lives, but they are constantly hearing about people who seem to have *no* family feeling. Thus, at the same time as Americans report high levels of satisfaction with their *own* families, they express a pervasive fear that other people's families are falling apart. In a typical recent poll, for example, 71 percent of respondents said they were "very satisfied" with their own family life, but more than half rated the overall quality of family life as negative: "I'm okay; you're not."

This seemingly schizophrenic approach does not reflect an essentially intolerant attitude. People worry about families, and to the extent that they associate modern social ills with changes in family life, they are ambivalent about innovations. Voters often defeat measures to grant unmarried couples, whether heterosexual or homosexual, the same rights as married ones. In polls, however, most Americans support tolerance for gay and lesbian relationships. Although two-thirds of respondents to one national poll said they wanted "more traditional standards of family life," the same percentage rejected the idea that "women should return to their traditional role." Still larger majorities support women's right to work, including their right to use child care, even when they worry about relying on day-care centers too much. In a 1990 *Newsweek* poll, 42 percent predicted that the family would be worse in ten years and exactly the same percentage predicted that it would be better. Although 87 percent of people polled in 1987 said they had "old-fashioned ideas about family and marriage," only 22 percent of the people polled in 1989 defined a family solely in terms of blood, marriage, or adoption. Seventy-four percent declared, instead, that family is any group whose members love and care for one another.

These conflicted responses do not mean that people are hopelessly confused. Instead, they reflected people's gut-level understanding that the "crisis of the family" is more complex than is often asserted by political demagogues or others with an ax to grind. In popular commentary, the received wisdom is to "keep it simple." I know one television reporter who refuses to air an interview with anyone who uses the phrase "on the other hand." But my experience in discussing these issues with both the general public and specialists in the field is that people are hungry to get beyond oversimplifications. They don't want to be told that everything is fine in families or that if the economy improved and the government mandated parental leave, everything would be fine. But they don't believe that every hard-won victory for women's rights and personal liberty has been destructive of social bonds and that the only way to find a sense of community is to go back to some sketchily defined "traditional" family that clearly involves denying the validity of any alternative familial and personal choices.

Americans understand that along with welcome changes have come difficult new problems; uneasy with simplistic answers, they are willing to consider more nuanced analyses of family gains and losses during the past few decades. Indeed, argues political reporter E. J. Dionne, they are *desperate* to engage in such analyses.

Few Americans are satisfied with liberal and feminist accounts that blame all modern family dilemmas on structural inequalities, ignoring the moral crisis of commitment and obligation in our society. Yet neither are they convinced that "in the final analysis," as David Blankenhorn of the Institute for American Values puts it, "the problem is not the system. The problem is us."

Despite humane intentions, an overemphasis on personal responsibility for strengthening family values encourages a way of thinking that leads to moralizing rather than mobilizing for concrete reforms. While values are important to Americans, most do not support the sort of scapegoating that occurs when all family problems are blamed on "bad values." Most of us are painfully aware that there is no clear way of separating "family values" from "the system." Our values may make a difference in the way we respond to the challenges posed by economic and political institutions, but those institutions also reinforce certain values and extinguish others. The problem is not to berate people for abandoning past family values, nor to exhort them to adopt better values in the future—the problem is to build the institutions and social support networks that allow people to act on their best values rather than on their worst ones. We need to get past abstract nostalgia for traditional family values and develop a clearer sense of how past families actually worked and what the different consequences of various family behaviors and values have been. Good history and responsible social policy should help people incorporate the full complexity and the tradeoffs of family change into their analyses and thus into action. Mythmaking does not accomplish this end.

Reflections on the History of Children and Childhood in the Postmodern Era

JOSEPH M. HAWES AND N. RAY HINER

Introduction

Our grandchildren enjoy a series of books in which they are asked to identify a rather outlandish character named "Waldo" who appears throughout the illustrations that make up most of the books. At first, Waldo can be hard to find, even for an adult. He does not bring attention to himself, preferring to take on the characteristics of his environment and recede into the background. Gradually, as one trains one's eyes to recognize Waldo, he begins to appear everywhere, in the fields, in the forest, in the streets, with animals and people, really in quite remarkable places.

Until recently, historians have found that children, like Waldo, are easy to overlook. Historians have traditionally been more interested in those who exercised power in society than in the masses of persons over whom power was exercised. Children were certainly not seen as important historical subjects except when they

Joseph M. Hawes and N. Ray Hiner, "Looking for Waldo: Reflections on the History of Children and Childhood in the Postmodern Era" (paper presented at the "History of Childhood in America" conference, Washington, D.C., August 5–6, 2000). Reprinted by permission of the authors.

were part of larger stories such as the movements to expand education, improve health, and regulate child labor. Otherwise, children were rarely seen or heard in the stories historians constructed about the American past. Fortunately, historians have begun to recognize children's ubiquitous historical presence and their surprising influence. Even so, searching for historical children, like looking for Waldo, is not always easy and may be an acquired taste.

In some respects, the relatively slow development of the history of children is surprising as it has now been at least thirty years since the pioneering work of Philippe Ariès, Lloyd deMause, and others first appeared. African American history, Native American history, and women's history, also relatively new areas of historical interest, though not without controversy, are now widely recognized as essential to any comprehensive history of American society and culture. Yet, in spite of an encouraging number of recent favorably reviewed works, children generally remain on the periphery of American historiography.

In retrospect, it is clear that much of the early, pioneering work in the history of children, though indispensable in stimulating interest in the field and establishing its legitimacy, suffered from a serious lack of definitional and theoretical clarity. This is understandable, given the complexity of the subject and the relative newness of the field, but if the history of children is to begin to reach its full potential, more attention should be devoted to clarifying the nature of the field and the questions that should direct inquiry. At the very least, the inconsistency and confusion that too often characterize the use of the term *childhood* should be addressed.

Defining the History of Children and Childhood

As historians we have been slow to make clear distinctions in our work concerning childhood as (1) an ideology or social construction, (2) an experience, and (3) a set of behaviors. Childhood as a social construction, that is, the ideals and expectations that adults establish for children, should not be confused with what children actually experience anymore than an experienced teacher assumes that what is taught is necessarily learned. Similarly, the ways children behave should not be confused with their experience or with childhood as an ideology. . . . We should keep in mind that children are, after all, complex human beings. Most reflective parents and caregivers understand this. Historians should do the same.

The complexity inherent in defining childhood as a social construction, as a set of expectations for children developed by adults, can perhaps be understood best through analogy. From this perspective, childhood is like a toy—something designed by adults and given to children. Toys contain coded messages or instructions to children. Consider, for instance, the not-so-subtle messages that a Barbie doll may send to an impressionable elementary school child. But consider also what two of our children did with their Barbies: one son set Barbie on fire (the hair is highly flammable), while a daughter routinely dismembered her Barbie. So what children actually do with their toys and how they experience them can be very different from what adults intended. So, too, the childhood constructed by adults for children is not necessarily what children actually experience, and a comprehensive history of children is not necessarily synonymous with the history of childhood.

Scholars in cultural studies often focus on childhood, which they rightly view as essential to their analysis, but children are not texts. This is why we make a distinction between the history of children and the history of childhood. We approach the history of children as an inclusive study of ideas, experiences, and behaviors, whereas the history of childhood as a social construction is by definition more limited in perspective. Thus, we see the history of childhood as an indispensable part of the more comprehensive history of children. Much of what is published in our field is actually about the ideology of childhood, while children, like Waldo, recede into the background. This is understandable because this is where records are most abundant, and what adults think and do is certainly vital to understanding children's lives. Nevertheless, children are too important for their history to be reduced to what adults said and did.

The Dangers of Chronocentrism and Antiquarianism

Regardless of how historians of children and childhood have defined their field, like other historians they have not always been able to avoid the myths, distortions, and half-truths associated with chronocentrism and antiquarianism. At least two varieties of chronocentrism deserve our attention: whiggism and nostalgia. Whiggism is based on the assumption that the past should be judged primarily by the standards of the present. Because whiggish historians tend to see the past as inferior to the present, they study the past to demonstrate its inferiority or to find the seeds, germs, or origins of the present. Whiggish historians often fail to appreciate the richness and integrity of the past as a world with its own reality that deserves to be understood and judged at least in part on its own terms. For example, some of Lloyd deMause's early work, which played a vital role in encouraging the study of the history of children, reflects whiggish assumptions. His pioneering work, *The History of Childhood,* begins with the following words: "The history of childhood is a nightmare from which we have only recently begun to awaken." He continued: "The further one goes back in history, the lower the level of childcare, and the more likely children are to be killed, abandoned, beaten, terrorized, and sexually abused." From the infanticide that characterized the ancient past, deMause believes that humanity has moved inexorably toward better treatment of children in the present, especially among the "psychogenically most advanced part of our population." Although deMause collected considerable evidence to support his "psychogenic theory of history," the whiggism inherent in his approach has tended to undermine its acceptance by other historians. . . .

A more direct example of whiggism in the history of children is the often-repeated shibboleth that children in the past (you pick the period) were viewed as miniature adults. This assertion is at best an oversimplification or half-truth. Even a cursory examination of the evidence for the assertions of miniature adulthood reveals their whiggish bias. For example, several historians have referred to the children of seventeenth-century Puritan New England as miniature adults. However, when one sets presentist, whiggish preconceptions aside, it becomes clear that Puritan adults made very clear distinctions between children and adults even though they sometimes made these distinctions in areas different from those commonly made by adults today.

Children in seventeenth-century New England certainly were expected to work at much earlier ages than children are today because the predominantly rural economy of seventeenth-century New England, unlike modern economies, offered many tasks that children could perform. On the other hand, Puritan children were rarely eroticized or exposed to adult sexuality in the countless ways that modern children confront daily in the print and electronic media. Puritans would no doubt be appalled by how modern children are expected to cope with adult sexual issues at such tender ages. From their perspective, they could reasonably assert that modern children are treated as "miniature adults." Thus, the assertion that Puritan children were viewed as miniature adults is at best a half-truth. In some ways, Puritan children were indeed treated more like adults than they are today, in work for example; but in other areas such as sexuality, the special needs of children were perhaps more respected in seventeenth-century New England than they are today. In any event, we would do well to heed Harvey Graff's conclusion that "there is no longer serious debate" about whether any people "in Western recorded history lacked a concept of childhood." They all had one. . . .

Even so, there are clearly important differences between being a child in the past and in the present. Significant progress has certainly been made in important aspects of children's lives. The history of child mortality, health care, access to formal education, attention to children with special needs, gender, and slavery all provide undeniable evidence that in very important ways children's lives have improved over time. Yet, progress for children rarely occurred along steady lines, was seldom distributed evenly across the population, and was hardly ever experienced without ambiguity. The point is that we should not assume that one trend represents the whole of children's experiences.

Chronocentrism can also lead in the opposite direction from the whiggish assumption that the past is essentially a deficient or unrealized present. Chronocentrism can encourage an unwarranted and oversimplifying nostalgia, which, unlike whiggism, sees the present as a descent from a superior, golden past. For example, Philippe Ariès' landmark work, *Centuries of Childhood,* expresses the author's nostalgic preference for the Middle Ages and his distaste for the politics and values of the modern world. Ariès argued that childhood did not exist until the early modern period when, he believed, children were segregated from adults and then treated as a special population and oppressively controlled and exploited by adults. Children were far better off, he implied, during the medieval period when they received no special treatment and were not separated as [a] group from adults. Few historians today accept Ariès' thesis that childhood was a creation of the early modern period, although some might agree with him on moral or pragmatic grounds that children today should have more opportunities to interact with adults.

Nostalgia is a normal human feeling. . . . Unfortunately, nostalgia, like all chronocentrism, tends to be very selective and simplistic. We usually yearn for only parts of our past, not all of it. In reality, the past and the present are made up of the good and the bad, the beautiful and the ugly. Nostalgia is too often a form of selective forgetting and remembering. Nostalgia can be a very useful motivating device and can encourage a critical reflection on our personal and collective experiences, but if we romanticize the past, we unnecessarily constrict its meaning and limit its usefulness to the present. . . .

Antiquarianism is closely related to chronocentric nostalgia. . . . The history of children is especially vulnerable to antiquarianism because of the natural nostalgia we all tend to feel for parts of our own childhood and because it is easy to assume that children were relatively inconsequential in our past. Moreover, the "quaintness" that is often attractive to antiquarians is similar to the "cuteness" that draws some to the study of children in the past. Children are often "cute," and their artifacts can be seen as "quaint," but children are hardly inconsequential, and there is far more to their history than quaint artifacts.

Questions to Guide Research

In 1985, we proposed five basic questions that we believed could help guide research in the history of children. . . . Below, we identify these questions and provide brief illustrations of how they can be used to organize and interpret information about children in the past. To ensure continuity and brevity, we generally restrict the illustrations to brief discussions of the implications of demographic research for each of the questions.

1. *What were the conditions that shaped the development of children?* This question encompasses a wide range of issues including the social indicators that determined the duration, scope, and intensity of childhood; the institutions in which children lived; and the complex relationships that occurred within these institutions.

We have learned a great deal about the demography of children, which is obviously fundamental to understanding the conditions that shaped their development. Mortality rates among American children ranged from ten to thirty times their current levels until late in the nineteenth century when greater awareness of the germ theory led to successful public sanitation programs and efforts to provide clean milk for infants. Within this regime of high mortality, there were great variations over time and among regions, classes, and ethnic groups. For example, in seventeenth-century New England, with its dispersed population and ample food supply, children experienced one of the healthiest environments in our history, while the seventeenth-century Chesapeake constituted one of the unhealthiest regions for both whites and black children because of widespread malaria and poor nutrition. This [resulted in a] pattern of death and remarriage [that] produced large numbers of families that resembled modern blended or reconstituted families created by divorce and remarriage. Stepparents and stepfamilies were very common in early America. . . .

2. *What were the social, cultural, and psychological functions of children?* Children, like members of all social groups, are assigned both implicit and explicit roles in American society and culture. Children are part of a larger system that places demands on them and shapes their behaviors in very precise ways that historians should investigate. What are some of the implications of high mortality rates for the functions of children?

America's high mortality rates and relatively high birth rates created a very young population. The average age of the American population was only sixteen in 1800 and did not rise above twenty-one until the twentieth century. Adults had to devote an enormous amount of time, energy, and resources to providing food, clothing, shelter, and education for children. Because labor was in very short supply, there was a very strong incentive to put children to work as soon as possible. Indeed, preparation for work was a normal part of life for virtually all American children, especially on farms, where the vast majority of American children lived before 1920. Throughout most of our history, American children, often very young children, worked on farms and plantations; in households, shops, and factories; and in the streets. As the American economy matured, and as mortality and birth rates declined, the economic role of children gradually shifted from that of producer to consumer until today, when children constitute a significant group of consumers whose preferences are carefully studied by advertisers and corporations. However, Viviana Zelizer has stated that as children became less valuable economically, they became more precious psychologically.

3. *What were the attitudes of adults toward children and childhood?* In one sense, this is the easiest question for historians to answer primarily because adults left voluminous records about their attitudes toward children. However, care must be taken not to confuse attitudes or rhetoric with actual behavior. Still, knowledge of what adults thought about children, what they expected children to do and be, how childhood was constructed, is fundamental to creating a comprehensive history of children.

Some historians have argued that high death and birth rates encouraged parents to see children as interchangeable and led them to delay making an emotional investment in their children until they could reasonably assume that they would survive. There is some evidence to support this view. Necronymic naming, or naming children after dead siblings, which might imply that children were seen as interchangeable, did not decline until the mid-nineteenth century when birth rates begin to drop and mortality rates improved. Certainly, few persons today have had experiences that would approach the enormous losses suffered by many parents in the past, such as Cotton Mather, who saw fourteen of his sixteen children die. How did parents come to terms with such losses? It seems reasonable to assume that some psychological defenses against the pain would appear. . . . However, many parents expressed deep pain when their children died. Cotton Mather compared the death of one of his children to having a limb torn from his body.

4. *What was the subjective experience of being a child in the past?* This is a very difficult question for historians to answer in part because children, especially young children, left relatively few records of their experiences. Yet with empathy, imagination, and careful attention to evidence, it is possible for historians to gain important insights into children's subjective worlds. Without this perspective, the history of children is not complete.

How did children experience the almost constant illness and death that characterized much of American history? Certainly, these conditions must have been very stressful to those who survived. To watch one's mother or father, brothers or sisters, or close relatives die slowly, painfully, without the benefit of modern pain-killing drugs, was no doubt traumatic for young children. If children today mourn the separation of parents through divorce, how did children in early America respond when the ravages of an epidemic took their loved ones from them? They had to come to terms with death in ways that we can hardly imagine. . . .

5. *How have children influenced adults and each other?* To understand this question, it is important not to confuse informal influence with formal authority or power

over others. Of all the impediments to the full development of the history of children and childhood, the assumed powerlessness of children has undoubtedly been the most important.

Because children have obviously had little formal power, scholars have too often assumed that most of the actual influence in adult-child relations flowed primarily in one direction, from adult to the child. However, all human relationships, even the most hierarchical, are inevitably reciprocal and dynamic. Although children have had little formal power, they have nevertheless exercised and continue to exercise great influence on virtually all aspects of American society and culture.

The Influence of the "Powerless"

In what ways were children influential? One part of the answer is undeniable. All adults were once children, an experience that obviously shaped their development in complex ways. Yet, children's influence goes far beyond the universality of childhood. Children were influential in our past in at least four additional ways: (1) as members of families, (2) as members of a distinct population group, (3) as producers and consumers, and (4) as cultural and political symbols.

As members of families, children exercised great influence over the lives of their parents, siblings, relatives, and caregivers. One does not need to tell parents that the birth or adoption of a child changes the fundamental dynamics of a family. Our archives are full of documents that testify to this influence. Moreover, few parents would deny that most children learn how to get what they want. An example of this point is the marketing strategy of the McDonald's restaurant chain, which pitches its ads directly to children, supplements those ads with a cartoon character like Ronald McDonald, and designs its retail outlets in ways that cater to children and make them feel welcomed. Thus, McDonalds uses the ability of children to influence their parents both as a way to sell hamburgers and to make a handsome profit for stockholders. Throughout our history, millions of parents and caregivers have by necessity and choice built their lives around providing for and caring for children, perhaps more then than now.

As members of a distinct population group, children have shaped society in ways that go far beyond their individual families. . . . One could argue with some justification that one of the most radical decisions ever made by our society was to confine large numbers of teenagers together in limited spaces for extended periods. We live with the consequences still. . . .

As producers and consumers, children played a significant role in the development of the American economy. Because children constituted such a large percentage of the early American population, adult labor was relatively scarce, and children, often very young children, were expected to work. Preparation for work was a normal part of life for early American children. While the many individual tasks performed by children in households, fields, and shops of rural and small-town America were not in and of themselves highly significant, collectively they represented a vital contribution to the economy. Children also worked the factories, mills, and mines of nineteenth- and early-twentieth-century America and thereby subsidized the industrialization of America by contributing to the production of cheap goods to compete in the growing international market. However, they did this at a very high cost in lost lives, ruined health, and lost opportunity for education and normal development. In spite of the intense campaign to eliminate child labor in factories, mills, and mines, it had little effect until the 1920s when social pressure, regulatory legislation, new technology, and compulsory education laws combined to reduce child labor. As more children went to school than went to work, their primary economic role gradually shifted until today, when children's predominant economic role is to consume the extraordinary range of products that are created for them.

As cultural and political symbols, children have had a remarkable influence on a wide range of public issues. As children constituted proportionally less of the population and as their economic roles shifted [from] production to consumption, their psychological and cultural importance in families and in society intensified. Thus, children have been increasingly placed at the center of American debates that express America's deepest feelings, hopes, and anxieties. Throughout our history, children have often been central to debates about family, religion, crime, education, citizenship, slavery, gender, race, sexuality, social justice, health, welfare, drug abuse, and day care, to name a few.

Conclusion

As scholars we have only begun to understand how consequential children have been in our history. Children should be taken seriously, now and in the past, because as human beings they deserve to be taken seriously but also because they have had and will continue [to] have a significant influence on who we were, who we are, and who we will become. . . . If as historians we want our future histories to be filled with children, we should heed Waldo's sage advice: "Keep looking for me. I'm out there, somewhere."

 F U R T H E R   R E A D I N G

Ariès, Philippe. *Centuries of Childhood: A Social History of Family Life*. Trans. Robert Baldick (1962).

Coontz, Stephanie. *The Social Origins of Private Life* (1988).

_____. *The Way We Never Were: American Families and the Nostalgia Trap* (1992).

Degler, Carl N. *At Odds: Women and the Family in America from the Revolution to the Present* (1980).

deMause, Lloyd, ed. *The History of Childhood* (1975).

Demos, John. *Past, Present, and Personal: The Family and the Life Course in American History* (1986).

Earle, Alice Morse. *Child Life in Colonial Days* (1899).

Elder, Glen H. Jr., John Modell, and Ross D. Parke, eds. *Children in Time and Place* (1993).

Farrell, Betty G. *Family: The Making of an Idea, an Institution, and a Controversy in American Culture* (1999).

Fass, Paula S., and Mary Ann Mason, eds. *Childhood in America* (2000).

Gordon, Michael, ed. *The American Family in Social-Historical Perspective,* 2d ed. (1978).

Graff, Harvey J., ed. *Growing Up in America* (1987).

Greven, Philip J. Jr. *Four Generations* (1970).

Hareven, Tamara K. *Family Time and Industrial Time* (1982).

Hawes, Joseph M., and N. Ray Hiner, eds. *American Childhood* (1985).

Hawes, Joseph M., and Elizabeth I. Nybakken. *American Families* (1991).

Lasch, Christopher. *Haven in a Heartless World* (1977).

Mintz, Steven, and Susan Kellogg. *Domestic Revolutions: A Social History of American Family Life* (1988).

Morgan, Edmund. *The Puritan Family* (1966).

Rabb, Theodore K., and Robert I. Rotberg, eds. *The Family in History* (1971).

Stone, Lawrence. "Family History in the 1980s: Past Achievements and Future Trends." *Journal of Interdisciplinary History* 12 (Summer 1981): 51–88.

_____. *The Family, Sex, and Marriage in England, 1500–1800* (1977).

Thorne, Barrie, and Marilyn Yalom, eds. *Rethinking the Family* (1982).

Vinovskis, Maris. "American Families in the Past." In James B. Gardner and George R. Adams, eds., *Ordinary People and Everyday Life* (1983), pp. 115–137.

_____. "From Household Size to the Life Course: Some Observations on Recent Trends in Family History." *American Behavioral Scientist* 21 (1977): 263–287.

Zelizer, Viviana A. *Pricing the Priceless Child: The Changing Social Value of Children* (1985).

CHAPTER
2

Marriage, Family, and Kinship in Early America

One of the first topics to gain interest among historians of family life was the colonial household. The family was the fundamental unit of society in British America. As John Demos pointed out in his 1970 book, A Little Commonwealth, *the colonial family functioned as nursery, church, hospital, school, penitentiary, and orphan asylum—services that in our own time have been removed from the family to be provided by public and private agencies. The family was also a vital symbol of society, a sort of society in microcosm. The principles of order that prevailed in the family, colonists believed, not only mirrored but also re-created the hierarchies that structured society as a whole. Precisely because the family was so central, it was a matter of public concern. Ministers devoted entire sermons to recommendations on proper family life, and church and government officials and neighbors all supervised— and often interfered in—family life. This intense interest in family life in the British colonies resulted in a rich array of sources on family life: sermons and advice books, laws and court cases, and letters and diaries. Yet the precise nature of family life in colonial America remains contested, in part because these different sources reveal distinct perspectives on family life. While prescriptive literature, such as sermons, dictates ideals, legal records indicate the failure of individuals to live up to these ideals and the need to compel them to do so by force. Personal writings suggest the ways in which individuals accepted, rejected, or modified prevailing norms of family life. Any comprehensive understanding of family life in colonial America must take all of these perspectives into account, but historians differ in the emphasis that they place on ideals and realities, laws and practice.*

If historians of families of European descent in the New World must contend with competing images in multiple sources, historians of Native American families and African American families face a different challenge. The written records for these families are scarce; moreover, they are authored by the European settlers who invaded Native Americans' land and enslaved African Americans. These writers had relatively little interest in documenting, much less understanding, the family lives of the people they sought to subjugate. Thus, historians of these groups must make creative use of such sources as travel accounts, slaveholders' inventories, and advertisements for runaways to find clues about Native Americans' and African

Americans' expectations and experiences of family life. Often, scholars combine these traditional historical sources with insights drawn from anthropologists. This poses a unique dilemma for researchers. While some may question to what extent anthropological studies of contemporary societies can yield insights about the past, a strict adherence to written sources from the period under study may come at the cost of even a limited or tentative understanding of nondominant cultures.

The diversity of families in seventeenth- and eighteenth-century America raises important questions about the nature and function of the family, such as: How do families adapt to different circumstances? Where does authority lie? Who is responsible for taking care of children? What, if anything, is constant about family life?

 ### D O C U M E N T S

In Document 1 three Europeans offer observations on marriage among Native Americans in the seventeenth and eighteenth centuries. These selections reveal the authors' biases, particularly their concerns about polygamy and infidelity, but these works also offer valuable clues about Native Americans' definitions of marriage, proper male and female work roles, and kinship. Document 2, a nineteenth-century recording of traditional Cherokee myths, suggests how Native Americans themselves transmitted values from generation to generation. Significantly, these myths suggest the centrality of matrilineal kinship among eastern tribes, a theme almost entirely missing from European accounts.

Documents 3 and 4 demonstrate the importance that English settlers in the New England colonies placed on "well-ordered" families. Colonial authorities—magistrates and ministers—are revealed as being in agreement that the family was the cornerstone of society and that an orderly family, under the governance of the male head of the household, was the key to social harmony. This assumption guided white Americans' responses both to the Native Americans that they encountered in North America (as seen in Document 1) and to the Africans that they brought to the American colonies (as seen in Document 5), although not always in consistent ways.

Document 5, a series of advertisements for runaway slaves that appeared in the *Pennsylvania Gazette* in the mid-eighteenth century, indicates the risks that enslaved African Americans took to rejoin family members from whom they had been separated by their owners' actions. In addition to suggesting the high value that black Americans attached to the family, the advertisements also indicate slaveowners' skepticism about blacks' ability to appreciate the institution that white Americans considered so central to their own lives.

1. Three Europeans Comment on Native American Marriage, Gender, and Kinship, 1600s–1700s

John Smith Describes the "Naturall Inhabitants of Virginia," 1608

The land is not populous, for the men be fewe; their far greater number is of women and children. Within 60 miles of *Iames* Towne there are about some 5000 people, but of able men fit for their warres scarse 1500. To nourish so many together they haue yet no means, because they make so smal a benefit of their land, be it never so fertill. . . .

Edward Arber, ed., *Travels and Works of Captain John Smith, President of Virginia, and Admiral of New England, 1580–1631* (Edinburgh: John Grant, 1910; originally published 1608), pp. 65, 67, 79–81.

The men bestowe their times in fishing, hunting, wars, and such manlike exercises, scorning to be seene in any woman like exercise; which is the cause that the women be verie painefull and the men often idle. The women and children do the rest of the worke. They make mats, baskets, pots, mortars; pound their corne, make their bread, prepare their victuals, plant their corne, gather their corne, beare al kind of burdens, and such like. . . .

Although the countrie people be very barbarous; yet haue they amongst them such government, as that their Magistrat[e]s for good commanding, and their people for du[e] subiection and obeying, excel many places that would be counted very civill.

The forme of their Common wealth is a monarchicall gouernement. One as Emperour ruleth ouer many kings or governours. Their chiefe ruler is called *Powhatan,* and taketh his name of the principall place of dwelling called *Powhatan.* But his proper name is *Wahunsonacock.* . . .

He hath as many women as he will: whereof when hee lieth on his bed, one sitteth at his head, and another at his feet; but when he sitteth, one sitteth on his right hand, and another on his left. As he is wearie of his women, hee bestoweth them on those that best deserue them at his hands.

When he dineth or suppeth, one of his women, before and after meat, bringeth him water in a wo[o]den platter to wash his hands. Another waiteth with a bunch of feathers to wipe them insteed of a Towell, and the feathers when he hath wiped are dryed againe.

His kingdome descendeth not to his sonnes nor children: but first to his brethren, whereof he hath 3. namely *Opitchapan, Opechancanough,* and *Catataugh;* and after their decease to his sisters. First to the eldest sister, then to the rest: and after them to the heires male and female of the eldest sister; but never to the heires of the males. . . .

Roger Williams Discusses Marriage and Divorce Among New England Indians, 1643

· · ·

Single fornication they count no sin, but after Mariage (which they solemnize by consent of Parents and publique approbation publiquely) then they count it hainous for either of them to be false. . . .

In this case the wronged party may put away or keepe the party offending: commonly, if the Woman be false, the offended Husband will be solemnly revenged upon the offendor, before many witnesses, by many blowes and wounds, and if it be to Death, yet the guilty resists not, nor is his Death revenged. . . .

They put away (as in Israell) frequently for other occasions beside Adultery, yet I know many Couples that have lived twenty, thirty, forty years together. . . .

God hath planted in the Hearts of the Wildest of the sonnes of Men, an High and Honourable esteeme of the Mariage bed, insomuch that they universally submit

---

Roger Williams, *A Key into the Language of America,* ed. John J. Teunissen and Evelyn J. Hinz (Detroit: Wayne State University Press, 1973; originally published London: Gregory Dexter, 1643), pp. 205, 208.

unto it, and hold the Violation of that Bed, Abominable, and accordingly reape the Fruit thereof in the abundant increase of posterity. . . .

Robert Beverley Defends the Morality of Virginia's Native Americans, 1705

The *Indians* have their solemnities of Marriage, and esteem the Vows made at that time, as most sacred and inviolable. Notwithstanding they allow both the Man and the Wife to part upon disagreement; yet so great is the disreputation of a Divorce, that Marry'd people, to avoid the Character of Inconstant and Ungenerous, very rarely let their Quarrels proceed to a Separation. However, when it does so happen, they reckon all the ties of Matrimony dissolv'd, and each hath the liberty of marrying another. But Infidelity is accounted the most unpardonable of all Crimes in either of the Parties, as long as the Contract continues.

In these Separations, the Children go, according to the affection of the Parent, with the one or the other; for Children are not reckon'd a Charge among them, but rather Riches, according to the blessing of the Old Testament; and if they happen to differ about dividing their Children, their method is then, to part them equally, allowing the Man the first choice.

Tho the young *Indian* Women are said to prostitute their bodies for *Wampom* Peak, Runtees, Beads, and other such like fineries; yet I never could find any ground for the accusation, and believe it only to be an unjust scandal upon them. This I know, that if ever they have a Child while they are single, it is such a disgrace to them, that they never after get Husbands. Besides, I must do 'em the justice to say, I never heard of a Child any of them had before Marriage, and the *Indians* themselves disown any such custom; tho they acknowledge at the same time, that the Maidens are entirely at their own disposal, and may manage their persons as they think fit.

Indeed I believe this Story to be an aspersion cast on those innocent Creatures, by reason of the freedom they take in Conversation, which uncharitable Christians interpret as Criminal, upon no other ground, than the guilt of their own Consciences.

The *Indian* Damsels are full of spirit, and from thence are always inspir'd with Mirth and good Humour. They are extreamly given to laugh, which they do with a Grace not to be resisted. The excess of Life and Fire, which they never fail to have, makes them frolicksom, but without any real imputation to their Innocence. However, this is ground enough for the *English,* who are not very nice in distinguishing betwixt guilt, and harmless freedom, to think them Incontinent: Tho it be with as little justice, as the jealous *Spaniards* condemn the liberty us'd by the Women of *France,* which are much more chast than their own Ladies, which they keep under the strictest confinement. . . .

Robert Beverley, *The History and Present State of Virginia, e*d. Louis B. Wright (Chapel Hill: University of North Carolina Press for the Institute of Early American History and Culture, 1949, originally published 1705), pp. 170–171.

2. James Mooney Records Traditional Cherokee Myths, 1900

The Owl Gets Married

A widow with one daughter was always warning the girl that she must be sure to get a good hunter for a husband when she married. The young woman listened and promised to do as her mother advised. At last a suitor came to ask the mother for the girl, but the widow told him that only a good hunter could have her daughter. "I'm just that kind," said the lover, and again asked her to speak for him to the young woman. So the mother went to the girl and told her a young man had come a-courting, and as he said he was a good hunter she advised her daughter to take him. "Just as you say," said the girl. So when he came again the matter was all arranged, and he went to live with the girl.

The next morning he got ready and said he would go out hunting, but before starting he changed his mind and said he would go fishing. He was gone all day and came home late at night, bringing only three small fish, saying that he had had no luck, but would have better success to-morrow. The next morning he started off again to fish and was gone all day, but came home at night with only two worthless spring lizards (*duwĕ′gă*) and the same excuse. Next day he said he would go hunting this time. He was gone again until night, and returned at last with only a handful of scraps that he had found where some hunters had cut up a deer.

By this time the old woman was suspicious. So next morning when he started off again, as he said, to fish, she told her daughter to follow him secretly and see how he set to work. The girl followed through the woods and kept him in sight until he came down to the river, where she saw her husband change to a hooting owl (*uguku′*) and fly over to a pile of driftwood in the water and cry, "*U-gu-ku! hu! hu! u! u!*" She was surprised and very angry and said to herself, "I thought I had married a man, but my husband is only an owl." She watched and saw the owl look into the water for a long time and at last swoop down and bring up in his claws a handful of sand, from which he picked out a crawfish. Then he flew across to the bank, took the form of a man again, and started home with the crawfish. His wife hurried on ahead through the woods and got there before him. When he came in with the crawfish in his hand, she asked him where were all the fish he had caught. He said he had none, because an owl had frightened them all away. "I think you are the owl," said his wife, and drove him out of the house. The owl went into the woods and there he pined away with grief and love until there was no flesh left on any part of his body except his head. . . .

The Man Who Married the Thunder's Sister

In the old times the people used to dance often and all night. Once there was a dance at the old town of Sâkwi′yĭ, on the head of Chattahoochee, and after it was

George Ellison, ed., *James Mooney's History, Myths, and Sacred Formulas of the Cherokees: Containing the Full Texts of* Myths of the Cherokee *(1900) and* The Sacred Formulas of the Cherokees *(1891) as Published by the Bureau of American Ethnology* (Asheville, N.C.: Historical Images, 1992), pp. 291–292, 345–347.

well started two young women with beautiful long hair came in, but no one knew who they were or whence they had come. They danced with one partner and another, and in the morning slipped away before anyone knew that they were gone; but a young warrior had fallen in love with one of the sisters on account of her beautiful hair, and after the manner of the Cherokee had already asked her through an old man if she would marry him and let him live with her. To this the young woman had replied that her brother at home must first be consulted, and they promised to return for the next dance seven days later with an answer, but in the meantime if the young man really loved her he must prove his constancy by a rigid fast until then. The eager lover readily agreed and impatiently counted the days.

In seven nights there was another dance. The young warrior was on hand early, and later in the evening the two sisters appeared as suddenly as before. They told him their brother was willing, and after the dance they would conduct the young man to their home, but warned him that if he told anyone where he went or what he saw he would surely die.

He danced with them again and about daylight the three came away just before the dance closed, so as to avoid being followed, and started off together. The women led the way along a trail through the woods, which the young man had never noticed before, until they came to a small creek, where, without hesitating, they stepped into the water. The young man paused in surprise on the bank and thought to himself, "They are walking in the water; I don't want to do that." The women knew his thoughts just as though he had spoken and turned and said to him, "This is not water; this is the road to our house." He still hesitated, but they urged him on until he stepped into the water and found it was only soft grass that made a fine level trail.

They went on until the trail came to a large stream which he knew for Tallulah river. The women plunged boldly in, but again the warrior hesitated on the bank, thinking to himself, "That water is very deep and will drown me; I can't go on." They knew his thoughts and turned and said, "This is no water, but the main trail that goes past our house, which is now close by." He stepped in, and instead of water there was tall waving grass that closed above his head as he followed them.

They went only a short distance and came to a rock cave close under Ugûñ'yĭ (Tallulah falls). The women entered, while the warrior stopped at the mouth; but they said, "This is our house; come in and our brother will soon be home; he is coming now." They heard low thunder in the distance. He went inside and stood up close to the entrance. Then the women took off their long hair and hung it up on a rock, and both their heads were as smooth as a pumpkin. The man thought, "It is not hair at all," and he was more frightened than ever.

The younger woman, the one he was about to marry, then sat down and told him to take a seat beside her. He looked, and it was a large turtle, which raised itself up and stretched out its claws as if angry at being disturbed. The young man said it was a turtle, and refused to sit down, but the woman insisted that it was a seat. Then there was a louder roll of thunder and the woman said, "Now our brother is nearly home." While they urged and he still refused to come nearer or sit down, suddenly there was a great thunder clap just behind him, and turning quickly he saw a man standing in the doorway of the cave.

"This is my brother," said the woman, and he came in and sat down upon the turtle, which again rose up and stretched out its claws. The young warrior still refused to come in. The brother then said that he was just about to start to a council, and invited the young man to go with him. The hunter said he was willing to go if only he had a horse; so the young woman was told to bring one. She went out and soon came back leading a great uktena snake, that curled and twisted along the whole length of the cave. Some people say this was a white uktena and that the brother himself rode a red one. The hunter was terribly frightened, and said "That is a snake; I can't ride that." The others insisted that it was no snake, but their riding horse. The brother grew impatient and said to the woman, "He may like it better if you bring him a saddle, and some bracelets for his wrists and arms." So they went out again and brought in a saddle and some arm bands, and the saddle was another turtle, which they fastened on the uktena's back, and the bracelets were living slimy snakes, which they got ready to twist around the hunter's wrists.

He was almost dead with fear, and said, "What kind of horrible place is this? I can never stay here to live with snakes and creeping things." The brother got very angry and called him a coward, and then it was as if lightening flashed from his eyes and struck the young man, and a terrible crash of thunder stretched him senseless.

When at last he came to himself again he was standing with his feet in the water and both hands grasping a laurel bush that grew out from the bank, and there was no trace of the cave or the Thunder People, but he was alone in the forest. He made his way out and finally reached his own settlement, but found then that he had been gone so very long that all the people had thought him dead, although to him it seemed only the day after the dance. His friends questioned him closely, and, forgetting the warning, he told the story; but in seven days he died, for no one can come back from the underworld and tell it and live.

3. Plymouth Colony Requires All Persons to Live in Families, 1669

Whereas great inconvenience hath arisen by single persons in the Colony being for themselves and not betaking themselves to live in well governed families, it is enacted by the Court that henceforth no single person be suffered to live of himself or in any family but such as the selectmen of the town shall approve of. And if any person or persons shall refuse or neglect to attend such order as shall be given them by the selectmen, that such person or persons shall be summoned to the Court to be proceeded with as the matter shall require.

William Brigham, ed., *The Compact with the Charter and Laws of the Colony of New Plymouth* (Boston, 1836), p. 156. This document can also be found in Robert Bremner, ed. *Children and Youth in America,* (Cambridge, Mass.: Harvard University Press, 1970), I: p. 49.

4. Puritan Minister Cotton Mather Describes "a Family Well-Ordered," 1699

As the Great God, who at the Beginning said, Let Us make man after our Image, hath made man a Sociable Creature, so it is evident, That Families are the Nurseries of all Societies; and the First Combinations of mankind. Well-ordered Families naturally produce a Good Order in other Societies. When Families are under an Ill Discipline, all other Societies being therefore Ill Disciplined, will feel that Error in the First Concoction. To Serve the Families of our Neighborhood, will be a Service to all our Interests. Every serious Christian is concerned, That he may be Serviceable in the World; And many a serious Christian is concerned, because he sees himself to be furnished with no more Opportunities to be Serviceable. But art thou not a Member of some Family? If that Family may by thy means, O Christian, become a Well-regulated Family, in that point thou wilt become Serviceable; I had almost said, Incomprehensibly Serviceable. . . . Saies the Lord, He will Command his Children, and They shall keep the way of the Lord. It seems, If every one that is Owner of a Family, would faithfully Command, and manage those that belong unto him, thro' the Blessing of God, they would generally Keep His Way, and His Law.

5. Slaves Escape in Search of Family Members, 1750s–1760s

October 26, 1758

Philadelphia, October 24, 1758.

Run away, on the 21st Instant, from Robert Wakely, of this City, a Negro Woman, named Anne, about 18 or 20 Years of Age, is short and well set, and had on a blue Jacket and Petticoat, Ozenbrigs Apron, and an old Cap, but no Shoes or Stockings. Also run away, at the same Time, a Negroe Man, named Frank, belonging to Alexander Collay, of Whitemarsh, about 30 or 35 Years of Age, is a slender middle sixed Fellow, and had on a new Wool Hat, Bearskin light coloured Coat, a Snuff coloured Jacket, without Sleeves, a striped Shirt, Leather Breeches, blue Stockings and good Shoes. They are Man and Wife, and supposed to be gone together. Whoever takes up said Negroes, and brings them to either of the Subscribers, shall have Fifty Shillings Reward for both, or if put into the next Goal where taken up Forty Shillings, paid by

Robert Wakely, or Alexander Collay.

Cotton Mather, *A Family Well-Ordered: Or, An Essay to Render Parents and Children Happy in One Another. Handling Two Very Important Cases. I. What are the Duties to be done by Pious Parents, for the promoting of Piety in their Children. II. What are the Duties that must be paid by Children to their Parents, that they may obtain the Blessings of the Dutiful* (Boston: B. Green and J. Allen, 1699), pp. 3–4, 6.

Billy G. Smith and Richard Wojtowicz, eds., *Blacks Who Stole Themselves: Advertisements for Runaways in the* Pennsylvania Gazette, *1729–1790* (Philadelphia: University of Pennsylvania Press, 1989), pp. 44, 50, 78, 84–85.

May 21, 1761

FIVE POUNDS Reward.

Run away from the Subscribers, living at Little-Elk, Caecil County, Maryland, a Servant Woman named Margaret Sliter (but probably will change her Name) about 28 Years old, fresh coloured, darkish brown Hair, born in England; had on when she ran away, two Bed-Gowns, one blue and white, the other dark Ground, both Callicoe, new Linsey Petticoat, and one of coarse Tow Cloth, new blue worsted Stockings, with white Clocks, good Shoes, two striped Linen Handkerchiefs, and one Silk one changing Colour, five Yards of about 700 Linen; and has stolen some Mens white Shirts.

Also a Negroe Man, named Charles, a lusty able Fellow, about 29 Years of Age, pitted with the Small-Pox, speaks good English, talks fast, is apt to get drunk, and pretends to be married to the aforesaid Margaret Sliter; had on when he ran away, a Pair of Thickset Breeches, a Pair of blue Yarn Stockings, old Shoes, with round Steel Buckles, a light coloured Jacket, an old brown Body-coat, a great Coat of a greyish Colour, and has a Pair of Breeches of the same (the great Coat has Metal Buttons on) some coarse Shirts, and one fine one, but may have more, two Pair of Trowsers, and two Pair of brown Yarn Stockings. Stole one white Gown of about 1200 Linen, one red and white striped Silk Handkerchief, some Womens Caps, a Ribbon, and a small Gun: Likewise a white Horse of about twelve Years old, branded on the near Shoulder R. and a bay Mare five Years old, bob tailed, some of her Feet white, a white Spot in her Face, a Man's Saddle with blue Housing, a Woman's old Saddle, the Seat of which is brownish, with Leather Skirts. Whoever takes up and secures said Woman and Negroe, with the Horse and Mare, and other Things, shall have the abovementioned Reward of Five Pounds, and all reasonable Charges, or Fifty Shillings for either the Woman or Negroe, and Fifteen Shillings for the Horse or Mare, with reasonable Charges, paid by

David Elder, Ann Holy.

N.B. The Negroe had two Felt Hats with him.

August 1, 1765

Lancaster, July 23, 1765.

Was committed to my Custody, on the 22d Day of this instant July, the following Negroes, viz. a Negroe Man, named Jack, alias Tobias, and a Negroe Woman, Named Jane, Wife to the said Jack, alias Tobias, and her two Children, a Boy, five Years old, or thereabouts, and a Girl about four Years old. The Man is about Thirty four Years of Age, and the Woman about Thirty; they have sundry good Clothes with them; they say they belong to James Campbell, in Conegocheague, near Fort Loudoun. The said Campbell is hereby desired to come and pay the Charges, and take them away, or they will be sold for the same, in four Weeks from this Day, by me

Matthias Buch, Goaler.

November 6, 1766

Run away, on the 7th of September, from the Subscriber, living in Baltimore Town, a Negroe Girl, named Hagar, about 14 Years of Age, of a brownish Complexion, has remarkable long Fingers and Toes, and a Scar under one of her Breasts, supposed to be got by Whipping: Had on, when she went away, an Ozenbrigs Shift and Petticoat, very much patched, and may now be very ragged, an Iron Collar about her Neck, which it is probable she may have got off, as it was very poorly rivetted; she is supposed to be harboured in some Negroe Quarter, as her Father and Mother encourage her in these Elopements, under a Pretence that she is ill used at home. Whoever takes up said Girl, and brings her to me, shall have, if taken ten Miles from home, Twenty Shillings Reward, if 20 Miles Forty Shillings, if further Three Pounds, and if out of the Province Five Pounds, paid by

William Payne.

N.B. All Persons are forbid to harbour the said Girl, as they shall answer the contrary at their Peril.

November 13, 1766

Somerset County, Maryland, October 19, 1766.

Run away, about the 16th of June last, from the Subscriber, living at Princess Ann Town, in Somerset County, Maryland, a Mulattoe Wench, named Ibbe, about 19 Years of Age, very fat and clumsy, with large Cheeks, short Nose, and Holes in her Ears; her Dress uncertain, as she had several Changes with her. She has been seen at Indian River with a free Negroe, pretended to be his Wife, and called herself Sabrah Johnson. Whoever takes up said Mulattoe, and secures her, so as her Master may have her again, shall have Five Pounds Reward, and reasonable Charges, paid by Captain George Noarth, in Philadelphia, or the Subscriber.

Arnold Elzey.

 E S S A Y S

The paucity of written sources on Native Americans—and the ethnocentrism of the Europeans who authored those sources—explains why, until recently, few historians have attempted to sketch more than a rough outline of Native family life. In the first essay, an excerpt from University of North Carolina Indian scholar Theda Perdue's 1998 book, *Cherokee Women*, Perdue weaves together accounts of travelers, traders, and missionaries to the seventeenth- and eighteenth-century American Southeast to depict the matrilineal kinship system of the Cherokees. Perdue's essay also suggests one reason that European observers were so unwilling—perhaps even unable—to understand Native family life: it was organized along principles that were diametrically opposed to the ideal of male authority that European newcomers brought to America.

The second essay uses personal letters to show that official pronouncements of patriarchy coexisted with affectionate, even passionate, relationships between husbands and wives in colonial America. Connecticut College historian Lisa Wilson's examination of colonial New England men's private writings suggests that prescriptive literature did not necessarily describe actual practices. Yet her discussion of court records reveals that issues of power remained central to colonial Americans' ideas about manhood, womanhood, and marriage.

The final essay, by demographer Allan Kulikoff of Northern Illinois University, uses plantation records to describe the early stages of family formation among African and African American slaves in eighteenth-century Maryland. Borrowing from anthropologists, Kulikoff distinguishes between families—persons related by blood or marriage—and households—persons sharing a residence. Like Perdue, he also suggests the possibility of multiple family forms (including polygamy) and inquires into the reasons for and the ramifications of matrifocal family life.

Matrilineal Kinship Among the Cherokee Indians in the American Southeast

THEDA PERDUE

[The native inhabitants of the American Southeast] defined themselves as a distinct people in ways that did not always make sense to European observers. Cherokees called themselves Ani-Yun Wiya, the Real People, which distinguished them from others with whom they had contact, but the bonds that held them together were obscure. Living in scattered villages separated by rugged terrain, Cherokees spoke several dialects of a common language, but no clear boundaries demarcated their territory and no political authority delineated citizenship. Only kinship seems to have bound Cherokees together in the early eighteenth century. Unlike the civic duties of European citizenries, the prerogatives and responsibilities of kinship extended to women as well as men. Furthermore, the Cherokees traced kinship solely through women. This circumstance gave women considerable prestige, and the all-encompassing nature of the kinship system secured for them a position of power.

Unfortunately, few early European observers managed to grasp the principle of matrilineal descent. In his otherwise perceptive account of Cherokee culture, J. P. Evans admitted that he simply could not comprehend "their mode of calculating clan kin" because "it appeared so incongruous." . . . Only the combination of primary source material and modern anthropological theory have enabled us to understand matrilineality and the complexity of Native American kinship. In aboriginal Cherokee society, matters of kinship affected social interaction, demography, internal order, and foreign policy, and the status of women derived in part from their place in the kinship system.

The basic unit of kinship in Cherokee society was the clan. All members of a clan supposedly descended from the same individual, and although the exact connection had long been forgotten, according to Evans, "this relationship seems to be as binding as the ties of consanguinity." Although there may have been other clans in earlier times, the Cherokees of the historic era had seven clans: *Aniwahiya* or Wolf; *Anikawi* or Deer; *Anidjiskwa* or Bird; *Aniwodi* or Paint; *Anisahoni,* perhaps

Theda Perdue, *Cherokee Women: Gender and Culture Change, 1700–1835* (Lincoln: University of Nebraska Press, 1998), pp. 41–51, 54–59. Reprinted by permission of the University of Nebraska Press. © 1998 by the University of Nebraska Press.

meaning Blue; *Anigotigewi,* perhaps Wild Potato; and *Anigilohi,* perhaps Twister. According to the principle of matrilineal descent, people belonged to the clan of their mother: their only relatives were those who could be traced through her. Blood relatives included siblings, the maternal grandmother (mother's mother), maternal uncles (mother's brothers), and maternal aunts (mother's sisters). The children of mothers' sisters were kin, but those of mother's brothers were not. Children were not blood relatives of their father or grandfather; a father was not related to his children by blood.

An entire clan did not live together, of course, but the stationary members of a household belonged to the same clan. A matrilineage, or subdivision of the clan descending from a particular known individual, formed the core of a typical Cherokee household. . . .

Generally, Cherokee households were quite large. [Englishman John] Norton described a multigenerational household he visited as "a little village." . . . A number of buildings including summer houses, winter houses, menstrual huts, corn cribs, and various storage buildings accommodated these people. Summer houses, where the family slept in the appropriate season, were large rectangular structures with gable roofs and clapboard sides. The size of the round winter houses, or hot houses, depended on the size of the family, with some as large as thirty feet in diameter and fifteen feet high. Constructed of wattle and daub, hot houses had no windows, no chimney, and only a small deerskin-draped opening for a door. Berths lined the walls, and a fire, which the women maintained, smoldered throughout the day to keep warm all those who had no reason to be out of doors.

The only permanent members of a household were the women. Husbands were outsiders; that is, they were not kinsmen. When a man married, he moved from the household of his mother to that of his wife. A man's move to his bride's residence did not mean that he became a part of her clan and lineage; in Alexander Longe's words, "Their wives is nothing akin to them." . . .

The Cherokees regarded marriage as a family affair. Both parties had to obtain the consent of relatives and while kinsmen sometimes strongly encouraged young people to marry, kin did not normally force mates on them against their will. . . .

Kin relationships played an important role in selection of marriage partners. Cherokees did not consider clan members to be appropriate mates. Longe reported that Cherokee men would "in no wise marry with a woman of their own family counting them their proper sisters." A person generally married into the clan of his or her grandfather, and such a marriage reflected a certain relationship between two clans. Love formulas, which rank second only to medicinal formulas in number, had phrases such as "I belong to the —————— clan, that one alone which was allotted into for you." In the marriage ceremony . . . the bride's male relatives undressed the groom and clothed him in new garments, confirming their relationship to him. When a spouse died, the survivor usually took as a new mate a close relative of the deceased.

Sometimes, a man did not wait for his wife to die in order to marry one of her female relatives. No evidence for multiple husbands exists (although some women changed husbands frequently), but the marriage of a man to more than one woman was relatively common. Practicality encouraged men to marry women of the same lineage, often sisters. That way, he only had to reside in one household rather than divide his time between the lineages of unrelated wives. Although early European observers decried polygamy and suggested that the practice "renders the women contemptible in the men's eyes and deprives them of all influence," some modern anthropologists have postulated that in societies where sororal polygamy is common, women enjoy a high degree of personal autonomy and suffer little from male domination or sexual competition.

In the event of divorce, the husband left his wife's house and returned to the household of his mother or sister. . . . Children always remained with their mothers and kinsmen rather than going with fathers to whom they were not related. John Lawson observed the consequences of marital separation among the matrilineal tribes of coastal North Carolina: "The Children always fall to the Women's Lot; for it often happens, that two *Indians* that have liv'd together, as Man and Wife, in which Time they have had several Children; if they part and another Man possess her, all the Children go along with the Mother and none with the Father."

The men who had a permanent connection to the household were the male members of the lineage, the brothers and sons of the female members. Whether the women of a household or their brothers were dominant on the domestic scene is uncertain. Most likely, few contests for hegemony arose. Brothers normally lived not with their sisters but with their own wives, and so opportunities for conflict were rare. . . . As a general rule even unmarried brothers and uncles spent little time in the household. They were either in the hunting grounds, at war, or in the council house.

Although brothers may occasionally have challenged the domestic authority of their sisters or uncles their nieces, men apparently never tried to dominate their wives. The eighteenth-century trader Alexander Longe wrote: "I have this to say that the women rules the roost and wears the breeches and sometimes will beat their husbands within an inch of their lives." According to Longe, who was given to hyperbole, husbands did not defend themselves against their wives' wrath: "The man will not resist their power if the woman was to beat his brains out; for when she has beat one side like a stalk fish, he will turn the other side to her and beat until she is weary. Sometimes they beat their husbands to that height that they kill them outright." . . .

In Cherokee society, home and hearth were part of a woman's domain. Whatever time she could spare from the fields was spent at the homestead with other women. Men probably felt somewhat uncomfortable there. If they were married, the lineage with whom they lived belonged to a clan different from theirs. If they were unmarried and lived with their own lineage, they had to contend with the presence of their sisters' husbands, who were men of another clan. This sort of intimacy between male members of different clans was awkward and, in the case of conflict between clans, disruptive. Consequently, a male presence in a household was irregular. The Cherokees, in fact, referred to the moon as male because it "travels by night" like men who paid only nocturnal visits to their wives' houses. While men did make appearances at the households of their wives and of their own lineages, they could be found most frequently at a communal site in the company of other men. Single men often preferred to sleep in the council house rather than in the houses of their mothers and sisters. But the control exercised by women over domestic matters did not stem merely from male abdication of authority. Matrilineality placed women in a unique position: they alone could convey the kinship ties essential to a Cherokee's existence.

Members of each of the seven matrilineal clans were dispersed throughout Cherokee territory, and every town usually had representatives of all clans. Although an individual might be personally unknown in a town, he or she always found a warm welcome from clan kin. [Trader James] Adair noted: "I have observed with much inward satisfaction the community of goods that prevailed among them, . . . especially with those of their own tribe [clan]. . . . When Indians are travelling in their own country, they enquire for a house of their own tribe; and if there be any, they go to it, and are kindly received, though they never saw the persons before—they eat, drink, and regale themselves, as at their own tables." The Cherokees based distinctions within clans on generation and gender and applied the same familial names to all those of roughly the same age and sex; wherever Cherokees traveled, therefore, they encountered parents and grandparents, brothers and sisters.

Clan members also cared for children whose parents had died. Longe observed that "if the mother dies before the child has left off sucking, any of the woman's relations that gives milk will take the child and give it to suck and they will make no distinction betwixt that child and their own proper children." . . . Clan members accepted children whose natural mothers had died because "mother" was a social rather than a strictly biological role. Children, in fact, had many "mothers," maternal aunts and other female clan members of their biological mother's generation. The same rules of behavior governed their interactions with all their "mothers."

Kin relationships determined how all Cherokees behaved toward one another. . . . Parents and children treated each other with respect, as did aunts or uncles and nieces or nephews, because the latter stood in the same social relationship as parents and children. Siblings and cousins were on familiar terms and could joke with and tease one another. People of the grandparent-grandchild relationship could be on terms of physical familiarity ranging from affection to sexual intercourse. This, of course, does not mean that elderly Cherokees had sexual relations with their grandchildren, but that the preferred mate was a person from grandfather's clan. Kinship terms and the relationship they entailed extended beyond close relatives to all members of one's clan. Consequently, the kind of relationship a person had with another depended on what they called each other. Evans reported: "An Indian can tell you without hesitating what degree of relationship exists between himself and any other individual of the same clan you may see proper to point out." Similarly, the clans of other people determined a person's behavior toward them: father's clan had to be respected, whereas sexual familiarity was permissible with grandfather's clan. . . .

The absence of kinship ties was a distinct liability in Cherokee society. First of all, people were unsure of how to behave toward someone who had no place in the kinship system. Consequently, the Cherokees once concluded a peace treaty with the Senecas by Cherokee women choosing Senecas for uncles and brothers. The Cherokees could interact peacefully with their old enemies only if they incorporated the outsiders into their kinship system. . . . In the event of illness, only a blood relative could summon the doctor; husbands and wives, being of separate clans, could not treat each other nor could a spouse send for the medicine man. . . . If a person died, the responsibility for burial rested with kinsmen. According to Adair, the Cherokees buried clan members together, and if a person died away from home, relatives collected the remains and properly interred them. Other clans played no role even in mourning the dead. . . .

The Cherokees may have regarded an individual without kin ties as something less than a person. Hostility to early traders probably stemmed from the Europeans' lack of relatives and place in the social structure. . . . This hostility was neither racially nor politically motivated, because the Cherokees distinguished themselves from others not by skin color or political allegiance but by their membership in a Cherokee clan. Any person, regardless of ancestry or nationality, who was born or adopted into one of the seven clans was a Cherokee; any person who did not belong to a Cherokee clan was not a member of the tribe and was liable to be killed almost at whim. Adair reported that "sometimes the Indians devote every one they meet in certain woods or paths, to be killed there, except their own people; this occasioned the cowardly Cherokee in the year 1753, to kill two white men on the Chikkasah warpath . . . for when they have not the fear of offending, they will shed innocent blood." The Cherokees had "fear of offending" fellow Cherokees because their relatives offered protection from and exacted vengeance for acts of violence.

By far the most important role that the matrilineal clan played was as the arbiter of justice. Cherokee jurisprudence was simple, and enforcement was swift and certain. An anonymous observer explained: "Retaliation is the principle of their criminal code. When an individual is killed, a relative of the deceased kills the murderer." The principle applied to lesser crimes as well. John Pridgett told [John Howard] Payne that "if in fighting one bruised the other, the same kind of bruise was made in his flesh. If one scratched the other, he was scratched in a similar manner. If one gouged the other's eye, his eye was gouged; and one knocked out a tooth, one of his teeth was knocked out &c." According to Adair the Cherokees inculcated the principle of retaliation in the very young: "A little boy shooting birds in the high and thick cornfields, unfortunately chanced slightly to wound another with his childish arrow; the young vindictive fox, was excited by custom to watch his ways with utmost earnestness, till the wound was returned in as equal a manner as could be expected. Then, 'all was straight,' according to their phrase."

If one Cherokee killed another, the clan kin of the slain person had the responsibility for avenging the death. Death upset the cosmic balance, and only the death of the person responsible or of a person from that same clan could restore order. When the clan of the victim had exacted vengeance, both clans involved considered the matter settled because harmony had been restored. Retaliation did not continue and consequently feuds between clans did not erupt. The clan of the offending party was, in fact, as disturbed by the disruption of order as was the clan of the victim. When a death was avenged, "all things were considered straight": order was restored.

Normally, the brother or nearest male relative of the deceased sought vengeance, but sometimes women may have participated in retaliation. One of John Howard Payne's informants claimed that the death of Doublehead, which other evidence indicates resulted from unscrupulous land deals, was an act of vengeance:

> Doublehead had beaten his wife cruelly when she was with child; and the poor woman died in consequence. The revenge against murder now became in the Indian's conscience, imperative. The wife of Doublehead was the sister of the wife of [James] Vann. Vann's wife desired with her own hand to obtain atonement for her sister's death. Vann acquiesced; and he and a large party of friends set away with his wife upon this mission of blood. . . .

The law of blood extended to anyone considered responsible for the accidental death of another. One observer wrote: "It is no excuse of a homicide, that it is accidental. A husband by mischance killed his wife with a ball that glanced obliquely from a tree; a brother of the wife thought it his duty to shoot the husband in retaliation." . . .

Some confusion exists over what happened when a person killed a fellow clan member. This was the most horrible of all crimes, almost unthinkable and consequently very rare. Adair suggested: "If indeed the murder be committed by a kinsman, the eldest can redeem: however, if the circumstances attending the fact be peculiar and shocking to nature, the murderer is condemned to die the death of a sinner [without anyone to mourn him]." Elias Boudinot, the nineteenth-century editor of the *Cherokee Phoenix,* disagreed and insisted that no man was entitled to kill a relative and so those responsible for killing kin suffered no penalty. The latter is probably accurate, but it is also likely that such murderers were ostracized or even exiled. Shoe Boots, for example, who became prominent in the nineteenth century, lived a number of years among northern Indians after he killed a kinsman.

Clans that were not involved in a fatal incident had nothing to do with it. No relationship, however close, other than that of clan kinship entailed or even permitted retaliation. Matrilineality and clan vengeance, for example, prohibited a child's revenge on behalf of a father or a father for his child: "A son therefore is not allowed to revenge the murder of a father, though he is required to punish that of a mother, a sister, or a brother." Fathers and children, of course, were not members of the same clan and so any retaliation would not be "blood" vengeance. The principle of clan vengeance also meant that no warriors, chiefs, priests, or any other recognized leaders of the community had anything to do with crime. The responsibilities that today we associate with police forces and courts rested with families. No one outside the family, however respected, had anything to do with providing protection or dispensing justice. . . .

Admission to a Cherokee clan derived from birth or adoption, and both depended on women. For this reason, the Cherokees included women in many activities, such as the Scalp Dance, that in terms of the rigid construction of gender seem appropriate only for men. Motherhood was not a trite sentimentality to Cherokees. Cherokee women invoked motherhood as the source of their power and used their status as mothers to make public appeals. In 1768 Cherokee warriors negotiating with Iroquoian peoples at Johnson Hall in New York presented a wampum belt, used to symbolize and record agreements, sent by Cherokee women to Iroquois women. Oconostota, a Cherokee war chief who was urging peace, relayed the women's message: "We know that they will hear us for it is they who undergo the pains of Childbirth and produce Men. Surely therefore they must feel Mothers pains for those killed in War, and be desirous to prevent it." Mothers also conveyed Cherokee identity; no one could be a Cherokee unless he or she had a Cherokee mother. When Attakullakulla, a distinguished Cherokee headman, appeared before the South Carolina Governor's Council, he demanded to know why no women were in attendance. After all, he pointed out to the governor, "White Men as well as the Red were born of Women." Women sat in Cherokee council meetings, and their presence led Timberlake to conclude that "the story of the Amazons [was] not so great a fable as we imagined, many of the Indian women being as famous in war, as powerful in the council."

The nature of Cherokee government made participation by women possible. . . . As mothers, women often had considerable influence on the debate: on occasion, they discouraged warriors from pursuing an enemy who had taken children hostage, or they prodded reluctant warriors into taking action.

Until late in the eighteenth century, the Cherokees had no national council: "Each town is independent of another. Their own friendly compact continues the union." The "friendly compact," of course, was kinship, but the Cherokees also found unity in an overarching principle that governed their behavior in both domestic and foreign affairs. Cherokees believed that human beings had the responsibility for maintaining cosmic order by respecting categories and maintaining boundaries. The Cherokee obsession with order and balance, or "harmony," as one anthropologist has called the fundamental ethic governing their behavior, extended to individual conduct as well as to relationships within the nation and with other peoples. A clan collectively avenged the deaths of members to restore balance, but Cherokees also expected each person to follow the rules and to govern his or her own behavior carefully. The result was considerable individual autonomy, particularly in terms of personal relationships.

Autonomy translated into sexual freedom for Cherokee women because no one controlled their sexuality. Unmarried women engaged in sex with whomever they wished as long as they did not violate incest taboos against intercourse with members of their own clans or the clans of their fathers. Married women also enjoyed considerable latitude. Their behavior provoked James Adair to conclude that "the Cherokee are an exception to all civilized or savage nations in having no laws against adultery; they have been a considerable while under a petticoat-government, and allow their women full liberty to plant their brows with horns as oft as they please, without fear of punishment." If the husband of an unfaithful wife took any action at all, he usually resorted to conjury.

Formulas existed to fix the affections of a wife who had a wandering eye, and priests had several methods, including colored beads and divining crystals, to determine whether she had been unfaithful. If the wife proved guilty and the husband desired revenge, the priest took some dead flies in his hand. If one came to life upon his opening the hand, it would burrow its way into the body of the wife and bring her a painful death on the seventh day. Payne, who recorded this practice, commented: "Whether the fly received any assistance from the husband or the priest is not reported."

The most acceptable course of action for the husband of a wayward wife, however, was to ignore the infidelity and, if he chose, take another wife. Louis-Philippe observed: "If a Cherokee's woman sleeps with another man, all he does is send her away without a word to the man, considering it beneath his dignity to quarrel over a woman." According to Norton, in the case of a wife's adultery, "the husband is even disgraced in the opinion of his friends if he seeks to take satisfaction in any other way, than that of getting another wife." . . .

Although female infidelity rarely perturbed men, husbands who strayed caused considerable disharmony in the community. Women whose husbands abandoned them for other women were "unreconcilable" according to Longe, who suggested that women had more of a proprietary interest in men than men had in women. He described a pattern of behavior that we are more accustomed to find in reverse in modern America: "Sometimes the young maids comes and steals away women's husbands. Then the wife, the first time she meets her, there is a bloody battle about it. Sometimes one gets the victory and sometimes the other. They that gets the upper-hand carried the husband. If these two women were to live a thousand years in the same town, nay, next door, they never will have any communication together, nor so much as speak the one to the other." Since such conflicts probably drew in family members as well, the results could be terribly disruptive. Such difficulties, however, never became the town's concern; they remained personal and familial.

Consequently, the Cherokees normally resolved sexual rivalries through divorce and remarriage. Louis-Philippe claimed that an Indian man who had several wives "takes them on and turns them away like servants, and similarly they leave him when it suits them to do so." Although many Cherokee marriages endured a lifetime, some ended in less than a fortnight, and [Lieutenant Henry] Timberlake maintained that a few Cherokees changed spouses three or four times a year. Adair placed the blame for the instability of Cherokee marriages squarely on the women: "Their marriages are ill observed, and of short continuance; like the Amazons, they divorce their fighting bed-fellows at their pleasure, and fail not to execute their authority, when their fancy directs them to a more agreeable choice." The Cherokees attached no stigma to those who dissolved their marriages. When Alexander Longe inquired about the reason for the divorce of a Cherokee couple, a priest told him "that they had better be asunder than together if they do not love one another but live for strife and confusion." In a similar vein, an Indian attempted to explain his people's philosophy of marriage to Adair: "My Indian friend said, as marriage should beget joy and happiness, instead of pain and misery, if a couple married blindfold, and could not love one another afterwards, it was a crime to continue together, and a virtue to part and make a happier choice." . . .

. . . Clans enabled Cherokees to place themselves in the world and establish appropriate relationships with the rest of the cosmos. Cherokees grounded their sense of self in the clan, and individual identity melded into clan affiliation. Women and men had equal claim on clan privileges, but both understood that women were the source of clan membership. Only those who belonged to Cherokee clans—regardless of language, residence, or even race—were Cherokee; only those who had Cherokee mothers were the Ani-Yun Wiya, the Real People.

Patriarchy and Marriage in Colonial New England

LISA WILSON

Benjamin Wadsworth, in his 1712 sermon *The Well-Ordered Family,* concluded "the Husband is ever to be esteem'd the Superior, the Head, and to be reverenc'd and obey'd as such." So powerful are such declarations to modern sensibilities that other, equally common colonial New England representations of marriage as a

---

Lisa Wilson, "A Marriage 'Well-Ordered': Love, Power, and Partnership in Colonial New England," in Laura McCall and Donald Yacovone, eds., *A Shared Experience: Men, Women, and the History of Gender* (New York: New York University Press, 1998), pp. 78–92. Copyright © 1998. Reprinted by permission of New York University Press.

partnership seem impossibly hypocritical. Men who recorded their feelings, however, felt that female subordination and affection were essential and complementary
parts of a successful marriage. In both the seventeenth and eighteenth centuries, a
husband was part of an interdependent family system that required mutual support
to function successfully. Cooperation, not simply coercion, kept a family "well-
ordered." Although the words came more freely by the end of the colonial period,
the tender language of love marked the writings of men in both centuries. For these
men, maintaining the delicate balance between household head and loving husband
was the key to domestic bliss as well as social acceptance.

Partnership in marriage was both an ideal and a reality in colonial New England.
This is not to suggest that men and women were equal. Rather, both had a stake in
their household and their children. Often their daily routines and duties were different, but both worked toward common goals. Men counted on their wives not only
to handle their own responsibilities, but to assist the men in their duties if needed.
In a happy union, the mutual support of marriage and the well being of the family
were central.

John Winthrop, like many husbands, described his third wife, Margaret, as his
"yokefellowe." G. Selleck Silliman and his wife, Mary, referred to each other in their
correspondence as "dear partner." In marriage a man entered a partnership that provided support for both husband and wife. In describing his vision of marital bliss to
his betrothed, Silliman pictured them passing "through all the Scenes of this Life
mutually supporting, blessing & assisting Each other in the Ways of Duty." . . . Together, husband and wife shared the joys and sorrows of life. William Dawes, in
defending his new wife to his doubting friend, Stephen Salisbury of Worcester, declared that with her he could "Share Equily in trouble & Afliction As Well As in Joy
& prosperty both is Equall." . . . Like friendly companions, husband and wife chatted
with one another, supported each other, and asked each other's advice. . . .

Silliman, a Fairfield, Connecticut, lawyer and Revolutionary general, consulted
his best friend [his wife] often about decisions great and small. Because of economic
difficulties brought on by his imprisonment during the Revolutionary War, he contemplated leaving public life.

> What shall I do my Love?—My late expensive Absence has cost me a great Deal of
> Mony,—should I again fall into the Enemy's Hands it would hurt me irreparably
> almost,—To reduce myself to a private Character would be my best Means of Safety, as
> the Enemy would make no Efforts after a Private,—[section deleted], were it not for the
> Advice of some great Characters, and for Fear that the People of my own County would
> be disgusted at it, I should most certainly do this,—What shall I do My Dearest? I wish
> I had Your Advice,—I am at a great Loss how to conduct.

. . . A man could gain a rare kind of friend in a successful marriage, one whose
faithfulness and loyalty surpassed all others.

Winthrop wrote to his wife while waiting for the *Arabella* to set sail for New
England. He began, "My Love, My Joy, My Faithful One." He also christened her
"dear heart," "my Most Sweet Heart," and "My Sweet Wife." Likewise, a few months
after signing the Declaration of Independence, William Williams of Lebanon, Connecticut, member of the Continental Congress, addressed his wife, Mary, as "my
Dear Love" and "my dear Child." Reeve called his "lovely Sally" "my Sweet girl"

and "innocent chicken." Silliman, in a letter to his father-in-law with news of his homecoming from the army, sent his love "to that Dear, Beloved Woman, whose uniformly endearing & Vertuous Conduct, deserves all the Tenderness that can possess a human Heart."

These men, despite the patriarchal realities of New England society, loved their wives with great intensity. Williams assured his wife Mary that he loved her as his "own soul." Similarly, Winthrop addressed one of his loving letters to "Mine Own Sweet Self" and often referred to his wife, Margaret, as "more dear to me than all earthly things." He read and reread his wife's letters aboard the *Arabella*. "I am never satisfied with reading, nor can read them without tears; but whether they proceed from joy, sorrow, or desire, or from that consent of affection, which I always hold with thee, I cannot conceive." Walley thanked God before his wedding in 1748 "that I have such abundant Reason to think that we have a sincere & fervent Love to each other." Soon after his marriage, Mather Byles confided to his father: "I enjoy all that full Satisfaction, which results from the tendrest Connexion of humane Life." He claimed to have "no romantic Ideas of visionary, unattainable Bliss: I really possess much more than I thought possible."

Husbands also freely wrote of their passion. The bed was a private place where a couple shared warmth, quiet conversation, and lovemaking. William Henshaw wrote to his wife, Phebe, during his sojourn in the Continental Army, "these Cold Nights I am Sensible of the want of a Bed fellow, I know not how long it will be before I enjoy the satisfaction of having you by my side." Benjamin Bangs, a Harwich, Massachusetts, trader, noted in his diary that his wife tended her sick mother all night with the sad notation, "I sleep alone." Reeve cautioned his beloved Sally to "not abuse my sweet Lips with your savage little teeth." Winthrop often ended his letters to Margaret with phrases like "I kisse my sweet wife," "kiss me my sweet wife," or "with many kisses and embraces." Finally, Silliman assured his lonesome wife that her passionate letters did not make her "a fond Hussey." He thanked her for "being so particular in your Letters the more prolix the better; are You not a married Woman my Dearest, may You not delight your Husband with saying to him just what you please?"

Men spoke most eloquently and passionately about their love for their wives on their wedding anniversaries, at the birth of a child, and when separated by the exigencies of war. An anniversary prompted a tender husband to thank God for his good fortune. When the fear and joy of childbirth loomed, a man again examined his heart. When war threatened his life, he recorded his most intimate thoughts about husbandly love and duty. These events made a man take pause and describe his deepest feelings.

Ezra Stiles, for example, reminisced in his diary in 1775: "This day 1757 I and my Wife were married. She has been a great Blessing to me; may the blessed God continue her a Blessing." The next entry in Stiles's diary acknowledged, "My wife very ill." A husband marked an anniversary when the happiness of his marriage day contrasted with the less happy present. John Tudor observed in 1748: "This day we have been Marred 16 Years, and by the goodness of God to our Family and Us, we have not had one Death in it til Yesterday Died our Negro Man Named Town." Although focusing on God's mercy, Tudor feared the separation that death brought.

Samuel Sewall recorded in 1711: "This being my Marriage-day, and having now liv'd in a married Estate Five and Thirty years," celebrated the event by retreating into his "Closet" for "Meditation and Prayer" and later attending a friend's funeral. The previous week he had lamented the recent deaths of "ancient Friends." His own successful life and marriage made his anniversary a time of solemn thankfulness. The unfortunate Cotton Mather marked his anniversary with the sorrow of impending loss: "When I had been married unto her just sixteen Years, (and as near as I can recollect, on that very Week, sixteen Years, that I was married unto her) God began to take her from me." His wife languished and later died from the complications of a miscarriage.

When husband and wife were apart on an anniversary, written expressions of love replaced private conversation. In September 1746, Ebenezer Parkman lamented the "Foul Weather" and the absence of his wife. Visiting her parents, she left him "dull without my Dear Consort." He reminisced,

> But how Ardent and United were we this Day Nine Year ago! when our Nuptials were Celebrated at Mr. Pierpoints at Boston. The Lord has pleas'd to overlook the many miscarriages and Defects which we have been chargeable with since, especially my own! and make us Mutually Blessings, and Helps to the Kin of God! O how soon the Time will come when there will be neither marrying nor giving in Marriage, but the Saints shall be as the Angels of God!

Silliman also found himself away from home on his wedding anniversary. He wrote to his disappointed wife:

> I am sorry to inform You, that I have no Prospect of keeping our happy Anniversary with You,—I hope You will have a Pleasure in observing it, in the Company of our Dear Sons, & Friends that I expect will be with You Each of whom I hope will think it an Anniversary that deserves Commemoration. My Love & Compliments to them respectively,—I regret the Occasion that keeps me from my Dearest at such a Time,—A Time ever to be observed by me with Delight & Pleasure.

An anniversary was properly shared and celebrated together. Separation left many a disappointed husband to record his private feelings alone.

Among the fortunate few, Tudor enjoyed his "beloved Wife of my Youth" for fifty years. On his anniversary in 1782, he recorded in his diary that "we have lived the whole time very comfortably and at this Day are so." He marked the dear legacies of their long life together: "In our Youthfull Days had Six Children, 3 Sons and 3 Daughters, but our two Eldest Sons died at Sea." His surviving children provided him with "12 Grandsons and 4 Granddaughters, but we have lost by Death 6 Grandsons" and one granddaughter. In fifty years this loving couple had "never, in all that Time, been absent from each other more than 5 Weeks at one time." They marked the day with "an Entertainment for our Children, and their Children, and a lovely Sight and Day we had of it."

Childbirth provided a husband with a fearful reminder of his love for his wife. A man remained strangely removed from the stage of this human drama, although his risk of loss was great. Childbirth was ultimately a female-centered experience; on most occasions, a woman had her friends and midwife, not her husband, by her side. The husband waited anxiously, often close by, listening to his wife's groans, awaiting the outcome. Men, although absent from the actual event, knew about pregnancy, child-birth, and its complications. Left on the periphery, however, a husband felt fragile.

A common hope expressed by both men and women was that a pregnant woman would become a "Living mother of a Living Child." Michael Wigglesworth received the news of his daughter's birth after his wife's thirty hours of hard labor. "After about midnight he [the Lord] sent me the glad tidings of a daughter that an the mother both living." Ebenezer Parkman recorded in his diary that "About 7 o'Clock a.m. a Fourth living Son was born, and my wife liv'd through it and becomes Com-fortable through the tender Mercy and Goodness of God."

Women appreciated only too well that childbirth meant potential death. Hus-bands also feared a wife's death, dreading the possible loss of their dearly beloved. Benjamin Bangs lay in bed with his wife in the spring of 1760. Husband and wife shared the same fears, and both had trouble sleeping.

> [M]y Dearest friend is much Concern'd being in and near a time of Difficulty & Dreamd a Dream that troubl'd Her much I put it off Slightly for fear of Disheartning Her but Directly upon it Dream'd much ye Same my Self of Being Bereft of Her & See-ing my Little motherless Children about me which when I awoke was Cutting to think of.

Many husbands coordinated the assemblage of birth assistants. When Parkman's wife went into labor, he went to get the midwife and the women who would attend her. Confronted with a snowstorm on his mission to "fetch Granny Forbush," the midwife, he found the snow so deep that it was "extraordinary difficult passing." When he found himself floundering in front of a neighbors' house, he enlisted the aid of two men of the house who "rode before me, by which means I succeeded." Local men brought their wives and a load of wood to help with the snowbound birth. Parkman, at another birth, summoned the midwife and other women when his wife "call'd Me up by her extreme pains prevailing upon her and changing into signs of Travail." The women came and stayed "all Day and Night." The following morning "the Women Scattered away to their several Homes" except the midwife, who stayed behind. Late that night he was again "call'd . . . with great earnestness to gather some women together." He "ran on foot," through bitter weather, to as-semble the women. Peter Thatcher realized his wife "was very ill" and sent a neighbor for the midwife. The midwife was attending another birth, and it took two hours for her to arrive. When "shee came shee sent for ye women." The young Samuel Sewall awoke at two in the morning and "perceived my wife ill." He lit a candle and raked the fire. At five, when his in-laws awoke, he informed his mother-in-law of his wife's condition. She "bad[e] me call the Midwife."

With the women assembled, the husband waited and prayed. As Parkman put it, "I resign my Dear Spouse to the infinite Compassions, allsufficiency and soverign pleasure of God and under God to the good Women that are with her, waiting Humbly the Event." Although peripheral, he remained aware of the delivery's progress. The overly sympathetic Michael Wigglesworth suffered mightily:

> The nearnes of my bed to hers made me hear all the nois. her pangs pained my heart, broke my sleep the most off that night, I lay sighing, sweating, praying, almost fainting through weariness before morning. The next day. the spleen much enfeebled me, and setting in with grief took away my strength, my heart was smitten within me, and as sleep departed from myne eyes so my stomack abhorred meat. I was brought very low

and knew not how to pass away another night; For so long as my love lay crying I lay sweating, and groaning.

This was their first child. If childbirth was so painful he pondered, "then how dreadful are the pangs of eternal death."

Sewall stayed with his mother-in-law in the kitchen during one birthing. She had joined his male vigil because "my wife was in great and more than ordinary Extremity, so that she was not able to endure the Chamber." At a previous birth, Sewall and his father-in-law waited in the "great Hall," where they "heard the child cry." The ever-industrious Cotton Mather tried to sleep through his wife's labor so that he could attend to his sabbath business the next day. He awoke "with a Concern upon my Spirit" and felt compelled to pray in his study. "While my Faith was pleading, that the Saviour *who was born of a Woman,* would send His good Angel to releeve my Consort, the People ran to my Study-door with Tidings, *that a Son was born unto mee.*"

With the child born, the women settled down to a repast organized by the grateful husband. Sewall feasted his wife's attendants with "rost Beef and minc'd Pyes, good Cheese and Tarts." The women assisting Parkman's wife finished eating before dark "tho some of them tarry'd in the Evening." Slowly, the women went home either by foot or by horse. Sewall "Went home with the Midwife about 2 o'clock, carrying her Stool, whoes parts were included in a Bagg. Met with the Watch at Mr. Rocks Brew house, who bad us stand, enquired what we were. I told the Woman's occupation, so they bad God bless our labours, and let us pass."

Even for a couple blessed with a strong union, conflicts proved disruptive. Arguments followed gender specific patterns. The worst that a disgruntled wife could do was to challenge a man's authority as family head. If he was cuckolded or beaten, the husband's mental anguish was severe because a wife took aim at his most valued commodity, his reputation. The sullying of his good name would lead to social humiliation. His livelihood, so dependent on personal networks, suffered if an ugly familial conflict became public. When men were challenged, they turned to the familiar rhetoric of male authority. Rather than suffer such humiliation, they tried to reassert their right to rule.

For men, an ideal wife did not disturb the peace of a household. Mather Byles informed his spinster sister, Mary, about the "Peace & Tranquility" of his new wife and home. If only she could be so happy in her marriage, "That your Husband may say of you, as I can of your Sister *Byles,* that he never saw your Brows wrinkled into a disagreeable Frown, or your Lips polluted by a peevish Syllable." Silliman listed the wonderful qualities of his first wife to the father of his second. Among her valued gifts was "a most happy, mild & calm Temper." With such a disposition "she never gave her Husband any Uneasiness by any Excess of her own Temper." He wanted to assure his new father-in-law that he had been happily married and that his new wife, miraculously, compensated him for his loss. On recalling the many merits of his recently deceased wife, Thomas Clap remembered that not "so much as Short Word ever pass between us upon any Occasion whatsoever." If they disagreed "about any lesser matters, we used to Discourse upon it with a Perfect Calmness & Pleasancy." Any expression of temper in a woman was a sign of trouble, and men, if Clap is any indication, diligently sought to avoid confrontation.

An angry wife, however, challenged a husband's right to rule. John Adams of Braintree, Massachusetts, Revolutionary leader and future president of the United States, recorded a "conjugal Spat" between his father and mother which caused such a ruckus that he was forced to leave the room and take "up Tully [Marcus Tullius Cicero, Roman statesman and author] to compose myself." The point of contention was the boarding of a young girl, Judah, in the household. The real issue was that John Adams the elder had made a commitment that increased Susanna Adams's workload but brought little to the family coffers. After heated discussion "My P[apa]. continued cool and pleasant a good while, but had his Temper roused at last, tho he uttered not a rash Word, but resolutely asserted his Right to govern." Mrs. Adams's response was less than deferential.

> My Mamma was determined to know what my P. charged a Week for the Girls Board. P. said he had not determined what to charge but would have her say what it was worth. She absolutely refused to say. But "I will know if I live and breath. I can read yet. Why dont you tell me, what you charge? You do it on purpose to teaze me. You are mighty arch this morning. I wont have all the Towns Poor brought here, stark naked, for me to clothe for nothing. I wont be a slave to other folks folk for nothing."—And after the 2 Girls cryed.—"I must not speak a Word [to] your Girls, Wenches, Drabbs. I'le kick both their fathers, presently. [You] want to put your Girls over me, to make me a slave to your Wenches."

Asserting his right to rule did little to diffuse the situation. According to John Adams the younger, this was the normal course of their disagreements—she raged and he remained cool. "Cool Reasoning upon the Point with my Father, would soon bring her to his mind or him to hers."

Richard Prey [or Pray] of Ipswich, Massachusetts, appeared in a Salem court in 1647/8 to answer charges that he had beaten his wife. Among the witnesses was Jabisch Hackett, who had seen him try to hit her with a large stick, kick her across a room, and throw a "porridge dish" at her. The provocation for this abusive outburst had been her public contradiction of him, declaring that he had, despite denials, profaned the Lord's Day with his swearing and cursing. This enraged Prey. One brave soul tried to intervene:

> Some one present told Prey that the court would not allow him to abuse his wife so, and he answered that he did not care for the court and if the court hanged him for it he would do it. It was said to him that the court would make him care, for they had tamed as stout hearts as his, and Prey answered that if ever he had trouble about abusing his wife, he would cripple her and make her sit on a stool, and there he would keep her.

His justification for his behavior was "that he would beat her twenty times a day before she would be his master." The court fined him "10s. for swearing, 10s. for cursing, 20s. for beating his wife, and 40s. for contempt of court, or to be whipped at the Iron works." Contempt of court, curiously, seemed the more serious charge. . . .

Women could upset the balance of power in a household most dramatically by sexual betrayal. A promiscuous wife not only publicly humiliated her husband, but threatened the legitimacy of his children. Cuckolded men were considered aberrant and despised. The law also considered a woman's sexual misconduct more heinous than a man's. The penalties applied to an adulterous woman exceeded the punishment meted out to her male counterpart. In the early laws of Massachusetts, for example, a woman who had sex with a man other than her husband was considered an adulteress, a crime punishable by death. For a man, such sexual impropriety was labeled simply fornication, penalized by a fine or whipping. Women were told that philandering husbands should be ignored or at least tolerated. A cuckold, however, received scolding rather than sympathy from his community. He was regarded as a fallen man unable to control his wife's behavior. . . . Men who suffered from their wives' adultery endured public ridicule as well as private pain.

Laurence Turner of Ipswich, Massachusetts, struggled to regain his honor in the face of his adulterous wife's flagrant behavior. He came to court in 1650 to try and end the gossip, if not her sexual betrayals. John Chackswell, a boarder in the Turner home, recounted a sexual dalliance that occurred in the husband's absence. Sarah Turner "in a sporting way, throw water at one Tobias Saunders," also a boarder in the Turner household. "Saunders, who was looking in at the window, ran into the house and took said Sarah in his arms and assaulted her." A female neighbor came to the door and was also assaulted by Saunders and John Smith. Thomas Billings "came in from the forge" and was pushed into the sexual fray. Chackswell "being troubled, rebuked them saying, 'Heere is good doeings, take heed wt you doe' and went to an upper chamber, not countenancing their lascivious acts."

Sarah Turner was also reported to have enticed Roger Tyler with her carnal language. She called to him as he left his house, "Tyler you have eaten Turnopps." He replied "Thou Lyest Turners Wife." She challenged him "Come hethr & let mee kisse thee & then I'le tell yee." Laurence Turner challenged his neighbors' testimony in court. He sought to redeem his reputation, if not his marriage.

William Beale went to court in Ipswich, Massachusetts, to end the gossip about his wife and their servant, Benjamin Chandler. Beale's wife went to a neighbor's house asking for Chandler after her husband "warned" him out of their house because "her husband was jealous of him." In his rage, Beale accusingly declared that "all her children were bastards save one." When Beale found his former servant, "he took an ax and beat down Benjamin Chandler's cabin to try to expel him." The court case, however, involved not adultery or assault, but slander and defamation. Beale brought William Hollingworth to court "in behalf of his wife" because Mary Doninge heard from Alexander Giligan that Mrs. Hollingworth "said to Beale's wife that her husband would not join the church so long as such as she was in it." Beale's concern was that his domestic difficulties had become a town scandal. He did not want the reputation of being a cuckold. The damage of the town rumormongers threatened these men as much if not more than their wives' alleged infidelities.

Not unlike a cuckolded husband, a man beaten by his wife suffered public ridicule. . . . [T]he man who endured such treatment reversed the natural order of things. The woman who did the beating rarely received social censure. To go to court to stop such abuse or even to acknowledge publicly such treatment was not an option for most men in early New England, either. Jacob Eliot suffered at the hands of his tormented and abusive wife, Ann. "She flew into the most Violent passion imaginable, & with her fist doubled, fell upon me & struck me with all her might, upon my Head & Breast, arm & shoulder, half a Dozen times or more." A similar outburst demanded his reaction, when his wife "flew into the utmost Rage & fury again, Calling me a Cursed Devil Kicked at Me, & struck me with her Fist again, & took up a Powder Horn, to strike me over the Head with, but defending my self, I warded off the blow." At the height of a confrontation that ended with her attempted suicide, Ann "Strook me with her Fist as hard as She could in the face, & about my Head & Belly several times & hurt me very much (especially with one Stroke in my face which I felt very sore for several Days after)." She even tried to kill him when she "took me by the throat, got both her hands into the handkerchief about my Neck, & try'd, with all her might, to twist it round to Choak me." Trying to contort the situation to her advantage, Ann Eliot threatened to tell neighbors about "my abuse to Her, twitching & halling her about to kill her, when only to defend my self & prevent Her running away to destroy her Self, I, as gently as I could Sometimes took hold of her Arms or Cloaths."

Ann relentlessly found fault in her husband: "I can't Speak loud to a Servant, or so much as mend the fire, but Snubbed and reproved Sharply." To Jacob, her railings were "all for nothing, or for the least trifle in the world." Eliot described what he considered the ridiculous circumstances that roused his wife's ire:

> my Singing to the Child to get him to sleep (being mad before) cry'd out with great Vehemence & Spight, o don't don't don't don't Mr. Eliot make that noise! I am almost killed with it already &c—Soon after She letting a rousing Fart, I pleasingly & Jocosely Said that was as bad a Noise I thought as my Singing, at which She flew into a prodigious Rage, & wished She had dy'd in her Cradle, before She had been bro't into so much Trouble &c.

Of course, her real provocations even the long-suffering Jacob knew only too well. From her cutting remarks, she clearly resented his absorption in his religious studies and his ministerial condescension toward her. She often vented her anger by "trifling, Jesting & playing with Sacred things" to provoke a response. He would quote scriptures during their confrontations "by way of Caution or advice, with a design to expound upon it—[she] not staying to hear me out, but turning quick & in great rage replying—Shitt on the Text."

In fact, Ann justifiably worried about her financial status and that of her child. Eliot had two children from his first marriage who would share part of their father's estate. Married in 1760, Ann and Jacob had two sons: Joseph, born in 1762, and John, born in 1764. Ann urged her elderly husband, who died in 1766, to rewrite his will to include his second family. After the birth of her first son, she became consumed with worry that "her & Jose [would be] . . . left destitute." Jacob dismissed her concerns saying, "I intended to take Care about [you] . . . as soon as I could Conveniently." But Jacob ignored her long-standing request, throwing Ann into a "most Violent & uncurbed passion." She protested that his son Jacob, by his first wife, "might be content with what he had got, for he should have no more. . . . He had much more than his part already, & She would Say it to all the World."

Jacob's fury was directed not only at his wife's violence, but also at his own weakness. He thundered back at her, but he considered even these responses as a defeat: "I shew'd some heat & anger (God forgive me)." When he answered her with "some Zeal," he justified himself with the aside, "it is marvelous I have born so much." He berated himself for giving in to her demands. When she refused to sleep with him he "(like a Fool for Peace Sake) Consented & Submitted." He preferred silence and Christian forbearance to confrontation, which may account for Ann's rage. After ordering him not to touch her in bed, saying he "Stank so Devilishly she could not bare me," he responded with cutting kindness:

I bore all with invincible patience & for the most part Silence—at last without the least Ruffle I faced my Dear—if by a few words you will say what will pacify you, & put an end to the Controversy, that we might go to Sleep in peace & love—otherwise, I was resolved by the Grace of Heaven, to Disappoint the Devil & Her, by not being Mad, let her say what She would.

Donning the mantle of God's servant, he could make sense out of his situation. He turned the other cheek because he was strong. But his Christian forbearance also left the martyred Jacob feeling that he was little more than "a page, or Servant" in his own home. After one of their bedchamber quarrels, Ann "with Sovereign Authority said, I command you to go & lie up Chamber." He "laugh'd, & reply'd, that she had expressly inverted the Sacred Text. . . . Husbands obay your Wives." His laughter was soon replaced by a "profound silence," which he broke by begging her "to admit me to bed." A furious wife could threaten the natural order. An abused man's shame could lead to silence and private humiliation.

When a man married, he risked his heart and his reputation. Marriages, particularly for the men examined here, were based on both a loving partnership and male dominance. The question of whether one or the other dictated marriage patterns in a given place and time overshadows the obvious: both were always present. For the men studied here, these two imperatives did not seem contradictory. By the end of the eighteenth century, more open expression of sentiment was certainly encouraged, but loving expressions characterized male writings throughout the colonial period.

Slavery and Family Life Among African Americans in Eighteenth-Century Maryland

ALLAN KULIKOFF

Sometime in 1728, Harry, a recently imported African, escaped from his master in southern Prince George's Country, Maryland, and joined a small black community among the Indians beyond the area of white settlement. The following year, Harry returned to Prince George's to urge his former shipmates, the only "kinfolk" he had, to return there with him. Over forty years later, another Harry, who belonged to John Jenkins of Prince George's, ran away. The Annapolis newspaper reported that "he has been seen about the Negro Quarters in *Patuxent,* but is supposed to have removed among his Acquaintances on Potomack; he is also well acquainted with the Negroes at Clement Wheeler's Quarter on Zekiah, and a Negro Wench of Mr. Wall's named Rachael; a few miles from that Quarter is his Aunt, and he may possibly be harboured thereabouts."

These two incidents, separated by two generations, are suggestive. African Harry ran away *from* slavery to the frontier; Afro-American Harry ran *to* his friends

Allan Kulikoff, "The Beginnings of the Afro-American Family in Maryland," in Michael Gordon, ed., *The American Family in Social-Historical Perspective,* 2d ed. (New York: St. Martin's Press, 1978), pp. 444–454, 456–462. Revised version of essay originally published in A. C. Land, L. G. Carr, and E. C. Papenfuse, eds., *Law, Society, and Politics in Early Maryland* (Baltimore: Johns Hopkins University Press, 1977). Copyright © Michael Gordon. Reprinted with permission of Palgrave Macmillan.

and kinfolk spread over a wide territory. The Afro-American runaway could call on many others to hide him, but the African had few friends and seemingly, no wife. These contrasts raise many questions. How did Afro-Americans organize their families in the Chesapeake colonies during the eighteenth century? Who lived in slave households? How many Afro-American fathers lived with their wives and children? What was the impact of arbitrary sale and transfer of slaves upon family life? How did an Afro-American's household and family relationships change through the life cycle?

This paper attempts to answer these questions. While literary documents by or about slaves before 1800, such as runaway narratives, WPA [Works Progress Administration] freed-slave interviews, black autobiographies, or detailed travel accounts are very infrequently available to historians of colonial slave family life, they can gather age and family data from probate inventories, personal information from runaway advertisements, and depositions in court cases. These sources, together with several diaries and account books kept by whites, provide a great deal of material about African and Afro-American family life in the Chesapeake region.

Almost all the blacks who lived in Maryland and Virginia before 1780 were slaves. Because his status precluded him from enjoying a legally secure family life, a slave's household often excluded important family members. Households, domestic groups, and families must therefore be clearly distinguished. A household, as used here, is a coresidence group that includes all who shared a "proximity of sleeping arrangements," or lived under the same roof. Domestic groups include kin and nonkin, living in the same or separate households, who share cooking, eating, childrearing, working, and other daily activities. Families are composed of people related by blood or marriage. Several distinctions are useful in defining the members of families. The immediate family include husband and wife or parents and children. Near kin include the immediate family and all other kin, such as adult brothers and sisters or cousins who share the same house or domestic tasks with the immediate family. Other kinfolk who do not function as family members on a regular basis are considered to be distant kin.

The process of family formation can perhaps best be understood as an adaptive process. . . . Blacks learned to modify their environment, learned from each other how to retain family ties under very adverse conditions, and structured their expectations about family activities around what they knew the master would permit. If white masters determined the outward bounds of family activities, it was Africans, and especially their descendants, who gave meaning to the relationships between parents and children, among siblings, and with more distant kinfolk. As a result, black family structure on the eve of the Revolution differed from both African and white family systems.

Africans who were forced to come to the Chesapeake region in the late seventeenth and early eighteenth centuries struggled to create viable families and households, but often failed. They suffered a great loss when they were herded into slave ships. Their family and friends, who had given meaning to their lives and structured their place in society, were left behind and they found themselves among strangers. They could never re-create their families and certainly not devise a West African kinship system in the Chesapeake. The differences between African communities were too great. Some Africans lived in clans and lineages, others did not; some traced their descent from women but others traced descent from men; mothers, fathers, and other kin played somewhat different roles in each community; initiation ceremonies and puberty rites, forbidden marriages, marriage customs, and household structures all varied from place to place.

Though African immigrants did not bring a unified West African culture with them to the Chesapeake colonies, they did share important beliefs about the nature of kinship. Africans could modify these beliefs in America to legitimate the families they eventually formed. They saw kinship as the principal way of ordering relationships between individuals. Each person in the tribe was related to most others in the community. The male was father, son, and uncle; the female was mother, daughter, and aunt to many others. Because their kinship system was so extensive, Africans included kinfolk outside the immediate family in their daily activities. For example, adult brothers or sisters of the father or mother played an important role in childrearing and domestic activities in many African societies.

Secondly, but far less certainly, African immigrants may have adapted some practices associated with polygyny, a common African marital custom. A few men on the Eastern Shore of Maryland in the 1740s, and perhaps others scattered elsewhere, lived with several women. However, far too few African women (in relation to the number of men) immigrated to make polygynous marriages common. Nevertheless, the close psychological relationship between mothers and children, and the great social distance between a husband and his various wives and children found in African polygynous societies might have been repeated in the Chesapeake colonies. In any event, African slave mothers played a more important role than fathers in teaching children about Africa and about how to get along in the slave system. Both African custom and the physical separation of immigrant men and women played a role in this development.

Africans faced a demographic environment hostile to most forms of family life. If African men were to start families, they had to find wives, and that task was difficult. Most blacks lived on small farms of less than 11 slaves; and the small black population was spread thinly over a vast territory. Roads were rudimentary. Even where concentrations of larger plantations were located, African men did not automatically find wives. Sex ratios in southern Maryland rose from 125 to 130 (men per 100 women) in the mid-seventeenth century to about 150 in the 1710s and 1720s, and to around 180 in the 1730s. In Surry County, Virginia, the slave sex ratio was about 145 in the 1670s and 1680s, but over 200 in the 1690s and 1700s. Wealthy slaveowners did not provide most of their African men with wives; the larger the plantation, the higher the sex ratio tended to be.

Africans had competition for the available black women. By the 1690s, some black women were natives, and they may have preferred Afro-American men. White men were also competitors. Indeed, during the seventeenth and early eighteenth centuries, white adult sex ratios were as high (or higher) than black adult sex ratios. At any period whites possessed a monopoly of power and some of them probably took slave women as their common-law wives. African men competed for the remaining black women who were mostly recently-enslaved Africans. These immigrant women often waited two or three years before marrying. Since the number of women available to African men was so small, many probably died before they could find a wife. In 1739 African men planned an uprising in Prince George's County partly because they could not find wives.

Foreign-born male slaves in Maryland and Virginia probably lived in a succession of different kinds of households. Newly imported Africans had no black kin in the Chesapeake. Since sex ratios were high, most of these men probably lived with other, unrelated men. African men may have substituted friends for kin. Newly enslaved Africans made friends with their nearest shipmates during the middle passage, and after their arrival in Maryland, some of them lived near these men. New Negroes could live with other recent African immigrants because migration from Africa occurred in short spurts from the 1670s to the late 1730s. The high sex ratios of large plantations indicate that wealthy men bought many of these Africans. Even if his shipmates lived miles away, the new immigrant could share the experiences of others who had recently endured the middle passage.

Despite the difficulties, most Africans who survived for a few years eventually found a wife. . . . By the 1690s, large numbers of Afro-American women entered their midteens and married Afro-American and African men. Because the plantations were small, and individual farm sex ratios likely to be uneven, the wives and children of married African men very often lived on other plantations. These men still lived mainly with other unrelated men, but at least they had begun to develop kin ties. A few African men lived with their wives and children, and some limited evidence suggests that the longer an African lived in the Chesapeake, the more likely he was to live with his immediate family.

Unlike most African men, African women commonly lived with their children. Some African women may have been so alienated that they refused to have children, but the rest bore and raised several offspring, protected by the master's reluctance to separate very young children from their mothers. Since the children were reared by their mothers and eventually joined them in the tobacco fields, these households were domestic groups although incomplete as families.

A greater proportion of African women than African men lived with both spouses and children. These opportunities usually arose on large plantations. There was such a surplus of men on large plantations that African women who lived on them could choose husbands from several African or Afro-American men. The sex ratio on large plantations in Prince George's during the 1730s, a period of heavy immigration, was 249. This shortage of women prevented most recently arrived African men from finding a wife on the plantation. For them the opportunity to live with a wife and children was rare. More Africans probably lived with their immediate families in the 1740s; immigration declined, large planters bought more African women, and the sex ratio on big plantations fell to 142.

Because African spouses were usually separated, African mothers reared their Afro-American children with little help from their husbands. Even when the father was present, the extended kin so important in the lives of African children was missing. Mothers probably taught them the broad values they brought from Africa and related the family's history in Africa and the Chesapeake. When the children began working in the fields, they learned from their mothers how to survive a day's work and how to get along with master and overseer.

Each group of Africans repeated the experiences of previous immigrants. Eventually, more and more Afro-American children matured and began families of their own. The first large generation of Afro-Americans in Maryland probably came of age in the 1690s; by the 1720s, when the second large generation had matured, the black population finally began increasing naturally.

The changing composition of the black population combined with other changes to restructure Afro-American households and families. Alterations in the adult sex ratio, the size of plantations, and black population density provided black people with opportunities to enjoy a more satisfying family life. The way masters transferred slaves from place to place limited the size and composition of black households, but Afro-American family members separated by masters managed to establish complex kinship networks over many plantations. Afro-Americans used these opportunities to create a kind of family life that differed from African and Anglo-American practices.

Demographic changes led to more complex households and families. As the number of adult Africans in the population decreased, the sex ratio in Maryland declined to between 100 and 110 by the 1750s. This decline gave most men an opportunity to marry by about age thirty. The number of slaves who lived on plantations with more than twenty blacks increased; the density of the black population in tidewater Maryland and Virginia rose; the proportion of blacks in the total population of Prince George's County, in nearby areas of Maryland, and throughout tidewater Virginia rose to half or more by the end of the century; and many new roads were built. The number of friends and kinfolk whom typical Afro-Americans saw every day or visited with regularity increased, while their contact with whites declined because large areas of the Chesapeake became nearly black counties.

How frequently masters transferred their Afro-American slaves, and where they sent them, affected black household composition. Surviving documents do not allow a systematic analysis of this point, but several conclusions seem clear. First, planters kept women and their small children together but did not keep husbands and teenage children with their immediate family. Slaveowner after slaveowner bequeathed women and their "increase" to sons or daughters. However, children of slaveowners tended to live near their parents; thus, even when members of slave families were so separated, they remained in the same neighborhood. Secondly, Afro-Americans who lived on small farms were transferred more frequently than those on large plantations. At their deaths small slaveowners typically willed a slave or two to their widows and to each child. They also frequently mortgaged or sold slaves to gain capital. If a slaveowner died with many unpaid debts, his slaves had to be sold. Finally, relatively few blacks were forced to move long distances. Far more blacks were affected by migrations of slaves from the Chesapeake region to the new Southwest in the nineteenth century than by long-distance movement in the region before the Revolution. These points should not be misunderstood. Most Afro-Americans who lived in Maryland or Virginia during the eighteenth century experienced separations from members of their immediate families sometime in their lives. Most, however, were able to visit these family members occasionally.

These changes led to a new social reality for most slaves born in the 1750s, 1760s, and 1770s. If unrelated people and their progeny stay in a limited geographic area for several generations, the descendants of the original settlers must develop kin ties with many other people who live nearby. Once the proportion of adult Africans declined, this process began. African women married and had children; the children matured and married. If most of them remained near their first homes, each was bound to have siblings, children, spouses, uncles, aunts, and cousins living in the neighborhood. How these various kinspeople were organized into households, families, and domestic groups depended not only upon the whims of masters but also upon the meaning placed on kinship by the slaves themselves.

The process of household and family formation and dissolution was begun by each immigrant woman who lived long enough to have children. The story of Ann Joice, a black woman who was born in Barbados, taken to England as a servant, and then falsely sold into slavery in Maryland in the 1670s, may have been similar to that of other immigrant women once she became a slave. The Darnall family of Prince George's owned Ann Joice. She had seven children with several white men in the 1670s and 1680s; all remained slaves the rest of their lives. Three of her children stayed on the Darnall home plantation until their deaths. One was sold as a child to a planter who lived a few miles away; another was eventually sold to William Digges, who lived about five miles from the Darnall farm. Both the spatial spread and the local concentration of kinfolk continued in the next generation. Peter Harbard, born between 1715 and 1720, was the son of Francis Harbard, who was Ann Joice's child. Peter grew up on the Darnall farm, but in 1737 he was sold to George Gordon, who lived across the road from Darnall. As a child, Peter lived with or very near his grandmother Ann Joice, his father, and several paternal uncles and aunts. He probably knew his seven cousins (father's sister's children), children of his aunt Susan Harbard, who lived on William Digges's plantation. Other kinfolk lived in Annapolis but were too far away to visit easily.

As Afro-American slaves were born and died, and as masters sold or bequeathed their slaves, black households were formed and reformed, broken and created. Several detailed examples can illustrate this process. For example, Daphne, the daughter of Nan, was born about 1736 on a large plantation in Prince George's owned by Robert Tyler, Sr. Until she was two, she lived with her mother, two brothers, and two sisters. In 1738, Tyler died and left his slaves to his wife, children, and grandchildren. All lived on or near Tyler's farms. Three of Daphne's siblings were bequeathed to granddaughter Ruth Tyler, who later married Mordecai Jacob, her grandfather's next-door neighbor. Daphne continued to live on the Tyler plantation. From 1736 to 1787, she had six different masters, but she still lived where she was born. Daphne lived with her mother until her mother died, and with her ten children until 1779. Children were eventually born to Daphne's daughters; these infants lived with their mothers and near their maternal grandmother. When Robert Tyler III, Robert senior's grandson and Daphne's fifth master, died in 1779, his will divided Daphne's children and grandchildren between his son and daughter. Daphne was thus separated from younger children, born between 1760 and 1772. They were given to Millicent Beanes, Robert III's daughter, who lived several miles away. Daphne continued to live on the same plantation as her four older children and several grandchildren. An intricate extended family of grandmother, sons, daughters, grandchildren, aunts, uncles, nieces, nephews, and cousins resided in several households on the Tyler plantation in 1778, and other more remote kinfolk could be found on the neighboring Jacob farm.

Family separations might be more frequent on smaller plantations. Rachel was born in the late 1730s and bore ten children between 1758 and 1784. As a child she lived on the plantation of Alexander Magruder; a large slaveowner in Prince George's; before 1746, Alexander gave her to his son Hezekiah, who lived on an adjoining plantation. Hezekiah never owned more than ten slaves, and when he died in 1769, he owned only two—including one willed to his wife by her brother. Between 1755 and 1757, he mortgaged nine slaves, including Rachael, to two merchants. In 1757, Samuel Roundall (who lived about five miles from the Magruders) seized Rachel and six other slaves mortgaged to him. . . . In 1760 Roundall sold Rachael and her eldest daughter to Samuel Lovejoy, who lived about nine miles from Roundall. At the same time, four other former Magruder slaves were sold: two to planters in Lovejoy's neighborhood, one to a Roundall neighbor, and one to a planter living at least fifteen miles away in Charles County. Rachael's separation from friends and family members continued. In 1761, her eldest child was sold at age three to George Stamp, a neighbor of Lovejoy. By the time Samuel Lovejoy died in 1762, she had two other children. She and her youngest child went to live with John Lovejoy, Samuel's nephew and near-neighbor, but her second child, about age two, stayed with Lovejoy's widow. Her third child was sold at age six, but Rachael and her next seven children lived with John Lovejoy until at least 1787.

These three examples suggest how Afro-American households and families developed in the eighteenth century. Husbands and wives and parents and children were frequently separated by the master's transfers of family members. At the same time, as generation followed generation, households, or adjacent huts, became increasingly complex, and sometimes included grandparents, uncles, aunts, or cousins, as well as the immediate family. Since other kin lived on nearby or distant plantations, geographically concentrated (and dispersed) kinship networks that connected numbers of quarters emerged during the pre-Revolutionary era.

How typical were the experiences suggested by the examples? How were families organized into households and domestic groups on large and small quarters? Data from three large planter's inventories taken in 1759, 1773–1774, and 1775, and from a Prince George's census of 1776 permit a test of the hypotheses concerning changes in household structure, differences between large and small units, and the spread of kinfolk across space. . . .

Kinfolk (immediate families and near kin) on large plantations [i.e., those with twenty or more slaves] were organized into three kinds of residence groups. Most of the slaves of some quarters were interrelated by blood or marriage. Domestic groups included kinfolk who lived on opposite sides of duplex slave huts and who shared a common yard and eating and cooking arrangements. Finally, most households included members of an immediate family.

The kinship structure of large plantations is illustrated by a household inventory taken in 1773–1774 of 385 slaves owned by Charles Carroll of Carrollton on thirteen different quarters in Anne Arundel County. Because Carroll insisted that the inventory be "taken in Familys with their Ages," the document permits a detailed reconstruction of kinship networks. Though the complexity and size of kinship groups on Carroll's quarters were probably greater than on other large plantations, the general pattern could easily have been repeated elsewhere.

The ten men and three women who headed each list were probably leaders of their quarters. Five of the quarters were named for these individuals. They tended to be old slaves who had been with the Carroll family for many years. While the mean age of all adults was thirty-seven years, the mean age of the leaders was forty-nine, and six of the thirteen were over fifty-five. The leader often lived with many kinfolk; he or she was closely related to about 36 to 38 percent of all the other slaves on the quarter. For example, Fanny, sixty-nine years of age, was surrounded by at least forty near kinfolk on the main plantation at Doohoregan, and Mayara James, sixty-five years of age, lived with twenty-three relatives on his quarter. . . .

Nearly half the slaves who resided on Riggs Quarter, Carroll's main plantation, were kinfolk (63/130). A network of this size could develop only on the home plantation of the largest Chesapeake planters. Each of the members of the group was either a direct descendant or an affine (in-law) of old Fanny. She was surrounded on her quarter by five children, nineteen grandchildren, nine great-grandchildren, four children-in-law, and three grandchildren's spouses. The network grew through the marriage of Fanny's children and grandchildren to children of other residents of the quarter. For example, Cooper Joe, his wife, and thirteen children and grandchildren were closely related to Fanny's family. By the early 1750s Cooper Joe had married Nanny of Kate, and about 1761 Fanny's son Bob married Frances Mitchell of Kate. Joe and Nanny's children were first cousins of the children of Bob and Frances, and thereby more remotely connected to all the rest of Fanny's descendants. The alliance of the two families was cemented in 1772, when Dinah, the daughter of Kate of Fanny, married Joe, the son of Cooper Joe.

The intraquarter kinship network was also a work group. Fanny's and Lucy's adult and teenage kinfolk worked together in the fields. Masters separated their slaves by sex, age, and strength, and determined what each would do, but blacks judged each other in part by the reciprocal kinship obligation that bound them together. Afro-Americans worked at their own pace and frequently thwarted their masters' desires for increased productivity. Part of this conflict can be explained by the Afro-American's preindustrial work discipline, but part may have been due to the desires of kinfolk to help and protect each other from the master's lash, the humid climate, and the malarial environment.

Landon Carter's lament upon the death of his trusted old slave Jack Lubbar suggests the dimensions of kinship solidarity in the fields. Lubbar had been a foreman over many groups of slaves. In his old age, he worked at the Fork quarter "with 5 hands and myself; in which service he so gratefully discharged his duty as to make me by his care alone larger crops of Corn, tobacco and Pease twice over than ever I have had made by anyone. . . ." Other blacks did not share Lubbar's desire to produce a large crop for Carter. "At this plantation," Carter writes, "he continued till his age almost deprived him of eyesight which made him desire to be removed because those under him, mostly his great grandchildren, by the baseness of their Parents abused him much." Lubbar's grandchildren and great-grandchildren, who worked together, were related in intricate ways: parents and children, maternal and paternal cousins, uncles and aunts, and brothers and sisters. They united against Lubbar to slow the work pace and conserve their energy.

When Afro-Americans came home each night from the fields, they broke into smaller domestic groups. Their habitat set the scene for social intercourse. On large plantations "a Negro quarter is a Number of Huts or Hovels, built at some distance from the Mansion House; where the Negroes reside with their wives and Families, and cultivate at vacant times the little spots allow'd them." Four early-nineteenth-century slave houses still standing in Southern Maryland suggest that slave families living on the same quarter were very close. Each house included two rooms of about sixteen-by-sixteen feet, separated by a thin wall. In three of the

homes, the two huts shared the same roof but had separate doorways. Two had separate fireplaces, the residents of one duplex shared a fireplace, and one quarter (which
was over a kitchen) did not have a fireplace. Neither family had much privacy, and
communication between them must have been commonplace. No activity could occur on one side of the hut without those on the other knowing about it. And the two
halves of the hut shared a common yard, where residents could talk, eat, or celebrate.

On the quarters the smallest local residence unit to contain kinfolk was the
household. Household members were not isolated from other kinfolk; they worked
with their relatives in the fields, associated with neighbors in the common yard,
and cooked meals or slept near those who lived on the other side of their duplex.
Nevertheless, kinfolk who lived in the same household were spatially closer when
at home than any other group of kin. . . .

Far less can be learned about families on small plantations. On these farms, the
slave quarter could be in an outbuilding or in a small hut. All the slaves, whether
kin or not, lived together, cooked together, reared children together, and slept in the
same hut. . . .

By the 1750s, a peculiar Afro-American life cycle had developed. Afro-
Americans lived in a succession of different kinds of households. Children under ten
years almost always lived with their mothers, and over half on large plantations lived
with both parents. Between ten and fourteen years of age, large numbers of children
left their parents' home. Some stayed with siblings and their families, others were
sold, the rest lived with other kin or unrelated people. Women married in their late
teens, had children, and established households with their own children. Over four-
tenths of the women on large plantations and a fifth on small farms lived with husbands as well as children. The same proportion of men as women lived with spouses
and children, but because children of separated spouses usually lived with their
mothers, large numbers of men, even on big plantations, lived with other men.

These life-cycle changes can perhaps best be approached through a study of the
critical events in the lives of Afro-Americans. Those events probably included the
following: infancy, leaving the matricentral cell, beginning to work in the tobacco
fields, leaving home, courtship and marriage, childrearing, and old age.

For the first few months of life, a newborn infant stayed in the matricentral
cell, that is, received his identity and subsistence from his mother. A mother would
take her new infant to the fields with her "and lay it uncovered on the ground . . .
while she hoed her corn-row down and up. She would then suckle it a few minutes,
and return to her labor, leaving the child in the same exposure." Eventually, the
child left its mother's lap and explored the world of the hut and quarter. In the
evenings, he ate with his family and learned to love his parents, siblings, and other
kinfolk. During the day the young child lived in an age-segregated world. While
parents, other adults, and older siblings worked, children were "left, during a great
portion of the day, on the ground at the doors of their huts, to their own struggles
and efforts." They played with age-mates or were left at home with other children
and perhaps an aged grandparent. Siblings or age-mates commonly lived together
or in nearby houses. On the Potomac side of Prince George's County in 1776, 86
percent of those zero to four years of age, and 82 percent of those five to nine years
of age lived on plantations with at least one other child near their own age. Many
children lived in little communities of five or more children their own age. Children

five to nine years old, too young to work full-time, may have cared for younger siblings; in Prince George's in 1776, 83 percent of all children zero to four years of age
lived on a plantation with at least one child five to nine years of age.

Black children began to work in the tobacco fields between seven and ten years
of age. For the first time they joined fully in the daytime activities of adults. Those
still living at home labored beside parents, brothers and sisters, cousins, uncles, aunts
and other kinfolk. Most were trained to be field hands by white masters or overseers
and by their parents. Though these young hands were forced to work for the master,
they quickly learned from their kinfolk to work at the pace that black adults set and
to practice the skills necessary to "put massa on."

At about the same age, some privileged boys began to learn a craft from whites
or (on the larger plantations) from their skilled kinfolk. Charles Carroll's plantations provide an example of how skills were passed from one generation of Afro-
Americans to another. Six of the eighteen (33 percent) artisans on his plantations
under twenty-five years of age in 1773 probably learned their trade from fathers and
another four (22 percent) from other kinfolk skilled in that occupation. For example,
Joe, twenty-one, and Jack, nineteen, were both coopers and both sons of Cooper Joe,
sixty-three. Joe also learned to be a wheelwright, and in turn probably helped train
his brothers-in-law, Elisha, eleven, and Dennis, nine, as wheelwrights.

Beginning to work coincided with the departure of many children from their
parents, siblings, and friends. The fact that about 54 percent of all slaves in single
slave households in Prince George's in 1776 were between seven and fifteen years
of age suggests that children were typically forced to leave home during those
ages. Young blacks were most frequently forced from large plantations to smaller
farms. The parents' authority was eliminated, and the child left the only community he had known. Tension and unhappiness often resulted. For example, Hagar, age
fourteen, ran from her master in Baltimore in 1766. "She is supposed to be harbor'd
in some Negro Quarter," he claimed, "as her Father and Mother Encourages her in
Elopements, under a Pretense she is ill used at home."

Courtship and marriage were highly significant *rites de passage* for many Afro-
American men and women. The process began earlier for women: while men probably married in their mid- to late twenties, women usually married in their late teens.
Men initiated the courtship. They typically searched for wives, visiting numbers of
neighboring plantations, and often found a wife near home, though not on the same
quarter. . . .

Marriage was more important for women than men. After the relationship was
consummated, the woman probably stayed with her family (parents and siblings)
until a child was born, unless she could form a household with her husband. Once
she had a child, she moved from her parents' home into her own hut. Though almost
all women were field laborers, their role as wives and mothers gave them a few
privileges. Masters sometimes treated pregnant women—and their children after
birth—with greater than usual solicitude. For example, Richard Corbin, a Virginia
planter, insisted in 1759 that his steward be "Kind and Indulgent to pregnant
women, and not force them then with Child upon any service or hardship that will
be injurious to them." Children were "to be well looked after."

There was less change in the life of most new husbands. Many continued to
live with other adult men. Able to visit his family only at night or on holidays, the

nonresident husband could play only a small role in childrearing. If husband and wife lived together, however, they established a household. The resident father helped raise his children, taught them skills, and tried to protect them from the master. Landon Carter reacted violently when Manuel tried to help his daughter. "Manuel's Sarah, who pretended to be sick a week ago, and because I found nothing ailed her and would not let her lie up she ran away above a week and was catched the night before last and locked up; but somebody broke open the door for her. It could be none but her father Manuel, and he I had whipped."

On large plantations, mothers could call upon a wide variety of kin to help them raise their children: husbands, siblings, cousins, and uncles or aunts might be living in nearby huts. Peter Harbard learned from his grandmother, father, and paternal uncles how his grandmother's indentures were burned by Henry Darnall and how she was forced into bondage. He "frequently heard his grandmother Ann Joice say that if she had her just right that she ought to be free and all her children. He hath also heard his Uncles David Jones, John Wood, Thomas Crane, and also his father Francis Harbard declare as much." Peter's desire for freedom, learned from his kinfolk, never left him. In 1748, he ran away twice toward Philadelphia and freedom. He was recaptured, but later purchased his freedom.

As Afro-Americans grew older, illness and lack of stamina cut into their productivity, and their kinfolk or masters were forced to provide for them. On rare occasions, masters granted special privileges to favored slaves. When Thomas Clark died in 1766, he gave his son Charles "my faithful old Negro man Jack whom I desire may be used tenderly in his old age." Charles Ball's grandfather lived as an old man by himself away from the other slaves he disliked. Similarly, John Wood, Peter Harbard's uncle, was given his own cabin in his old age.

Many old slaves progressed through several stages of downward mobility. Artisans and other skilled workers became common field hands. . . . As slaves became feeble, some masters refused to maintain them adequately, or sold them to unwary buyers. An act passed by the Maryland Assembly in 1752 complained that "sundry Persons in this Province have set disabled and superannuated Slaves free who have either perished through want or otherwise become a Burthen to others." The legislators uncovered a problem: in 1755, 20 percent of all the free Negroes in Maryland (153/895) were "past labour or cripples," while only 2 percent (637/29,141) of white men were in this category. To remedy the abuse, the assembly forbade manumission of slaves by will, and insisted that masters feed and clothe their old and ill slaves. If slaveholders failed to comply, they could be fined £4 for each offense.

As Afro-American slaves moved from plantation to plantation through the life cycle, they left behind many friends and kinfolk, and established relationships with slaves on other plantations. And when young blacks married off their quarter, they gained kinfolk on other plantations. . . .

Since husbands and wives, fathers and children, and friends and kinfolk were often physically separated, they had to devise ways of maintaining their close ties. At night and on Sundays and holidays, fathers and other kinfolk visited those family members who lived on other plantations. Fathers had regular visiting rights. Landon Carter's Guy, for instance, visited his wife (who lived on another quarter) every Monday evening. Kinfolk, friends, and neighbors gathered in the yard around the slave cabins and talked, danced, sang, told stories, and drank rum through many an evening and special days on larger plantations. These visits symbolized the solidarity of slave families and permitted kinfolk to renew their friendships but did not allow nonresident fathers to participate in the daily rearing of their children.

The forced separation of Afro-American kinfolk by masters was not entirely destructive. Slave society was characterized by hundreds of interconnected and inter-locking kinship and friendship networks that stretched from plantation to plantation and from county to county. A slave who wanted to run away would find kinfolk, friends of kinfolk, or kinfolk of friends along his route who willingly would harbor him for a while. As Afro-American kinship and friendship networks grew ever larger, the proportion of runaways who were harbored for significant periods of time on slave quarters seemed to have increased in both Maryland and Virginia.

There were three different reasons for slaves to use this underground. Some blacks, like Harry—who left his master in 1779, stayed in the neighborhood for a few weeks and then took off for Philadelphia—used their friends' and kinfolk's hospitality to reach freedom. Others wanted to visit. About 27 percent of all run-aways from southern Maryland mentioned in newspaper advertisements from 1745 to 1779 (and 54 percent of all those whose destinations were described by masters) ran away to visit. . . . [I]n 1756, Kate, thirty years old, ran away from her master, who lived near Georgetown on the Potomac. She went to South River about thirty miles distant, where she had formerly lived. Friends concealed her there. Her master feared that since "she had been a great Rambler, and is well known in *Calvert* and *Anne Arundel* Counties, besides other parts of the Country," Kate would "indulge herself a little in visiting her old Acquaintances," but spend most of her time with her husband at West River.

Indeed, 20 of 233 Maryland runaways (9 percent) left masters to join their spouses. Sue and her child Jem, eighteen months old, went from Allen's Freshes to Port Tobacco, Charles County, a distance of about ten miles, "to go and see her husband." Sam, age thirty, lived about thirty miles from his wife in Bryantown, Charles County, when he visited her in 1755. Will had to go over a hundred miles, from Charles to Frederick County, to visit his wife, because her master had taken her from Will's neighborhood to a distant quarter. . . .

This article has attempted to portray African and Afro-American family life among slaves in the eighteenth-century Chesapeake. It is based upon all the available evidence and upon speculations from that evidence. Many important questions about black family life in the colonial period remain to be answered. In the first place, we need to know more about household and family structure. Could the same structures be found in other parts of the region? In South Carolina? In the northern and middle colonies? Was the pattern of change described here repeated in other areas? Secondly, we must go beyond this essay and describe in greater detail the nature of the Afro-American developmental cycle and the emotional content of relationships among kinfolk in various places at different times.

 F U R T H E R   R E A D I N G

Anderson, Karen L. *Chain Her by One Foot: The Subjugation of Women in Seventeenth-Century New France* (1991).

Cott, Nancy F. "Eighteenth-Century Family and Social Life Revealed in Massachusetts Divorce Records." *Journal of Social History* 10 (Fall 1976): 20–43.

Daniels, Christine, and Michael V. Kennedy, eds. *Over the Threshold: Intimate Violence in Early America* (1999).

Day, Joy, and Richard Buel. *The Way of Duty: A Woman and Her Family in Revolutionary America* (1984).

Demos, John. *A Little Commonwealth: Family Life in Plymouth Colony* (1970).

Glover, Lorri. *All Our Relations: Blood Ties and Emotional Bonds Among the Early South Carolina Gentry* (2000).

Gutiérrez, Ramón A. *When Jesus Came, the Corn Mothers Went Away: Marriage, Sexuality, and Power in New Mexico, 1500–1846* (1991).

Gutman, Herbert G. *The Black Family in Slavery and Freedom, 1750–1925* (1976).

Kulikoff, Allan. *Tobacco and Slaves: The Development of Southern Cultures in the Chesapeake, 1680–1800* (1986).

Levy, Barry. *Quakers and the American Family: British Settlement in the Delaware Valley* (1988).

Morgan, Edmund. *The Puritan Family: Religion and Domestic Relations in Seventeenth-Century New England* (1966).

———. *Virginians at Home: Family Life in the Eighteenth Century* (1952).

Perdue, Theda. *Cherokee Women: Gender and Culture Change, 1700–1835* (1998).

Smith, Daniel Blake. *Inside the Great House: Planter Family Life in Eighteenth-Century Chesapeake Society* (1980).

Smith, Daniel Scott. "Parental Power and Marriage Patterns: An Analysis of Historical Trends in Higham, Massachusetts." *Journal of Marriage and the Family* 35 (August 1973): 419–428.

Ulrich, Laurel Thatcher. *Good Wives: Image and Reality in the Lives of Women in Northern New England, 1650–1750* (1982).

Van Kirk, Sylvia. *Many Tender Ties: Women in Fur-Trade Society, 1670–1870* (1980).

Wall, Helena M. *Fierce Communion: Family and Community in Early America* (1990).

Wilson, Lisa. *Ye Heart of a Man: The Domestic Life of Men in Colonial New England* (1999).

CHAPTER
3

Children and
Childrearing in a
Developing Democracy

Since the publication of Bernard Wishy's influential study The Child and the
Republic, *in 1968, scholars have seen childrearing as the key to the American
character. Whereas colonial parents, convinced of the inherent sinfulness of their
offspring, sought to subdue their children's will to their own, parents in the newly
formed United States of America understood that in the absence of external controls,
children would require internalized discipline. A uniquely American literature
about and for children emerged to meet this need, capitalizing on new ideas about
children's capacity for good as well as evil.*

*Advice books for parents and didactic fiction for children offer historians ample
scope for exploring ideas about childhood and child nurture between European settlement and the Civil War, but such sources leave important questions unanswered. The
experiences of fictional children may not have accurately reflected those of flesh-
and-blood youngsters, and the extent to which parental practice coincided with
prescription remains unclear. Moreover, literature for and about children was generally aimed at America's privileged families, so that the experiences of children
and parents in poor families are obscured, rather than revealed, by relying on such
sources. Historians have attempted to overcome these difficulties by augmenting
literature on* childhood *(adults' ideas about children) with sources on* children
*(children's own accounts of their lives). Letters, diaries, and autobiographies offer
insight into the lives of well-to-do children, while exploring the assumptions behind
laws pertaining to children or the clothing children wore can help scholars to explore
the lives of less fortunate children.*

*In the popular imagination, two images of childrearing in early America are
persistent: the idea that colonial Americans believed in the adage, "spare the rod
and spoil the child" and the idea that they treated children as "miniature adults."
Scholarly inquiry has called both of these assumptions into question, yet these
notions have remained remarkably resistant to revision. Indeed, scholars confront*

difficulties in presenting the significant shift from "premodern" to "modern" childrearing without perpetuating these stereotypes. In their attempts to counter simplistic understandings of early American childhood, historians of childrearing implicitly or explicitly question how different early Americans' attitudes and actions toward children were from those in our own time.

In addition to demonstrating the rise of modern childrearing in the United States, the study of childhood in the early republic raises interesting questions about the sources that historians use and the conclusions that they draw from these sources. Where have Americans gotten their ideas about childrearing in early America? What alternative readings of these sources are possible? How much difference was there between childrearing in colonial America and childrearing in the newly formed United States? And why do we know so much more about the lives of well-to-do children than we do about the lives of less privileged children?

 ## D O C U M E N T S

Colonial Americans' concern for order manifested itself in a desire to control children's behavior closely. Document 1, consisting of two New England colonies' laws permitting harsh corporal punishment for disobedient youth, illustrates this trend. The practice of breeching, described in Document 2, likewise reflects colonial Americans' preoccupation with maintaining social order. While all small children, boys as well as girls, were dressed in long skirts, which restricted movement, older boys—and only boys—traded dresses for breeches, giving them greater freedom of movement and symbolizing their adult destiny as heads of households.

While colonial parents, who believed in the doctrine of original sin and infant depravity, sought to impose their will on their children through fear and punishment, parents in the emerging nation were influenced by the writings of English philosopher John Locke. Parents in revolutionary America eagerly read Locke's theories of child nurture, excerpted in Document 3, as well as his treatises on political economy. Describing children as innocent and malleable, Locke recommended that parents guide their children gently through affection and reason.

The remaining documents illustrate the effects of Lockean thinking on American families between the American Revolution and the Civil War. In Document 4 Virginian Laura Wirt's parents, Elizabeth and William, evince the optimism and affection that typified childrearing in the new republic. Their letters also indicate the new importance of mothers in the milder form of government recommended by advice book authors such as John J.C. Abbott, whose 1834 manual, *The Mother at Home,* is excerpted in Document 6. The goal of this new form of childrearing was the creation of an active conscience; the workings of this internal guide to proper behavior are evident in Document 7, in which Lucy Larcom recalls her girlhood in antebellum New England. Yet the echoes of an earlier emphasis on subduing children's will, rather than cultivating their consciences, are visible in the account of minister Francis Wayland, who shared his childrearing methods with the readers of the *American Baptist Magazine* in 1831. This article is reprinted as Document 5.

1. Colonial Legislatures Permit Harsh Punishment for Disobedient Children, 1642, 1646, 1654

Connecticut, 1642

Forasmuch as incorrigeableness is also adjudged to be a sin of death, but no law yet amongst us [has been] established for the execution thereof: For the preventing [of] that great evil it is ordered, that whatsoever child or servant within these liberties shall be convicted of any stubborn or rebellious carriage against their parents or governors, which is a forerunner of the forementioned evil, the Governor or any two Magistrates have liberty and power from this Court to commit such person or persons to the house of correction, and there to remain under hard labor and severe punishment so long as the Court or the major part of the Magistrates shall judge meet.

Massachusetts, 1646

If any child[ren] above sixteen years old and of sufficient understanding shall curse or smite their natural father or mother, they shall be put to death, unless it can be sufficiently testified that the parents have been very unchristianly negligent in the education of such children, or so provoked them by extreme and cruel correction that they have been forced thereunto to preserve themselves from death or maiming. . . .

   If a man have a stubborn or rebellious son of sufficient years of understanding, viz. sixteen, which will not obey the voice of his father or the voice of his mother, and that when they have chastened him will not harken unto them, then shall his father and mother, being his natural parents, lay hold on him and bring him to the magistrates assembled in Court, and testify to them by sufficient evidence that this their son is stubborn and rebellious and will not obey their voice and chastisement, but lives in sundry notorious crimes. Such a son shall be put to death.

Massachusetts, 1654

Forasmuch as it appears by too much experience that divers children and servants do behave themselves too disrespectively, disobediently, and disorderly towards their parents, masters, and governors, to the disturbance of families and discouragement of such parents and governors: For the ready prevention whereof it is ordered

---

J. Hammond Trumbull, ed., *Public Records of the Colony of Connecticut* (Hartford, Conn.: Case, Lockwood and Brainard Company, 1850–1890), I:78. This document can also be found in Robert Bremner, ed., *Children and Youth in America: A Documentary History* (Cambridge, Mass.: Harvard University Press, 1970), I: p. 37. Nathaniel Shurtleff, ed., *Records of the Governor and Company of Massachusetts Bay, 1628–1686),* 5 vols. (Boston: W. White, 1853–1854), III:101, 355. This document can also be found in Robert Bremner, ed., *Children and Youth in America: A Documentary History* (Cambridge, Mass.: Harvard University Press), I: p. 38.

by this Court and the authority thereof that it shall henceforth be in the power of any one magistrate, by warrant directed to the constable of that town where such offender dwells, upon complaint, to call before him any such offender, and upon conviction of such misdemeanors to sentence him or them to endure such corporal punishment by whipping or otherwise as in his judgment the merit of the fact shall deserve, not exceeding ten stripes for one offence, or bind the offender to appear at the next Court of that county. And further, it is also ordered, that the commissioners for the town of Boston, and the three commissioners for towns where no magistrate dwells, shall have the like power, provided the person or persons so sentenced shall have liberty to make their legal appeal to the next County Court, if they desire it in any of these cases.

2. A Colonial Mother Describes the Custom of Breeching, 1679

Dear Son:

You cannot beleeve the great concerne that was in the whole family here last Wednesday, it being the day that the taylor was to helpe to dress little ffrank in his breeches in order to the making an everyday suit by it. Never had any bride that was to be drest upon her weding night more handes about her, some the legs, some the armes, the taylor butt'ning, and others putting on the sword, and so many lookers on that had I not a ffinger amongst I could not have seen him. When he was quite drest he acted his part as well as any of them for he desired he might goe downe to inquire for the little gentleman that was there the day before in a black coat, and speak to the man to tell the gentleman when he came from school that there was a gallant with very fine clothes and a sword to have waited upon him and would come again upon Sunday next. But this was not all, there was great contrivings while he was dressing who should have the first salute; but he sayd if old Joan had been here, she should, but he gave it to me to quiett them all. They were very fitt, everything, and he looks taller and prettyer than in his coats. Little Charles rejoyced as much as he did for he jumpt all the while about him and took notice of everything. I went to Bury, and bo^t everything for another suitt which will be finisht on Saturday so the coats are to be quite left off on Sunday. I consider it is not yett terme time and since you could not have the pleasure of the first sight, I resolved you should have a full relation from

Yo^r most aff^{nate} Mother
A North.

When he was drest he asked Buckle whether muffs were out of fashion because they had not sent him one.

Paula S. Fass and Mary Ann Mason, eds., *Childhood in America* (New York: New York University Press, 2000), p. 82.

3. English Philosopher John Locke Recommends a Rational Approach to Childrearing, 1693

If what I have said in the beginning of this Discourse be true, as I do not doubt but it is, *viz.* That the difference to be found in the Manners and Abilities of Men, is owing more to their *Education* than to any thing else; we have reason to conclude, that great care is to be had of the forming Children's *Minds,* and giving them that seasoning early, which shall influence their Lives always after. For when they do well or ill, the Praise or Blame will be laid there: And when any thing is done unto-wardly, the common Saying will pass upon them, That it is suitable to their *Breeding*.

As the Strength of the Body lies chiefly in being able to endure Hardships, so also does that of the Mind. And the great Principle and Foundation of all Vertue and Worth, is placed in this, That a Man is able to *deny himself* his own Desires, cross his own Inclinations, and purely follow what Reason directs as best, tho' the appetite lean the other way.

The great Mistake I have observed in People's breeding their Children has been, that this has not been taken care enough of in its *due Season;* That the Mind has not been made obedient to Discipline, and pliant to Reason, when at first it was most tender, most easy to be bowed. Parents, being wisely ordain'd by Nature to love their Children, are very apt, if Reason watch not that natural Affection very warily, are apt, I say, to let it run into fondness. They love their little ones, and 'tis their Duty: But they often, with them, cherish their Faults too. . . .

. . . Thus Parents, by humoring and cockering them when *little,* corrupt the Principles of Nature in their Children, and wonder afterwards to taste the bitter Waters, when they themselves have poisoned the Fountain. For when their Children are grown up, and these ill Habits with them; when they are now too big to be dandled, and their Parents can no longer make use of them, as Play-things; then they complain, that the Brats are untoward and perverse; then they are offended to see them wilful, and are troubled with those ill Humours, which they themselves infused and fomented in them; And then, perhaps too late, would be glad to get out those Weeds, which their own hands have planted, and which now have taken too deep root to be easily extirpated. For he that has been used to have his Will in every thing, as long as he was in Coats, why should we think it strange, that he should de-sire it, and contend for it still, when he is in Breeches? . . .

. . . For if the Child must have Grapes or Sugar-plumbs, when he has a Mind to them, rather than make the poor Baby cry, or be out of Humour; why, when he is grown up, must he not be satisfied too, if his Desires carry him to Wine or Women? They are Objects as suitable to the longing of one of more Years, as what he cried for when little was to the inclinations of a Child. The having Desires accommodated to the Apprehensions and Relish of those several Ages is not the Fault; but the not having them subject to the Rules and Restraints of Reason: The Difference lies not in the hav-ing or not having Appetites, but in the Power to govern, and deny our selves in them. He that is not used to submit his Will to the Reason of others, *when* he is *young,* will

John Locke, *Some Thoughts Concerning Education,* ed. John W. Yolton and Jean S. Yolton (New York: Oxford University Press, 1989; originally published 1693), pp. 103–105, 107–110.

scarce hearken or submit to his own Reason, when he is of an Age to make use of it. And what a kind of a Man such an one is like to prove, is easie to foresee. . . .

It seems plain to me, that the Principle of all Vertue and Excellency lies in a power of denying our selves the satisfaction of our own Desires, where Reason does not authorize them. This Power is to be got and improved by Custom, made easy and familiar by an *early* Practice. If therefore I might be heard, I would advise, that, contrary to the ordinary way, Children should be used to submit their Desires, and go without their Longings, even *from their very Cradles*. The first thing they should learn to know should be, that they were not to have any thing, because it pleased them, but because it was thought fit for them. If things suitable to their Wants were supplied to them, so that they were never suffered to have what they once cried for, they would learn to be content without it; would never with Bawling and Peevishness contend for Mastery; nor be half so uneasy to themselves and others as they are, because *from the first* beginning they are not thus handled. If they were never suffered to obtain their desire by the Impatience they expressed for it, they would no more cry for other Things, than they do for the Moon. . . .

Those therefore that intend ever to govern their Children, should begin it whilst they are *very little;* and look, that they perfectly comply with the Will of their Parents. Would you have your Son obedient to you when past a Child? Be sure then to establish the Authority of a Father, *as soon* as he is capable of Submission, and can understand in whose Power he is. If you would have him stand in awe of you, imprint it *in his Infancy;* and, as he approaches more to a Man, admit him nearer to your Familiarity: So shall you have him your obedient Subject (as is fit) whilst he is a Child, and your affectionate Friend when he is a Man. . . .

I imagine every one will judge it reasonable, that their Children, *when little,* should look upon their Parents as their Lords, their Absolute Governors; and, as such, stand in awe of them: And that, when they come to riper Years, they should look on them as their best, as their only sure Friends; and as such, love and reverence them. The Way I have mentioned, if I mistake not, is the only one to obtain this. We must look upon our Children, when grown up, to be like our selves; with the same Passions, the same Desires. We would be thought Rational Creatures, and have our Freedom; we love not to be uneasie, under constant Rebukes and Browbeatings; nor can we bear severe Humours, and great Distance in those we converse with. Whoever has such Treatment when he is a Man, will look out other Company, other Friends, other Conversation, with whom he can be at Ease. If therefore a strict Hand be kept over Children *from the Beginning,* they will in that Age be tractable, and quietly submit to it, as never having known any other: And if, as they grow up to the Use of Reason, the Rigour of Government be, as they deserve it, gently relaxed, the Father's Brow more smooth'd to them, and the Distance by Degrees abated; his former Restraints will increase their Love, when they find it was only a Kindness to them, and a Care to make them capable to deserve the Favour of their Parents, and the Esteem of every Body else.

Thus much for the Settling your Authority over your Children in general. Fear and Awe ought to give you the first Power over their Minds, and Love and Friendship in riper Years to hold it: For the Time must come, when they will be past the Rod, and Correction; and then, if the Love of you make them not obedient and dutifull, if the Love of Vertue and Reputation keep them not in Laudable Courses, I ask, What Hold will you have upon them, to turn them to it? Indeed, Fear of having a scanty Portion if they displease you, may make them Slaves to your Estate, but they will be never the less ill and wicked in private; and that Restraint will not last always. Every Man must some Time or other be trusted to himself, and his own Conduct; and he that is a good, a vertuous and able Man, must be made so within. And therefore, what he is to receive from Education, what is to sway and influence his Life, must be something put into him betimes; Habits woven into the very Principles of his Nature; and not a counterfeit Carriage, and dissembled Out-side, put on by Fear, only to avoid the present Anger of a Father, who perhaps may dis-inherit him.

4. Laura Wirt's Parents Offer Instruction and Advice, 1810

Elizabeth Wirt to Laura Wirt, June 8, 1810

My dear Laura

Your Father and myself are both extremely anxious to see you again, because we love you dearly. And we almost regret having permitted you to go so far away from us. We know your Aunt Nancy will be very kind & attentive to you, but we long to have you with us, to see you every day, & to hear your racket through the house.

I hope you had an agreeable journey up and have gained a good appetite; and that you will not loose it by eating too many cherries. You know your promise, To let your Aunt see every cherry you eat?

You have before this commenced your studies. And I hope you read a great deal. And remember to hold your pen properly when you write. I shall expect soon to have a letter from you. And that you will tell me everything you do. That you behave kindly to Emma, & never quarrel with her, not even when she may have taken your play things from you, for you know she is much younger than you, & does not know so well how to behave herself. You must write me how you spend the day—who dresses you in the morning, what you do before dinner; how you pass the evening, what walks you take; And if any Visitors come to the house, whether you always answer prettily when spoken to? not hanging your head and muttering, but holding it up, & listening politely to whatever they may say, & then answering like a lady. I hope you are learning to draw handsomely and remember not to put the painting Brush in your mouth. You must hem shaving clothes for Uncle Cabell. And ask Miss Eliza to teach you to darn your own stockings. Every night when you undress for Bed, fold all your clothes smoothly on a chair by themselves—And mind to keep your trunk in neat order. But above all things my dear child remember to Pray to your Father in Heaven every night, & every morning. Do it gravely & seriously that God may hear you & bless you: which he will not do if you laugh and trifle about your Prayers.

. . . Be [a] mighty good girl until I see you again[.] Father sends his love to you, and six (kisses). . . .

your affectionate Mother
E. W. Wirt.

William Wirt Papers, Maryland Historical Society, Baltimore, Maryland.

William Wirt to Laura Wirt, July 14, 1810

My dear daughter.

I cannot let Doct. Hare go away without carrying you some token of my love: and as I could find nothing in the stores that pleased my taste, I have sitten down to write you a letter. A letter from an affectionate father ought to be far more precious in a daughters eyes than jewels and diamonds—for jewels and diamonds cannot make you happy, but the love of your parents can always do it, if you are a good girl and have no fault to find with yourself, and know that you have done nothing to displease your father who is in Heaven.—I hope to hear from your mother that you are a fine, sweet girl and are very industrious in your studies, which is the only way to make your parents happy and to make them love you dearly: and it is the only way to reward your mother for the great trouble she is taking with you: you ought to consider how few mothers there are who take so much care of their daughters—for almost all of them, to get rid of the trouble themselves, send their daughters to school with a whole parcel of other children some of whom will be very bad, and then their daughters learn bad words and wicked tricks and plant thorns in the bosoms of their parents; displease their heavenly father, and sometimes are so much despised that they have to turn beggars & go about in rags, begging their bread from door to door—I dare say your dear good mother can tell you a pretty story about such a girl, that, at last, was ruined by the wicked tricks she learnt at school—and then you will understand how kind your mother is, to take all the trouble of teaching you, herself, that you may be kept out of harm's way while you are young, and grow up in virtue & religion. There are very few mothers in this world who will take so much trouble, and therefore you ought to love yours most dearly and try to lessen her trouble as much as possible by being very industrious and taking a great deal of pains in your learning— If you will always try your best, every body will say by & bye that you are the most sensible and fine girl in Virginia for if you will learn fast, I will spare no expense to get masters to come and teach you under your mother's eye—I am going to send directly to Philadelphia for globes, a telescope and an Orrery for you—Mama will tell you what these are. . . . May God bless you prays your affectionate father

Wm Wirt

William Wirt to Laura Wirt, July 22, 1810

My dear Laura.

I thought, while I was writing to your mother, that I should not find time to write to you: but, on second thoughts, I have determined to write even if I have to work for it, 'till midnight—for it would not be right for me to recieve such a pretty letter from my daughter without answering it. Major Clarke has just been here: and I shewed both Robert's letter and yours to him: and he was so much pleased that tears of pleasure came into his eyes—"what fine children these will be," he said "if they keep on in learning, as they have begun"—and you do not know how it delights your fathers heart to hear his children praised. . . .

Yes, indeed; I shall be delighted to hear you play a tune on the piano: for I am desirous of your being the best performer on the piano & harp, the best Latin,

French, Italian & Spanish scholar in the Unites States and the best & sweetest girl too: for if you played every so well and were ever so good a scholar, still nobody would love you unless you were also a sweet-tempered, kind-hearted girl to every body & every thing. I can tell you a story of a girl who was very beautiful and could play upon the harp like an angel and yet no-body loved her, because she was proud, fretful and crosstempered—always scolding at the servants—always saying ill-natured things of people behind their backs—or saying cruel things to modest, bashful, good-tempered people, to hurt their feelings & make them unhappy; 'till at last she was turned into a wasp, without a sting—always spitefully trying to sting and yet hurting no body, 'till once in flying at a snow-white bird of paradise to sting that to death, she was caught in a swallow's beak and dropped down in a chimney into a kitchen fire. . . .

Heaven bless you—
your affectionate father Wm Wirt

5. The Reverend Francis Wayland Describes Discipline, 1831

Mr. Editor, . . .

My youngest child is an infant about 15 months old, with about the intelligence common to children of that age. It has for some months been evident, that he was more than usually self willed, but the several attempts to subdue him, had been thus far relinquished, from the fear that he did not fully understand what was said to him. It so happened, however, that I had never been brought into collision with him myself, until the incident occurred which I am about to relate. Still I had seen enough to convince me of the necessity of subduing his temper, and resolved to seize upon the first favorable opportunity which presented, for settling the question of authority between us.

On Friday last before breakfast, on my taking him from his nurse, he began to cry violently. I determined to hold him in my arms until he ceased. As he had a piece of bread in his hand, I took it away, intending to give it to him again after he became quiet. In a few minutes he ceased, but when I offered him the bread he threw it away, although he was very hungry. He had, in fact, taken no nourishment except a cup of milk since 5 o'clock on the preceding afternoon. I considered this a fit opportunity for attempting to subdue his temper, and resolved to embrace it. I thought it necessary to change his disposition, so that he would receive the bread *from me,* and also be so reconciled to me that he would *voluntarily* come to me. The task I found more difficult that I had expected.

I put him into a room by himself, and desired that no one should speak to him, or give him any food or drink whatever. This was about 8 o'clock in the morning. I visited him every hour or two during the day, and spoke to him in the kindest tones,

William G. McLoughlin, "Evangelical Child-Rearing in the Age of Jackson: Francis Wayland's View on When and How to Subdue the Willfulness of Children," *Journal of Social History* 9, 1 (Fall 1975): Appendix 1:35–39.

offering him the bread and putting out my arms to take him. But throughout the whole day he remained inflexibly obstinate. He did not yield a hair's breadth. I put a cup of water to his mouth, and he drank it greedily, but would not touch it with his hands. If a crumb was dropped on the floor he would eat it, but if *I* offered him the piece of bread, he would push it away from him. When I told him to come to me, he would turn away and cry bitterly. He went to bed supperless. It was now twenty-four hours since he had eaten any thing.

He woke the next morning in the same state. He would take nothing that I offered him, and shunned all my offers of kindness. He was now truly an object of pity. He had fasted thirty-six hours. His eyes were wan and sunken. His breath hot and feverish, and his voice feeble and wailing. Yet he remained obstinate. He continued thus, till 10 o'clock A.M. when hunger overcame him, and he took from me a piece of bread, to which I added a cup of milk, and hoped that the labor was at last accomplished.

In this however I had not rightly judged. He ate his bread greedily, but when I offered to take him, he still refused as pertinaciously as ever. I therefore ceased feeding him, and recommenced my course of discipline.

He was again left alone in his crib, and I visited him as before, at intervals. About one o'clock Saturday, I found that he began to view his condition in its true light. The tones of his voice in weeping were graver and less passionate, and had more the appearance of one bemoaning himself. Yet when I went to him, he still remained obstinate. You could clearly see in him the abortive efforts of the will. Frequently he would raise his hands an inch or two, and then suddenly put them down again. He would look at me, and then hiding his face in the bedclothes weep most sorrowfully. During all this time I was addressing him, whenever I came into the room, with invariable kindness. But my kindness met with no suitable return. All I required of him was, that he should come to me. This he would not do, and he began now to see that it had become a serious business. Hence his distress increased. He would not submit, and he found that there was no help without it. It was truly surprising to behold how much agony so young a being could inflict upon himself.

About three o'clock I visited him again. He continued in the state I have described. I was going away, and had opened the door, when I thought that he looked somewhat softened, and returning, put out my hands, again requesting him to come to me. To my joy, and I hope gratitude, he rose up and put forth his hands immediately. The agony was over. He was completely subdued. He repeatedly kissed me, and would do so whenever I commanded. He would kiss any one when I directed him, so full of love was he to all the family. Indeed, so entirely and instantaneously were his feelings towards me changed, that he preferred me now to any of the family. As he had never done before, he moaned after me when he saw that I was going away.

Since this event several slight revivals of his former temper have occurred, but they have all been easily subdued. His disposition is, as it never has been before, mild and obedient. He is kind and affectionate, and evidently much happier than he was, when he was determined to have his own way. I hope and pray that it may prove that an effect has been produced upon him for life. . . .

I. From this incident, which is in every respect literal fact, without any embellishment, parents may learn the intensity of the obstinacy of children. When they find their children stubborn, they need not be surprised. Let them hold out in a mild yet firm course of discipline until this obstinacy is subdued. This is real kindness. There can be no greater cruelty than to suffer a child to grow up with an unsubdued temper. Let us strive, by the grace of God, to cure the evil as early as possible. I do not make these remarks, by way of telling how much better I govern my family than other people. I believe no such thing. Far from it. God has seen fit to call me to bring up a child of unusually unyielding temper. I have related the effect of this method of treatment, in the hope that it might be an encouragement to those who may be required to undergo a similar trial.

II. But secondly, I could not avoid looking upon the whole of this little incident, as illustrative of the several steps in the ordinary progress of a sinner's conversion.

1. I remarked that my child was about 15 months old, and yet I had never been obliged thus to treat him before. The fact is, I had never before required anything of him, which was directly contrary to his will. Hence there had never occurred anything to test the question, whether he was disposed to consider my will or his own as of supreme authority. But as soon as a case occurred, which brought him and myself into direct and naked collision, his disposition was revealed in an instant. How unyielding that spirit of disobedience was, I have already related.

I have thought that this part of the incident illustrates the reason why so many sinners *are not,* and why some sinners are in a state of conviction. So long as they do not feel anything to be *immediately* required of them, which is at variance with their own wishes and pursuits, they are at ease in sin. They feel no distinct opposition to the law of God, and are not in fact *convinced* that they are sinners. Let God grant a sinner's desires, and require of him only external service, and he would be entirely content. But let the Holy Spirit present before him the law in all its broadness, let him see that he must submit his will unreservedly and universally to the will of God, and he is at once in open rebellion. He was living without the law before, but let the commandment thus come and his sinful disposition revives; that is, comes forth in its power, and he dies, that is, yields himself at once to its deadly influence. Thus the commandment which was unto life, that is, would have secured his happiness had he obeyed, is in consequence of his disposition found to be unto death. We see, therefore, why it is that men are not, when in a state of thoughtfulness, conscious of their enmity to God: namely, because they do not feel that his law is opposed to their will, and we see how it is, that their real character at once is revealed, when the real character of God is brought into immediate collision with their desires.

2. It will be remembered, that I offered my child food, and he would not take it. I offered to receive him to my arms, if he would renounce his hostility to me, and evince it by simply putting forth his arms to come to me. I would not force him to come, nor would I treat him with favor until he submitted. I was right and he was wrong. He might at any moment have put an end to the controversy. He was therefore inflicting all this misery voluntarily upon himself.

Here several things are to be observed.

1. The terms I offered him were perfectly kind. I was willing to pass by all that he had done, if he would only evince a right disposition. 2. I could offer no other terms. To have received him on any other terms would have been to allow that his will was to be my rule of action, and whenever he set out to have his own way, I

must have obliged my whole family to have conformed in all their arrangements to his wishes. He must have been made the centre of the whole system. A whole family under the control of a child 15 months old! How unjust this would have been to all the rest, is evident. Besides, my other children and every member of my family would have been entitled to the same privilege. Hence there would have been as many supreme authorities as there were individuals, and contention to the uttermost must have ensued.

Again, suppose I had subjected all my family to this infant's caprice, and had done so whilst he remained under my roof, how could I have afflicted him with a more grievous curse? He would soon have entered a *world where other and more powerful beings than he* would have opposed his will, and his disposition which I had cherished must have made him miserable as long as he lived.

Or again, if all this had been done, he could not have been made happy. He did not *know enough* to be able to secure his own happiness. Had I let him do as he pleased, he would have burnt and scalded himself a dozen times a day, and would very soon have destroyed his life. Seeking, therefore, his good, and the good of the family, I could do nothing else than I did. Kindness to him as much as to them, taught me not to yield to him on any other terms than a change of disposition.

On the contrary, by yielding to me, my whole family has been restored to order; he is happier by far than he has ever been before, and he is acquiring a disposition which will fit him for the wide world, which, if he lives, he will enter upon.

So, to apply all this to the case of a sinner, *God* can offer a sinner *no other terms than repentance.* To yield to the sinner's will, and save him without the unconditional surrender of his will, would be to make the sinner's will the centre of the moral universe. How would you like amoral government founded on your neighbor's caprice? It would be to throw down the government of law, and make this universe a hell.

It would be unkind to the sinner himself. He does not know enough of the universe to secure his own happiness, if he were permitted to act without control. He would make a hell for himself, even if God left him entirely alone. It is, therefore, infinitely kind in God to resist him, for if he were not resisted, he would destroy the happiness of the universe and himself together. By resisting him, he only ruins himself.

To avoid all these evils, God only requires of him to surrender his own willful and wicked opposition, and be happy. Is it not exceedingly reasonable that he should do so? Is there anything to cause his pain but his own willful obstinacy? Does he not inflict all his misery upon himself? In one word, the creature is trying every possible means of escape from the wrath to come, except submission, and this it obstinately and most sensitively avoids. Ought we to tell a sinner in such a state to wait, to use the means or to submit to God, while yet he was holding out the sceptre of mercy?

3. Again. When very hungry, my child accepted of bread from my hand while yet his opposition to me was unchanged. Extreme distress produced a forced yielding, so far as to secure an immediate alleviation, but his heart was the same as ever.

Thus we fear it is with many a convicted sinner. He sees that eternal destruction is before him, and he must yield or perish. He yields as it were *to force.* He gives up this and that and the other external sin. He surrenders the objects on which his heart is set, rather than his heart itself. The stream is changed rather than the fountain. He gradually convinces himself that God has pardoned him, and settles down too frequently in a false hope. At other times God reveals to him again the deceitfulness of his heart with still greater clearness, and he is yet more distressed than ever. Happy are they who are thus led to surrender their whole body and soul and spirit a living sacrifice to their God and Redeemer.

4. The change, as I remarked, was instantaneous. He might have obeyed me as well twenty-four hours before. It produced an instantaneous change in his whole character.

So in the case of conversion. The sinner has only to submit himself to the righteous government of God, and accept of the Saviour's sacrifice, and the agony is over. There is no reason why he should delay. You may do it now, reader, whilst your eyes rest upon this trifling relation. The moment of your doing so, will introduce you to a new world. You will be filled with love to God. The peace that passeth understanding will be shed abroad in your heart. Your bosom will glow with love to the whole family of the redeemed on earth and in heaven. You will find that happiness can never be obtained by obeying your own will, but that it is obtained only by relinquishing it, and making God the centre of your affections, the eternal rest of your soul.

I will close with a very few words of address.

1. We frequently hear persons declare that they are not opposed to God, and therefore need not a change of heart. My dear friend, should God set his law before you in the full exactitude of its enactment; should he cut you off from every thing you love until you obeyed his law, and loved him with all your soul, and mind, and strength, how would it be with you? How would you love such a God, and such a government? In such a condition you will soon find yourself. Is it not true then that you must be born again?

2. To the convicted sinner I would say, that all your distress results from the conviction that you must submit your will to God, or perish. Unqualified submission, is, to an unhumbled heart, the most grievous of all things. But I pray you consider that it is just. God's throne would be iniquitous unless he required it. You cannot be happy without it. You will be happy as soon as you do it. The whole redeemed universe will rejoice to welcome you to their family. *Submit yourself unto God.*

Not only is God just in this, he is infinitely compassionate. He gave his own Son to suffer, to render this offer possible. Now is his day of grace. He only asks you to be his dear child. His language during all your obstinate resistance to the strivings of his Spirit is, How can I give thee up, Ephraim? How can you resist so compassionate a Redeemer any longer?

3. But beware of a false peace. It is not giving up the objects of our regard, it is the surrendering of the will itself that is repentance. It is the renouncing our own will, and placing the will of God on the throne of our hearts. Let us pray for the searchings of his Spirit, that we may not, in so important a question, be deceived.

4. The evidence of this change is found in a life conformed to the will of God. It our wills are carnal and selfish, our lives will be so too. If the will of God rules in us, our lives will exemplify the holiness of his law. We shall love his society. We shall love to please and obey him. We shall love all holy beings, and derive much of our happiness from communion with the saints.

A Plain Man
[Francis Wayland]

6. John J. C. Abbott Gives Advice to Mothers, 1834

. . .

Mothers have as powerful an influence over the welfare of future generations as all other causes combined.—Thus far the history of the world has been composed of the narrations of oppression and blood. War has scattered its unnumbered woes. The cry of the oppressed has unceasingly ascended to heaven. Where are we to look for the influence which shall change this scene, and fill the earth with the fruits of peace and benevolence? It is to Christianity as taught from a mother's lips. In nine cases out of ten, the first six or seven years decide the character of the man. If the boy leave the paternal roof uncontrolled. turbulent and vicious, he will, in all probability, rush on in the mad career of self-indulgence. There are exceptions. But these exceptions are rare. If, on the other hand, your son goes from home accustomed to control himself, he will most undoubtedly retain that habit through life. If he has been taught to make sacrifices of his own enjoyment, that he may promote the happiness of those around him, he will continue to practise benevolence, and consequently will be respected and useful and happy. If he has adopted firm resolutions to be faithful in all the relations of life, he in all probability will be a virtuous man, and an estimable citizen, and a benefactor of his race.

When our land is filled with virtuous and patriotic mothers, then will it be filled with virtuous and patriotic men. She who was first in the transgression, must be yet the principal earthly instrument in the restoration. Other causes may greatly aid. Other influences must be ready to receive the mind as it comes from the mother's hand, and carry it onward in its improvement. But the mothers of our race must be the chief instruments in its redemption. The brightest rays of the millennial morn must come from the cradle. This sentiment will bear examining; and the more it is examined the more manifestly true will it appear. It is alike the dictate of philosophy and experience. The mother who is neglecting personal effort, and relying upon other influences for the formation of virtuous character in her children, will find, when it is too late, that she has fatally erred. The patriot who hopes that schools, and lyceums, and the general diffusion of knowledge, will promote the good order and happiness of the community, while family government is neglected, will find that he is attempting to purify the streams which are flowing from a corrupt fountain. It is maternal influence, after all, which must be the great agent, in the hands of God, in bringing back our guilty race to duty and happiness. O that mothers could feel this responsibility as they ought! Then would the world assume a different aspect. Then should we less frequently behold unhappy families and broken-hearted parents. A new race of men would enter upon the busy scene of life, and cruelty and crime would pass away. O mothers! reflect upon the power your Maker has placed in your hands. There is no earthly influence to be compared with yours. There is no combination of causes so powerful, in promoting the happiness or the misery of our race, as the instructions of home. In a most peculiar sense, God has constituted you the guardians and the controllers of the human family. . . .

John J. C. Abbott, *The Mother at Home* (London: John Mason, 1834), pp. 165–167.

7. Lucy Larcom Remembers the Pangs of Conscience, 1889

Although the children of an earlier time heard a great deal of theological discussion which meant little or nothing to them, there was one thing that was made clear and emphatic in all the Puritan training: that the heavens and earth stood upon firm foundations—upon the Moral Law as taught in the Old Testament and confirmed by the New. Whatever else we did not understand, we believed that to disobey our parents, to lie or steal, had been forbidden by a Voice which was not to be gainsaid. People who broke or evaded these commands did so willfully, and without excusing themselves, or being excused by others. I think most of us expected the fate of Ananias and Sapphira, if we told what we knew was a falsehood. . . .

I could not deliberately lie, but I had my own temptations, which I did not always successfully resist. I remember the very spot—in a footpath through a green field—where I first met the Eighth Commandment, and felt it looking me full in the face.

I suppose I was five or six years old. I had begun to be trusted with errands; one of them was to go to a farm-house for a quart of milk every morning, to purchase which I went always to the money-drawer in the shop and took out four cents. We were allowed to take a "small brown" biscuit, or a date, or a fig, or a "gibraltar," sometimes; but we well understood that we could not help ourselves to money.

Now there was a little painted sugar equestrian in a shop-widow down town, which I had seen and set my heart upon. I had learned that its price was two cents; and one morning as I passed around the counter with my tin pail I made up my mind to possess myself of that amount. My father's back was turned; he was busy at his desk with account-books and ledgers. I counted out four cents aloud, but took six, and started on my errand with a fascinating picture before me of that pink and green horseback rider as my very own.

I cannot imagine what I meant to do with him. I knew that his paint was poisonous, and I could not have intended to eat him; there were much better candies in my father's window; he would not sell these dangerous painted toys to children. But the little man was pretty to look at, and I wanted him, and meant to have him. It was just a child's first temptation to get possession of what was not her own,—the same ugly temptation that produces the defaulter, the burglar, and the highway robber, and that made it necessary to declare to every human being the law, "Thou shalt not covet."

As I left the shop, I was conscious of a certain pleasure in the success of my attempt, as any thief might be; and I walked off very fast, clattering the coppers in the tin pail.

When I was fairly through the bars that led into the farmer's field, and nobody was in sight, I took out my purloined pennies, and looked at them as they lay in my palm.

Lucy Larcom, *A New England Girlhood, Outlined from Memory* (Boston: Houghton Mifflin, 1889), pp. 74–77.

Then a strange thing happened. It was a bright morning, but it seemed to me as if the sky grew suddenly dark; and those two pennies began to burn through my hand, to scorch me, as if they were red hot, to my very soul. It was agony to hold them. I laid them down under a tuft of grass in the footpath, and ran as if I had left a demon behind me. I did my errand, and returning, I looked about in the grass for the two cents, wondering whether they could make me feel so badly again. But my good angel hid them from me; I never found them.

I was too much of a coward to confess my fault to my father; I had already begun to think of him as "an austere man," like him in the parable of the talents. I should have been a much happier child if I had confessed, for I had to carry about with me for weeks and months a heavy burden of shame. I thought of myself as a thief, and used to dream of being carried off to jail and condemned to the gallows for my offense: one of my story-books told about a boy who was hanged at Tyburn for stealing, and how was I better than he?

Whatever naughtiness I was guilty of afterwards, I never again wanted to take what belonged to another, whether in the family or out of it. I hated the sight of the little sugar horseback rider from that day, and was thankful enough when some other child had bought him and left his place in the window vacant. . . .

E S S A Y S

In the first essay, Philip Greven of Rutgers University, one of the pioneering historians of American family and childhood, addresses the childrearing methods of evangelical Protestants—from colonial Puritans to antebellum Methodists. While Greven's chronological scope is broad, his emphasis on the importance of subduing children's wills resonates with the themes that other scholars associate with childrearing practices before the American Revolution. Given popular assumptions about early American childrearing, Greven's analysis of children's attire and discipline deserves special attention.

In the second essay, Anne Scott MacLeod of the University of Maryland, who has written extensively on the "moral tales" authored and read by antebellum Americans, uses children's fiction as a backdrop to the lived experiences of American children in the decades leading up to the Civil War. Like other scholars of childrearing in the new nation, she emphasizes the development of conscience through careful, loving parenting. She also explores the relationship between ideal and reality by drawing comparisons between stories *for* children (short stories and novels) and stories *by* children (autobiographies and memoirs).

Breaking Wills in Colonial America

PHILIP GREVEN

Evangelical family government was authoritarian and rigorously repressive. Parental authority was absolute, and exercised without check or control by anyone else within the household. Obedience and submission were the only acceptable responses for children. Over and over again, from the early seventeenth century through at least the

Philip Greven, *The Protestant Temperament: Patterns of Child-Rearing, Religious Experience, and the Self in Early America* (Chicago: University of Chicago Press, 1977), pp. 32–38, 42–46, 49–55. Copyright © 1977 by Philip J. Greven Jr. Used by permission of Alfred A. Knopf, a division of Random House, Inc.

early nineteenth century, the same themes appear in the writings of evangelicals about discipline and family government. . . .

. . . The authoritarianism of evangelical family government—unquestioning obedience on the part of the ruled—did not imply that parents had to "play the tyrant in order to enforce their [children's] obedience," however. "Habitual obedience has no need of such severities; it is yielded readily, and as a matter of course. Nothing short of very obstinate and habitual disobedience can bring matters to such extremities." As was clear to other evangelicals also, "Parents, who govern well, never suffer their children to arrive at such a pass, that nothing short of torture will coerce them. They commence the business in season, and enforce obedience by gentler methods; they master the disease at its first appearance, and so avoid the necessity of desperate remedies." . . .

From the earliest months of life through the subsequent years of childhood, evangelical parents acted upon the assumption that parental authority was unlimited and incontrovertible. Parents systematically imposed their own wills upon their infants and small children without interference from servants or grandparents. Total power of parents, total dependency and obedience of children—this was the persistent polarity. The parent-child relationship thus was shaped by a stark and sharply defined gulf between the generations—an enormous and unbridgeable distance between parents and children, which implicitly denied to children any rights to their own desires, needs, or wishes that might be at odds with those designed for them by their parents. . . .

With remarkable consistency and persistence, evangelicals through the centuries insisted that parents must control and break the emerging will of children in the first few years of life. The central issue, as they perceived it, was this: the autonomous will and self-assertiveness of the child must be reduced to impotency, be utterly suppressed and contained, or the child ultimately would be damned for eternity. "Break their wills," urged John Wesley, "that you may save their souls." This simple injunction, reiterated again and again, was the keystone to the evangelical method of child-rearing. Everything in the subsequent lives of these children depended upon the success or failure of this policy of unrelenting repression, which shaped their personalities and provided the foundations in experience early in life of the denial of self and self-will that formed the innermost core of evangelical religious experience and belief. To understand evangelicals and evangelicalism, it is imperative to understand the goals and practices of discipline that dominated the earliest years for the children of evangelical families. As the Reverend George Whitefield observed, when only twenty-three years old himself, if parents "would but have resolution to break their [children's] wills thoroughly when young, the work of conversion would be much easier, and they would not be so troubled with perverse children when they are old."

The imposition of parental wills, and the disciplining of children's wills, undoubtedly began very early in life, often within the first year, although very few sources survive to describe precisely how such control might have been exerted. Two mothers, one English and the other American, one the mother of evangelicals and the other the daughter of an evangelical, did leave a few observations about their practices during the infancies of their children. Esther Edwards Burr, a daughter of Jonathan Edwards and the wife of the Reverend Aaron Burr, an early president of Princeton, wrote in 1754 to her intimate friend Sarah Prince (daughter of the

Reverend Thomas Prince of Boston) that "I had almost forgot to tell you that I have begun to govourn Sally [her firstborn child]. She has been Whip'd once on *Old Adams* account, and she knows the differance between a Smile and a frown as well as I do. When She has done any thing that She Suspects is wrong, will look with concern to See what Mamma Says, and if I only knit my brow, She will cry till I Smile, and altho She is not quite Ten months old, yet when She knows so much, I think tis time She should be taught." Such discipline and early government of an infant was not always easy for a parent, essential though it was deemed to be. As Esther Burr added, "none but a parent can conceive how hard it is to chastise your *own most tender self,* I confess I never had a right idea of the mothers heart at such a time before, I did it my Self too, and it did her a vast deal of good. If you was here I would tell you the effect it had on her." For all her affection for her child, she was too much the daughter of an evangelical Christian not to know that a beginning must be made early, in order to subdue sin and self-will in the child while still in the cradle.

Similarly, Susanna Wesley recalled her own methodical ways of nursing, rocking, and disciplining her children from their infancy—but with none of the tenderness and affection evident in the comments by Esther Burr:

> The children were always put into a regular method of living, in such things as they were capable of, from their birth; as in dressing and undressing, changing their linen, etc. The first quarter commonly passes in sleep. After that they were, if possible, laid into their cradle awake, and rocked to sleep, and so they were kept rocking till it was time for them to awake. This was done to bring them to a regular course of sleeping, which at first was three hours in the morning and three in the afternoon: afterwards two hours, till they needed none at all. When turned a year old (and some before) they were taught to fear the rod and to cry softly, by which means they escaped abundance of correction which they might otherwise have had: and that most odious noise of the crying of children was rarely heard in the house, but the family usually lived in as much quietness as if there had not been a child among them.

From the mother of the founder of "Methodism," these words leap off the page as testimony to the carefully controlled pattern of daily life governing the infants in her family from the day of their birth. "A regular method of living," "a regular course of sleeping" require no imagination to infer the imposition of parental goals. Every aspect of the infant's life was controlled by the mother, or by the servants who did her bidding. Strictly maintained schedules of sleep and feeding assured that the infant's needs and desires would be shaped into conformity with the intentions and plans of the parents. In the Wesley household, at least, there was to be no such thing as demand feeding or uninterrupted sleep. The shaping and breaking of the child's will had begun during the first months of life.

Like Susanna Wesley and Esther Edwards Burr before him, John Witherspoon knew that the process of subjugation had to begin as early as possible, starting in infancy. "I would therefore recommend to every parent to begin the establishment of authority much more early than is commonly supposed to be possible; that is to say, from about the age of eight or nine months." "You will perhaps smile at this," he acknowledged, "but I do assure you from experience, that by setting about it with prudence, deliberation, and attention, it may be in a manner completed by the age of twelve or fourteen months."

Nevertheless, successive generations of evangelicals knew that breaking a child's will, even in infancy, was not easy. The imagery of repression and conquest which persists through the centuries in evangelical discussions of early childhood testifies to the difficulties and the constant challenges posed by the necessity of breaking children's wills. As John Wesley observed, "A wise parent . . . should begin to break their [children's] will, the first moment it appears. In the whole art of Christian education there is nothing more important than this. The will of a parent is to a little child in the place of the will of God. Therefore, studiously teach them to submit to this while they are children, that they may be ready to submit to his will, when they are men." "But in order to carry this point," he acknowledged, "you will need incredible firmness and resolution. For after you have once begun, you must never more give way."

Evangelical parents were engaged in war with their children, a war which could end only with total victory by the parents and unconditional surrender by the child. The imagery of their warfare is the language of conflict, of conquest, of breaking, crushing, subduing, destroying; the language of power unchecked and of resistance quelled. Might and right—the prerogatives of parenthood—faced defiance and rebellious willfulness—the characteristics of the unbroken child. Generation after generation of evangelical parents wrote about their battles with the pride and contentment that sprang from success. Their children, conquered, submitted and forgot their own early efforts at independence and selfhood.

Early in the seventeenth century, John Robinson observed that "surely there is in all children, though not alike, a stubbornness, and stoutness of mind arising from natural pride, which must, in the first place, be broken and beaten down; that so the foundation of their education being laid in humility and tractableness, other virtues may, in their time, be built thereon. This fruit of natural corruption and root of actual rebellion both against God and man must be destroyed, and no manner nourished, except we will plant a nursery of contempt of all good persons and things, and of obstinacy therein." In order to do this, he said that parents must see to it that "children's wills and wilfulness be restrained and repressed, and that, in time."

A century later, the same assumptions and similar imagery pervade the advice offered by Susanna Wesley to her son John for rearing children as she herself had raised her own:

> In order to form the minds of children, the first thing to be done is to conquer their will and bring them to an obedient temper. To inform the understanding is a work of time, and must with children proceed by slow degrees, as they are able to bear it; but the subjecting the will is a thing that must be done at once, and the sooner the better; for by neglecting timely correction they will contract a stubbornness and obstinacy which are hardly ever after conquered, and never without using such severity as would be as painful to me as to the child. . . . When a child is corrected it must be conquered, and this will be no hard matter to do, if it be not grown headstrong by too much indulgence. And when the will of a child is totally subdued, and it is brought to revere and stand in awe of the parents, then a great many childish follies and inadvertencies may be passed by. Some should be overlooked and taken no notice of, and others mildly reproved; but no wilful transgression ought ever to be forgiven children without chastisement less or more, as the nature of circumstances of the case may require. I insist on the conquering of the will of children betimes, because this is the only strong and rational foundation

of a religious education, without which both precept and example will be ineffectual. But when this is thoroughly done, then a child is capable of being governed by the reason and piety of its parents till its own understanding comes to maturity, and the principles of religion have taken root in the mind.

What is most striking about successive generations of evangelicals is their exceptionally fierce response to the emergent will of their children, and their insistence, over and over again, that parents must break the child's will in order to make the child obedient. . . . Breaking the child's will was the crucial step toward a lifelong experience of submission and self-denial.

Submission extended beyond the initial confrontations of infancy and very early childhood to dominate the lives of children throughout the years in which they remained under their parents' roof and tutelage. Parental discipline and the constant control exercised by parents over their children's lives never ceased entirely. As John Wesley noted, not even marriage "cancels or lessens the general obligation of filial duty," nor did obedience cease or lessen "by our having lived one-and-twenty years." "I never understood it so in my case," he acknowledged. "When I had lived upwards of thirty years, I looked upon myself to stand just in the same relation to my father as I did when I was ten years old. And when I was between forty and fifty, I judged myself full as much obliged to obey my mother in everything lawful, as I did when I was in my leading-strings"—from the time he could first walk. Obedience, first securely obtained by the successful conquest of the child's will, remained the central preoccupation of both parents and children in evangelical families.

Breaking children's wills was vital for discipline within evangelical families. But it was only the first stage in the imposition of rigorous parental control over the lives of children as they emerged from infancy and passed through childhood. From the time children could walk and talk, their outward lives were subject to daily discipline in diet, dress, and manner. Outward appearances counted even when parents acknowledged that godliness was not subject to external confirmation. But their actions implied over the generations that they were intent upon seeing that the outward lives of their children bore witness to the discipline and the self-denial which marked the true Christian. What one ate, how much one ate, how one dressed, and how one behaved mattered profoundly to evangelical parents, who sought to govern the outer lives of their children according to the values which dominated their inner lives as well.

Restrictions upon food and habits of eating probably began in infancy for many evangelicals, but little information has survived about the first year or so of life. The more general attitudes toward food as an agency of discipline, however, are apparent in some of the writings by evangelicals. John Robinson recommended that parents inure their children "from the first, to such a meanness in all things, as may rather pluck them down, than lift them up: as by plain, and homely diet, and apparel." Susanna Wesley, too, knew the importance of food in shaping the character of her children, and used it as a basic weapon in her armory of domestic discipline. Her description of her method of feeding her own children merits close attention:

> As soon as they were grown pretty strong they were confined to three meals a day. At dinner their little table and chairs were set by ours, where they could be overlooked; and they were suffered to eat and drink [small beer] as much as they would, but not to call for

anything. If they wanted aught they used to whisper to the maid that attended them, who came and spake to me; and as soon as they could handle a knife and fork they were set to our table. They were never suffered to choose their meat, but always made to eat such things as were provided for the family. Mornings they always had spoon meat; sometimes at nights. But whatever they had, they were never permitted at those meals to eat of more than one thing, and of that sparingly enough. Drinking or eating between meals was never allowed, unless in case of sickness, which seldom happened. Nor were they suffered to go into the kitchen to ask anything of the servants when they were at meat: if it was known they did so, they were certainly beat, and the servants severely reprimanded. . . .

They were so constantly used to eat and drink what was given them, that when any of them was ill there was no difficulty in making them take the most unpleasant medicine; for they durst not refuse it, though some of them would presently throw it up. This I mention to show that a person may be taught to take anything, though it be never so much against his stomach.

Her words tell it all: "confined," "suffered," "never permitted," "never allowed," "made to eat"—the language of control and conscious repressiveness. Food was a focal point for discipline in the Wesley household, as it undoubtedly was in other evangelical households as well. The advice of her son, in later years, simply confirmed her own practices. Noting that "Next to self-will and pride, the most fatal disease with which we are born, is *love of the world*," John Wesley observed disapprovingly that many parents "cherish 'the desire of the flesh,' . . . by studying to *enlarge the pleasure of tasting* in their children to the uttermost: not only giving them before they are weaned other things besides milk, the natural food of children, but giving them both before and after, any sort of meat or drink that they will take." To take pleasure in eating was an invitation to lust and unbridled sensuality in general. To discipline the palate and to govern the stomach, therefore, were important elements in shaping character. That was why evangelicals assumed that food was too important to permit children from infancy on to determine their own wishes and needs in this respect.

Clothing, too, was an indispensable focal point of discipline in evangelical households. Quakers, of course, beginning in the first generation of the mid-seventeenth century and persisting for generations thereafter, were particularly concerned about dress, as their plain style testified over the years. But the same was true of other evangelicals as well. As John Wesley said, "Whenever . . . I see the fine-dressed daughter of a plain-dressed mother, I see at once the mother is defective either in knowledge or religion." Since clothing provided visible clues to the inner person, rich and costly clothing could only mean one thing. "I am pained continually," Wesley said again, "at seeing religious parents suffer their children to run into the same folly of dress, as if they had no religion at all." . . .

While simplicity was considered to be indispensable to evangelicals, the actual clothing which their children wore was taken so much for granted by parents that the issue was rarely discussed in letters or diaries. Yet for the purposes of both discipline and the formation of temperament, the clothing of infants and small children was actually of profound importance. Throughout the Anglo-American world, probably at all levels of society from the poorest to the wealthiest, children were dressed in the clothing of females regardless of their actual gender. From infancy until about the age of six, both girls and boys wore petticoats or gowns, thus appearing almost indistinguishable on the basis of their clothing until boys were breeched, when they abruptly shifted to the clothes characteristic of young and adult men, giving up forever the feminine dresses and gowns they had worn throughout the formative years of childhood. The portraits of children from genteel and wealthy families which survive from the seventeenth and the eighteenth centuries . . . provide clear evidence of this practice among the upper ranks of early American society—a practice that continued throughout at least the first half of the nineteenth century and, in some families until the early twentieth century. There is no reason to assume that evangelicals and others did not share these practices, for rural families with large numbers of children would have found it very easy to pass the gowns from one child to the next, regardless of gender, as they were still doing in the late nineteenth century in the Middle West and probably elsewhere as well. Gowns of simple homespun were the clothing of farmers' boys and girls, while the genteel dressed in silks and satins. But every child before the age of six seems to have been dressed in clothing appropriate to females.

Clothing symbolized the feminization of children; and since being female meant being perceived as weaker, inferior, submissive, and obedient, the clothing of children became a part of the overall process of discipline by parents who sought to control and dominate the wills of their offspring. By having both boys and girls wear long dresses, with aprons and petticoats, their physical movements would be restricted and inhibited from the first stages of motion—crawling, walking, running, and climbing. Perhaps one of the major purposes of such clothing was to limit the play of very young children, as dresses so clearly limited the activities of girls and young women for the rest of their lives. Only boys eventually would be freed from these encumbering clothes, enabled to participate actively in the physical life of the world outside and beyond the household.

The choice of identical clothing for boys and girls also suggests that, by beginning life as visibly female, all children could be governed in the same ways and with the same goals in mind. All had wills that needed breaking and desires that needed to be subdued and suppressed. Girls would never have any outward sign of release from the submission of early childhood. Boys, once they took off their gowns, would see that they were different—and superior. Clothing was only a facet of these deeply engrained assumptions and beliefs; but the original experience of being conquered, broken, and feminine bound both sexes together in ways that would continue to shape their temperaments, values, and experiences throughout their lifetimes.

The attitudes toward food and clothing were symptomatic of a pervasive preoccupation with discipline that governed all aspects of children's lives. Their manners and deportment toward parents, siblings, and other persons both within and outside the household were also constantly subject to parental injunctions and oversight. Children's behavior in general was shaped by parental discipline long after the initial confrontations had been resolved successfully in favor of parental authority and the child's submission. . . .

The enduring symbol of the exercise of external authority and discipline by early American parents was the rod, the use of which is often thought to have been characteristic of discipline in evangelical families century after century. Severity did mark the conduct of some parents, of course, and the rod or physical punishment of various kinds were manifestations of discipline, sometimes even from infancy. . . .

Yet the use of the rod in fact usually testified to the failure of discipline rather than its success. The rod punished disobedience and external behavior which did not conform to the wishes of parents; but the actions themselves revealed a failure of parental discipline. The whole point of breaking a child's will early, as evangelicals knew, was to make the child's obedience habitual and "natural" from infancy, so that physical punishments and the use of the rod would be rarely necessary. If a child's will were broken successfully, obedience would not depend upon external coercions and threats. As John Witherspoon recognized, "The more complete and uniform a parent's authority is, the offences will be more rare, punishment will be less needed, and the more gentle kind of correction will be abundantly sufficient." "We see every where about us examples of this," he noted. "A parent that has once obtained, and knows how to preserve authority, will do more by a look of displeasure, than another by the most passionate words, and even blows." Successfully imposed discipline implemented from the earliest years of childhood minimized the need for the rod.

The most effective discipline of all, however, was not external—in response to parental punishments—but internal—in response to self-discipline. The use of the rod in discipline, which has been exaggerated in our portraits of the early American past, was probably the *least* effective method of all for the encouragement of self-discipline and conformity to the standards of behavior set by evangelical parents for their children. Important as outward behavior was to evangelicals, and preoccupied as they always were with the obedience of their children, their principal methods of discipline, once the children's wills had been conquered, focused upon the most effective source of control over their children's actions, feelings, and thoughts: their consciences.

The continuous pressure exerted by parents upon their children for perfect compliance with parental standards was augmented, from a very early age, by the pressures exerted by children upon themselves. Evangelical discipline was most successful when it was least dependent upon external commands and oversight. What made most evangelical children behave properly—whether or not any adult was around to notice—was their continuously active conscience, the inescapable inner disciplinarian, which governed their lives from early childhood through adulthood, monitoring, checking, censuring, and controlling their thoughts, feelings, and behavior. True discipline, for evangelicals, was self-discipline, and self-discipline was internal and inescapable. For this, a powerful conscience was essential, and the methods of child-rearing characteristic of evangelical families were designed to ensure the formation of such a conscience.

The interplay between conscience as an inner disciplinarian and parents as outer disciplinarians shapes the recollections of John Dane, the Ipswich tailor, who remembered: "When I was but a lettell boy, being edicated under godly parents, my Conshans was veary apt to tell me of evells that I should not doe. Being now about aight yers ould, I was given mutch to play and to run out without my fathers Consent and againe his comand. One a time, I haveing gone out most parte of the day, when my father saw me cum home, he toke me and basted me. I then cept home, and followed my busenes two or thre[e] dase. My father and mother Comended me, and told me that god would bles me if I obeyed my parents, and what the contrary would ishew in. I then thout in my harte, o that my father would beat me more when I did amis. I fard, if he did not, I should not be good." . . .

For evangelical children, conscience served as the inner voice for external authority—the expectations and commands of both parents and God. Their obedience was thus assured by the permanent presence within themselves of the internalized rules and restrictions upon feelings, thoughts, and behavior constantly invoked and enforced by their own consciences. But conscience often was a stricter disciplinarian than even parents, so that self-discipline proved much more effective in shaping the behavior of evangelical children than the prospects of punishment by parents.

The techniques used by Cotton Mather to shape the consciences and temperaments of his children were designed to foster both a sense of guilt and of shame. As he observed in 1706,

> I first begett in them an high Opinion of their Father's Love to them, and of his being best able to judge, what shall be good for them.
>
> Then I make them sensible, tis a Folly for them to pretend unto any Witt and Will of their own; they must resign all to me, who will be sure to do what is best; my word must be their Law.
>
> I cause them to understand, that it is an *hurtful* and a *shameful* thing to do amiss. I aggravate this, on all Occasions; and lett them see how *amiable* they will render themselves by well doing.

Mather's basic premise of discipline was the absolutism of his own paternal authority within the family, and the totality of submission on the part of children to their parent's will and wishes: "my word must be their law." But Mather knew that the most effective method for ensuring the compliance of children with the wills of their parents was not beatings but guilt and shame. The hurtfulness of doing "amiss" would be felt both by the parents and by the children, whose consciences would cause them intense inner pain; while the shamefulness of doing amiss would embarrass them in their own eyes and make them eager to be accepted once more by conforming to the will of their parents. Only by so doing could they ensure that they would be loved.

Love and fear were a potent combination in the disciplining of children. Jonathan Edward's grandfather, Richard Edwards, ruled his own family on these principles. As his son, Timothy Edwards, recalled: "God gave him not only wisdome to Govern himself, but also to Govern others, that he in his providence had put in Subjection to him. His Children and Servants, alwayes both Lov'd and fear'd him, and never despis'd him." Fear arose not from the use of the rod, but from the awesomeness of parental power directed against misbehavior. Richard Edwards "hated vice and wickedness wherever he Saw it. He abhorr'd to plead for, Justify, or make Light of Sin, because Committed by them that were nearly Related to him. . . . If his Children did amiss they must expect no favour from him, no more then if they were Strangers. Yea his Spirit (though he Lov'd them dearly) was more Stir'd against that which is evil in them then in Such as were but Neighbours." The Reverend Thomas Prince of Boston recalled that his own father had been "a very affectionate Husband and Father: In his former years, pretty severe in Governing his Family; of later, rul'd them with great ease and Gentleness." As Cotton Mather said, "I wish that my *children* may as soon as may be, feel the principles of *reason* and *honor,* working in them, and that I may carry on their education, very much upon those principles. Therefore, first, I will wholly avoid, that harsh, fierce, crabbed usage of the children, that would make them tremble, and abhor to come into my presence." "I will so use them," he added, "that they shall *fear* to offend me, and yet mightily *love* to see me, and be glad of my coming home, if I have been abroad at any time." . . .

There are hints throughout the generations that evangelical parents—and others too—used the threat of disownment as an ultimate weapon against disobedient children. This technique of discipline is suggested, for instance, in the example of Richard Edwards dealing with his disobedient children as if "they were Strangers." Cotton Mather noted that "I would have it looked upon as a severe and awful *punishment* for a crime in the family, to be *forbidden for awhile to come into my presence.*" Given the intensity of the relationship between parents and children, such a threat, even briefly and infrequently made, could evoke profound fear in a small child. There is no way of knowing how significant such threats and such techniques might have been. But a reasonable guess is that the frequent experience of anguish and terror reported by evangelicals who felt themselves cast out or banished from the sustaining presence of God implies that banishment from the presence of one's parents, and the withdrawal of their love, could be potent sources of fear indeed.

The reactions of Joseph Pike to his children suggest the power of the withdrawal of love and approval, as well as the potency of reproof and correction. "I love those of them who deserve it, very dearly; and, when I have observed them sober and religiously inclined, I thought them as near and dear to me as my own life"; "on the other hand," he added, "when I have observed anything in them that tended to hurt, such as wildness, rudeness, evil words, or actions, bad company, or an inclination to pride or height, or to this, or the other new fashion,—these things, I could not see in my children, without duly discountenancing, and advising, reproving, or correcting, as the nature of the offence required." And he continued—significantly for the impact of parental disapproval on their children's behavior—that "I bear my dear wife witness, that she has been of the same mind with me, in all these respects." When both parents joined together in offering love to children on the condition of exact compliance with their wishes and wills, the impact upon the child could be profound.

If displeasure came from the parents themselves, and no grandparents were around to intercede on the child's behalf, the loss of parental love and parental approval left children bereft of support, isolated within the family and totally at the mercy of their own desires and their own self-will, which got them punished in the first place. When their wills could only exist in conformity to the wills of their parents, who alone could decide "what shall be good for them," evangelical children left on their own and disapproved of by their parents could feel utterly devastated and destroyed. The loss of love left only fear. The options presented to children were clear and simple: either obey the wills of parents, or be cast away—left alone without other wills to guide and sustain them. For children whose wills had been broken early, such punishment—which focused upon their inner need to obey without deviation—indeed would be severe. What ultimately guaranteed their obedience was their inability to exist comfortably on their own. Conscience therefore provided them with internalized rules, which mirrored their parents' wishes and wills more faithfully than even parents might have thought possible. The methods of discipline most favored by evangelicals therefore had their most profound impact upon the moral consciences of evangelical children. For the rest of their lives, they would never be entirely freed from the pangs of guilt and the embarrassments of shame implanted within them during their earliest years.

Developing Character in Antebellum America

ANNE SCOTT MACLEOD

Americans have a long history of fervent aspiration for their children and about as long a tradition of making those aspirations publicly known. From the sermons and catechisms of the seventeenth century to the pop psychology of the twentieth, a record of American hopes for the next generation exists, in detail and in print. In the early nineteenth century, when the republic was young and national feeling ran high, concern for the future of the new nation and for the children who would soon be its active citizens became thoroughly intertwined. Together, these preoccupations produced a flood of advice literature for parents and instructive fiction for children, most of which said nearly identical things about ideal child management, on the one hand, and ideal child behavior, on the other. Both literatures were prescriptive, the fiction no less than the advice books, and the prescriptions were quite remarkably consistent. The image of the well-managed child and of the ideal home that was to produce him or her shine forth everywhere in the admonitory writing of the new American republic.

How closely reality fit these images is a great deal harder to know. The experience of children is difficult to penetrate at any time, the more so when it is the experience of a childhood long past. Children leave few accounts of themselves; we must almost always reconstruct their lives and ways from evidence supplied by adults.

Probably the most direct path we can find to a remote childhood is through autobiography, in spite of the fact that it is written by adults. Personal memoirs are no more free of distortion than other sources, of course. Memory is imperfect, and recall of childhood may well be colored by nostalgia, exaggeration, resentment, or any number of other emotions. Adults may remember their youth as harder or harsher than it was, or they may see it through a haze of sentiment that softens or romanticizes past reality. All the same, used with reasonable respect for its limitations, autobiography can be immensely revealing. If patterns appear, if the experience in one account is echoed in others, then it seems fair to assume some reality in what we read. . . .

. . . Accounts of this kind . . . can help a curious reader of the present day explore what match there was—if any—between prescription and the realities of child nurture. And autobiographies can also suggest some answers to the even more elusive question of how children responded to prescribed methods of child training.

Prescription, of course, includes the children's fiction of the early nineteenth century, which was written never to beguile children but always to teach them. More

Anne Scott MacLeod, "Child and Conscience," in *American Childhood: Essays on Children's Literature of the Nineteenth and Twentieth Centuries* (Athens: University of Georgia Press, 1994), pp. 99–113. Reprinted by permission of The University of Georgia Press.

specifically, children's fiction taught moral values; stories imparted the many lessons a child must learn if he was to become a responsible citizen and a moral human being. Since authors generally agreed on both the values they held and on the literary model . . . they followed, their stories sounded much alike.

At the center of each tale was a child character intended as a model for the child reader to emulate. This fictional ideal was generally good, which is to say obedient, industrious, affectionate to parents, and respectful toward authority; yet he or she was not (or at least not usually) a prig. Fictional children had faults and lapses from grace: they sulked or shirked or disobeyed their parents; they lost their tempers and teased their sisters, doubtless like children the authors really knew. What made them models was not their perfection, which did not exist, but their sensitive consciences, which did. The fictional child who did wrong was quick to repent and eager to reform, and of all the qualities the authors tried to implant in children, these were perhaps the most important. Early nineteenth-century children's fiction was too close to eighteenth-century thinking to postulate perfection in human form, especially in children. What could be hoped for and, more to the point, inculcated, was an active conscience capable of correcting inevitable missteps and serving as a steadying guide in a far from perfect world.

"Inculcated" was the operative word. Whatever the fictional child's strengths, they were not his by simple birthright. Though the Calvinist view of children receded after 1820, and so the nineteenth-century child was (generally) absolved of innate depravity, romantic notions of childhood perfection did not reach children's fiction until the latter half of the century. If few antebellum authors looked on children as limbs of Satan, fewer yet saw them as flawless. Quite the contrary, in fact; a major point in early nineteenth-century juvenile books was that the sound moral character of model children was a product, not a natural endowment. A good child represented the triumph of wise and loving parental guidance.

In fact, most children's stories were didactic in two directions. On the one hand, they instructed the child reader in the value of goodness and the doleful consequences of disobedience, carelessness, pride, and a host of other moral failings. At the same time, they offered models of correct child nurture for parents. Most early nineteenth-century children's fiction reflected the transforming influence of [French philosopher Jean-Jacques] Rousseau and [English philosopher John] Locke, who had taught that experience, rather than admonition, was the most effective teacher. Children's authors endorsed this philosophy wholeheartedly. They advised parents to forbid and warn as little as possible, in favor of allowing children to learn from the consequences of their own decisions, and they designated stories to show the method in practice.

In fiction, therefore, children discovered the error of their ways through the sad experience that inevitably followed wrongdoing in the books. Eight-year-old Sophia Morton, for example, hated sewing, and said so. Her rational mother did not argue or demand but quietly locked up Sophia's workbasket until she should ask for it again. It is only fair to record that Sophia's was not a simple case of laziness. With the time she gained by giving up sewing, Sophia turned her mind to learning Greek and catching up with her brother in Latin, and very happy she was, at first, without her seams to stitch. But the day inevitably came when Sophia began to be tired of "looking like a slut." Then events moved swiftly, as they always do in these stories. Sophia was invited to a dance, where she overheard the other children criticize her roundly for her "shabby" and "sluttish" dress. As the philosophers had promised, experience spoke and Sophia heard: "How foolishly, how wrong, I have acted! said Sophia," enlightened at last. It is typical of the literature, however, that Sophia's own conclusions were firmly reinforced by her mother: "You will one of these days, my daughter, become a woman; and you will then discern . . . how happy you were to have been taught . . . when you were young, all those things which every woman ought to know. . . . Let her be ever so learned or so wise, she will always be laughed at, if she is found to be ignorant of them."

Since Providence did not always oblige with suitable as well as timely punishment, parents also had to discipline children. But discipline was to be rational, combining love and firmness in judicious proportion. Lydia Maria Child recommended gentleness toward children in *The Mother's Book:* "It's effects are beyond calculation, both on the affections and the understanding." But, she added, "that is not all; there should be united with [gentleness] firmness—great firmness." Affection and reason were the twin pillars of family management, in children's books as in advice literature, both of which assumed that children were rational as well as affectionate by nature. Authors counseled that quiet meditation was more effective than punishment, since it allowed a child's own powers of reasoning to bring about reform; many a fictional child improved his character by solitary contemplation of his sins. While lonely reflection was usually imposed by parents, it could also be self-administered. In one of the numerous "contrast" stories of the time, a bad boy, "hooted" by the other boys in the village, retires alone to seek the cause. "He . . . confined himself to his room, for some days. There he reasoned with himself on the cause that could produce such treatment. . . . 'For what reason,' said he to himself, 'could my little neighbors . . . hoot me?' . . . On comparing the good boy's behavior with his own, he very soon discovered the reason. To become sensible of our errors is half the work of reformation."

Catherine Sedgwick's *Home* draws the thinnest of fictional veils over detailed instruction on the subject of family government. In an early chapter of this rather solemn story, Wallace Barclay, a ten-year-old lad with a terrible temper, kills his sister's kitten in a fit of rage. Father despairs of his son's character ("the boy is hopeless!"). Though Mother is more optimistic ("my dear husband! Hopeless at ten?"), she agrees that it is time for stern measures. "'Go to your own room,' Mr. Barclay tells Wallace, 'You have forfeited your right to a place among us.'"

Wallace spends the next two weeks in silence: "[He] went to school as usual, and returned to his solitude, without speaking or being spoken to." When his aunt protests because he is "mewed up" so long, his mother explains the family philosophy: "We do not keep him mewed up . . . nor does he continue mewed up, for a single flash of temper, but because, with all his good resolutions, his passionate temper is constantly getting the better of him. There is no easy cure for such a fault. If Wallace had the seeds of consumption, you would think it the extreme of folly not to submit to a few weeks' confinement, and how much worse than a consumption is a moral disease!"

Most of the assumptions and all of the purposes of these stories can be found many times over in children's fiction of the period. Writers pressed parents to take the moral lapses of their children seriously yet they also urged them to treat children as rational beings. They condemned physical punishment and constant reproach as useless—or worse, as Lydia Maria Child observed: "Constant reproof may lead a child to conceal faults; but it seldom leads one to overcome them." And if harsh words were a mistake, still less helpful was harsh physical punishment. Jacob Abbott, one of the most influential children's authors of his time, remarked many times in his stories on the evil effects of overseverity. The "wild and reckless character" of a boy in one of Abbott's *Franconia* tales is explained as "partly his father's fault, who never gave him any kind and friendly instruction, and always treated him with a great degree of sternness and severity." A child badly reared, wrote another author, "had so much to unlearn; so much of hardness and unkindness, falsehood and indolence, that he did not know where to begin."

Better than "hardness," the writers counseled, was the "law of love." The only right way to govern any one is by giving them confidence in your kindly feelings toward them—by love." Sedgwick's Mr. Barclay brought the two halves of the philosophy together: "[He] held whipping on a par with such nostrums in medicine as peppermint and lavender, which suspend the manifestation of the disease, without conducing to its cure. He believed the only effectual and lasting government—the only one that touches the springs of action, and in all circumstances controls them, is *self*-government. It was this he labored to teach his children. The process was slow but sure. It required judgement, and gentleness, and above all, patience on the part of parents, but every inch of ground gained was kept. The children might not appear so orderly as they whose parents are like drill-sergeants . . . but; deprived of external aid or restraint, the self-regulating machine shows its superiority."

What the stories said was said again, and at length, in the many advice books on child management. As stern admonitions about "breaking a child's will" early in life gave way to kinder assumptions about child nature, a less rigorous—and less anxious—form of nurture became possible. If it was no longer necessary to see childish misbehavior as evidence of inborn evil, then correction of it could be milder and, doubtless, more optimistic. "What we call a natural love of mischief," said *The Mother's Book,* "is, in fact, nothing but activity. . . . If [children] are not furnished with what is useful or innocent, they will do mischief." With some rock-hard exceptions, child nurture authors agreed with fiction writers that the true source of obedience was love, rather than fear, and that the soundest family order built upon affection and respect between parent and child. Throughout the first half of the nineteenth century, orthodox and reform writers alike counseled parents that "environment, persuasion, example, precept and carefully formed habits" were the best instruments of home training. "The most efficient family government may be almost entirely administered by affection," according to John S. C. Abbott, "if it be distinctly understood that disobedience cannot pass unpunished. . . . It is ruinous to the disposition of a child, exclusively to control him by [fear.]" When Lyman Cobb published a book called "The Evil Tendencies of Corporal Punishment" in 1847, he was not breaking new ground but summarizing several decades of advice literature.

To authors of children's books and advice literature, the advantage of self-regulation was as apparent as it was to Mr. Barclay, and the best possible argument for firm but gentle parenting. Harsh training might produce a child—and ultimately an adult—obedient to *external* restraint, but external restraints were few in nineteenth-century American society. An upbringing that produced a sensitive conscience, on the other hand, made for *internal* control; independent, individual, and reliable. Nineteenth-century parents would not have understood the twentieth-century dread of guilty feelings; to them guilt was the signal that conscience was at work. "Guilt fixes . . . the sting of remorse within the bosom," and remorse, most nineteenth-century Americans believed, would spur improvement.

Didactic fiction and admonitory advice literature are easy to dismiss as tracts whose examples are idealized beyond any connection with reality. It is certainly true that the children who emerge from autobiography are not much like either the pattern children of fiction or the exemplary models of advice literature. If nothing else, their mischief was more creative than the feeble pranks that didactic authors invented for their characters. The children of autobiography did not sin and learn in equal measure; indeed, they often created havoc without necessarily supplying a moral text for their mentors. The enterprising children of Samuel Gridley and Julia Ward Howe were immortalized in two autobiographies by Laura E. [Howe] Richards, one for children, one for adults. Richards tells of being up-ended in a horse trough at age four by her brother Harry, age six, who felt no malice toward her; he only wanted to know what would happen. True, scientific curiosity also moved Harry to drop wet sponges down the stairwell of the tall Boston house where the Howes lived onto the bald heads of his father's distinguished visitors. Years later, when he was a celebrated scientist, Harry sighed a little because he could afford orchestra seats at the opera, which offered less scope than the balcony for experimentation. It is hard to find the moral here. In fact, few of the Howe children's many and varied escapades (Flossy and Julia drinking train oil under the impression it was syrup, Laura falling into the sugar barrel while trying to satisfy her sweet tooth) seems to have promoted much moral reflection.

Jeanette Gilder's memoirs are a lively catalog of her childhood scrapes, only a few of which improved her character noticeably. She certainly felt remorse from time to time; however, as neither she nor anyone else knew what she might do next time, her education by experience proceeded slowly. When she ran away (at nine) to join the Union army, the colonel of her chosen regiment hastily sent her back to her family, but she was not discouraged. "I was marched promptly off to bed, but I made a tent of my sheets, and with a broom for a musket, drilled myself till I was so tired that I fell asleep." Autobiography is full of such rowdy, inventive, scapegrace children, girls and boys alike, who were not always preoccupied with the pursuit of goodness.

Nevertheless, the fiction is not altogether misleading and the advice writers not entirely unvindicated. There is plenty of evidence in autobiography that American child nurture was often as mild and as reasonable as the experts recommended and as effective in developing a child's conscience as the fiction promised. Many American parents took their family obligations as seriously as any advice writer could wish. Alice Kingsbury's parents did not send their children away to school, because they "believed that their influence over us, their companionship, was more important in our development than that of strangers, and they consciously exerted themselves to provide what they considered the right influence to be true companions." In Kingsbury's memory, this approach was a success: "As a family, we were great comrades, great talkers, great laughers." William Dean Howells remembered a home "serenely bright with a father's reason and warm with a mother's love."

Frequent or severe physical punishment seems to have been rare, whether the family was rich or not, country or city, pioneer or settled gentility, northern or southern. Autobiographers remarked often on their parents' tolerance, sometimes with an air of faint surprise. If young Harry nearly drowned his little sister, even in a scientific spirit, he needed correction, but Julia Ward Howe was as rational and restrained as any fictional model. "We were almost never whipped," wrote Richards, "but for this misdeed Harry was put to bed at once, and our mother, sitting beside him, gave him . . . a 'talking to' which he did not soon forget."

Adela Orpen, child of pioneer Kansas, observed that "such a thing as father being unkind to his child was unheard of, and was in fact non-existent. No father was unkind, the children were too few and too precious." There must have been exceptions, but they are hard to find in autobiography. In quite a different setting, Cornelia Morse Raymond's father, who was president of Vassar College in the 1860s, had plenty of children—nine, in fact, who rocketed in and out of his study at will. Yet he, too, was patient and kind. When a visitor asked (cautiously) whether the noise bothered him, he said, "Good noise never bothers me." Raymond recorded that her father "never scolded" and "always understood," just as Laura Richards said that her father though "absorbed in high works," was "never out of patience" with his children. Caroline Creevey defused her own vivid imaginings of the Judgement Day by hoping that God was as forebearing as her mother: "God might be very like my mother who did not scold or punish severely, even when deeply offended. I could, generally, make her smile when she reproved me."

Indeed, the limits of parental tolerance could be quite surprisingly elastic. Eleanor Abbott and her sister, Madeline, granddaughters of the sage and famous Jacob, grew up in Cambridge, Massachusetts, where they were known in the neighborhood as "The Fighting Abbotts." "Our technique was simple. I caught and tripped the victim. Madeline sat on him. And we both pounded him. Most always it was only boys that we fought. I don't know why." After one especially stirring encounter, the fighting Abbotts returned home somewhat damaged. Their father met them at the gate "with rather a grave mouth but a twinkle in his eye. 'One might almost infer' he said, 'that there has been an accident.' 'There was!' I said, 'But we won it!'" The Abbotts, of course, knew everyone of intellectual consequence in Cambridge, and it is satisfying, somehow, to learn that enterprising Eleanor and her brother put a toad in James Russell Lowell's mailbox.

Tradition often holds that boys were punished more sternly than girls, but the memoirs furnish little evidence of it. James Weldon Johnson recorded that his mother spanked him sometimes (though "the force applied was never excessive") but his father never did so. "My Richmond grandmother's advice . . . about not sparing the rod and spoiling the child had no effect on him; not once in his life did he lay a finger in punishment on me or my brother." "There was never any scolding or punishing by my parents," wrote Ulysses S. Grant, "no objection to rational enjoyments, such as fishing, [or] going to the creek. . . . I have no recollection of ever being punished at home, either by scolding or by the rod." William Dean Howells's father admonished his sons when they had done wrong and "then ended the matter, as he often did, by saying 'Boys, consider yourselves soundly thrashed.'"

None of this meant that children lived their lives outside adult control. Though they so often called their childhood years "happy," "indulgent," or "carefree," autobiographers also remembered discipline. Of his father, Johnson wrote, "By firmness and sometimes by sternness, he did exercise strong control over us." Isabella Alden's parents were gentle and understanding but not all flaccid: "My mother was by no means given to changing her mind; having once spoken firmly, I had not the slightest hope of getting [what I wanted.]" As fiction and advice literature recommended, the discipline recorded in most autobiography aimed at the inner control of conscience, not the obedience of fear. "Mother never locked us in the closet for our misdeeds," observed Henrietta Skinner, "but she would say, 'Go upstairs to my bedroom, take a chair into the closet and sit there half an hour. You may leave the door open six inches for light and air.' It was never *said* that we were to take neither books nor toys to amuse ourselves . . . but it was 'understood.' We were *trusted,* and so it became impossible to do anything but carry out our punishment in its implied spirit."

The "law of love" *was* powerful: though her father never scolded, Cornelia Raymond recalled that "one word from [him] . . . always sank into my mind to become a moral principle influencing my whole life." Virginia Terhune Van de Water was an extremely sensitive child, painfully vulnerable to ridicule or thoughtless criticism. Her parents protected her when they could and themselves treated her with great gentleness. Affection gave them all the authority they needed over her. "To a loving child," her memoirs observe, "a parent's unhappiness means more than that parent's anger. . . . Love and faith had greater restraining power over me than had anger and fear." Una Hunt also admitted that her parents' loving, rational rule was successful, if not always welcome. "The matter was always explained to us and left to our better natures to decide—how I detested my Better Nature!"

Autobiography suggests that the longer-range results of this approach were all the moralists hoped for. Children did indeed develop tender consciences at an early age. Looking back, adults often remembered with dramatic clarity the first time they knowingly violated the moral standards they had learned from birth and experienced the pangs of a conscience they had not quite known they had. . . .

. . . Rachel Butz [, an Illinois girl, recalled that she] and her mother were visiting with Aunt Margaret and Rachel had been left alone with her supper. She found four apples in a box. "The temptation proved too great. . . . I took one, shut the box and ran out into the yard to eat the coveted fruit." Guilt spoiled her pleasure immediately. "I choked on the fruit"; it lay "like a heavy burden on my heart." Aunt Margaret wondered out loud who could have taken the apple and ended by deciding that the hired man must have been the culprit. "But I had not read the story of George Washington and his Little Hatchet in vain," wrote Butz. "I made full confession of my sin . . . sobbing meanwhile." Aunt Margaret offered to give the repentant sinner another apple, but "I had enough for that time and ever since then have I had the slightest inclination to take what was not my own."

James Weldon Johnson, raised in Florida, remembered that "one evening after dark [when] I and my brother, being in possession of a few pennies, conspired to run around the corner to Mrs. Handy's grocery store and buy two "prize" boxes of candy. We went without giving notice or asking permission. On starting back I became immediately aware of the gravity of the situation. With each step homeward my foreboding increased. . . . When I entered the house it was with as heavy a sense of sin as any infant conscience could carry."

Conscientious children were full of good resolutions, but they found perfect virtue hard to sustain. William Dean Howells and his brother read a boy's story in the *New York Mirror* that showed "how at many important moments the hero had been balked of fortune by his habit of lying. They took counsel together, and pledged themselves not to tell the smallest lie, upon any occasion whatever. It was a frightful slavery, for there are a great many times in a boy's life when it seems as if the truth really could *not* serve him. . . . My boy and his brother groaned under this good resolution, I do not know how long, but the day came when they could bear it no longer, though I cannot give just the time or the terms of their backsliding."

That memoirs often mention children's fiction in their accounts of moral crisis is not, I think, incidental. Didactic fiction repeated to children the same values they learned at church, at home, and at school. For most American children, the moral universe presented to them by adults was, at least in theory, coherent to a degree we would scarcely recognize. No one would argue that adult society always lived up to the moral code found in children's books; for that matter, neither the fiction or advice literature ever pretended it did. Literature was rife with warnings to children that the world was full of temptation and downright wickedness. But whatever its lapses in action, society endorsed the code in precept: honesty, industry, charity, self-control—such standard virtues received universal lip service. If children's fiction was not often unflinchingly realistic, neither was it wholly unconnected with its society. The family life it described was highly idealized, to be sure, but it was an ideal many American families acknowledged and some achieved.

Nor was advice literature just an abstraction, though it must have seemed irrelevant at some parental moments. The dominant Protestant, middle-class culture of the early United States took it as given that self-regulated citizens formed the basis of social order and that self-control, a commitment to the work ethic, and a reasonable concern for the good of the community were virtues indispensable to the young Republic. That these values were best instilled in children by rational means was a conviction that had taken root in the broad and varied American middle class of the late eighteenth century, planted, assuredly, by Locke and Rousseau but cultivated by the didactic children's stories of Maria Edgeworth and Hannah More. Henrietta Skinner wrote that her mother "had been brought up on the ideas of . . . Maria Edgeworth and . . . Hannah More, that children should be educated mentally and morally through lessons drawn pleasantly and easily from the practical things of life." If so, she was typical of many American parents whose mode of child rearing at least approximated the ideal set out in both books of advice and children's fiction, and whose success at creating self-regulated children acutely sensitive to the rule of conscience is recorded in many American memoirs of the early nineteenth century.

 F U R T H E R   R E A D I N G

Ariès, Philippe. *Centuries of Childhood: A Social History of Family Life.* Trans. Robert Baldick (1962).

Calvert, Karin. *Children in the House: The Material Culture of Early Childhood, 1600–1900* (1992).

Demers, Patricia. *Heaven upon Earth: The Form of Moral and Religious Children's Literature to 1850* (1993).

Greven, Philip. *The Protestant Temperament: Patterns of Child-Rearing, Religious Experience, and the Self in Early America* (1977).

Hawes, Joseph M., and N. Ray Hiner, eds. *American Childhood: A Research Guide and Historical Handbook* (1985).

Hoffert, Sylvia D. *Private Matters: American Attitudes Towards Childrearing and Infant Nurture in the Urban North, 1800–1860* (1989).

Kiefer, Monica. *American Children Through Their Books, 1700–1835* (1948).

Kuhn, Anne L. *The Mother's Role in Childhood Education: New England Concepts, 1830–1860* (1947).

Locke, John. *Some Thoughts Concerning Education.* Ed. John W. Yolton and Jean S. Yolton (1989).

MacLeod, Anne Scott. *American Childhood: Essays on Children's Literature of the Nineteenth and Twentieth Centuries* (1994).

_____. *A Moral Tale: Children's Fiction and American Culture, 1820–1860* (1975).

Murray, Gail S. "Rational Thought and Republican Virtue: Children's Literature, 1789–1820." *Journal of the Early Republic* 8 (Summer 1988): 159–177.

Nelson, Claudia, and Lynne Vallone, eds. *The Girl's Own: Cultural Histories of the Anglo-American Girl, 1830–1915* (1994).

Reinier, Jacqueline. *From Virtue to Character: American Childhood, 1775–1850* (1996).

Strickland, Charles. "A Transcendentalist Father: The Child-Rearing Practices of Bronson Alcott." *Perspectives in American History* 3 (1969): 5–73.

West, Elliott, and Paula Petrik, eds. *Small Worlds: Children and Adolescents in America, 1850–1950* (1992).

Wishy, Bernard. *The Child and the Republic: The Dawn of Modern American Child Nurture* (1968).

CHAPTER
4

Marriage and Family
in Victorian America

The ideal of romantic love is one that has fascinated Americans for generations. His-torians have traced the origins of the quest for fulfillment in marriage in the Anglo-American world to the seventeenth century, although examples of the romantic ideal can be found much earlier—in the tradition of courtly love in medieval Europe, for instance. But in the United States, the ideal of "companionate marriage," emphasiz-ing mutual respect and romantic love between the marriage partners, flourished after the American Revolution. Courtship rituals, wedding rites, and divorce regulations all underwent significant changes as men and women in the new nation looked to marriage as the ultimate source of personal satisfaction. By the mid-nineteenth cen-tury, the companionate ideal was widely embraced by white, well-to-do Americans.

The pervasiveness of the romantic ideal was reflected in a wide range of pub-lished and private writings. Etiquette guides and advice books offered young people advice on forming a marriage based on romantic love. In letters and diaries, women and men recorded their innermost feelings and intimate interactions. And when the quest for mutual satisfaction proved unsuccessful, husbands and wives brought their complaints to divorce court, revealing through their petitions what their expectations of marriage had been and how reality had fallen short of those expectations.

While white, well-to-do Americans generally agreed on the desirability of com-panionate marriage, the books they read, the letters they wrote, and the divorces they demanded all indicate that achieving the ideal was a difficult proposition. Men and women in nineteenth-century America—perhaps especially women, who had few sources of satisfaction beyond the home—struggled to resolve the contradictions of companionship. Husbands and wives puzzled over how to achieve equality in marriage in a society in which male dominance was the rule. They wrote countless letters that paid homage to the ideal of marital "oneness" at the same time that they testified to the reality of men's and women's separate lives. And they celebrated children as the tokens of their shared love and unity of purpose even as they con-tended with the fact that childbearing and child care imposed greater burdens on women than on men. In the quest to understand love, marriage, and family life in Victorian America, historians must grapple with these same difficulties.

While historians generally agree on the importance of the ideal of romantic love in marriage, they have not reached consensus on the degree to which Americans achieved this ideal. Several important questions remain unanswered: What is the relationship between prescription and practice? How did women's and men's different roles in marriage shape their attempts to achieve the companionate ideal? And why did women write so much more about their expectations and experiences of marriage than did men?

D O C U M E N T S

Nineteenth-century Americans aspired to the romantic ideal; they wanted to marry for love. In Document 1, a letter that seventeen-year-old New Englander Eliza Southgate wrote to her cousin, Moses Porter, in 1800, Southgate reveals both the pervasiveness of this ideal and her skepticism about its achievement. Her reflections illustrate that while both women and men longed for love, their roles in courtship were strictly differentiated—as they would continue to be in marriage.

Documents 2 and 3 suggest that nineteenth-century Americans' heightened expectations of matrimonial bliss might well have increased their chances for disappointment. In Document 2, written in 1815, Connecticut wife and schoolteacher Emma Willard offers her younger sister Almira Hart some sobering advice, warning her against hoping for too much happiness in marriage. South Carolina wife and author Caroline Gilman echoes these concerns in her 1838 autobiographical novel, *Recollections of a Southern Matron,* which is excerpted in Document 3.

A series of letters written between 1841 and 1846 from Virginia-born Martha Hunter Hitchcock to her cousins makes up Document 4. Hitchcock's marriage to a physician in the U.S. Army (whom she referred to as "the Dr.") resulted in frequent moves; in the five-year span covered by these letters, the Hitchcocks lived in five states: New York, Florida, North Carolina, Georgia, and Texas. Like many women who accompanied their husbands west, Hitchcock mourned the loss of her family and friends back home. Loneliness exacerbated Hitchcock's emotional dependence on her husband and, after a series of miscarriages (hinted at in the second letter), on her only child, Lillie, born in 1845.

Texan Elizabeth Scott Neblett's "Review of the past eight years," written for her husband, Will, in 1860, is included as Document 5. Neblett offers an oblique critique of Will's emotional distance, but at the same time she assumes primary responsibility for the marriage. Neblett's discussion of motherhood is likewise fraught with tension; while she regards children as the tangible evidence of her love for her husband, she also sees pregnancy and childbirth as a terrible source of suffering.

1. Eliza Southgate Expresses Her Opinion of Love Matches, 1800

September, 1800

. . . As I look around me I am surprised at the happiness which is so generally enjoyed in families, and that marriages which have not love for a foundation on more than one side at most, should produce so much apparent harmony. I may be censured for declaring it as my opinion that not one woman in a hundred marries for love. A woman of taste and sentiment will surely see but a very few whom she could love,

Clarence Cook, ed., *A Girl's Life Eighty Years Ago: Letters of Eliza Southgate Bowne.* New York, 1887. This document can also be found in Nancy Cott, ed., *Root of Bitterness: Documents of the Social History of American Women* (New York: Dutton, 1972), pp. 103–105.

and it is altogether uncertain whether either of them will particularly distinguish her. If they should, surely she is very fortunate, but it would be one of fortune's random favors and such as we have no right to expect. The female mind I believe is of a very pliable texture; if it were not we should be wretched indeed. Admitting as a known truth that few women marry those whom they would prefer to all the world if they could be viewed by them with equal affection, or rather that there are often others whom they could have preferred if they had felt that affection for them which would have induced them to offer themselves,—admitting this as a truth not to be disputed,—is it not a subject of astonishment that happiness is not almost banished from this connexion? Gratitude is undoubtedly the foundation of the esteem we commonly feel for a husband. One that has preferred us to all the world, one that has thought us possessed of every quality to render him happy, surely merits our gratitude. If his character is good—if he is not displeasing in his person or manners— what objection can we make that will not be thought frivolous by the greater part of the world?—yet I think there are many other things necessary for happiness, and the world should never compel me to marry a man because I could not give satisfactory reasons for not liking him. I do not esteem marriage absolutely essential to happiness, and that it does not always bring happiness we must every day witness in our acquaintance. A single life is considered too generally as a reproach; but let me ask you, which is the most despicable—she who marries a man she scarcely thinks *well* of—to avoid the reputation of an old maid—or she, who with more delicacy, than marry one she could not highly esteem, preferred to live single all her life, and had wisdom enough to despise so mean a sacrifice, to the opinion of the rabble, as the woman who marries a man she has not much love for—must make. I wish not to alter the laws of nature—neither will I quarrel with the rules which custom has established and rendered indispensably necessary to the harmony of society. But every being who has contemplated human nature on a large scale will certainly justify me when I declare that the inequality of privilege between the sexes is very sensibly felt by us females, and in no instance is it greater than in the liberty of choosing a partner in marriage; true, we have the liberty of refusing those we don't like, but not of selecting those we do. This is undoubtedly as it should be. But let me ask you, what must be that love which is altogether voluntary, which we can withhold or give, which sleeps in dullness and apathy till it is requested to brighten into life? Is it not a cold, lifeless dictate of the head,—do we not weigh all the conveniences and inconveniences which will attend it? And after a long calculation, in which the heart never was consulted, we determine whether it is most prudent to love or not.

How I should despise a soul so sordid, so mean! How I abhor the heart which is regulated by mechanical rules, which can say "thus far will I go and no farther," whose feelings can keep pace with their convenience, and be awakened at stated periods,—a mere piece of clock-work which always moves right! How far less valuable than that being who has a soul to govern her actions, and though she may not always be coldly prudent, yet she will sometimes be generous and noble, and that the other never can be. After all, I must own that a woman of delicacy never will suffer her esteem to ripen into love unless she is convinced of a return. Though our first approaches to love may be involuntary, yet I should be sorry if we had no power of controlling them if occasion required. There is a happy conformity or pliability in the female mind which seems to have been a gift of nature to enable them to be happy with so few privileges,—and another thing, they have more gratitude in their dispositions than men, and there is a something particularly gratifying to the heart in being beloved, if the object is worthy. . . . Indeed, I believe no woman of delicacy suffers herself to think she could love any one before she had discovered an affection for her. For my part I should never ask the question of myself—do I love such a one, if I had reason to think he loved me—and I believe there are many who love that never confessed it to themselves. My Pride, my delicacy, would all be hurt if I discovered such *unasked* for love, even in my own bosom. I would strain every nerve and rouse every faculty to quell the first appearance of it. There is no danger, however. I could never love without being beloved, and I am confident in my own mind that no person whom I could love would ever think me sufficiently worthy to love me. But I congratulate myself that I am at liberty to refuse those I don't like, and that I have firmness enough to brave the sneers of the world and live an old maid, if I never find one I can love. . . .

2. Emma Willard Gives Marital Advice, 1815

Emma Willard to Almira Hart, July 30, 1815

Dear Sister:

You think it strange that I should consider a period of happiness as more likely than any other to produce future misery. I know I did not sufficiently explain myself. Those tender and delicious sensations which accompany successful love, while they soothe and soften the mind, diminish its strength to bear or to conquer difficulties. It is the luxury of the soul; and luxury always enervates. A degree of cold that would but brace the nerves of the hardy peasant, would bring distress or death to him who had been pampered by ease and indulgence. This life is a life of vicissitude. A period of happiness, by softening and enervating the soul, by raising a thousand blissful images of the future, naturally prepares the mind for a greater or less degree of disappointment, and unfits us to bear it; while, on the contrary, a period of adversity often strengthens the mind, and, by destroying inordinate anticipation of the future, gives a relish to whatever pleasures may be thrown in our way. This, perhaps you may acknowledge, is generally true; but you cannot think it applies to your case—otherwise than that you acknowledge yourself liable to disappointment by death. But we will pass over that, and we will likewise pass over the possibility of your lover's seeing some object that he will consider more interesting than you, and likewise that you may hereafter discover some imperfection in his character. We will pass this over, and suppose that the sanction of the law has been passed upon your connection, and you are secured to each other for life. It will be natural that, at first, he should be much devoted to you; but, after a while, his business must occupy his attention. While absorbed in that he will perhaps neglect some of those little tokens of affection which have become necessary to your happiness. His affairs will

John Lord, *The Life of Emma Willard.* (New York: Appleton, 1873), pp. 44–45. This document can also be found in Nancy Woloch, ed., *Early American Women: A Documentary History, 1600–1900* (New York: McGraw-Hill, 1997), pp. 156–157.

sometimes go wrong, and perhaps he will not think proper to tell you the cause; he will appear to you reserved and gloomy, and it [will] be very natural in such a case for you to imagine that he is displeased with you, or is less attached than formerly. Possibly you may not in every instance manage a family as he has been accustomed to think was right, and he may sometimes hastily give you a harsh word or a frown. But where is the use, say you, of diminishing my present enjoyment by such gloomy apprehensions? Its use is this, that, if you enter the marriage state believing such things to be absolutely impossible, if you should meet them, they would come upon you with double force. We should endeavor to make a just estimate of our future prospects, and consider what evils, peculiar situations in which we may be placed, are most likely to beset us, and endeavor to avert them if we can; or, if we must suffer them, to do it with fortitude, and not magnify them by imagination, and think that, because we cannot enjoy all that a glowing fancy can paint, there is no enjoyment left. I hope I shall see Mr. L————. I shall be very glad to have you come and spend the winter with me, and, if he could with propriety accompany you, I should be glad to see him. I am involved in care. There [are] forty in our family and seventy in the school. I have, however, an excellent house-keeper and a very good assistant in my school. You seem to have some wise conjectures floating in your brain, but, unfortunately for your skill in guessing, they have no foundation in truth.

Little John says I must tell you he has learned a great deal. He goes to a little children's school, and is doing very well. Doctor has not yet gone to Pittsfield after mother, but expects to set out this week. We both feel very unpleasantly that he could not have gone before, but a succession of engagements made it impossible.

Yours affectionately,
Emma Willard

3. Caroline Gilman Recommends Wifely Submission, 1838

The planter's bride, who leaves a numerous and cheerful family in her paternal home, little imagines the change which awaits her in her own retired residence. She dreams of an independent sway over her household, devoted love and unbroken intercourse with her husband, and indeed longs to be released from the eyes of others, that she may dwell only beneath the sunbeam of his. And so it was with me. After our bustling wedding and protracted journey, I looked forward to the retirement at Bellevue as a quiet port in which I should rest with Arthur, after drifting so long on general society. The romance of our love was still in its glow, as might be inferred by the infallible sign of his springing to pick up my pocket-handkerchief whenever it fell. . . .

For several weeks all kinds of droll associations were conjured up, and we laughed at anything and nothing. What cared we for fashion and pretension? There we were together, asking for nothing but each other's presence and love. At length

Caroline Howard Gilman, *Recollections of a Southern Matron.* (New York: Harper & Brothers, 1838), pp. 250–257. This document can also be found in Nancy Woloch, ed., *Early American Women: A Documentary History, 1600–1900* (New York: McGraw-Hill, 1997), pp. 158–160.

it was necessary for him to tear himself away to superintend his interests. I remember when his horse was brought to the door for his first absence of two hours; an observer would have thought that he was going a far journey, had he witnessed that parting; and so it continued for some days, and his return at each time was like the sun shooting through a three days' cloud.

But the period of absence was gradually protracted; then a friend sometimes came home with him, and their talk was of crops and politics, draining the fields and draining the revenue. . . . I was not selfish, and even urged Arthur to go to hunt and to dinner-parties, although hoping that he would resist my urging. He went frequently, and a growing discomfort began to work upon my mind. I had undefined forebodings; I mused about past days; my views of life became slowly disorganized; my physical powers enfeebled; a nervous excitement followed: I nursed a moody discontent, and ceased a while to reason clearly. Wo to me had I yielded to this irritable temperament! I began immediately, on principle, to busy myself about my household. The location of Bellevue was picturesque—the dwelling airy and commodious; I had, therefore, only to exercise taste in external and internal arrangement to make it beautiful throughout. I was careful to consult my husband in those points which interested him, without annoying him with mere trifles. If the reign of romance was really waning, I resolved not to chill his noble confidence, but to make a steadier light rise on his affections. If he was absorbed in reading, I sat quietly waiting the pause when I should be rewarded by the communication of ripe ideas; if I saw that he prized a tree which interfered with my flowers, I sacrificed my preference to a more sacred feeling; if any habit of his annoyed me, I spoke of it once or twice calmly, and then bore it quietly if unreformed; I welcomed his friends with cordiality, entered into their family interests, and stopped my yawns, which, to say the truth, was sometimes an almost desperate effort, before they reached eye or ear.

This task of self-government was not easy. To repress a harsh answer, to confess a fault, and to stop (right or wrong) in the midst of self-defence, in gentle submission, sometimes requires a struggle like life and death; but these *three* efforts are the golden threads with which domestic happiness is woven; once begin the fabric with this woof, and trials shall not break or sorrow tarnish it.

Men are not often unreasonable; their difficulties lie in not understanding the moral and physical structure of our sex. They often wound through ignorance, and are surprised at having offended. How clear is it, then, that woman loses by petulance and recrimination! Her first study must be self-control, almost to hypocrisy. A good wife must smile amid a thousand perplexities, and clear her voice to tones of cheerfulness when her frame is drooping with disease, or else languish alone. Man, on the contrary, when trials beset him, expects to find her ear and heart a ready receptacle. . . .

I have not meant to suggest that, in ceasing to be a mere lover, Arthur was not a tender and devoted husband. I have only described the natural progress of a sensible, independent married man, desirous of fulfilling all the relations of society. Nor in these remarks would I chill the romance of some young dreamer, who is reposing her heart on another. Let her dream on. God has given this youthful, luxurious gift of trusting love, as he has given hues to the flower and sunbeams to the sky. It is a superadded charm to his lavish blessings; but let her be careful. . . .

Let him know nothing of the struggle which follows the first chill of the affections; let no scenes of tears and apologies be acted to agitate him, until he becomes accustomed to agitation; thus shall the star of domestic peace arise in fixedness and beauty above them, and shine down in gentle light on their lives, as it has on ours.

4. Martha Hunter Hitchcock Complains of Loneliness and Illness, 1840–1846

Martha Hunter Hitchcock to Martha Hunter,
January 28, 1840

If I had never married how much of pain, and dissatisfaction, should I have escaped—at all events I should never have known what jealousy is. You must not betray me, dear cousin, for in despite of all my good resolutions, I find it impossible always to struggle against my nature—the school of indulgence, in which I was educated, was little calculated to teach me, those lessons of forbearance, which I have had to practise so frequently, since my marriage—it is ungrateful in me to murmur, if perchance a little bitter is mingled in my cup of life, when it is given in kindness, to render the draught more wholesome—too much happiness, might intoxicate, and a few disappintments, a few ills, such as mine, are like a good medicine, given at a good time—

Martha Hunter Hitchcock to Martha Hunter,
September 20, 1840

I verily believe, that, in the whole course of our correspondence, I have never written you a letter, which did not contain some account of my ill health, or the consequences thereof:—and I, as firmly believe that should it continue (as I trust it will) to the end of my existence, you will never receive one, which will not inform you, either of my being, or of my having been very sick—for never, since I arrived at woman's estate, have I enjoyed three months, of uninterrupted health—and repeated illnesses, have so broken down my constitution, that I have little reason to hope, for any permanent exemption, from the sickness, and suffering, to which I have so long been the unwilling heir. . . . Thus you see my dear Cousin, that my sky is not always bright, tho I make the most of the sunshine, which sometimes gleams across my pathway—and I have sometimes fancied, that these occasional glimpses of happiness, are brighter, for the long, dark, intervals between—

Martha Hunter Hitchcock to Sarah Hunter,
March 8, 1841

I have been very sorely tried of late—and have been obliged to endure many things which I once thought, could never have fallen to the share of one, whose life had hitherto been but one series, of love and affection—I remember, when I first grew

---

Hunter Family Papers, Virginia Historical Society, Richmond, Virginia.

up, I should have looked with horror upon anyone, who had even suggested the probability of my ever leaving my parents—it would have been so revolting to my feelings—I never had thought of such a thing in my life, until after my marriage—and even then, I looked upon it, as only temporary—and thought, that like young birds, when weary of wandering, we would return to our nest again, and fold our wings forever, at home—how crude and erroneous, such ideas were, my subsequent life, has proved. So little, do we know of ourselves! and so shortsighted are we, whenever we attempt, to penetrate the mystery, in which our destiny in shrouded!!

Martha Hunter Hitchcock to Sarah Hunter, January 27, 1841

I have lived so long among strangers since my marriage, that when I contrast it with the old warm affection, in which I was nurtured, the contrast is so terrible, that I cannot refrain from weeping at the thought of it—I hope my dear cousin, that yours, will be a happier destiny than mine, in that respect—only think of it! nearly a year and a half have passed away, since I have seen, a single relation! . . . I have not the least idea, of seeing my friends, and my home, for years—The journey is so long—and so fatiguing—and the difficulty of procuring a leave of absence, so great to a Physician, whose services are constantly in requisition, and I could not think of undertaking so long a journey without my husband—my health is so precarious, that I should not dare to incur the dangers, and exposures of such a trip, without him, for the world—So that you see I have, not the remotest prospect of seeing them for a long time—perhaps never again!—The thought is so terrible, that I dare not dwell upon it.

Martha Hunter Hitchcock to Martha Hunter, February 12, 1845

I would have written to you before, my dear cousin Martha, but Lillie has been so very unwell, and I have been so much occupied with her, and so ill myself, that I could not make the necessary effort—I think that in all my bitter experience, I have never been so entirely, and hopelessly miserable, as I have been, during the past month—Uneasiness about Lillie, and very great sorrows of my own, which I cannot commit to paper, have almost weighed me down to the grave; and indeed, without any affectation, I look forward to that, as the only real rest, I shall ever know—

Martha Hunter Hitchcock to Sarah Hunter, July 22, [1845]

It is almost impossible to go [to Texas], without sacrificing every comfort, and leaving behind me, every trace of civilization—Still I am willing to undertake it, if the Dr will consent—Nothing is so terrible to me, as separations from the Doctor—You my dear cousin, who live quietly at home, with a pretty accurate knowledge of where you will be at the end of a month, can form little idea, of the state of suspense, in which us poor army folk live—It is a very trying life, yet like every other life, it has its spots of sunshine, as well as its shadows—I begin to believe that the good, and evil, of this world more equally distributed, than I used to think it—every situation has its trials—all have their advantages and their counterbalancing disadvantages—

When I see any one who is perfectly happy, and contented with his lot in life, I shall perhaps think differently—

**Martha Hunter Hitchcock to [?] Hunter,
November n.d., 1845**

I wonder if I shall ever be so blest, as to have a house, and home, which I can call my own—where I can sow the seed, and expect to gather the flower—plant the tree, and expect to reap the fruit—There are many pleasant things, in our Army life; and for a man, it must be preferable to all others—but for a woman, there are many drawbacks, to its enjoyments, and not the least, is the breaking up of all those local attachments, which in a woman's nature, are so strong.

**Martha Hunter Hitchcock to Martha Hunter,
June 25, 1846**

I have long been anxious to write to you, dear Cousin, but unfortunately, I have had so much sickness, and sadness in my family, for a month or two past, that I have been unable to do so—Lillie had the scarlet fever, during our visit to Alabama, and she has never recovered from the effects of it—My life is a constant vigil—and there is nothing which wearies mind, and body, so much, as watching a sickly child. . . . Every day, she becomes more, and more necessary to my happiness—almost to my existence—And now that the Dr is absent, for an indefinite time, and I have nothing but her, to cling to, it really seems, as if she was my life. . . . It is a very trying situation for me, to live alone as I do, with all the cares of a troublesome household upon my hands—a sick child, about whom I feel the greatest anxiety—and a husband, absent on the most perilous enterprise. . . . Yet all this I have to endure, and may have to suffer more—for I know not, what Fate may have in store for me, of further suffering—for I have long since ceased, to anticipate anything else—But you must not dear cousin imagine, from this letter, that I am discontented with my lot, painful as it is—It is my destiny, and I must fulfil it—

5. Lizzie Neblett Describes Marriage and Motherhood in Texas, 1860

A Review of the Past Eight Years

It has now been almost eight years since I became a married woman. Eight years of checkered good and ill, and yet thro' all it seems the most of the ill has fallen to my lot, until now my poor weak cowardly heart sighs only for its final resting place, where sorrow grief nor pain can never reach it more. Through these eight years I must say that you my husband have been kind to me much kinder than I perhaps deserved, but you will have the approving conscience to sustain you when I am no more.

Erika L. Murr, *A Rebel Wife in Texas: The Diary and Letters of Elizabeth Scott Neblett, 1852–1864* (Baton Rouge: Louisiana State University Press, 2001), pp. 74–75.

I feel that I have faithfully discharged my duty towards you and my children, but for this I know that I deserve no credit nor aspire to none; my affection has been my prompter, and the task has proven a labor of love. You have not rightly understood me at all times, and being naturally very hopeful you could in no measure sympathize with me during my seasons of gloom and despondency—and your conduct which may have been only indifferent, has appeared to my excited imagination harsh, and caused a thrill of anguish in my bosom, that I hope yours may never feel. I know I am full of faults, and feel that you are much better than the most of men to have borne with [my] many faults as kindly and leniently as you have, for which I pray God that you may have your reward both here and hereafter. And here above all other thoughts arises the conviction that I have not made you as happy as some other woman, combining a happier disposition with a better mind than I have, could have done, and that often this truth forces itself upon you. But marriage is a lotery and that your draw proved an unfortunate one on your part is not less a subject of regret with me than you, and Heaven send that your next trial may prove fortunate, in every respect. I do not wish you to remain single when I am gone, a widowed life is a lonely one, and you need the tongue of a sensible woman to occasionaly awake you from a revery, that if indulged in continually might lead to we don't know where, certainly not to happiness. I think you have undergone a gradual change and that the present finds you a far different man from what you were eight years ago. It seems to me that you regard all things that approach towards sentiment or sentimentality as beneath your notice, and that the wife of [to]day is a far different creature from the bride of eight years ago, that she has not the same call upon your love and sympathy that she had then. If she has proven herself unworthy, surely the thought that she is the mother of your children [who] has suffered greatly in giving them to your arms should at least encircle her name with thoughts of tenderness and feelings of sympathy.

You never tell your feelings, and if subject to spells of mental depression I never know it and you often seem very indifferent, about me in particular. It seems to me that could we change places, I would feel great solicitude and anxiety about you.

It is useless to say that during these eight years I have suffered ten times more than you have and ten times more than I can begin to make you conceive of, but of course you can not help the past, nor by knowing my suffering relieve it, but it might induce you to look with more kindness upon [my] faults. I feel different and am more afflicted now than ever before, and think it probable, (tho' I fear not,) that my desire to die will be gratified, but oh the suffering that lies between me and the port of death, and who knows I may suffer it all, and yet live to go thro' with the same again in [a] few years? No, my hand shall be raised to take my own life first. I will never dread death as much as I dread the suffering of my coming confinement, for deaths pangs are, methinks, as nothing compared with the pains of labor, and I look forward to a very tedious one and painful one, more than an ordinary degree. But let me banish the thought[.] I can benefit it in no way by thinking of it, and God knows the suffering will be sufficient when I reach it. The 17th of this month I was 27 years old—and I think my face looks older than that, perhaps I'll never see an other birth day and I don't grieve at the idea.

Corsicana Navarro Co Texas,
Jan 22nd 1860

◤ *E S S A Y S*

In the first essay, an excerpt from E. Anthony Rotundo's 1993 book, *American Manhood*, Phillips Academy historian Rotundo explores the competing concepts of marriage in nineteenth-century America. Using the personal correspondence of middle-class northeasterners, he demonstrates how these concepts played out in daily life, revealing the power relationships and gender roles that characterized marriage in the Victorian North.

In the second essay, Anya Jabour of the University of Montana uses the diary and letters of plantation mistress Elizabeth Scott Neblett to offer a case study of marriage in the mid-nineteenth-century South. Where Rotundo emphasizes the difficulties posed by gendered "spheres" and unequal power, Jabour focuses on the tensions that resulted from women's inability to control their own—or their husbands'—sexuality.

Men, Women, and Marriage in the Nineteenth-Century North

E. ANTHONY ROTUNDO

The modern wedding ceremony is so elaborate and so fully enveloped by myth and custom that it seems to be centuries old. The ceremony as we know it, however, did not exist in 1800. Northerners of that day married in a civil ceremony which followed Puritan tradition. Performed by a local magistrate, the wedding was held in a private home before a few witnesses. In the world of 1800, marriage created a household, which was the basic unit of society. The community had a vital interest in the stability of every marriage, and so each wedding united a couple in mutual duty and bound it solemnly to the community through the presence of legal authority.

During the first third of the nineteenth century, a new ceremony emerged. It focused not on the place of marriage in the community but on the two individuals being wed. The bride and groom stood together at the center of the ceremony. They dressed in clothing they chose especially for themselves and for the occasion. Each of them was flanked by a few attendants of the same age and sex—the people who were closest to them in their own individual worlds of friendship and support. Larger numbers of relatives, friends, and associates formed an audience to watch the bride and groom in their special moment. A minister presided over the ceremony, which—by the 1830s—was usually held in a church. Instead of invoking the legal authority of the community over this marriage, he united the hearts and souls of two individuals into one couple.

The new focus of the wedding ceremony reflected the new focus of marriage. In the nineteenth century, matrimony was viewed increasingly as a union of two unique individuals. As this ideal gathered strength, the actual occurrence of intimacy within marriage became more common, but it never became the dominant experience of middle-class husbands and wives. The ideal was too difficult for many people to achieve, and the social conditions of nineteenth-century marriage—the distribution of power and the separation of spheres—proved too much of a barrier.

E. Anthony Rotundo, *American Manhood: Transformations in Masculinity from the Revolution to the Modern Era* (New York: Basic Books, 1993), pp. 129–140. Copyright 1993 by Perseus Books Group. Reproduced with permission of Perseus Books Group in the format textbook via Copyright Clearance Center.

Concepts of Marriage

Nineteenth-century marriage, with its emphasis on the individual husband and wife, was based on two different ideas about the fundamental nature of the bond. In one of these concepts, wedlock represented a union of two persons. Though this was an old idea, it had new resonance in a world where the individual had become the basic unit of society. The second concept was one of marriage as a power relationship based on male dominance. In the era of hierarchy that was now fading, this second idea of marriage had been the prevailing one. During the nineteenth century, the idea of marriage as a union of individuals mounted steadily in importance. It grew up alongside the hierarchical concept of marriage without really supplanting it. The two could be quite compatible—but during the century, as people began to develop the egalitarian possibilities of marital union, the two concepts sometimes came into conflict.

In an era when love was a matter of full and lasting sympathy, marriage was easily cast in the same terms. The "right idea of marriage," according to Elizabeth Cady Stanton, was a bond of "deep fervent love and sympathy." . . .

Thus, the common notions of love and empathy created a constant pressure toward oneness. This notion of unity had roots in religious belief. Men and women of the nineteenth century saw "holy matrimony" as a sacred arena where man and woman practiced the Christian virtues of love and self-denial, where spiritual union transcended selfishness and lust. The shift from civil ceremonies to church weddings made a statement: marriage was a hallowed union, not merely a business contract. Daniel Wise, an author of advice to young women, defined his ideal of matrimony in spiritual terms: "Marriage, properly viewed, is a union of kindred minds,—a blending of two souls in mutual, holy affection,—and not merely or chiefly a union of persons."

Even the most secular of people spoke in terms of union when they described the ideal marriage. In 1809, Massachusetts bachelor George Tuckerman described with envy the marriage of his newlywed brother, Joseph. Writing to their sister, George pronounced Joseph "a fortunate man" and said of the new couple: "Their thoughts, and feelings, dispositions and inclinations, and almost every throb of the Heart, appear to move in unison." George asked wistfully: *"Am I* ever to ever to enjoy anything like this—[?]" Tuckerman's yearning expressed the dominant ideal of wedlock in his century.

Still, it is important to stress how the ideal of union rested on the foundation of nineteenth-century concepts of gender. Charles Van Hise stated the gender issue clearly in a letter to his fiancée, Alice Ring. "Man and woman will love," he wrote, "because the mind of one is the complement of the other." Thus, when Van Hise said that each lover "harmonizes the life of the other" and that there are "deep, sweet harmonies" between them, he meant that love brought together natures of very different construction and made of them an agreeable whole.

Van Hise was writing about two individuals who were complementary opposites in many ways. The notion of woman and man as creatures with opposing qualities was, after all, the very essence of nineteenth-century bourgeois thinking about gender. Marital oneness was more than a merger of two kindred spirits—it was a union of opposites.

The gender differences which blended in marriage were familiar ones. Midwesterner Champion Chase explained to his fiancée that "true female character was perfectly adapted and designed by its influence often exerted to soften and beautify the wild rough and turbulent spirit of man." But men saw marriage as more than a way to make up for their lack of self-restraint. They saw it as a way to remedy their own clumsiness in matters of love and tenderness. One man wrote that women possessed "affection and all the finer sensibilities of the heart and soul . . . needed for comfort and consolation." Men imagined that they could turn to women for a kind of nurturant understanding that other males would not provide. As the hero of Francis Parkman's novel *Vassall Morton* put it: "I would as soon confess to my horse [as to a man]." Men turned to women to make them whole, to provide them with means of living and being which they believed they could not provide for themselves. . . .

The concept of marriage as a union of two people was a romantic—even spiritual—notion. The other dominant view, which envisioned wedlock as a relationship of power and duty, was decidedly earthbound. As different as these two conceptions were, though, they shared one important quality: both rested on common beliefs about the fundamental traits of manhood and womanhood. These common assumptions about gender kept the two dominant concepts of marriage closely linked even when they seemed to point toward very different sorts of relationships.

The structure of power and duty in marriage, as nineteenth-century men and women thought of it, began with basic characteristics. The belief that women were clean and domestic suited them by nature to maintain a home, and the assumption that they were pious and pure fitted them to raise the children and act as a conscience to their husbands. A man's duties in marriage were envisioned by a similar process. Since men were considered naturally active and courageous, it followed readily that they should go out into the world to play the role of breadwinner. Byron Caldwell Smith, a young college professor, stated the basic expectation: "A home is the work of husband and wife, but the unequal positions of women and men make the husband responsible for the support of this home." . . .

Beyond this sex-typed division of labor, there lay another vital question: In this marital arrangement, who held ultimate authority? Middle-class men and women had no doubt as to the answer. James Jameson, an early nineteenth-century writer on the family, put it flatly: "In the domestic constitution the superiority vests in the husband; he is the head, the lawgiver, the ruler . . . he is to direct, not indeed without taking counsel with his wife, but to his decision the wife should yield." By giving the power in marriage to the husband, middle-class culture was passing on a traditional arrangement. The very language Jameson used betrays his adherence to the time-honored notion of the man as the head of the household. . . .

Married Life: Roles and Realities

Henry Poor, the business publicist, believed that women gave up everything when they married. This fact helped to form the basis for the inequality in nineteenth-century marriage. By marrying, a woman lost her name, her home, and, in most cases, the control of her property. She surrendered her social identity and put in its place a new one: essentially, that of her husband. Much of who she was became submerged in who her husband was.

Young men and women knew this even when they were single. A Connecticut law student, George Younglove Cutler, wrote in his diary that "besides leaving everything else to unite themselves to one man they [women] subject themselves to his authority." The structure of the marriage relationship also empowered the husband to determine his wife's social status. Elizabeth Hill, a young Ohio woman, realized that "a lady could not shape the future . . . she went down or up as her husband did . . . he led the way, made the reputation, the fortune of both." A man's power to shape a wife's fortune gave him the upper hand in deciding matters of mutual concern. We can see this process at work by examining two domestic issues: where the family would live, and who would manage its finances.

Choice of residence was an issue even before the wedding. The experience of an engaged couple, Augusta McKim and Alexander Hamilton Rice, shows how a man used his breadwinner's role to make this decision his own. As Alexander's college graduation approached, he accepted a job in Virginia. Augusta, his fiancée, lived in Boston. She did not want him to move so far away and accused him of being "too ambitious for worldly distinction." He replied by pointing out to her that a good first job was important to his future, and that the position in Virginia was the best that he could find. Then, he reminded her that he was the "one upon whose arm you are to lean thro' life, upon whose reputation your own will also rest and upon whose effects your happiness as well as his own will mainly depend." As long as the wife depended on her husband's economic support and all that came with it, he could treat his needs as those of the entire family and demand prime consideration. . . .

Family finance was another area in which a man's right to decide was undoubted. Men, we know, wrangled with their fiancées over the expense of setting up a household. Typically, the future bride did most of the shopping herself, but, as long as the groom provided the money, her purchases needed his approval. This pattern continued into marriage. The Poor family of New York City and Massachusetts dealt with earning and spending in a revealing way. Henry signed blank checks and gave them to his wife; she then used them to buy goods and services for the household. This system provided Mary with daily flexibility but left Henry with final oversight.

The example of the Poor family also shows the persistence of this form of gender arrangement. For all his acumen as a business analyst, Henry turned out to be a thoughtless manager of household finances. He was slow to pay bills, he often put too little money in the family checking account, and he gave Mary too few signed checks for the purchases he expected her to make. Mary protested this behavior frequently, but she never moved to take over Henry's role. Although he demonstrated his lack of fitness for the task and even showed an "unmanly" want of rationality in the process, it was unthinkable that he should be replaced.

Beyond these specific tasks, the larger pattern of mundane duties and behaviors in a marriage reflected male power. The experience of Will and Elizabeth Cattell shows how this power expressed itself in the lives of one couple. Will was a minister, a college president, and an official of the Presbyterian Church, while Elizabeth was the organizing force that made Will's professional life possible. A letter from Will to their son James makes this dynamic clear. Writing on a Sunday morning, Will noted that the hour had come when Elizabeth ("dear Mama," as he referred to her) always told him to hurry so they would not be late for church. A few sentences later, he interrupted himself: "Yes!—there's the call from dear Mama!! So goodbye till after church:—and Mama is calling to Harry 'Would you see that Papa has his cuffs!'"

This telepathy in the Cattells' marriage took place on the common ground of Will's needs. It was Elizabeth who knew that Will wanted a reminder about the time before church, it was she who knew that he would forget his cuffs. She monitored his health, his work hours, and his sleeping habits as well. As she said, "I know you so well . . . you need someone to watch you." For his part, Will accepted his wife's help with childlike passivity ("dear Mama"). He waited happily for her call, instead of stirring himself to activity at the right time; he counted on her reminder about his cuffs instead of taking his own responsibility for them. While the details of these interactions played themselves out through the individual personalities of Elizabeth and Will Cattell, the fact that their thoughts merged around Will's needs is a sign of the power in the husband's role. A woman depended on her husband's income, and she cleared a path for him through the mundane business of life so that he could concentrate on his work.

Yet, as much as patterns and expectations in marriage were heavily skewed in favor of male power, those factors did not determine the outcome of any one decision, nor did they set the habits of authority in any given marriage. Rather, they established conventional limits within which the unique needs and distinctive traits of particular wives and husbands determined their own routines for the exercise of power.

Perhaps the most revealing statements on this subject come from passing remarks made by husbands and wives about decisions in their marriage—remarks that are tossed off so casually that they suggest a description of daily habit. In 1848, Theodore Russell, a prominent Boston lawyer, wrote to his father about the vacation he was going to take. "I suppose I am little tired out," he wrote, "I dislike to go away just now but my wife presses me hard to do so—and I have concluded to." This brief comment shows three revealing facts about power and choice in the Russells' marriage. First, Sarah Russell felt free to give her husband advice. Secondly, Theodore listened to her advice and took it seriously. Third, the ultimate power to decide lay with Theodore. She may have pressed him hard to take a vacation, but he was the one who "concluded" to do it. . . .

To put this in somewhat more abstract terms, social expectation gave husbands most of the power to make decisions for the couple and the family. Depending on the individuals and their own unique needs and arrangements, a wife could have an influence on her husband's decisions. The degree of influence could vary from minimal to overwhelming; the influence of most middle-class wives fell well between those two extremes. Even in cases where the wife's influence was overwhelming, however, she had to overwhelm her husband because he was the one empowered to make the decisions. . . .

What happened when men ceded large amounts of power to their wives? Some people viewed this practice with tolerance and a few even admired it. More generally, social convention worked to discourage such violations of prevailing norms. In his diary, New Englander John Barnard denounced a woman who "told me how she managed her husband and a great deal of nonsense which was interesting only as it was not pleasing." Barnard asserted that this woman was "sowing the seeds of strife." While Barnard criticized only the wife in this case, some men also belittled husbands who let their wives make the decisions.

In 1846, Massachusetts shoe manufacturer Arial Bragg described a couple in which the man took orders from his wife. Bragg wrote that "she wore the breeches, as the vulgar saying is." That phrase is revealing in many ways. Most obviously, it points out the fact of a gender role reversal with the most dramatic symbolism possible. The saying poked fun at women, especially in an era when women could never wear pants. It also degraded the husband. The word *the* in "the breeches" stresses the notion that there was *one* pair of pants to be worn in a marriage. If the husband was not wearing the pants, then he must have been wearing the dress. The clear meaning is that the man was a woman, which implied that he was foolish, confused, and (like a woman) not worthy of respect. He was, in short, a contemptible figure.

In the context of nineteenth-century gender meanings, there was a second layer of contempt in saying that a man did not wear the breeches in his marriage, as it recalled the attire he had worn in earliest boyhood. At that point, he was small and powerless. He was dominated by other people, most often his mother, and was dressed in a fashion that made him indistinguishable from a little girl. Thus, to say that a man's wife wore the breeches (and Bragg's use of the phrase makes clear that it was a common saying) was not simply to belittle him by calling him a woman; it was to call him a little boy, which meant, in turn, a powerless creature who resembled a little girl. This popular phrase hit a man in many spots at once. It served as a forceful reminder that a man made himself contemptible if he let his wife exercise the power in their marriage.

Thus it was that norms of proper gender behavior were enforced. Yet there were counterpressures toward allowing women greater influence in a marriage. When a husband was usually gone from the household and the wife was there running it, men must have found it difficult to avoid turning over power to their wives. Moreover, the ideal of union in marriage may have encouraged men to share their power with women. A man who identified deeply with his wife was bound to appreciate her needs and her point of view more than a man who was content to be distant from his wife. Such empathy on a husband's part might readily yield a process of marital decision making in which the wife took an active part.

But the social force that played the largest role in increasing a wife's influence was the rise in woman's moral stature during the nineteenth century. The very way in which young men pleaded with their fiancées for moral guidance indicates that the new valuation of a woman's character gave her increased leverage in dealing with her husband. The wife's replacement of the husband as the parent who would mold their children's character offered her another source of power within the marriage. . . .

The power relationship between husband and wife seemed at once changed and unchanging. In describing spousal roles under the new domestic-relations law of the nineteenth century, legal historian Michael Grossberg has noted that courts and commentators came to recognize "separate legal spheres in the home" with "enlarged . . . rights" for the wife and mother. Yet there was no doubt as to who held the final power. "Patriarchy," writes Grossberg, "retained its legal primacy." While a new "domesticated concept of patriarchy . . . distinguished between male authority to govern the household and female responsibility to maintain it and nurture its wards," such new distinctions "perpetuated patriarchy in republican society."

In the law, in printed counsel, and in the actual behavior of men and women, the nineteenth century marked a change but not a revolution in the power relations of husband and wife. Man's primacy in the home was modified and circumscribed but not denied. All parties recognized the man as head of the household—and one dimension of his power was his dominion over his wife. . . .

Marriage and Family in the Nineteenth-Century South

ANYA JABOUR

On a wet, rainy evening in May 1852, nineteen-year-old Elizabeth ("Lizzie") Scott retired to her room to write in her diary. Lizzie, the daughter of wealthy Texas slaveowners, was engaged to be married to William Henry ("Will") Neblett, a man seven years Lizzie's senior. As her wedding day approached, Lizzie recorded her thoughts about the impending event in her diary with phrases that indicated that she regarded marriage with mixed emotions. "My life will be entirely changed," she reflected. "All my cherished recreations of mind & body must in part be abolished. I will have much to do, and I hope much happiness, if not, miserable will be my exchange." Unfortunately for her own peace of mind, Lizzie's words would prove prophetic. Eight years later, in 1860, she reflected, "Eight years of checkered good and ill, and yet thro' all it seems that most of the ill has fallen to my lot, until now my poor weak cowardly heart sighs only for its final resting place, where sorrow grief nor pain can never reach it more." Indeed, throughout her marriage, Lizzie complained that sorrow, grief, and pain, rather than happiness, characterized her life as "a married woman." Lizzie Neblett's private writings, including her antebellum diary and her wartime letters to her husband, reveal a vast contrast between the ideal of romantic love and affectionate family life and the reality of married life and motherhood in the nineteenth-century South.

Like many Americans born between the American Revolution and the Civil War, Lizzie believed that romantic love was the surest route to personal happiness. As a teenager, she described herself as being formed for love. "Nature seems to have assigned my heart for loving ardently truly," she reflected, "& has implanted the longing[,] I may say holy desire[,] to be loved." Lizzie's urgent need to be loved reflected her society's beliefs about women's special affinity for the qualities of "the heart," but it also grew out of her personal experiences. Hints about Lizzie's childhood suggest that her parents were at best cold, and at worst abusive, toward their daughter. Unhappiness at home may well have facilitated the nineteen-year-old's decision to marry Will Neblett in 1852. After a stormy exchange with her parents in May of that year, she wrote furiously in her diary: "I am done being cursed and threatened to be *cow hided.* . . . Well now, even if I did not love Will, I should be tempted to marry him, if I had the chance to get away from here."

In the mid-nineteenth century, the women's rights movement was just getting started, and a few exceptionally educated, talented, and determined women were postponing their wedding dates or avoiding marriage entirely to pursue careers as writers or reformers. But such developments were largely limited to the urbanizing, industrializing Northeast; for southern women, the only respectable option to marriage was to become a "spinster aunt" dedicated to the care of younger siblings, cousins, nieces, and nephews. Clearly, remaining a dependent daughter in the home of her parents was an unattractive alternative for Lizzie, and her desire to escape an unhappy home may well have facilitated her decision to marry.

Written for this volume by Anya Jabour.

While the Scotts' relationship with their daughter may have hastened her wedding day, their relationship with each other probably contributed to her ambivalence about marriage. Like many young women in nineteenth-century America, Lizzie longed for a marriage of mutual love and respect—what historians have labeled "companionate marriage." Yet the experience of her parents had shown her that, all too often, an impassable gulf yawned between the ideal and the reality. Her own father, she reflected, had destroyed her mother's chances for marital bliss through his unkind words and his indulgence in "illicit love." While in the nineteenth-century North, state legislatures increasingly passed new divorce laws permitting wives to escape unhappy marriages, southern courts and congressmen continued to uphold the doctrine of marital unity except in cases of extreme physical cruelty, the wife's adultery, or the husband's inability to provide for his family or to produce heirs. With few escapes from unhappy marriages, southern wives simply had to adapt to their husbands' behavior, including affairs with slaves and prostitutes. Lizzie knew from personal experience that while marital happiness was vulnerable to male "passion[s]," wives had little recourse when their mates proved uncaring or unfaithful. Even as she reassured herself, "I have no cause to murmur[.] I love, and am beloved!" she continued to worry about Will's constancy.

Concerns about her relationship with her intended husband were only one factor in Lizzie's evident reluctance to commit herself to marriage. Despite her youth, Lizzie also was keenly aware of the legal ramifications of marriage. The evening before her wedding day, which she spent with her betrothed, she commented that it was "the last evening I will spend with him as Lizzie Scott," and again, on the day itself, she wrote, "Six hours to be Lizzie Scott." Lizzie's repeated references to her impending name change reflected her awareness of the principle of *coverture*—the legal invisibility of married women—that was symbolized in the practice of wives taking their husbands' name. She reflected one evening: "I will become a wife—a great responsibility. My identity, my legal existence will be swallowed up in my husband." Indeed, as Lizzie well knew, married women had no "legal existence"; they were unable to sign contracts, to own property, or even to appear in court without their husbands' permission. On a woman's wedding day, any property she brought with her to the marriage became her husband's. Marriage simply obliterated a woman's existence in the eyes of the law.

Married women's legal disabilities made them dependent on their husbands for daily necessities, encouraging them to accede to their husbands' preferences in determining where to settle. Lizzie agreed to her husband-to-be's plan to live with his parents for the first six months after their wedding, even though this would delay her desire for "a home of our own." "I am willing to go any where, put up with any thing do anything for Will, and with him," she explained. Women's legal and economic powerlessness—what Lizzie called "the stern realities of life"—dictated that women "submit to any privations" to ensure their husbands' success.

The privations of married life included more than simply leaving behind familiar surroundings. Childbearing—the inevitable aftermath of marriage in an age before reliable contraception—also endangered women's health. This biological reality was heightened in the antebellum South by the social expectation that women bear many children. Although the national birthrate fell by one-half during the nineteenth century, from 7 children per woman in 1800 to 3.56 in 1900, southern women continued to average 6 or more live births up to the Civil War. Many southern women bore still more children; Lizzie's sister-in-law Susan Womack Scott, who had married Lizzie's older brother John in 1844, gave birth to thirteen children. Moreover, maternal death rates were higher in the South than in the North; in 1850, one in twenty-five southern women died in childbirth, twice as many as in the North. Lizzie, like most young women in the Old South, doubtless knew someone who had died in childbirth. The bride-to-be was well aware that, as one historian has remarked, "a possible death sentence came with every pregnancy."

Marriage would mean many things for Lizzie: the wifely responsibility "to prevent love dying," legal and economic dependence on a young man just beginning his career, and risking life and health to bear children. Not surprisingly, Lizzie regarded marriage with some trepidation. "I have a thousand fears, and misgivings whether I should marry or not," she admitted. Indeed, she broke her engagement to Will twice in a three-year time period. Even after she had firmed her resolve to be "eternally launched on the shores of Matrimony," Lizzie continued to record doubts and fears in her diary. "Sometimes I think really that I cannot marry so soon," she wrote less than three weeks before her wedding. "I am not ready." As her wedding day approached, Lizzie seemed equally determined and terrified. "I had better get married at once," she resolved, "and have it over with."

Initially, Lizzie's marriage lived up to, even surpassed, her most hopeful expectations. On her wedding day, the bride pronounced herself "happy as I ever thought to be," and on the eve of her two-week anniversary, she penned an entry in her diary that suggested that she and Will had achieved the romantic ideal: "I am so deeply happy. Will is such a good, kind husband I feel loves me devotedly. I think it will last, always. We have been married now two weeks tommorrow, and really it seems scarcely a week. I have been so happy. . . . I find Will better than I thought he was, and I love him ten times better than I did before we were married, and I believe he loves me better."

But it was not to last. Only two weeks later, although she insisted that "married life so far goes very well," Lizzie admitted that "Will makes me cry sometimes, and vexes me too." While she tried to shrug off her misgivings, noting that "it is over in a moment," the future would give Lizzie many more moments of grief and vexation.

One of Lizzie's most persistent problems would prove to be an unending cycle of pregnancy, childbirth, and child care. According to one historian of southern women, "the most widespread source of discontent" among the South's planter-class women "was the actuality of the much glorified institution of motherhood." Much like marriage, motherhood was idealized in nineteenth-century America. Yet also like marriage, motherhood was not really a choice; most women had no alternative to marriage, and once married, most women had no alternative to motherhood. The birth control methods available in the nineteenth century—primitive contraceptives (forerunners of today's condom, diaphragm, and sponge), periodic abstinence (today's "rhythm method"), and coitus interruptus (withdrawal before ejaculation)—were either unreliable, dependent on men's cooperation, or both. Thus, while some women in both North and South successfully managed to control their family size through close cooperation with their husbands, most nineteenth-century women bore children at regular intervals until they reached menopause.

Less than a year after becoming a wife, Lizzie became a mother. "I expect to be confined about the middle of April," she wrote in December 1852. Like many young women in the antebellum South, Lizzie regarded the birth of her first child as a significant event, one that marked her full assumption of the responsibilities of adulthood. She looked forward to motherhood even as she feared the dangers of childbirth, which made her "low spirited" and gave her the "histericks." "The coming event occupies my mind continually," she confided to her diary; "'tis the one great thought of my brain the one joy of my heart." Trying to ignore the pain and risk that awaited her, Lizzie concentrated on the fulfillment she anticipated from her new role. In only a few months, she wrote optimistically, "I will be a Mother— and feel all a mothers love, the holiest passion in the human breast."

But Lizzie was destined for disappointment. Although both she and the baby—a girl, named Mary Caroline—survived, Lizzie suffered a double blow. First, the child was a girl (Lizzie had hoped for a boy), and second, both mother and child were struck down with measles, making the adjustment to the multitudinous responsibilities of motherhood especially difficult. Although Lizzie and Will were slaveholders, Lizzie, like most of her counterparts, was the principal caregiver for all six of her children—a role that included both health care and breastfeeding. While Lizzie successfully nursed her "sweet little babe" through a five-week illness, she could not recover from her other disappointment so quickly. Lizzie, who had "suffered greatly" in childbirth, no longer regarded motherhood with pleasure. "How time changes all things!" she exclaimed. "How time has changed me. My pursuits, my tastes, my feelings have all changed. And when I think how I once felt, and thought, I could weep that those feelings are forever fled." Although she loved Mary dearly, Lizzie hoped to spare her from a like fate: "I think of what the future may have in store for her, what her lot may be, and I feel sad. Oh my daughter I would that you had been a boy, for 'womans lot is hard to bear' and I would save you from what I have endured, and should life be prolonged must still endure."

Lizzie's life was indeed "prolonged," and by 1860 she had given birth to two more children—Robert Scott (b. 1855), known as Bob, and William Teel (b. 1857), called Billy—and was pregnant yet again. Lizzie ceased keeping a diary shortly after Mary's birth, perhaps because of the demands of motherhood, but in January 1860 she penned "A Review of the past eight years," written to Will. While she did not blame her husband for her unhappiness, calling him "kinder than I perhaps deserved," Lizzie expressed deep dissatisfaction with both marriage and motherhood. She spoke of her children in terms of "duty" and "suffering" rather than love or affection; her highest hope for them was that they would earn her Will's love. Yet even that last, she doubted. "You never tell your feelings," she complained to her husband, "and you often seem very indifferent, about me in particular." Insecure in her husband's affection, burdened by the care of three young children, and anticipating what would prove to be a "very tedious" and "painful" delivery—in May 1860, she would give birth to her fourth child, a boy named Walter—Lizzie sank into "gloom and despondency." Death, she wrote, was preferable to repeated pregnancies and childbirth: "I will never dread death as much as I dread the suffering of my coming confinement, for death pangs are, methinks, as nothing compared with the pains of labor. . . . Perhaps I'll never see an other birth day and I don't grieve at the idea."

Three years later, Will left home to serve as a private in Company I of the Twentieth Texas Infantry in Galveston, where he served as a guard for the gunboat *Bayou City* before obtaining a post as a Confederate clerk. For the rest of the Civil War, between 1863 and 1865, Lizzie and Will wrote to each other several times a week. Their correspondence offers additional insights into this southern couple's marriage and into the sources of Lizzie's unhappiness.

While Will, who never saw active duty, complained of "the laziest and most monotonous life that can well be imagined," Lizzie described herself as "desolate and bereaved," sentiments that were heightened by being left alone while pregnant with a fifth—and clearly unwanted—child. Although Lizzie and Will apparently had tried using contraceptives—what Lizzie called "preventives"—their efforts to control their family size were unsuccessful. Much to Lizzie's consternation, even the couple's attempt to prevent pregnancy via abstinence failed when Lizzie, in an abandoned moment, yielded to her husband's entreaties and engaged in sexual intercourse with him. Throughout the rest of the war, Lizzie frequently (and bitterly) would allude to the encounter that had produced the Nebletts' fifth child, a daughter they named Bettie. But in 1863, while she anticipated her fifth parturition, Lizzie wrote, "No worse calamity could befall me, than to be doomed to have an other child." Alternately hoping for death in childbirth and oblivion in drug abuse, she asserted, "It seems to me that no martyr bound to the stake ever dreaded the devouring flames worse or more than I do the coming pains of labor."

Even after she had passed safely through labor, Lizzie's resentment of motherhood and fear of childbirth pervaded all her letters. Although relieved of a "mountain of anxiety and dread" by her safe delivery, Lizzie found herself unable to love her fifth child, whom she described as "an ugly little thing." "I can take no pleasure in her," she wrote. "The very sight of her is a pain to me." Even though the infant was named for her mother, Lizzie distanced herself from the baby emotionally, telling her husband: "I always think of her as your baby and not mine. I reckon that is because she was so unwelcome to me." Moreover, she almost immediately began to worry that she would once again become pregnant once Will came home. Throughout her husband's absence, Lizzie continued to express her deep anxiety about the ever-present possibility of repeated pregnancies—what she movingly referred to as "the constant dread & fear of a calamity ten thousand times worse than death."

For Lizzie, the inability to control her reproduction—what she called "the misery & pain of woman's lot"—was a major obstacle to achieving the happiness that she had hoped for in marriage. Her frustration with the realities of nineteenth-century marriage was no doubt heightened by her related fear that Will might prove faithless. Although Lizzie claimed not to doubt Will's constancy—"I have unbounded confidence in your moral conduct & character," she told him in June 1864—she was understandably alarmed when she learned that he had contracted hydrocele (the accumulation of bodily fluids in the scrotum), a condition associated with veneral disease. In addition, her skepticism about men's self-control reflected the sexual double standard that was pervasive in nineteenth-century America, particularly in the South: "Man's nature in this particular," she wrote with evident distaste, "is so well known that we never marvel, nor doubt much, when we hear of the best of men going astray." Even while lauding Will's "sound sense & judgment," which she believed raised him above the generality of men, Lizzie may well have worried that the obvious solution to her dilemma—complete abstinence—might give her husband an excuse to indulge in "vile passion." Lizzie was thus caught in a double bind: to keep her husband's love, she felt compelled to risk her own health and happiness.

Lizzie's dread of pregnancy emerged as a major theme in her wartime correspondence. "The *horrible* nightmare" of pregnancy, she wrote, "would always frighten away any little happiness that might occasionally cross my path. So I am a doomed creature any how, and my only hope is a speedy death."

Lizzie's lack of control over sexuality—her own and her husband's—not only caused her personal unhappiness, but also drove a wedge between husband and wife. Most obviously, Lizzie's deathly fear of pregnancy interfered with the couple's physical relationship. "This constant & never ceasing horror I have of childbearing constantly obtrudes itself between me & my desire & longing to see & clasp you round the neck once more," she wrote to Will, "& thus my longing wears a curb."

Although Will expressed his willingness to cooperate with his wife in practicing birth control—even offering to abstain from further marital relations—actual practice did not follow this plan. Following a brief furlough at home in spring 1864, when Will returned to his post he was deluged with letters from Lizzie worrying that the "risk" she had taken during his visit—unprotected sex—might result in yet another pregnancy. Despite her desperate desire to avoid pregnancy, Lizzie regarded sex as a way of binding her husband's affections. In the midst of one of her many reflections on whether she deserved Will's love, she demanded, "Ask yourself if some body did not forget self a few times for your pleasure." Clearly, however much Lizzie wished to avoid pregnancy, she did not think it was possible to avoid sex. "The love I have for you," she told her husband, "would over come the awful dread I have of a certain thing, not over come it either, but make me willing for your sake to risk a certain event happening." Recognizing that her often-distant husband found it difficult to express affection verbally, she yielded, against her better judgment, to what she pointedly called "*your sort of love*"—that is, physical passion.

Indeed, Will's rare love letters usually focused on his physical attraction to his wife—precisely the sort of attention she dreaded. In one "rather romantic" letter in 1864, for instance, he related a dream he had about Lizzie in her nightgown with her feet and legs bare. Moreover, Will shared his wife's assumption that their relationship was strengthened by her repeated sacrifices for his happiness. Writing fourteen years after the couple's first meeting, he assured Lizzie that his love endured: "Time has added a bond of esteem and respect for the many self sacrifices you have made for me, and my comfort and happiness," he wrote.

Because preventives had failed and abstinence had proved to be an impossible goal, the Nebletts' only remaining options were abortion or separation. Abortion—inducing a miscarriage through the ingestion of poisonous substances or the insertion of foreign objects into the uterus—was, as one historian has described it, "woman's last resort" in nineteenth-century America. At several points during Will's wartime absence, Lizzie demanded that he acquire "devilish things"—the instruments for inducing an abortion—before returning home. While not yet stigmatized by organized religion or criminalized by state courts, abortion was, in Lizzie's mind, a sin.

Nevertheless, by 1864, the mother of five saw it as the lesser of two evils: if she was unable to avoid repeated childbirth, she vowed, she would either abort the fetus or "kill myself and run the risk of going to the devil." Lizzie asked Will to find and purchase a large syringe and a supply of ergot, a mold that grows on grain and brings on violent contractions and that was sometimes used as an aid in difficult deliveries in the nineteenth century. But the tools necessary for a self-induced abortion proved difficult to obtain, particularly since Lizzie had to rely on her husband, who did not share her sense of urgency, to procure these items. In May 1864 a frustrated Lizzie proposed that the couple separate permanently in order to avoid the threat of pregnancy.

As Lizzie's final solution indicated, the couple's difficulties extended beyond sexual tension to emotional dissatisfaction. In most cases, of course, the two were linked, as when Lizzie told her husband—much to his chagrin—that she did not want him to return home before they had found a sure means of preventing conception. In the absence of insurance against pregnancy, Lizzie dreaded her husband's safe return as much as she desired it. "I had rather meet a woods full of Bare than meet you after a long absence," she wrote in 1863. "I dread to see you, tho' I love you far better than I do my own life."

For his part, Will seemed unable—or perhaps unwilling—to grasp the depth of Lizzie's dissatisfaction with motherhood and horror of childbirth, an inability that created emotional, as well as physical, distance between husband and wife. While he attempted to sympathize with Lizzie during her wartime pregnancy—"I am so much grieved at your helpless and unfortunate state of body," he once remarked—and asserted that he felt "painful interest" in his wife's welfare, he refused to acknowledge the extent of Lizzie's distaste for motherhood. In reply to her "thoughts of melancholy and trouble," he wrote: "You say you do not like children and that ours is a cause of unhappiness. Now I do not believe all of this." More often, Will simply overlooked his wife's misery, responding to her most plaintive letters with silence. Will's "very silent manner," Lizzie wrote, caused her "very bitter unhappy & miserable thoughts." The difficulty, as Lizzie knew, was that Will simply did not understand her feelings: "You never could seemingly comprehend how utterly wrecked the prospect of happiness was with me," she accused him in April 1864.

Lizzie's complaints distressed Will, but he regarded himself as helpless to change the situation. Lizzie often complained of Will's "coldness" and reluctance to express his feelings, a reluctance that caused her to feel awkward expressing her own. While his silence was most noticeable at the times when his wife's need was greatest, Will's habitual reserve made it difficult for him to reassure his wife of his love at all times. "I am sorry Lizzie that you cannot take my love for you on trust without frequent renewal of the pledge," he wrote dispiritedly, adding that he was not to blame for the "matter of fact & reflective cast" of his personality that "dictates the style of my letters."

Although Lizzie criticized her husband for his "coldness," she also blamed herself for her own unhappiness. Measuring herself against nineteenth-century society's feminine ideal—cheerful in the face of adversity—she repeatedly found herself wanting. Throughout her marriage, she obsessively worried that her husband's love for her would fail in the face of her own failure to be the "patient, loving and faithful wife" that Victorian Americans regarded as a "true woman." "I have not made you as happy as some other woman, combining a happier disposition with a better mind than I have, could have done," she concluded sadly.

Lizzie also castigated herself for her inability to find happiness in motherhood. "I am not a true mother," she once worried, because she did not want to suffer on behalf of her children. Nineteenth-century Americans believed that a true woman would be not only a satisfied wife, but also a selfless mother. One Victorian advice book summed up conventional wisdom with these words: "The care of children requires a great many sacrifices, and a great deal of self-denial, but the woman who is not willing to sacrifice a good deal in such a cause, does not deserve to be a mother." Like other women in mid-nineteenth-century America, Lizzie regarded motherhood as a sacred duty. "The education of our children, and the proper cultivation of their hearts," she wrote, were "the chief end & aim of my life." But Lizzie also resented the sacrifices that motherhood entailed, and she did not find the fulfillment that she had expected in caring for her children. "I know it is wrong & unfortunate for me to feel so," she reflected, "but children have lost their charm for me, & in the sober hour of reflection I regret that I ever had a child."

Lizzie's distaste for motherhood coexisted with her anxious desire to perform her role well. "I am the unwilling mother of five helpless and dependent children," she mused. "That they are here, in this world is not their fault," she acknowledged, and thus, despite her own unwillingness, it was Lizzie's "duty to provide, to educate, both brain and heart, and fit them to take their place in the world as useful & good citizens." Acknowledging her responsibilities as a mother did not help Lizzie to accept the role gracefully, however, particularly after giving birth to an unwanted child. "Our children trouble me greatly," she wrote sadly. "I once felt differently about children & I sigh that that time has past, & then the labor I had to perform was one of love, & did not crush me, like the labor of duty—but my last child was the feather that broke the cam[el]'s back, I will never *recover* from it. My good sense teaches me to feel ashamed of these feelings & thoughts, but does not teach me to discard them," she summed up the situation. As with her marriage, Lizzie's conviction that she was inadequate to her assigned role only exacerbated the problem. "Above all things," she wrote in 1864, "I regret that I have lost all pride in the children, and view them more as a curse than a blessing."

Lizzie's conflicted feelings about motherhood caused her to regard her children—"the little torments," she called them in 1864—with ambivalence. "My conduct & my words about my children do contradict each other," she reflected late in the war; "no mother ever felt more anxiety, or was more unwearied in her attention to her sick children than I am, & ever have been." Indeed, Lizzie was, at times, a caring and attentive mother who nursed her children tenderly through illnesses, a fact she frequently recalled when attempting to convince herself that she was not a failure as a mother. Yet while Lizzie could be concerned and caring, she could also be cruel and manipulative. "No doubt you often think as I do that your children's greatest misfortune is in having such an unwilling mother," she wrote to Will in 1864. Indeed, as an unwilling mother, Lizzie responded to her children's demands with impatience, frustration, and even abuse. "God fixed me to have children in pain & sorrow," Lizzie once wrote, but in truth, this unwilling mother visited pain and sorrow on her children as well.

Lizzie's anger at her fate sometimes exploded into violence directed toward the children, even—and especially—the youngest, baby Bettie. For Lizzie, Bettie served as a constant reminder of her own lack of control over her fate. "It does seem this baby tries me more than all the others put together did," she complained. "Her coming was so out of place and season, & I feel it so sensibly yet, & that makes the matter worse." Every time she looked at Bettie, she told her husband, she found herself thinking of "the terrible *nine months*" of pregnancy and "their excruciating termination."

While Lizzie's initial reaction of disgust was soon mixed with fondness—"I find myself loving her better & better every day," she reflected a few days later; "no one can withstand the sweet winning ways of their own innocent babe"—she continued to grieve at her own misfortune at having given birth to a second girl and at Bettie's misfortune of being born female. "Altho, I cant wish her dead, and could not neglect one iota of my duty to her, yet I can't help feeling that her death would be a blessing to me & her," she wrote. Indeed, "the bitterness of having given birth to one of my sex to suffer, be humiliated, and to bear in hopeless misery the fate that her kind, loving and obliging heart led her into" tinged all of Lizzie's comments on her youngest child.

Lizzie repeatedly bewailed her misfortune at having given birth to daughters, expressing the belief that death was preferable to the misfortune of being born female. She responded with despair, rather than with pride, to evidence of Bettie's intellectual potential: "How I sigh and think what is it when we sum up all her little tricks, her evidence of sense, and expansion of brain, when she is only a poor miserable wretch of a female, doomed to bear children[,] suffer, and if like me in her disposition, doomed to go to hell at last. I declare it would be a relief to me to know she and Mary were both dead."

Lizzie's despair at her own fate also shaped her attitudes toward her older daughter. She found it impossible (or impractical) to encourage Mary, a bright girl who was eager to learn, in her lessons: "I haven't the heart to stimulate Mary to apply herself to her books, or learn anything," she explained. "The idea of her fate here after if she lives to marry spoils every thing with me." For a woman, Lizzie had concluded from sad experience, it was "better [to] be a fool than educated": "Poor devil of a woman has no business knowing any thing in the way of accomplishments, her life business is to bear & nurse children, & it is time labor & money thrown away, to try and give her accomplishments fit for the parlor & a life of ease & enjoyment."

Lizzie's negative attitudes and actions were not limited to her daughters. Her childrearing methods—a combination of shame and punishment—offer a striking counterpoint to the affectionate childrearing in vogue in nineteenth-century America. Rather than relying on love and reason to motivate the children to proper behavior, Lizzie offered them withering scorn and brutal whippings. Bob, "the best child we have," she treated with barely disguised contempt. "I have taken occasion to mortify Bob about his conduct all the time," she told Will; "I want to make him feel it as keenly as possible." Billy, whom Lizzie described as "a mean, bad child," suffered still more. "He grows worse all the time," Lizzie said of the six-year-old boy in 1863, "and you can't appeal to his feelings, he is too flinty to care for any thing, & stubborn as ever. I can't get him to do any thing unless I get the cowhide in hand." Indeed, nearly all of Lizzie's descriptions of the children revolved around punishment; she "whipped" all the children—including ten-month-old Bettie—often, justifying her conduct by saying that they were ill-behaved and unresponsive to appeals to reason.

A victim herself, Lizzie became a victimizer. Unable to extricate herself from an untenable situation—unable even to imagine an alternative—she directed her anger at her own weakness and dependence toward those weaker and more dependent than herself: her children. From the modern vantage point, it is unsurprising that Lizzie's behavior fed a cycle of abuse. Billy responded in kind by striking and scratching his siblings until he left scars, while Walter, "a high tempered fractious little fellow," went about the house smashing furniture and "popping" the cat with a whip. But Lizzie, who suffered so much physical and emotional anguish for the sake of her children, was aggrieved at their lack of affection for each other and for her, and she predicted (accurately, as it turned out) that they would desert her once they reached adulthood. "I have no doubt but several of my children have inherited my unhappy disposition," she reflected soberly, "and I fear my conduct influenced by my unfortunate views of marriage & children will cause my children to love and respect me less than I deserve. I know and feel all this," she added, "and yet I fear it is beyond my power to reform."

"The fate of the greater part of womankind," Lizzie reflected much later in her life, was marriage and motherhood. Yet in these roles, which were supposed to bring unalloyed happiness, Lizzie found only misery. Because she knew that she was supposed to find fulfillment as a wife and mother, she regarded her inability to do so as a personal failing. "My whole life has been a grand mistake," she lamented. If Lizzie's life was a grand mistake, it was one that was repeated many times over in the nineteenth-century South. Indeed, according to one renowned scholar, southern women's dissatisfaction "centered on women's lack of control over many aspects of their own sexual lives and the sexual lives of their husbands"— precisely the problems that Lizzie wrestled with in her own marriage. Lizzie may have been, as she put it, a "poor weak contemptible woman," but it was a fate she shared with many others.

Although nineteenth-century southerners, no less than northerners, looked to marriage and family as the ultimate sources of happiness, they were often disappointed. For women in particular, the romantic ideal demonstrated itself to be only an illusion, flawed at its inception by its refusal to acknowledge or challenge the persistent and profound differences in husbands' and wives' roles and status.

 F U R T H E R   R E A D I N G

Basch, Norma. *Framing American Divorce: From the Revolutionary Generation to the Victorians* (1999).

———. *In the Eyes of the Law: Women, Marriage, and Property in Nineteenth-Century New York* (1982).

Bleser, Carol, ed. *In Joy and in Sorrow: Women, Family, and Marriage in the Victorian South, 1830–1900* (1991).

Brodie, Janet. *Contraception and Abortion in Nineteenth-Century America* (1994).

Cashin, Joan E. *A Family Venture: Men and Women on the Southern Frontier* (1991).

Censer, Jane Turner. *North Carolina Planters and Their Children, 1800–1860* (1984).

Cott, Nancy F. *The Bonds of Womanhood: "Woman's Sphere" in New England, 1780–1835* (1977).

————. *Public Vows: A History of Marriage and the Nation* (2000).

Degler, Carl N. *At Odds: Women and the Family in America from the Revolution to the Present* (1980).

Frank, Stephen M. *Life with Father: Parenthood and Masculinity in the Nineteenth-Century American North* (1998).

Griswold, Robert L. *Family and Divorce in California, 1850–1890: Victorian Illusions and Everyday Realities* (1982).

Grossberg, Michael. *Governing the Hearth: Law and the Family in Nineteenth-Century America* (1985).

Hartog, Hendrik. *Man and Wife in America: A History* (2000).

Hoffert, Sylvia D. *Private Matters: American Attitudes Toward Childrearing and Infant Nurture in the Urban North, 1800–1860* (1989).

Jabour, Anya. *Marriage in the Early Republic: Elizabeth and William Wirt and the Companionate Ideal* (1998).

Johansen, Shawn. *Family Men: Middle-Class Fatherhood in Early Industrializing America* (2001).

Leavitt, Judith Walzer. *Brought to Bed: Childbearing in America, 1750 to 1950* (1986).

Lewis, Jan. *The Pursuit of Happiness: Family and Values in Jefferson's Virginia* (1983).

Lewis, Jan, and Kenneth Lockridge. "'Sally Has Been Sick': Pregnancy and Family Limitation Among Virginia Gentry Women, 1780–1830," *Journal of Social History* 22 (Fall 1988): 5–19.

Lystra, Karen. *Searching the Heart: Women, Men, and Romantic Love in Nineteenth-Century America* (1989).

May, Elaine Tyler. *Great Expectations: Marriage and Divorce in Victorian America, 1880–1920* (1980).

McMillen, Sally G. *Motherhood in the Old South: Pregnancy, Childbirth, and Infant Rearing* (1990).

Mintz, Steven. *A Prison of Expectations: The Family in Victorian Culture* (1983).

Riley, Glenda. *Divorce: An American Tradition* (1997).

Rothman, Ellen K. *Hands and Hearts: A History of Courtship in America* (1984).

Rotundo, E. Anthony. *American Manhood: Transformations in Masculinity from the Revolution to the Modern Era* (1993).

Ryan, Mary P., *Cradle of the Middle Class: The Family in Oneida County, New York, 1790–1865* (1981).

Sklar, Kathryn Kish. "Victorian Women and Domestic Life: Mary Todd Lincoln, Elizabeth Cady Stanton, and Harriet Beecher Stowe." In Kathryn Kish Sklar and Thomas Dublin, eds., *Women and Power in American History.* 2 vols. (1991): I:229–243.

Smith, Daniel Scott. "Family Limitation, Sexual Control, and Domestic Feminism in Victorian America." In Nancy F. Cott and Elizabeth H. Pleck, eds., *A Heritage of Her Own: Toward a New Social History of American Women* (1979), pp. 222–245.

Smith-Rosenberg, Carroll. *Disorderly Conduct: Visions of Gender in Victorian America* (1985).

Wertz, Richard W., and Dorothy C. Wertz. *Lying In: A History of Childbirth in America* (1989).

Wilson, Lisa. *Life After Death: Widows in Pennsylvania, 1750–1850* (1992).

CHAPTER
5

Families in Bondage

Until quite recently, scholarly discussion of family life in slavery has been dominated by the impulse to counter stereotypes of the black family as unhealthy and unstable. Cultural critics have characterized contemporary African American family life as marred by the matriarchy and illegitimacy that are the twin legacies of slavery, which denied slaves the right to marry and severely curtailed men's authority over their offspring. While sociologist Franklin Frazier and historian Stanley Elkins were among the first to identify these alleged defects in the African American family and to trace the origins of these tendencies to slavery, concern about the "pathological" nature of the black family became widespread in the wake of Senator Daniel Patrick Moynihan's 1965 report on the modern black family, which linked the problems of blacks in the inner cities—including drug abuse, high crime rates, and skyrocketing unemployment—to the female-headed African American household that, according to the Moynihan report, originated in the slave era and continued to characterize black neighborhoods. The timing of the report, which coincided with the Black Power movement and with a wave of revisionist slavery scholarship, ushered in a wave of studies that sought to demonstrate that slave families were, in fact, healthy and stable—characteristics that defenders of the black family identified with a nuclear family headed by a strong male. Not until two decades later, in the 1980s, did scholars such as Deborah Gray White, using feminist theory and a comparative anthropological perspective, call into question the sexist and ethnocentric assumptions that underlay these attempts to defend the black family by portraying it as adhering to white, middle-class norms.

In the past two decades, research on the slave family has moved beyond questions of family structure (nuclear or "incomplete") and authority (male-headed or "matriarchal") to consider the conflicted relationship between slave families and the whites who claimed ownership of them and the complex interactions within slave families, households, and communities. In this effort, historians have benefited from the ready availability of oral histories of former slaves, the result of the depression-era Works Progress Administration's (WPA) interviews with elderly blacks. Although these firsthand accounts are plagued by methodological problems, such as the nature of the questions posed by the interviewers, the interviewers' race (often white) and bias (reflected in their decision to render responses in dialect), and the subjects' nostalgia, they remain valuable sources for the study of the slave family. The emerging history of slave childhood, in particular, has benefited from the WPA interviews. By combining these recollections with contemporaneous accounts by travelers, slave owners, and runaway slaves, scholars are able to investigate some of the most troubling aspects of family life in bondage, including infanticide, domestic violence, and the breakup of families by sale or migration.

Ultimately, the study of the slave family revolves around issues of control. While slave owners had the ultimate authority over slave families, slaves contested this authority in a variety of ways. This power struggle affected the dynamics of family life in ways that scholars are only beginning to understand. Many questions are still unresolved: How successful were slaves in asserting control over their own lives? To what extent were their options limited by the master's power? Who suffered most from the constant battle for control?

 D O C U M E N T S

Although it was against the law to teach slaves to read and write, a privileged few received instruction from sympathetic whites and free blacks. Document 1 is composed of two rare letters between slave husbands and wives. These letters, written by Virginia slaves in the two decades preceding the Civil War, poignantly reveal the grief that the domestic slave trade caused individuals and families.

The next two documents present the testimonies of two slave runaways, both of whom published accounts of their lives in an attempt to rouse antislavery sentiment. Frederick Douglass's 1845 *Narrative of the Life of Frederick Douglass*, excerpted in Document 2, highlights the twin themes of the separation of family members (in this case mother and child) and the sexual abuse of slave women.

Selections from Harriet Jacobs's 1861 *Incidents in the Life of a Slave Girl*, originally published under the pseudonym Linda Brent, make up Document 3. Jacobs, like Douglass, raises the spectre of sexual assault. She also illuminates the contest for control over children's loyalties and destinies that took place between masters and slaves. Finally, she reveals the mixed emotions with which she regarded motherhood.

English-born actress turned plantation mistress Fanny Kemble's descriptions of slave women, written in 1838–1839 and published as *Journal of a Residence on a Georgia Plantation* in 1863, compose Document 4. Kemble, an abolitionist sympathizer, documents the appallingly high rates of infant mortality and maternal debility on her husband's plantation.

Document 5 comprises a selection of interviews with former slaves conducted under the WPA in the mid-1930s. Hannah Chapman's recollections highlight the heroic efforts that some slave men in "abroad" marriages (marriages in which the husband and wife lived on different plantations) made to maintain contact with their children, while Jordan Johnson painfully recalls slave men's inability to protect their wives from abuse. Caroline Hunter reveals how slave men's powerlessness could lead them to abandon their families and demonstrates that slave mothers, no less than slave fathers, saw their ability to care for other family members severely compromised under slavery. Fannie Moore, while illustrating that mothers shared child care responsibilities with other adults, emphasizes that her own mother put her children's interests first, risking punishment to protect them from harm. Mingo White's story illuminates the long-lasting effects of the forced separation of family members, and Rose Williams offers a powerful firsthand account of the despicable practice of slave breeding.

1. Slave Husbands and Wives Correspond, 1840s–1850s

Sargry Brown to Mores Brown, October 27, 1840

Dear Husband—

this is the third letter that I have written to you, and have not received any from you; and dont no the reason that I have not received any from you. I think very hard of it. the trader has been here three times to Look at me. I wish that you would try to see if you can get any one to buy me up there. if you dont come down here this Sunday, perhaps you wont see me any more. give my love to them all, and tell them all that perhaps I shan't see you any more. give my love to your mother in particular, and to mamy wines, and to aunt betsy, and all the children; tell Jane and Mother they must come down a fortnight before christmas. I wish to see you all, but I expect I never shall see you all—never no more.

I remain your Dear and affectionate Wife.

Sargry Brown.

James Phillips to Mary Phillips, June 20, 1852

Dear Wife—I will now write to you to inform you where I am and my health. I am well, and I am in hope when you receive this, it may find you well also. I am now in a trader's hands, by the name of Mr. Branton, and he is agoing to start South with a lot of negroes in August. I do not like this country at all, and had almost rather die than to go South. Tell all of the people that if they can do anything for me, now is the time to do it. I can be bought for $900. Do pray, try and get Brant and Mr. Byers and Mr. Weaver to send or come on to buy me, and if they will only buy me back, I will be a faithful man to them so long as I live. Show Mr. Brant and Mr. Weaver this letter, and tell them to come on as soon as they possibly can to buy me. My master is willing to sell me to any gentleman who will be so kind as to come on to buy me. They have got poor James Phillips here with leg irons on to keep him from getting away; and do pray gentlemen, do not feel any hesitation at all, but come on as soon as you can and buy me. Feel for me now or never. If any of you will be so kind as to come on to buy me, inquire for Cochron's Jail. I can be found there, and my master is always at the Jail himself. My master gave me full consent to have this letter written, so do not feel any hesitation to come on and see about poor James Phillips. Dear wife, show it to these men as soon as you get it, and let them write back immediately what they intend to do. Direct your letter to my master William A. Branton, Richmond, Va. Try and do something for me as soon as you can, for I want to get back very bad indeed.—Do not think anything at all of the price, for I am worth twice that amount. I can make it for any person who will

---

John W. Blassingame, ed., *Slave Testimony: Two Centuries of Letters, Speeches, Interviews, and Auto-biographies* (Baton Rouge: Louisiana State University Press, 1977), pp. 46–47, 95–96.

buy me, in a short time. I have nothing more to write, only I wish I may be bought and carried back to Harrisburg in a short time. My best love to you, my wife. You may depend I am almost dying to see you and my children. You must do all you can for your husband.

Your husband,

James Phillips.

2. Frederick Douglass Describes Separation and Sexual Abuse, 1845

I was born in Tuckahoe, near Hillsborough, and about twelve miles from Easton, in Talbot county, Maryland. I have no accurate knowledge of my age, never having seen any authentic record containing it. By far the larger part of the slaves know as little of their ages as horses know of theirs, and it is the wish of most masters within my knowledge to keep their slaves thus ignorant. I do not remember to have ever met a slave who could tell of his birthday. They seldom come nearer to it than planting-time, harvest-time, cherry-time, spring-time, or fall-time. A want of information concerning my own was a source of unhappiness to me even during childhood. The white children could tell their ages. I could not tell why I ought to be deprived of the same privilege. I was not allowed to make any inquiries of my master concerning it. He deemed all such inquiries on the part of a slave improper and impertinent, and evidence of a restless spirit. The nearest estimate I can give makes me now between twenty-seven and twenty-eight years of age. I come to this, from hearing my master say, some time during 1835, I was about seventeen years old.

My mother was named Harriet Bailey. She was the daughter of Isaac and Betsey Bailey, both colored, and quite dark. My mother was of a darker complexion than either my grandmother or grandfather.

My father was a white man. He was admitted to be such by all I ever heard speak of my parentage. The opinion was also whispered that my master was my father; but of the correctness of this opinion, I know nothing; the means of knowing was withheld from me. My mother and I were separated when I was but an infant—before I knew her as my mother. It is a common custom, in the part of Maryland from which I ran away, to part children from their mothers at a very early age. Frequently, before the child has reached its twelfth month, its mother is taken from it, and hired out on some farm a considerable distance off, and the child is placed under the care of an old woman, too old for field labor. For what this separation is done, I do not know, unless it be to hinder the development of the child's affection toward its mother, and to blunt and destroy the natural affection of the mother for the child. This is the inevitable result.

I never saw my mother, to know her as such, more than four or five times in my life; and each of these times was very short in duration, and at night. She was hired

Frederick Douglass, *Narrative of the Life of Frederick Douglass, an American Slave, Written by Himself* (New York: Signet, 1968; originally published 1845), pp. 21–23.

by a Mr. Stewart, who lived about twelve miles from my home. She made her journeys to see me in the night, travelling the whole distance on foot, after the performance of her day's work. She was a field hand, and a whipping is the penalty of not being in the field at sunrise, unless a slave has special permission from his or her master to the contrary—a permission which they seldom get, and one that gives to him that gives it the proud name of being a kind master. I do not recollect of ever seeing my mother by the light of day. She was with me in the night. She would lie down with me, and get me to sleep, but long before I waked she was gone. Very little communication ever took place between us. Death soon ended what little we could have while she lived, and with it her hardships and suffering. She died when I was about seven years old, on one of my master's farms, near Lee's Mill. I was not allowed to be present during her illness, at her death, or burial. She was gone long before I knew any thing about it. Never having enjoyed, to any considerable extent, her soothing presence, her tender and watchful care, I received the tidings of her death with much the same emotions I should have probably felt at the death of a stranger.

Called thus suddenly away, she left me without the slightest intimation of who my father was. The whisper that my master was my father, may or may not be true; and, true or false, it is of but little consequence to my purpose whilst the fact remains, in all its glaring odiousness, that slaveholders have ordained, and by law established, that the children of slave women shall in all cases follow the condition of their mothers; and this is done too obviously to administer to their own lusts, and make a gratification of their wicked desires profitable as well as pleasurable; for by this cunning arrangement, the slaveholder, in cases not a few, sustains to his slaves the double relation of master and father. . . .

3. Harriet Jacobs Remembers Growing Up a Slave, 1861

Dr. Flint, a physician in the neighborhood, had married the sister of my mistress, and I was now the property of their little daughter. It was not without murmuring that I prepared for my new home; and what added to my unhappiness, was the fact that my brother William was purchased by the same family. My father, by his nature, as well as by the habit of transacting business as a skilful mechanic, had more of the feelings of a freeman than is common among slaves. My brother was a spirited boy; and being brought up under such influences, he early detested the name of master and mistress. One day, when his father and his mistress had happened to call him at the same time, he hesitated between the two; being perplexed to know which had the strongest claim upon his obedience. He finally concluded to go to his mistress. When my father reproved him for it, he said, "You both called me, and I didn't know which I ought to go to first."

Harriet A. Jacobs, *Incidents in the Life of a Slave Girl, Written by Herself,* ed. Jean Fagan Yellin (Cambridge, Mass.: Harvard University Press, 1987; originally published 1861), pp. 9, 27–29, 60–62.

"You are *my* child," replied our father, "and when I call you, you should come immediately, if you have to pass through fire and water."

Poor Willie! He was now to learn his first lesson of obedience to a master. . . .

During the first years of my service in Dr. Flint's family, I was accustomed to share some indulgences with the children of my mistress. Though this seemed to me no more than right, I was grateful for it, and tried to merit the kindness by the faithful discharge of my duties. But I now entered on my fifteenth year—a sad epoch in the life of a slave girl. My master began to whisper foul words in my ear. Young as I was, I could not remain ignorant of their import. I tried to treat them with indifference or contempt. The master's age, my extreme youth, and the fear that his conduct would be reported to my grandmother, made him bear this treatment for many months. He was a crafty man, and resorted to many means to accomplish his purposes. Sometimes he had stormy, terrific ways, that made his victims tremble; sometimes he assumed a gentleness that he thought must surely subdue. Of the two, I preferred his stormy moods, although they left me trembling. He tried his utmost to corrupt the pure principles my grandmother had instilled. He peopled my young mind with unclean images, such as only a vile monster could think of. I turned from him with disgust and hatred. But he was my master. I was compelled to live under the same roof with him—where I saw a man forty years my senior daily violating the most sacred commandments of nature. He told me I was his property; that I must be subject to his will in all things. My soul revolted against the mean tyranny. But where could I turn for protection? No matter whether the slave girl be as black as ebony or as fair as her mistress. In either case, there is no shadow of law to protect her from insult, from violence, or even from death; all these are inflicted by fiends who bear the shape of men. The mistress, who ought to protect the helpless victim, has no other feelings towards her but those of jealousy and rage. The degradation, the wrongs, the vices, that grow out of slavery, are more than I can describe. They are greater than you would willingly believe. Surely, if you credited one half the truths that are told you concerning the helpless millions suffering in this cruel bondage, you at the north would not help to tighten the yoke. You surely would refuse to do for the master, on your own soil, the mean and cruel work which trained bloodhounds and the lowest class of whites do for him at the south.

Every where the years bring to all enough of sin and sorrow; but in slavery the very dawn of life is darkened by these shadows. Even the little child, who is accustomed to wait on her mistress and her children, will learn, before she is twelve years old, why it is that her mistress hates such and such a one among the slaves. Perhaps the child's own mother is among those hated ones. She listens to violent outbreaks of jealous passion, and cannot help understanding what is the cause. She will become prematurely knowing in evil things. Soon she will learn to tremble when she hears her master's footfall. She will be compelled to realize that she is no longer a child. If God has bestowed beauty upon her, it will prove her greatest curse. That which commands admiration in the white woman only hastens the degradation of the female slave. I know that some are too much brutalized by slavery to feel the humiliation of their position; but many slaves feel it most acutely, and shrink from the memory of it. I cannot tell how much I suffered in the presence of these wrongs, nor how I am still pained by the retrospect. My master met me at every turn, reminding me that I belonged to him, and swearing by heaven and earth that he would compel me to submit to him. If I went out for a breath of fresh air, after a day of unwearied toil, his footsteps dogged me. If I knelt by my mother's grave, his dark shadow fell on me even there. The light heart which nature had given me became heavy with sad forebodings. The other slaves in my master's house noticed the change. Many of them pitied me; but none dared to ask the cause. They had no need to inquire. They knew too well the guilty practices under that roof; and they were aware that to speak of them was an offence that never went unpunished. . . .

O, what days and nights of fear and sorrow that man caused me! Reader, it is not to awaken sympathy for myself that I am telling you truthfully what I suffered in slavery. I do it to kindle a flame of compassion in your hearts for my sisters who are still in bondage, suffering as I once suffered. . . .

When my babe was born, they said it was premature. It weighed only four pounds; but God let it live. I heard the doctor say I could not survive till morning. I had often prayed for death; but now I did not want to die, unless my child could die too. Many weeks passed before I was able to leave my bed. I was a mere wreck of my former self. For a year there was scarcely a day when I was free from chills and fever. My babe also was sickly. His little limbs were often racked with pain. Dr. Flint continued his visits, to look after my health; and he did not fail to remind me that my child was an addition to his stock of slaves. . . .

As the months passed on, my boy improved in health. When he was a year old, they called him beautiful. The little vine was taking deep root in my existence, though its clinging fondness excited a mixture of love and pain. When I was most sorely oppressed I found a solace in his smiles. I loved to watch his infant slumbers; but always there was a dark cloud over my enjoyment. I could never forget that he was a slave. Sometimes I wished that he might die in infancy. God tried me. My darling became very ill. The bright eyes grew dull, and the little feet and hands were so icy cold that I thought death had already touched them. I had prayed for his death, but never so earnestly as I now prayed for his life; and my prayer was heard. Alas, what mockery it is for a slave mother to try to pray back her dying child to life! Death is better than slavery. . . .

4. Fanny Kemble Reports on Slave Women's Health, 1863

. . .

. . . I have a mind to transcribe . . . the entries for today recorded in a sort of daybook, where I put down very succinctly the number of people who visit me, their petitions and ailments, and also such special particulars concerning them as seem to me worth recording. You will see how miserable the physical condition of many of these poor creatures is; and their physical condition, it is insisted by those who uphold this evil system, is the only part of it which is prosperous, happy, and compares well with that

Frances Anne Kemble, *Journal of a Residence on a Georgian Plantation in 1838–1839,* ed. John A. Scott (New York: Knopf, 1961; originally published 1863), pp. 229–231.

of Northern laborers. Judge from the details I now send you; and never forget, while reading them, that the people on this plantation are well off, and consider themselves well off, in comparison with the slaves on some of the neighboring estates.

Fanny has had six children; all dead but one. She came to beg to have her work in the field lightened.

Nanny has had three children; two of them are dead. She came to implore that the rule of sending them into the field three weeks after their confinement might be altered.

Leah, Caesar's wife, has had six children; three are dead.

Sophy, Lewis's wife, came to beg for some old linen. She is suffering fearfully; has had ten children; five of them are dead. The principal favor she asked was a piece of meat, which I gave her.

Sally, Scipio's wife, has had two miscarriages and three children born, one of whom is dead. She came complaining of incessant pain and weakness in her back. This woman was a mulatto daughter of a slave called Sophy, by a white man of the name of Walker, who visited the plantation.

Charlotte, Renty's wife; had had two miscarriages, and was with child again. She was almost crippled with rheumatism, and showed me a pair of poor swollen knees that made my heart ache. I have promised her a pair of flannel trousers, which I must forthwith set about making.

Sarah, Stephen's wife; this woman's case and history were alike deplorable. She had had four miscarriages, had brought seven children into the world, five of whom were dead, and was again with child. She complained of dreadful pains in the back, and an internal tumor which swells with the exertion of working in the fields; probably, I think, she is ruptured. She told me she had once been mad and had run into the woods, where she contrived to elude discovery for some time, but was at last tracked and brought back, when she was tied up by the arms, and heavy logs fastened to her feet, and was severely flogged. After this she contrived to escape again, and lived for some time skulking in the woods, and she supposes mad, for when she was taken again she was entirely naked. She subsequently recovered from this derangement, and seems now just like all the other poor creatures who come to me for help and pity. I suppose her constant childbearing and hard labor in the fields at the same time may have produced the temporary insanity.

Sukey, Bush's wife, only came to pay her respects. She had had four miscarriages; had brought eleven children into the world, five of whom are dead.

Molly, Quambo's wife, also only came to see me. Hers was the best account I have yet received; she had had nine children, and six of them were still alive.

This is only the entry for today, in my diary, of the people's complaints and visits. Can you conceive a more wretched picture than that which it exhibits of the conditions under which these women live? Their cases are in no respect singular, and though they come with pitiful entreaties that I will help them with some alleviation of their pressing physical distresses, it seems to me marvelous with what desperate patience (I write it advisedly, patience of utter despair) they endure their sorrow-laden existence. Even the poor wretch who told that miserable story of insanity, and lonely hiding in the swamps, and scourging when she was found, and of her renewed madness and flight, did so in a sort of low, plaintive, monotonous murmur of misery, as if such sufferings were "all in the day's work."

I ask these questions about their children because I think the number they bear as compared with the number they rear a fair gauge of the effect of the system on their own health and that of their offspring. There was hardly one of these women, as you will see by the details I have noted of their ailments, who might not have been a candidate for a bed in a hospital, and they had come to me after working all day in the fields.

5. Former Slaves Recall Family Life, 1930s

Hannah Chapman

. . .

My father wuz sold 'way from us when I wuz small. Dat wuz a sad time fer us. Mars wouldn't sell de mudders 'way from deir chillun so us lived on wid her wid out de fear ob bein' sold. My pa sho' did hate ter leave us. He missed us and us longed fer him. He would often slip back ter us' cottage at night. Us would gather 'round him an' crawl up in his lap, tickled slap to death, but he give us dese pleasures at a painful risk. When his Mars missed him he would beat him all de way home. Us could track him de nex' day by de blood stains. . . .

Jordan Johnson

Husbands allays went to de woods when dey know de wives was due fo' a whippin', but in de fiel' dey dare not leave. Had to stay dere, not darin' even look like dey didn't like it. Charlie Jones was one slave dat had his wife workin' in de same fiel' wid him. Was plantin' tobacco—he was settin' out an' she was hillin.' Annie was big wid chile an' gittin' near her time, so one day she made a slip an' chopped a young shoot down. Ole man Diggs, de overseer, come runnin' up screamin' at her an' it made her mo' nervous, an she chopped off 'nother one. Ole overseer lif' up dat rawhide an' beat Annie 'cross de back an shoulders 'till she fell to de groun.' An' Charlie he jus' stood dere hearin' his wife scream an' astarin' at de sky, not darin' to look at her or even say a word.

Caroline Hunter

I ain' got no education and I don' know when I was born, but I do know I was born a slave. I was born near Suffolk, Virginia. My moma was a slave, but my papa was free. I had thirteen chillun, an' all died but four. One ain' never took breath. I had three brothers to live. My mama, papa, me an' my three brothers all live in one room back of my mastah's house. We et, slep an' done ev'ything in jus' dat one room. My papa didn't stay wid us ve'y long. He left 'cause my massa beat him. It happen

Ira Berlin, Marc Favreau, and Steven F. Miller, eds., *Remembering Slavery: African Americans Talk About Their Personal Experiences of Slavery and Freedom* (New York: New Press, 1998), pp. 129–130, 132–134, 139–140, 144–145, 161–164. Copyright © 1998. Reprinted by permission of The New Press, (800) 223-4830.

lak dis, honey. Pa love dogs an' kep' one wid him all de time. One day he was out gatherin' up sheep, an' de dog was wid him. Somehow, de dog kilt one sheep; papa didn't know it. When massa found it out he beat my papa till he bled. Papa was free, an' he didn' think massa had no business beatin' him, so he left an' came to Norfolk an' jined de army. . . .

Lord, I done been thew somepin'. When I'se five years ole I had to wuk. I had a job cleanin' silver an' settin' de table. A few years after dat I was put out in de fiel's to wuk all day. . . . I can' never forgit how my massa beat my brothers cause dey didn' wuk. He beat 'em so bad dey was sick a long time, an' soon as dey got a smatterin' better he sold 'em. Two of 'em I seen agin after we was freed, but de oles' one I ain' never seen since. If de massa couldn' rule you dey would sell you, an' if you got so you couldn' wuk dey'd take you in a boat dey had an' dump you in de water. . . .

During slavery it seemed lak yo' chillun b'long to ev'ybody but you. Many a day my ole mama has stood by an' watched massa beat her chillun 'till dey bled an' she couldn' open her mouf. Dey didn' only beat us, but they useta strap my mama to a bench or box an' beat her wid a wooden paddle while she was naked.

Fannie Moore

Nowadays when I heah folks a' growlin an' a' grumblin bout not habbin this an' that I jes think what would they done effen they be brought up on de Moore plantation. De Moore plantation b'long to Marse Jim Moore, in Moore, South Carolina. De Moores had own de same plantation and de same niggers and dey children for yeahs back. . . .

Marse Jim own de bigges' plantation in de whole country. Jes thousands acres ob lan'. An de ole Tiger Ribber a runnin' right through de middle ob de plantation. On one side ob de ribber stood de big house, whar de white folks lib and on the other side stood de quarters. . . .

De quarters jes long row o' cabins daubed wif dirt. Ever one in de family lib in one big room. In one end was a big fireplace. Dis had to heat de cabin and do de cookin too. We cooked in a big pot hung on a rod over de fire and baked de co'n pone in de ashes or else put it in de skillet and cover de lid wif coals. We allus hab plenty wood to keep us warm. Dat is ef we hab time to get it outed de woods.

My granny she cook for us chillens while our mammy away in de fiel. Dey wasn't much cookin to do. Jes make co'n pone and bring in de milk. She hab big wooden bowl wif enough wooden spoons to go 'roun'. She put de milk in de bowl and break it [*the cornpone*] up. Den she put de bowl in de middle of de flo' an' all de chillun grab a spoon.

My mammy she work in de fiel' all day and piece and quilt all night. Den she hab to spin enough thread to make four cuts for de white fo'ks ebber night. Why sometime I nebber go to bed. Hab to hold de light for her to see by. She hab to piece quilts for de white folks too. Why dey is a scar on my arm yet where my brother let de pine drip on me. Rich pine war all de light we ebber hab. My brother was a holdin' de pine so's I can help mammy tack de quilt and he go to sleep and let it drop.

I never see how my mammy stan' sech ha'd work. She stan' up fo' her chillun tho'. De ol' overseeah he hate my mammy, case she fight him for beatin' her chillun. Why she git more whuppins for dat den anythin' else. She hab twelve chillun.

I member I see de three oldes' stan' in de snow up to dey knees to split rails, while de overseeah stan off an' grin.

My mammy she trouble in her heart bout de way they treated. Ever night she pray for de Lawd to git her an' her chillun out ob de place. One day she plowin' in de cotton fiel. All sudden like she let out big yell. Den she sta't singing' an' a shoutin', an' a whoopin' an' a hollowin'. Den it seem she plow all de harder. When she come home, Marse Jim's mammy say: "What all dat goin' on in de fiel? Yo' think we sen' you out there jes to whoop and yell? No siree, we put you out there to work and you sho' bettah work, else we git de overseeah to cowhide you ole black back." My mammy jes grin all over her black wrinkled face and say: "I's saved. De Lawd done tell me I's saved. Now I know de Lawd will sho me de way, I ain't gwine a grieve no more. No matter how much yo' all done beat me an' my chillun de Lawd will show me de way. An' some day we nevah be slaves." Ole granny Moore grab de cowhide and slash mammy cross de back but mammy nebber yell. She jes go back to de fiel a singin'. . . .

Mingo White

I was born in Chester, South Carolina, but I was mos'ly raised in Alabama. . . . When I was 'bout fo' or five years old, I was loaded in a wagon wid a lot mo' people in 'hit. Whar I was boun' I don't know. Whatever become of my mammy an' pappy I don' know for a long time. . . .

I was jes' a li'l thang; tooked away from my mammy an' pappy, jes' when I needed 'em mos.' The only caren' that I had or ever knowed anything 'bout was give to me by a frein' of my pappy. His name was John White. My pappy tol' him to take care of me for him. John was a fiddler an' many a night I woke up to find myse'f 'sleep 'twix' his legs whilst he was playin' for a dance for de white folks. My pappy an' mammy was sold from each yuther too, de same time as I was sold. I use' to wonder if I had any brothers or sisters, as I had always wanted some. A few years later I foun' out I didn't have none. . . .

De nex' time dat I saw my mammy I was a great big boy. Dere was a 'oman on de place what ever'body called mammy, Selina White. One day mammy called me an' said, "Mingo, your mammy is comin'." I said, "I though dat you was my mammy." She said, "No I ain't your mammy, yer mammy is 'way way from here." I couldn't believe dat I had anudder mammy and I never thought 'bout hit any mo'. One day I was settin' down at de barn when a wagon come up de lane. I stood 'roun' lack a chile will. When de wagon got to de house, my mammy got out an' broke and run to me an' th'owed her arms 'roun' my neck an' hug an' kiss me. I never even put my arms 'roun' her or nothin' of de sort. I jes' stood dar lookin' at her. She said, "Son ain't you glad to see your mammy?" I looked at her an' walked off. Mammy Selina call me an' tol' me dat I had hurt my mammy's feelin's, and dat dis 'oman was my mammy. I went off an' studied and I begins to 'member thangs. I went to Selina an' ast her how long it been sence I seen my mammy. She tol' me dat I had been 'way from her since I was jes' a li'l chile. I went to my mammy an' tol' her dat I was sorry I done what I did an' dat I would lack for her to fergit an' forgive me for de way I act when I fust saw her. After I had talked wid my real mammy, she told me of how de family had been broke up an' dat she hadn't seed my pappy sence he was sold. My mammy never would of seen me no mo' if de Lawd hadn't a been in de plan.

Rose Williams

Dere am one thing Massa Hawkins does to me what I can't shunt from my mind. I knows he don't do it for meanness, but I allus holds it 'gainst him. What he done am force me to live with dat nigger, Rufus, 'gainst my wants.

After I been at he place 'bout a year, de massa come to me and say, "You gwine live with Rufus in dat cabin over yonder. Go fix it for livin'." I's 'bout sixteen year old and has no larnin', and I's jus' igno'mus chile. I's thought dat him mean for me to tend de cabin for Rufus and some other niggers. Well, dat am start de pestigation for me.

I's took charge of de cabin after work am done and fixes supper. Naw, I don't like dat Rufus, 'cause he a bully. He am big and cause he so, he think everybody do what him say. We'uns has supper, den I goes here and dare talkin', till I's ready for sleep and den I gits in de bunk. After I's in, dat nigger come and crawl in de bunk with me 'fore I knows it. I says, "What you means, you fool nigger?" He say for me to hush de mouth. "Dis am my bunk, too," he say.

"You's teched in de head. Git out," I's told him, and I puts de feet 'gainst him and give him a shove and out he go on de floor 'fore he knew what I's doin'. Dat nigger jump up and he mad. He look like de wild bear. He starts for de bunk and I jumps quick fer de poker. It am 'bout three feet long and when he comes at me I lets him have it over de head. Did dat nigger stop in his tracks I's say he did. He looks at me steady for a minute and you's come tell he thinkin' hard. Den he go and set on de bench and say, "Jus' wait. You thinks it am smart, but you's am foolish in de head. Dey's gwine larn you somethin'."

"Hush yous big mouth and stay 'way from dis nigger, dat all I wants," I say, and jus' sets and hold dat poker in de hand. He jus' sets, lookin' like de bull. Dere we'uns sets and sets for 'bout an hour and den he go out and I bars de door.

De nex' day I goes to de missy and tells her what Rufus wants and missy say dat am de massa's wishes. She say, "Yous am de portly gal and Rufus am de portly man. De massa wants you-uns for to bring forth portly chillen."

I's thinkin' 'bout what de missy say, but say to myself, "I's not gwine live with dat Rufus." Dat night when him come in de cabin, I grabs de poker and sits on de bench and says, "Git 'way from me, nigger, 'fore I busts yous brains out and stomp on dem." He say nothin' and git out.

De nex' day de massa call me and tell me, "Woman, I's pay big money for you and I's done dat for de cause I wants yous to raise me chillens. I's put yous to live with Rufus for dat purpose. Now, if you doesn't want whippin' at de stake, yous do what I wants."

I thinks 'bout massa buyin' me offen de block and savin' me from bein' sep'rated from my folks and 'bout bein' whipped at de stake. Dere it am. What am I's to do? So I 'cides to do as de massa wish and so I yields. . . .

I never marries, 'cause one 'sperience am 'nough for dis nigger. After what I does for de massa, I's never wants no truck with any man. De Lawd forgive dis cullud woman, but he have to 'scuse me and look for some others for to 'plenish de earth.

◢ *E S S A Y S*

In the first essay, Brenda Stevenson of Ohio State University examines the challenges that confronted slaves as parents and partners. Utilizing WPA interviews with Virginian ex-slaves, she explores the explosive issues of breeding, rape, infanticide, child abuse, and miscegenation. In the process, she calls attention not only to the external pressures brought to bear on slave families, but also to the internal strife that slavery fostered.

In the second essay, Stephanie J. Shaw of UCLA highlights the paradoxical nature of motherhood in slavery. By seeking to protect and to provide for their children, slave mothers, ironically, helped to perpetuate the system that oppressed them. At the same time, however, slave mothers and their partners in child care—husbands, sisters, neighbors, and kin—disproved racist whites' assertions that blacks had neither the desire nor the ability to create and sustain family ties.

Marriage in Slavery

BRENDA STEVENSON

The family was an institution that was by all measures vitally important to every faction of the population of antebellum Virginia, white and black, slave and free. Moreover, the family was important to these various groups of Southerners for quite similar reasons. They believed that a positive family life was necessary to both individual and group survival—emotional, physical, cultural, economic, and social. For many, its existence implied an assurance of comfort in a world that more often than not proved to be harsh, unpredictable, and violent. Regardless of one's racial or cultural identity, political status, social class, or religious beliefs, "family" was an ideal and a reality that antebellum Southerners prodigiously sought and fought to protect. Family was for them the most natural of institutions, and within its confines the most fundamental human events—birth, life, marriage, and death—took on a legitimacy that guaranteed one's humanity and immortality. The family institutions that antebellum Southerners erected provided organization and structure to their lives and resources.

Yet, for many residents of pre–Civil War Virginia, the opportunity to live, act, and take comfort within the physical and emotional boundaries of one's family were privileges that were often elusive, if not impossible to obtain. No group of early nineteenth-century Virginians found it more difficult to create and maintain stable marriages and families than did slaves. This essay is an examination of Virginia slave families during the latter half of the antebellum era. Of primary concern are the problems that adult slaves encountered within their families, particularly as marital partners and parents.

Blacks suffered greatly from the constant pressures attendant to living and working within a slave society. . . . [W]hite Virginians tried to impose their authority on every aspect of slave life, including the family in order to fulfill their need to

Brenda Stevenson, "Distress and Discord in Virginia Slave Families, 1830–1860," in Carol Bleser, ed., *In Joy and in Sorrow: Women, Family, and Marriage in the Victorian South, 1830–1900* (New York: Oxford University Press, 1991), pp. 103–118, 120–124. Copyright © 1992 by Carol Bleser. Used by permission of Oxford University Press, Inc.

control the labor of their human chattel. It was not unusual for slave masters to choose their slaves' marital partners, to separate those couples they had united, to force extramarital sexual partners on them, and even to sell off their children when it became economically advantageous, promoted discipline in the quarters, or helped to secure their own authority.

The negative implications of such actions for slaves who were trying to maintain functional family groups were, of course, substantial. An acutely detrimental phenomenon was the forced outmigration of slaves from Virginia in the antebellum period to other parts of the South as part of the lucrative domestic slave trade. This mandatory and often indiscriminate exodus which separated husband from wife, and mother from child, stripped many slaves of the kin- and community-based networks that they had managed to construct over generations of residence in Virginia. Slave owners sold and shipped literally hundreds of thousands of slave men, women, and children representing all age groups with various family and marriage commitments out of the state. Richard Sutch conservatively estimates that during the decade from 1850 to 1860 alone, slaveholders and traders exported almost sixty-eight thousand Virginia slaves to the lower South and Southwest. More often than not, masters sold their slaves without regard to family groups or marital status. Even those slaveholders who wanted to keep slave families united had little control over their future unity once the slave family was purchased by someone else. Donald Sweig's survey of the marital histories of slaves in northern Virginia, for example, indicates that as many as 74 percent of those exported left the state without accompanying family members. Moreover, one can reasonably surmise that since most of the slaves exported were between twenty and forty-nine years old, many of them were spouses and parents at the time of their departure. Regional studies substantiate this generalization. When Jo Ann Manfra and Robert Dykstra reviewed a survey of late antebellum slave marriages in southern Virginia, for example, they found that at least one-third of those couples who separated did so as a result of slaveholder demands. Manfra and Dykstra's analysis also documents that mandatory division was the predominant reason young married slave couples separated. Separated slave couples and the breakup of families also produced orphans. The disruption of family ties and its consequences (such as orphaned children) were especially serious problems for Virginia bondsmen and women during the latter half of the antebellum period.

Other information descriptive of Virginia slave life in the last decades before the Civil War also documents these phenomena. When one considers the recollections of ex-slaves, many of which record the personal histories of the last generation of slave children, adolescents, and young adults, the scope of these problems is obvious. Charles Perdue, Thomas Barden, and Robert Phillips provide the largest collection of published Virginia slave narratives in *Weevils in the Wheat: Interviews of Virginia Ex-Slaves* (1976). Of the 142 autobiographical statements found in this compilation, 87 include both impressionistic and detailed statistical information that ex-slaves provided about their parents. Among this group of former slaves, fully 18 percent suggested that neither their mothers nor their fathers contributed significantly to their rearing. . . .

Slave kin groups and communities on large holdings ideally provided alternative means for slaves to exchange and share emotional and economic support with loved ones in spite of the potentially destructive power of the owners to separate slave families. Regardless of the many Virginia slave family groups that had some characteristics of a nuclear structure, extended and stepfamilies persisted in slave communities as innovative sources of socialization, social intercourse, material aid, and cultural expression.

Within the arena of the slave community, child rearing was a shared responsibility. In the absence of a parent, other nuclear and extended family members and sometimes fictive kin took on the major responsibility of rearing children. Adult female siblings or maternal female kin were the first choices as surrogate primary care-givers. . . .

The importance of any one person's particular contribution to the rearing of children within slave families was determined by a number of variables. Generally, physical proximity to the child, the closeness of the consanguinal tie, and gender implied one's responsibility in this familial matter. Another important variable was the size of the slave child's nuclear and extended family. Slave children who were members of large families and slave communities, for example, were surrounded by a number of kin who could serve as child rearers. Other considerations which affected this decision were the age of possible care-givers and the status of these nurturers' physical and mental health, the other domestic responsibilities of these potential rearers, and, relatedly, their willingness to accept the responsibility of helping to raise the youngsters. . . . Slave owners, however, *ultimately* decided who would assume such responsibilities, and slaves, in general, had to act accordingly.

Slave masters insisted on the importance of the slave mother in the slave family, particularly in regard to child rearing. In so doing, they helped to sustain both African and European cultural traditions that slaves drew upon when deciding how to order their social world. Accordingly, slave mothers took on the most significant long-term obligations of child care. Virginia slave owners promoted matrifocal and matrilocal families among their slaves in several ways. First, a Virginia law dated 1662 stipulated that black children take the status of their mothers. This legal association between slave mother and child reinforced, within the slaveholder's perception of an ordered domestic world, the cultural dictates of their society concerning gender differentiated responsibility. Masters believed that slave mothers, like white women, had a natural bond with their children and that therefore it was their responsibility—more so than that of slave fathers—to care for their offspring. Consequently, young slave children routinely lived with their mothers or female maternal kin, thus establishing the matrilocality of slave families. Moreover, masters compiling lists of their human property routinely identified the female parent of slave children but only sometimes indicated paternity. Also, when prompted to sell a group of slaves which might include parents and their children, owners sometimes tried to sell a mother with her small children as a single unit but rarely afforded slave fathers this same consideration.

At the same time that slaveholders promoted a strong bond between slave mothers and their children, they denied to slave fathers their paternal rights of ownership and authority, as well as denying them their right to contribute to the material support of their offspring. Undoubtedly, slave masters felt that if it became necessary for them to challenge the power that slave parents had in the lives of their children, it would be much easier to do so if the parent with whom the child most readily identified as an authority figure was a female rather than a male.

Slaveholders' insistence on the importance of the slave mother by identifying her as the head of the slave family and primary care-giver of the children, along with the derivation of the slave child's status from that of the mother, firmly established the matrifocality of most slave families. Thus, while slave fathers had a significant presence in the consciousness of their children, mothers obviously were much more physically and psychologically present in the children's lives.

A review of the slave narratives can elucidate further these issues of slave family structure and membership. If one considers the sample Perdue provides in his compilation, it is clear that the large majority of Virginia ex-slaves identified their mothers as the primary providers of care and socialization during their childhood. Significantly, 82 percent spoke of the physical presence of their mothers during most of their childhood years, while only 42 percent recalled continuous contact with their fathers. Moreover, fully one-third of those who did make mention of the presence of their fathers during their childhood indicated that these men did not live with them but only visited on their days off. . . . Many Virginia slave children born in the last decades before the Civil War, therefore, grew up without fathers or black male role models and nurturers, while women bore and reared children without the comfort and support of their husbands or other male kin.

Virginia Bell, an ex-slave from Louisiana, recalled her parents' personal histories: "Both of them was from Virginny, but from diff'rent places, and was brought to Louisiana by nigger traders and sold to Massa Lewis. I know my pappy was lots older than my mother and he had a wife and five chillun back in Virginny and had been sold away from them out there. . . . I don' know what become of his family back in Virginny, 'cause when he was freed he stayed with us." Katie Blackwell Johnson was a Virginia ex-slave who never had the privilege of living with her father. As an adult, Johnson recalled very little about her male parent. "I only remember seeing him once," she stated. "He was stretched on the floor. He took me in his arms and I went to sleep. My mother said he was a great gambler and he never came to see us without a jug of liquor."

Although many of the ex-slaves interviewed obviously knew and lived with their mothers, some slaves also grew up without their mothers. This was particularly so for the last generations of Virginia slaves who were born and reared between 1830 and 1860 when masters increasingly were selling women to traders who took them out of the state. Information descriptive of the slave exports from the state documents this activity. Richard Sutch estimates that by 1850, slaveholders were selling equal numbers of adult women and men and actually more adolescent and young adult females than males within those broad age cohorts. Because the average age at first birth for Virginia slave women was between nineteen and twenty years, large numbers exported were probably young mothers, many of whom were forced to leave without their young. Liza McCoy recalled that her Aunt Charlotte, a slave who lived in Matthews County, "was sold to Georgia away from her baby when de chile wont no more three months." Ex-slave Fannie Berry included in her autobiographical account of life in late antebellum Virginia a tragic scene of slave mothers separated from their infants. She described the incident in part as:

> Dar was a great crying and carrying on 'mongst the slaves who had been sold. Two or three of dem gals had young babies taking with 'em. Poor little things. As soon as dey got on de train dis ol' new master had de train stopped an' made dem poor gal mothers

take babies off and laid dem precious things on de groun' and left dem behind to live or die. . . . [the] master who bought de mothers didn't want gals to be bothered wid dese chillun 'cause he had his cottonfields fer new slaves to work.

Berry went on to explain the fate of the abandoned infants that "some po' white man would take dem an' raise dem up as his slaves and make 'em work on his plantation and if he wanted to, would sell 'em."

Unfortunately, the socialization of slave youth was a difficult task for slaves regardless of the composition of their individual families. Slave child rearers faced obstacles to success that most whites did not. The most important deterrent was a legal one which had negative implications for all aspects of the relationship between rearer and child. Simply, slave parents were not the legal guardians of their children—white owners were. Moreover, since slaveholders were quite willing to share their authority with persons other than slave kin, particularly nurses, overseers, drivers, and other whites residing on their property, slave family members had many threats to their influence over the lives of their youngsters. Slave children were confronted with a variety of authority figures, white and black, each with his or her own priorities, demands, and contributions to their upbringing. These youths had to learn to assess the power and value of each of these adults as well as to appease their demands, often simultaneously.

Slave kin and white owners held the most important positions of power in the lives of slave children. Yet, as the balance of power was both a delicate and complex phenomenon that could shift quite suddenly, slave kin had to work diligently to retain some control in the face of unsolicited interference from others. White owners balked at attempts by slave kin to gain control over the lives or allegiances of black children in opposition to their authority as masters. They understood that such challenges to their authority showed that their slaves did not accept their assigned inferior status and were teaching their slave children to resist as well. Masters met such trials with extreme hostility and often open brutality. . . .

Caroline Hunter's recollections about her life as a child with her slave mother and three brothers on a small farm near Suffolk, Virginia, at the end of the antebellum era include a telling example of the frustration that slave kin felt in response to the intrusion of white authority in the lives of their children. The scene she describes also suggests important questions about the slave child's general perception of black adult authority:

During slavery it seemed lak yo' chillun b'long to ev'ybody but you. Many a day my ole mama has stood by an' watched massa beat her chillun 'till dey bled an' she couldn' open her mouf. Dey didn' only beat us, but dey useta strap my mama to a bench or box an' beat her wid a wooden paddle while she was naked.

Stripped naked and beaten before her daughter, other family members, and the slave community, Caroline Hunter's mother must have known that such an example of her obvious helplessness in the face of slaveholder power would jeopardize her authority within her own domestic sphere—authority that she needed in order to rear Caroline and her other children. Nevertheless, the owner's demonstration of control did not destroy the bond between child and parent or the respect that Caroline had for her mother. On the contrary, the experience seemed to have deepened the young girl's appreciation for her mother's plight and helped to further instill in the daughter a profound hatred for their cruel owner. Yet, these expressions of white dominion and control that slave youth repeatedly witnessed had some impact on the ways in which slaves differentially identified and related to white and black authority.

Ex-slave Nancy Williams of Yanceville, Virginia, recounted an experience which demonstrates the influence that owners could have on a slave child's perspective of parental authority. Williams explained that as a young child, she was a favorite of her master who, consequently, did not beat her and frowned on the strict disciplinary policy of her parents. Her parents probably believed that their master was spoiling Nancy and resented his intrusion in their domestic affairs. It was clear to slave parents that children reared in such a manner eventually would face harsh confrontations with whites and also risk alienation from their slave peers. As such, slave child rearers like the Williams's had to fight a war of wits with their owners to gain the necessary authority to properly socialize their own children.

Not surprisingly, slave children did not always cooperate with their parents' efforts. Nancy Williams sometimes tried to manipulate her master's "benevolence" in order to avoid the stinging punishments that her parents often inflicted. The ex-slave recalled that on one such occasion, she had refused to do a task that her mother had assigned her. Nancy was fleeing from her parent and the inevitable beating she was to receive when she decided that the best place to hide was between her owner's legs. Nancy, mindful of her master's fondness for her, knew that her mother would not whip her in his presence. "I run up de stairs rit 'tween marsa's legs," Williams remembered, "an ask him for 10 [cents]. She couldn't ketch me den." Mrs. Williams, however, was not about to let her child get away with this obvious act of disrespect or her original offense. Years later, the errant daughter noted her mother's eventual triumph: "[W]hen she did [catch me,] she beat de debil outa me."

One can expect that with the decline of the viability of the extended slave family and the nonrelated surrogate kin network in the wake of increased exportation of slaves, the overall socialization of many slave youth suffered. One must also concede, however, that even under optimum conditions for success, slave kin rarely were able to rear children that were not affected to some degree by the actions and ideologies of whites who held so much power over their physical, psychological, and intellectual developments. Obviously, slaves sometimes internalized prevalent racist views which created tension within their families and communities. Color stratification was a problem which posed particularly negative consequences for those slaves touched by it, because of the explosive issues of force, sex, female purity, and marital sanctity that it evoked. Color consciousness and stratification among blacks resulted from a combination of factors, such as a consistently high rate of miscegenation and, relatedly, a large biracial population among slaves and free blacks, as well as the popularity of racist ideologies concerning race difference and hierarchy and their practical application in antebellum Virginia society.

Much of the interracial sexual activity that resulted in the state's biracial population involved white-male coercion and rape of black females. Consequently, the children born of these assaults were potent symbols of the immense power that whites held over the most intimate spheres of black life. They were a constant reminder to their mothers and her kin of their powerlessness in the face of white male domination and violence. "My mama said that in dem times a nigger 'oman couldn't help herself," May Satterfield recalled, "fo she had to do what de marster say. . . . she had to go." Consequently, the presence of racially mixed children in homes of slaves sometimes engendered feelings of shame, humiliation, and anger.

Slave families and communities usually attached an even deeper stigma to those children conceived as a result of the voluntary sexual relations between black women and white men. Although slaves were very empathetic to those women who were the victims of coercion, they often ostracized slave women who openly consorted with white men. Many bondswomen and men viewed these concubines as promiscuous and disloyal. Their children shared, to a certain extent, the dishonor of their mothers.

It is not surprising, therefore, that many racially mixed children felt shame and confusion about their white parentage. Patience Richardson Avery, for example, immediately rejected the notion that Thomas Hatcher, Jr., a white resident of some prominence in Chesterfield County, was her father. When her mother first introduced Mr. Hatcher to their small daughter, Patience remembered that she screamed: "I ain't got no father; . . . He no father o' mine! He white!" Although she was only a few years old at the time, Patience profoundly understood the sociopolitical distinction between "black" and "white" and was horrified that she might be related to a white man. . . .

Mothers and other family members were sensitive to the kinds of teasing, insults, and rough treatment that their mulatto children might receive at the hands of blacks and whites. They often lied to them about their paternity or taught them to avoid the issue when questioned about it. "Who's yo' pappy?" was the question that slaves often asked Candis Goodwin; the illegitimate daughter of a neighboring slave owner and a slave woman. Goodwin often quipped back at those teasing her: "Tuckey buzzard lay me an' de sun hatch me," but she secretly knew her "pappy" was "Massa Williams."

Despite the obvious hostility with which many slaves responded to miscegenation, the reaction in the slave quarter to racially mixed children often was a complex and contradictory one. While many felt uneasy with the presence of these children and a few openly rejected them, unresolved feelings of black inferiority caused some to treat racially mixed and generally light-skinned children as superior to their darker peers. . . .

Certainly, many male and female slaves viewed African-Americans with light skin and eye color, straight hair and noses, and thin lips as exceedingly attractive. When the mulatto Candis Goodwin was a young woman living on the Eastern Shore, she was considered "de purties" girl in the area. Virginia Haynes Shepherd of Churchland was the daughter of a domestic slave and a white doctor. Although she was embarrassed when asked about her paternity, Mrs. Shepherd was quite forthcoming with her impressions of black feminine beauty. Describing one slave woman of local acclaim, Shepherd noted: "Diana was a black beauty if there ever was one. She had this thin silk skin, a sharp nose, thin lips, a perfect set of white teeth and beautiful long coal-black hair."

Thus, while Patience Avery and other mulattoes were uncomfortable with an ancestry that was partially white, other racially mixed African-Americans . . . were proud of it, considered themselves superior to other blacks, and believed they were the elite within their families and their communities. Many blacks must have accepted these notions of entitlement that some light-skinned slaves promoted—few racially mixed slaves could have afforded to prolong such pretensions of superiority otherwise.

Of course, other problems related to the flaws in the antebellum South also haunted the families of bondsmen and women. Reared in a society that was extremely violent, even by standards of the nineteenth century, slaves sometimes also chose brutal force as a means of control of their families and among their peers. . . .

The violence and brutality that whites imposed on their slaves undoubtedly influenced the ways in which bondsmen and bondswomen treated their own children and other dependents. The ability to beat someone, to hold that kind of physical control over another human, was a sadistic expression of power that blacks learned repeatedly from their interaction with and observation of white authority figures. This expression of control was meant to impress children with their parents' ability to command some power over their offspring's behavior. Also, adult slave kin wanted to demonstrate to whites, who often tried to usurp or demean slave parental authority, that they claimed a right to control and chastise their own children regardless of the legal guardianship that white owners possessed. Perhaps it was this demonstration of black slave power within their own domestic sphere rather than the concern for the actual physical pain the children endured that really offended whites.

As "contraband of war," for example, Virginia slaves who took refuge behind Union lines and went to reside in the federal army and freedmen aid-society camps quickly claimed their freedom which they, in part, defined as a right to make vital decisions regarding their own children. It is obvious that they were no more receptive to the judgments that Northern teachers and missionaries made about their methods of child discipline and rearing than they were of their former owners' "interference." One Northern white teacher of the "contraband" in Virginia's southern coastal area wrote in 1864, "we have our sympathies called out, almost every day, for the innocent children who are harshly beaten by their willful enemies[,] their harsh mamas. . . . close by us lives a black woman who lashes her little boy with a rawhide. We have remonstrated repeatedly, but she 'Reckons I shall beat my boy just as much as I please'; . . . and she does beat him till his cries wring the anguish from our hearts." . . .

Abuse in slave families was not limited to children alone. Spousal ill-treatment was another serious problem. Relationships between husbands and wives suffered from slaveholders' usurpation of control in slave marriages even more profoundly than those relationships between parents and children. Verbal and physical abuse among married partners were sometimes responses to complex issues of discord within slave marriages. This prevalence of mistreatment among some antebellum blacks toward their spouses prompted one ex-slave to comment that "some good masters would punish slaves who mistreated womenfolk and some didn't."

Unfounded in Virginia law, slave marriages were tenuous relationships in which couples struggled to survive among the immense and divisive pressures of slave life. Slaveholders had the final say as to which slaves would marry and whom they could marry and when and, therefore, exercised immense dominion over this most intimate of decisions affecting adult slaves. Because they controlled vital aspects of slave marriage, owners' actions often meant the success or failure of these relationships.

Concerned with economic and logistic issues that slaves were not privy to, masters sometimes imposed marriage partners on slaves whom the individual bondswoman or man might not have chosen if given the opportunity to decide otherwise. Charles Grandy, an ex-slave from Norfolk recalled that on the farm where he resided:

> Marsa used to sometimes pick our wives fo' us. If he didn't have on his place enough women for the men, he would wait on de side of de road till a big wagon loaded with slaves come by. Den Marsa would stop de ole nigger-trader and buy you a woman. Wasn't no use tryin' to pick one, cause Marsa wasn't gonna pay but so much for her. All he wanted was a young healthy one who looked like she could have children, whether she was purty or ugly as sin.

Although Grandy spoke specifically of the lack of choice male slaves had in acquiring wives, it is evident from his description of the process that the women involved—young women recently sold away from families and perhaps husbands—had absolutely no choice in the matter whatsoever. . . . The emotional and sexual exploitation of some women slaves forced to marry men whom they did not love undoubtedly increased their resentment toward their masters and their husbands, which then sparked marital discord. Likewise, those males forced to marry women they did not know or even think physically appealing hindered the development of a loving, respectful marital relationship. . . .

Clearly, the marital forms and relationships of slaves were related in part to their owners' desires to increase their slave holdings. Many antebellum Virginia slaveholders insisted that their slaves exercise their procreative powers to the fullest extent and encouraged various forms of marriage or sociosexual bonding between male and female slaves to insure high rates of birth. Slave breeding in Virginia is well documented through child-to-women ratios, the personal papers of owners, and the testimonies of slaves. As one ex-slave noted: "The masters were very careful about a good breedin' woman. If she had five or six children she was rarely sold." . . .

. . . In order to promote the rapid birth of slave children, slave masters not only offered material incentives and may have threatened those slaves who refused to cooperate, but they also usurped the slaves' decision as to whether or not to participate in monogamous marital relationships. Thus, some slaveholders forced slave women and men to have several sexual partners outside of their marriage. Elige Davisson of Richmond, for example, stated that he was married once before he became free, but his owner still brought "some more women to see" him. Davisson insisted that his master would not let him have "just one woman" but mandated that the young male slave have sexual relations with several other female slaves so that they would bear children. Such demands to participate in their owner's breeding schemes brought a great deal of pain and anger to the individual slaves and to the couples involved.

Undoubtedly, slave marriages varied in terms of quality, length, and ideals even in the most supportive environment. Most slaves wanted long-standing, loving, affectionate, monogamous relationships with their spouses. Yet, they could not expect that their partners would be able to protect them from some of the most violent and abusive aspects of slave life. Most could only hope that their spouses would understand the lack of choices they had with regard to labor, attention to domestic responsibilities, and to their relationships with whites. The inability of slave wives and husbands to actualize their ideals of gender differentiated behavior, even those which were obviously unrealistic given their positions as slaves, often was the source of marital discord.

Slave women with "abroad marriages" usually had no alternative but to take on the role of the central authority figure within their immediate families, especially as child rearers, while their husbands lived on separate plantations. In doing so, however, they challenged Western tradition concerning gender specific behavior and power in nineteenth-century households that slaves often respected. Consequently, matrifocal families were common among late antebellum Virginia slaves but were not always acceptable to the couples who comprised them. Since many slave women and men hoped to function in their families according to the proposed ideal of the larger Southern society, their inability to do so engendered resentment, frustration, and anger.

Thomas Harper, for example, a slave blacksmith in Alexandria, Virginia, decided to escape to Canada because he was not allowed to support his family. It was, he explained too "hard to see them in want and abused when he was not at liberty to aid or protect them." . . . Dangerfield Newby became so frustrated in his attempts to secure his family's freedom that he helped plan and execute the raid of John Brown on Harpers Ferry in 1859. His need to offer his wife and children the security of freedom was enhanced by his wife's constant appeal. "I want you to buy me as soon as possible," she wrote to him in August 1859. "I want you to buy me as soon as possible, for if you do not get me somebody else will. . . . Do all you can for me, which I have no doubt you will," she begged. The blacksmith's desire to "protect" and "support" his family as well as Mr. and Mrs. Newby's feelings about his duty to provide the security of freedom to his family suggest that some slaves held ideals of manhood also popular in some European and African cultures.

Slave husbands sometimes imposed nearly impossible ideals of womanhood on their wives as well. . . . Not surprisingly, ideals concerning female purity and marital chastity presented extreme challenges to slave couples.

The instances of white male sexual aggression toward married slave women created a great deal of tension and discord in the marital relationships of slaves. Although slave husbands theoretically understood the inability of their wives to protect themselves against the sexual overtures and attacks of white men, they resented and were angered by such occurrences. Their reactions were in response equally to their own sense of powerlessness to defend their wives and to a recognition of the physical and psychological pain their spouses experienced. When slave husbands did intervene, they suffered harsh retaliation—severe beatings, sometimes permanent separation from their family, or even murder. Many probably felt, as did Charles Grandy, who spoke of the murder of a male slave who tried to protect his wife from the advances of their overseer, that a "Nigger ain't got no chance."

Consequently, some slave husbands targeted their helpless wives to be the recipients of their frustration, pain, guilt, and rage rather than the white men who attacked them. Regardless of whom the slaves struck out at, however, their responses had little effect on modifying the behavior of those white men who raped female slaves. "Marsters an' overseers use to make slaves dat wuz wid deir husbands git up, [and] do as they say," Israel Massie noted. "Send husbands out on de farm, milkin' cows or cuttin' wood. Den he gits in bed wid slave himself. Some women would fight an tussel. Others would be 'umble—feared of dat beatin.' What we saw, couldn't do nothing 'bout it. . . . My blood is bilin' now [at the] thoughts of dem times. Ef dey told dey husbands he wuz powerless."

Many slave women were ashamed that they had been victimized by their white masters and were afraid of the consequences for themselves, their families, and the children they might have conceived. They tried to conceal the sexual assault from their husbands. "When babies came," Massie went on to explain, "dey [white fathers] ain't exknowledge 'em. Treat dat baby like 'tothers—nuthing to him. Mother feard to tell 'cause she know'd what she'd git. Dat wuz de concealed part." Some slave wives went to great lengths to keep the truth from their husbands, claiming that mulatto children actually belonged to their spouses. "Ole man, . . . stop stedin' [studying] so much foolishness," responded one frightened slave wife when her husband noted that their youngest child was very physically distinct from their other children. She was able to end her husband's open suspicions by constructing a story, but few could hide the obvious.

Faced with such overwhelming problems, some slave couples responded in ways that further augmented the destruction of their marriages and families. Alcoholism, domestic violence, jealousy, and adultery were internal problems which sometimes plagued these relationships. More than a few slave couples voluntarily separated. Manfra and Dykstra's review of a survey of late antebellum slave couples who resided in the south of Virginia, for example, indicates that of those marriages terminated before general emancipation, 10.1 percent ended as a result of mutual consent and another 10.8 percent because of the desertion of a spouse. . . .

The forced separation of slave couples, of course, had the most devastating impact on slave marriages. Large numbers of loving commitments ended in this manner. When slaveholders separated husbands and wives by long distances, it was almost impossible for these couples to retain close ties to one another. The difficulty was a result of the emotional and sociosexual needs of adult slaves as well as of the insistence of their owners that they remain sexually active and thus naturally reproductive. Some masters expected these separated couples to form new relationships as soon as possible. Many did eventually remarry, but the pain and sense of loss that they felt must have been a source of continual anguish for them and their children, who had to adjust to the authority of stepparents and to their inclusion in stepfamilies.

When one Virginia "contraband" woman found her first husband in a refugee camp in 1864, she testified that the two, "threw [them]selves into each others arms and cried." The husband as well as the woman, however, had remarried since their forced separation. While his new wife looked on the touching scene of reunion with obvious jealousy, the older wife was disturbed for other reasons. Although she described her present husband as "very kind" and she was determined not to leave him, she had to admit that she could not be happy after seeing her first husband. The thought of the source of their permanent separation still angered and frustrated her, even though she claimed she was pleased with her present spouse. "White folk's got a heap to answer for the way they've done to colored folks! So much they wont never *pray* it away!" she concluded in disgust.

The voice of this one ex-slave in condemning of those slaveholders who purposefully destroyed slave marriages and families is no doubt representative of the voices of many who were similarly hurt. Their personal testimonies as well as the plantation records of their owners document the destruction that came to many

Virginia slave families during the last decades of the antebellum era. Involuntary separation and the dispersal of husbands and wives from the rest of their families, sexual abuse, material deprivation, and forced marriages were some of the tremendous problems faced by slave families. Domestic violence, color stratification, spousal abandonment, and adultery were some of the manifestations of the internal strife within black slave families and marriages which were caused in large measure by their oppressive living conditions. . . .

Motherhood in Slavery

STEPHANIE J. SHAW

Mothering under slavery was truly contested terrain. The process of mothering in the antebellum South serves as one of many useful case studies for examining social constructions of mothering from a variety of viewpoints. Questions related to single parenting, women's working outside the home, surrogacy, and reproductive rights have historical antecedents in the political economy of slavery. While aspects of this essay reflect consideration of many of these questions, the focus is on the mothering of enslaved children by women who sought to define the process for themselves while living in a system where others claimed control of the process outright.

Because the successful operation of a political economy of slavery depended on the effective management of both productive labor (physical labor related to the production of ordinary goods and services) and reproductive labor (all the tasks related to the generation of and maintenance of human life), it was not possible for any aspect of slave life, including mothering, to develop entirely under the control of and based on the desires of those who were enslaved. But perhaps more significantly, because mothering, as the philosopher Sara Ruddick suggests, involves the protection and preservation of life, the fostering of emotional and intellectual development, and the preparation of a child for his or her expected social roles, slave owners and enslaved women participated in the process of mothering in ways that often, ironically, reinforced each others' interests. . . .

The history of antebellum slavery is fraught with paradoxes. In the first instance, slaveholders had routinely to demonstrate their power or control over those who were enslaved; yet absolute rigidity would only reveal the slaveholders' tenuous grip. Slaveholders had to provide some food, clothing, and shelter to those they claimed to own, because a semblance of dependency was critical to maintaining the system. But they could not provide too much because they also wanted to turn as handsome a profit as possible. And, at a time when slavery had been abolished in the rest of the Western world, slaveholders had to argue that the system was a benevolent one with one purpose—the protection and support of a class of people not competent to provide for themselves. Yet all the while, slaveholders had to count on those very slaves they claimed paternalistically to protect to use wit and skills to provide the

Stephanie J. Shaw, "Mothering Under Slavery in the Antebellum South," in Evelyn Nakano Glenn, Grace Chang, and Linda Rennie Forcey, eds., *Mothering: Ideology, Experience, and Agency* (New York: Routledge, 1994), pp. 237–254. Copyright © 1992. Reproduced by permission of Routledge/Taylor & Francis Books, Inc.

many services and necessities they demanded for themselves. These contradictions, and the ways in which both slaveholders and the women they enslaved supported them, are especially apparent in the process by which all those involved sustained the lives of children born into the system.

Anna Bishop, born a slave in 1849 in Alabama, remembered during her old age that "all de women on Lady Liza's place had to go to de fiel' ev'y day an' dem what had suckerlin' babies could com in 'bout nine o'clock in the mawnin' an' when de bell ring at twelve an' suckerlin' 'em." The women were not relieved of their productive responsibilities simply because they had children, but because of the productive consequence of their reproductive labor, adjustments had to be made. Enhancing the survival of those newborns would eventually add to the labor force, because those children would be in the field, too, before the age of ten, pulling up weeds, carrying buckets of water back and forth to the field hands, or otherwise employed in some productive capacity, and thus contributing to the system. Consequently, allowing the women to leave the fields to nurse not only enhanced the survival of the children but also relieved the owners of the obligation to provide extra food for the infants and to place more women in the nursery (losing their labor elsewhere) in order to feed the babies. Nursing mothers fulfilled the job requirement and in so doing gained some relief from the demands on them for physical labor. Some women, no doubt, also saw these feedings not as another work assignment, but as an opportunity to bond with and nurture their children. Thus, the women fulfilled both their own interest in mothering and the owner's interest in their productive and reproductive responsibilities.

Though many former slaves remembered their owners as compassionate people who showed special concern for women, infants, the elderly, and families, most available documentation is of a nature that makes it difficult to draw out slave owners' compassion and separate it from their business interests. In an especially clear example, Virginian Robert Snead expressed concerns to his wife, Octavia, about the health of one slave child: "You should be more than cautious, and especially with the children and Effia; Effia is often complaining with her throat and it may go hard with her. I should dislike for you to lose her as she is handy about sewing and our family is getting so large it would be a great loss on [?] her." Most examples, however, are more ambiguous. Slave owners, for example, regularly supplemented the diet of pregnant and nursing women by giving them extra food. In some instances, doing so was an act of generosity, but such acts also helped to protect the economic investments in human chattel while allowing enslaved women to provide better for the nourishment of their children.

Enslaved women, however, did not always depend on slaveholders to provide the means for sustaining the children's lives. . . . Enslaved women regularly demonstrated their ability to provide a higher standard of life for their children than their owners were willing to provide. Rose, whose family name is not known, was separated from her mother when she was a child in Virginia, but partly because she was not a great distance from her mother and because they both remained in the same white family, her mother regularly sent money and fruit with the white family members, who visited back and forth. Many slaves maintained small gardens in order to supplement their own and their children's diets. And while hunting and fishing are regularly characterized as a part of male slave efforts to support their families, Addie Vinson, born in the 1840s, remembered his mother performing these duties. She fished for her family at night after working all day at her other required tasks. "Many's de time," he recalled, "i'se seed my mammy come back from Barbers Crick wid a string of fish draggin' from her shoulders down to de ground." Moreover, his mother did not take the four days after Christmas as holidays, as did most of the adults in the slave community; instead, she used the four days to weave and wash for white people who lived in the area, and with the meager pay was able to provide materially for her children beyond what their owner provided.

The ability of slaves to earn money, buy fruit, plant a garden, or catch a fish made some difference in the lives of their children. But if those opportunities were not present, and often that was indeed the case, all was not lost, at least not for ingenious and daring slaves. Especially willful, courageous, clever, and perhaps lucky ones succeeded at "taking" some of what they needed to sustain themselves and their families. Georgia house servant Charlotte Raines accomplished the feat by wearing a flour sack tied around her waist under her skirts, into which she dropped so much food on a day-to-day basis that it bumped her knees when she walked. Alice Marshall, a Virginia woman who was nearly grown when the Civil War ended, also remembered her mother appropriating food for the children.

> I tell you, honey, mistiss Sally had a plenty, but we ain' fared de bes' by no means. She ain' never give us 'nough to eat; so my mother had to git food de bes' way she could. I 'member one way special. When de preacher come to mistiss' for Sunday morning breakfast, de white folks all git together an' have prayers. Den' tis my mother tek basket, go in de smoke house, git all de meat she want. When de preacher der, mistiss ain' bother 'bout nothing. Minds you, we ain' 'lowed to ever put our foot inside de meat house. Ole mistress kept de floor covered wid sawdus' an' dat smoothed off even. An' she better not find nary track in dat sawdus'. Anyhow my mother gwan in der, but she ain' never fergit to rub out her tracks. We got meat an' my mother ain' got caught neither.

From the point of view of slave owners, clothing for young children was as unnecessary a luxury as meat. They were, after all, nonproductive beings and would not begin to pay for their upkeep (through work) until they were about ten years old. Slave owners at first allocated children two shirts a year—a lightweight one for the warm seasons and a heavier one for the winter. Boys and girls wore this pullover sliplike shirt and received no other clothing from their owners until they were nearly teenagers. Delia Garlic, who was separated during her childhood from her mother, never even owned an undershirt until just before the birth of her first child. She possessed but a "shimmy an' a slip for a dress . . . made out of de cheapes' cloth that could be bought." Frederick Douglass and other male slaves recalled receiving their first pairs of pants as historic events. And sometimes even the cold weather of winter had little effect on this practice unless other slaves undertook the task of providing additional clothing for the children.

Former Alabama slave Sara Murphy, born in the early 1850s, noted that the mothers of enslaved children where she lived regularly wove long underwear from cotton for the children. Linda Brent's grandmother provided her with most of her clothing during her childhood and adolescence, giving her an alternative to the linsey-woolsey dress that she received every winter as her clothing ration, which, incidentally, marked her as a slave. Brent's grandmother also bought her a new pair of shoes one winter, but Mrs. Flint, her young mistress's mother, took them because they squeaked, and it disturbed her. Slaveholders rarely allocated shoes to slave children before they were capable of performing productive labor. But even when the children were fortunate enough to have leather shoes, they were usually very crude items, and special care had to be taken of them if they were to protect the children's feet, which often went without socks. Horace Muse, who was nearly thirty-two years old at the end of the Civil War, remembered that "no matter what tasks mother got to do, fo' she go to bed she clean dem shoes an' grease em' wid tallow grease. Git stiff as a board in cold weather, an' lessen you grease 'em dey burn your feet an' freeze 'em too."

Where enslaved women and men provided necessary food and clothing for their children, slave owners did not have to worry about deficiencies. This regular demonstration of resourcefulness proved the fallacy of slave owners' claims that the institution served a necessary and benevolent purpose. In the owners' views, those whom they enslaved were not capable of caring for themselves. But women's interest in their children, and their ability to raise them to some extent by their own standards, regularly gave the lie to the slaveholders' claims. These women's efforts, however, also simultaneously supported the owners' interest and made it possible for owners to continue to neglect the needs of these women and children whom they claimed to own. . . .

There is much evidence to suggest enslaved women's interest in mothering their children, but often women's efforts were brutally conditioned by the structure of the larger political economy, and by the slaveholders who worked to sustain it. For example, scholars have presented substantial evidence to prove the persistence of the nuclear slave family, traditionally defined, but tradition had little to do with how those families survived intact. At a time when femininity was defined by motherhood and mothering in the larger society, slave owners frequently did not allow slave women to mother their children. The women's productive labor was often viewed as much more valuable to their owners than the reproductive labor involved in rearing a child who, as yet, had no value. As a consequence, new patterns of child care emerged, with a variety of people mothering slave children. The historian Deborah Gray White has demonstrated the importance of an existing network among enslaved women that helped to facilitate adequate child care. When slave owners chose the ones to perform these tasks, they usually called upon people whose own productive capacities had significantly diminished but who could still perform the (presumably) less physically demanding tasks of mothering.

All children where Phoebe Faucette lived were cared for by "some old man or some old woman." Georgia Baker, born in the 1840s in Georgia, was cared for by her grandfather, about whom she said "all he done was to sit by the fire all day with a switch in his hand and tend the children whilst their mammies was at work." Allen Sims, who was probably not yet ten years old at the end of the Civil War, recalled that "Aunt Mandy, what was too old to work, looked atter all de little nigger chilluns, whilst dey mammy's working." . . . Callie Williams's mother kept slave children in a small cabin with homemade cradles while the other women worked in the fields. The mothers returned from the fields to feed their nursing infants twice a day. And while both the nurse and the mothers shared some time with the children, both were limited in what they could do, for in this case the mothers had to return to the fields, and the nurse usually had other tasks to perform as well.

The assignment of extra tasks seems to have been common in the case of women nurses. Williams's mother had to spin two to four cards of cotton while she watched the children. The Tennessee planter Benjamin Bedford's nurse tended the children in addition to her main duties as a laundress and cook. Bedford advised his overseer that "the negro woman who cooks and washes when not engaged in that business [is] to churn, work butter, work in the garden, make up negro clothing or attend to little negroes or such needful employment about the yard that is necessary and proper because it does not consume all her time to cook and wash." Many of those who cared for slave children had other major work responsibilities, because slave owners rarely considered child care an activity requiring all of the nurse's time.

Particularly in cases where those assigned to care for children had many other responsibilities, there was a great chance the children would not receive close attention; they might even unavoidably be neglected. While Mandy McCullough Cosby's recollection about slavery, "de way de chillun rol roun' in the big nurses room," could indicate that the children enjoyed a carefree and uninhibiting environment, for example, it could also suggest the lack of attention they received. McCullough, born in the 1830s, witnessed these events as an adult, and her memory of what might have been haphazard child care was not all that different from the memory of slightly younger George Womble, who characterized mealtime in the nursery. The horrible scene involved children eating with animals from a trough, a popular method of feeding when there were a lot of children. The children gathered around the trough were not allowed to hit the animals, and they ate with their hands up to the sides of their heads so that the dogs and pigs could not lick them in the face as they ate. While this form of feeding might not have been typical for most slave children, it probably inspired many mothers to devise alternatives to the child care arranged by their owners. They knew that the nursery was not necessarily the best place for their small children.

One alternative involved requiring older children to care for the younger ones. Sylvia Witherspoon's mother left Sylvia in charge of her siblings when she (the mother) had to report to the fields. "She would tie the smalles' baby on my back so's I could play wid out no inconvenience," Witherspoon recalled. Joseph Holmes's mother had eight children, and she made each one of them responsible for another. Holmes remarked: "We was raised in pairs. I had a sister who come along wid me, an' iffen I jumped in the river she done it too. An' iffen I go th'ough a briar patch, her[e] she come along too." Mary Smith's mother left her in charge of her younger siblings. Smith, who reported being only seven years old at the time of surrender, was but a child herself. In order to help her with her large responsibilities, she noted that her mother would "pin a piece of fat back [meat] on my dres' before she went to de fiel' and when de baby cry I tek him up and let 'em suck 'em." . . .

. . . [U]nder some circumstances, . . . slave women took their children to the fields with them, though doing so represented no small amount of danger. During the early nineteenth century, women on Saint Simons Island carried their infants with them to the field in baskets they carried on their heads. According to Julia Rush, a former slave, Oliver Bell's mother was a plow hand, but she took him to the field with her every morning and sat him under a post oak tree, where he usually remained until she called or went for him. "Dat tree was my nurse," Bell recalled. Sara Colquitt, who was born in the 1830s, took her two children with her to the field as well; she tied the youngest to a tree limb (perhaps making a swing, in effect) to keep him or her away from bugs on the ground. And Roxy Pitts, born in 1855, whose mother succeeded in escaping from her owner, was taken to the field along with her younger sister by her father, who "kep' a bottle of sweeten water in he shirt to keep [it] warm to gib de baby when it cry." To a large degree, it was simply not possible for those who were enslaved to determine totally for themselves the method by which or the extent to which their children would be cared for. But as some of the above examples suggest, the extent to which these children were nurtured (or the extent to which they could be) depended not only on their owners' whims and resources but on the women's needs, willingness, and ability to improvise. . . . [N]ot all slave children experienced the benefits of mothering.

Enslaved adults often worked from sunup to sundown at one task, and after that, they attended to weaving, spinning, shucking corn, mending tools, and other indoor work assignments. And as Cordellia Thomas said, "Come day, go day, no matter what happen, growin' chillun had to be in bed at deir reg'lar time." Former Georgia slave Will Sheets noted that the most he ever saw of his mother was when she came to the cabin at night, and "den, us chilluns was too sleepy to talk. Soon as us et, us drapped down on a pallet and went fast asleep." More to the point, and indicating both adult and childhood work responsibilities, Tom Singleton remembered that the adults "were too busy to talk in de daytime, and at night us wuz so wiped out from hard work [us] just went to sleep early and never talked." Mandy McCullough, reared in Alabama, recalled that children who did not yet have work responsibilities played all day, ate their supper at the trough in the yard, and "some of dem jes' fall ovah on de groun' asleep, and is picked up, and put on dey pallet in de big chillen's room." During the work week at least, these children were, by necessity, mothered by others or not at all.

Perhaps the most difficult aspect of slavery for mothers came with the breakup of families because of being sold or hired out. Under these circumstances, sometimes the best that they could do was to ask and hope that someone else would care for their children. Mingo White, probably born in the 1840s, moved to Alabama with his family when he was four or five years old. He was "jes' a li'l thang; tooked away from my mammy an' pappy jes' when I needed 'em mos'. The only caren' that I had ever knowed anything 'bout was give to me by a frien' of my pappy. His name was John [W]hite. My pappy tol' him to take care of me for him. John was a fiddler 'n many a night I woke up to find myse'f 'sleep 'twix his legs whilst he was playin' for a dance for de white folks." Laura Clark, only a few years younger than White, was one in a group of children sold from their North Carolina home to an Alabaman. The new owner either bought or hired elder slaves Julie Powell and Henry to care for them during the trip by wagon to the Deep South. "Wa'n't none of dem ten chillin no kin to me," Clark recalled, "and he never brout my mammy so I had to leave her behine. I recollect mammy said to ond [aunt] Julie, 'take keer my baby chile . . . and iffen I never sees her no mo' raise her for God." Clark's referral to Julie as aunt should be read not simply as the traditional respect that slaves showed for elders by giving them kinship titles but also as an indication that there developed a bond between them based on a caring, familial relationship.

In spite of the extensive efforts of all those who mothered slave children, the overall conditions of slavery were often not conducive to preserving the lives of slave children. While infant mortality rates generally declined over the decades, some mothers experienced death rates among their children that were as high just before the demise of slavery as they were at the end of the eighteenth century.

Slaveholders sought solutions to protect their investments, which were not only a source of their wealth, of course, but a source of their political power and social status as well. One London businessman who owned slaves in the United States wrote to his correspondent, probably a relative who was acting as his overseer:

> I am grieved to hear of the mortality among the negro children, and am very much afraid there is not proper care taken of them. You tell me there were ten born last year, and but one of them is living, and that [one] but three days old. . . . [I]s there no method to be fallen on to prevent it; suppose something by way of [illegible] was given to such of them as raise their children and to wenches that took care of them in the lying in aft[?] the children were brought you [illegible] to make them more careful and attentive.

More than fifty years later, Nicholas Edmunds recorded the following vital statistics for his slave woman Harriet: She gave birth to Washington on August 28, 1851, and he died on November 14, 1851. Dolly was born on March 4, 1853, and died on August 31, 1853. Luke, born on March 20, 1854, died on September 17, 1854. Sally, born on April 5, 1857, died six months later. A son, not named, was born on August 25, 1860, and died four days later. And Albert was born on November 1, 1861, and died nine months later (on August 10, 1862). Four of Harriet's children were listed with no death dates (b. 1850, 1855, 1858, and 1859) and therefore quite possibly lived to be set free. Still, five of her ten children did not see the first anniversary of their births, and one made it only to his first birth anniversary.

Notwithstanding all the possible "natural" factors contributing to high infant mortality rates in the eighteenth century and isolated problems in the nineteenth, the letter from the British slaveholder cited above suggests other considerations. He proposes that enslaved women could be induced to take better care of the infants and raises a question about the extent to which adults deliberately contributed to the deaths of their children. Undoubtedly, many women made choices not to preserve the lives of slave children. And in these instances the evidence of contested terrain is vivid.

A Fairfax County, Virginia, court convicted Ally, the slave of George Miller, for "exposing [her child] as causing its death" in 1835. A Buckingham County Court convicted Polley of murdering her child in 1818. Kesiah allegedly killed her infant daughter on April 13, 1834. The courts sentenced all of the women to hang. Between the 1840s and the 1860s, William Massie, the prominent Virginia planter and diarist, regularly noted his suspicions regarding the deaths of slave children on his plantation. In one instance he noted that Gabriel, the sixteen-month-old child of Lizzie, "was murdered right out by his mother's neglect and barbarous cruelty." At another point he wrote that Rhoda's fourteen-month-old son "was neglected . . . by its mother and died like a dog." And about Lucy's children, Romulus and Remus, born in 1844, Massie wrote that Remus died of neglect, and "Romulus died by waste caused by the natural neglect of his infamous mother."

The accounts of alleged infanticide cases may, of course, be suspect in the light of more recent medical discoveries that indicate the importance of their contexts. Poor nutrition, low birth weights, poor pre- and postnatal care, and even genetic disposition quite possibly caused some or all of these infants to fall victim to Sudden Infant Death Syndrome (SIDS). When the Mississippi farmer T. S. Jones wrote to a relative in Tennessee in 1852 about his slave woman Milly, who had recently "overlaid" her child, he noted that this incident made "three out of four children [that] she has killed in that way in eight years. This last one was a fine, likely, healthy child about seven months old." Milly could have, in her exhaustion, unknowingly "overlaid" her children. She might even have deliberately killed them. The only thing certain is that children who succumb to SIDS are likely to have siblings who suffer the same fate. And, consequently, Milly might simply have been destined to suffer the loss of her children.

Still, there are many irrefutable examples of infanticide. Amey, slave of John Grisham from King and Queen County, Virginia, killed her two infant children, Isbell and Harrison, on April 13, 1799. She cut their throats with an ax. Sixteen years later, Jenny (Powhatan County, Virginia) killed her three children. And Hannah, a Granville County, North Carolina, slave, killed her child Soloman. One witness at her trial testified that after Hannah cut her child's throat, she attempted to slit her own and, upon failing, asked Bob, another slave, to "put her away."

On occasion, slave women threatened infanticide in an attempt to affect an owner's behavior. One often cited example involves a woman who successfully prevented her owner from selling her away from her child as punishment for some offense. Upon hearing that she could not take her child with her, the woman raised the infant into the air by its feet, threatening to smash its head into the ground rather than to leave it behind. She fully understood her master's value system and his proprietary interest in her child, and she used that understanding to ensure the maintenance of her values and to take the child with her. Though the latter example is an important one to the contrary, one must also acknowledge the possibility that some of these women suffered from postpartum depression and acted as a result of some psychological trauma beyond their control.

Certainly there remain many questions about the extent to which slave mothers killed their children. Undoubtedly some did, and many did not. Where they did, infanticide sometimes represented a powerful example of women's opposition to this form of sexual and economic exploitation. But these examples could also reflect that the women possessed such a reverence for humanity and a level of self-determination that they simply decided to prevent a child, whose life they felt responsible for, from growing up in a system in which their owners demonstrated little respect for either. Vincent Harding provides a chilling example of this, in which a husband and wife "shut up in a slave baracoon and doomed to the southern market . . . did by mutual agreement send the souls of their children to Heaven rather than have them descend to the hell of slavery." Both parents killed themselves after killing their children.

Several scholars have noted the records of Southern physicians who remarked on the high rate of abortion among slave women. (No doubt some spontaneous abortions or miscarriages were included here.) One physician said planters believed "that the Blacks are possessed of a secret by which they destroy the fetus at an early stage of gestation." Another noted with some surprise that "whole families of women . . . fail to have any children." One planter claimed to have discovered that "the slaves had concocted a medicine with which they were able to terminate their unwanted pregnancies." And another said he had "an older female slave [who] had discovered a remedy for pregnancies and had been instrumental in all . . . the abortions on his place."

Women's decisions to have abortions might represent a political act of defiance if they determined that they would not give birth to children in a system that allowed no consistent recognition of them as those children's mothers. That is, after some analyses of their situations, they could have decided not to have children because those children would belong to slave owners, not to themselves. The famous successful runaway Ellen Craft, at least, at first refused to marry because "marriage meant children—children who would belong to Robert Collins" rather than to her and her husband. But Ellen Craft's ability to decide, while enslaved, not to marry and not to conceive might represent an unusual case. Rather, what is most evident is that many women did not have a choice. Many were "married up" against their will. And whether "married" or not, many were raped. Still, even when slave women had abortions, refused to conceive, or committed infanticide in order to protect children from a lifetime of slavery, they often did so in the interest of mothering. And even when they made such decisions without considering the child's future, they made mothering decisions—decisions not to mother.

Probably, most slave women allowed children they conceived to be born, to live, and to grow up in the slave system. And just as these adults often provided children with more food and clothing than their owners allowed, they also attempted to nurture the youngsters and to minimize their encounters with the most brutal aspects of the system. . . .

Parents began very early to discipline children in ways that would be important for their survival as they matured, and as their contact with owners and overseers increased. The process began during childhood and in the "nursery," where lessons could be taught clearly but gently. Aunt Mandy, who took care of Allen Sims and numerous other children while their mothers worked in the fields and elsewhere, would "pop" him and the others with a brush when they did not obey her. But Sims added, "she fuss more dan she whipt." It was important for the children not only to respect the authority of their Black elders but also to learn to respect authority figures in general if they were to survive under the supervision of slaveholders and overseers. . . .

Martha Showvley's mother made concerted efforts to teach her children not to meddle in the affairs of others. The importance of such a lesson is illustrated by the death of a Richmond County, Georgia, slave women whose owner beat her to death after hearing a child's innocent conversation. The woman had given birth to twins one day and on the next day was ordered to scrub the floors of her owner's home. After she fainted while working, her mistress had a slave take her to her cabin and another one finish the scrubbing. The mistress's husband was satisfied that the work was done when he returned, but a slave child innocently told him what had happened in his absence. The owner mercilessly beat the woman because, he said, she was lazy and deceitful, and she died the same day while still tied to the whipping post. Teaching children to hear and not repeat, to see and not disclose, was critical to controlling the conditions of their survival, and to survival itself, because many of things that happened in the slave quarters would not have been acceptable to the owners.

Probably most important, in terms of their preparation for future roles, slave children were taught to work and to work well. From birth, the futures of these children were geared toward work, and it was the job of their parents and other adults to see that they were able to fulfill that responsibility. But as much as it was the job of adult slaves to socialize children to their roles as workers, the adults' commitments to mothering also motivated them to psychologically prepare the children for this work. The adults provided with their strict disciplinary measures some protection for the children because, as the historian Eugene Genovese observes, "parents knew that soon enough the indulgence [of slave owners] would give way to the whip. Better they instill elementary habits and discipline in their children early and according to their own measure."

Jennie Kendricks's mother probably took her oldest daughters with her to the spring to wash at night, not simply to have their help and their company, but to teach them how to wash and to convey to them that, being girls, that is what they would eventually have to do, even after working all day at something else. Ferebe Rogers said she virtually "come up twix the plow handles" because her mother took her to the fields and began to teach her how to plow when she was quite young. Will Sheets learned from an older slave woman named Mandy to drive cattle to and from the pasture. And Mary Smith's mother provided Smith, when she was only seven years old, with her first lessons in chopping cotton. Many children learned to spin thread from their mothers who were weavers. And Charlie Dink, when he was seven or eight years old, walked the rows in the field with his mother "totin' cawn for her to drap." By this process, he not only began to learn to work but also relieved his mother of concerns about his care while she worked.

Because the work roles slave children faced very early came under the direct supervision of sometimes sadistic owners and overseers, teaching children to work hard and well was, quite possibly, the best way in which their parents could protect them—short of running away with them. By the time many of these children were five years old, they were assigned to fanning flies away from slave owners or their visitors. At a very young age many children began to carry food to the fields and water to both the house and the fields from nearby wells and springs. Between the ages of five and ten, they set and waited on tables in the big house, threaded needles, spun thread, picked up cow chips, swept yards, and performed a variety of other work details. Doing these tasks diligently and effectively could save them from severe punishment.

Mollie Mitchell, born around 1845, went to work hoeing in the field at the age of seven, but she got whipped often because she could not "keep in the row." Tom Singleton, born in 1838, had occasional childhood whims that caused him to neglect his work role; he received his only beating as a child because he got involved in a marble game after his mistress had sent him to get thread. Easter Jones, a dishwasher in her owner's house, had to remove the dishes from scalding water, but she knew, even as a youngster, that "if I drap it dey whip me. Dey whip you so hard your back bleed." One ex-slave woman claimed to have had bones broken as a child on more than one occasion by her mistress, who beat her with a fire iron for not waking up quickly enough to see to the crying white infant to whom she was supposed to attend. And Delia Garlic's mistress ran a hot iron down Delia's arm and hand after she accidently hurt the white child to whom she attended.

Those who mothered slave children had good reason, then, to work hard at preparing the children for their eventual work assignments. These children would too soon be caught between the labor requirements inherent in the system and their own natural inclinations and abilities as children. Thus it is not surprising that Emmaline Kilpatrick vividly remembered Black children growing up faster than white children did. Jasper Battle noted that slave children grew so fast that most of those assigned to nursing "warn't no older dan de white chillun dey tuk keer of." He also claimed that slave children "12 or 14 years old [in] dem days was big as a white child 17 or 18 years old." Battle was around 21 years old upon emancipation and therefore spoke not only from personal experience but also from years of observation. Clearly, Battle was equating responsibility with age and size, because slave owners subjected the children they owned to an accelerated passage from childhood to adulthood. Very early in the children's lives, owners began to characterize them as "grown" or "most grown," thereby justifying putting them to work at a young age. The children's parents and others who mothered them could do little to alter this reality. And so they reared their children in a way that would better prepare them for it.

The exigencies of day-to-day life, in fact, necessarily resulted in a type of mothering that often reinforced the oppressive system of which it was a part. As women provided food, clothing, and shelter for children beyond that provided by slave owners, they helped to fortify the system. And as they taught those children to work in fields, in kitchens, at sewing and spinning machines, they prepared the children for a future of work and possibly a future as slaves. When they devised alternative child-care arrangements that allowed them to keep up their work in the fields, the big houses, or on some property other than that of their owners, the slaveholders' proprietary interest in these children was further protected at no additional expense to themselves.

But mothering under slavery was not always a matter of women's indirect and unavoidable support of the system. When women engaged, directly and indirectly, in abortions and infanticide, they picked away at one of the bases of the system's life itself—reproduction. And even as they performed mothering tasks that reinforced the system of slavery, they also chipped away at institutional assumptions about dependency (cultural, material, and political) and thereby helped to prepare their children for freedom.

They did this in part by transmitting a set of values and traditions to the children that reinforced a kind of self-sufficiency, community culture, and group identity that could help to sustain them within and beyond their enslavement. When mothers left their older children in charge of younger ones, they not only answered their child-care problems but also provided the children with important lessons in assuming responsibility for one another. When women taught children to address other Black people not related to them by blood as "aunt," "uncle," and "granny," they taught children that "family" had a basis not only in kinship but in community as well. When members of the slave community devised the means or took advantage of opportunities to supplement their allotted rations of food, clothing, or shelter, they demonstrated their ability to care for themselves despite persistent portrayals of them as perpetual dependents. And ultimately, while the teaching of children to work effectively prepared those children for work as slaves, it also prepared them for freedom. More profoundly than slaveholders could have predicted, the efforts of enslaved women who mothered children in the antebellum South simultaneously served the interests of both slaveholders and slaves.

F U R T H E R   R E A D I N G

Blassingame, John W. *The Slave Community: Plantation Life in the Antebellum South* (1972).

Burton, Orville Vernon. *In My Father's House Are Many Mansions: Family and Community in Edgefield, South Carolina* (1985).

Clinton, Catherine. "'Southern Dishonor': Flesh, Blood, Race, and Bondage." In Carol Bleser, ed., *In Joy and in Sorrow: Women, Family, and Marriage in the Victorian South, 1830–1900* (1991), pp. 52–68.

Davis, Angela. "Reflections on the Black Woman's Role in the Community of Slaves." *Black Scholar* 3 (December 1971): 2–15.

Elkins, Stanley M. *Slavery: A Problem in American Institutional and Intellectual Life* (1959).

Farnham, Christie. "Sapphire? The Issue of Dominance in the Slave Family, 1830–1865." In Carol Groneman and Mary Beth Norton, eds., *"To Toil the Livelong Day": American Women at Work, 1780–1980* (1987), pp. 68–83.

Frazier, E. Franklin. *The Negro Family in the United States* (1939).

Genovese, Eugene. *Roll, Jordan, Roll: The World the Slaves Made* (1974).

Gutman, Herbert G. *The Black Family in Slavery and Freedom: 1730–1925* (1990).

Hine, Darlene Clark. "Female Slave Resistance: The Economics of Sex." *Western Journal of Black Studies* 3 (Summer 1979): 123–127.

Johnson, Michael P. "Smothered Slave Infants: Were Slave Mothers at Fault?" *Journal of Southern History* 47 (November 1981): 439–520.

Jones, Jacqueline. *Labor of Love, Labor of Sorrow: Black Women, Work, and the Family from Slavery to the Present* (1985).

King, Wilma. *Stolen Childhood: Slave Youth in Nineteenth-Century America* (1995).

Malone, Ann Patton. *Sweet Chariot: Slave Family and Household Structure in Nineteenth-Century Louisiana* (1992).

McLaurin, Melton A. *Celia, a Slave* (1991).

Moynihan, Daniel Patrick. *The Negro Family in America: The Case for National Action* (1965).

Rawick, George. *The American Slave: A Composite Autobiography* (1972).

Schwarz, Marie Jenkins. *Born in Bondage: Growing Up Enslaved in the Antebellum South* (2000).

Stevenson, Brenda. *Life in Black and White: Family and Community in the Slave South* (1996).

White, Deborah Gray. *Ar'n't I a Woman? Female Slaves in the Antebellum South* (1985).

C H A P T E R
6

Fathers and Children
in the Civil War Era

The Civil War, often referred to as a "brothers' war" since men from the same family sometimes fought on opposite sides, has long fascinated the American public. Yet it is only recently that social historians have turned their attention to the Civil War, which had previously been regarded as the domain of military historians. The 1992 publication of a book of essays edited by Catherine Clinton and Nina Silber, evocatively titled Divided Houses, *marked the convergence of military and social history and located that convergence squarely in the study of the American family.*

In the effort to uncover the personal side of this country's greatest conflict, scholars have been aided by the ready availability of published primary source materials, including the writings of soldiers at war and families on the homefront. During and after the war, men, women, and children self-consciously kept diaries, wrote memoirs, and preserved correspondence as a record of what they recognized as a pivotal turning point not only in their own lives, but also in the course of national history. Prior to the 1970s, many of these materials were privately published and directed chiefly at a local audience. In the past three decades, however, as social historians have recognized the value of these sources, academic presses have issued (or reissued) an astounding number of Civil War letters, diaries, and memoirs, and scholars have eagerly seized on these sources for insights into the lives of American families during a time of tremendous uncertainty and upheaval.

The resulting reexamination of the Civil War has had its greatest impact on the study of the men who served, fought, and died in the Union and Confederate Armies. While elite officers—and, to a lesser extent, common soldiers—have long gained attention from Civil War buffs and military historians, the study of men in blue and gray has been fundamentally changed by the insights of family historians, who look at the experiences of soldiers through the lens of gender and recognize military service as one of many ways in which society constructs masculinity.

Studying the wartime family—and men's roles within it—raises fundamental questions about male gender roles and the nature of war: Were men's civilian and military roles complementary or contradictory? Did the Civil War significantly alter Americans' ideas about masculinity, or did it simply intensify preexisting notions of manhood? What can studying families in a time of crisis teach us about family life under ordinary circumstances?

DOCUMENTS

The men who fought in the Civil War were not only soldiers; they were also members of families. A series of letters from Confederate soldier Edgeworth Bird to his teenaged daughter, Saida (known as Sallie), reveals a man eager to maintain his role as a father even from afar. Written between 1861 and 1864, these letters constitute Document 1.

Young Sallie Bird was fortunate; her father returned home to his Virginia plantation even before the war's conclusion in 1865. In some cases, of course, the Civil War permanently deprived children of their fathers. A poem by C. Chauncey Burr that appeared in a northern magazine for children, *The Student and Schoolmate,* in 1865, included as Document 2, dramatizes the death of a soldier-father.

Boys as well as men were caught up in the military conflict. A short story by N. L. E. that appeared in a northern periodical, *The Little Pilgrim,* illustrates children's fascination with the war. The 1863 tale, reprinted as Document 3, also hints at the complicated dynamics of gender, class, and ethnicity that emerged during children's play.

Such fictional depictions had their real-life counterparts, as excerpts from the Civil War diary of Louisianan Kate Stone, included as Document 4, suggest. Stone records her brothers' eagerness to join the Confederate Army and their departures for war: twenty-one-year-old William in May 1861, eighteen-year-old Coleman in March 1862, seventeen-year-old Walter in September 1862, and seventeen-year-old Jimmy in August 1864. Of the four, two (Coleman and Walter) died in the line of duty. Stone's uncle, Bohanan Ragan, also enlisted in the armed forces in May 1861, at the age of twenty-two.

North and South, boys and men of all ages were enthralled with military service because serving in the army functioned as a coming-of-age ritual for young men, blurring the boundaries between "boys" and "men." Document 5, the memoir of Union soldier Alfred S. Roe of his early days with the Tenth Regiment of the Massachusetts Volunteer Infantry, originally published in 1909, demonstrates how raw recruits were transformed into brave soldiers; the farewell speeches he recalls suggest how important this identity was to honorable manhood.

1. A Confederate Father Writes to His Daughter, 1861–1864

Edgeworth Bird to Sallie (Saida) Bird

Camp Walker [Va.], 19 August 1861

I wrote and mailed today a letter for Mama and another for Grandpa, my dear little daughter, and now comes your turn. You asked for just a "little letter" and you shall have it, tho' somewhat longer than your emphasis called for. Three or four days elapsed without my writing Mama, a very unusual thing nowadays, and I hasten to supply the defiency by sending home two today and this to you tomorrow.

I was suddenly detailed as officer of the guard to supply the place of a sick man, and its duties, being very fatiguing from loss of sleep, unfitted me for anything but

John Rozier, ed., *The Granite Farm Letters: The Civil War Correspondence of Edgeworth and Sallie Bird* (Athens: University of Georgia Press, 1988) pp. 14–16, 57–58, 137–139, 162–163, 184–185.

sleep. I have received from you two very nice letters, and one wee little fellow from Bud. I gave Bud's letter to Jimmy Alfriend to read, and his reply on returning it was, "I tell you, Mr. Bird, he writes a mighty nice letter for a little fellow." He has written Wilson and will look anxiously for an answer. He must be sure and answer it. Tell him to take his time, and write nicely, and a good deal about Jimmy's sweethearts. And you, dear daughter, remember I always show both your letters to a half dozen gentlemen, and you both should take a great deal of care in composition and neat penmanship.

All the news I might send you is contained in the letters to Mama and grandpa and would be stale the third reading. Just while I am writing General Toombs has arrived. He makes his headquarters at our camp and his tent will be pitched in 30 yards of our tent. So we shall breathe the atmosphere of distinguished men, and its being Brigade Headquarters will make our encampment quite a place of resort. Just here darkness came on and I stopped rite after supper. I perceive General Toombs has erected his tents about a hundred yards from us in the open field. He has four much larger than Mama saw us have in Atlanta, all placed in a row and a servants tent in the rear. They present a very nice appearance. The view from a neighboring hill is very beautiful. I wish my little daughter could stand with me and see it. One can see for many miles in every direction and, at one *coup d'oeuil,* no less than the encampments of sixteen Regiments. Think what a splendid view they present, how the white canvass glistens in the sunlight; and the white tents far away in the distance, dotting the green plain of pines, seem like great white swans on some far off water. But we've had no sun of late, nothing but rain, rain and slush. We've a good many sick from colds and measles in the regiment tho' few in our two companies.

Now for a word of advice. Do you love your Papa so far away from you? Will you and Wilson value his commendation if God spares him to come to you again? If so, then try and perform all your duties honestly and faithfully. Be *truthful,* never attempt deceit in *anything* or with *anybody.* Never neglect to say your prayers, and study your lessons well that you may never fret Mama, who makes so many sacrifices for you both. Obey your grandpa as you would me. Do these things, my little ones, and God will bless you both, as I do. Kiss Mama for me a hundred times, and Bud and grandpa. Bud shall have a letter soon. Remember me to Jule Alfriend and any of your little friends that care for it. Howdye to all the servants. Tell Allen I think of him often, and how anxious he was to come with me. Sam sends a heap of love to them and is in good health. Mama must write to me very often, bless her darling heart. Her letters are half my life nowadays and I must have them every day or so. So far I am in good health. Goodbye, my darling child. Remember, be pure in heart and truthful. Your affectionate Father, Wm. E. Bird

Edgeworth Bird to Sallie (Saida) Bird

Camp Georgia near Bull Run, 12 January 1862

Dear Daughter,

I have received from you at different times various letters which have remained unanswered, but have always been acknowledged in my letters to Mama. I have always fully appreciated the affectionate tone of your letters, my child, and have noted with increased pleasure your improvement in penmanship and style, and have not failed always to thank the good God who gave me so capable a daughter, and her so efficient and admirable a Mother.

Tho' you've never been to school from home a day in your life, yet you've had advantages that few are lucky enough to meet up with, and if Bud and yourself had failed to improve them, you would indeed be very censurable. The very best teacher, who has twenty or more pupils to instruct, could never have taken the same pains or been near so thorough as your dear Mama has been, and you both owe her *double* duty and love during life.

As the saying goes, you are just entering your "teens," young lady, and it behooves you to begin to prepare yourself in earnest to face the stern realities of life. Hitherto you have been as a little machine, entirely under the direction and control of another motive power. In a few short years your happiness, both in this life and the one to come, will depend upon your own sound judgement and good conduct. The day may come when you may have neither Mama or Papa to counsel you, and it is *now* time that you were fitting yourself to steer your own bark through life's troubled waters, relying upon the chart of your own good sense and virtue to direct you.

Learn always, be the consequence life or death, to speak the truth and to *love* the truth; to practice virtue and to *love* virtue. Truth and virtue are twin sisters, and if personified in heaven, would be seated there on golden thrones as queens. A young girl's heart and mind should be as pure and spotless as a field of snow. As a shower of muddy water would stain and deface the one, so do the gusts of Passion, Untruth, Deceit, defile and corrupt the other. Try then, daughter, to love and practice every virtue—to exercise a calm control over any evil prompting of your nature. Be cheerful, be lively, be jubilant if you will, but never let there be malice or ill nature in your mirth. Try never to be giddy; never let reason lose her sway. Be studious; Knowledge is power; store your mind with useful knowledge. Cultivate a literary taste and the light accomplishments if you wish; they sit gracefully on a woman, but lean not on them as a staff to make your way happily through life. Patience, Purity, Humility, a stern sense of duty—these will bear you up and o'er every wave of trouble, and hurl back every billow of misfortune that Satan's rage or a world's envy may cast at you.

My dear little daughter, I find I have produced more a lecture than a letter, and will speak of other things. I am quite well; only anxious to get home and take you and Bud and Mama and Grandma all in my arms, and Grand Pa, too. Won't I have a great armfull? Kiss Mama a thousand times for me, dear sweet Mama, and love and obey her well. Kingdoms of love to Bud and Grandma and to Grandpa and Mr. Edwards. Howdy to all the servants. Goodbye, daughter. Your own loving Papa, W. E. Bird

Edgeworth Bird to Sallie (Saida) Bird

Camp near U.S. Ford, Va., 21 August 1863

My dear Daughter,

The different letters you have written me are very deserving of an answer long since, and it has ever been in my mind to send you a "wee" letter. But then you know, Daughter, Mama must be served first, and she keeps me very busy answering her letters, and I reply to every letter that she sends me, at that. Your last was received last night and was very nicely written for the first two pages, then you had to dress to go visiting. You must be a great visitor. Nearly all your letters begin well and neatly, but your industry and perseverance give out before you have finished. Now, daughter, I have referred to this several times and don't do it in a spirit of fault finding, but for your improvement.

Laying aside that motive, it would make very little difference to me that one part of a letter should be written less neatly than another. To write a letter is not so easy a matter to you as to your Mother, but still it is a slight job, and you should show more perseverance. If you are going visiting today, don't write; tomorrow write, and don't go visiting. Try and acquire the habit in your youth of resolutely carrying out what you undertake. There's a lecture for you, young Damsel. I'm quite a lecturer nowadays. In my last to Mama, I believe I lectured you and her and Bud and the teachers. It may be that my lectures may gain me the sobriquet of "Grumbler." But young people must have someone to point out their faults.

I can't say I am delighted that you are going to school. I fear for you that you are about to pass from the sure, loving guidance of your Mother and mingle with those who care so much less for you. You will have many temptations to do wrong, many trials to your good temper, and small troubles innumerable. But if you will govern yourself by a few simple rules, you will come through unscathed. Always be truthful, also always act the lady, and preserve your own self-respect. Never hurt another's feelings, and if you do so inadvertently, never be ashamed to apologize openly. Try and be first, always, but don't let ambition be your first motive, but a solid improvement of your mind. Be kind and approachable to all and try to gain the good will even of the humblest. Love your neighbour as yourself. Try to act up to that great precept of our Redeemer.

If Latin is taught you, I wish you to study it by all means, and, daughter, do so willingly, and cheerfully. Your argument against doing so is easily met. Your Cousin Lucie and Sallie Casey are undoubtedly very sweet, but would they have been less so had they studied Latin? Mama is sweeter than any of them and she *did* study Latin. It is not difficult to attain, and you can never have a correct knowledge of your own language until you have acquired a good knowledge of Latin. I wish you to go at it with an intention to master it, and so with French, which is the universal language. Indeed both, one or other, will take you over Europe.

There is nothing of interest happening now. We are lying quietly in camp. I believe the Q.M. Department is the only one kept very busy. We have to send long distances for supplies and forage. From what Mama says, I expect your prospect of going to Mrs. Ford's is broken up. I'm sorry for it, from the account given of the school, I would prefer much that you be there. Tell Bud to slave ahead and study hard. Always go to school prepared to recite a good lesson. You will have to lay aside your evening dresses and promenades to accomplish that. You have but few years in which to store your mind with book knowledge, and you'll have to be diligent.

Pray write me as often as you can. T'will improve you, for as I prove such a critic, you'll take pains. Richard said his Mother must send his books, clothing, etc., by Sam Hayes. I ask for messages to his mother but his modesty keeps him silent. Give my love to any of your young friends whom you think will value it, among others to Miss Kate Rucker, and oceans of love to Mama. I've just written her. Love to Grandma and the Hayes cousins.

Your Uncle John, I presume, will have left before this reaches you. Kiss Bud, and Mama, and Grandma for me. Love to our Yancey kinfolk. All your friends here are generally well. The health of the troops is unusually good. Goodbye, Daughter, God bless you and guide you, your affectionate Father,

Wm. E. Bird

Edgeworth Bird to Sallie (Saida) Bird in Athens

Granite Farm, 19 April 1864

My dear Daughter,

. . . Are not you and Grandma both surprised to find me not yet gone? Circumstances have so transpired that I still breathe the flower scented air of Granite Farm, to the great joy of Mama and no small gratification to myself. Recent movement's of Longstreet's Corps have quite changed our plans. Only the night before I was to set out to join the party at Washington, Col. DuBose's boy reached here, telling me of the late army news and the change in programme. Robert left early Monday morning with him. He is to take my horse on with Col. D's horses under charge of one of the 15th.

Our party now all go on by the cars. I leave for Mayfield tomorrow, and Mama was so elated at my staying two days longer that she promised to behave beautifully tomorrow. It is her greatest trial to be left alone. It is scarcely less a burden to me, but we all have our duties and must perform them faithfully.

You, too, must bear this in mind and try to do well in every obligation of life. Be truthful under all circumstances, and to be this means to be true and good in a thousand ways. Study, study, study; an enlightened, well polished mind, well regulated and stored with useful knowledge, is the greatest blessing you could prepare for yourself, after a true piety. Unite the two and you have the Philosopher's Stone. I must slip in a little lecture. Can't you persuade that kind Miss Lipscomb to get underway a Latin class? I do so much desire you to understand Latin thoroughly and consider it indispensable to a polite education.

Give oceans of love to dear Grandma and make her understand how much I regret not seeing her. I have a bright hope it will not be long before Dick is back to rejoice her heart and dear Miss Kate's. Give her, too, my kindest love. Mama is now packing my trunk and stowing away a small box of good things, a pleasing but sad task to her. The last day at home will always be gloomy in spite of one's resolves.

Bud has been making prodigious efforts to capture a wild turkey, but his early risings and patient sittings have hitherto been in vain. Mrs. Wiley is decidedly better, and there are hopes of her recovery. Give love for me to all our family kindred. Kind regards to Dr. Linton. Kiss Grandma and Cousin Caro for me. Write me quite often and take pains to compose well. Be kind and loving to Mama and *cheerfully* obedient and you will always have the warmest love of your affectionate Father.

William E. Bird

Edgeworth Bird to Sallie (Saida) Bird

Near Richmond, 10 August 1864

Dear Daughter,

Your letter and Bud's under the same envelope reached me quite recently. I am always pleased to get your letter and the young man's, the more so as they, in one sense, resemble angel's visits, being "few and far between." . . .

I should be very sorry to know that you had lost the benefit of Miss Lipscomb's instruction, for tho' I do not know her personally, Mama's high opinion of her and your affection convince me of her great worth. . . I am too far off to have a finger in the pie of your education . . but there's one ingredient I shall insist be under the pastry (where the real good things are), that is a thorough knowledge of Latin. . . .

In French you are doing well, I presume. Try to be perfect in it. I would have you neglect nothing, my child, that will contribute to giving you a vigorous and cultivated mind. . . . Your opportunities are none of the best, owing to the stormy times we live in, and any great progress must be owing to *your own industry and perseverance.*

I hear frequently from Mama, as she writes nearly every day—her letters are an inexpressible comfort and pleasure, by far the greatest I experience in this miserable war life. She has many trials and burdens at home; the care of a plantation is a new onus and not properly belonging to her department, but under necessity she assumes it bravely, and right ably and skillfully does she direct. Little one, you may well be proud of your Mother. Imitate her energy and faithful performance of all duties. You can never be *half so beautiful,* so I won't try to create an emulation on that point.

Have you written Colonel Waddell? He urges you to do so; will reply and send his photograph as promised. You will be amply repaid if you can coax him out of spare time for occasional correspondence. He is peculiarly happy in letter writing. . . . Your Cousin Sammie Wiley is sitting nearby at the desk. . . . His health was never better. He hasn't been at home since little Lizzie was a wee baby of a few days. . . . Mr. Pete Harris is absent most of the time . . . to procure forage for the Brigade. Benning's [Brigade] and the Texas Brigade of Field's Division are on the north side of the James, and for some weeks have been having quite a period of rest. Balance of Division are at Petersburg.

Our men hold the trenches all the while and keep an active watch for any demonstration against Richmond from this side. . . . Our army in North Georgia seems unfortunate. Reverse after reverse falls to its share. It is composed of splendid material and was effective in the hands of a master mind like Johnston. Hood is a nice fellow, but isn't owner of sufficient mental calibre for the crisis. . . . General Lee spent nearly a whole day in consultation with the President, t'is said, so tell your Grandma to feel easy. It is all arranged to gobble up Sherman. If the old "Butcher" [Grant] wasn't so pertinacious along the Weldon Road, we'd send our Lee down to solace the Georgians for a week or so, but Johnston would do equally if our pig-headed President would replace him [Hood]. . . .

You seem greatly attached to Miss Emma Huger. In view of your mutual friendship I claim that you present her my respectful compliments and desire to meet and know well my daughter's friend. How does Bud come on with his studies? You are the senior, Miss Sallie . . . remember you are to look after and advise him and generally play the role of "Big Sis." . . . I was very much distressed to hear of the death of poor George Hays and most fully sympathize with his mother. . . . Ah! the hearts that are bleeding today from this cruel strife. . . . Tell Bud "Gavroche" has gone home carried by Bill Alfriend, but he is not to think of him till his study time has passed. God bless you, dearest daughter, and care for you in all things.

Your affectionate Father, William E. Bird

2. A Popular Poem Mourns a Soldier-Father's Death, 1865

The Soldier's Baby

A baby was sleeping,
Its mother was weeping,
Pale vigil was keeping,
For slumber had fled.

Sad news from the battle,
Where death's cannon rattle,
Of news from the battle!
Its father was dead.

The wife still is weeping,
The baby is sleeping,
Good angels are keeping
Watch over its bed.

Too young to know sorrow,
Or life's woes to borrow,
Must learn some to-morrow,
Its father is dead.

3. Children Play at War, 1863

The Children's Attic

It certainly looked very much like a rainy day: the clouds were gray and leaden, and already a few drops were falling into the brook and making little circles all over it.

Johnnie stood at the window and watched it all with rather a sorry face, for mamma said if it rained the boys must not go to school, and there were those new, thick shoes, with shiny tops and slippery soles that he wanted so much to wear today.

C. Chauncey Burr, "The Soldier's Baby," *The Student and Schoolmate* 12 (August 1865), 239. This document can be found in James Marten, ed., *Lessons of War: The Civil War in Children's Magazines* (Wilmington, Del.: Scholarly Resources, 1999), pp. 102–103.

N. L. E., "The Children's Attic," *The Little Pilgrim* 10 (July 1863), 93–94. This document can be found in James Marten, ed., *Lessons of War: The Civil War in Children's Magazines* (Wilmington, Del.: Scholarly Resources, 1999), pp. 76–78.

He would not believe that the circles in the water were made by rain drops—they were "lucky bugs," he said, so he went out and stood on the piazza, but one drop came down plump on his nose as he looked up at the sky, and another, and yet another, till a whole shower of them came dashing into his eyes and on his hands to make him believe his mother. It certainly was a rainy day; "going to be a hard storm, too," papa said, as he came up from the post office, reading the morning paper; so Johnnie came into the house, quite pleasantly, and said, "Well, mamma, I suppose we shall have to play in the attic today."

Happy for Johnnie that he could say "we"; that he was not obliged to play alone that stormy day; so far from that, the Brooks' children were for all the world like a flight of stairs, of which Master Johnnie was the top stair. The next step down came Alfred, a rogue of a boy, always ready for a laugh and a frolic, but whose feet went rather laggingly to school, even though they had new shoes on them.

Next in order came solemn, four-year-old Benjamin, with hard, round cheeks, and chubby legs. Julie, her brothers' pet, is two years old, and baby Alice still stares with unmeaning eyes at the top of her cradle.

"Come, boys," said Johnnie, "let's go to the attic," so away clattered the six little feet, up to their own special domain, and there let us follow them.

Was there ever a nicer place for little boys to spend a rainy day in? All the cosier because the rain came down now hard and fast, making a great noise on the roof above them, and making it seem so good to have a home of their own to spend stormy days in.

Now do not suppose that this attic is a finished chamber, with plastered walls and painted floor. Not at all. It is a large, old-fashioned, open garret, where the boys can drive nails all day long in the naked boards and beams, and have things pretty much their own way. The walls are partly covered with pictures, that they have cut out of newspapers and pasted up themselves. A rocking horse, all saddled and bridled, stands in one corner; a nice little swing hangs from the beams overhead; a low shelf on one side answers for a carpenter's bench, and is covered with carpenter's tools—got up in miniature. A table, jut high enough for the children, and made on purpose for them, is there too, and around it are three little chairs; while playthings of all kinds are lying about the floor.

"Let us play school," said Johnnie, "and I'll be the teacher."

"Ho! school!" said Alfred, "'tis bad enough to go to school really, without playing it at home! No, we'll play soldiers, and I'll be first lieutenant." Alfred's ambition was quite equal to the post of captain, but Johnnie always claimed that as his birthright.

It was nothing new for the boys to play soldiers. On one side of the garret was a queer looking tent, which they had set up for themselves, made of a worn-out carpet; this they called "Camp Brooks." An odd-looking tent it was; so low, that not even chubby little Benjamin could stand upright in it, but perhaps no foot-sore, battle-worn soldier ever enjoyed the rest of a tent more than they did this, as they crept in at one end and sat under its shadow on the hard garret floor.

Happy little soldiers, to know nothing of war but its mimicry—nothing of camp life but their own "Camp Brooks!" Their mother had made them paper caps, with tassels of red, white and blue, and putting these on, they marched off sturdily round the attic, Captain Johnnie ahead, the gallant lieutenant following, and the only private trying hard to make his short legs keep step with his brothers'.

"Halt!" shouted the captain. "Form in line!" and the line was formed as straight and long as the one small boy composing it could do it. "Forward on the double quick!" and away they ran, till poor Benny, catching his toe in a crack, came ingloriously to the ground.

"He must be carried to the hospital," said Ally, but just as his officers were tugging him off to the tent, mamma appeared at the door with little Julie, who came pattering in, shouting—

"Hurrah for stripes and blues! Julie will be sojer with Johnnie."

"Oh no, Julie, you'll spoil all our fun! Girls can't be soldiers, can they mamma?"

"Not often," said mamma, "though there was a girl once who led a great army to battle and to victory; but you can call Julie the daughter of the regiment, or as you have a wounded man here for the hospital, you will want her for a nurse."

"Mamma," said Alfred, "I wish we had some rations."

"Oh ho!" laughed mamma, "you want to put me at the head of the commissary department, do you? Well, I must make a raid on the pantry then"; so going downstairs she sent up Bridget with a nice tray, holding four little white mugs, a pitcher of milk, and a plate of hot, light gingerbread. Did ever soldiers fare better—and would it not be for the comfort of soldiers of a larger growth, if the mothers and the Bridgets could go with the army?

"Bless the childers!" said the good-hearted Bridget, "I'll bet they are having a good time."

"Oh, Bridget," said Benny, his round eyes full of reproof, "you must not say bet—'tis very wicked; but perhaps," he added by way of apology, "you did not have a mamma to tell you it was wicked."

"O hone, what a boy!" said Bridget, setting down the tray, and going off with a laugh playing about her mouth for the boy, and a tear in her eye for the old mother lying dead under the green grass of "swate Ireland."

And so, while the rain came dashing against the windows, and pattering on the roof, making some poor homes desolate and cold, chilling through the real soldiers as they lay wounded and dying on the wet ground after a dreadful battle—these little make-believe soldiers, with their paper caps and wooden guns, laughed and played through the rainy day in the children's attic.

4. A Southern Girl Records Her Brothers' Eagerness to Fight, 1861–1862

May 15 [1861]: My Brother [William] started at daybreak this morning for New Orleans. He goes as far as Vicksburg on horseback. He is wild to be off to Virginia. He so fears that the fighting will be over before he can get there that he has decided to give up the plan of raising a company and going out as Captain. He has about fifty men on his rolls and they and Uncle Bo have empowered him to sign their names as members of any company he may select. Mamma regrets so that My

John Q. Anderson, ed., *Brokenburn: The Journal of Kate Stone, 1861–1868* (Baton Rouge: Louisiana State University Press, 1972), pp. 13, 16–18, 94, 143–144.

Brother would not wait and complete his commission. He could get his complement of men in two weeks, and having been educated at a military school gives him a great advantage at this time. And we think there will be fighting for many days yet. . . .

May 25: My Brother returned this evening. He did not succeed in joining the Monticello Guards from Carroll Parish. They had gone up the river, but he joined the Jeff Davis Guards at Vicksburg and was elected 3rd lieutenant. It is an Irish company officered by Americans. It was raised by Dr. Buckner and Capt. Manlove, and if My Brother had seen either of them on his way to New Orleans, they would have given him the captaincy. Tom Manlove is a captain. Uncle Bo cannot join it as a private, as the association would not be pleasant; and he is so disappointed not to be with My Brother. He hopes to get into the Volunteer Southerns, which will leave Vicksburg in a few days.

The Jeff Davis Guards leave for Richmond [Va.] on Monday, and so My Brother and Uncle Bo get off in the morning as early as possible. My Brother told us much of the soldiers he saw in New Orleans: the Zouaves, with their gay, Turkish trousers and jackets and odd drill; the Tiger Rifles, recruited from the very dregs of the City and commanded by a man who has served a term in the penitenitary; and the Perrit Guards, the gambler's company—to be admitted one must be able to cut, shuffle, and deal on the point of a bayonet.

My Brother is in extravagant spirits. He is so glad to get off, and then he saw Kate and I think they have made it up again. Uncle Bo is very sad for he so wanted for them both to be in the same company. Now they can only hope to be in the same regiment. I can see them go, for I feel I know they will return. The parting will be dreadful for Mamma. She so depends on My Brother, her oldest and best beloved. The boys are disgruntled because they cannot go too.

May 26: Our two loved ones left us this morning, but we cannot think it a last farewell. My heart tells me they will come again. They go to bear all hardships, to brave all dangers, and to face death in every form, while we whom they go to protect are lapped safe in luxurious ease. But oh! the weary days of watching and waiting that stretch before us! We who stay behind may find it harder than they who go. They will have new scenes and constant excitement to buoy them up and the consciousness of duty done.

Mr. Catlin came over to tell them good-bye. My Brother explained everything to him and gave him a letter for the men Brother had been drilling. I hope they will not blame him.

Mamma fitted them out with everything she thought they could need. And their three horses were well loaded down. Wesley [a slave] went to wait on them and was very proud of the honor of being selected to "go to battle with Marse Will." We hope he will do, though he has not been much about the house. Uncle Bo would not take a man for himself. He says a private has no business with a body servant, but if he changes his mind, a boy can be sent to him at any time.

Both will belong to infantry companies, and they will be fitted out with uniforms in Vicksburg. Brother Coley went with them as far as Vicksburg. They left so quickly that none of their friends knew in time to come over to say good-bye. Mr. Valentine will be sorry. He is such a friend of My Brother's.

They said good-bye in the fairest, brightest of May mornings. Will they come again in the summer's heat, the autumn's grey, or the winter's cold?

Mr. Newton and the boys rode out to the river with them. As they rode away, out of the yard and through the quarters, all the house servants and fieldhands watched them go. And many a heartfelt "Good-bye, Marse William and Marse Bo—God bless you" went with them.

I hope we put up everything they need. We lined their heavy blankets with brown linen and put pockets at the top for soap, combs, brushes, handkerchiefs, etc. The linen is tied to the blankets with strong tapes so that it can be easily taken off and washed. And we impressed it on Wesley that he must keep everything clean and take the best care of both our soldiers as long as they are together. He promised faithfully to do his best. Mamma has been very brave and stood the separation better than I hoped.

March 1 [1862]: . . . Another soldier is leaving our fireside. Brother Coley has joined Dr. Buckner's cavalry company, and long before the month is over he will be on the field fighting to repel the invader. The first March winds find him safe in the haven of home. April will find him marching and counter-marching, weary and worn, and perhaps dead on the field of battle. He is full of life and hope, so interested in his company, and eager to be off. He says chains could not hold him at home. He has been riding ever since his return Wednesday trying to get the horses, subscriptions, and recruits for his company. Robert Norris goes with a sad foreboding heart to perform a dreaded duty. Brother Coley goes as a bridegroom to his wedding with high hopes and gay anticipations. Robert's is really the highest type of courage. He sees the danger but presses on. Brother Coley does not even think of it—just a glorious fight for fame and honor. . . .

Sept. 24: . . . Brother Walter goes on Monday to join Dr. Buckner's company in Bolivar County [Miss.] and all are busy preparing him for the start. The house will be desolate indeed when he is really gone, following in the perilous paths his brothers are treading before him. If he would only wait until he is eighteen or until there is another requisition for troops, but "No, no, he cannot wait. The war might be over before he gets there, and he would feel disgraced forever if he had not fought in the good Cause." So runs his logic. There are so many victories he fears even now peace may be proclaimed before he is enrolled as a soldier fighting with his brothers. . . .

5. A Union Veteran Remembers
Military Drills and Farewells, 1909

. . .

These were days of somewhat dull camp routine. To young men entirely unused to restraint, they were irksome, yet just such experience was necessary to transform them into serviceable soldiers. From six to eight hours a day were spent in drill, the remaining time being devoted to the various incidents of camp life, such as roll-call,

Alfred S. Roe, *The Tenth Regiment Massachusetts Volunteer Infantry, 1861–1864* (Springfield, Mass.: Tenth Regiment Veteran Association, 1909), pp. 13, 16, 19–20, 26–28.

partaking of meals, fatigue duty, etc. No soldiers were permitted to leave camp without a pass from headquarters and of these only five per company could be issued in a single day. The regular daily routine appears in the following scheme: 5.00 a.m., reveille and roll-call; 6.30, breakfast; 7.30, guard-mount; 8.30, regimental drill; 12.30 p.m., dinner; 3.00, company drill; 5.30, supper; 6.30, battalion line and dress parade; 10.00, tattoo; 10.30, taps, at which time lights were extinguished and quiet reigned. The camp had the advantage of the first two regimental officers, both doing their best to bring their diverse elements into military form. . . .

July 2d [1861] marked a step forward, since then the Regiment marched to the U.S. Armory and each man was supplied with a new gun from the Arsenal. It took only seven hundred and forty to go around, since more than two hundred of the men had not returned from their leave of absence, or were on duty in the camp. The weapon itself was of the common make, model of 1842, and was soon replaced with the Enfield rifle. This musket was thus given out for purposes of drill and parade and, with them in hand, the men felt a hundred fold more like real soldiers as they marched back to their quarters. . . .

Departure from Springfield was impending and on the 15th [of July 1861] all were aware that the morrow would end their stay in camp No. 1. There were many things to be done before going, but a part of the afternoon was devoted to the presentation of a stand of colors to the Regiment by the ladies of Springfield. Once more all the available space of the park was filled as never before. The men were in line opposite the assemblage when the bearers of the colors approached the platform. Mrs. James Barnes represented the ladies and Col. James M. Thompson, who had been active in aiding the ladies in all their efforts to enhance the comfort of the soldiers, presided. Mrs. Barnes in presenting the colors to Colonel Briggs said:

> Colonel Briggs: I have been requested by the ladies of Springfield to present through you, to the Tenth Regiment of Massachusetts Volunteers, these colors, National and Regimental. I am also charged with the delivery of a letter which accompanies them, in which the ladies have expressed the sentiments which they deemed appropriate to the occasion.

As she paused briefly the letter was read by Colonel Thompson as follows:

> *To. Col. Henry S. Briggs, and the Tenth Regiment of Massachusetts Volunteers under his Command:*
>
> The ladies of Springfield, feeling a deep interest in their country's cause, desire to testify the same to you, by presenting you with these colors, the emblems of her glory as a republic, and of that State which has given you to be the defenders and upholders of her most sacred rights. Let these banners, differing in design, yet one in sentiment, be your reverence as they are ours; and wherever the fortunes of war may lead you, we hope, as we believe, that their lustre may never be dimmed by any neglect on your part. May the sight of them ever fill your hearts with new zeal and strengthen in you the determination to defend them to the death.
>
> To you, sir, who have the honor to command, and to our brave brothers who compose the Tenth Regiment of Massachusetts Volunteers, we commit this precious charge. We accompany it with our prayers for your safe and honorable return to your families and friends. And may a gracious God, who is powerful to protect you amid the dangers of the battle, as amid the peaceful retirement of your homes, have you constantly in His holy keeping.
>
> Ellen Phelps, Elizabeth D. Rice, E. S. Merriam, Bell C. Saxton, Mary A. Sargent, Sarah M. Bliss, *Committee.*

Mrs. Barnes then resumed:

> I trust, sir, that these sentiments will find a ready response in your own heart and in the heart of every man under your command. As you are now about to enter upon the solemn duties for which you and your Regiment have been enrolled, you will always remember that the heart of many a wife and mother and child and sister, will beat anxiously for your *safety,* but, remember, no less anxiously for your *honor.* Not only personal friends, but the whole people of the State of Massachusetts will share these feelings. I take great pride, sir, in having been selected by the ladies to present to you these beautiful emblems of our Nation and State, and I am happy to believe they could not be placed in more honorable hands. . . .

Rapid proficiency had been made in drill, and the dress parades were daily witnessed by multitudes from Medford and adjoining towns. . . . [On July 23] Captain Marshall visited the camp and administered the oath to about one hundred men who quite filled the Regiment. Among these was Drummer-Boy Myron P. Walker of Company C, who had been absent June 21st. Only fourteen years old, he was unqualifiedly the youngest "man" in the Tenth Regiment. To crown all the experiences of this eventful day, and to indicate the esteem in which the Regiment was held by the Medford people, the ladies of East Medford, Pleasant and Ship streets visited the camp in the evening, bringing with them four barrels of doughnuts, besides baskets of cake, currants and other luxuries. Each company received four pailfuls, enough for a good sample of home cooking and, through well-filled stomachs, to attest the kindness of their Medford friends for whom they rent the air with enthusiastic cheers.

The breaking of camp began the 24th, with the sending to Boston of the extra baggage of the Regiment that it might be loaded on the steamers *S. R. Spaulding* and *Ben De Ford,* then waiting at the dock, vessels to be pretty well known in following years as transports for soldiers all along the Atlantic coast. Thursday, the 25th, saw the remainder of the baggage and equipage packed early in the morning. At 7:30 a. m. tents were struck, loaded upon the wagons and everything was made ready for a start. Again the great hearts of the Medford citizens appeared in that they served the "boys" with a farewell breakfast of baked beans and brown bread, not a few of them coming on the ground to say "Good-bye;" there was also a considerable showing of friends from the towns of the western part of the state. At 2:00 p. m. the Regiment marched to the village of Medford, less than a mile away, where, after forming a hollow square, prayer was offered by one of the village clergymen, after which Ex-Gov. George N. Briggs, father of the Colonel, addressed the men in an impressive manner. There is no other similar incident recorded during the war. Himself renowned for the purity of his character, the excellence of his long administration, his words were heard by appreciative listeners, none of them thinking how soon those instructive lips were to be stilled in death. Beginning with a statement of why the men were leaving their homes with hostile intent, pointing out the duty of the President and their own, he proceeded to address them in a paternal spirit, touching upon the value of character, the vices he would have them shun, and concluded with the following personal appeal:

> You are going to meet active and earnest opponents Never underrate the power or bravery of an enemy. If you come in conflict with them, show yourselves to be *men* and *New England men.* If your enemies are brave and gallant, imitate and excel them in those qualities.

If they are cruel and inhuman to their wounded foes, avoid and abhor their example. Such conduct disgraces humanity. Should they fall into your hands as prisoners, remember they are your brethren, and treat them with kindness and magnanimity. Show them that it is not your purpose nor the purpose of the Government you defend to subjugate them as enemies, but to restore them to the dominion of the laws, and the benign and just power of the Constitution, to the enjoyment of the same privileges which you claim for yourselves. Never raise your weapons upon a fallen foe, never stain those bright bayonets with the blood of wounded and disabled foes.

Officers and soldiers of the Tenth Regiment: whilst you rally around and defend the standard of your country, never forget that you owe allegiance to a Higher Power. We must all render an account of our conduct here to the Supreme Ruler and Judge of heaven and earth. The soldier, of all men, should feel that he is in the presence of God and humbly implore His protection. He is a God of battles, and will be a shield and buckler to those who put their trust in Him. Trust in his mercy and rely on his mighty arm for protection. May He preserve and bless you all.

When the army of an ancient republic were going forth to battle a mother of one of the soldiers said to him, "My son, return home *with* your shield or *on* your shield." Adopting the sentiment of that noble mother, let me say to the commander of this Regiment: My son! and to the true and brave officers associated with you, and to the resolute, hardy and intelligent men under your command, bring back those beautiful and rich colors presented you by the ladies of Springfield, the emblems of your country's power and glory, waving over your heads, unstained, or return wrapped in their gory folds. . . .

 E S S A Y S

In the first essay, Marquette University historian James Marten, the author of *The Children's Civil War* (1998), discusses Confederate soldiers as fathers. In addition to describing the parenting roles that these men undertook (as well as those that they did not, or could not, undertake), he suggests that the separation and danger of war may well have heightened these men's awareness of the importance of fatherhood to their identities.

In the second essay, Reid Mitchell of the University of Maryland explores soldiering as a coming-of-age ritual. Focusing on Iowan Cyrus F. Boyd, Mitchell demonstrates that enlisting in the armed forces often coincided with adolescence and early adulthood and that serving in the Union Army became an important way for northern youths to stake their claim to manhood. Drawing on his 1993 study of northern soldiers, *The Vacant Chair*, Mitchell also discusses Americans' use of familial imagery to describe the Civil War.

Fatherhood in the Confederacy

JAMES MARTEN

Children often invaded the sleep of Confederate fathers. Winston J. T. Stephens had been in the army for only a few months when he "had a regular soldiers dream" about his one-year-old daughter. "I thought I had returned" home, he wrote his wife. "Rosa called Pa Pa & smacked her lips for a kiss, but alas I awoke & had a

James Marten, "Fatherhood in the Confederacy: Southern Soldiers and Their Children," *Journal of Southern History* 63, 2 (May 1997): 269–281, 283–292. Copyright by the Southern Historical Association. Reprinted by permission of the Managing Editor.

soldiers bed & bed fellow." William E. Stoker served with the 18th Texas in Arkansas until his death at Jenkins' Ferry in April 1864; soon after he left Texas, he began dreaming about his wife Elizabeth and their little daughter Priscilla. "It appears to me just as natural to be talking to you & Priscilla," he told Elizabeth. "When I wake, it nearley kills me for to think it aint so." An army doctor taking morphine to help him rest—"I can hardly sleep the half of these long lonesome nights for thinking of *you all*"—experienced dreams "so life-like & natural that I could hardly realize that I was not *at home* when I awoke in the morning. I seemed not only to see *your faces*—loving faces—but I heard & distinguished the *voices*. . . . I saw & heard you all *so plainly!*"

The grief and longing haunting these soldiers' statements stand in stark contrast to a dominant historical interpretation. Historians have frequently argued that nineteenth-century fathers distanced themselves emotionally from the lives of their children. Colonial fathers had apparently taken charge of child rearing, especially of boys, soon after the children were weaned—exerting discipline, guiding offspring toward careers and marriage, even feeding and putting them to bed; however, as the nineteenth century progressed, the twin developments of urbanization and industrialization separated the workplace from the home and carried fathers out of their children's daily lives. Early in the century, mothers gained preeminence in the raising of children as women sought rewarding and vital roles in the new republic, as the "Cult of Domesticity" and numerous child-rearing guides assigned primary responsibility for child care to mothers, and as stern colonial assumptions about child development gave way to a less rigid, more empathetic style that stressed the importance of maternal affection. Antebellum fathers, so the argument goes, retained their roles as enforcers of discipline and arbiters of family morals but left "child-nurture" to their wives.

Yet the assumption that all families shared in the admittedly far-reaching transformations of the nineteenth century overlooks the fact that the conditions producing such fatherly detachment were not spread evenly throughout the country. Especially among working-class Americans and residents of rural areas of the South as well as the North, fathers were deeply involved in many facets of their children's lives. In parts of the South fathers and mothers together created the kind of child-centered families that historians often assume were limited to the urban middle class. . . . Confederate soldiers filled their letters with reminiscences and vignettes of their lives before the war—chats and playtimes, rowdy suppers and cozy winter evenings—that clearly suggested that when at home they interacted intimately and wholeheartedly with their children and that they found extended separation from them intolerable.

But Civil War correspondence did not merely reveal pre-existing behavior and assumptions; there is, in fact, reason to believe that the war prompted more intense relationships among family members. . . .

The conditions bred by the war—separation, sacrifice, loss—not only helped to shape the tone and content of their correspondence but also inspired Americans to a greater appreciation of their families. Victorians—especially northerners and urban dwellers—had already begun to view the family as an institution threatened by the modern age. It became a haven from stress, a conduit of moral values, and a prominent component of what their descendants would call "quality of life," and its disruption was to be avoided. Although industrialization and urbanization had made few inroads in the South by 1861, the separation and stress of war fostered similar anxieties among Confederate fathers. In addition, even as children became less important as contributors to household economies (and in slaveholding families, children were less apt to have been considered economic assets), they became more important as sources of emotional, even sentimental, satisfaction. One could argue that at the same time that the war heightened the importance of masculinity as a valuable component of manhood, it also increased the social value of concerned fatherhood.

Confederate fathers displayed at least three separate conceptions of fatherhood. The first and simplest related to the daily care of children, which they could enjoy only in their dreams and remember in nostalgic letters with which many modern fathers can easily identify. The second—the notion that their duty to their country and to their families' honor superseded their duty to provide emotional and material support to their families—actually deprived them of the physical closeness to which they were accustomed. The third—a paternal, even patriarchal, insistence on providing wide-ranging guidance and instruction—reflected their attempt to reconcile the former with the latter. Duty and honor may have torn them from the arms of wives and children, but distance alone could not cause them to forsake their responsibilities completely. As a result, Civil War fathers desperately sought to project their authority and love through the erratic mails, remaining fathers in function as well as in name. They poured concern and affection into their letters, explained their absence as best they could, and instructed their children about beliefs, behavior, and assumptions—shaded by traditional gender considerations—that they believed carried more weight when propelled by paternal authority.

Confederate fathers hated the powerlessness imposed upon them by distance and military duty, and the most ubiquitous and affecting portions of their letters demonstrated their concern for the physical and mental well-being of their children. A Mississippi cavalryman scolded his wife for failing to send him all the details about his newborn daughter's crippled hand. "My imagination has given wings to my anxiety," he exclaimed, "until my sleep has been disturbed and my waking hours rendered gloomy in consequence of all kind of vague suppositions."

Even the pronounced formality of the letters of Jedediah Hotchkiss, a Confederate engineer who fretted for several days after word arrived of his daughter Nelly's serious illness, could not obscure his pain and feelings of helplessness at being away from his family during an emergency. He "read with streaming eyes by the camp fire" his wife's recent letters. Although resigned to the possibility of his child's death, he waited "in painful solicitude the further news." Obviously trying to share the burden of worry with his wife, he spent "much of the sleepless nights in thinking of her and your sorrowing condition." Luckily, the crisis passed in a few days, and he soon received a letter with a violet Nelly had picked from the garden. "I was very happy," he sighed with relief, "to think my little daughter was reviving and getting new life again just as the sweet flowers are opening under the influence of the vernal sun."

The birth of a son or daughter inspired elation tempered by dismay at the miles separating father from newborn. When Lt. Col. James Williams, commanding the garrison of Fort Morgan near Mobile, heard of the birth of his son George in May

1863, he wrote to his wife that "It is well that I have some control of my very restive and excitable nerves or they might have led me into extravagancies . . . that would ill accord with the dignity of the post commander." Williams attempted "to keep my mind on my work—but my wife and the black haired baby charge into my thoughts—break my lines of battle—harass my columns and demolish my squares in four ranks in a manner unknown before to military art." He managed a furlough during the summer of 1863 but was still distracted in August. "Whenever I go to write to you I am always so overcome by my thoughts of you and baby," he confided to his wife, "that I am almost unable to compose myself. . . ." His efforts to put pen to paper would be diverted by "pictures of Master George asleep and awake, in bed and perched like a bird on his mothers arm—and in-all kinds of temper, from violence of baby passion down to the good nature that lies on the bed and crows by the hour." . . .

The death of a child caused equally strong, if opposite emotions. The importance placed by Victorians on infant nurture and on the family, combined with the less harsh Protestantism of the Second Great Awakening, often led bereaved parents to practice a series of ritualized responses when a child died. Fathers in the army could participate only through aching letters to their wives. During the month after Edwin Fay's oldest son, William Edwin, died in 1862 at the age of five, the despondent sergeant issued a stream of self-pitying letters to his wife. "My heart is bursting," Fay cried, drunk with misery, "I almost fear I shall go crazy—I don't see how I can stand it." He blamed his wife, who negligently allowed the boy to run outdoors too often and to eat too much fruit; the Yankees, whose "accursed villainy took me away from my family"; and himself. Fay bitterly regretted his decision to join the Confederate army. Perhaps he could have prevented Will Ed's death; he could at least "have been at home to see him die." He pleaded with his wife to "take care of our last one, do not let it die," then closed almost hysterically with "I cannot stand it here—I shall desert or do something worse—I cannot stand it. I cannot write— My heart is broken—I don't deserve or crave to live—Oh Mother what shall I do. . . . My heart is bursting, my brain on fire." Drained and heartbroken, Fay seemed to retreat from this kind of emotional investment in his surviving son, for he rarely mentioned Thornwell in his letters during the remainder of the war.

Praying that their children would survive the numerous diseases and accidents that frequently claimed young victims in the nineteenth century, soldiers also pleaded for good news from home. Theophilus Perry wanted to hear about "the sports & tricks of the children. Nothing is better calculated to shed light & smiles over my face" or to "lift a great load from my heart." Wives kept their husbands up to date on new words and recent pranks that were no doubt funnier to read about than to clean up. "Bam" Gordon of Georgia, for instance, had played with a tub of water, a tea kettle, and cold ashes from the stove. "You can judge for yourself," his mother wrote to his father, "how he looked." Like toddlers of any era, Bam was "no sooner stopped from one piece of mischief, before he does something else equally as bad." Mothers dutifully reported on the comings and goings and the social, academic, and moral development of their offspring, obviously hoping to close the distance between soldiers and their children through detailed descriptions. John Davidson had been gone to the army for over a year and a half when his wife Julia wrote early in 1863, "The children are well. Hetty is very hearty & as red as a rose," while Bascom "is still learning his book though it is hard to keep him at it as he is so anxious to play." Bascom and his older brother Charley "are very much afraid of bad boys. if they are out side & see any boys coming that they think are bad they will come in. . . . they have heard a great deal of Swearing but have not taken it up." C. L. Burckmyer's wife frequently wrote from France to her officer-husband in South Carolina to report on the progress of their ten-year-old daughter, including the many awards she received at school. Although she once apologized for going into such detail about Mamie's studies, "I know how interested you have always been in everything concerning your only child."

As Confederate fathers worried about the health and activities of their children, they also instinctively pondered deeper elements of their relationships with their offspring. Civil War fathers feared that their small children would forget them, even as they demonstrated that their sons and daughters laid tender claims to their thoughts. Indeed, one Texas soldier's fear took on a special urgency because, lacking photographs of his wife and child, he worried that he might actually "forget how you & priscilla looked." "Does she know my photograph yet," asked another Confederate about his eight-month-old daughter, "or does she look upon it as a toy?" "Train up the little fellows in the way th[e]y should go," John Davidson urged his wife, "and talk to them of there [*sic*] absent Father. I hope th[e]y will not forget him that thinks of them so often and loves them so dear." Dorsey Pender had two sons—Turner, age two, and the infant Dorsey—when the war began. The young colonel urged his wife Fanny, "Don't let Turner forget me. Make him talk of papa . . . [even] if he is too little to know anything about [me]. It is a hard thing to think that our own child does not know anything about [me]; to feel that he may never." Another Confederate was even more upset at the thought of never again seeing his children. In a dramatic letter to his wife, Shephard Pryor pleaded that if he died on the battlefield, "don't let them forget that they had a father and [to] my dear boy speak of me frequently and learn him to love me, though I may be dead to this world." A brief visit to his Georgia home suggested to a frustrated George W. Peddy that his daughter Laura might forget him; "she looked so strange at me. . . ."

Wives and mothers insisted that children had certainly not forgotten their fathers. Letters from home provided breaks in camp routine and at least temporary respites from the fear and weariness that burdened southern soldiers; perhaps the most satisfying news for Confederate fathers were tales of the ways that children kept their memories alive. Willis Jones's children, according to their mother Martha, "talk of you constantly" and "are always making preparations for your return." A Lamar County, Texas, woman wrote to her husband that their little boy Eddy "shed tears when he heard that you could find no little boys to hug you around the neck," and "talked a great deal about you. For weeks after you left when he would get anything good he would say lets keep some for fodder [father]." Matty, the youngest, "cant talk to say any thing about you but tell her that Father is coming and she will run to the door and hollow as loud as she can then she looks disappointed and sad." Little Rosa Stephens was only a year or so old when her father Winston joined a Florida unit; her mother Octavia testified that, when going to bed the night after Winston left, Rosa "looked all around and kept calling for Pa Pa and made me feel right sad. . . ." A young Texas named Willy Bryan proved that he had not forgotten his father when he named a new pig "Guy." His mother wrote to Willie's father—

Guy Sr.—that it was "Rather a funny namesake, but it showed his feelings toward you." Helen Chunn, the daughter of a lieutenant in the 40th Georgia, made "a great fuss" over his ambrotype and, when she received a letter from her father, "went dancing all over the house, showing it to every body and delivering your respects" to neighbors and friends. She vowed "to keep your letter as long as she lives."

Harriet Perry of Marshall, Texas, filled letters to her husband Theophilus with heartbreaking images of how much their daughter Mattie missed him. One day Mattie convinced herself that her father was coming; "I never heard her laugh out so loud or seem so delighted as she was." Other times she held her doll up to the window to look for "Papa," and one day she donned her bonnet and headed out the door "to see papa." Harriet reported that little Mattie "talks of you every day, particularly at meals." When she kissed the page on which her mother was writing, Harriet circled the spot and labeled it "daughter kissed here." (The letter still bears a yellow stain well over a century later.) Harriet apparently found her frequent descriptions of Mattie's doings therapeutic. "She is the sweetest little creature in the world," Harriet wrote in the fall of 1862. "I could not live without her. . . . I seldom let her go out of my sight; she is a great deal of company for me—in fact all I have & I cant bear for her to be away from me. . . . I shall almost fill my letter about our little darling but I know that is more interesting to you than any thing I could write."

Even better than children's affection and concern filtered through their mothers' correspondence were letters from children themselves, who told their fathers about daily events and concerns, showed off new-found writing skills, and stressed how much they wanted to see their fathers. A typical note came from young "Dump" Hall to his Confederate father at Vicksburg. "I am going to have a letter written to you to let you know that I have not forgotten you yet," he began. He mentioned his spelling efforts, his need for a new book, the doll his sister Molly wanted, and his own preference that "you would come home and shoot birds for me [rather] than stay there and shoot them yankees." . . . Louisa Gilmer, no more than ten years old but staying at a Savannah boarding school, wrote her Confederate father Jeremy about home news and asked him what he had named his horse. "I do want to see you so much," she mourned, especially in the evening, "when I come in and no one is in, and I am so lonesome by my self and if you where [*sic*] here you would tell me stories and so I would not be so lonesome."

A collective portrait of southern fathers emerges from these letters. They were not only concerned parents but also sources of comfort and affection; children were accustomed to a wide range of intimate connections with their fathers, who tucked them in, chattered easily about daily concerns, and provided companionship and humor. But this instinctive, natural response to their children clashed with a more abstract, yet in the long run perhaps more important, function. In the minds of southern men, the war had made being a good and loyal soldier one of the duties of being a good father. In fact, although there is no reason to doubt the sincerity of soldiers' longing to be with their families or their interest in the mundane details of child rearing, their devotion to the concept of honor and the belief that patriotic sacrifices were necessary to maintain their families' good names overcame such sentimental attachments. In effect, they were saying that the love they felt for their families mandated their continued absence in Confederate service. The difficulty of their decisions to leave wives and youngsters in exposed and potentially dangerous situations led many to attach great significance to their own actions. Some remarked on the typical south-ern determination to defend their homes and families from invading Yankees. Most, however, yielding to the powerful strain of southern honor that defined themselves and their families, asserted that their loyal service would bring prominence to their families and offered as the only alternative the shame their descendants would suffer if the soldiers shirked their duty. Southerners seemed to believe that such a blot of dishonor would be particularly damaging to their sons' futures.

This insistence that honor and paternal responsibility meshed cut across rank and class lines. An Alabama private clearly missed his seven young children when he wrote his wife shortly after joining the army that "I would bee glad to see little ginny and give her a kiss and see the rest of the children frolic around and play on my lap and see babe suck his thum. . . ." Yet, his duty to his country and to his family kept him in the field: "if it had not have been the love I have for them and my country I would have been ther now." Nearly a year later, he assured his wife that he would not give up the cause: "I dont want it throwed up to my children after I am dead and gone that I was a deserter from the confederate army I dont want to do anything if I no it that will leave a stain on my posterity hereafter." . . . Josiah Patterson of Georgia expressed his own commitment to the southern cause with a homely analogy aimed at his sons. A soldier had "many hard, disagreeable duties to perform," but "the true soldier does not grumble and complain but does all that his country's service demands willingly and cheerfully like a good little boy that obeys his father and mother for the love he bears them and the kindness he has received from them." In the same letter, he added that, despite the dangers and hardships, it was "better that your Father should leave you and become a soldier than that you should become slaves and serfs. . . . Love for my offspring, so far from being a happiness, is but torture to me, if their prospects in future are blasted. No, my little ones," he ended his extended soliloquy on patriotism and responsibility, "I love you too dearly to permit the ruthless footsteps of the invader to crush out your liberty while I am en-joying an inglorious inactivity or ease at home."

Confederate fathers clearly believed that part of their paternal duty would be fulfilled if they served their country well, a concept that fit easily into a southern gentleman's notion of public service. They also sought to educate their children about the patriotic crusade. . . .

. . . [I]n addition, most fathers also engaged in instruction that covered the whole gamut of mid-nineteenth-century values. Denied daily contact with their sons and daughters and convinced that their sacrifice would benefit their families and enhance their fatherly roles, Confederate fathers continued to participate in educating their children by offering far-ranging advice on schooling and careers, morality and ethics, behavior and etiquette. In normal times, these lessons might have been spread out over several years and delivered in a variety of subtle ways. The war, however, forced men to concentrate their advice and to exert their paternal authority through the formal medium of the written word. Although they grimly accepted the need to do their political and military duty for their county, they also believed that they had a duty to guide and counsel their progeny. Some saw the heightened strain and uncertainty of war as an opportunity to focus their children's attention on the lessons it could teach them. A Confederate surgeon emphasized to his children that "these are times such as one *sees only once*—when we are all dead

& gone many lifetimes hence—they will be spoken of as the '*bloody age*'—the times of horror—of famine—misery—wretchedness." Yet something good could come of the crisis, if only the children would imagine the diseased, cold, hungry, blighted soldiers living and dying in "*camps* all over the land," and "*resolve* never to *complain* of the little difficulties & troubles that come in your way."

As these admonitions indicate, southern fathers did at times attempt to use their own harrowing experiences to set forth standards of behavior for their children. Letters from Confederate fathers written in this vein demonstrate that Bertram Wyatt-Brown's complex and useful analysis of the antebellum South can be applied to the war years. Although Wyatt-Brown highlights "shame"—whereby threats to family status and the possibility of community disapproval shaped behavior—as a parental tool, he also argues that "conscience"—a set of values more at home in the Puritan North in which children's guilt could be used to force them to internalize ideas of right and wrong—was not ignored in the honor-bound South. He suggests that during the antebellum period there began a transition from the traditional focus on honor to an increasing emphasis, especially among evangelical southerners, on conscience. Civil War fathers clearly demonstrated this mixture of the old and new in their wartime parenting. Wyatt-Brown also detects a "haphazardness in Southern father-child relations," an inconsistent concern for their children's well-being and upbringing. Yet he also shows that southern fathers did step up their paternal intervention during times of crisis such as illness. That the Civil War became, for Confederate fathers, a family as well as a political crisis is reflected in their wartime correspondence, which shows them intensely—if rhetorically—involved with every aspect of the lives of their sons and daughters.

The endurance of hardships gave some fathers leverage to induce good behavior by inspiring a healthy dose of guilt. David Coon hoped that "my sorrow at parting with family and friends may not be increased by unfavorable reports from home, so that in after years you will not have to look back with sorrow and remorse for what could then be mended." If he could "hear a good report" of his nine children, "it will be the best keepsake I could wish to remember you by." Theodore Montfort of Georgia also expected that his sacrifices would inspire his children to follow his good advice. In a letter written early in the war, he described the illness and difficult conditions he faced and then reminded them that "while you are all at home where you can keep dry with a good room, fire and bed to sleep in, you should feel grateful and take care of everything as your Father is undergoing these hardships and dangers that you might remain at home and be comfortable as you are." He urged them to mind their mother, offered presents for good behavior, and expressed his desire that when he returned from the war, "I want to find that you have done everything right and have improved in every respect."

The correspondence between members of three different southern families shows the application of both honor and conscience. For instance, Col. John L. Bridgers Sr. of Tarboro, North Carolina, portrayed a classic southern patriarch when he issued stern orders to thirteen-year-old John Jr., who was attending boarding school. Critiquing one of the boy's recent letters, the colonel pointed out that "Restless[ness] and dissatisfaction Johnny are the weak points in your character. . . . When difficulties beset you work them out of your way" or "endure them. . . . son I appeal to you to become firm and to throw away that feeble determination of yours." Subsequent letters addressed his son's troubles with teasing classmates ("In trying to teach you more control I have often told you if you did control yourself more the boys would pet you. . . . Learn not to be teased.") and with the "hatred" young John felt toward them. ("Such a wholesale hatred would be more worthy of [a] Yankee than my son.") The elder Bridgers also pointedly announced that "Your cousin Henry is the most popular boy at Dr. Nelson's School. He is a universal favorite and the thought renders his father so proud and happy." Of course, that was not the case with John. "You do not know what that idea causes your mother and myself to feel, to have raised a son the hated object of school. For your own sake, for our sake render yourselve more agreeable." In another letter, he reminded his son that "I never had the pleasure of receiving a letter from a father as you are *now* doing."

In contrast to the Bridgerses' hard-edged correspondence are the long, loving letters exchanged by Edgeworth Bird and his Georgia family. Of course, the fine points of getting along in the world—the central concern of Bridgers's letters—meant different things for boys and girls, and Bird's detailed and sympathetic counsel to his teen-aged daughter Saida steered her toward entirely different personal goals than the business-like, almost political, goals urged upon young John Bridgers. Bird wrote Saida that, as she entered her " 'teens,' . . . it behooves you to begin to prepare yourself in earnest to face the stern realities of life." She would soon have to depend less on other people's advice and direction and more on her "own sound judgement and good conduct." In preparation for her parents' inevitable deaths, "it is *now* time that you were fitting yourself to steer your own bark through life's troubled waters, relying upon the chart of your own good sense and virtue to direct you." He praised the "twin sisters" of truth and virtue and urged her to be cheerful but not giddy, studious and literary, patient, humble, and dutiful. These characteristics "will bear you up and o'er every wave of trouble, and hurl back every billow of misfortune that Satan's rage or a world's envy may cast at you." Although he apologized for producing in this letter "more a lecture than a letter," other letters encouraged Saida to be "truthful under all circumstances" and to "Study, study, study," for "an enlightened, well polished mind, well regulated and stored with useful knowledge, is the greatest blessing you could prepare for yourself, after a true piety." She was also to act "the role of 'Big Sis' " to her younger brother Bud, "to look after and advise him," since she "was the senior, Miss Sallie. . . ."

In a similar effort, Confederate surgeon Samuel D. Sanders encouraged his thirteen-year-old daughter Mary, a student at Columbia Female College in South Carolina, to pursue knowledge as well as piety. In late 1861 he asked her not to "think too much about visiting" nor to "associate much with bad girls." She must "trust in your blessed Savior for salvation," which would lead her to "have a good, honest, pure soul." "It will break my heart if you are not a very good girl," he reminded her. A year later he passed along advice more commonly given to boys—to prepare herself for a future career—but qualified it as a necessity brought about by the war and directed her toward the decidedly feminine occupation of teaching drawing and painting. "If the Abolition army conquer us in this war," he explained, "we will all be poor, and you may have to support yourself by teaching something." She must not anticipate an inheritance but should "get ready to be an earnest worker yourself" rather than one of the "idle drones in the great hive of life."

Although soldiers like Bird and Sanders proudly advised their daughters, many soldiers who took their patriotic and paternal responsibilities seriously revealed the same sense of urgency felt by the South Carolinian Franklin Gaillard. Early in the war he wrote his son that he "never thinks of going into battle and being shot, but right off he thinks of his little David being left without him to impress upon [him] those principles which he would like to have govern and guide him when he grows to be a man." Although his younger sister would be advised by the aunt with whom they were both staying, young David would have to mature without paternal influence. Gaillard summarized his advice in a few sentences: he wanted his son "to be always obedient and grateful," and "kind and polite to all, study hard at school, tell the truth always," and "make no friends with mean and untruthful boys." In addition, "he must always be brave," and "never do wrong to anyone—nor let others do wrong to him." If he followed that advice, "when he grows up to be a man, if war should come again . . . he will make a good and faithful soldier." David and Maria Gaillard were orphaned when their father fell during the battle of the Wilderness.

Many Confederate soldiers shared Gaillard's assumption of a special relationship between father and son. Southern men of the planter and middle class had long taken over the education and socialization of their six- and seven-year-old boys—mothers, of course, mentored their daughters—regarding career choices, racial and sexual relationships, and public service. Even in nonrural areas, by mid-century, as mothers became identified as the primary caregivers for young children, fathers retained their duties as their sons' instructors and guides to a moral life, productive work habits, and healthy ambition.

American fathers in the mid-nineteenth century extended the same types of advice to boys and girls—be good, mind your mother, do your schoolwork—but they frequently placed different emphasis and used different tones in the directives aimed at boys and girls. Just as their war records would mean more to their sons' future than their daughters', one of the chief concerns of both Union and Confederate fathers was for their sons to develop honorable characters and respected names. For instance, Joseph W. Young, a Union officer from Indiana, wanted his daughter Mary to mind her mother and to "learn her Book" and extended affectionate greetings to Martha Ann and to Willey—"God bless her little Rosey cheecks"—but instructed his wife "to take good care of Little Jake for [I] have a great deel of confidence in him if he has the proper Raising he will make a man that will make his mark in this world." Showing the same regard for his son, Willis Jones, a Confederate soldier from Kentucky, worried to his wife that sixteen-year-old Willis Jr. "was just at the age when my supervision of him is indispensable" but hoped that "he will be like myself after losing my father . . . and feel the importance of conducting himself as a gentleman." Willis Sr. asked his wife to tell their son "how much I think of him and if I ever live to see him, that I hope to find him an educated, modest, accomplished gentleman. . . ."

Other soldiers limited their words of wisdom to homely and straightforward counsel. Thomas Brady's last letter before he was killed in April 1865 asked his wife to tell his only son that "I want him to be a good boy . . . be carefull of him self and . . . not go too close to the Horses & Mules." Writing from the hospital cot that would become his deathbed, J. G. Meacham of Kentucky ordered Toby and Billy to mind their mother "and for the lords sake if I never do see you all no more keep out of bad company and grog Shops." Ciny was to obey her mother and all the children were to "shum bad company and bee kind to each other." The Hall sisters, staying with their father's parents, were instructed to "take plenty of exercise in the open air," carry wood chips for their aunt, and "talk loud to Grandpa." . . .

Reinforcing their paternal guidance and their customary places as heads of families, southern soldiers frequently offered advice to their wives about health and discipline issues. . . . An Arkansas captain proffered extremely detailed advice to his wife regarding their only child, a three-year-old son. Ostensibly limiting his discussion to education, "the subject that is upermost in my mind," he ranged broadly across many facets of behavior and training. "Teach him to place a proper estimate upon whatever he can comprehend, and to exercise his owne good sense. Direct him as a reasonable beeing, capable of seeing and judging the rights and wrongs of things. . . ." Young Willie needed to learn the value of neatness and to take pride in his common sense. "Be careful how and for what you Praise him," the proud father and demanding husband warned, "but be shure to give him some to-ken of your approbation when he deserves it." Discipline was necessary but must not be too harsh, since "the frowns of a judisious and loved Mother is better than many stripes or much scolding." Indeed, "let him make you his friend and confi-dential companion, then you will find ample opportunity for teaching him the great and important Truths. . . ." A similar refrain appeared in Joel Blake's recommenda-tions to his wife in Florida. He applauded her practice of praying with their son Willie whenever he disobeyed her: "shame him & talk with him seriously. Teach him to fear God as well as the rod, and you will find no doubt he will require less whip-ping and be a better child." "A soft word," he predicted, "may often touch the heart, make an impression, which years can never wipe out."

Thoughts of a postwar future in which they would be reunited with their children and allowed to fulfill all the duties of fatherhood often, at least temporarily, pushed aside martial and political ideals and concerns about education and discipline. Two long years before the end of the war, a North Carolinian wished only "to make a comfortable living and raise & Educate our little children & raise them up in the way they should go and see them grow up to perfection and if they do right what a source of happiness it would be to us in our declining days." In a letter to his wife, another southerner dreamed of a postwar "home where the vanities and troubles of the outside world are barred out," where their children "will live [to] be a comfort to us and useful members of society. I am looking far ahead," he admitted, "but these tempting scenes of the future, when the present is so dreary, cannot be dispensed with." Doubts that they would ever see their cherished offspring sometimes over-came generally optimistic references to the future. In the summer of 1864, Marion Fitzpatrick calmly talked about his son Henry's new breeches. "I want to see him so bad," he wrote, "But it seems doubtful now about ever seeing him again. Men are killed and wounded around me nearly every day and I know not how soon my time may come." Fitzpatrick was mortally wounded at Petersburg late in the war. . . .

Confederate fathers believed that their roles as parents followed them into the army—indeed, for many, their military service was an integral, if painful, part of parental duty. The war did not create within a single generation a new concept of fatherhood. Separation did, however, become a lens that helped fathers focus more completely and determinedly on their progeny, inspiring them to extend advice and counsel—as well as love and humor—to the youngsters behind the lines. The affection that leaps from their letters transcends Victorian rhetoric and indicates how important to their self-images were their roles as fathers.

Like modern parents, Confederate fathers loathed missing birthdays and childhood milestones such as first steps and new words; they agonized over their inability to witness the innocent pranks of toddlers, small accomplishments of schoolchildren, and growing maturity of adolescents. For some, the experiences of war—separation, danger, loss or the potential for loss—confirmed fathers' interest in their families and in the joys and responsibilities of fatherhood. For others, the crisis awakened ideas they had not yet fully grasped when they were torn from the bosoms of their families. Perhaps they realized that they had been taking their children for granted, perhaps—surrounded by men, cut off from home and hearth—they merely sought to lighten their loneliness by exploring a facet of their personalities and character that army life all but overwhelmed. Whatever their reasons, sons and daughter rarely strayed far from the thoughts of privates and generals. As John West lay in an encampment far from his Texas home one cold, clear night, he gazed up from his blanket and thought of his children's favorite song, "Twinkle, twinkle, little star." He wondered "if Stark has taught it to Mary yet," then communicated in a few words the often unspoken desire of fellow soldiers, a longing that clearly shows the importance of fatherhood to Confederate fathers, but rarely emerges from scholarly studies of child rearing and family relationships: "I want to see them grow up and love each other. . . ."

Coming of Age in the Union Army

REID MITCHELL

When Abraham Lincoln first ran for President, Cyrus F. Boyd was already twenty-four years old. Nevertheless he would later say that he and the other Republican boys of Palmyra, Iowa, "organized a company of young men just young enough and strong enough to do some tall yelling." They must have been a sight—each one wearing blue overalls, white shirts, and "a chip hat," riding horseback to electioneer for Lincoln. "We were supposed to be assisting Abraham Lincoln to be elected President and everybody now knows that he was elected." The horses, he later confessed, were really colts. "We not only had to break and drill ourselves but had to break the *colts* also and at the same time."

This frolicking lot of young politicians became one of the companies Iowa contributed to the Union war effort. "When our man Lincoln called for men to suppress the insurrection we did not respond the first time but at the next call we left the colts at home and went almost to [a] *boy*." The word "boy" and indeed the emphasis are not mine but Boyd's himself, when he looked back years later at the events of the Civil War. Later in life, Boyd took his wartime diary and rewrote it into an account of his months in the Fifteenth Iowa Infantry Regiment, the regiment in which

Reid Mitchell, "Soldiering, Manhood, and Coming of Age: A Northern Volunteer," in Catherine Clinton and Nina Silber, eds., *Divided Houses: Gender and the Civil War* (New York: Oxford University Press, 1992), pp. 43–54. Copyright © 1992 by Catherine Clinton and Nina Silber. Used by permission of Oxford University Press, Inc.

he served until he left to become an officer in another outfit. This autobiography, a mixture of a young man's diary and an old man's reflections, he sent to a friend of his who had soldiered with him in the Fifteenth Iowa. Cyrus F. Boyd self-consciously molded his autobiographical tale of service in the army into a story about a boy becoming a man—making soldiering a coming-of-age experience. He obviously expected his friend would recognize this story and share this understanding of their youthful joint service in the Union army.

This vision, this credo of masculinity, maturation, and military service, was hardly unique to Cyrus F. Boyd or to the Civil War. Both during the years 1861 through 1865 and all through the postwar period, as Americans tried to make sense of their war, they linked the transformation of the civilian into soldier and the passage of a boy into adulthood. At the minimum, the relationship was twofold. First, with a great number of American youth—defined roughly as those still living within a parental household—joining the army, those who lived through the war emerged at the age traditionally associated with full manhood. They "came of age" during the war and the war had to be part of that experience. Second, the very ideas of man, soldier, and citizen were inextricably linked. Remaining a civilian was thought unmanly; going to war a proof of manhood. Since coming of age means not simply becoming an adult but assuming adult gender roles—becoming a man—popular thought sometimes conflated the two transformations. And so did many of the young men who served in the armies.

Considering the age of many Union soldiers, as well as that of their Confederate counterparts, the stress on war as a maturing process is hardly surprising. Gerald Linderman notes that "in both armies, eighteen-year-olds constituted the single largest age group the first year of the war." The men who served in the Union companies habitually referred to themselves as the boys, as did their officers and civilians, and nobody seems to have taken offense at the term. What strikes us now is how elderly Civil War armies were compared with the ones produced by mass conscription in the twentieth century. But nonetheless, from 1861 to 1865, many American men spent in the army the period of late adolescence and early adulthood usually associated with coming of age.

Cyrus F. Boyd felt the change begin in his initial weeks of service. The first sign that the young soldier was entering man's estate may have come from the flattering attention of the young women both back home and in other Iowa towns. In his diary, Boyd began noting how well the girls treated him. The company was mustered in Keokuk and there Boyd could scarcely make up his mind which young lady appealed to him most—"very shy" Lizzie Sullivan whose eyes were "sparkling black," or the Johnston girls, who gave him and his friends gingersnaps when the regiment went down river. When attending church, he principally noticed the women: "The people are very sociable—especially the young ladies who seem to take a great interest in the soldiers." All of his stepping out with Maggie, Aggie, and Lizzie seems to have been given zest by the fact that he was a soldier soon to be off to the war. One night, "We had a good dinner and a pleasant time not unmarred however by the ever present thought this might be the *last* time we should meet these kind people." The romantic soldier paying court before the army moves on was a role that Boyd took to with no trouble. While it may have marred the good times, it also added to their appeal. On the day the regiment boarded the boat that began their journey to the battle of Shiloh, they marched down the Main Street to Keokuk under the eyes of the women of the town. "1000 strong we marched that afternoon in the pride and glory of youthful soldiers. The sound of the music—the cheering shouts of the people robbed [us] of all regrets and we marched proudly away. I saw some of our good friends on the side walks—but it would not do to look back."

While Boyd and other decent young men were sparking the local girls, other Iowa soldiers enjoyed the saloons and brothels of Keokuk. Boyd complained of their fascination with the pleasures of the river town. But these unrepentant soldiers were claiming man's estate just as Boyd was, although in less respectable ways. These young men asserted their freedom from home and their new sense of masculinity with liquor and prostitutes. Soon Boyd recognized that this type of coming-of-age would be typical of his fellow soldiers, although he never learned to approve. "Whiskey and sexual vices," he claimed, "carry more soldiers off than the *bullet.*"

This escape from small-town morality seemed to be an inescapable part of sol-diering. Old soldiers told a young recruit in another part of the Union army that "unless a man can drink, lie, steal, and swear he is not fit for a soldier." The men who pursued these vices and others—gambling and swearing were even more common-place than drinking and fornication—disturbed Cyrus Boyd most by their enthu-siasm: "How eager they seem to abandon all their early teachings and to catch up with everything which seeks to debase." Entering into the heavily masculine world of the army, they prided themselves on these thoroughly masculine vices. But to Boyd, who believed that true manhood required not release but restraint, the speed of his fellow soldiers' degradation was appalling.

Part of masculinity was achieving a self-discipline within the institutional disci-pline of the army. Cyrus F. Boyd and other northerners were as proud of their ability to withstand the temptations to which other soldiers gave in as they were of their service to the Union. Indeed, virtuous self-discipline was in itself a kind of service. When secession and rebellion were perceived as hot-headed and impulsive—the re-sult of unrestrained passion—self-discipline had political implications. During the war with the emotional, treacherous—feminine, childlike—South, the son of the ra-tional, loyal—masculine, adult—North should be manly and upright.

Yet part of the transformation necessary to become a soldier was hardening. While Boyd worried about men whose morals coarsened, he himself became less sensitive than he had been, more inured to suffering—both his own and others. Hard-ening was a process that ranged over all aspects of Boyd's life, from the common-place to the most serious. It included getting used to a variety of discomforts and privations. His diet became coarser and simpler. "We have bid farewell to Bakers bread, cow's milk and such soft things. Had a piece of meat and a hard tack for breakfast—we are gradually breaking in." He learned to live outdoors; on the com-pany's first night camping, "some of the boys began to think of their *mothers* and to talk of returning to their comfortable homes in the western counties."

Hardening also included becoming accustomed to death and violence. The Fif-teen Iowa Infantry's introduction to bloodshed was perhaps more sudden than most. On April 6, 1862, they were aboard a steamer at Pittsburgh Landing, having breakfast, when the order came to go ashore. Once there, they ran into the battle of Shiloh. They hurried for three miles, "meeting hundreds—yes thousands of men on the retreat who had thrown away their arms and were rushing toward the Landing—

most of these were *hatless* and had nothing on them except their clothes." Some of those who fled had been shot; some ran and others were being carried off on stretchers. As they passed, the Iowans could not help noticing that some of the men were "covered with blood from head to foot."

"Here we were a new Regt which had never until this morning heard an enemies gun fire thrown into this *hell* of a battle—without warning." This was what the Civil War generation and others before and since called "the baptism of blood"—a phrase that connoted not only sudden and complete maturation but a radical transformation in character and experience. In telling his story, Boyd deliberately contrasted the innocence of the recruits to the horror of the baptism.

The general horror of battle quickly became more specific. The Fifteenth Iowa came to the edge of a large field with a ravine at one end. They crossed the ravine and deployed into line of battle, all in clear view of the Confederates. The rebels fired on them. "Here I noticed the first man shot. . . . He was close to us and sprang high in the air and gave one groan and fell *dead.*" Then the hardening began. Boyd and his fellow soldiers each had to step over the newly dead man. "Each man as he came up seemed to hesitate and some made a motion to pick him up." But they could not stop to tend to the man. Instead, the officers "sternly" ordered a charge, the men responded with a cheer, and they moved forward—only to be pushed back and to retreat over that same open ground. Masculinity meant restraining both their instincts to flee— to be a coward was to be no man—and their instincts to minister to the corpse.

As they were recrossing the field, a soldier came to Boyd and told him that his brother Scott was being left behind. Exhausted, Scott had collapsed on the ground. Boyd ran back to rescue his brother, only to be told "he never could go any farther and that I had better save myself and let him go." Pleading with his brother had no effect, so Cyrus Boyd grabbed Scott Boyd "by the *nap of the neck* and jerked him upon his feet and told him to *come* or I should help him with my *boot.*" Scott stood up and Cyrus helped him seek cover in the ravine. There he left his brother, confident he could work his way to safety, and returned to his company.

They continued to fight and fall back, ending up on the bluffs back at the landing where they had disembarked that morning. From the bluffs, they witnessed the arrival of Buell's army—all, in Boyd's opinion, that saved Grant, his army, and themselves. There was a final rebel charge but the Union forces held. Then came night, in many ways more horrible than the day had been. As the rain came down, Boyd and his company tried to sleep, listening to the groans of the other men, wounded and dying, who surrounded them, and to the sounds of wounded horses "running through the darkness." Morning came and they were thankful to be held in reserve through the second day's fighting.

After the battle was finally over, Boyd and his friends went out and examined the field where they had fought. In just a few days war had changed them forever: "By this time we had become accustomed to seeing *dead* men and the *shock* had passed." They walked unmoved through the camp of the Fifty-second Illinois, looking at the bodies of dead and wounded soldiers, Union and Confederate, "alternately scattered over the ground." Some of the wounded were "so near dead from exposure they were mostly insane." Elsewhere on the field, Boyd came across a dead rebel lying "on his back with his hands raised above his head"; the man "had died in great agony. Boyd reached down and, for a memento, took a button off his coat.

"War is *hell* broke loose and benumbs all the tender feelings of men and makes of them *brutes.*" This was one conclusion Boyd drew after experiencing battle— presumably he included himself in his observations. He also concluded, "I do not want to see any more such scenes and yet I would not have missed this for any con- sideration." Being a man meant risking horrors that might unman an individual— not by feminizing him but by making him inhuman. The hardening process was painful but it was well begun.

Boyd noticed his own hardening most when it centered on his reaction—or growing lack of reaction—to suffering and death. He also found himself, despite his fears of moral degradation, taking food—chickens, pigs, roasting ears—from southern civilians. This was a more traditional form of masculine assertion that usually characterized the modest Boyd: being one of a group of armed men invad- ing a homestead and taking what they wanted because nobody there could stop them. For Boyd, this food was due to the soldiers because they were loyal and self- sacrificing, while southerners were neither, and because, well, because they were soldiers. But he still responded to peacetime values that held foraging was theft. When Company E slaughtered a rebel sheep, Boyd noted approving that, "Major Purcell gave them a healthy old lecture and told the men they would not be allowed to *kill sheep* even if they were away from *home* and that hereafter such men would be severely *punished.*"

Finally, the hardening required a kind of mental vigor. Even as he inveighed against whisky and fornication, Boyd believed the real enemy to the soldier was internal. "More men *die* of homesickness than all other diseases—and when a man gives up and lies down he is a *goner.*" His strategy for surviving the war was not simply military discipline—the ability to march, fight, obey orders, and keep oneself clean—not just moral discipline—the avoidance of temptation and degradation— but mental discipline as well. "Keep the mind occupied with something new and keep *going all the time* except when asleep." This pursuit of action and Boyd's prac- tice of positive thinking was another duty required by manliness.

That Cyrus F. Boyd should look back and choose to shape his life in the Union army into a tale of his coming-of-age is hardly surprising. This understanding of manhood, with its complex layers of definition, was commonplace among northern- ers of the Civil War era. Ideas about true manliness were central to the experience of northern men enlisting in the army, serving through the war, and remembering their service. In fact, the image of the young soldier coming of age was so central to later understanding of the war that it became, through a kind of cultural metonymy, a fig- ure for both true manhood and for the nation itself.

Becoming a man was no simple step for a middle-class northerner like Cyrus F. Boyd. Sexual assertion by itself was insufficient; indeed, the young man might re- gard it as a sign that he was unmanly because he failed to exercise manly restraint. Physical violence—hunting and killing his fellow man in what seemed to be an ex- tension of a primitive, perhaps savage, role—might be masculine, but true manhood required self-discipline and civilized morality. Both sexuality and violence had to be domesticated before a male became a true man—the one could be fulfilled only within the family, the other had to be directed purposefully toward a licensed enemy. Yet the demands of familial duty—defending family, home, and country—threat- ened to undercut the emotive ties that should bind a man to wife, parents, children, and friends: could a man harden himself enough to survive the war yet remain a son and a husband? True men recognized the role of emotions. An Illinois soldier confessed to his wife, "I cannot sing yet those songs such as, the vacant chair, the tears come." He went on, however, to invoke the ideal of manliness to justify his tears. "A man that cannot shed a tear when he thinks of those he left at home, is no man." Shedding a tear might be easy or painful or meaningless; what should a man do when his brother is lying exhausted on the battlefield of Shiloh while his company is rushing on? Is he first a sergeant or a sibling?

Volunteering in itself was a sign of coming into manhood—it meant accepting a man's duties to defend his home and country. It was also, for many soldiers, the first time they had been away from parental supervision. Besides, military service had long been regarded as a climacteric. Sidney O. Little, an Illinois soldier, sounded as if he doubted his mother could believe in his transformation—he told her "you may think me jesting"—but he assured her that "my coming into this war has made a man of your son." As Benjamen F. Ashenfelter put it, deciding not simply to enlist but re-enlist in August 1863, "A man that is afraid to face his Countries foe on an open field would not Defend A wife & children from the Midnight Assassin." Another, boringly predictable attitude toward the relationship of soldiering and manliness was the claim that those who refused to fight weren't men at all—they might as well be women. As one soldier said, "Any young man who is drafted now and forgets his manhood so far as to hire a substitute is'nt [*sic*] worthy the name of man and ought to be put in petticoats immediately." When the soldier Wilbur Fisk, an unofficial correspondent of his newspaper back home, explained why he sometimes wrote at length on the minutiae of soldier life, he spoke to the children of the community. "I thought perhaps some of the boys who read the *Freeman,* but are not old enough yet themselves to be soldiers, and some of the little girls too, perhaps, who never can be soldiers, but who almost wish sometimes they had been born boys so that they could, would be interested to read all about the little affairs in a soldier's common everyday life."

Soldiers and other northerners frequently talked about fighting for the Union in specifically familial terms. Burage Rice, a New York captain, predicted the sure defeat of rebellion. "By the sacrifice and blood of our fathers was the Republic founded and by the treasure, faith, honor, and blood of their sons shall the same glorious flag forever wave over us." The Union was a fragile legacy handed down by the fathers of the Revolutionary generation: their sons owed it protection.

But the long chain of familial responsibility did not end with the Civil War generation. The soldier's manhood required him to be a dutiful father as well as an obedient son. Henry H. Seys attributed his patriotism to "all the teachings of my boyhood—the very milk that nourished me in my infancy." This childhood education forced him to serve; otherwise "I should despise myself and be *ashamed to answer the questions of my children.*" Preserving the Union was the duty he owed both the generation behind him—particularly, it would seem, his mother—and the generation to come. He further told his wife, "teach our children that their duty to the land of their birth is next to their duty to their God. And that those who would desert *her* in the hour of danger, should be deserted by Him when *their* final calamity comes." Fathers expected mothers to inculcate their children with patriotic values; the feminine, domestic sphere was the ground for the masculine, public world.

Henry H. Seys—and many others like him—saw himself as part of an extensive family, one that included generations of Americans, not just his own parents and children. To put it simply, many northerners considered the Union itself a family. Fighting for the Union was, in that sense, much like fighting for one's family.

This metaphor influenced more than just the experience of the young men of the North who joined the Union army. It underlay a lot of thinking about the Union's war goals. One way to sum up Union war motivations succinctly was to say that the South needed to be taught a lesson. The North was the schoolmaster, the army the rod, and the South the disobedient child. The Vermont Yankee Wilbur Fisk, looking back in 1894, remembered the enthusiasm with which "we boys" had greeted the war. "We were ready to shout hurrah because now there would be a chance to teach the South a lesson, but we didn't realize how much it would cost us to teach it."

Americans had a habit of talking about the body politic in terms of family relationships. Even antiwar northerners used familial imagery—"let the erring sisters depart in peace." Sisterhood, in this case, wasn't powerful—the image provoked a sad aura of weakness. Northerners who were prowar used the image of unruly children who had to be made to obey. Sometimes this way of thinking about the South even reached the battlefield. Usually the specific familial imagery was hidden—northerners discussed southerners in terms of irrationality, emotion, savagery. One soldier wrote after the battle of Shiloh, "We showed them on the 2d day that northern obstinacy and coolness was more than a match for southern impetuosity"—northern obstinacy and coolness making up a critical part of manliness. Occasionally, northern imputations of southern childishness could be detected overtly. Henry C. Metzger wrote his sister, "I hate to hear the Rebles cheerre when they make a charge, they put me in mind of small schoolchildren about the time school is out." And indeed, sometimes men at war sound as if they have schoolboy notions of honor behind all the bloodshed and policy. A perfectly sensible Wisconsin soldier wrote his wife this, as he visited with defeated Confederate soldiers in Johnston's army in 1865: "They are willing to admit that we have whipped them, and that is all that we want of them, is to acknowledge that we are too much for them, and we will also get along very finely." The soldier knew that behind the war had been issues of the nature of the American Republic, the fate of democratic institutions, the place of slavery in a free society— yet he was able to write as if getting the Confederates to cry uncle had been the whole point of the conflict.

The family analogy for understanding southern rebellion and northern response—the notion that the southern states might best be understood as disobedient children, the northern ones as filial—was woefully inadequate, indeed nonsensical. I am not suggesting that anyone who seriously thought about politics entertained it for a minute or ever pushed the analogy into an identification. But in a period when political duties were so often expressed in familial imagery, it is striking that an armed rebellion of grown men was sometimes made to sound like a squabble in a kindergarten. The family metaphor provided perhaps the most common image by which people thought about the political world.

Volunteer soldiers were dutiful sons of both their parents and their Revolutionary forefathers. Rebels challenged the mild parental authority of the national government—and thus defied the Revolutionary generation as well. In that sense, the good sons of 1861 went to war against the bad sons. Perhaps there is a hint of this, however attenuated, in the way we continue to call the Civil War "the Brothers' War." And if there is not, at least there is little doubt we still think of the war as a family tragedy.

Thinking about the Civil War experience as a rite of passage also continued into the next generation, as the sons of 1861 became the fathers of the Gilded Age. Once war becomes the defining experience for manhood, how can sons grow up in its absence? Just as the sons and grandsons down the line of the revolutionary generation knew that they might never measure up to the heroes of 1776, the children of the postwar era faced the knowledge that the ultimate courage was shown not by them but by their fathers. (Or perhaps worse—as in the lifelong case of Theodore Roosevelt—had *not* been shown by their fathers.) Mrs. C. E. McKay, a Civil War nurse, said in 1876, "And ought we not carefully to teach the children of the present generation,—charging them not to let their children or their children's children forget what it cost their fathers to leave to them a united country?"

Men who had suffered through and survived the war told their children that military experience was crucial to manhood—in fact, they spoke of war not only as a burden to be borne manfully but as a piece of luck. "Through our great good fortune," Oliver Wendell Holmes, Jr., said, "in our youth our hearts were touched with fire." Both the veterans and the younger men coming after them worried that with no equivalent experience, the youth of America would never grow into men. College athletics—played, at Harvard, on Soldier's Field—were just one way that postwar society tried to reproduce the manly experience of war for their children. Stephen Crane, in his great novel *The Red Badge of Courage,* imaginatively seized the Civil War—and can we not hear, in its subtle ironies, a rebellious protest against turning frightened young men into heroes? Theodore Roosevelt literally seized upon war, pursuing the strenuous life up the slope of Kettle Hill. It took a generation of men uncertain of their manhood to find in the quick and nasty war with Spain in 1898 "a splendid little war."

Talking about and presumably thinking about Civil War soldiers coming of age eventually influenced thinking about the war itself. Some saw—and still see— the Civil War as a coming-of-age experience for the nation entire. The war unified the country; it created strong institutions, including a powerful if short-lived army, and a long-lived sense of American power; it made Ohioans and New Yorkers as well as South Carolinians and Alabamians realize that they were Americans. It is as if the nation could not really mature without a massive bloodletting inflicted on itself, as if six hundred thousand deaths were some kind of adolescent rite of passage.

And Cyrus F. Boyd? He completed the romance of war by returning to Keokuk after Appomattox and marrying Maggie Johnston, one of the young ladies who had presented him gingersnaps. He had already become a soldier and an officer. Becoming a husband and a father—becoming in that sense, as well, a man—was for him part of his Civil War experience. Nothing in the diary he left us suggests that he would have been surprised that his years spent fighting for the Union could be interpreted as years he spent growing up. He wrote as if the war that swept down on him and his companions was as natural and expected and necessary as childbirth, love, and death. This synchrony of public and private lives was how a generation of soldiers—and their children who followed—made sense of the painful, fumbling, demotic heroism and the remarkable unremarkableness of the men who fought for the Union.

F U R T H E R   R E A D I N G

Bardaglio, Peter W. *Reconstructing the Household: Families, Sex, and the Law in the Nineteenth-Century South* (1995).
Berlin, Ira, Steven F. Miller, and Leslie F. Rowland et al. *Freedom: A Documentary History of Emancipation* (1982–).
Bleser, Carol. *The Hammonds of Redcliffe* (1981).
———, ed. *In Joy and in Sorrow: Women, Family, and Marriage in the Victorian South, 1830–1900* (1991).
Burr, Virginia Ingraham, ed. *The Secret Eye: The Journal of Ella Gertrude Clanton, 1848–1889* (1990).
Clinton, Catherine, and Nina Silber, eds. *Divided Houses: Gender and the Civil War* (1992).
Faust, Drew Gilpin. *Mothers of Invention: Women of the Slaveholding South in the American Civil War* (1996).
Fleet, Betsey, and John D.P. Fuller, eds. *Green Mount: A Virginia Plantation During the Civil War* (1962).
Marten, James. *The Children's Civil War* (1998).
———, ed. *Lessons of War: The Civil War in Children's Magazines* (1999).
Mitchell, Reid. *The Vacant Chair: The Northern Soldier Leaves Home* (1993).
Mohr, James C., ed. *The Cormany Diaries: A Northern Family in the Civil War* (1982).
Myers, Robert Manson, ed. *The Children of Pride* (1972).
Pease, Jane H., and William H. Pease. *A Family of Women: The Carolina Petrigrus in Peace and War* (1999).
Rozier, John, ed. *The Granite Farm Letters: The Civil War Correspondence of Edgeworth and Sallie Bird* (1988).
Throne, Mildred, ed. *The Civil War Diary of Cyrus F. Boyd, Fifteenth Iowa Infantry, 1861–1863* (1977).
Whites, LeeAnn. *The Civil War as a Crisis in Gender: Augusta, Georgia, 1860–1890* (1995).
Wiley, Bell. *The Life of Billy Yank* (1952).
———. *The Life of Johnny Reb* (1943).
Woodward, C. Vann, ed. *Mary Chesnut's Civil War* (1981).

CHAPTER
7

Families on the Frontier

Since the publication of Frederick Jackson Turner's "frontier thesis" in 1893,
Americans have been fascinated by the "Wild West." For Americans of European
descent, the iconography of hardy settlers bringing plows and pews to the West has
proved to be both popular and enduring. The first wave of family histories of the
frontier, published in the 1970s, modified this popular image, pointing out that
most pioneers were members of families rather than rugged individualists, but
these histories did not challenge the ethnocentric thinking that shaped their studies
of predominantly white settlers moving westward.

In the 1980s and 1990s, historians of the West began to pioneer a new approach,
regarding the frontier less as a boundary between "civilization" and "wilderness"
and more as a space where cultures came into contact—and, sometimes, into conflict.
Benefiting from the insights of this group of scholars, scholars who currently study
families in the West now regard the region as a place where ideas about and experiences of family life are complex and contested. Differences of gender, ethnicity, and
generation are now at the forefront of family studies on the frontier.

Reflecting this wider definition of frontier families, scholars of the West consult
a broad range of sources. In addition to such traditional sources as the personal
writings of white settlers, historians investigating families in the West turn to official
records of the federal government and to oral histories of subjugated peoples. These
changes in the study of families on the frontier have allowed scholars to examine
different groups—white settlers, Native Americans, and Hispanic colonists—both
on their own terms and in relation to one another.

Scholarship on families and children on the frontier suggests broader questions
about westward exploration, assimilation, and people's ability to adapt both to their
environment and to the presence of other peoples: How does the process of western
"settlement" appear differently depending on the vantage point adopted? What
contradictions were encapsulated in government-sponsored "civilization" programs?
Would members of the younger generation be better prepared to live in a diverse
society than their elders?

 D O C U M E N T S

For white Americans who moved west, work was a necessity for all members of the
family. The need for labor pressured settlers to modify their ideas about what activities
were age and gender appropriate; as the first two documents illustrate, pioneer girls

201

often took on significant work responsibilities. In Document 1, Harriet Taylor Upton, born in Portage County, Ohio, in 1853, describes her girlhood on the frontier. In Document 2, Montanan Margaret Bell recalls the work she performed on the ranch of her stepfather, Hedge, at ages nine and ten in the early twentieth century.

Work also emerges as a major theme in the recollections of Mexican American women in the Southwest. In Document 3, American-born Esperanza Montoya Padilla describes her mother's work as a ranch wife, a boarding-house keeper, and a *partera* (midwife) in the mining town of Mascot, Arizona, in the 1920s. Dolores López Montoya's involvement in the community was not exceptional, as Socorro Félix Delgado's memories, included as Document 4, demonstrate. Delgado, who was born in Tucson, Arizona, in 1920, describes her extended family and her grandmother's active role in church and community life.

Community life was a contested idea on the Indian reservations that the federal government established in the West. As the policy recommendations included as Document 5 show, children bore the brunt of government officials' intervention into Native American life. These conflicting plans for the education of Indian children suggest tension between Indian identity and assimilation into the Anglo-American mainstream.

1. Harriet Taylor Upton Recalls Pioneer Life, ca. 1870

. . . Men had so much to do outdoors that they couldn't bother with things in the house, and women were in great despair over the inconveniences. One sturdy mother became so enraged because her husband procrastinated in building an oven, saying that she could no longer bake bread and do all her cooking in one big iron kettle, that she fashioned some bricks of mud and built an oven which was such a success that people travelled out of their way to see it in action. . . . When these early housewives got their ovens to going, they would bake fifty mince pies at a time, put them in a cold room, often "the parlor chamber" as the guest room was called, where they would freeze and would bring them out as occasion required, reheating them by the fire. The woman who made the oven of bricks once had it full of pies when the Indians came along in the night and carried them all off. . . .

Grandfather approved of my energy. I used to follow him around as he worked, sometimes stumbling along behind the plow, hoping he would let me drive. Grandmother always made me remove my dirty shoes on the porch after I had been on one of these plowing expeditions. I drove the hay rake occasionally, but was not a real success at it. I grew so excited under the responsibility that I would forget to release the hay at the proper time. Hours I have sat in the barn with him as he thrashed out the wheat with a hand flail. . . . Then the straw would be forked up, the wheat and the chaff scraped together and later put through a machine called a fanning mill, where the chaff was separated from the grain. I was often allowed to turn the wheel which worked the machine. It was easy to do, but it was a dirty job and my grandmother required me to brush myself and comb my hair before I could go inside the house, and even then bits of straw would remain in my hair for days.

I helped to churn and carried water to the men in the field during harvest time, and fed the chickens and rode into the barn from the field on the hay load. I cut and

Rosalyn Baxandall, Linda Gordon, and Susan Reverby, eds., *America's Working Women* (New York: Random House, 1976), pp. 72–74.

twisted lamp lighters to be used in the winter to save matches, and sewed carpet rags, and enjoyed doing all these things. I have little respect for the person who invented a do-less Heaven.

Perhaps I like the sugar making time the best of all seasons on the farm. My spring vacations were always spent there. . . . I spent most of my waking hours and some of my sleeping ones in the sugar bush, as the sugar camp was then called. My uncles were patient with me and allowed me to follow them in their work all day. When they drove through the woods gathering up the sap from the buckets hung to the trees and pouring it into casks which were on a sort of sledge with 6-inch boards for runners, I would romp along at their side, falling down at times, drinking out of the full pails at others and riding on the vehicle when I cared to do so. . . .

Just as my grandfather allowed me to run the fanning machine to free the chaff from the wheat, so my grandmother let me reel the yarn she had spun from the spindle to the reeling machine. . . .

Grandmother dried berries, corn, pumpkin; raised her babies, and took into her family anyone unfortunate in the neighborhood. She nursed the sick at their homes when she could leave her own; and when she could not, she brought the well children or the convalescent to her home and cared for them. . . .

After a long hard day, she would gather me in her arms and croon me to sleep, for she could not carry a tune. I thought she was the most beautiful old woman I had ever seen, especially when she wore a cap. Regardless of what she was doing—washing, baking or churning,—she stopped work each morning at ten o'clock, sat down, opened her Bible and read that which her eyes first fell upon. She believed she was led to these verses. Her plain face glowed with love. To be near her was to receive a benediction. She had great sorrows, among them the death of her only daughter, her youngest child, but she never complained. When other women were lamenting about how hard they worked or what troubles they had, she would give a sort of a grunt of disapproval and say, "Oh, shucks!" . . .

2. Margaret Bell Describes Children's Work on the Montana Frontier, ca. 1910

That winter [1909–1910] was hard on me and the poor half-starved dogies [i.e., calves]. Hedge often left us children alone, and I was always in difficulties or getting hurt. Both our pitchforks were big four- or five-tined forks, too heavy and awkward for me. I found a little three-tined fork without a handle and a discarded handle, and I thought I might rig up a nice little fork for myself, but there was a piece of wood in the furl of the fork. I tried burning the wood out, then tried digging it out with a spike, driving the spike in and pulling it out, but finally I drove it in too far and couldn't budge it. I hammered and pulled and jerked, and the spike flew out, hit my mouth, and broke a front tooth. When the cold air struck that broken tooth, it felt as though I'd been shot. After that, I had to keep my mouth shut when I was outside, and I learned not to holler at the horses or cattle until the tooth got over being so sensitive.

Margaret Bell, *When Montana and I Were Young: A Frontier Childhood,* ed. Mary Clearman Blew (Lincoln: University of Nebraska, 2002), pp. 112–116, 121–122.

Another time when Hedge was away, one of the yearlings fell into the spring and couldn't get out. I didn't know if you could pull an animal out by the head without breaking its neck, but I had to do something. I harnessed old Jess (she stood high, and the harness was heavy, but I finally got it on, bridle and all), and then I got a single-tree off the wagon and rode her to the spring. After getting all wet and muddy, I managed to get the rope around the yearling's middle and tied to the singletree. I was ready to hitch it to Jess, but when I looked at the ice around the spring, all jagged with cattle tracks, I thought I might tear the hide off the calf if I dragged him over it. I remembered a hide we had, hanging on the haystack fence, so I ran and brought it back to spread over the ice, but it spooked Jess, and she was off.

Down the brushy slope she went with me and the yearling bouncing behind her. The hide scraping over the ice and then over the brush made such a racket that Jess was too scared even to notice my hold on her bridle. Finally, we lost the calf hide on the brush, and as soon as that noise stopped, Jess stopped and looked around to see what it was all about. I took a look at my legs to see whether the rosebush scratches looked as bad as they felt.

The yearling was covered with black mud and looked as though he was about to die. I led Jess up to the hay corral gate. It was tight even in warm weather and almost impossible for me to open in the cold, but by getting down on my knees and opening the bottom first, I could manage it. I led Jess around to the sunny side of the haystack and unhooked her and left her eating hay, shut the gate to keep the other cattle from getting into the hay, and then rushed back to see if the calf was still alive. He was, but he lay inert, rolling his eyes till only their whites showed. A native range steer would have used his last bit of strength to struggle to his feet, but not a dogie. His spirit had been broken when he was a calf, and it wouldn't take much to finish him off. I rubbed some of the mud off him with dry hay and covered him with more hay, then dashed back to the house to prepare something warm for him to drink, if he would drink it.

I poured about three quarts of hot water into a bucket and threw in several cupfuls of oatmeal and a handful of salt. Beck went with me to help pour it down the calf, but as soon as he got a taste of the warm mixture he showed signs of life and stuck out his tongue to lick it. He tried to raise his head, and with our help, he got his front feet under him. Beck and I braced him up with frozen chunks of cow manure.

After he got his head up, he drank up the oatmeal and water and even licked the thick part on the bottom of the bucket. I picked out some good hay, and he ate that, too. I was happy. I had accomplished a big job and could go home now, take off my frozen, muddy clothes, and have something to eat myself.

I might not have gone to school, but I had to solve more problems than most children. There was nobody to go to for help when Hedge left us alone, and I had to try everything until I found a way that would work. . . .

In the summer, Beck and I milked a lot of cows. Hedge milked, too, when he was home, but we were forty miles from the creamery, and it usually took him four days to make the round trip to town and back. He went once a week with the cream, so for four days out of every week, we children were on our own, with all the work to do.

I thought I was very systematic about managing during the four days Hedge was away. I would milk the cows, feed the calves, and set the milk in the spring for the cream to rise. We used tall cans with a faucet close to the bottom and a glass in the side where we could see when the milk had run out the faucet and the cream was down to the bottom of the can. The skim milk we fed to the calves, and the cream we poured into barrels provided by the creamery. These barrels were wood, lined with tin, with a float to keep the cream from churning on the way to the creamery. They were tough to wash. The creamery sent them back dirty, and I almost had to stand on my head to wash the bottoms. . . .

When Hedge was away, it was my job to check the traps twice a day during cold weather. If a trapped coyote's foot froze, it might break off and let him get away. I had to kill the trapped coyotes by hitting them over the head with a club. If they showed fight, I didn't feel so bad, but usually they didn't, and I had to prime myself by thinking about the dirty work of coyotes, killing little calves and lambs, and how often they scared me when I was alone on the prairie at night. A man might kill a coyote without a qualm, but I dreaded it.

After I learned to shoot a gun I didn't mind killing badgers, rock chucks, prairie dogs, chicken hawks, and rattlesnakes. A rattlesnake was the first thing I learned to kill. I felt sorry for other animals, but never once did I feel sorry for a rattler.

I was never a good enough shot to kill a coyote on the run, which would have seemed different from clubbing one that was helpless in a trap. But no one ever wasted a bullet on a trapped animal because of the cost and also because a bullet made a hole in the hide.

Coyote traps had a spring on each side and were hard for me to set in cold weather. I would jump on the springs to press them down and then try to catch them. It usually took me several times. Once in my haste I caught my thumb in the trap. For a minute I was panicky. I examined the wire on the trap and saw it was too neat a job to be unwound without a pair of pliers and both hands. I tried to spring it by jumping on it with my knees, but I couldn't get enough force that way and only hurt my throbbing thumb. There was nothing else to do but unwire the trap from the tree before my thumb froze.

It didn't take long. I took off my scarf and wrapped it around my hand and the trap. I knew what happened to a cow's foot if she froze it, and I was three quarters of a mile from the house. I hurried all I could, planning just how I would get the trap open: I would have Beck get two monkey wrenches and open the jaws of the trap wide enough to fit over the springs.

The scheme worked, and what a glorious feeling as we screwed the wrenches down, the trap fell open, and my thumb was free! It hurt worse than ever, but I kept shaking it furiously and running around so I wouldn't feel it so much. Still, it was a sore thumb, badly bruised and slightly frosted. . . .

3. Esperanza Montoya Padilla Details Her Mother's Home and Community Work in the 1920s

My name is Esperanza Montoya Padilla. I was born in Mascot, Arizona, on August 28, 1915. Mascot was a mining town in the Chiricahua Mountains above Dos Cabezas, which is near Willcox. My mother's name was Dolores López Montoya; she came from a small town called Huepac close to Cananea, Sonora, Mexico. . . . My father

Patricia Preciado Martin, *Songs My Mother Sang to Me: An Oral History of Mexican American Women.* (Tucson: University of Arizona Press, 1992), pp. 101–107. © 1992 The Arizona Board of Regents. Reprinted by permission of the University of Arizona Press.

was from Santa Fe, New Mexico. I think my dad married my mother in Mexico and brought her over here. I believe that she was about fourteen years old. . . .

As long as I can remember, my mother always had a boarding house. In the very early days in Mascot, before my father passed away, there was a mine across the road from our house. . . . All the men that worked there used to come and eat at our house because there was no other place for them to eat in Mascot. In those years the miners did not sleep at our house. There was another house across from our home that was our property, too, and that's where the miners slept. It was a nice house with big wood-burning heaters and stoves where they made their coffee. Across the road, also, was a well that belonged to us. My dad was always very fussy about the well. When cars arrived up the hill from Dos Cabezas the drivers had to get permission from my dad to use the well to get water. Later on he put a lock on the well because the people were not taking care of it the way they should.

The boarding house was always part of our home. There were trees all around— fruit trees, mostly. Apricot and peach. My mother made jam. There were *trincheras* (rock retaining walls) that my father had built. The door that was the entrance to the kitchen faced the road that went between Dos Cabezas and Mascot. On the other side of the kitchen was a dining room, and a hall to one side of the kitchen where the miners washed their hands to get ready for dinner. At the entrance to the hall there was a chiffonnier with a pitcher and bowl and two little doors on the bot- tom where the towels were hung. One of my jobs was to go and check and make sure that there were fresh towels hanging there. On the other side of the hall was a room like a pantry; it was very dark and cool in that room, and that is where they kept the *carne seca* and *carne adobada*. There was a porch on the side of the house that faced the road, and the living room and our bedrooms were on the other side of the house. All of the windows of the bedrooms were completely covered with ivy so thick that you couldn't see in or out. I always figured that my dad planted that ivy so that no one could look inside. . . .

They had a garden—they grew tomatoes and chile and a few other things. And of course we had our fruit trees. But one of my brothers, Juan, had a farm in Bowie, and he used to bring a lot of produce—corn, chile verde, sartas of chile, watermelons, melons—up to Mascot for our boarding house.

And they had animals, of course. My dad had goats, and he sold the wool. He kept a cow for fresh milk, and goats and pigs and chickens and even turkeys! He slaughtered so we would have fresh meat, and we had to have the chickens for the eggs, of course. My mother sold the chickens and turkeys, too. It was rare to have them; other people did not have these things. I think she used to sell the carne seca, too. She was always in business!

Most of the slaughtering was done during the winter when it was time for tamales. When my father slaughtered a pig, my mother would make *carne adobada*. She made a sauce with red chile, garlic, onions, oregano, and other spices and then dipped the meat in the sauce and let it drain and dry. This is the way that the meat was preserved—there were no refrigerators in those days. I remember, also, that when an animal was slaughtered, they collected the blood, and they would take it to Mother in the kitchen. She put garlic and onion in it, and then she cooked it and stirred it until it thickened and curdled; it looked like chopped liver. They made *chicharrones* also. They cut up the pork skins outside and then cooked them in a kettle on an open fire. Everyone pitched in—there was a lot of action! The fat would be strained and collected in cans and saved. That is the lard that my mother used for cooking. I tell my kids that I love all those foods because I was raised with them. . . .

Everybody had a job. We had big tinas that we filled with water so that the garden could be watered when my dad came home from work. We filled the tinas with water for the laundry and got the wood and made the fire for heating it. The boys fed and watered the animals. The patio had to be swept and cleaned. My dad was very fussy about the kerosene lamps; that was one of my jobs. I cleaned the chimneys. Wood had to be gathered for the stove and for the big wood-burning heaters. It snowed a lot in the winter, and it got very, very cold. . . .

My sisters helped my mother a lot—setting the table, washing and putting the dishes away, helping with the cooking. There must have been about ten men who ate there, but they would never all come at the same time because they had different shifts.

My mother had a lot of beautiful dishes. In those days there was no plastic. The dishes used to come in a great big barrel, and my mother would take orders for dishes from different women. For doing this she would get a set of dishes free—the little cream pitchers. the butter plates, the whole bit!

My mother had a great big wood-burning stove, and there was a big tank on one side that was used for heating the water. On the other side was a box for the wood. It had a pretty shelf for the salt and pepper shakers. The stove was set against a wall of solid rock. Our house was built against the hill, and my dad must have made that wall with dynamite. From the stove there was a step down to a big table against the other wall. That's where my mother did her cooking and baking. Under this table she kept great big cans of lard and flour. And there was another little table there where my dad used to sit and drink his coffee and look out the window.

My mother was a very good cook, and she could make almost anything— American as well as Mexican-style food. She made a lot of *guisados* (stews) and caldos, and of course, tortillas. She had to make pies and cakes and cupcakes for the miners' lunches. She made puddings. Lemon pies were her speciality. Oh, how my brother Manuel was after her to make lemon pies—his favorite! She made the best *empanadas de calabaza* (pumpkin turnovers)! In fact, I still make them myself, but I wonder if I'm doing it the right way.

Mother would get up very early and put on the coffee and make breakfast and pack lunches for the men. She made fried eggs and potatoes. It was very rare that we would have ham, but she made her own chorizo. She also made pancakes and baking-powder biscuits in the mornings. And then, of course, she had to get an early start on the evening meal—caldos and guisados and tortillas or whatever. In the evening after dinners she baked bread and rolls. I guess that is when she had the time.

When it was Mother's rest time, she would sit down in her chair. I don't know what she was thinking. I was little—running around, jumping around—and she would say to me, "Abre el horno para ver como está el pan." ("Go open the oven door to see how the bread is doing.") And I would go and look and then go and tell her that it looked this way or that. My brother-in-law Cipriano Trillo used to say that Mother made the best bread! My kids always say, "My mother makes the best bread!" But I still think my mother's was better. Maybe it's because when you are a child everything your mother makes tastes so good.

She was never too busy or too tired to help me with my childish things. I used to gather walnuts, and with the patience of a child I would sit and crack the walnuts until I had a cupful. Then I'd tell my mother that I wanted to make candy. She'd tell me, "You put in so much sugar and so much of this and so much of that and stir and stir and then you add the walnuts." We'd make taffy and when people were visiting we'd have taffy pulls.

Mother was also a *partera*. Whatever babies were born in Mascot, she delivered them. The men came to the house and picked her up. "Ay, Doña Lolita, mi esposa está con dolores!" ("Ay, Doña Lolita, my wife is having pains!") And she would get up in the middle of the night and go wherever she was needed. She never complained. We'd go to New Mexico to deliver my sisters' babies. I always wondered how in the world she knew all this. I don't think she ever had any problems, thank God. I guess God was with her, because everything went right, and they would call her again for the next baby.

Poor Mother, I remember when I had my babies, I went by the book. Everything the book said, I did. And my mother would tell me to give the babies tea when they got sick, and I would say, "No, no, no! I don't want to start your medications!" And she would get upset with me and say, "How do you think that all of you were raised?" "Well, I'm going to bring mine up different," I would tell her. "I'm going to be the modern one!"

Anyone that needed help would come to her. If they were sick, or if their babies were sick, they came to her for advice. She gave them medicines and comforted them. She gave the babies teas *cuando estaban empachados* (when they had indigestion or colic). She had all kinds of little jars with herbs. In fact she used to buy the herbs from the Arab and Jewish merchants who came from Douglas and El Paso to sell their wares, all kinds of things from a truck. She was always *curando* [curing].

. . . She also gave massages to everyone who was sick. She made this stuff that was so stinky from turpentine and I don't know what in the world! It smelled worse than Ben Gay. People had faith in her healing. . . .

4. Socorro Félix Delgado Describes Family and Religion in Arizona, ca. 1930

My name is Socorro Delgado. I was born on September 9, 1920, in Tucson at my grandparents' home at 443 S. Meyer. My parents' names were José Delgado and Carlota Félix Delgado. My mother was born in Tucson on December 26, 1892, and died in 1985 at the age of ninety-three. My father was from the area of San Ignacio and Magdalena, Sonora; he came to Tucson as a young man to find work. My maternal grandparents' names were Jesús Félix and Andrea Arreola Félix. My grandmother Andrea, Manina we called her, was born in Ures, Sonora, in 1871; she came to Tucson when she was three years old and died in 1968 at the age of ninety-seven in her home at 447 S. Meyer. My grandfather Jesús was from Pitiquito, Sonora. I

Patricia Preciado Martin, *Songs My Mother Sang to Me: An Oral History of Mexican American Women* (Tucson: University of Arizona Press, 1992), pp. 53–55, 59–63, 66–69. © 1992 The Arizona Board of Regents. Reprinted by permission of the University of Arizona Press.

remember *his* mother—my great-grandmother. Her name was Apolonia Félix; we called her Grande. She had come from Spain, and when I was little she was already very *ancianita* [a very old woman]. She died in 1934 at the age of 103! My grandfather was her only child, and, you know, in those days the older people stayed with the family. I lived with my grandmother Andrea when I was growing up, and at one time we had four generations living in our house at the same time.

My great-grandmother Grande was a seamstress. She was very independent and liked to work and earn her own money. She even left for California once to do sewing; she was told she could earn a lot of money there. When she came back she brought a railroad car full of furniture and china and pictures, some of which I still have in my apartment. The first house my grandparents bought was at 443 S. Meyer. It was big—five or six bedrooms. Grande had her own sewing room in that house. She used her bedroom as a fitting room—I remember the mannequin. She made dresses for the whole wedding party, the *madrinas* (bridesmaids), and for the flower girls, as well as the bride. She also knew how to crochet; she embroidered. She did *deshilado*. That is an old-fashioned needlework where you pull the threads in cloth. She had a wooden frame for stretching the cloth. She pulled the threads (woof) and gathered the other threads (warp) into a design using a needle. She did needlepoint and made pillows for chairs out of velveteen and colorful yarn. I still have a little cushion that she made. . . .

Grande used to sew for us kids. When I graduated from the eighth grade at St. Augustine Cathedral School, the old Marist College on Ochoa, she made me my graduation dress—silk organdy, pale pink, with a big sash. She was already over one hundred years old when she made me that dress. . . .

The day she died I was in the house. My mother and grandmother always went to mass at the cathedral—every day, rain or shine. They asked me if I wanted to stay with Grande. They told me that if she had trouble breathing to give her a little spoonful of water. So I sat with her; I didn't want to leave her side because I was afraid that something might happen to her. I guess she was dying, but I didn't know it. I could see her hand moving over the ribbon trim on the blanket, and I asked myself, "What is she doing?" She always made me thread needles for her because she could not see too well; she made me thread a needle on the very day that she died because she could feel that a thread was unraveling on her blanket and she wanted to make it right. That's the kind of person she was.

I remember that she was constantly at her machine—an old Singer treadle. She would get up in the morning and sit at her machine before breakfast, and Manina used to have me go and get her and help her up so she could come to eat. She had sat so long at her sewing machine through all those years that when she got up she was all bent over her cane. . . .

My mother was always very hardworking, even as a child. She would get up real early in the morning and wash the dishes in a tina. They had to draw water from a well because they had no sink. She'd make little baking powder biscuits from scratch every morning for herself and her brothers, and they would take sandwiches to school. She made tortillas early in the morning when she was very young also. She made burritos and they took them to school for lunch. She made breakfast. They always had potatoes scrambled with eggs. It took a lot of time to cook because they made everything from scratch. If they were going to make a caldo, they had to go out and pick the vegetables in the garden, the corn, squash, carrots, potatoes, and they had to wash everything real well. I remember my mother saying, "What's to it (cooking) now that all this prepared food has come into being? Everything is in the refrigerator and freezer!" They roasted their own coffee beans—I did that, too—in a big pan on top of the stove until they browned to a certain color and it smelled very good. They stored the roasted coffee in a can and ground it fresh whenever they made coffee. They boiled the grounds in water and then filtered it. My mother and Manina made such wonderful coffee.

Of course, they had the carne seca. They put it in the oven to roast it a little bit, soaked it, and then pounded it to make carne machaca. This is what they did in their "spare time." They stored the meat in their "refrigerator"—a cabinet with screen that they would put outside in the fresh air. And then they would fry the machaca with potatoes or eggs.

Workers on my grandfather's farm made the *sartas* (strings of chile), but my mother and grandmother would take the chile from the sartas and clean it well—not wet it, but wipe it dry with a clean dish towel. They roasted it in the oven—all this was done with mesquite wood—in that big stove. Then they took it outside to let it cool and dry well. I did that, too. And then they ground the chile with a hand grinder and covered it and had the chile ready. All this had to be done after the evening meal—roast the coffee, ground the chile, and pound the meat. . . .

After the ranch was sold, my parents moved to Tempe where my father worked as foreman on a farm. When my grandfather died, I lived with my grandmother in town to keep her company. Later, when my parents moved, I stayed with her because I was going to St. Joseph's Academy. So I was raised by my grandmother—*por eso aprendí de ella* (that's why I learned so much from her).

My grandmother was very religious. She told us that she was raised by *her* grandmother and that *she* was also very religious and that's where she learned all this. Her grandmother's name was Lolita and she used to call her Malita.

My grandmother had a special devotion to the rosary, and we used to pray the rosary every night, on our knees. And after the rosary she prayed to each and every saint whose picture she had up there on her wall. So when she would say, "Let's pray the rosary," I used to think, "Oh, no!" because it would take forever! And we had to stay on our knees. If we dared to squirm or slouch she would give us "that look"—straighten up, keep still, stay quiet.

. . . [S]he had a *velación* [vigil] in thanksgiving to Los Dulces Nombres [the saints] because they had granted her prayer when they wanted to buy the ranch. She had the velación from the first year they moved to the ranch. My mother told me they would be a whole week in preparing for it. So Christmas was always very special to her because, although people would say, "That's not the day of the Holy Family," she would say "That's the day the baby was born." She always had this little altar, a little statue of Los Dulces Nombres which I still have and the two candles. But on Christmas Eve she would dress it up special. She covered the little table with beautiful crocheted and embroidered cloths that my great-grandmother had made. For many years I helped her decorate. We hung sheets on the wall and pinned a lot of paper flowers on them. She made the flowers herself. And in the backyard we had a big palm tree. She would have somebody cut the palm fronds, and we cleaned them and put them this way and that way. And then she would buy four *big* candles at the cathedral and put two on each side of Los Dulces Nombres. I used to buy things at Kress'—little birds and little bells—anything to hang to make it more colorful. And Manina would supervise and make sure that everything was done just so, that everything matched, that nothing was crooked. When we finished, she would say, "Tenemos que tener los claveles frescos [We have to have fresh flowers]." She would always buy six fresh carnations to put on the altar. It was a *big* spending.

The important thing was the family. My parents, my sisters, Carmen and Andrea, and my brother, José, my uncles and aunts and cousins and neighbors and friends also came to my grandmother's house early on the twenty-fourth. Christmas Eve was a day of abstinence—you don't eat meat—so they made enchiladas and potato salad with egg. And she made biscochuelos and wine out of dried figs. She fermented the figs in a big crock, covered it with a clean dish towel, stirred it on different days, and put it in little bottles. That was a special treat on the night of the twenty-fourth. . . .

Under the little altar table she had hidden little gifts—a little doll or a little car or some candy from the dime store. She told us that the Baby Jesus had left it there because we had been good. We didn't know Christmas trees; we didn't know Santa Claus. . . .

She was a very *Cristiana* [Christian woman]—everybody loved her. She used to tell me about her life, and she would say: "Don't just ask God for help; you have to do your part; don't just sit and wait for things to come from Over There." And she taught me to always be kind to people; it didn't matter who came to the door. "Even if you don't have anything, if it's a real hot day, then give them a cold glass of water and people will say, 'It's good!' And if it's cold and you don't have any coffee, just heat some water." And she told me, "Remember that there is only one God, and He is my Father and He is your Father and He is the Father of the drunk man going by and the Father of that little *viejita* (elderly woman) who is sick, so that makes us all brothers. So always be kind to people, no matter who they are."

At that time there were no rest homes, and the older people stayed with their family and died at home. The family came running to my grandmother. "Andreita, Andreita, my mother says to come because my father is very sick!" It was all a neighborhood thing there on Meyer Street—everybody knew each other—and she would take her rosary and go and pray. She walked everywhere. She said that a person who was dying was in great need of prayer because the devil was always around trying to tempt them even on their deathbed. She prayed to help them die peacefully. I remember once a little girl ran and said, "Andreita, come quick, quick." Manina ran with her apron still on. She not only prayed but also was very good at counseling and comforting people.

She also said the rosary at the *velorio*—the night before the burial. In those days they used to do that in the homes with the casket. They did it that way for my grandfather and my Tío Ramón, and for my great-grandmother, *esa viejita,* Apolonia. After the funeral there was the *novenario*—nine days of the rosary—at the family's house. She liked to begin the novenario on a Monday so that she had two Mondays during the nine days because she said that Monday was the day of souls in purgatory. . . .

She knew three generations of Carrillos at the mortuary. In those days the priests and deacons didn't say the rosary like they do now, and Arturo Carrillo, the father of Leo, Sr., used to come and get her. She made many friends like that. They never forgot her because she had prayed for them and she used never to charge for anything. . . .

My grandmother was always very active in the church. She knew three generations of bishops. She remembered when Bishop Gercke came in 1924. She went to the reception that they had for him at the university in the old auditorium. Way back, when she still lived at La Providencia, she went around to the ranchos collecting money for the first San Augustín Church—they were remodeling. She said that there was this lady who told her, "Andrea, I don't have any money, but I have these two chickens. Do you want to take them and sell them?" And she said yes. That's the way it was. She ended up with I don't know how many chickens because *she* bought them and then donated that money to the church. She used to go around with my uncle in that boquecito [i.e., horse-drawn buggy]—who could tell her no!

After she moved into town she always belonged to the cathedral. Back in those days it was the ladies who had the St. Vincent de Paul Society. My grandmother did that. Padre Pedro Timmermans gave them money and they bought groceries and filled little boxes with food to give to the poor people who came to the rectory asking for food.

She was a *veladora*—she belonged to the Society of Perpetual Light. They had adoration every day so that the Blessed Sacrament was not alone. Margarita King and Concepción Rebeil also belonged to that society. My grandmother was also a *celadora*—there was a day in the month that she was responsible for twelve ladies who would come from six in the morning until six at night. My grandmother used to stay all day in case someone didn't show up. We were in school, and we loved that day because she took lunch—little burros and things from the Trujillos' Guaymense Bakery.

When school was out at noon we ran and had lunch with her! They don't have the veladoras anymore. All those things have ended. . . .

5. The U.S. Government Makes Contradictory Proposals for Educating Indian Children, 1940s

Willard W. Beatty Recommends Education for Leadership, 1942

Before it will be possible to realize fully the present administration's objective of reëstablishing Indian self-government, it will be necessary to facilitate the preparation of native leaders. If there is any phase of the human relationship problem which government and missionary groups have sadly muffed, it is the training of leaders. . . .

It is generally believed that leaders are born, or at least possess innate qualities which are responsive to social impact. It is within our power to influence such leaders through education or through experience, but it is very doubtful whether leaders can be made from those who lack the innate capacity. Yet the need for

Willard W. Beatty, "Preparation of Indians for Leadership," in Oliver La Farge, ed., *The Changing Indian* (Tulsa: University of Oklahoma Press, 1942), pp. 139–143. Copyright © 1942. Reprinted with permission of the publisher, University of Oklahoma Press. This document can also be found in Robert Bremner, ed., *Children and Youth in America: A Documentary History* (Cambridge, Mass.: Harvard University Press, 1974), III: pp. 1722–1733.

informed native leadership has never been greater. We are far from sure that we know how to meet the need. Just sending an intelligent young Indian to college does not seem to be enough.

Sometimes the college experience results only in a profound feeling of inferiority or insecurity. So many conflicting pressures are encountered and so little intelligent guidance is available. Attitudes toward Indians vary so from state to state, or from region to region, that the young Indian almost inevitably encounters racial or social prejudice at one time or another. Even among many who are sympathetic with Indians, the student may find it taken for granted that he is intellectually inferior because of his race. In many groups an Indian who adheres to the religious beliefs of his tribe will find himself subject to criticism, attack, or maudlin sentimentality. With no frame of reference against which to evaluate these conflicting pressures, he is likely to be swayed in one direction or another without ascertaining the reasons.

As a result, some young Indians return to their tribal groups completely convinced that the only future for an Indian lies in denial of his race and acceptance of white culture and religion, while others who have experienced rejection from race-proud whites return to the Indian home hoping to resolve their conflicts and doubts by accepting the Indian pattern unquestioningly. Neither tendency is healthy or well balanced. Somewhere in the educational pattern it appears necessary to insert a training period which can be devoted to helping the young Indian understand himself and his racial heritage, the white races and their heritage, and the industrial culture which dominates America.

The leadership for such a training program is not going to be easy to find, for the objective in such an institution, as I see it, will be to create an atmosphere of self-analysis and curiosity which will permit the young Indian ultimately to formulate his own personal pattern without any attempt upon the part of the staff to dictate the conclusions at which he will arrive. To be effective and helpful, such a period should probably be post–high school, or, to adopt a designation which already has some acceptance, be a junior college program. High school graduates, from Indian and public high schools, who have shown leadership potentialities should be carefully selected for development. Courses in anthropology, race psychology, and comparative religions should be offered, which would enable each youngster to compare himself and his tribal group with other races or groups. He would then learn that cultural, racial, and religious differences are common among the races of men, and that differences therefore are not necessarily stigmata of inferiority.

Indian history and the present legal status of Indians should be thoroughly investigated. English should be taught by someone with an unusual facility for enriching and vitalizing the study of language, so that a young Indian after two or three years in such an atmosphere would be thoroughly at home both in understanding and expressing himself in English. At the same time opportunity should be given to study effective transposition of ideas from English into native Indian languages. Science would have an important place in such a program, not in its quantitative aspects, but as a way of thinking, and in its historic influence upon white culture and civilization. For the student who has need for it, there should be an opportunity to gain some insight into mathematics and possibly one or two other disciplines, but the place allotted to these would be minor.

After two or three years, students from such an institution might return to their own areas to follow a vocation learned in high school, or might go on to college. Careful guidance would determine professional study and the institution selected for further work. While such a program would not be guaranteed to answer all of our needs for leadership, it should at least produce a group of emotionally well-adjusted young people who are aware of the serious problems confronting their tribal groups. So far this proposal has not even entered the blueprint stage. It is submitted here for analysis and discussion just as it has been among employees of the Indian Office and leaders of the Indians. If it weathers criticisms, more effort will be made to give it reality in the developing education program of the Indian Office.

Congress Suggests That Schools Promote Assimilation, 1944

Education of Indian children.—In large part, the eventual liquidation of the Indian problem and the dismantling of the Indian Bureau depends upon the degree of success achieved in the proper education of the Indian children. . . . The real hope of eliminating the need for an expensive and extensive Indian Bureau at some future date lies in the universal and judicious education of the Indian children.

One hopeful sign on the horizon is the fact that your committee found an almost universal desire among adult Indians that their children should receive proper education. Less hopeful, however, are some of the results presently being obtained under the heading of "Indian Education."

By and large, the physical equipment of Indian schools is in good condition and is fully as adequate as that provided white children in adjacent areas. Likewise, the teachers in the Indian Service are as amply if not better paid than similar teachers in the schools of white citizens. On certain reservations, however, inadequate school facilities still exist.

The inadequacies existing in Indian education grow out of such factors as the following rather than from inadequate school equipment and insufficient teachers: (*a*) Irregular and indifferent school attendance on the part of many Indian children; (*b*) inferior and impossible home conditions to which many Indian children are compelled to return after school hours and during the summer vacation; (*c*) courses of study which fail either to equip an Indian child to practice, successfully, a vocation or to inspire and equip him to seek higher education; (*d*) a tendency in many reservation day schools to "adapt the education to the Indian and to his reservation way of life" rather than to "adapt the Indian to the habits and requirements he must develop to succeed as an independent citizen earning his own way off the reservation"; (*e*) inadequate opportunity for Indian students to secure standard high-school education and training in junior and senior colleges or universities so that the Indian

U.S. Congress, House of Representatives, Select Committee to Investigate Indian Affairs, *An Investigation to Determine Whether the Changed Status of the Indian Requires a Revision of the Laws and Regulations Affecting the American Indian,* 78 Cong., 2d sess. (1944), Report No. 2091, pp. 8–10. This document can also be found in Robert Bremner, ed., *Children and Youth in America: A Documentary History* (Cambridge, Mass.: Harvard University Press, 1974), III: pp. 1717–1719.

can develop talented leaders of his own race and so that able Indian students can enter the professions or secure advanced vocational training.

To stimulate and improve Indian education so that greater results may be secured from the sizable sums now being spent for it, your committee makes the following recommendations:

(1) All reservation day schools in the lower grades should be so operated that their eighth-grade graduates are eligible to enter standard 4-year accredited high schools on or off the reservation. All Indian high schools should be so operated that their twelfth-grade graduates are eligible to enter the State university and the colleges of the States in which they are located, or advanced vocational or agricultural schools.

It is not the thought of your committee that all Indian youths will go through high school or that all Indian students should attend colleges or universities but we do feel that their elementary training should be at a level which will enable those who have the aptitude and desire for higher training to acquire it.

(2) Compulsory school attendance should be enforced on every reservation either by the Indian Bureau officials, tribal officials, or public school officials operating in cooperation with Federal authorities. It cannot have anything but an unwholesome effect upon America as a whole if large groups of Indian children continue to grow up in ignorance through the failure to enforce compulsory school attendance regulations.

(3) The goal of Indian education should be to make the Indian child a better American rather than to equip him simply to be a better Indian. The goal of our whole Indian program should be, in the opinion of your committee, to develop better Indian Americans rather than to perpetuate and develop better American Indians. The present Indian education program tends to operate too much in the direction of perpetuating the Indian as a special-status individual rather than preparing him for independent citizenship.

(4) Scholarships, student loan funds, and other educational stimuli should be provided so that Indian students will attend institutions of higher learning in greater numbers. One of the disappointing features of our Indian education record is the fact that so small a percentage of Indian students ever graduate from high school to say nothing of attending or graduating from colleges or universities.

(5) The Indian Bureau is tending to place too much emphasis on the day school located on the Indian reservation as compared with the opportunities afforded Indian children in off-the-reservation boarding schools where they can acquire an education in healthful and cultural surroundings without the handicap of having to spend their out-of-school hours in tepees, in shacks with dirt floors and no windows, in tents, in wickiups, in hogans, or in surroundings where English is never spoken, where there is a complete lack of furniture, and where there is sometimes an active antagonism or an abysmal indifference to the virtues of education.

If real progress is to be made in training the Indian children to accept and appreciate the white man's way of life, the children of elementary school age who live in violently substandard homes on reservations should be encouraged to attend off-the-reservation boarding schools where they can formulate habits of life equipping them for independent citizenship when they reach maturity. . . .

ESSAYS

The first essay, by Elliott West of the University of Arkansas and author of *Growing Up in the Country* (1987), reflects scholars' growing interest in the history of children. Focusing on the children of white settlers on the plains frontier, West uses the experiences that western children recorded in their memoirs and autobiographies to challenge traditional interpretations of western settlement and childhood in the late nineteenth century. In the process, he also calls attention to the emergence of a "generation gap" much earlier than has been generally supposed.

In the second essay, an excerpt from Sarah Deutsch's 1987 book, *No Separate Refuge*, University of Arizona historian Deutsch examines the central place of women in the Hispanic families of the American Southwest at the turn of the century. Shifting the focus of scholarship from Anglo-American pioneers to Hispanic villagers, she questions stereotypes of Hispanic women as secluded and oppressed and presents them instead as both independent of and integrated into the larger community.

In the third essay, Katherine M.B. Osburn of Tennessee Technological University, who has written about Native American women in her 1998 book, *Southern Ute Women*, explores the changing and contested meanings of manhood for Ute Indians under the reservation system. Using Ute fathers' correspondence with and concerning their children in the early twentieth century, she calls attention to the ways in which Native American fatherhood was conditioned by the program of assimilation and by the policies of agents for the Office of Indian Affairs.

Children on the Plains Frontier

ELLIOTT WEST

Frances Fulton found much to impress her when she moved to northern Nebraska early in the 1880s. She marveled at the rugged and beautiful valley of the Niobrara River, with its rich grasses and occasional splash of wild roses. Less pleasant, but still remarkable, was the brutal winter wind that moaned southward out of the Dakotas. The young woman sometimes found the people of the plains as unusual as her new homeland. They lived in holes in the ground called dugouts and faced an uncertain future with a dogged optimism. And they were forever behaving in ways she would never have expected in her native Pennsylvania: "It has been a novel sight to watch a little girl about ten years old herding sheep near town, handling her pony with a masterly hand, galloping around the herd if they begin to scatter out, and driving them into a corral."

Like Fulton, many transplanted easterners noted that children seemed to live differently on the Great Plains. Just as she had, many observed that boys and girls also played prominent roles in meeting the daily needs of families on that part of the far-western frontier. Historians, however, have paid less attention to young people who came west to occupy the plains.That is a pity, for the children of the plains frontier have much to tell us about the pioneer experience and the history of American families.

Elliott West, "Children on the Plains Frontier," in Paula Petrik and Elliott West, eds., *Small Worlds: Children and Adolescents in America, 1850–1950* (Lawrence: University Press of Kansas, 1992), pp. 26–33, 35–41. Reprinted by permission of the publisher, the University Press of Kansas.

Paying attention to children of the plains frontier can teach us three broad lessons. The first concerns the pioneer conquest during the second half of the nineteenth century. The invasion of the plains—a region larger than western Europe, from the Dakotas and Montana on the north to the *llano estacado* of Texas on the south—involved a variety of forces and figures: soldiers, freighters, and merchants, land speculators, railroad promoters, and corporate kingpins. But most significant, both in numbers and in sheer impact upon the region, were the farming and ranching families who began arriving by the thousands on the eve of the Civil War.

This huge army of families began a radical transformation of vast stretches of the plains, destroying the economic base of Indian inhabitants and laying the foundation for long-term growth of population and political development. The efforts by families to begin making a living then, was the key event in the Euro-American conquest of this region. And in that grabbing hold of the land roles played by children were essential.

In describing the economic conquest of the plains, historians typically have concentrated on the tasks of "production." This rather misleading term focuses on those labors most celebrated in descriptions by journalists and travelers, in lithographs and chromos of the day. On the farming frontier, "production" meant breaking and plowing and planting the land, caring for the crops, and gathering the harvest. As with most frontier work, these accomplishments usually are attributed to those stalwart, barrel-chested pioneer males who, we are told, were most responsible for transforming the West.

Men did take part in all these tasks, of course, but they were not alone. In most aspects of farm production, women and children also had a hand, and boys and girls had some jobs all to themselves. The initial breaking of the sod, woven thick with the roots of grasses, was difficult work typically done by men. This first assault on the land, however, left a field full of large clods and matted soil that had to be broken up. In poorer families this work was done by hand. Everyone, young and old, took part. After Linneus Rauck broke up part of his Oklahoma homestead with a borrowed plow, he and his wife each took up an axe and his three children were handed butcher knives. Together they hacked their way through several acres to prepare the soil for a garden and their first seed bed of kaffir corn. Once a field was broken, children's help was more substantial. Accounts tell of girls and boys as young as eight plowing fields in the spring. R. D. Crawford of North Dakota, who plowed his first field at eleven, later claimed to have walked thirty thousand miles behind a plow during the next dozen years. His claim, although surely exaggerated, still emphasizes an important point. The revolution in agricultural technology during these years was allowing children to take over some jobs previously done only by men. Before moving to Kansas as a boy, Percy Ebbut had seen land plowed in his native England, a heavy labor performed by full-grown men using old-style plows. But on the plains, Ebbut wrote, a boy behind a new steel-tipped plow could handle the job easily: "I have plowed acre after acre from the time I was twelve years old."

Fully capable of planting most crops, children were especially useful in the next stage—the care of the growing crops. Here, in fact, girls and boys probably played their most prominent part in pioneer production. During the long hot summer months, men often turned away from the fields to build and repair outbuildings, to fence gardens and fields, and to work in towns or at railroad construction for desperately needed cash. That left their children to protect the crops against a variety of threats. A Kansas farmwife filled her diary with similar entries, day after day, during June 1880: "The children was working in the corn field," and, "The children pull the weeds." Youngsters drove simple cultivators, or "go-devils," to throw a fresh layer of dirt against the plants and keep weeds on the defensive. They worked as living scarecrows, patrolling the fields for hours a day, disbursing the grazing cattle and horses and shooing away the whirling birds that threatened to devour the family's future. No tasks demanded a greater perseverance and outlay of time; none was more essential. For many families, the children's help was indispensable.

At harvest time the entire family typically took to the fields, racing against the coming of fall hailstorms or an early frost that could wipe out the year's effort. Boys and girls cut and shucked corn; on the eastern fringe of the plains they picked cotton. Edna Matthews remembered blistering August days of her Texas girlhood, when the rows of cotton and corn stood "like a monster" before her. "Sometimes I would lay down on my sack and want to die," she wrote. "Sometimes they would pour water over my head to relieve me." Children helped at harvesting by centuries-old techniques and by the newest mechanized methods. When wheat was cut by hand, children tossed the stalks into a wagon bed, then beat it with flails so the grain and chaff could be separated by tossing it on a winnowing sheet. When modern harvesting and threshing machines were used, children also played their parts. A boy would "turn bundles," handing sheaves of cut wheat to a man who built them into dome-shaped stacks. Next the thresher arrived. If it was horsedriven, a small girl might lead the animals around their circle, while one brother cut the bands of sheaves about to be threshed and another kept the machine cleared of straw to keep it from clogging. Haymaking was essential to the survival of herds on many ranches and stock farms. Here, too, young boys and girls were fully integrated into the tasks, both in the ancient forms of cutting and gathering by hand and in the new, mechanized methods used increasingly in the pastoral West.

So in all the labors of farm production, from sodbusting to harvesting, whatever the techniques, with the simplest tools to the most sophisticated, plains children played essential roles in their families' efforts to transform the country and to make it pay.

But this was only the start of the youngsters' contributions. The work of production was possible only because of a wide range of other work, much of it highly productive in its own way. In this, the "subsistence" side of the family economy, the role of girls and boys was if anything even more important.

Most obviously they helped in preparing and caring for the gardens that provided much of the family's food after the first year. Even before the melons and squash had matured, however, children were putting food on the table, first by a job rarely mentioned in most histories of farm life—the gathering of wild plants. The meadows and watercourses offered a remarkable bounty for those who knew how to find it. Along the creeks were chokecherries, dewberries, elderberries, creek plums, fox and winter grapes, red and black haws. On higher ground were currants, wild onions, lamb's quarters, purslane and pigweed. At times this natural smorgasbord provided most of a family's food, and in any case it gave their diet a healthy diversity. Children grew up calling these plants "vegetables out of place," and they agreed with the O'Kieffe family's policy toward weeds: "If you can't beat 'em, eat 'em."

Children put meat on the table as well. Common impressions to the contrary, grown men usually had little time for hunting. That job was left to sons and daughters, some as young as seven or eight, who stalked and killed antelopes, raccoons, ducks, geese, deer, prairie chickens, bison, wild hogs, and above all, rabbits. Young people came to love this work more than any other. Before she moved to western Kansas, the teenager Luna Warner apparently had done little of this work, but soon she was boasting to her diary of bringing down a variety of game. She accompanied friends and her father on a two-day bison hunt, and she took advantage of other situations not necessarily within the bounds of the hunter's code, once killing a steer mired in a nearby creekbed. "Hunting seemed to me the greatest sport in all creation," wrote Frank Waugh of his early years on the Kansas plains. "Compared with it, everything else was as dust in the cyclone."

There is a nice irony here. As they brought the land under cultivation, farm families liked to think of themselves as redeeming this country from the native peoples who were retreating before the advancing fields. Yet even as they congratulated themselves, they were surviving by a kind of hunting-and-gathering economy quite like that of the Indians. During those first few years of settlement, when produce from the fields and gardens was least reliable, wild plants and animals were most abundant. By bringing them in, children in many cases were supplying most of their families' sustenance.

Children, in fact, generally labored at a wider variety of tasks than either mothers or fathers. They were in that sense the most accomplished and versatile workers of the farming frontier. These jobs inevitably brought a broad range of responsibilities as well. Together, the diversity of their physical chores and of their responsibilities demanded considerable adaptability—a willingness to wrestle with previously unconfronted problems and to call on unexplored individual resources. . . .

Throughout rural America, of course, young people helped in the labors and other duties of family farms. To some extent, the story of the plains frontier is merely a variation of a larger one that includes children of Alabama sharecroppers and of New York dairy farmers. Yet conditions in Kansas and the Dakotas after the Civil War were in some ways distinctive. Pioneer families were starting from scratch, building houses and outbuildings and fences, preparing soil for cultivation, and establishing their herds. They did these jobs in a demanding country that posed unfamiliar challenges, including an erratic, highly unpredictable climate. In the more settled regions to the east, networks of relatives and time-tested neighbors often were available to help families through the many labors of the annual agrarian cycle. On the frontier, however, these systems of support frequently had been left behind. All this meant that a typical plains family was thrown back more on its own resources to accomplish an extraordinary job of work. To meet such a challenge, children were probably even more important on the frontier than elsewhere in rural America.

The children's story offers a second lesson, besides broadening our understanding of westward expansion and young people's part in it. There is an "outer" and an "inner" history of the frontier. One concerns the process of conquest and transformation of the land; the other describes how people responded to that country and to what was happening there. The emotional dimension to the western settlement is just as important as the economic, and in understanding that inner history, the children's perspective is once again essential.

In particular, the responses of boys and girls suggest how the pioneer experience helped create a distinctive generation. In some ways, of course, the children of any time and place grow up with perspectives and attitudes different from those of their parents. But the peculiar nature of the frontier experience—and the distinctive angles of vision of adults and young people—deepened and widened those inevitable generational differences.

"The West" meant one thing to adults and something else to children. Adults had grown up someplace else—whether New York, Alabama, Ireland, or China. To them, the West was the "new" country. Typically they headed west in search of the better chance, but they knew they were leaving much behind: family, friends, the millions of details that made up the familiar world of their origins. This step was usually painful. Recent books about the great westward migration have emphasized the trauma of separation, a sense of loss and dislocation that was especially acute among pioneer women. The titles of these books often make the point: *A Scattered People* and *Far From Home.*

In a sense the emotional base of these pioneers remained in the East. As their writings show, they were continually pulled between their hopes and their memories, now predicting a glorious future in the new country, now missing what they had put behind them. On the trip onto the plains, parents marveled at strange new sights, then longed for the spiritual solace of a familiar elm tree or an ivy-covered wall. Once settled in, mothers and fathers set out to change their new surroundings, not only for profit but also to make their world resemble the one they had left. Mothers strove to make their soddies and cabins "home like"; men lavished enormous energy on fragile maple and walnut saplings so these eastern trees might survive and flourish where nature obviously never meant them to be. These tasks were expressions of an emotional tug-of-war that parents never fully resolved. For the rest of their lives they remained psychologically disjointed.

But pioneer children, whatever other difficulties they faced, did not have to grapple with this irresolvable conflict. Growing up in the West, they felt no tug from another place. To understand the child's experience, we have to adopt a perspective different from virtually all books written about western settlement. Children did not see themselves as a "scattered people" since one must be scattered *from* someplace, and the West was the only place they had ever known first-hand. They were not "far from home"; they *were* home. . . .

Not surprisingly, these young people acquired a remarkable knowledge of this country. Only four months after her arrival in western Kansas, Luna Warner had collected and cataloged 117 plants she had found around her family's homestead. Young settlers often seemed to know their surroundings far better than their elders. The Montanan Lillian Miller would write of the coloration patterns of curlews, finches, thrushes, and swallows. She also learned scores of wild-bird calls, although she specialized in domestic fowls, chickens in particular; she claimed to be able to crow in eight different keys. Ellison Orr described the flying and feeding habits of grouse, partridges, quail, pigeons, cowlinks, and shrikes.

Children took pride in this knowledge, and often they made it clear that what they knew set them apart from their elders. Frank Waugh, who came to the Kansas plains at four, filled more than twenty pages of his memoir with descriptions and comments on plants and animals. He wrote not only of the differences between big and little bluestem but also on how compass plant could be told from rattle weed and where each stood in relation to buffalo pea, milk weed, flowering thistle, and wild aster. The adults he knew had been ignorant and uncaring about such things. His neighbor, a successful farmer, could identify only two plants: sunflowers and cockleburrs. To grown-ups, Waugh thought, "the stars above and weeds underfoot were equally nameless and therefore insignificant. Every wild plant was a weed. All wild plants, like all wild animals, had to be destroyed to make way for farms."

This exploration continued from early infancy into and through adolescence. Children were finding and naming the many parts of their world; they were also discovering what they enjoyed and disliked and were testing their own abilities. The two processes were not only simultaneous; in a way, they were the same. In that, western boys and girls were making a special claim of possession. As children shaped who they would become, they did so in a world that was in a sense becoming more theirs than their parents'.

As children grew older, much of this exploration occurred as they played with friends and siblings and performed the multitude of jobs that were part of their annual regimen. The circumstances of this work and play, like the range and variety of labors, were in some ways distinctive to the frontier. Those circumstances in turn encouraged certain traits of personality in children. The same conditions that required children to work at many different tasks—a lack of outside help in establishing a farm from scratch—often left a child working largely on his own, frequently in the great yawning spaces of the plains. . . . When Marvin Powe was nine, for instance, his father told him to find and return some runaway horses, assuming the animals were close by. In fact they had wandered miles from the ranch, and when Marvin could not find them, he just kept going, living off the land and camping for a while with some cowboys. It took him a week to locate the horses, yet his father was just starting out to look for Marvin when the boy showed up. Experiences like Marvin's suggest these sons and daughters developed a remarkable independence and self-reliance that surprised and sometimes shocked visitors from the East. In later years, at least, these children often attested to a confidence and self-respect. From traveling to supply the family's water and helping her father to build fence during her Oklahoma girlhood, Allie Wallace recalled, she first learned to know and trust her "established capability."

Yet these same patterns of interaction may have had other, more troubling results. Frontier children seem often to have grown toward adulthood with contradictions inherent in their complicated relationships with their parents, with their peers, and with the country around them. So much of their work, for instance, brought children close to their families—not always physically, but in their perspectives and emerging identities. Girls and boys necessarily knew much about the state of family affairs and tribulations; they knew well their own worth and the part they played in family survival. Yet the particulars of their work and play took them away from the homestead, often to spend hours or even days by themselves. Nine-years-old Cliff Newland was hired to haul supplies every week to cowboys in line camps, a round-trip of seventy-five miles. Cliff knew that the pay—fifty cents a day—helped him and his widowed father pay for necessities on their small West Texas ranch. The experience suggests that Cliff, like thousands of other plains youngsters, was being pulled, emotionally and psychologically, in different directions. His responsibilities and sense of worth bound him to his father; the particular actions with which he gained those feelings bred an isolation and an acceptance of separation from other people as the norm.

Many other lessons they learned seemed always to be bumping into each other. A lot of their work and play taught them to be independent, to rely on their own devices, and to move easily and confidently among adults. At the same time, their parents, especially their mothers, were trying to rear them by Victorian values, and these values told them that childhood was a precious time that should be prolonged as much as possible, that they should spend most of their time under their parents' close watch, that they should defer to their elders' opinions, and that they should step into adult roles only gradually. It must have been confusing.

Growing up western could be especially troubling for girls on their way toward womanhood. As children, they were expected to spend much of their time laboring at jobs typically assigned to men—plowing, planting, harvesting, hunting, herding. They often came to identify with this work. Even when they complained of its hardships, they usually enjoyed its freedom of movement, and they took pride in its highly visible accomplishments—the transformation of the land that was celebrated so lustily at the time.

Often they identified less with their mothers' labors, those essential, complex tasks of the household. Sometimes they resented it. Edna Clifton's mother used to tell her of her own girlhood in Tennessee, where she had spent much of her time sewing, cleaning, cooking, and tending the baby, chores impeccably feminine by the standards of the day. Edna, who spent her time herding, weeding, hunting, gathering fuel, and hauling water, was irate: "I thought my grandmother must have been the meanest woman in the world." The Oklahoman Susie Crocket, with her several brothers, supplied much of her family's income by trapping, then curing and selling the hides. Once, when she found a wolf in her trap, her brothers taunted her, saying she would have to ask for their help. "I won't," she said; then she beat the animal to death with a tent pole. She recalled all that with some affection, but she said, "I hated to see Ma come in with a big batch of sewing, for I knew it meant many long hours sitting by her side sewing seams." It was unfair, she wrote: "I could help the boys with the plowing or trapping, but they would never help me with the sewing."

Then as they entered adolescence these girls received very different messages from their parents and elders. They had earned their confidence and their "established capability" by doing certain kinds of labor; they had gained a sense of themselves by confronting and learning from the country around their homes. Now they were told to put behind them the work and play they had known so long and to concentrate instead on jobs traditionally assigned to women: domestic tasks of rearing children and keeping the house and its immediate environs. They were told, quite literally, to come indoors. The result, naturally, was a dissonance between these women's pasts and futures. Some of these young women made this transition willingly; some did not.

Such contradictions—and other aspects of the inner history of frontier childhood—were not necessarily unique to the developing West. Certain tendencies among plains children, however, were accentuated by the special conditions of pioneer life: an identification with a new physical environment, the range of work and responsibilities, and the isolation in which much of that work took place. The resulting traits of personality may have contributed in turn to the formation of a distinctive regional character. During the late nineteenth and early twentieth centuries, as plains communities matured and political and social institutions took root, these boys and girls would mature to become many of the area's political and economic leaders, its farmers and ranchers, its housewives and schoolteachers, its drifters and crooks. Studying the emotional development of plains children can help us trace and define the emergence of the modern West.

The distinctive nature of plains childhood suggests the third lesson that these young people can teach us. This lesson concerns the history of American families generally and in particular the ways that history has often been oversimplified. Much has been written lately about the family, childrearing, and the relations between parents and their daughters and sons. Historians have given particular attention to the generations of the late nineteenth and early twentieth centuries, the same years in which much of the plains was being invaded by westering pioneers. Supposedly, American childhood was "reconstructed" during those decades, to use one scholar's word. Specifically, parents were encouraged to exert more control over the particulars of their children's lives. In the home, which was seen as a haven in a corrupted world, mothers especially were to use their superior virtue to nurture the nobler sensitivities of sons and daughters. Away from the hearth, public schools were to encourage those same higher values and to instill respect for dominant political and economic institutions.

Essential to this "reconstructed" childhood was an orderly, controlled introduction of young people into adult society, and vital to that was the withdrawal of children from America's workplaces. Only then could youngsters be shielded from adult vices and be tutored properly in personal and civic virtue. Besides, in an increasingly industrialized world of specialized, often highly technical occupations, a young boy or girl simply had less to offer. These changes were basic to the making of the contemporary ideal of the "child-centered" family, in which parents dedicate substantial time and resources to the careful, choreographed upbringing of the "economically useless child."

This scenario is familiar to every student of American social history, and properly so. It is crucial in understanding the system of values and expectations in which both children and adults have come to live during this century. But this story of childhood's "reconstruction" is much less helpful in describing the ways most American families in fact have lived. In the first place, its focus is less on behavior than on goals—those of proper childrearing—as expressed mainly by social and educational reformers. On the question of how closely parents actually lived by these ideals, most examples have come from upper-middle-class families in towns and cities of the northeastern quadrant of the forty-eight contiguous states. In short, the story as now told essentially describes a rather small minority of Americans and the ideals to which they aspired.

Nothing close to a full picture of American children will be possible until we apply general notions—in this case that of a thoroughgoing remaking of childhood—to the many settings of national life. On the plains frontier many parents did seem to embrace such new ideals as a concern for youngsters' moral development, especially as directed by mothers and such public institutions as the common school. But these ideals were continually colliding with the necessities of life on this fringe of an expanding national economy. Most pioneer families faced a dilemma: They would have to take on the increased burden of labor associated with starting farms from scratch, yet the move west often left them with fewer resources and less help to meet the demands of the day. Given this situation—and the fact that most of the essential work of pioneer farming was within the children's abilities—most parents relied heavily on their sons and daughters in dealing with their load of labor. Far from being withdrawn from the workplace, children were, if anything, involved in a broader range of labor than their parents. Some of that work was done close to their parents, but much was not. That meant mothers and fathers were in no position to oversee closely how their girls and boys passed their days, to guide with much precision their steps into adulthood. Other frontier conditions—the high rate of mobility among its people, the newness of its shallow-rooted public institutions, its legendary vices often openly displayed—further complicated the task of implanting modern ideals of childrearing. As a result, plains children grew up shaped by a confusion of influences that reflected both emerging national values and the peculiarities of their place and time.

Surely the same general observation could be made of children elsewhere. Families of the rural South and in urban immigrant neighborhoods of the Northeast and Midwest also relied on their youngsters' wide-ranging labors, but other conditions set those places apart from pioneer settlements of Kansas and the Dakotas. Life in all these places, furthermore, differed from that in Maine lumber towns, in Hispanic villages along the Rio Grande, and in well-to-do suburbs of Atlanta. Always a nation of dazzling diversity, the United States was experiencing some of the most profound changes of its history—great tidal movements of population, a prodigious industrial expansion that revolutionized national economic life, a splintering and reformation of class lines, and a blurring and refocusing of social distinctions. Seldom has so much in the lives of so many Americans changed so rapidly and in so many different ways.

The lesson for anyone trying to reconstruct the lives of children is clear: Be careful. Generalizing about the history of children, based mainly on the experiences of the boys and girls of one social class in one part of the country, tells us as much (or as little) as looking at the history of the United States entirely through the eyes of adults. The identities of plains children—their behavior and characters, who they were and who they became—all reflected in some ways the peculiar settings in which they found themselves. The same could be said of their cousins throughout the United States. Only when that diversity is recognized can we begin to bring children fully into the American story.

Women, Work, and Community in Hispanic New Mexico and Colorado

SARAH DEUTSCH

Looking back on a New Mexico village of the early twentieth century, Luisa Torres recalled:

> I watched my maternal grandparents a lot. . . . On the day that my grandmother was seventy, I saw her open the doors of her little adobe house. It was a spring day and there were millions of orange and black butterflies around the corn plants; my grandmother ran towards the butterflies and gathered so many of them in her apron that she

Sarah Deutsch, *No Separate Refuge: Culture, Class, and Gender on an Anglo-Hispanic Frontier in the American Southwest, 1880–1940* (New York: Oxford University Press, 1987), pp. 41–62. Copyright © 1987 by Sarah Deutsch. Used by permission of Oxford University Press, Inc.

flew up in the air, while she laughed contentedly. I wanted to know all that my grand-mother knew.

Like many grandmothers of the time, Luisa's grandmother knew particularly about medicinal plants, "remedios." But in wanting to know all that her grandmother knew, Luisa was expressing more than a desire to share in the knowledge of herbal medicine. At the southern end of the regional community, in the Hispanic heartland's communal villages, women had their own world. They had realms of expertise which served the entire village, and a society and economy that coexisted with those areas they shared with men and areas men held alone.

Nestled between mountain peaks, arid and relatively inaccessible, the villages seemed to many observers changeless and idyllic. Yet the rise of the regional community and the increasing migration of men affected relations even here. To understand the resilience of the villages, how they survived that migration and how they faced an Anglo presence not only at the edge of the region but in the villages themselves, requires a deeper understanding of village dynamics, the social organizations there, and, in particular, the activities of women. For as the men migrated, the women's world and the world of the village began to merge.

This world of village women has scarcely appeared in the historical literature of Chicanos except as overgeneralized and stereotyped images of submissive, cloistered, and powerless women. The focus has been on a rigidly patriarchal ideology, articulated only by those peripheral to or outside this world, by the Hispanic elite or Anglo observers of the time, or by later authors imposing views derived from other sites and times. Their vision and the concentration on ideology have not only distorted our view of village life, but marred our understanding of the dynamics of inter-cultural relations. Recently, authors have cast doubt on these stereotypes, exposing their roots. But the work of historical reconstruction for the period covered here is only beginning.

It is against a more concrete village background that the developments of the regional community must be seen, and that the Chicanas' and Chicanos' experiences as they moved into Anglo enclaves and cities must be judged. Only by examining this world and the gender structure of the village as it was lived, in the family, the neighborhood, religion, and work, can the impact of cross-cultural relations in the village and outside it be understood.

At the center of the family stood Hispanic women, and they dared not move beyond it, or so runs the common wisdom. According to this wisdom, sexual divisions and the separate women's world served to keep women subordinate, cloistered, and protected within the family. But the family was more complex than a woman's kingdom or her prison. An examination of village women's lives as daughters, wives, mothers, and widows reveals more subtle nuances regarding their status, even within the realm of family.

At age eight or nine, the separate women's world began. Before that, villagers expected boys and girls to behave in much the same way and share the same chores. But after their first Communion, they could dance at "bailes" and learn adult tasks. By age sixteen, girls had received enough training from their mothers or grandmothers to be ready for marriage. At this crucial stage, the village insisted on monitoring male/female relations. Unmarried males as well as females found that "almost the only recognized means of contact" outside their own homes and away from their families was the informal ritual of the village dance. Adolescent girls went out always accompanied, whether by mother, aunt, little sister, grandmother, or, later, a number of girlfriends. So between fiestas and weddings, the young men used their earnings to sponsor dances in the hope of finding a mate.

At dances, women and children seated themselves on benches around the walls, and men stood outside the dance hall except when requesting a dance or dancing. Conversation was theoretically forbidden between unmarried partners, but acquaintance from a dance could lead to a courtship conducted through furtive letters if the parties were literate, by studiously fortuitous visits with the family, or by communication through siblings. Sometimes secret engagements resulted. Even for adolescents, the distance between theory and reality permitted a degree of autonomy.

Village girls more often than boys were the targets of warning stories which depicted the dire and often supernatural consequences of walking out with mysterious strangers. But these stories did not simply reflect a double standard. They told of village mores: the young man was never a local village youth, the girl was always in her grandmother's care. The tales reveal as much about expectations for village boys and the trials of elderly widowed grandmothers raising none-too-submissive young girls, as they reveal about definitions of female virtue. And reality was often more lenient. Of the family and the village, it was only Jesusita Aragon's grandmother who never forgave her the two illegitimate children Jesusita had while under her roof. The children's father escaped equal shame only because Jesusita, who did not want to marry him, refused to identify him. Marriage might, in a sense, have liberated Jesusita. After marriage, a woman might "act as she pleases," and some went to dances and traveled without their husbands, but before marriage ritualized meetings were designed to minimize potential complications and unresolvable conflicts within the village.

When a village youth decided to make a public offer of marriage, he required the consensual participation of a panoply of villagers, male and female. He had his father, or occasionally his mother, and a godparent visit the girl's parents and leave a written offer. The girl's father and mother discussed the matter and sent for the "madrina," the godmother. The madrina acted as an intermediary between the parents and the girl, who was "at liberty to accept or refuse." Women within the family were acknowledged to have a mind of their own, and not socially forbidden to exercise it. Both the boy and the girl communicated through their parents and grandparents. Age determined one's actions more than sex.

The groom or his family provided the wedding, trousseau, and reception, which helps to explain why males tended to marry later than females. But this was not a purchase of the bride by the groom's family. The bride often brought property into the marriage; the new couple was equally likely to live with the bride's as with the groom's parents, and after the wedding ceremony the "entregada de los novios" symbolized the giving of the groom to the bride's family and the bride to the groom's. The marriage created not just binary ties, but networks.

In a rigidly patriarchal society, one would expect consistent and sizable age differences between spouses, but in the villages there were no strong norms as to age difference in first marriage. Women tended to marry between the ages of 15 and 21, men between 19 and 26. But every village had women who had married younger men as well as the occasional woman married to a man twenty years older than she.

Lack of strict norms regarding age at marriage, of course, is hardly proof that marriages were not rigidly patriarchal. But there is other evidence. In the northern New Mexico and southern Colorado villages, molestation of women and wife-whipping were considered punishable crimes and cause for divorce. In 1903, for example, a Hispanic man in a Hispanic southern Colorado county was arrested merely for quarreling with his wife. Arbitrary male behavior was considered deviant; decisions, particularly major ones such as moving for work or school, or regarding the marriage of a child, were made jointly by husband and wife.

Even child-rearing, even of daughters, did not fall solely to the mother or to women. The whole family—father, mother, aunts, uncles, and grandparents—participated in bringing up the children. Fathers and grandfathers dealt with girls as well as boys not merely to discipline them, but to teach them about such things as farming and horseback riding, to tease them and tell stories, and to take them to school and town. "My grandfather," recalled Patricia Luna, "always spoke to me as a strong person, capable of doing just about anything." Living on his farm with her uncles, she said, she "used to do everything they did, work in the fields, whatever. If there was something I didn't know how to do, they wouldn't do it for me, they'd teach me." Girls growing up in this cooperative atmosphere looked forward to companionable and not rigidly hierarchical marriages.

Property relations in marriage testified to this lack of rigid stratification. That husband and wife shared rights in property acquired during marriage was the rule for Hispanic families long before it became so for Anglos, as was equal inheritance by sons and daughters. Unlike early agricultural settlers in the eastern United States, at death Hispanic men tended to leave the bulk of their property to their wives rather than to their daughters or sons. This pattern created a number of widowed females in almost every village who were more than titular heads of household. These women were listed in the census as general farmers who owned their own land and used the labor of their married and unmarried children, or planted the land themselves. This inheritance norm was strong enough for a Señora Martinez in southern Colorado to contest the disposition of her husband's estate even though in this case all the property had been in his name. She claimed a right to half the property "because," she explained in 1900, "all know that I worked as much as my husband and spent less than he and our son. My husband always told me that for my work half was for me, that it was not owed me except that I had earned it." Women who pulled their own weight economically in these Hispanic families expected the fact to be acknowledged in tangible as well as intangible ways.

When women did enter marriage with their own property, particularly women who were better-off than average, they often quite consciously kept the property separate from their husband's and managed it themselves. John Lawrence's Hispanic wife let her sheep out on partido contracts separately from his sheep, and Cleofas Jaramillo noted that her "husband had borrowed the money from [her] and had never paid it back" when he died unexpectedly. Less wealthy women joined their husbands in taking out mortgages and partido contracts, but affixed their name separately. These women also participated, with or without their husbands, as heirs in land-grant litigation. And one woman, "of her own separate means," added a few hogs and chickens valued at $150 to an estate the total value of which was only $700. A married couple's identity of interest was a desirable but not always assumed state in these Hispanic villages.

Even an unhappily married Hispanic woman, however, when asked why she had married, responded, "Where else could I have gone?" The norm in the villages was a household headed by a married couple. Women, even propertied women, would not want to grow old in the village alone. Marriage provided a means to integrate the individual once more into the group and to perpetuate that integration through children. In villages as interdependent for labor and subsistence as the Hispanic communal villages of New Mexico, such reinforced networking was crucial to ensure mutuality and harmony. Whether male or female, the individual found that multiplying the ties to the group increased his or her security, and remarriage after widowhood was common for both sexes.

Widowed women nonetheless engaged actively in business enterprises and defended their interests in court beyond the traditional geographic bounds of Hispanic women's activities, the village. They bought, homesteaded, or rented land, or entered and continued business on their own or with their children. As widows, their role as head of the family made the enlarged scope legitimate. Since these women had often retained the management of their own property throughout their marriage—unlike, for example, the colonial New England farm wives described by Laurel Ulrich—what was new was less the nature of the activities than their occasional location outside the village.

Widows were not the only women who broke the bounds of women's usual behavior with impunity. So, too, did midwives. Indisputably in the women's realm alone was childbirth. And the partera, the midwife, stood at the apex of the community of women, and at the same time transcended it. As a key figure in the community she had no male equivalent and was not bound by many of the strictures which applied to male/female interactions. When the men came to fetch the partera for childbirth, none cast aspersions on her for traveling alone with a man even for thirty miles. The midwives themselves recognized a danger "because," as Jesusita Aragon admitted, "sometimes you go out when you don't know the guy who comes to get you, and you don't know if you can trust him or not. But," she concluded, "you have to go, and any hour night or day." Both men and women realized the village relied on children to perpetuate itself, and that in the partera's hands lay the well-being of mother and child.

Any adult woman could become a midwife, but relatively few did so, and they were never, in this period, entirely self-selecting. They tended to be middle-aged or older women, women who did not have young children to mind, who could come day or night, and whose family could take care of their other work while they were gone. And they could be gone for some time. Midwives were called when labor began and stayed until the mother was settled after the birth, which might take two or three days.

Expectant women selected parteras and their selection created parteras from neighbors. The process usually began simply by a sequence of village women asking a particular neighbor for help in childbirth. They asked a woman known to be somewhat altruistic, one who did not seek the post too actively, who was trustworthy, strong, fearless, and intelligent—all considered female as well as male virtues—and, most important, who had great experience and success with childbirth.

Because of the responsibility for life involved, because of the heavy demands on one's time, and because it was never, until at least the 1920s, a full-time profession, women tended to be diffident toward the opportunity to become midwives. As they gradually realized, however, that they had been chosen—and a call to assist in childbirth could be refused only in case of physical disablement, and would be answered "regardless of time, weather, distance, and the parents' economic, marital, or religious status"—these women set about apprenticing themselves informally to other midwives, eager to learn all they could to alleviate the uncertainty and lighten the responsibility.

This was strictly a female apprenticeship, women passing knowledge to women; just as childbirth itself was restricted to the women's community, the knowledge and the personnel were defined and controlled by women alone. Older midwives were happy to pass on the responsibility, if not the authority, to the next generation. Jesusita Aragon found that the three midwives in Trujillo "were glad when I started because they were getting old. . . . And they talk to me, how to do this and how to do that."

The mode and ritual of payment were also significant and reinforced communal values. In contrast to the set fees of Anglo male doctors, the compensations "were called gifts, because they were free-will offerings," a WPA investigator discovered in the 1930s. Like curanderas (herbal healers), when the patient "asked how much was owed her—they knew she would not charge them—she would reply that it was nothing, 'just what you want to give me.'" As neither curanderas nor parteras could refuse to treat destitute villagers, the recompense varied from a value of fifty cents to a maximum of ten dollars, and was almost always in kind. The villagers never lost sight of the personal nature, the community aspect, of midwifery and health care, and except among rich and Anglicized families, the busy, impersonal, non-communicative, and very expensive doctors could not compete. As midwife Susana Archuleta explained, "you can't look at midwifery in terms of dollar signs. You have to be sympathetic." Rejecting the ability of men to make good midwives, she insisted, "delivering a baby is not just a business. It's a personal thing, a very personal thing. It's a woman-to-woman experience."

The midwife's specialized knowledge and vital function gave her a respected place in the community as a whole. It was not just that her calling exempted her from certain mores. According to one observer:

> The midwife was the only type of leader in a village community except for the men who were politically inclined, and, of course, except for the religious teachers. People would go to the midwife because there was no other leader.

For women, the midwife became "a general counselor." But the men, too, recognized her importance and took pains to assure her contentedness in the village. Mothers and fathers often chose the partera as godmother to the children she delivered, creating a multitude of connections to bind her to village families. In a communal society where illiteracy was common, respect depended on knowledge, character, and function. Parteras combined the three in high order, and although their authority had its base in the community of women, it was not limited to that community.

For almost all women, relations between sexes within the family were characterized not by rigidity and hierarchy, but by flexibility, cooperation, and a degree of autonomy. Important family decisions were made jointly, parteras' families and widows filled in for those absent, and wives managed their own property and created and per-petuated the all-important partera system. Yet family was only one facet of women's lives. Female experience even here varied according to age, marital status, and call-ing. If the calling of midwife could so affect the status of parteras in the larger society, it is clearly worth looking beyond family life to discover women's village experience and, inseparable from it, the village's social organization and dynamics.

In addition to the community of family, women shared in the larger community of the village. This wider world displayed many of the same patterns that characterized relations between the sexes in the more intimate realm of the home. As mothers, wives, and daughters, women bound the community with ties of kinship. They also, however, entered the community as women and as individuals, unmediated by fam-ily, particularly in religion and production. Indeed, women not only shared in the community, they were instrumental in creating it, socially and physically, and in sustaining it.

As girls played "comadres," or co-mothers, in the dusty soil near the house, promising to choose each other as "madrina" or godmother for their children, they pledged, as one woman recalled, "not to quarrel, or be selfish with each other." Be-tween Hispanic women, the comadre relationship was among the most significant of relations. The natural mother and the comadre, natural father and copadre, shared the parenting, but co-parents' ideas on child-raising prevailed in any dispute. They named the child, sponsored the christening, acted as surrogate chaperones, consulted on the choice of a mate for the child, and were the only witnesses at the child's wed-ding. The parents usually asked the wife's parents to be co-parents for the first child, and the husband's for the second, and then other relatives and friends. In this way, the comadre relationship created a dense network of care and obligations in the village.

Besides reinforcing close relations and fostering a special relationship between grandmother and granddaughter, the madrina relationship provided insurance. The grandmother/madrina frequently ended up raising her godchild, sometimes because the mother had died and the widowed father had married a woman who did not want the extra child, or, as one Anglo observer put it, because "the grandparents must have some children to be with and work for them in old age." From their grandmothers these girls learned such skills as healing and midwifery, and in turn they provided lifelong care and devotion. Sometimes the girls were their grandmothers' only com-panions. The madrina system worked to ensure companionship, to prevent isolation, and to provide care.

The clustered settlement pattern so chaotic to Anglo eyes further fostered the sense of neighborhood created by networks of co-parents and other relatives. It encouraged cooperative labor and aid in difficulties such as illness, and provided mutual benefits and responsibilities which "neighborhood" implied. Many married children built houses on their parents' land, often attached to their parents' house. Occasionally entire plazas or village squares were enclosed. Butchering, house raising, harvesting, and funerals became community-wide social events for both men and women.

As in other agricultural communities, however, women had more of a hand in creating the neighborhood than men did. Their daily visiting, sustaining social net-works, far exceeded that of the men. Observers in one village home counted as many as fourteen different visitors in a single afternoon. Women also maintained the links with kin in other villages; wives went on visits for weeks at a time, traveling sometimes with the whole family, other times alone.

These neighborhood and kin networks provided temporary or permanent care for children whose own parents could not support the extra mouths. They provided farm labor in case of old age, illness, or widowhood; employment (in exchange for food and services) for widowed mothers or their children, or children living with destitute grandparents; and temporary homes for children in villages with schools. In maintaining community ties, women ensured the cohesiveness of the village as well as the welfare of themselves and their families.

Women maintained the community through their participation in religion, also, although the most visible sign of Hispanic Catholicism in northern New Mexico was the widespread male religious society known as the Penitentes. The Penitentes, with their mutual benefit aspects and flagellant practices, involved the entire village, members and nonmembers, in their Holy Week rituals. While it was not their show, women were not entirely excluded from Penitente rituals. Some women performed physical penance privately or at separate times. Other women, members of Penitente auxiliaries, made Lenten meals, cleaned the moradas or chapter chapels, and cared for sick members. A third way in which women participated was in the village-wide aspects of the Holy Week's events: preparing feasts, participating in church services, and following in procession the image of Mary carried out of the church by women to meet the image of Jesus carried into the village by the Penitentes for a ritual embrace.

In Penitente functions, women acted mainly as auxiliaries, but they had their own answer to the male-dominated Holy Week. They had the month of May, which was devoted to Mary. During the month many women met daily for prayer meetings, and in some villages they gathered twice daily. Women led a procession carrying an image of Mary from house to house and conducting prayers. One Hispanic convert tried to explain to his fellow Protestants the importance of Mary among the villagers: "They need and they deeply seem to feel that need of merely a human justified and glorified person to plead their cause before God, as they dare not approach him by any other means."

The importance these Hispanics attributed to Mary provided a basis and legitimation for woman's role in what has often seemed a male-dominated church. Where the tangible symbol of that male dominance, the priest, appeared monthly at best, there was little to enforce a subordinate role for women. Indeed, in many villages a local woman, usually an older woman or one prominent for some other reason, led services in the weeks between priestly visits. Most of the villagers, male and females, attended. Religion in the Hispanic villages was clearly the property of both sexes. While the men led the Penitente Holy Week services in the morada and Penitentes performed special funeral services for members, the women's activities sustained the ongoing, year-round church.

Women had a prominent, distinct, and organized role in religion. Their church services, their month of May, and their auxiliary functions did not set them apart from the community of men but rather provided an integrating force for the community, just as their building of networks based on kinship did. In both religion and the neighborhood, women functioned as community builders and sustainers, using the family at times, but not bound by it, and creating a central place for themselves in the community as they built it.

In their productive work, as in religion and in the family, women achieved an autonomous base and, simultaneously, integration into the village. Both mutuality and parallelism characterized the sexual division of labor here as well. Moreover, work and religion were not entirely separate. That most vital of village work, agriculture, demanded religious faith for success. In turn, such faith manifested itself through active participation in production, helping other producers, and placing God's will above one's own desires, for women as well as for men. Village religion fostered a communal ethos in production, and women played a vital role in sustaining both.

Perhaps the most fundamental work of women, the one most obviously allied to maintenance, centered around food in all its stages: production, processing, provision, and exchange. Hispanic women were responsible for the garden, a plot of irrigated land usually close to the house. As loss of land led to a decline in livestock, the garden grew in significance. Women controlled this land, and planted, weeded, irrigated, and harvested such items as melons, chili, onions, garlic, native tobacco, sweet corn, green beans, radishes, and pumpkins with or without the help of men. Often a widow who had no other land survived on the produce of her garden. Where families owned a few goats and chickens, these too fell under the care of the women or the children under their supervision, and produced eggs and milk from which women made cheese. The garden provided Hispanic women with an autonomous base, a source of subsistence independent of but not in competition with men. In addition, women's participation in the essential production phase of food—though they also helped process men's crops and livestock—legitimized their participation in ownership and minimized status differences between sexes.

Sometimes there was little to harvest. As two anthropologists cogently explain, "During years when late frosts killed spring blossoms people didn't eat fruit. During years when insects or other causes diminished the crops or decimated the herds, people didn't eat much of anything." The uncertainty of harvest underlined the actual as well as the ritual significance of produce for the villagers and the vital role of its distribution in ensuring village harmony.

The effort and time involved in processing, the vagaries of the harvest, and the love of the land which had produced it for generations, as well as its life-giving properties, imbued food at times with a symbolic significance. Cooking was usually simple. Once the foods were all milled or dried, a single pot of beans, vegetables, and occasionally meat would be put on the fire and would serve as the day's meals. On special occasions, the women gathered to bake bread. It was not the cooking itself, but what women did with the food after it was cooked that mattered. During Holy Week in particular, when the women were preparing feasts, "little girls had to carry the trays of food to many houses and bring others back before they could eat their dinner." Observer Olen Leonard found it was "a day when homemakers vie with one another in the preparation and exchange of food." But this was no mere rivalry in housewifely tasks. Sociologist Antonio Goubaud-Carrera revealed that "exchange, borrowing, and sharing of food among members of the extended family and friends is a definite and important means making for the integration of the society." The significance went even further than village integration, however, and involved the definition of female virtue, as is best revealed by a Hispanic mid-wife's story.

The midwife had come to deliver a child and found the labor lasting an unusually long time. Exhausted, she went to borrow something from a neighbor and there discovered the apparent reason for the difficult birth. It seemed the woman ate her meals standing in her doorway, but gave nothing away. Children who were hungry asked for bread and stood watching her eat, but to no avail. The midwife concluded that the mother was so stingy the child did not want to be born to her, so the mid-wife took the woman's wheat flour (considered a luxury and kept for feast days) and made a large number of tortillas. Then she had the mother-to-be call in all the children she could find and dispense the tortillas with her own hands. The child was finally born, and the woman became very generous.

Food was a woman's own product, the disposal of which she controlled, and her treatment of it defined her character both as a woman (one worthy to be a mother) and as a member of a communal village. Men could and did share their butchered meat with their neighbors, and their field produce with those who helped harvest and with those in need. As individual participants in the same community, women and men shared a set of values in regard to production and distribution, and female as well as male virtue required this generosity and degree of selflessness. Women did not enter the community simply as wives whose place there depended on the behavior of their husbands. They entered as producers, and it was in part through the distribution of their own produce that they held a place in their own right.

This definition of virtue did not preclude either the men of the women from producing food for exchange. One woman "sold" her cheese "to the village people who did not have cows or goats of their own." She sold it within an informal women's network; mothers sent their children for it and bought it "not for money, but traded" for "flour, cornmeal, and sometimes a bar of home made soap." In addition, women paid church dues with hens and, when they could, children's schools fees with their produce. Trading for cash, however—outside the village almost by definition and certainly outside a woman's network—usually remained in the hands of either married men or widows.

The allocation of dealing with outsiders to men was at least in part a legacy of bad roads, inadequate transportation, and women needing to stay near their children in the village. Just as women processed some of men's produce, men sold some of women's cash crops, such as chili peppers or goat kids. But food remained distinct from other products, and there were separate requirements for its legitimate sale. It was more like village land, whose preferred buyers were always relatives, than like, for example, weavings or sheep. A woman from Cordova rejected the opportunity to sell her homemade ice cream through a local merchant. "It would be dishonest to sell food you make in your home for profit at a store," she explained, and her husband concurred, "she is right, because to make food is part of our life as a family and to start selling that is to say that we have nothing that is *ours* . . . better to have less money and feel we own ourselves, than more and feel at the mercy of so many strangers." Exchange for trade, even sale for cash by the producer, retained the intimate connection between producer and subsistence-product and retained the producer's control over that product, but by introducing a middle-man, one lost control of one's virtue. Women's production of food, like women's creation of neighborhood, was thus both inbued with the communalism of the village, and vital to it.

Women had a hand more literally, also, in the construction of the community. While men made adobes and built the basic structure of the houses, women plastered them each fall, inside and out, with plaster made by mixing burnt and ground rock with water, and they built their own fireplaces and outdoor ovens. Plastering was usually a communal event, both for individual homes and for community structures. In 1911 at Embudo, New Mexico, forty women joined together to plaster the new school and build two fireplaces. In 1901 at San Pablo, Colorado, the village women working on the church divided their services among child care, kitchen work, and plastering. This was not work strictly within the home, nor work strictly for their own family. Plastering involved women as members in their own right of a larger community, in a service which required work both inside and outside the home, and it allowed them a share in shaping the village environment.

Much of this women's economy of production and exchange has remained invisible to historians, made so less by its unsalaried and often informal nature than by male recorders and census takers. It is highly significant that in the 1910 census for Rio Arriba County, whereas male or Anglo female enumerators listed ten females with occupations for every one hundred males in communities they covered, Sophie Archuleta, a public school teacher in Truchas whose father was a general farmer, whose mother was a seamstress, and whose sister and brother performed labor on the home farm, listed seventy-nine females with occupations for every one hundred males. To Hispanic women, their own work was highly visible and, in terms of value, on a par with that of the men.

But even the basic outlines of acceptable women's work had always depended more on the composition of the family than on sexual norms. Anthropologists Paul Kutsche and John Van Ness noted that within the household, tasks were divided by sex and age "in a marked but not rigid fashion," adding that "the division of labor is not absolute. If age and sex distribution in a family, or illness, or jobs away from home, makes it inconvenient to go by custom, then anyone does anything without stigma." Men could wash, cook, and iron; women could build fences, hoe corn, plant fields, and herd and shear sheep. In Chimayo, the men usually did the carding of wool, the women spun, and both wove. Prudence Clark recalled visiting a house in Chimayo in 1903 where, while twelve women sat spinning, in the adjoining room the men smoked, gossiped, and looked after "the little people." The women, too, would stop occasionally "and have a smoke." As men increasingly migrated for labor, both women's work and the traditional, flexible sexual division of labor were increasingly exploited, and their prior existence eased the transition to a migratory community whether or not the norms changed.

Both Anglos and Hispanics noted the relatively rapid spread of "bedsteads, tables, chairs, sewing machines, and cooking stoves" into Hispanic homes between 1880 and 1900, and that the men's newly available wage labor paid for it. They noted the technological cross-cultural contact, but gave less notice to the concomitant extension of women's work. Not the new technology but the patterns of the regional community it signified, extended the women's world and strained its usual patterns and mores in ways both similar to and different from the strains placed on the migrating men.

That women often enjoyed the new technology, in particular the cookstoves, is not in dispute. In 1901, two women were sufficiently attached to a single cookstove to bring the case to court. But the alterations in women's labor were not limited to their work within the home. In most villages, the women's gardens lay closer to the home than the men's grain fields did, so that the women could tend the children and the garden at one time. When the men left the village for wage labor each spring, gathering at the local store with their families and bedding and departing "moist-eyed" for the railroad station, the women were left with the care of the men's crops. In the 1930s, Cordova resident Lorin Brown reflected back on this "new order":

> There was no abandonment of the land; rather a new order saw the women taking charge of the planting of crops aided in part by their children and men too old to seek work outside the valley. . . . During the long summers, the women tended their gardens and fields with perhaps more care than even their menfolk might have done.

When the men returned with the summer's wages, they found they needed to purchase only sugar, coffee, salt, and possibly some white flour and clothing. Women were moving from a shared position at the village center as village producer, to sole tenancy of that position.

Not everyone found that ends met easily. In an increasingly cash-dependent economy, some women found the new pattern required them to go even further afield, beyond adopting the men's farm work. Whether because of declining fertility of home fields, an early or late frost, loss of land, or other reasons, wives and daughters even of farmers found themselves working as seamstresses and laundresses away from home. Their cash income supplemented whatever the men's crops brought. In isolated Truchas, many of the nine out of sixteen laundresses who worked away from home were daughters and wives of landowning farmers. To an even greater degree did the wives of those wage earners (usually sawmill, railroad, or farm laborers) who had moved off the land permanently and now lived in rented housing in the villages, perform wage labor either in or away from the home.

The women who had not only joined their husbands in the new wage sector, but had moved off the land, whether from desire to live with their husbands year-round or from inability to keep up the farm alone, found their community status altered. In their new home they lived divorced from their traditionally intimate relationship with the land and what they produced on it, and often from the village itself.

Still, in all of these scenarios, though the sexual structure of work was altered, men and women retained a mutuality of production without either sex's activities becoming more critical than the other to the survival of the family and community. And, in many cases the altered patterns could be seen as perpetual "emergencies," which, like the lack of male children, legitimized departures from the norm at the same time they produced strains. In this way, new facets of women's work could alter women's place within the community while affecting their relations within marriage to a lesser degree.

Within the villages, subtle shifts occurred in the nature of women's work. For the most part plastering had been performed for exchange or as community service, though it was acknowledged as a skill if not an art. By 1910, however, census records show that some women had become professionals, making their living by plastering.

Similar trends emerged in sewing, weaving, and later, mattress-making. By 1910, Chimayo held fourteen men and twenty women whose primary occupation was weaving; none had been so listed in 1880. Women were crossing the fine line between the traditional provision of labor for others for the maintenance of community and the newer trend of providing the same services within the community for maintenance of self.

There were other departures from the communal norm which did not necessarily originate with the renewed Anglo activity of the 1880s but were exacerbated by it. For example, between 1895 and 1905, Hispanic men brought seven divorce cases and Hispanic women brought six into Rio Arriba County's district court; from 1905 to 1910, the men brought seven and the women thirteen, more than keeping pace with the increase in population. By 1913, in the court's June term alone there were fourteen Hispanic divorces; eight of them brought by men.

For both men and women, desertion was the most common reason for divorce, although at least two women brought charges of cruel and inhuman treatment, and three men of adultery. Countersuits appeared occasionally. One man in Rio Arriba County hotly denied that he had mistreated his wife, and in retaliation accused her of adultery. In Santa Fe County, another man countered his wife's claims of abandonment with his own complaints that she "continually and shrewishly quarrelled with him" and "told him that she did not care or wish to live with him any longer and that he must leave the house." Whoever brought the suit tended to get custody of the children, but only the father—as the one with more lucrative options in the wage sector—paid child support, and regardless of who brought suit, the husband usually paid the court costs.

According to the census records almost every village had at least one Hispanic divorced person, usually female, and there were frequently more. In 1910, for example, Chimayo had one divorced man and four divorced women, Coyote had four divorcées and Truchas had two divorced men and five divorced women. In rare cases, a divorced woman would live with her parents. Usually these women lived alone as heads of households with their children and occasionally a widowed mother or grandmother. The pattern did not vary remarkably for divorced men.

Sometimes the divorced women owned property. If it were a farm, and they had grown sons, life could continue more or less in its old patterns. But if it were only a house, which was far more often the case, and particularly if the children were young, the women had to enter the cash sector, which usually meant work as poorly paid washerwomen inside or outside the home. Widows and single women who had become heads of households usually had done so as property owners, with adult male wage-earners or farm labor in the house. They remained within the mutually essential sexual structure of family labor. In contrast, propertyless divorced women with young children, as limited wage earners without a land base, found themselves struggling to keep afloat in a lopsided household.

Divorce and separation were thus acceptable when either partner deviated from the norms of mutual support and respect, but such disruptions in the network of village life could not be encouraged. One woman who left an abusive husband and eventually moved to Cordova became "Tia Lupe" (Aunt Lupe), to the whole village, providing healing and counseling services and receiving fuel and other compensation, but she lived there alone. Divorced women and men may not have been shunned by the community, but neither were they fully reincorporated through, for example, a return to their landowning parents. Many parents lacked the resources to maintain the enlarged household. Instead, incorporation and survival in the community for the divorced often came to rest on wage labor or monetary relations with fellow villagers or outsiders, rather than on the communal exchange of produce and services. The plight of these families underscored the essential nature of the integration of men's and women's labor, village and cash economies, neighborhood and migration, for the survival of the Hispanic communities.

In these less than perfectly harmonious communal villages, also, lived single women with illegitimate children. In the late 1930s, Daniel Valdez commented, "this is common throughout the Valley. Every year brings a score of illegitimate babies with it. This is no more common now than it was a generation past." Illegitimacy was not the product of cultural breakdown or of a new modernism, but a long-term phenomenon of an agricultural society. But length of tradition did not necessarily mean smooth acceptance, and the increasingly dominant cash economy placed extra burdens on unwed mothers. While Ruth Barker claimed that "even the illegitimate child inherits no town censure. . . . the unmarried mother . . . [is] treated with kindness, leaving social errors to the wisdom of the confessional," there is no evidence that unwed mothers had an easier life than divorced or separated mothers. While most illegitimate children seem to have been accepted by the community, there were husbands who refused to recognize them, and mothers whose washing work could not support them or who fostered them to couples who abused them. Perhaps these are the children who fell through the social net of the northern Hispanic villages and landed in St. Vincent's Orphans' Home for girls in Santa Fe, which had forty-seven Hispanic girls in 1909, and 116 (at least 23 from Rio Arriba County alone) in 1913. Of the fifty-nine Hispanic women in the New Mexico State Penitentiary between 1884 and 1917, nine were separated wives, three were single women, and two were widows. Forty-two had been charged with sexually related crimes, including thirty-seven cases of adultery. Of the forty-two women charged, ten were laundresses, seven seamstresses, seven servants, two laborers, and one was a farmer. It is a measure of the difficulty of these women's lives that of the eight who gave reasons for their "crime," two listed desertion by husband, five claimed "necessity," and only one claimed "love."

There was another set of women who found no comfortable place in village society. These were the "brujas" or witches. Egalitarianism and communalism do not necessarily exist at the expense of individuality. Rather a broad-minded tolerance may characterize such a group, limited only by perceived threats to the village's existence. For the Hispanic villagers, broken marriages and brujas provided such threats. Divorced people and witches existed not simply as eccentric individuals, but as individuals unattached and possibly even hostile to the dense and vital network of family relations that sustained the community.

Ironically, belief in witchcraft could operate to ensure tolerance of a certain degree of eccentricity. New Mexico's Writers' Project investigators in the 1930s found that "brujas were taken for granted by all. The men as well as the women believed in brujas, and were careful not to offend anyone they were not sure of." Eccentric behavior in these cases was safest dealt with politely. As with witchcraft elsewhere, in New Mexico these beliefs also provided a forum for the relief of social tensions, as when Hispanics told Charles Briggs, "all *Indios* are witches." Witches in New Mexico could be either male or female, but they were usually female, and in a classic juxtaposition of good woman/bad woman, the color blue, associated with Mary, was used to protect against witches, while "I go without God and without the Holy Virgin" was the incantation which allowed witches to fly.

According to historian Marc Simmons, it was only after Hispanics realized that the United States courts would not hear witchcraft cases that vigilante-style reprisals occurred. In 1884, a woman near Chimayo "was taken from her lonely adobe hut by three roughs . . . and murdered," apparently for suspected dealings with the devil; and in 1882 a woman from Abiquiu was whipped until near death by the henchmen of her supposed victim. Those suspected of witchcraft in the villages tended to be older women, usually of somewhat mysterious origins, women, whether widowed or never married, who lived alone with few if any kinship ties to the villagers. The village women's fear of growing old alone which led them to adopt and foster small children thus had far more than economic or even affectional roots, and the loss of ties to the village had more than economic consequences.

Some of these village tensions were less a sign of cultural breakdown or even of the adjustment to the new economic context than a witness to the perpetual distance between the ideal aspired to and the reality in any society, and to the perceived fragility of the corporate community. They represented the ways in which villagers had long dealt with elements that threatened the family economy and communal virtues, elements potentially too disharmonious to incorporate safely into their small mutually dependent society of one hundred to five hundred people. Into this pattern of dealing with village tensions they thrust the newer tensions, the potential problems, caused by the adaptation to the regional community and the Anglo-dominated larger economy: the professionalization of former services, the cash-dependent widows. As they held the disruptive elements of Anglo society at bay, beyond the village, the villagers also relegated their own disruptive elements, including witches and divorcées, to the village periphery if not beyond.

At the orderly center of the village, on the other hand, lay a closely knit community of women. It encompassed informal hierarchies of skill, age, knowledge, and spirituality, and it fostered communal virtues. Women's social existence was not cloistered, not limited to the home and family or even to the community of women, nor did they participate in the village solely as wives, mothers, and daughters. They performed communal labor and religious services for the entire village, work that took them out of the house, as well as autonomous labor in the garden and in the home. In the northern New Mexico and southern Colorado villages, the parallelism of Hispanic men's and women's work on the land, in religion, and in building was not competitive and stratified but mutually supporting. Neither men nor women were as effective economically on their own as they were together. Yet neither was powerless or completely dependent.

The rise of the regional community had not placed women at the center of village life. They were already there. But it did create a situation where they held that spot increasingly alone. Others have commented on the autonomy and power of women in primarily subsistence economies with small-scale exchange. Anthropologist Alice Schlegel has explained, "each sex in any society has primary control over certain activities, and the rewards and power accruing to each sex depend upon the centrality of these activities to the society as a whole." In a village increasingly divided into village women and migrant men, women's activities sustained the community physically and spiritually. The integrative function of women in the village grew in importance, and more frequently women provided the continuity for the village, as they did for the church during the absences of the priest. As women's work was not limited to hidden and reproductive work in the household, the work of both sexes remained visible and essential to subsistence itself. That the Hispanic village as a whole, not just the women, acknowledged the equally vital nature of men's and women's work was attested by property-holding and -use practices, marital and inheritance norms, and religious practices, which recognized and perpetuated women as autonomous beings.

The men's purview of external affairs included not just the cash sector and migrant labor, but Anglos, investigators or tourists, who came to the village. Most likely it was this allocation of external affairs to men which led to the first distortions in depictions of village sexual structure. This division of labor meant that when Anglos dined at Hispanic village homes, they ate with the men while the women and children ate later, whereas when the family was alone they usually all ate together. It also meant that virtually all impressions of Hispanic society received by Anglos were received through Hispanic men, who naturally had a stake in creating an image for themselves acceptable to Anglo notions of gender and to whom, most likely, it would not occur to volunteer information about the women's world. This is brought out particularly in obvious gaps in some sociological literature. Olen Leonard, for example, places the labor of the woman firmly in the home, ignoring her garden duties, and insists that the father "is definitely the head," handling, for example, finances and provisions for the family. But what happens when, according to Leonard himself, the father is gone from six months to a year is a question Leonard does not tackle.

The women made up the stable core of the village. The society and economy of women was inextricably linked to the ability of Hispanics to survive in their new cultural economic patterns, just as the lack of a rigid sexual division of labor allowed women to compensate for men's seasonal absences. Through their visiting, their sharing of food, plastering, childbearing, and, most important, their stability, production, and earnings as non-migrants, women provided for increasingly mobile villagers not only subsistence, but continuity and networks for community, health, and child care, for old age and emotional support. As leaders both within and outside the community of women, as churchwomen and parteras, willing to act independently and even combatively in legal struggles over property and marriage, and as property owners and producers in their own right, Hispanic village women were hardly, after all, cloistered, powerless, or even, necessarily, submissive. It was these women who would have a crucial role, not just in maintaining the larger structure of the regional community—that human network extending the ties of the village over hundreds of miles so that the village could survive—but in resisting whatever Anglo cultural threat manifested itself within the village.

Fatherhood and Assimilation
Among the Southern Utes

KATHERINE M. B. OSBURN

In pre-reservation times, when a child was born to the Ute Indians of Southwestern Colorado, the baby's father and mother lay in separate shallow troughs filled with warm ashes covered in cedar bark and green brush. The mother remained on this "hot bed" for thirty days, abstaining from eating meat and fish lest she spoil her husband's abilities to hunt and fish. The father had a four-day lying-in. At the end of this period, the newborn's grandparents (or older relatives acting as grandparents) cooked meat for the father and, as they ate, admonished him to provide for the child, blessing him to increase his prowess as a hunter. After the meal, the father went on a mock hunt lasting several days. During this ritual he ran frantically through the surrounding countryside in the exaggerated motions of a skillful hunter. This ceremony ensured that he would have the speed and endurance to be a successful provider. Ute rituals surrounding the mother and child also focused on their important productive roles and were crucial to the family's survival. These ceremonies continued for a time after the Ute people were confined to a reservation, indicating that the father's role as provider remained critical to tribal survival. Yet, by the late nineteenth and early twentieth centuries, men had lost their role as hunters and struggled to provide for their families by farming, stock raising, and wage labor.

In studying how Indians adjusted to reservations, historians and anthropologists have analyzed the public roles of Indian men. The emphasis has been on men's political behavior as they coped with the government's assimilationist programs and the degrees to which they cooperated with or resisted the government agenda for their tribes. Native American men, however, also interacted with reservation officials for more personal reasons. Among the Southern Utes, Native American men attempted to enlist the help of agents and boarding school superintendents to protect their children's health and safety in government schools. In so doing, they created a public caretaking role for themselves. Deprived of their traditional activities and identities as hunters and warriors, Ute men nonetheless created a means to continue their traditional role of family protector and provider by using new skills such as literacy. Ute men took up the pen to maintain their traditional roles of monitoring their children's progress and their health.

Historical Background

Before confinement to a reservation, the Ute Indians moved throughout the present states of Colorado, New Mexico, and Utah in seasonal migrations, hunting, fishing, and gathering berries and roots in the mountains from early spring until late summer and then moving to lower elevations for the winter. Hunting and foraging

Katherine M. B. Osburn, "'I Am Going to Write to You': Nurturing Fathers and the Office of Indian Affairs on the Southern Ute Reservation, 1895–1934," in Laura McCall and Donald Yacovone, eds., *A Shared Experience: Men, Women, and the History of Gender* (New York: New York University Press, 1998), pp. 245–251, 254–265. Copyright © 1998. Reprinted by permission of New York University Press.

groups, consisting of small groupings of bilateral extended families, tended to stay in the same areas and were thus identified as territorial bands. The entire tribe numbered about eight thousand at the time of contact with Europeans. There were seven Ute bands; the southernmost bands—the Capote, Mouache, and Weminuche—were known as the Southern Utes. The Utes acquired horses sometime in the mid-seventeenth century. Several bands then began hunting buffalo, which provided tipis, clothing, blankets, and horn implements.

Gender relations in pre-reservation Ute culture were egalitarian. Men and women participated equally in all important decisions concerning both the family and the band. Individual families acted as the primary unit of social control, settling all interpersonal disputes and violations of Ute social and moral codes. Within their families, Utes recognized a gendered division of labor, but valued the contributions of men and women equally. Men hunted, fished, butchered meat, cleared campsites, gathered tipi poles, conducted raids and defensive warfare, and made all implements for their tasks. Women gathered and processed wild plants, tanned hides, made tipis and camp household equipment, and cared for children. They also sometimes accompanied men on raids to scalp and gather loot. Although men usually directed military and communal subsistence activities, women could participate in public decision-making. Male leadership depended upon the consent of the entire group. If anyone disapproved of a collective decision, he or she was free to leave the group. Ultimately, authority within the band was based on age rather than gender, and no one had the power to coerce behavior from another. Egalitarian gender roles held even after contact with Europeans.

The United States took control of Ute territory in 1848 after the Mexican War. Beginning in 1849, the U.S. government signed a series of treaties with the Utes, creating and—as conflict occurred between Utes and settlers—continually redefining a reservation for them. In 1868, the Great Ute Treaty outlined a reservation containing about one-fourth of the Colorado Territory. In 1873, under the Brunot Agreement, the Utes surrendered six thousand square miles of their land (about one-quarter of the reservation) to the United States in return for a perpetual $25,000 annual payment. Finally, in 1880, Congress created the current Southern Ute reservation, a narrow strip of land in the extreme southwestern corner of Colorado. There, the Office of Indian Affairs (OIA) carried out a program of forced assimilation.

From 1887 to 1934, the federal government, through the OIA, used legislation known as the Dawes Act to compel Native Americans to adopt Euro-American culture. The OIA hoped to transform Native Americans into yeoman farmers and farm wives through the assignment of individual land holdings known as allotments. The Dawes Act outlawed Native American culture and established a code of Indian offenses regulating individual behavior according to Euro-American norms of conduct. Violations of the code were tried in a Court of Indian Offenses on each reservation. The plan also included funds to instruct Native Americans in Euro-American patterns of thought and behavior through Indian Service schools. The government implemented the Dawes Act on a tribe-by-tribe basis; in 1895, Congress passed the Hunter Act, administering Dawes among the Southern Ute.

An important objective of the Dawes program was to restructure Native American gender roles. The *Rulebook for the Court of Indian Offenses,* published in 1883, outlined the OIA's agenda for male gender roles. The new code of conduct prohibited feasts and dances that celebrated warrior culture because they taught children to value the warrior role. Because policymakers viewed Indian men as lazy and irresponsible, the OIA established policies to force Indian husbands and fathers to provide for their families and act as the heads of their households. Any man who failed "without proper cause to support his wife and children" lost his rations until he could prove to the Court of Indian Offenses that he would "provide for his family to the best of his ability." The OIA compelled able-bodied men to support their families through their own efforts at farming, forbidding them from leasing their lands. Procedures for establishing annuities rolls further defined the husband-father as the head of his household. "The father and head of the family will be allowed to receive and receipt for the shares of himself, his wife, and minor children." . . .

The OIA expected Indian men, as heads of their households, to place their children in schools. . . . Educational facilities available to the Ute included day and boarding schools. The OIA conducted a "boarding camp" school on the reservation from 1885 to 1890. Two Presbyterian mission schools also opened on the reservation around the turn of the century. While mission schools claimed some pupils, reservation personnel pressured Ute men to send their children to OIA institutions; in the late nineteenth and early twentieth centuries, this generally meant boarding schools. The OIA opened several schools near the reservation: the Fort Lewis Boarding School in 1892; the Southern Ute Boarding School in 1902 (which closed in 1920); the Allen Day School in 1909; and the Ute Mountain Boarding School in 1915. Because these schools did not offer instruction beyond the third grade, many Ute children attended schools out of state. One of these institutions was the Santa Fe Indian Boarding School.

The Santa Fe School: Parents and Administrators

The Office of Indian Affairs opened the Santa Fe Indian Boarding School in Santa Fe, New Mexico, in 1890. Between 1910 and 1934, twenty-seven boys and thirty-two girls from the Southern Ute reservation attended the school. Student folders housed in the National Archives from these years contain extraordinary letters from Ute parents and children to other family members and to Santa Fe and Ute Agency superintendents. The letters of Ute men to reservation and boarding school officials in the early twentieth century reveal a poignant inner world of men struggling to create a tolerable life for their children under extremely difficult conditions.

Eight Ute fathers contacted Santa Fe superintendents during this period, either by writing directly or requesting that the Ute agent write. . . . Several themes appear in these letters. Fathers communicated their desire to participate in decisions concerning their children and resonated hopes for their children's futures. They expressed sadness over their separation and continually inquired when and under what conditions the children would be sent home. Children who wrote letters either to their families or the reservation agent expressed profound homesickness. The most frequently mentioned concern of Ute fathers, however, was their children's health. Utes had lost children to disease in government schools from their establishment in the nineteenth century. Of the twenty-five Ute students sent to boarding school in Albuquerque in 1883, twelve died. When the Utes grudgingly sent sixteen children to the Fort Lewis Boarding School in 1894, three of them died and three returned home blind. This pattern continued in the early years of the twentieth century, as nine girls sent to Santa Fe between 1919 and 1925 died of either influenza or tuberculosis. Most parents who wrote to the Santa Fe superintendents, Frederick Snyder (1910–18), John D. DeHuff (1919–28), and Burton L. Smith (1928–30), had lost some member of their extended families to diseases contracted in boarding schools. Consequently, these men had great anxiety about the health of their children. When fathers heard rumors of their children's illness, they immediately attempted to have them sent home.

School and reservation administrators, however, were more likely to deny these requests than to honor them. Unless a child's illness was clearly life-threatening, superintendents generally refused to allow children to leave, despite fathers' pleas. . . . Once parents signed papers admitting their children to Indian Service schools, the school superintendent assumed the primary authority over the child. With the advice of their school physicians, superintendents decided what sickness warranted a child's leaving. In serious cases, such as tuberculosis, they often sent the children to sanatoriums rather than grant permission for them to return home. Although administrators followed this procedure in hopes of aiding the students' recovery, the decision sometimes cost a child its life. For example, in 1919, Santa Fe superintendent John D. DeHuff sent Euturpe Bancroft to the tuberculosis sanatorium in Dulce, New Mexico, where she subsequently died. In 1921, he sent Alice and Nudza Clark there; Alice recovered, but Nudza died. Parents' heartbreak at not being able to see their children before they died is a frequent theme in agents' correspondence on this topic.

School officials, somewhat sympathetic to this consideration, assured parents that they would be notified immediately should their offspring become ill. In 1920, when Southern Ute agent Edward McKean inquired after Ute pupil John Frances Taylor (at the request of his father, John Taylor), Superintendent DeHuff replied that the boy only had a cold. "You may assure this boy's father," he wrote, "that it is our invariable rule at this school that whenever any child is sick enough to warrant any feeling of anxiety or alarm upon the part of anybody, the parents or the home superintendent will be duly notified from this office." Despite these assurances, Ute parents sometimes suspected the worst if their children failed to write. . . .

[Tribal elder] Jacob Box wrote letters for his children and for the children of friends. Four of his eight children attended the Santa Fe school during this period: Marjorie, who entered school in 1917; Florence, in 1918; Ellen, in 1924; and Fritz, in 1927. A former pupil of the school, Box believed in education. In 1919 he wrote superintendent DeHuff: "We must make an honest living[.] [T]here is no choice in such a matter[,] for it is one of the common necessities and obligations of nature." Box believed this "obligation of nature" extended to girls as well as boys, saying, "I like to see my girls got [*sic*] graduates." In another letter he wrote: "The girls [will] soon be over there again. I send [Marjorie's] sister [Florence] to you this fall. [Would] [y]ou like more girls[?]" When Marjorie graduated in 1923, Box sent her to Haskell Junior College in Kansas. He proudly advised DeHuff of her progress.

> I am going to write to you[.] Marjorie B. Box [is] getting along alright at Haskell Inst[titute]. . . . I like to see my tribe['s] boys and girls try like Marjorie B. Box. I like to see so big [a] school [for] some girls [of] my tribe. I think Marjorie [will] stay [at] Haskell till [she] finish[es] over there. I am glad [to] see my daughter working [for the] Indian service.

Box also recommended the school to other Ute children and inquired after those he had persuaded to go. DeHuff praised his diligence and asked him to please "use your good influence to get more Ute pupils."

Enthusiastic for education, Box was nevertheless cautious for his children's well-being. His letters reflect his role as family protector and the assertiveness of his writing suggests confidence in dealing with OIA personnel. Almost immediately after Marjorie's admittance, Box wrote Superintendent Snyder: "If my little girl [gets] sick bad[,] send [her] home if you please[.] I forgot to tell you all about it[.] I [will] be over there some time in the Christmas day." Snyder did not reply, Box frequently asked if his children needed anything or directed the superintendents to purchase clothing. He sent money every year so that they could come home for the summer: "I am going to write to you. How is [*sic*] all my daughters getting along with her study [*sic*] [?] When school [is] out[,] you send the girls home. [N]ow you let me know when school [is] out [at] Santa Fe. You send these girls because her [*sic*] mother[']s not well[.] [H]er mother like to see the girls." Box always assured the superintendents that he would "send them back again when school opens" and, true to his word, he did, accompanying the children on several occasions. "I [let] you know we be over there in Sept. 22. Five girls and one boy [will come]. I like to see you about the girls['] matters. I am glad to see you again."

Both DeHuff and McKean seemed to respect Box, probably because of his co-operation in procuring children for OIA schools. Box's decisive letters exemplified this relationship: he knew his inquiries would be taken seriously. When Florence fell ill in March 1921, McKean advised DeHuff: "Her parents are anxious for her to return and I believe, under the circumstances, that the best interests of your school and the future cooperation of these Indians will thus be served." DeHuff suggested that Florence instead be sent to the Jicarilla Tuberculosis Sanatorium, but she insisted on going home. Unlike some other cases, DeHuff allowed Florence to go home immediately. Within one month, a telegram from McKean arrived at Santa Fe: "Florence Box very sick, the father requests you send Margaret home to leave in the morning [on] Saturday." Margaret left for home without delay, but Florence died before she got there.

Despite Florence's death, Box returned his daughters to Santa Fe, but he did not take any further chances with them. In May 1923, Marjorie took sick and Box went to Santa Fe and brought her home. Marjorie recovered and entered Haskell Junior College in the fall. In March of the following year, Ellen came down with a skin disease and Box informed DeHuff:

> I am going to write to you. To want to know about my daughter Ellen Bent Box. [H]ow [is] she getting along[?] [S]he [is] not sick[,] if she sick send her home. Mary Graves died yesterday afternoon. If Ellen [is] alright at school I am glad. One boy died from over there at Ute Mountain, Towaoc, Colo. I [would] like to hear from you soon.

DeHuff replied respectfully, asking Box "to convey an expression of my deepest sympathy" to Mary's parents, and assuring him that Ellen's condition was not serious. He informed Box that he would personally "keep close watch on Ellen's case and, if she fails to make proper progress toward recovery, I shall not keep her here." In May, Mable Spencer, a Ute student at Santa Fe, returned to the reservation due to tuberculosis and told Box that Ellen was still sick. Box advised DeHuff: "If she sick yet we [would] like to have her here at home to tak[e] care of her. Maybe she [will] get well now." DeHuff again reassured Box: "If at any time Ellen's case should take a serious turn, I will let you or Mr. McKean know promptly and endeavor to send the child home." In June, Box's anxiety over Ellen spilled over in poignant prose.

> I am thinking about my daughter Ellen[.] She never write to me for a long time[,] about three months now. [I]f she [is] sick don't . . . give her too long. I'[ll] take care of her. Because [if you] send children too late home, [they] can['t] get well. Mabel got bad again. [N]ow I want to know [to] be sure how she was now and get bad and well. God knows. Light of the world.

Although he again assured Box that "your daughter Ellen is not suffering from any dangerous skin disease," DeHuff nonetheless sent Ellen home. Apparently the intensity of Box's pleas, with their heartfelt references to Christian scripture, moved him. Ellen recovered after her return but, for undocumented reasons, never went back to Santa Fe. She instead attended the Albuquerque Indian School until her father's death in 1928.

The problem of student illnesses grew worse in the spring and summer of 1925, when five female students at Santa Fe became gravely ill. Mable Spencer (who had apprised Box about his daughter), Jane Thompson, Annie Snow, Alice Brown, and Mary Grove all died after they were sent home, Mabel with tuberculosis and the others with the flu. In the fall, Cyrus Grove, Mary's father, wrote DeHuff, frantic about his other daughter, Margaret. These letters, born of a father's grief, declared Grove's disquiet most assertively: "I am asking you if it[']s time that Margaret Grove is sick. I want to know right away if she [is] sick or not. I don't want her to get too sick or we don't want to lose her like we did Mary. [I] [w]ould like to hear from you soon." DeHuff replied that Margaret was indeed ill and he was sending her home. He telegraphed McKean to meet her train. Margaret died nonetheless, confirming her father's worry and disproving the superintendents' oft-repeated claims that they "immediately" notified the parents of any child who was seriously sick. . . .

. . . When B. L. Smith took over at the Santa Fe school in 1926, the level of cooperation between the school and Ute fathers declined. Student deaths in 1925 had frightened the pupils, who conveyed alarming letters home. Rose Thompson (sister of Jane, who had died in the flu epidemic) wrote a plaintive letter to McKean in September 1926.

> Dear sir[,]
>
> I am going to write to you and let you know how I am down here at school[.] [Y]ou, know[,] Mr. McKean[,] I am going to let you know I am very lonesome and I always think of home and I want to go home[.] [Y]ou know how lonesome this school is and I want to go home and when the girls get sick here and get [sore] when they go home and die[.] I am not going to do that and die[.] [P]lease Mr. McKean[,] send for me[.] I know [the students] always get blind when the children that [*sic*] get sick and die when they go home[;] and I want to go home[.] I must close here[.]
>
> [F]rom[,] Rose Thompson

McKean requested information but Superintendent Smith answered dismissively, "Rose is homesick. She has a very pronounced case of the itch and has been regularly treated in the hospital ever since this was discovered." Smith saw no reason to allow Rose to return home. . . .

Similarly, Mary Baker's request to return to the reservation was dismissed as mere homesickness. Julian Baker, a tribal leader, began asking for his daughter's return in September 1928 when she advised him of her illness. He had the Southern Ute agent, W. F. Dickens, inquire after Mary's health. Dickens assured Smith that this was not an idle request. Baker, he noted, "is a very good Indian and anxious for her to go on with her studies." Smith replied that there was "not a word of truth in [Mary's] statement that she is not well" and said that she was "just homesick." This answer did not satisfy Baker, however, and he sent Smith a letter on October 3. Like Jacob Box, Baker wrote forcefully, explaining to Superintendent Smith exactly what he wanted him to do: "Am dropping you this letter to let you know that I want my daughter Mary to come home." He included a check to cover Mary's travel expenses and instructions concerning what hotel to use on the journey. Smith answered that there was "no reason whatever for Mary to go home. She is just homesick and will get over it—hundreds of students do." Dickens urged Mary to stay, as did Mellie Daniels, matron at the Southern Ute Boarding School at Ignacio, Colorado. Daniels sent Mary a cheerful letter asking her to "try to feel good about it all if you can." All the OIA personnel seemed united to keep Mary at Santa Fe.

Baker, however, was tenacious. He wrote twice in late October and both times Smith again replied that Mary was "doing quite well." He asked Baker to please write her letters encouraging her to stay. Annoyed, Baker wrote again on November 14.

> I am going to write to you again for the third time to ask you again to send my girl Mary back to home. . . . I have been to Mr. Dickens so many times and I don't want to bother him so much and one thing that I don't want to do is write to you so many times. Because you might say what is the matter with me. I am very sorry for her even that it was I who sent her to there. I am not feeling very good. So I am trying to get her back again through all you peoples so you will know that I am asking with my own mind. I made up my mind to let her be send [*sic*] back to home. So I am going to look for her this week and I want you to let her come home and start from there on Saturday. . . .

On December 6 Mary was still in Santa Fe, and Baker's next letter became pleading:

> Please send Mary to home. I hear she is very sick and I am very anxious and so I wish that you let her come home please do that please let her get on the train Saturday so that she get[s] home on Sunday. And [she will] go [to] school here on Monday.

. . . . On December 26, Smith finally conceded that Mary had contracted the flu. Although her illness was "not serious," they were sending her home as soon as they deemed it safe for her to travel. On January 3, 1929, Baker expressed his irritation with the OIA. "I am sorry to hear that my girl is sick and that is why I always try to get her back home before she gets worse. Because she was not very strong. I will wait for her on Saturday." The very next day Baker . . . sent another letter declaring his intention to get Mary himself, fearing that she was not strong enough to travel alone. "And I hope I will find my girl in good condition," he warned, and "I don't want to wait long for her. I want to see her as soon as I can." Baker retrieved his daughter, who eventually recovered and never returned to Santa Fe. . . .

While their children attended the Santa Fe Boarding School, Ute fathers monitored their children's lives and attempted to look out for their best interests. Responding to their children's letters or to reports about their offspring, these men made their wishes known to the school superintendents. In encouraging education, they sought to provide for their children's futures. In requesting their return upon hearing rumors of illness, they also sought to protect their children from epidemic diseases. While their behavior might be expected from a concerned parent in any culture, it may also be viewed as a continuation of their traditional roles as protectors and providers. Reflecting the complicated nature of acculturation, however, Ute fathers combined traditional parenting roles with government farming programs. Any analysis of their behavior and their ability to fulfill their parental goals thus requires sorting out several complex variables. What does the interaction of Ute men and school officials disclose about the process of assimilation and the ability of administered peoples to retain a measure of autonomy over their families?

The eight Ute fathers in this sample represent some of the more "assimilated" Indian men at Southern Ute reservation. All were farmers, cultivating anywhere from 10 to 160 acres. Jacob Box, Robert Burch, and Joe Price were on the 1909 "honor roll," giving them the right to lease their property without agency supervision. Julian Baker was such a successful farmer that in 1932 agent Edward Peacore chose him to testify on Indian farming for a Senate subcommittee on Indian affairs. Moreover, they were stable husbands and fathers. Although this stability in itself is not an indicator of assimilation, it happened to correspond with the OIA agenda. Of the eight, only one, the former slave John Taylor, was separated (and that was due to his wife's actions); six remained married to the same women for the entire Dawes period, and one was widowed and remarried. Several of them were educated and all were anxious for their children to attend school. They were, to the best of their abilities, meeting the government's expectations of them as heads of their households and as fathers. . . .

. . . Both the OIA and the Utes viewed fathers as protectors and providers. Yet, in the larger context of the reservation, fathers' power to help their children was circumscribed by the government. For all the OIA rhetoric about training Indian men to assert leadership and assume responsibility for their families, agents and boarding school superintendents controlled these children's lives. On some level, naming Indian men as "heads of their households" represented a formality that sanctioned their colonization—it was a method of bringing them into the dominant culture without giving them substantive power and responsibility. Additionally, while some anxious fathers received reassurances when their children became ill, other men's concerns were dismissed. Even when agents attended to the men's worries, they rarely respected the fathers' wishes. Ute fathers, therefore, were up against powerful political forces far beyond their control. A closer examination of Indian policy during this period reveals the conditions that limited Ute men's ability to parent effectively.

For all of their cooperation with the assimilationist agenda, Ute fathers' success in supervising their children's lives seems largely to have been contingent on the personality of school superintendents. . . . With school superintendents holding the ultimate power to direct these children's lives, Ute fathers' parenting role was severely restricted. . . .

Although the men's correspondence was usually ineffective, it provides a fascinating glimpse into the activities of Ute fathers in the early reservation years. The letters reveal Ute men to be thoughtful, caring, concerned parents who were active in their children's lives. In this, they continued their traditional domestic roles as protector and provider, and refuted the OIA's characterization of Indian men as lazy, irresponsible, and unconcerned fathers. Additionally, each of these men made a decision to help his family adjust to the changes brought about by confinement to a reservation. He accepted the new role of farmer and recognized the necessity of education for his children. Thus, each embraced assimilation as a means of continuing his traditional parental role.

Nonetheless, the voices of Indian fathers seeking to protect and provide for their offspring were often lost in the cacophony of conflicting policies set forth by the Indian Service. On the one hand, the OIA attempted to force Indian men into a Euro-American patriarchal role, designating them as heads of their households. On the other, they constrained Ute fathers' effectiveness by reserving nearly absolute power over Indian families for OIA adminstrators. For all their rhetoric about inculcating Indian men with a sense of familial responsibility, the paternalism of Indian policy meant that there was really only room for one father on the reservation: the Great Father in Washington.

 # FURTHER READING

Adams, David Wallace. *Education for Extinction: American Indians and the Boarding School Experience, 1875–1928* (1999).

Cashin, Joan. *A Family Venture: Men and Women on the Southern Frontier* (1991).

Deutsch, Sarah. *No Separate Refuge: Culture, Class, and Gender on an Anglo-Hispanic Frontier in the American Southwest, 1880–1940* (1987).

Ellis, Clyde. *To Change Them Forever: Education at the Rainy Mountain Boarding School, 1893–1920* (1996).

Faragher, John Mack. *Sugar Creek: Life on the Illinois Prairie* (1986).

———. *Women and Men on the Overland Trail* (1979).

Garceau, Dee. *The Important Things of Life: Women, Work, and Family in Sweetwater County, Wyoming, 1880–1929* (1997).

Griswold, Robert. *Family and Divorce in California, 1850–1890: Victorian Illusions and Everyday Realities* (1982).

Gordon, Linda. *The Great Arizona Orphan Abduction* (1999).

Hampsten, Elizabeth. *Settlers' Children* (1991).

Hyer, Sally. *One House, One Voice, One Heart: Native American Education at the Santa Fe Indian School* (1990).

Jeffrey, Julie Roy. *Frontier Women* (1998).

LeConte, Janet. "The Independent Women of Hispanic New Mexico, 1821–1846." *Western Historical Quarterly* (January 1981): 17–35.

Martin, Patricia Preciado. *Songs My Mother Sang to Me: An Oral History of Mexican-American Women* (1992).

Mihesuah, Devon A. *Cultivating the Rosebuds: The Education of Women at the Cherokee Female Seminary, 1851–1909* (1993).

Myres, Sandra. *Westering Women and the Frontier Experience, 1800–1915* (1982).

Osburn, Katherine M.B. *Southern Ute Women: Autonomy and Assimilation on the Reservation, 1887–1934* (1998).

Pascoe, Peggy. *Relations of Rescue: The Search for Female Moral Authority in the American West, 1874–1939* (1990).

Peavey, Linda, and Ursula Smith. *Frontier Children* (1999).

Petrik, Paula. *No Step Backward: Women and Family on the Rocky Mountain Mining Frontier* (1987).

Riley, Glenda. *The Female Frontier* (1988)

———. *Frontierswomen: The Iowa Experience* (1981).

———. *Women and Indians on the Frontier* (1984).

Schlissel, Lillian. *Women's Diaries of the Westward Journey* (1981).

———, ed. *Far from Home: Families of the Westward Journey* (2002).

Stratton, Joanna. *Pioneer Women: Voices from the Kansas Frontier* (1981).

Szasz, Margaret Connell. *Education and the American Indian: The Road to Self-Determination, 1928–1973* (1973).

Trennert, Robert A. Jr. *The Phoenix Indian School: Forced Assimilation in Arizona, 1891–1935* (1988).

West, Elliott. *Growing Up in the Country* (1987).

C H A P T E R
8

Children and Child-Savers
in Progressive-Era America,
1880–1920

*In the contemporary United States, many Americans accept as commonplace the
notions that childhood is an innocent stage of life and that adolescence is a turbulent period of transition. Given these assumptions, it seems no more than common
sense to expect adults—parents, educators, and professionals—to provide children
with protection from physical harm and immoral influences and adolescents with
guidance along the perilous path from childish innocence to adult responsibility.
Yet scholars' investigations have revealed that both these assumptions and the
conclusions that Americans have drawn from them are historical creations, shaped
by the rise of the new human sciences (psychology and sociology) and the new
helping professions (education and social work) and conditioned by well-to-do,
white, native-born Americans' anxieties about urbanization, industrialization,
and immigration.*

 *The Progressive Era—the decades spanning the transition from the nineteenth
century to the twentieth—was the heyday of the "child-saving" movement. Spurred
by concerns about the urban poor and the plight of children in the cities, reformers
sought to rescue and rehabilitate the city's youth in a variety of organizations, including orphanages, "houses of refuge," and reformatories. Their academic counterparts created the "child-study" movement in the late nineteenth century, culminating
in what Joseph F. Kett, in his influential 1977 book,* Rites of Passage, *has dubbed
the "invention of adolescence." In a parallel development, child-savers, public officials, and social scientists defined a new social problem among the nation's urban
poor: juvenile delinquency. While for nineteenth-century reformers the solution was
to remove immigrant, black, and working-class children from their presumably
deleterious home environments, in the twentieth century the emphasis shifted from
"saving" children from their families to reforming the families themselves, often
through the mechanism of the newly instituted juvenile court system. The notion
that private agents and state officials could and should intervene in family life
prefigured the rise of the modern welfare state.*

250

Progressive-Era child-study professionals, charitable societies, and public agencies produced a flood of information—sociological studies, investigative reports, and case files—detailing their efforts on behalf of children and youth. In the process, they also revealed contests over definitions of work, sexuality, and family between the child-savers and their clients. The outcome of these contests would shape the lives of children and the form of the institutions designed to serve them for decades to come.

The Progressive Era's child-saving movement, then, is dominated by power struggles: between men and women, parents and children, middle-class reformers and working-class families. These contests for control raise complex questions about the sources and nature of social change: Were reformers motivated by a greedy desire to exercise social control over immigrants and poor people or by a genuine wish to improve the lives of families and children? How did the interests of middle-class reformers and working-class families collide—and converge? What insights can the child-saving movement of a century ago yield into today's concerns about "at-risk" youth?

 # D O C U M E N T S

From the mid-nineteenth century through the 1920s, state agencies and private charities around the country sponsored an array of institutions to care for orphaned, abandoned, and delinquent children and youth. Document 1, taken from New York State's annual report on charities, describes one such institution, the New York Catholic Protectory. Founded in 1863, the Protectory was the largest institution of its kind in the United States by the time of this report in 1876. The report suggests how reformers' interest in improving children's lives converged with the public's interest in reducing the costs of caring for dependent members of society.

Some poor families surrendered their children to institutions to reduce the financial burden of supporting them; others sent their children to work. Middle-class reformers and working-class parents often clashed over the issue of children's work, as an 1896 report by a special committee on female labor in New York City, included as Document 2, indicates.

While child-savers called attention to the claims of innocent children, other Progressive-Era reformers warned of the dangers posed by juvenile delinquents. Children's need for protection and adolescents' need for discipline came together in the late-nineteenth-century movement for a juvenile justice system. Judge Ben Lindsey, who was admitted to the Colorado bar in 1894, was one of the most influential proponents of the juvenile court movement. In Document 3, he recalls his earliest encounter with youths caught in the adult prison apparatus.

The theories of psychology professor G. Stanley Hall, who published his magnum opus, *Adolescence,* in 1904, contributed to Americans' heightened concern about the potential—and the problems—of the teen years. An excerpt from this landmark book constitutes Document 4.

Although Hall's theories concerned middle-class white youth, Progressive-Era reformers saw the greatest threat as emanating from the crowded immigrant neighborhoods of the country's urban centers. Document 5, derived from a report on juvenile delinquency among Polish American children in Chicago published in 1918, reveals reformers' attitudes about class, ethnicity, and family life. It also suggests the gendered dimensions of delinquency: petty theft for boys, precocious sexuality for girls.

1. William P. Letchworth Visits the New York Catholic Protectory, 1876

The object of this society is "to provide for the education and support of such idle, truant, vicious, or homeless children of both sexes, from seven to fourteen years, as may be properly surrendered to its protection, or committed to its custody by the order of any magistrate of New York, or by the Commissioners of Public Charities and Correction." In addition to the class of children sent to the Protectory under commitment, the officers are allowed to take children who may be intrusted to them by their parents.

The Protectory is located in the town of Westchester, in Westchester county, eleven miles from the City Hall in New York. Its postoffice is Westchester. The institution may be reached by a short ride upon the Harlem Railroad, leaving the train at Tremont station. A ride of about two miles from the depot brings one to the extensive group of large buildings which comprise the Protectory establishment. Prominent among these, and first arresting the attention, is the boys' department, an imposing brick structure, four stories high, with basement and mansard roof, having a central tower containing a fine tower clock. The architectural design of the tower, as well as of the entire building, is quite elaborate, the whole presenting a stately appearance. The edifice is situated in the midst of extensive grounds, which are being improved. The site is an eligible one, the land in front gently sloping away from the main building. The soil is desirable for agricultural purposes, and the location is healthful.

A visitation with Commissioner Hoguet was made to this institution October 15, on which occasion the boys' department was found to be under the care of Brother Teliow, assisted by thirty of the Roman Catholic Order of Christian Brothers, and the girls' department under the charge of Sister Helena, with twenty-two other Sisters of Charity of Mt. St. Vincent associated with her in the work.

Although it will be difficult to convey to the reader, in the short space allotted to it in this report, an adequate idea of the system and arrangement of this immense establishment, yet a brief sketch of its noteworthy features which came under our observation will be attempted. The various parts of the institution were visited in the following order, beginning with the

Boy's department.—There were here at the date of visitation about thirteen hundred and forty boys. In the large printing room there were between seventy and eighty, under the supervision of a foreman, himself once an inmate, but now a superior workman. In this room are three steam-power presses. Stereotyping is carried on to an extent enabling the establishment to make all the castings used in its printing. About fifty-five boys were setting type, whose ages averaged about fourteen, and twenty little fellows were folding paper, none of whom were older than

William P. Letchworth, "Orphan Asylums and Other Institutions for the Care of Children," in *Ninth Annual Report of the New York State Board of Charities* (Albany: 1876), pp. 264–274. This document can also be found in Robert Bremner, ed., *Children and Youth in America: A Documentary History* (Cambridge: Mass.: Harvard University Press, 1971), 2: pp. 456–460.

eleven years. There were also ten, between fourteen and eighteen years of age, working at the presses.

In the tailoring department were about thirty boys sitting cross-legged on a platform, like tailors, and very busy at work; others were operating sewing machines, in all about sixty boys. The boys make every thing they wear, and in addition do a great deal of work for employers.

In the room appropriated to the boys' clothing are cases containing fourteen hundred small compartments, one of which is allotted to each boy. These are numbered, and the clothes that are in them are also numbered to correspond. The garments are of a warm woolen material, and of various colors. The President remarked: "I will not permit the boys to wear uniform clothes. I never buy two pieces of cloth alike."

In the shoemaking department there were nearly four hundred boys, ranging in ages from eleven to seventeen years. There are two shops in this department, one for making nailed and the other for making sewed shoes. The work is done largely by machinery. The boys wrought with alacrity, and seemed cheerful and attentive to their duties. The Brother says: "They have stated hours for labor and for education, and a given space of time for recreation. They have certain tasks to do, and when these are done they can go and play." . . .

About two hundred boys were employed in the cane-seating department, their ages varying from nine to eleven years. The work here seemed to be well done, and the boys' movements were brisk and orderly.

In a room in the basement were found about four hundred boys engaged, some in blocking out soles, and all working with a will.

The laundry contains four steam washing machines. The washing for the institution is all done by the boys, under the supervision of one of the Brothers and an assistant.

In the cabinet making department the boys were engaged in making bureaus, chests of drawers, wash-stands, etc. Many creditable specimens of their handiwork were there for inspection. Attached to the establishment is a blacksmith's shop, a wheelwright's shop, a horse-shoeing and a wagon-making department, and a machine shop, in which the machinery is repaired. The iron bedsteads used in the establishment are also made here. Bedsteads are likewise made to supply outside orders.

In the box-making department the boxes for packing shoes are made. All the carpentry about the institution, the Brother says, is done by the boys, and two buildings have been put up by them. In addition to the trades taught in all the departments named, the boys are instructed in gardening and farming. About seventy-eight were engaged in this kind of work. . . .

Thirty-five cows are kept on the place. All their milk is used in the institution, but even this, we were informed, is insufficient for the inmates. All the vegetables used are raised in the extensive gardens of the Protectory, except a full supply of potatoes. The lands of the institution cover one hundred and forty-seven acres. One hundred and thirty-five acres are under cultivation, twenty acres being laid out in garden.

The domestic part of the house is on the same large plan as the industrial. The kitchen, with its huge caldrons and polished boilers for coffee and tea, and with its other appurtenances, is on a scale commensurate with the requirements for feeding fifteen hundred mouths at a single meal, and is suggestive of the hospitality of baronial times.

The refectory is capable of accommodating eleven hundred boys at a sitting. In addition to these, a considerable number of the foremen sit here on a dais at one end of the room, and eat with them. A smaller refectory for the little boys could seat about three hundred. A Brother sat at one end, and the clerks and foremen of departments at the other. The boys were well supplied with a meat stew, bread, turnips, potatoes and apples. Before eating, the form of grace usual in Roman Catholic Asylums was repeated, and after the meal thanks were in like manner returned.

Beeves are butchered on the place to supply meat for the table. A very large and well-constructed slaughter-house, furnished with all the necessary conveniences for butchering the animals required for the sustenance of the children, has been erected during the year.

The dietary is as follows:

For ordinary days: Breakfast—Coffee, bread, butter and meat.

Dinner—Soup, meat, vegetables, bread and fruit in its season.

Supper—Bread, butter, tea and dessert.

For Fridays: Breakfast—Coffee, bread, butter and cakes.

Dinner—Soup, fish, potatoes, bread and coffee.

Supper—Bread, butter, tea and biscuits.

In the Junior Department meat is served but once a day; and as a substitute gruel of Indian or oaten meal, rice, etc., is given in the morning.

The dormitories are very large, containing about three hundred and fifty beds each, and are all similarly furnished. They are lighted on four sides. The windows are large and mullioned. In an alcove off each room, and separated from it by curtains, are beds for three of the Brothers. The boys' bedsteads are of iron, single, two feet four inches wide, having head and foot rails. Straw beds are used; the straw being changed every three months; the pillows are some of husks, some of sponge and some of hair. The beds were square and regularly made; they were very thick, the depth of straw in the ticks being fully fourteen inches. The Brother remarked on this point: "It pays us to buy straw to make decent beds for the boys. As soon as it becomes broken and inelastic we send it off and use it in the stables." Each bed had two sheets, two blankets and a coverlet. The covering is increased as the weather becomes colder. The rooms are lighted by gas. A spacious gas-house, with all its necessary dependencies, retorts, iron receivers, tank, storehouse for coal, and full complement of service pipes for all buildings of the institution, has been constructed.

Night closets adjoin each dormitory.

The chapel is of old Saxon-Gothic architecture, and has a capacity for seating fifteen hundred. It contains a large central altar, a confessional at each end, a gallery and a piano. The piano when used is accompanied by music upon stringed instruments.

The infirmary is on the same floor as the chapel. There was here one inmate, suffering from consumption; another from pneumonia; and a third from a swollen foot. This department is in charge of a Brother, and contains twenty beds. In connection with it is an apothecary shop. A large gas jet is kept burning in a flue in the center of the infirmary, for the purpose of ventilation.

The halls of the Protectory are ten feet wide, and extend through the whole length of the building. In addition to the central staircase are four other flights of stairs, rendering easy egress from the building in case of fire. Each floor has a water-pipe and a number of leather buckets ready for use in case of fire.

Girls' Department. . . . The number of girls on the day of visitation was six hundred and one, their ages ranging between seven and sixteen years. They were dressed neatly and differently, the Sisters preferring variety in color and material as a matter of taste. The girls' hair was mostly tied up with ribbons, and their faces looked clean and bright.

Care is taken in the arrangements for ablutions. Each inmate has her own towel. This is numbered with her own number. Every girl in the house, Sister Helena informed us, has a number, and this number is on her clothes, her books, and every thing allotted to her, and each is held responsible for her own. In this way an opportunity is more readily afforded for observing and rewarding those who show the most neatness in the care of what belongs to them.

The school comprises ten classes of about fifty each in the primary departments, and sixty or seventy in the classes of the older pupils. The rooms are furnished with patent desks and all modern appliances. The personal cleanliness of the inmates was marked. The Sister says: "The mornings and evenings are devoted to the school, and the afternoons to work. Young children of either sex are not expected to work. Their day is divided between the school and the play-ground. Special pains is taken to give young girls ample out-door recreation. About three hundred and seven girls, comprising all of the junior classes, are kept in school five hours per day. Those girls who are engaged in the industrial departments during part of the day, are kept in school two hours in the morning, and those employed in house labor are kept in school two and one-half hours in the afternoon."

In one of the classes we found about sixty-eight girls engaged in finishing off shirts. In the "operating room" there were sixty-two machines, all worked by girls, who are paid according to their capacity. The following figures will better explain the extent of the industrial features of this department: About ninety-six girls are engaged at shoe-fitting, about one hundred and seventy-six in plain sewing, and about twenty-five in house-work. . . .

The house was found to be very clean and tidily kept and the order prevalent throughout in all the housekeeping as well as industrial departments, it would seem, must have a beneficial effect upon the children, many of whom, before coming here, were brought up in the utmost neglect, and left to habits of heedlessness. The demeanor of the Sisters appeared to be that of earnest women, engaged in a work undertaken as a duty, investing them with a dignity that seemed to inspire respect among the children.

The whole number of children, both boys and girls, in the Protectory at the date of October 1, 1875, was 1,944. Of these, 538 were orphans, 1,021 half-orphans, and 365 had both parents living. There were of native parentage, 147, and of foreign parentage, 1,797. Of the entire number, fifty-three were partially supported by parents or friends. The number of children transferred from Randall's Island Nursery and the county poor-house of Westchester at the time the system of rearing children in these institutions was broken up, was 108. The whole number of children received during the year was 941; the number discharged, 839. Of the latter, 84 were indentured, 643 returned to parents or guardians, 79 left without permission, 19 were transferred to other institutions, and 14 died. . . .

2. The Reinhard Committee
Investigates Child Labor, 1896

The opinion of the committee presented in its preliminary report, that large numbers of children were employed in manufacturing places contrary to law, has been amply confirmed by its further and fuller investigations. The committee stamps the employment of child labor under the statutory age as one of the most extensive evils now existing in the city of New York, and an evil which is a constant and grave menace to the welfare of its people. Many children were found by the diligent efforts of the committee's subpoena servers and brought before the committee, who were under the requisite age, and many others were seen by members of the committee upon their investigation tours. These children were undersized, poorly clad and dolefully ignorant, unacquainted with the simplest rudiments of a common school education, having no knowledge of the simplest figures and unable in many cases to write their own names in the native or any other language.

Fannie Harris, who earned two dollars per week, of which her mother allowed her two cents a week for spending money, testified:

Q. Now, have you been to school in this country? *A.* No.

Q. Can you read? *A.* I can read a little, not much.

Q. What can you read—can you read "dog?" *A.* No. sir.

Q. Do you know how to spell dog? *A.* I went to night school.

Q. Do you know how to spell dog? *A.* I have forgotten it since night school stopped.

Q. Can you spell "cat?' *A.* Yes, sir.

Q. How do you spell it? *A.* I have forgot.

Q. When did you have a birthday; did you have a birthday lately? *A.* No, sir.

Q. Did you ever have a birthday? *A.* No, sir.

Q. You know what a birthday is, don't you Fannie? *A.* Yes, sir.

Q. What is that? *A.* The day that you were born.

Q. Now, didn't you have a birthday? *A.* I never had a birthday because we have not any money to make a birthday.

Q. That is, you never had a little party? *A.* No, sir.

Q. A birthday is a day when you have a little party, is it not? *A.* Yes, sir.

Q. Does your mamma work? *A.* Now she ain't working, because I am working, but before, when I didn't work, she worked.

Q. Your mamma is not sick, is she? *A.* No, sir.

Q. And your mamma wants you to go to work? *A.* Yes, sir; sure she does; and I want to go to work myself.

Q. And if you don't go to work then your mamma will have to go to work? *A.* Sure.

"Report and Testimony Taken Before the Special Committee of the Assembly Appointed to Investigate the Condition of Female Labor in the City of New York," *New York Assembly Documents, 1896,* 23, no. 97, part I, pp. 5–8. This document can also be found in Robert Bremner, ed., *Children and Youth in America: A Documentary History* (Cambridge, Mass.: Harvard University Press, 1971), 2: pp. 674–675.

Q. Now, Fannie, when will you be 15 years of age? *A.* I don't know.

Q. Are you 15 now? *A.* No, sir.

Q. And this paper (showing age certificate) your mamma gave you, did she? *A.* I went to a lawyer and paid twenty-five cents and he gave me it . . .

Parents and mercenary and corrupt notaries alike connive at the employment of children under the statutory age. A parent who is willing to permit its child to work in a factory at an age under 14 is ordinarily just as willing to perjure himself as to the age of the child. To carry out his purpose he has little difficulty in obtaining the assistance of a notary, who is willing, for the illegal fee of twenty-five cents, to be a party to the crime. . . .

3. Judge Ben Lindsey Encounters Youthful Criminals, 1894

The clerk gave me the numbers of the cases. I got the pleadings and went into the old West Side jail to see my clients. The Warden smiled when I told him their names. I followed him through clanging iron doors with their rattling bolts and bars to the back part of the building.

At the end of a corridor I came in front of a cage on the floor of which were two small boys engaged in gambling with two grown men who had been brought in from some outlying section of Arapahoe county, a sparsely settled empire that then ran clear to the eastern state line.

I found that these boys had already been in jail more than 60 days and had learned to play poker from their older cell mates, a safe cracker and a horse thief, upon whom they had come to look as great heroes.

My first thought was that the judge in assigning me to defend two such men from serious crimes had given me a pretty tough job but my concern was soon relieved as the Warden explained:

"It's the kids the judge wants you to look after. He was over here the other day and he didn't like it very much that they're still here. He said he knew a young fellow who was just the one to look after the case. I guess it must be you."

"Then," I asked, to make doubly sure, "it's not those two men who are my clients?"

"No," he drawled. "Those guys have got two real lawyers to defend 'em."

"But," I persisted, "I am appointed to defend two burglars."

The kids looked like such real boys that in my confusion I had been unable to visualize them as criminals—my mind just refused to work that way.

"Sure you are," said the Warden, "but them's the burglars."

A number of things shot through my mind as this first step in my difficulties cleared up. One was that it, perhaps, took "two burglars" like these boys to make

---

Benjamin B. Lindsey and Rube Borough, *The Dangerous Life* (New York: Horace Liveright, 1931), pp. 49–53. This document can also be found in Robert Bremner, ed., *Children and Youth in America: A Documentary History* (Cambridge, Mass.: Harvard University Press, 1971), 2: pp. 515–517.

"one burglar." And so my pride that had soared from the flattery of two assignments when any young fellow would have been tickled to death with one was a bit humbled.

My first task—that was afterward to become my task in so many thousands of cases that I then little knew were to follow—was to get acquainted with the prisoners. It was my first appearance before the bench of youth but its lesson was to stay with me even in the days when I had long ceased to be a lawyer and had become a judge. For there by those bars that would have shamed the King Tiger of the Jungle I was able to begin a lasting friendship with the little prisoners.

They were typical boys from the realm of Gangville, as I was to come to know it so well. They were about twelve years of age.

The one that impressed me most was a little freckle-faced Irish lad with a sense of humor. He was charged with having gone into a railroad section house and taken a lot of tools.

"Sonny," I said, "you are charged with burglary."

"I ain't no burglary," he countered.

"I guess you don't know what burglary means," I ventured. And I explained to him that the long rigamarole in the complaint papers meant to charge him with breaking and entering a tool house and THAT constituted burglary.

"I never stole 'em, I just took 'em," he answered heatedly. "So I ain't done no burglary—I ain't done nothin'."

"Well, one thing you can't deny," I went on, getting chummy with my client. "You've got the dirtiest face I ever saw on a kid."

"'Tain't my fault," he shot back with a grin. "A guy threw water on me and the dust settled on it."

When I protested to the Warden against this good-natured boy being held in jail with two hardened old criminals, he admitted it was "a damned outrage."

"How many boys are there in jail?" I asked.

"Oh, quite a number," he answered. "Most of them don't stay so long as these two boys—they're waiting for the fall term of court. Their families couldn't afford to put up bonds."

"But why do you put them in with that horse thief and safe cracker?"

"The jail is crowded," he said. And he gave various other excuses.

Well, in answering the charge against those kids, I did a thing that was perhaps purely artless, the direct reaction from my rage complexes, my indignation at injustice.

I prepared an answer that was an indictment against the state of Colorado for its crime against those two boys. The thing got a lot of public discussion and raised quite a furor.

Here were two boys, neither of them serious enemies of society, who were about to be convicted of burglary and have felony records standing against them for the remainder of their lives. And, pending the decision of their cases, they were associating generally with criminals and particularly with a horse thief and a safe cracker. The state was sending them to a school for crime—deliberately teaching them to be horse thieves and safe crackers. It was outrageous—and absurd.

My first fight then was with the state of Colorado. I was determined that those boys should have their chance. I saw only vaguely then what afterward became clearer to me—that my first fight with the state was not just for those two boys but for millions like them. Even then, however,—before I had formulated any plan to change the things that were or had written any of the hundreds of laws I afterward wrote for my own and other states and foreign countries—I had made up my mind to smash the system that meant so much injustice to youth.

Although I did not know it, I was well on the road to "The Dangerous Life," with its sorrow and disappointment, and its satisfaction in achievements marred by the consciousness of a goal never fully reached.

How little the judge knew the real size of that first little case to which, in a whimsical moment, he had assigned me!

I went back to him. I talked and he listened. I found him in a measure sympathetic, though he did not fully share my indignation over the situation and warned me against taking it too seriously.

However, he gave me to understand that he would not be bound too much by rule and rote, technicality and precedent, but would cooperate with me as far as he could to do what was "best for the boys" even though, according to the conventions of that time, it might not seem to be the "best for the state." (Of course, I was to know in time that, when properly understood, whatever is "best for the child" is really "best for the state.")

He was not just sure that he had authority to do what he thought he ought to do. But he finally agreed I might continue the case from time to time that we might spare these boys from the blight of conviction for felony and its drag and handicap in after years—provided I would look after them in the meantime.

And, of course, I agreed to that.

I became the Juvenile Judge and Probation Officer.

Such was my first juvenile case.

4. Psychologist G. Stanley Hall
Defines Adolescence, 1904

Adolescence is a new birth, for the higher and more completely human traits are now born. The qualities of body and soul that now emerge are far newer. The child comes from and harks back to a remoter past; the adolescent is neo-atavistic, and in him the later acquisitions of the race slowly become prepotent. Development is less gradual and more saltatory, suggestive of some ancient period of storm and stress when old moorings were broken and a higher level attained. The annual rate of growth in height, weight, and strength is increased and often doubled, and even more. Important functions previously non-existent arise. Growth of parts and organs loses its former proportions, some permanently and some for a season. Some of these are still growing in old age and others are soon arrested and atrophy. The old moduli of dimensions become obsolete and old harmonies are broken. The range of

G. Stanley Hall, *Adolescence: Its Psychology and Its Relation to Physiology, Anthropology, Sociology, Sex, Crime, Religion, and Education* (New York: 1904), I, xiii–xviii. This document can also be found in Robert Bremner, ed., *Children and Youth in America: A Documentary History* (Cambridge, Mass.: Harvard University Press, 1971), 2: pp. 81–83.

individual differences and average errors in all physical measurements and all psychic tests increases. Some linger long in the childish stage and advance late or slowly, while others push on with a sudden outburst of impulsion to early maturity. Bones and muscles lead all other tissues, as if they vied with each other, and there is frequent flabbiness or tension as one or the other leads. Nature arms youth for conflict with all the resources at her command—speed, power of shoulder, biceps, back, leg, jaw,—strengthens and enlarges skull, thorax, hips, makes man aggressive and prepares woman's frame for maternity. The power of the diseases peculiar to childhood abates, and liability to the far more diseases of maturity begins, so that with liability to both it is not strange that the dawn of the ephebic day is marked at the same time by increased morbidity but diminished rates of mortality. . . .

The momentum of heredity often seems insufficient to enable the child to achieve this great revolution and come to complete maturity, so that every step of the upward way is strewn with wreckage of body, mind, and morals. There is not only arrest, but perversion, at every stage, and hoodlumism, juvenile crime, and secret vice seem not only increasing, but develop in earlier years in every civilized land. Modern life is hard, and in many respects increasingly so, on youth. Home, school, church, fail to recognize its nature and needs and, perhaps most of all, its perils. . . .

The functions of every sense undergo reconstruction, and their relations to other psychic functions change, and new sensations, some of them very intense, arise, and new associations in the sense sphere are formed. Haptic impressions, appetite for food and drink, and smell are most modified. The voice changes, vascular instability, blushing, and flushing are increased. Sex asserts its mastery in field after field, and works its havoc in the form of secret vice, debauch, disease, and enfeebled heredity, cadences the soul to both its normal and abnormal rhythms, and sends many thousand youth a year to quacks, because neither parents, teachers, preachers, or physicians know how to deal with its problems. Thus the foundations of domestic, social, and religious life are oftenest undermined. Between religion and love, God and nature have wrought an indissoluble bond so that neither can attain normality without that of the other. Secondary sexual qualities are shown to have an ever-widening range, and parenthood to mean more with every upward step of development. The youth craves more knowledge of body and mind that can help against besetting temptations, aid in the choice of a profession, and if his intellect is normal he does not vex his soul overmuch about the logical character of the universe or the ultimate sanction of either truth or virtue. . . . There are new repulsions felt toward home and school, and truancy and runaways abound. The social instincts undergo sudden unfoldment and the new life of love awakens. It is the age of sentiment and of religion, of rapid fluctuation of mood, and the world seems strange and new. Interest in adult life and in vocations develops. Youth awakes to a new world and understands neither it nor himself. The whole future of life depends on how the new powers now given suddenly and in profusion are husbanded and directed. Character and personality are taking form, but everything is plastic. Self-feeling and ambition are increased, and every trait and faculty is liable to exaggeration and excess. It is all a marvelous new birth, and those who believe that nothing is so worthy of love, reverance, and service as the body and soul of youth, and who hold that the best test of every human institution is how much it contributes to bring youth to the ever fullest possible development, may well review themselves and the civilization in which we live to see how far it satisfies this supreme test.

Never has youth been exposed to such dangers of both perversion and arrest as in our own land and day. Increasing urban life with its temptations, prematurities, sedentary occupations, and passive stimuli just when an active, objective life is most needed, early emancipation and a lessening sense for both duty and discipline, the haste to know and do all befitting man's estate before its time, the mad rush for sudden wealth and the reckless fashions set by its gilded youth—all these lack some of the regulatives they still have in older lands with more conservative traditions. In a very pregnant psychological sense ours is an unhistoric land. Our very Constitution had a Minerva birth, and was not the slow growth of precedent. Our ideas of freedom were at the outset fevered by the convulsion of the French Revolution. Our literature, customs, fashions, institutions, and legislation were inherited or copied, and our religion was not a gradual indigenous growth, but both its spirit and forms were imported ready-made from Holland, Rome, England, and Palestine. To this extent we are a fiat nation, and in a very significant sense we have had neither childhood nor youth, but have lost touch with these stages of life because we lack a normal development history. It is not merely that we have no antiquity rich in material and spiritual monuments that is the best nursery of patriotism in the young, but our gallery of heroes is largely composed, not of glorious youth but of sages advanced in age or old in wisdom for their years. Our immigrants have often passed the best years of youth or leave it behind when they reach our shores, and their memories of it are in other lands. No country is so precociously old for its years. . . . In this environment our young people leap rather than grow into maturity. . . . We are conquering nature, achieving a magnificent material civilization, leading the world in the applications though not in the creation of science, coming to lead in energy and intense industrial and other activities; our vast and complex business organization that has long since outgrown the comprehension of professional economists, absorbs ever more and earlier the best talent and muscle of youth and now dominates health, time, society, politics, and law-giving, and sets new and ever more pervading fashions in manners, morals, education, and religion; but we are progressively forgetting that for the complete apprenticeship to life, youth needs repose, leisure, art, legends, romance, idealization, and in a word humanism, if it is to enter the kingdom of man well equipped for man's highest work in the world.

5. Sociologists Describe Juvenile Delinquency Among Polish Immigrants, 1918

Joe and John Kasperek. Mr. and Mrs. Kasperek were married in Galicia and came to Chicago in 1902. John was born 1903, Joe in 1905, Mary 1908 and Stanley 1910. Mrs. Kasperek died in 1911 and Kasperek married again in 1912. A girl was born in 1913. In July, 1913, John and Joe left home separately. After 8 days John was picked up by an officer, but Joe was gone 5 weeks. Joe had a record for repeatedly running away during the last 2 years. Once he had taken his little sister and kept her 4 days. They slept in sheds and under sidewalks. The truant officer said he

William I. Thomas and Florian Znaniecki, *The Polish Peasant in Europe and America,* 2d ed. (New York: Knopf, 1927). This document can also be found in Robert Bremner, ed., *Children and Youth in America: A Documentary History* (Cambridge, Mass.: Harvard University Press, 1971), 2: pp. 591–597.

had had trouble with the boys for years but would not bring them to Court because their father was too anxious to have them placed in an institution. Father and step-mother both worked, the latter leaving at 5:30 A.M., and returning at 7 P.M. The children were locked in the dirty, miserable house. She did not stay home when or-dered to by the Court, but continued to work, saying she had no money for food. The officer wrote: "I always find the 2 youngest children sitting on a bench, never talk, appear frightened." John frequently stayed home and looked after the younger children, but Joe was wilder and was soon sent to an institution. The father was ordered to pay $5 a month board. This he never did and when arrested always claimed he was out of work. John was picked up later and sent to the Parental School also. The parents did not go to see the children or send them any clothes, though ordered to do so by the court. The father pretended he did not know where they were. When they were released Joe and another boy broke into a dry-goods store and stole some things. Joe skipped out of the State, but was brought back and sent to St. Charles School. John about the same time was arrested for stealing $1 from his father and leaving home.

Neighbors complained that the stepmother was neglecting the children and even mistreating them, made them all sleep on the floor, and that the house was a rendezvous for drinking people, as both father and stepmother were heavy drinkers. Joe and John were found stealing potatoes from the railroad. Dr. Healy reported Joe in general poor physical condition, enlarged tonsils and defective vision. He had run away from his father while leaving court and told the judge he did it to escape a whipping. The father said: "I do not whip him so bad." Father made $1.75 a day working in a box-factory. Mother said she worked to help pay off debts. Both boys were again paroled to their parents. The Parental School refused to receive Joe back saying he didn't need "correction," only "permanent care" and it must have been by mistake he was sent there in the first place. The family was entirely indif-ferent to him, neither visited him, nor provided him with anything.

Joe and John both disappeared soon. Once in mother's absence they entered house through pantry-window and took 60 cents. A man reported that he had picked up Joe, given him clean clothes and offered him a home, but he had run away again. Officer called at home one Monday: "I found Mr. Kasperek at home playing the accordion to his wife (he was perfectly sober but very sentimental). Said he worked all day Sunday so was entitled to stay home Monday." Soon he was out of work and Mrs. Kasperek was picking potatoes off the railroad tracks. The landlady said she beats her children. "There was a girl's new bicycle in the bed-room. She said he had bought it. I doubt this very much . . . Her own girl was well dressed. I censured her for not putting more clothing on the other children.

"Joe was picked up in front of Detention Home . . . had slept for 3 nights in a wagon almost in front of Detention Home. When found was almost starved, dirty and with a very sore foot. Was kept in bed for a week or 10 days. This child had a good record at the Detention Home [always behaved well when there]. Asked him why he will not stay home. He says he does not get breakfast at home. Talked to father and mother. Both . . . have tried to do better and in a measure have succeeded, but for some reason their boys won't stay home."

John was not yet 14 years old and was sent back to Public School. He attended regularly except when it was stormy, "he had a very long walk and was always poorly clothed." Joe was released and went to school regularly too for awhile. The family moved to better rooms. Joe soon disappeared. The stepmother developed tuberculosis. At first she refused treatment but was soon so ill that she was taken to the County Hospital, where she died. John and Joe were sent to St. Charles School.

The documents, as we see, corroborate our assumption that in studying the delinquency of children there is no need to ask what are the factors of demoralization, for there is no morality to start with . . . A well furnished and cleanly kept house—a point on which much stress is now being laid by American social agencies—shows a certain economic stability and an interest of the woman in housekeeping but does not permit us to conclude that vital moral traditions or active educatory interests are present in the parents, nor even that strong bonds unite the marriage-group. Even the preservation of active solidarity between husband and wife does not necessarily argue in favor of their ability or willingness to educate their children. Assumptions of this kind are based upon the mistaken idea that the family (by which always the marriage-group is here meant) is by its very existence a constructive social agency and bound to have a positive educatory influence if only the parents are not completely demoralized and do not actually teach the children evil ways. In fact, the marriage-group organization is a good instrument for imparting to the young generation schemes of behavior with the help of which their life-organization can be built; but this instrument is worthless unless properly used, *i.e.,* unless the parents have a well ordered set of schemes of behavior to impart and know how to do it. And these are precisely the weak points in an average immigrant family.

We must realize that in Polish peasant life the educatory rôle of the marriage-group was something entirely different, much richer in content and better ordered than it is here. The marriage-group was an integral part of the wider social milieu and shared its stock of traditions and schemes of behavior. The children were early made to participate in all the activities of the parents—economic, hedonistic, social, religious—and thus unreflectively absorbed and imitated their entire life-organization. Further, the parents gradually, without effort or reflection, introduced the children into the accumulated body of traditions of the community and into the present active life of the latter and thus prepared them to supplement later from the principles and examples offered by the community whatever deficiencies there might have been in their early education. The parents did not need to be expert educators nor even to be conscious of their moral standards and planfully follow an educational system. All they had to do was to act themselves in accordance with the morality of their social milieu and to mediate between the traditions and social opinion of the community and the consciousness of their children.

All this is radically changed in America. The children no longer take part in the activities of their parents. They go to school or run the streets while the parents work, or play in their own separate milieux. There is still some community of interests and occupation left between the girl and her mother but the boy has very little in common with his father. Education by action is no longer possible. And even if the boy had any opportunities of participating in his father's activities he would not gain much by it for these activities have little social meaning left in them—unless, of course, the father is one of the active builders of the Polish-American social system. Furthermore, the marriage-group is no longer the medium through which the child is introduced into the social life of his wider milieu. On the contrary, not only are his contacts with this milieu for the most part direct and independent of the selective control of his elders but he is often called to mediate between his parents and American institutions whose real meaning he may not understand any better than they, but with which he has a better superficial acquaintance. Any authority which the parents might claim as bearers of social traditions of the wider milieu is thus definitely undermined.

Under these circumstances the immigrant's home could acquire an educatory influence only if the older generation were trained in moral ideals, if their intellectual horizon were widened, if they were taught how to follow a system of rational education and were willing to do it. In other words, reflective, voluntary, planful educational methods would have to be substituted in each home for the unreflective, spontaneous "natural" ways by which social education successfully proceeded in the Polish peasant life. But this is clearly, at the present stage of development of the lower classes in all countries and under the present economic and social conditions, for the immense majority of mankind, an unattainable aim. The immigrant would have an incomparably more difficult task in this respect than the average native American who has still a large stock of traditions and whose old unreflective educational methods still work. How large is the proportion of intelligent American homes where these traditional methods are supplemented or supplanted by a new, rational, planfully organized system of education?

If now a practically a-moral boy who has no efficient life-organization inculcated in him is put in contact with the complex life of an American city, it is only natural if he simply follows his instincts and moods, and it depends on the nature of these instincts and moods and on the values which happen to come within his reach whether he will approximately "behave himself," *i.e.,* do things which usually do not fall under the attention of the agencies maintaining public order, or will "misbehave," *i.e.,* transgress the limits of the permissible imposed by law and police ordinances and earn a reputation for wildness or even viciousness. Regular work in school or shop is not a form of life which would temperamentally appeal to him any more than to anybody else, for the habit of work requires a control over temperamental impulses which can be only implanted by social training. He may be frightened into it, if temperamentally cowardly or passive, by continuous threats of punishment, but if he thinks that he can avoid punishment it is only natural that he should be a truant during his school years and later leave every "job" after its novelty has worn off. If his home is associated with unpleasant experiences—lack of freedom, penalties deserved or undeserved, uncongenial family atmosphere—it is not strange that he should run away from home and try to avoid these unpleasant experiences, for filial love and obedience and even ordinary foresight, which would make him prefer the smaller evils at home to the greater evils awaiting him outside, are institutional, not temperamental attitudes. If he sees things which he covets displayed in shopwindows or pleasures which he enjoys to be obtained with a little money, it is perfectly natural for him to steal, burglarize or rob, since respect for property is not a matter of instinct but of long and complex social education. If he is of a fighting or revengeful disposition, there is nothing to prevent him from fighting or even killing except compassion and fear which may depend on the mood of the moment and in general require an active, socially trained imagination. If the spirit of adventure stirs in him, with or without the cooperation of dime novels and moving pictures, there is no reason in his eyes why he should not launch into the wide unknown world, full of new and marvelous experiences. There is from the standpoint of his own consciousness nothing immoral in whatever he may do, for he knows only conflicts between momentarily opposing wishes but no moral conflicts between a wish and a general norm of behavior voluntarily accepted as binding.

Of course, usually such an a-moral boy, if his temperamental impulses are not particularly strong, becomes step by step adapted to the practical conditions of life by the mere pressure of the social machinery which forces him to develop a minimum of foresight, to choose the lesser evil of work rather than the worse evil of prison or hunger, to keep away from too dangerous adventures, to imitate the example or to obey the will of other, already settled, members of society and thus to acquire a set of habits just sufficient to keep him floating with the current of social life. He does not become thereby any less a-moral, only learns to remain within the limits of the legally permitted, or more exactly, unlearns to transgress these limits. This kind of passive adaptation is prevalent among the second generation. It produces a large mass of individuals who from the social standpoint are not definitely negative, since they do not actively disturb the social order, but are simply worthless.

The position of a girl in an immigrant family differs from that of a boy in the fact that the claims which the family puts upon her are greater. She is supposed to be under stricter control even after school-age. She is expected to help in housework if she does not work outside, and to turn all of her earnings into the home. Moreover, the old rule prohibiting sexual relations before marriage is still enforced upon her. Thus a few remnants of the traditional life-organization are preserved for her benefit; her rearing is on the average not as a-moral as that of a boy.

But there are many exceptions. When the parents themselves are demoralized sexually the traditional rule, of course, cannot be efficiently enforced and cases are not rare when the girl is actually pushed into sexual demoralization by her parents. And even when the marriage-group keeps a minimum of respectability and the parents wish the girl to remain "straight," applying to her the old social schemes, the latter have little if any educational value, for the social meaning which they had in the old country is lost in the new conditions and the schemes are empty forms with no vital power of regulating conduct. The participation of the girl in the household activities of her mother has no constructive influence because . . . these activities have no longer the same positive significance for the mother herself that they had in the old country and because the feeling of familial solidarity which made individual cooperation in family affairs interesting has for the most part disappeared. Therefore also the claim of the parents to the girl's earnings seems no longer socially justified and is apt to appear to the girl's individualized consciousness as unjust exploitation. It was perfectly normal for a girl in the old country to turn over all her earnings to her father or mother, but then she knew that these earnings went toward her future dowry or marriage outfit, and even if the family was too poor to give her a dowry—it was never too poor to make an outfit—she was positively interested in keeping its economic standing above the level of misery, for its standing was her own standing as well. All this is lost here. Finally, the demand of sexual purity was there really a demand of the most vital importance. A girl who lost her "virginal wreath" discredited for ever herself and to a certain degree also her family in the eyes of the community and impaired or even destroyed her chances of marriage, *i.e.,* the only possible form of normal life in her own eyes and in those of her relatives and acquaintances. The possibility of her actions remaining a secret was exceeding small, and she knew it. The only course left to her under normal conditions was to leave for the city or for a foreign country, which meant breaking all the strongest and most deeply implanted social ties. Whereas here the weakness of social control, the feeling of personal independence early developed by the numerous contacts outside of home, the innumerable suggestions of sexual life pervading the city atmosphere and—perhaps most of all—the looseness of sexual mores in the immigrant community, all cooperate in depriving sexual relations before marriage not only of most of their traditional social "badness" but even of any really deep personal importance. The whole matter acquires the character of an incident, important only when either resulting in pregnancy and childbirth or when leading to a more or less lasting life-policy—concubinage, with possible marriage later, or a prostitute's career.

Under these circumstances the rulings to which the girl is subjected at home—and which are certainly neither rationally explained to her nor tactfully suggested—appear often arbitrary and tyrannical, and not infrequently, instead of helping to restrain her instincts, stir her to a more radical revolt and from merely a-moral make her distinctly anti-moral.

Stella Kurowska. Stella was 15 years old when she told this story to the Juvenile Court: "On the night of June 7, 1916, about 8 o'clock Helen Sikowska and I were standing at the corner . . . Mike and Tomczak and another Mike came along in an automobile and Helen asked them for a ride. We went quite a ways, and then Tomczak said he wanted to [have intercourse with] me. He said if we did not do it he would not take us home . . . They drove up in front of a saloon and all three of the fellows went in the saloon and stayed there about one hour. Helen and I sat in the car and waited for them. They came out and we started back for home. We drove for a ways, and when we came to a place where there was no houses they stopped the machine and said it was broke. Tomczak went to sleep. Mike, the driver of the car, got out and took me with him and walked me over the prairie. There he knocked me down and . . . did something bad to me . . . Then they took us back home."

Mike was a chauffeur, 19 years old. His parents had died when he was young and a friend, a married woman, had cared for him since. She stated that he had never been in any sort of trouble before and was always a good boy. Others corroborated this.

Shortly after Helen Sikowska, who was 18 years old, ran away from home sending word to her mother that she would not return. The home conditions were excellent and the mother said that Helen had always been a good girl until she met Stella.

Marien Stepanek. Marien was arrested for acting "obstreperous" with another girl in a railway waiting room. She had no underclothing on when arrested [in June]. She was 16 years old, had left home before Easter and had been going much to shows and moving picture theaters. She told a police woman that she had been drugged on the North side and carried to a room by two men on different nights. She had been in the habit of receiving mail at the General Delivery and frequented the Boston Store with a man about 45 years of age whom she claimed was her husband.

Marien said she had "no fault to find" with her home, her father and mother were kind to her but she met a lady by the name of Le Mar and told her she lived in Milwaukee. "And she asked me to live with her, said she was getting a divorce from her husband, and I stayed with her for awhile . . . assisted her with the work." When asked where she met her girl friend she said: "Met her at the Boston Store and did not want to talk to her. And she came up to me and she wanted me to fix it up for her. Said she wanted to get away from home and said I should call up her mother and tell her that she was doing housework and told me to talk as if I was an elderly lady, and I went and did that."

The following letter was received from her while she was away: "Dear Mother, I am feeling fine. Everything is all right, don't worry about me. I am leading high life because I am an actress. I got swell clothes and everything, you wouldn't know me. I had Clara down town one day I was out with the manager. She had a nice time . . . I never had just nice times in all my life. Everybody says that I am pretty. I paid 65 dollars for my suit and 5 dollars had [hat], 6 dollars shoe 3 gloves 2 dollar underwar 5 dollar corest. Know I have hundred dollars in the bank but I want you to write a letter and say youll forgive me for not telling the truht but I will explain better when I see you and will return home for the sake of the little ones. I will bring a hundred dollars home to you and will come home very time I can its to expensive to liv at a hotel now sent the letter to me this way Genarel Devilery Miss Marion Stephan."

Her father testified: "After Easter got a letter from her something like that one only more in it. She was rich and everything else, which is not so. So she says answer me quick as you can because I go to Milwaukee tomorrow. And I answer it right away to come home as soon as possible. Thought maybe the letter would reach her and heard nothing more until 3 weeks ago and then this letter come and I begging her to come home and be a good girl. She come home and asked if wanted to stay home now and she feel very happy that she is home and thought maybe she would behave . . . Next day she said she was going for her clothes . . . and I says I go with you. And I could not go and left my boy and girl to go with her Sunday. And she left them in the park and did not come home. Then she was back again Tuesday and in the evening when I come home from work she was not there . . ."

Marien said she kept company with men for quite awhile, giving three names, but she denied immoral relations with any of them. She said she had been going out with another fellow "but he is a gentleman in every way."

"*Court:* With whom have you had immoral relations?

"*A.* Cannot remember.

"*Q.* Have you been to a hotel at any time since you have been away?

"*A.* Been to a hotel one time with Helen . . . and a girl, Freda Jones. She lives under a different name, Freda Jarvis . . .

"*Q.* Did you hear anybody offer $2 at this hotel?

"*A.* I heard that what Freda said. She was kind of sore . . . She said about it: "What they think I am anyhow, stingy fools. Think I am doing anything for $2 . . . Helen and I laughed at her . . .

"*Q.* What did you understand by that?

"*A.* I understood what she meant by it . . .

"*Q.* What did you mean by the statement that you are leading a 'high life'?

"A. Meant had been to cabarets and dance halls. Been going to Morrison Ball room . . . and I went to the 'Booster's Club,' that's the old Morrison place."

Marien was sent to the reform school in Geneva but released in September, as her home conditions were good.

The conclusion as to the significance of sexual immorality in girls of the second generation is perfectly obvious. Illicit sexual tendencies are simply a component—sometimes predominant, oftener subordinate—of a powerful desire for new experience and for general excitement which under the given conditions cannot be satisfied in socially permitted ways. It depends in some measure on individual temperament whether in a given case this desire for new experience will be successfully counteracted by a desire for security which tends to make the girl stay in the beaten path and follow the rules laid down by society. But this depends also, perhaps in a still larger measure, on the question what attractions are offered by society to those who stay in the beaten path. And these attractions are certainly neither many nor strong for the daughter of a Polish immigrant. First school, which to her mind does not lead anywhere, is not a means to any definite end. Then dependent and meaningless housework at home or tiresome shopwork with no profit to herself. Later marriage and, after a few short new experiences, continuation of the same meaningless work from day to day without any new outlook for the future, with children as the only important genuine interest—and this has to be bought at the cost of pain, ceaseless toil, increased poverty and diminished chances for personal pleasure. There is little response at any period of her life from parents, husband or children, little recognition, for in a loose community recognition does not come as a reward of "sterling moral qualities" and "honest labor" but goes to all kinds of superficial brilliancy and show.

Perhaps the girl would settle down unrevoltingly to this steady life, however dull, if the apparent possibilities of an entirely different life, full of excitement, pleasure, luxury and showing-off were not continually displayed before her eyes in an American city. Shop windows, theaters, the press, street life with its display of wealth, beauty and fashion, all this forms too striking a contrast to the monotony of the prospect which awaits her if she remains a "good girl." If she felt definitely and irremediably shut off from this "high life" by practically impassable class barriers, as a peasant girl in Europe feels, she might look at all this show of luxury as upon an interesting spectacle with no dream of playing a rôle in it herself. But even aside from the idea of democracy—which though it does not mean much to her politically, teaches her to think that the only social differences between people are differences of wealth—she feels that some small part at last of this gorgeousness actually is within her reach, and her imagination pictures to her indefinite possibilities of further advance in the future. Sooner or later, of course, she will be forced back into her destined channel by society, by the state, by economic conditions, will be forcibly "reformed" and settled, not into a satisfied, positively moral course of life but to a more or less dissatisfied acceptance of the necessary practical limitations of her desires and of the more or less superficial rules of *decorum*. But before her dreams are dispelled she tries to realize them as far as she can. We have here, of course, only one specification of the unrest which characterizes America and American women.

▲ E S S A Y S

In the first essay, excerpted from her 1988 book on the history and politics of family violence, *Heroes of Their Own Lives,* Linda Gordon of New York University details the "discovery" of child abuse in late-nineteen-century Boston. Using the records of Boston's premier child-protection organization, the Massachusetts Society for the Prevention of Cruelty to Children (MSPCC), she explores reformers' definitions of child abuse and shows that these definitions undermined parental authority in immigrant families at the same time that they allowed native-born reformers to bring attention to the problems of poverty, alcoholism, and domestic violence.

In the second essay, Mary E. Odem of Emory University and author of the 1995 book, *Delinquent Daughters,* examines generational conflict among California's working poor through the lens of the juvenile court system. Focusing on statutory rape prosecutions in the early twentieth century, she describes young women's sexual activity as both an avenue to autonomy and a route to ruin. Along the way, she illuminates points of difference and agreement between working-class parents' and middle-class reformers' attitudes about female chastity.

Child Abuse and Child Protection in Boston, 1880–1910

LINDA GORDON

Child abuse was "discovered" in the 1870s. Surely many children had been ill-treated by parents previously, but child abuse had not been considered a social problem. Deviant behavior becomes a "social problem" when policymakers perceive it as threatening to social order, and generate the widespread conviction that organized social action is necessary to control it. In just such a manner the social problem of child abuse was constructed by reformers and charity workers. The evidence of that new social concern was the rapid worldwide establishment of Societies for the Prevention of Cruelty to Children [SPCCs]: by the end of the decade there were thirty-four such societies in the United States and fifteen elsewhere.

The modern history of family violence is not the story of changing responses to a constant problem, but, in large part, of redefinition of the problem itself. The nineteenth-century interpretation of child abuse, "cruelty to children," did not focus on *family* violence. The reformers who established the SPCCs did not conceive of family as the root of the problem, or as the logical jurisdictional boundary. In the twentieth century a cultural anxiety about the breakdown of the "traditional" family—specifically about gender and generational relations—influenced the child-protection movement, but nineteenth-century reformers were more affected by class, ethnic, and cultural anxieties. They were reacting above all against urbanism and the new immigration, which jointly created an urban underclass threatening to their whole vision of a good society. They saw cruelty to children as a vice of inferior classes and cultures which needed correction and "raising up" to an "American"

Linda Gordon, *Heroes of Their Own Lives: The Politics and History of Family Violence: Boston, 1880–1960* (New York: Penguin, 1988), pp. 27–30, 32–52, 54–57. Copyright © 1988. Reprinted by permission of the author.

standard. Their emphasis on cruelty made children's mistreatment seem willful rather than structural, a view which in turn grew from their unexamined confidence that their own family patterns were better because they practiced self-control. One of the most poignant ironies of their project is that their clients turned around the meaning of their phrase and labeled their agency, the MSPCC, "the Cruelty." Poor children said to their immigrant parents, mothers-in-law said to mothers, feuding neighbors said to each other, "Don't cross me or I'll report you to the Cruelty."

In the late-nineteenth-century cities, child abuse appeared worse than before, and indeed it may well have been worse. Urban poverty was more stressful in many ways than rural poverty: housing was overcrowded and overpriced; homes and neighborhoods were filthy, without adequate facilities for disposing of wastes; the air and water were polluted; the food in the markets was often adulterated and rotten, and the urban poor could not grow their own; there were new dangers from fires, traffic, and other urban hazards; wage-earners were at the mercy of periodic unemployment and grinding hours and conditions. Immigration separated many newcomers from potentially supporting kinfolk, created neighborhoods that were not communities, left mothers more alone with children than they had been in the "old country." The anonymity of urban life promoted more theft, vandalism, and violence.

We can only speculate about how these stresses contributed to child abuse, since we have no way to determine its incidence in agrarian societies. We can, however, explain why child abuse was more visible and more disturbing in the late nineteenth century than it had been previously. On the one hand, the moral reformers who defined the social problem were influenced by a growing sensibility of tenderness toward children and revulsion against personal violence; on the other hand, the rough ways of the poor were more visible—in big cities people of different classes lived and worked in proximity and the poor, particularly children, lived much of their lives on the streets. Reformers considered child abuse not only a moral wrong but also a kind of pollution, poisoning the stock of future citizens and the daily order of civil society. Child protection was one of a range of campaigns to control social disorder.

In the "gilded age," as the 1870s through 1890s are often called, in reference to the fortunes amassed by new industrial magnates, charity work took on a greater class consciousness—and class fear. In cities like Boston such fears were nearly inseparable from xenophobia as the working class became increasingly Catholic and foreign. A native-born Protestant elite was fearful of losing political and cultural control of their society to the immigrants, largely Catholic, streaming into the cities. The feared sources of social disorder now included not just disease, laziness, and depravity, but also organized resistance: labor unrest, even revolution, threatened, especially after the strike-ridden summer of 1877. As the threat to social order appeared to come not just from random deviant individuals but from entire social groups, so the response shifted from random individualized acts of charity, persuasion, and threat to organized collective action.

Helping children assumed a special resonance in part because of these new aspects of charity in industrial society. Because children were thought to be innocent (in contrast to previous Calvinist anxiety about children's capacity to be possessed by evil), they could easily be victimized. Because children were thought to be malleable (a view of children itself a product of "bourgeois" society, not characteristic of traditional peasant cultures), they could be molded into good citizens. The images of proper childhood that the child-savers sought to impose had class content, as we shall see, expressed in a sensibility about how children should behave in the present and toward what goals they should be directed. Protecting children from the wrongs of adults unified the charitable and the controlling impulses.

I do not wish, however, to offer here a functional argument, that child protection was seized upon because it fit some need outside its expressed purposes. The fit between child-saving and other social anxieties was an historical fact, not a causal explanation. Their concern about children was not merely a mask for intervention whose "real" purposes were other—such as labor discipline. The child protectors were primarily motivated to rescue children from cruelty. However, their own values and anxieties made that cruelty more visible and disturbing than it once had been.

While child protection was a national, even international movement, this study focuses on one city. In most ways, Boston's experiences in the late nineteenth century were not fundamentally different from those of many United States cities: its geography and age may have made its poverty and the growing distance between rich and poor more vivid and more extreme, but basic conditions were similar throughout the United States. Still, Boston's peculiarities shaped not only its own child-protection organization—the Massachusetts Society for the Prevention of Cruelty to Children—but also the national movement, since the MSPCC was so influential.

Two major features of Boston's history affected the MSPCC: the relative strength, rootedness, and stability of its Protestant establishment, and the relatively early arrival of large groups of immigrants who were not Protestant or Anglo-Saxon. . . .

Child protection grew out of a more general child-saving charitable activity, dating from early in the century, devoted primarily to placing poor and abandoned children in asylums and in apprenticeships. Child-saving drew heavily on women's reform and philanthropic energy, and was influenced by feminist interpretations of social ills. . . . These early child-saving efforts were characterized by what psychiatrist John Bowlby has called the "rescue fantasy." The reformers saw themselves as gracious, privileged big sisters, not only of children but of adult women of the lower classes. Their sense of what they had to offer was deeply religious and evangelical; they considered Catholicism as hardly better than superstition. The rescue fantasy reflected not only their class condescension but also their search for an arena in which to feel powerful, and, as has often been the case with women, their religious conviction justified their stepping out of their domestic sphere. . . .

The influence of this feminist vision was strengthened in Boston by the integration of upper-class charity and women's activism within the reform community, and then by the integration of another upper-class cause: campaigns against cruelty to animals, which had organized SPCAs [Societies for the Prevention of Cruelty to Animals] several decades previously, Some SPCCs arose as additions to pre-existing SPCAs. (Many "humane" societies continue to connect the two functions today.) The legal basis for prosecuting animal abusers existed where there were no such means against child abusers, an irony appreciated by 1870s reformers, who used it as an argument for child protection. . . .

In Boston, SPCA men and child-saving women cooperated in forming a new organization, and the women retained substantial influence for several decades. . . . Women were tremendously important in financial support for charities such as the MSPCC. A study of fund-raising for Boston's charities, done in the early twentieth century, showed that women were responsible for more than half the contributions. While we have no equivalent date for the nineteenth century, the available evidence suggests the same pattern prevailed then. Individual women contributed 36 percent of the funds raised, in contrast to individual men's 37 percent, a remarkable proportion considering how much more money men had than women. Moreover, women solicited most of the contributions from both men and women. . . .

In the MSPCC's first few decades, upper-class women not only raised money but also participated actively in the work of the Society. They found placements for children, became guardians of children, investigated farm and boarding homes. . . .

The MSPCC's images of good and bad child-raising were deeply influenced by the sensibility of these upper-class women. In their fund-raising they sentimentalized the sufferings of children, and found a sure touch for evoking tears and money from their audiences. They produced "before and after" photographs in which neglected immigrant children (the women liked to call them "waifs") were pictured first as they had been found and then dressed in Victorian finery to show how they could be "saved." The way they conducted the temporary home expressed their mission, too. Emphasizing cleanliness, fine dress, good food, order, and quiet, they self-righteously used it to expose by contrast the inadequacy of the children's parental homes.

Although women were active in organizing and fund-raising for the MSPCC, its managers, staff, and public spokesmen were all men. The men, too, were generally upper-class and had roots in the reform tradition as well as anti-cruelty-to-animals work. . . .

It is remarkable how quickly the Society became very busy. By the end of 1881, after three and a half years of work, it had handled 2,017 cases involving 3,660 children. Its agents had filled up 3,600 ledger pages and 3,000 pages of a letter book. It is not surprising that there was so much cruelty to children, but that a new organization received such a heavy caseload in such a short time makes one ask, How did the MSPCC find the cases?

Its success was largely due to the zeal of its agents, as its workers were then called. In these early years MSPCC agents went out onto the streets seeking abuses to correct. They looked for children begging, children outside when they should have been in school or inside, children improperly dressed or excessively dirty, children peddling. During two months of the summer of 1880, for example, 45.2 percent of new cases were initiated by agents themselves. The agents saw themselves as a street police for children, supplementing the inadequate resources of the police and truant officers. The first General Agent, Dixwell, became a virtual ambulance chaser. He scanned the Boston newspapers for items that suggested mistreatment of children. When he read in the *Boston Daily Globe* of a "waif" begging without socks or shoes, he set out to find him, and did—on Washington Street, selling pins while his mother watched from a hiding place. Dixwell arrested the boy, who was sentenced to a reform school for two years—for what offense is unstated. . . . When the *Boston Herald* reported that a boy playing in the street had been injured in his eye by something his companion had thrown, Dixwell wrote to the Superintendent of Boston City Hospital to find out how badly he was injured, collecting evidence to prosecute the parents for neglect. . . .

Soon the majority of MSPCC cases came from non-staff, known as complainants. Increasingly they were family members, who initiated 34 percent of complaints in 1880 and 61 percent by 1890. . . . Other agencies and authorities—Overseers of the Poor, truant officers, police officers, other Boston charity agencies, the Associated Charities, teachers and school headmasters, agencies in other towns seeking to trace people or to hand over responsibility for roving clients—also began to make regular referrals to the MSPCC.

Not all complaints turned into "cases." Informants sometimes gave wrong addresses; or agents, unfamiliar with densely populated working-class neighborhoods and unaided by the residents, could not find the people in question. Boston's poor in this period were extremely transient. . . . Furthermore, agents often found no evidence of wrong-doing despite a complaint. Hostile neighbors and relatives often turned in false accusations. In 1880 56 percent of complaints were dismissed by the agency for lack of evidence; in 1890 65 percent, and the proportation was at least that high every year thereafter, sometimes reaching almost 3:1. Some complaints were withdrawn by complainants. This was particularly common when family members were the initiators, because they were acting out of anger, which then subsided, or because they began to see dangers to themselves if the MSPCC became involved. For example, in one 1890 case, a woman complained that her husband had "wasted" $900 left to her by her former husband, and when she remonstrated with him, he struck and threatened her and refused her the rent money. But a few days later, when the MSPCC wrote to the man, she hid the letter from him and turned away an agent trying to see him. Such ambivalence was most frequent in wife-beating cases, but also evident in many others. . . . The MSPCC took on not only cases that would today be considered child abuse but also other social problems that its leaders saw as cruelty to children.

One such problem was the *padrone* system, a form of indentured labor. Beginning in the 1860s, children from Italian families, particularly in the poor southern provinces, were recruited for labor in the United States in return for payments to their parents. In exchange, the *padrone* kept the children's earnings, thus gaining incentive for severe exploitation of the children. As historian Robert Bremner has pointed out, "From the standpoint of [poor] parents . . . the boys and girls would be better provided for than under their own roofs; there would be fewer mouths to feed at home, and a little money coming in each month from across the sea." In fact, the *padrone* system had counterparts among many nationalities, including the Irish and later the Chinese, but these reformers believed it to be uniquely Italian.

The *padrones* usually sent the children out as street musicians, sometimes with organ-grinders. . . . The SPCCs sponsored legislation limiting street trades, even for adults. . . .

In Boston the MSPCC took credit for wiping out the *padrone* system and the work of children with organ-grinders, but this claim was self-serving and disregarded what Italians themselves were doing. The Italian legislature outlawed this form of indenture and an active Italian-American campaign helped stimulate, in

1874, a federal law against "Italian white child slavery" and several well-publicized convictions. . . .

The complaints against child performers and the *padrone* system were sometimes put in terms of child labor. However, there is reason to doubt the seriousness of this concern, given the Society's infrequent attempts to monitor child labor in other situations. . . . The MSPCC lobbied for and took credit for improvements in the state's anti-child-labor legislation. However, considering the class basis of support for the MSPCC, it is not surprising that its activity concerning child labor in industrial or large commercial establishments was minimal. Major campaigns about the overwork of children were always directed against the poor, not the rich. Agents worried about immigrant children overworked by "lazy" parents or greedy *padrones*. Here the child-savers came into conflict with immigrants' traditional expectations that children ought to work and to contribute to a family economy.

The MSPCC also took on the problems presented by children without parents— lost, orphaned, or abandoned. Only the last group fits into contemporary concepts of child abuse, but for the early MSPCC all these problems seemed parallel, putting children in need of care. Many orphans left alone were reported to the Society. "[Agent] Smyth . . . to see B . . . children. Father & mother dead some years. [thirteen-year-old boy] in bed—so called—to keep warm. He got up and when dressed looked like a 'scarecrow.'" This boy was responsible for three younger siblings, even though he had kinfolk nearby: uncles in Dorchester, Hingham, and South Boston. In December 1896 two children, ages six and five, were found alone, their mother having died in January 1895, their father being in jail for drunkenness. In 1894 a school headmaster reported that a ten-year-old boy was alone, his foster mother having been imprisoned for running an "idle and disorderly house." . . .

Babies abandoned at hospitals, police stations, or other institutional places were usually sent directly to asylums. Older lost children, however, were often brought to the MSPCC. . . . The numbers of lost children were substantial—in Boston averaging five per thousand population in 1874. Some children may have been recorded "abandoned" without adequate searches for their parents. However, the MSPCC also received complaints of abandonment of a less ambiguous sort: from women hired to board infants or even older children for periods of time, who reported that the parents had absconded. Inversely, parents often came to the MSPCC to find boarding homes for their children—or even permanent homes, because of poverty or illegitimacy, for example.

Boarding mothers figured ominously and ambiguously in the sensationalized issue of baby farming. . . . Many poor women supported their own families by caring for children, in an occupation partly an extension of wet-nursing. Their poverty combined with the helplessness or indifference of parents to leave the babies vulnerable to mistreatment. Some advertised publicly that they desired to "adopt" babies, then "got rid" of them either themselves or through farming them out to yet others. In 1905 the New York SPCC prosecuted a child-care operator who allegedly subcontracted 700 babies out to other women. The accused, Mrs. Letizia Tombarina, took babies into her care for $10 per month and then farmed them out to other Italian women for $5 per month. Many of these children had been sent to her by established child-saving groups. She and her agents found the "subcontractors" by reading the death notices in the Italian papers; when a nursing infant had died, the mother would be approached and offered a baby to nurse. . . .

Child protectors saw another form of abuse in the widespread practice of insuring children. The practice originated as burial insurance, organized by working-class mutual-aid societies. Many child-savers considered insurance at best "an offensive symbol of the prevalent materialistic orientation toward childhood"; at worst as an incentive to murder. But the child protectors were less unified on this issue than on others, and some SPCC spokesmen defended the insurance of children. . . .

The child protectors' division on this issue indicated their confusion about what children were being insured for, and their disdain for working-class families. Prosperous reformers often disapproved of the poor's spending substantial sums on funerals and wakes, while to many people anything less than a generous funeral was a statement of disregard for the child who had died. A pauper burial "confounded tragedy with degradation." At the same time children often produced regular income on which their families were dependent, and for this reason insuring children was no more cynical than insuring their fathers. It was of a piece with the practice, common at this time, of suing for damages in the "wrongful death" of a child, damages often awarded in exact replication of the child's expected earning power.

In identifying the problems in need of correction, early child protectors saw the mistreatment of children through their own cultural lenses. Indeed, their sense of mission was more powerful because it came from a feeling of unquestioned superiority to the masses among whom child neglect and abuse were so widespread. . . .

Social workers' bias in their view of clients has been a consistent problem in child-protection work. In the nineteenth century, it was at its worst, because the social distance between clients and workers was greatest. The fact that agency workers commonly visited clients in their homes in this period only widened the distance, since the clients' home lives seemed repulsive to the child protectors, who saw only their filthy, ill-furnished apartments, their unkempt and odorous persons, their dirty verminous children, their shouting and profanity, their diets of bread and beer (or wine, as Italians clients became more frequent) and stew. The agents hated the garlic and olive-oil smells of Italian cooking, and considered their food unhealthy, overstimulating, aphrodisiac. Their languages were so different, even when the clients spoke English, that there was little opportunity for clients to make their individual personalities known to agency workers.

Such bias and social distance affected the diagnoses of the causes of cruelty to children. In the nineteenth century, two themes dominated child protectors' analyses: drunkenness and the cultural inferiority of the immigrants. Moreover, they believed the two to be connected, despite the fact that some immigrant groups, such as Italians, Portuguese, and Southeast Europeans, did not have patterns of high alcohol consumption.

Until Prohibition the MSPCC consistently cited intemperance as the main causal factor in cruelty to children. . . . Heavy drinking did in fact create great misery among Boston's poor, causing illness, greater impoverishment, violence, and depression, but the child protectors were unable to distinguish it from moderate drinking. The presence of any alcoholic drinks or bottles, including wine and beer, in the homes of their clients was evidence of alcoholic depravity, and any woman who touched spirits was considered *ipso facto* unfit.

MSPCC agents also traced child mistreatment to vices inherent among inferior nationalities and cultures, a problem usually called "depravity." Their conviction that "Americans" were superior, as evidenced in their more humane treatment of children, was explicit: for example, "mother will never bring up her children according to American standards," a caseworker wrote of a recalcitrant client. . . .

If the early child protectors were insensitive to the power relations in their work, if they saw their clients as helpless and grateful, that very ignorance left them a clear emotional path on which to follow their kind and helping impulses. They responded like the amateurs they were—personally. In many cases, agents, or equally often their wives, paid from their own pockets to help children, or intervened personally in family problems. In the winter of 1879, one reads, Mrs. Dixwell gave breakfast and warm clothes to a boy, and Mrs. Otis (an MSPCC director) gave him warm mittens. In 1883 a fifteen-year-old boy was placed informally with an MSPCC agent's uncle who had an estate in Waltham. Or, later that year, Agent "A. J. Smyth at the request of [a father] took his son from the grandparents . . . and carried him to the fa[ther] . . . ."

Society workers, influenced both by the traditions of "friendly visiting" and by the need to investigate cruelty allegations, spent a great deal of time on the streets and calling upon families in their homes. Agents were detectives, looking for absconded fathers, finding runaway or lost children, verifying addresses, checking marriage, death, birth, and divorce records. In their detecting, MSPCC agents acted far more like police than like friendly visitors. Like police, they were not always law-abiding. As an *Annual Report* put it, delicately, "It is true we have taken risks on the margin of legal liability which seemed needful to rescue the child . . . but without cost to the society." Agents visited homes late at night or early in the morning—at times calculated to find wrongdoing. Unable to gain entry, they climbed in windows. They searched without warrants. Their case notes frequently revealed that they made their judgments first and looked for evidence later.

Agents relied very largely on warnings and threats in their efforts to help mistreated children, believing that the specter of action would be enough to reform parents. Even among our random sample—which includes only cases in which cruelty was confirmed by the agency—no action was taken in many cases: 47 percent in 1880, down to 32 percent by 1893.

Somewhere between action and inaction was "advice and referral." This was used increasingly as the MSPCC delineated its jurisdiction and refused to accept certain cases. For example, many came to the Society for relief (i.e., financial aid), which it never provided. Nevertheless, clients were often clever to do so. Sometimes an agent's referring a client elsewhere resulted in a run-around, but at other times an MSPCC referral was practically as good as cash. Thus a father came in with eight young children, asking for vaccinations for the children, rent money, and employment. When he went on to the Overseers of the Poor, the Provident Association, and the Industrial Aid Society, he came with an MSPCC recommendation. Similarly, the MSPCC had the power to get children released from other institutions. In one case a widow was able to persuade the MSPCC that her child had been mistakenly taken. She earned her living doing garment-finishing work and like all home workers had to travel to and from jobbers to pick up and deliver bundles, and to look for jobs. While thus temporarily absent she had taken sick and gone to a friend's home to recuperate, she claimed. When she returned, she found that her children had been taken to the Chardon Street Home, a shelter run by the Overseers of the Poor. The MSPCC agent gave her a letter to get her children back.

The MSPCC's influence over other agencies was thus an important aspect of its power and function.

The MSPCC also assumed substantial authority to arrange adoptions, trustee-ships, child support, custody, and guardianship agreements; it became, in modern terms, both an arbitration and a mediation agency. . . . Many men came to get help in finding wives and children who had left them. Mrs. Sarah E. Dawes, the president of the Nickerson Home (a private nonsectarian Roxbury home for children), called about a fourteen-year-old girl who had lived there eleven years, Her mother, about to be released from prison, had declared her intention of coming to get her daughter, but Dawes sought to prevent this and asked MSPCC help. The agent advised her on how to seek guardianship. . . .

The MSPCC also negotiated private placing-out agreements. . . . An excerpt from one private placing-out agreement illustrates the form of parents' sacrifice of their rights:

> For and in consideration of expenses incurred, or to be incurred, by Mass. Socy PC to C in behalf of my child eleven years of age, and to enable said Society to procure for said child a suitable home . . . I hereby delegate to said Society my authority over said child; and I . . . give up said child to said Society unreservedly . . . or such other disposal as may seem to said Socy best for its welfare, agreeing that I will neither seek to discover its home, attempt its removal therefrom nor in any way molest the family in which it may be placed, or other parties interested.

When the Society decided upon legal action against child abusers it had relatively few options: It could prosecute a child abuser for assault and battery, drunkenness, or rape; alternatively, it could have the children adjudged neglected and committed to a city-run institution. Among the MSPCC's earliest actions was lobbying for increased legal powers. Legislation of 1882 gave the MSPCC two important new powers: (1) a probate court judge could appoint the Society as guardian for any neglected, ill-treated, or abandoned child under fourteen, for a period of time during which the MSPCC could retain or assign custody; and (2) any judge could give the MSPCC immediate thirty-day custody of abandoned or deserted children under five. With these powers the MSPCC could remove children immediately to its own temporary home, without the delays of trials; it could place children for long periods in other homes or in foster or even adoptive homes. . . .

The MSPCC also obtained legislation against particular behaviors which it deemed cruel to children. Against baby farming an act of 1882 required that local boards of health register all boarding homes, and that the Overseers of the Poor register any illegitimate child given out to board. Against child performers, the MSPCC won the removal of all exceptions to the ban on children in "public exhibitions," and a prohibition on the admission of children under thirteen to shows. Exhibiting deformed children in circuses was specifically prohibited. The sale or gift of tobacco to minors was prohibited, as was the sale of firearms. A whole series of acts regulated peddling by minors. Tougher laws were passed against sexual abuse, including raising the age of consent to fourteen. Truancy laws, too, were toughened. . . .

. . . In its first two decades the MSPCC was a key force behind the increased state regulation of children's activities and parents' child-raising. . . . Even more important was their day-to-day assumption of authority over the definition of appropriate treatment of children and punishment of violators. . . .

MSPCC agents gathered information from the police, asked police officers to bring cases to them, conscripted police officers as supervisors in cases where mistreaters of children had been warned but not punished, and took referrals from the police. Boston MSPCC agents did not themselves make arrests; rather, if they thought an arrest likely, they stopped first at the local police station to bring an officer with them. Once on the scene, the police deferred to the MSPCC agent as the expert on domestic law, and followed his directions.

Otherwise, MSPCC agents acted like police in countless small ways. They called people to their office with letters that sounded like legal summonses, and their recipients usually complied. They threatened families with arrest or with taking custody of children. They regularly interviewed neighbors and relatives, attempting to entrap them into damaging statements about those under investigation. They searched homes, confiscated unacceptable objects, such as liquor bottles, and ejected "unwholesome" visitors. . . .

. . . Previously, child-savers such as the Children's Aid Societies directed their efforts at "dependent" children—meaning those reliant on the public or community for support. Children became dependent through orphanage, desertion, the impoverishment of their parents, or by running away (becoming "little wanderers," in the language of the time). While the earlier child-savers probably did "steal" some children from poor parents, they did not publicly claim the right to do so. Following the activist lead of the SPCAs, the SPCCs proclaimed their intention to intervene in existing, not necessarily "dependent," families.

In claiming this right to intervene into intact families, child protection was challenging patriarchal relations. A pause to consider the definition of patriarchy is necessary here. . . . I use the term in its . . . historical . . . sense, referring to a family form in which fathers had control over all other family members—children, women, and servants. . . . That historical patriarchy defined a set of parent-child relations as much as it did relations between the sexes, for children rarely had opportunities for economic independence except by inheriting the family property, trade, or craft. While women were subordinated, mothers too benefited in some ways from patriarchal parent-child relations: their authority over daughters and young sons was an important value when women lacked other kinds of authority and independence, and in old age they gained respect, help, and consideration from younger kinfolk.

The SPCCs' claim to speak on behalf of children's rights, and to intervene in parental treatment of children, was an attack on patriarchal power. At the same time, the new sensibility about children's rights and the concern about child abuse were signs that patriarchal family expectations and realities had already been weakening, particularly in the United States. . . .

Early child-protection work did not, of course, envision a general liberation of children from parental control. On the contrary, the SPCCs aimed as much to reinforce a failing parental/paternal authority as to limit it. Indeed, SPCC spokesmen viewed excessive violence against children as a symptom of *inadequate* parental authority. If assaults on children were provoked by children's insubordination, this showed that parental weakness, children's disobedience, and child abuse were mutually reinforcing. Furthermore, by the turn of the century, the SPCCs discovered that the majority of their cases concerned neglect, not assault, and neglect to them exemplified especially vividly the problems created by inadequate parental supervision and authority.

In sum, the SPCCs sought to reconstruct the family along lines that altered the old patriarchy, already economically unviable, and to replace it with a modern version of male supremacy. This new system included state (later, professional) regulation limiting parental rights and prescribing new standards for proper child-raising. Children were to be disciplined with patience and indulgence. Fathers, now as wage laborers rather than as slaves, artisans, peasants, or entrepreneurs, were to have single-handed responsibility for economic support of their families but little direct participation in domestic life. Women and children were not to contribute to the family economy, at least not monetarily. Children instead were to spend full time in learning—cognitive lessons from professional teachers, psychological and moral lessons from the full-time attention of a mother. Children's respect for parents was to be inculcated moralistically and psychologically, because it no longer rested on an economic dependence lasting beyond childhood. The family as a whole became an object of ideology, no longer just a given. In the next century the concept of "family violence" gained resonance because it seemed to represent a contradiction, a violation of a space and a set of relations that were to be inherently peaceful. . . .

Female Sexuality and Juvenile Delinquency in Early-Twentieth-Century California

MARY E. ODEM

The social and sexual autonomy of daughters was a major source of conflict in working-class families in the early twentieth century and led many parents to seek the assistance of the legal system. Working-class parents made use of recent changes in statutory rape laws to control their rebellious teenage daughters. Middle-class purity reformers had carried out a successful national campaign to make sexual intercourse with teenage girls a criminal offense by raising the age of consent in rape statutes. Their demand was based on the belief that sexual exploitation by adult men was the major cause of moral ruin among young working-class women and girls. When the campaign began in 1885, the age of consent in most states was ten or twelve years; by 1920, nearly every state in the country had raised the age of consent to sixteen or eighteen years. Through this campaign, reformers aimed to control both male sexual license and the social and sexual behavior of working-class teenage girls that conflicted with middle-class moral standards.

Middle-class reformers may have been responsible for raising the age of consent, but once this legislation was in place, working-class parents used it for their own needs and purposes. In the California counties of Alameda and Los Angeles,

Mary E. Odem. "Teenage Girls, Sexuality, and Working-Class Parents in Early Twentieth-Century California," in Joe Austin and Michael Nevin Willard, eds., *Generations of Youth: Youth Cultures and History in Twentieth-Century America* (New York: New York University Press, 1998), pp. 50–60. Copyright © 1998. Reprinted by permission of New York University Press.

working-class parents initiated approximately half of the prosecutions for statutory rape in the early decades of the twentieth century. They, along with middle-class reformers, were greatly disturbed by their daughters' assertions of social and sexual autonomy. As traditional forms of moral regulation proved less effective, some parents turned to the courts to control teenage daughters and their male partners. This chapter explores the struggles over teenage sexuality in working-class families through an analysis of statutory rape prosecutions in the Alameda County Superior Court for the decade 1910 to 1920 (112 cases), and in the Los Angeles County Juvenile Court for the years 1910 and 1920 (31 cases). . . .

Like many urban areas in the rest of the country, Alameda and Los Angeles counties witnessed tremendous population growth and economic development in the late nineteenth and early twentieth centuries. The principal cities of the two counties, Oakland and Los Angeles, grew at a rapid pace. Between 1880 and 1920, the population of Oakland increased from 34,555 to 216,261, and the population of Los Angeles grew from 11,183, to 576,673. The great expansion of transportation, trade, and industry in California drew a succession of native-born and foreign-born workers to both cities. In the late nineteenth century, native-born white Americans and northern Europeans made up the bulk of the working-class population in these cities. After the turn of the century, thousands of southern and eastern Europeans, Mexicans, Asians, and African Americans joined these earlier migrants to California.

This diverse population of working people in Alameda and Los Angeles counties exhibited a range of sexual norms and practices. Many adhered to strict moral codes that placed great importance on the chastity of daughters. Some of the parents eventually turned to the legal system to enforce these moral codes and to punish rebellious daughters and their male partners. Virtually all of the parents who filed statutory rape complaints in these counties were working class; that is, they and/or their spouses were employed as skilled, semiskilled, or unskilled workers. This group of parents reflected the diversity of the working-class populations of the two counties. They included native-born whites and blacks; skilled workers and common laborers; rural migrants and seasoned urban dwellers; and immigrants from Germany, Ireland, Italy, Portugal, Russia, and Mexico.

Historians have usually associated the emphasis on female sexual purity with bourgeois Protestant culture and have drawn clear distinctions between the sexual behavior and norms of middle-class and working-class people. They have shown that middle-class Americans in the nineteenth century developed an ideology of sexual restraint that emphasized female purity and male continence and relied on individual self-control to regulate the passions. We know far less about the sexual mores of white, immigrant, and black working-class people during this period, but it is generally assumed that they were not bound by middle-class moral reticence. They supposedly had more fluid definitions of licit and illicit behavior, were more tolerant of sex outside of marriage, and did not stigmatize children born out of wedlock.

Although there clearly were important differences between middle-class and working-class expressions of sexuality, one has to be careful not to overgeneralize about the working-class experience or to neglect the strict moral codes that operated within many working-class and immigrant communities. Concern with female chastity was not rooted in middle-class Protestant culture alone. It was also based in the patriarchal family structure of preindustrial societies, in various religious traditions, and in a code of honor that linked family reputation to the morality of wives and daughters. Many of the migrants to California came from rural communities and small towns in Europe, Mexico, and parts of the United States in which fathers had controlled the labor and sexual lives of wives, children, and servants in ways that best supported the family economy. The stability of the patriarchal household demanded particularly close control of the sexuality of wives and daughters. Out-of-wedlock births threatened the limited economic resources of the family and the need to insure "legitimate" male heirs.

Religious teachings reinforced the importance of premarital chastity in preindustrial communities. According to the Judeo-Christian ideal, sexual intercourse before marriage, and after marriage except with one's spouse, was sinful. The Catholic Church, in particular, placed great value on virginity. Catholic doctrine forbade sex outside of the bonds of marriage and held that sex between married partners was strictly for the purposes of reproduction.

In theory, religious strictures on chastity applied to both sexes, but religion competed with a popular ethos that expected moral purity in women yet tolerated and even encouraged male sexual license. This double standard of morality was deeply rooted in Anglo-American culture and shaped both law and social custom in Britain and the United States. The insistence on female chastity was particularly pronounced in the Mediterranean societies from which Italian and Portuguese immigrants came, and also in Mexico, where a code of honor linked a family's status and reputation to the sexual purity of its daughters and wives. Here again, though, the double standard was in operation, for whereas sexual promiscuity destroyed a woman's honor, it enhanced a man's prestige and status in society.

Other working-class and immigrant groups came from communities that were somewhat less vigilant about guarding female chastity. In some small towns and rural villages of northern and western Europe and the United States, families tolerated sexual play and sometimes intercourse among young couples in the context of betrothal. Such courting practices were permitted because it was expected that marriage would follow, particularly if pregnancy resulted. Families and community leaders could usually pressure a reluctant father to marry his pregnant girlfriend.

To regulate the sexual behavior of youth, preindustrial and rural societies relied on external methods of control that operated best in relatively small, close-knit communities. Family, community, and church worked together to monitor young couples and to channel sexuality into marriage. In the small towns and rural villages of the United States, Europe, and Mexico, most daughters worked in farm households or small workshops and family businesses, under the close supervision of their parents or other relatives. The familial context of such work not only insured that parents retained control over their daughters' labor and services, but also enabled them to monitor the young women's social activities and relations with men. Families generally were well acquainted with the young men who courted their daughters. Couples usually met at the young woman's home or at community events and celebrations under the watchful eyes of neighbors. In southern European and Mexican villages, daughters were usually chaperoned by family members whenever they left home to go to the market, attend religious services, or take part in social events.

Even among experienced urban workers, as well as among migrants from rural areas and small towns, a preoccupation with female morality was evident. By the late nineteenth century, certain sectors of the American working class had embraced standards of sexual respectability that resembled those of the middle class. This was particularly true of the aristocracy of skilled laborers—made up primarily of native-born Americans and workers of Canadian and northern or western European backgrounds—and of the small elite in African American society. However, this development should not be read as a passive acceptance of bourgeois values, the end result of decades of moralizing by middle-class reformers and ministers. Rather, these white and African American workers reformulated dominant standards of respectability in response to their particular needs and social experiences. Many skilled workers and their wives embraced values of female domesticity and moral purity, yet at the same time mounted a radical critique of industrial capitalism which, in their view, destroyed the home by forcing women and children to work for wages, thereby threatening their physical and moral well-being. These workers and their unions fought for a "family wage" that would enable them to keep their wives and young children out of the paid labor force. This strategy aimed both to protect male wages and the family's standard of living and also to preserve the moral respectability of wives and daughters.

For a range of economic, cultural, and religious reasons, then, diverse groups of native-born and immigrant working people in Alameda and Los Angeles counties valued female chastity and used various means to enforce it. Traditional expectations of daughters and controls over their social interactions and relations with men, however, were seriously challenged in the rapidly growing and changing urban environments of Oakland and Los Angeles. In such large cities, earlier methods of regulating the sexuality of youth through family, community, and church were far less effective than they had been in villages and small towns. The great geographical mobility of workers, the crowded, ethnically diverse neighborhoods, and the growing number of young people living away from home made it difficult for parents or community leaders to ensure that marriage would automatically ensue when young women engaged in sex or got pregnant. Religious and communal sanctions did not have the same power to control deviant sexual behavior in large, heterogeneous cities as they had in small, face-to-face communities.

Compounding the problem, working-class daughters began to challenge familial expectations and roles as a result of new forms of work and recreation that drew them increasingly into the public sphere, where they experienced greater freedom from family constraints. Daughters continued to play a vital role in the family economy, for most working-class fathers did not earn enough to support the whole household on their wages alone. But the context of women's labor had changed dramatically. Instead of domestic work or industrial home work in family settings, the principal forms of female employment in the nineteenth century, daughters now worked in department stores, offices, factories, canneries, and restaurants. In Los Angeles some also had access to a variety of jobs in the burgeoning movie and entertainment industry. Most of these changes in employment opportunities did not apply for African American women, who were barred from the higher-status female jobs and compelled to work mostly in domestic service. But even young black women experienced greater social autonomy during this period as they left their families and farm households in the rural South to live and work in new urban environments.

Working out from under the supervision of family members, young women formed casual acquaintances with men they met on the streets and in the workplace. They used their status as wage earners to assume privileges such as staying out late, going to dance halls, and using part of their earnings to buy stylish clothes, makeup, or movie tickets. Some daughters took advantage of their new economic power to move away from home and live with friends or coworkers. Although most wage-earning daughters continued to live with parents or relatives, a growing number boarded in apartments and rooming houses with their peers.

The expansion and commercialization of leisure activities in Oakland and Los Angeles at the turn of the century created a youth-oriented, mixed-sex world of amusement that altered courtship patterns and further undermined family control of daughters. Urban youth spent many of their leisure hours with peers in the dance halls, movie theaters, and cafes that sprang up in the downtown areas, and they also flocked to the amusement parks built in the early years of the twentieth century in both cities. Opened in 1903, Oakland's Idora Park covered seventeen acres and offered numerous attractions to the thousands who visited daily: a carousel, a roller-coaster, a vaudeville theater, a dance pavilion, and a skating rink featuring a Tunnel of Love. In Los Angeles, young men and women could ride the trolley from almost anywhere in the county to the beachside amusement parks at Venice and Long Beach, which featured roller-coasters, merry-go-rounds, penny arcades, shooting galleries, and brightly lit promenades with cafes and dance pavilions. These new recreational facilities provided social space for unsupervised flirtation and intimate encounters with members of the opposite sex.

In response to these changes, immigrant and working-class families pursued various strategies to monitor their adolescent daughters as they worked and played in American cities. Mexican and Italian families attempted to maintain a system of chaperonage by having a relative, often an older brother, accompany daughters when they left home. Some parents also tried to supervise their wage-earning daughters by having them work in establishments with other family members. In the rapidly growing cities of Oakland and Los Angeles, however, such careful supervision was difficult to maintain. Over the objections of their families, daughters still went out in the evenings on their own and formed intimate relationships with young men they met at work, on the streets and beaches, and in the various amusement centers.

When familiar methods of sexual regulation proved ineffective in modern urban environments, some working-class parents turned to the courts for assistance. They used the statutory rape law to restrain daughters and their male partners who violated traditional moral codes. Numerous working-class parents sought legal intervention to end intimate relationships their daughters had formed with male companions. In one case, a fifteen-year-old Portuguese girl left home and stayed in a hotel for several days with a young man she had been dating. When her father found out, he confronted the man in his place of employment and then had him arrested for statutory rape. He explained to court officials, "You know how I felt towards him, what I wanted to do when he ruined my home." One working-class mother called on the court when she learned that her fifteen-year-old daughter, Louise, was involved in a sexual relationship with a young man nineteen years of age. The couple first met at the Majestic Dance Hall in Oakland and had been seeing each other for several months without the mother's knowledge. When the mother discovered a letter from the young man that revealed the nature of the relationship, she beat her daughter, reported her to juvenile authorities, and had the young man arrested for statutory rape.

In numerous cases, parents used the law to retrieve runaway daughters and their male companions. During the late nineteenth and early twentieth centuries, female runaways presented a serious problem to families in Oakland and Los Angeles, as well as other urban areas in the country. The local newspapers contained daily notices about teenage girls missing from home. Parents and police often suspected that the girls had been kidnapped and forced into prostitution by white slavers. A typical notice in the *Oakland Tribune* read: "Grace Logan goes to pay a visit to friends in Alameda and drops from sight. . . . It is the opinion of the girl's brother that she was either 'spirited away or has been the victim of white slavers.'"

Court records and newspapers, however, reveal that the young women and girls had more complex reasons for leaving home. Some were seeking greater independence and freedom from strict parental supervision. The *Oakland Tribune* reported that the mystery surrounding one seventeen-year-old girl's disappearance was solved when her friend reported "she was tired of restrictions placed on her by parents and planned to leave home and seek employment to make her own way in the world." There was great conflict in many families over how late daughters remained out at night, whom they dated, and where they spent their leisure time. Such a dispute led to the case of two female cousins who, frustrated with strict familial control of their behavior, ran away one Sunday afternoon. They headed immediately for the dance pavilion in Oakland's Idora Park, where they met a young man who worked as a sales clerk at a local store. After spending the evening with them at the amusement park, the man invited the teenagers to stay in his room for the night. The next evening, as the girls were on their way to another dance, they were apprehended by the police.

A number of other cases involved teenage girls who had run away to escape unhappy or abusive home situations. One Russian Jewish girl left her father's house because of his constant beatings. She moved in with her boyfriend, a young man who had previously boarded in her home until he was kicked out of the house because he tried to prevent the father from beating his daughter. The parents sent the police after the couple and had the young man arrested. Other young women also left home without parents' permission to live with their boyfriends. In one such case, sixteen-year-old Sara Gardner, who worked as a sales clerk, met a young Frenchman, a musician, at a dance pavilion in San Francisco. Over the next few weeks, the man visited her home, met her parents, and took her out several times to the movie theater and ice-cream parlor. Then he persuaded her to leave home and live with him in his Oakland apartment,and helped her find a job in the same theater where he worked. Within a week Sara's mother, uncle, and the police tracked down the couple at the theater and had the man arrested for statutory rape.

A number of parents turned to the court when confronted with a daughter's out-of-wedlock pregnancy, a problem which threatened both the economic stability and the social standing of many working-class families. Parents also worried about the humiliation and limited marriage prospects their daughters would face as unmarried mothers. Such were the concerns of Mrs. Alvarez, when she learned of her teenage daughter's pregnancy. Attempting to salvage her daughter's reputation, Alvarez enlisted several female relatives and neighbors to confront the suspected father where he worked and urge him to marry the girl. When he still refused, Alvarez had him arrested. As she explained in court, "I did it because I didn't want my daughter that way, because when a girl is that way, nobody thinks good of her . . . I told him I wanted him to marry the girl just to give her a name."

As working-class parents turned to the court to enforce traditional moral codes, their daughters struggled to assert their own social and sexual autonomy. The sexual encounters they described in court did not fit the image of male lust and female victimization described by purity reformers in the age-of-consent campaign. Instead of being the helpless victims of evil men, most of the young women were willing participants in a more complicated sexual drama. In 72 percent of the Alameda cases prosecuted between 1910 and 1920 and 77 percent of the Los Angeles cases in 1920, young women said they had consented to sexual relations with their male partners. The desire for pleasure, adventure, companionship, marriage, and economic support all figured in young women's decisions about their sexual choices. Most of their male partners were young working-class men. Seventy-three percent of the defendants in Alameda County were between the ages of eighteen and twenty-nine, the bulk of them between eighteen and twenty-four. Seventy-four percent of those whose occupation is known were skilled or unskilled laborers. The young men charged with statutory rape in the Los Angeles Juvenile Court were between thirteen and nineteen years of age, with 74 percent between the ages of fifteen and seventeen. They were employed in various working-class occupations such as store clerk, agricultural laborer, and teamster.

The young women in these court cases also challenged prevailing conceptions of female sexual innocence through their dress, language, and behavior. Many had flirted openly with young men on the street, dressed in the latest fashions, and attended dance halls, movie theaters, and amusement parks unchaperoned, often "picking up" young men once they arrived. In so doing, working-class daughters undermined the rigid classification of women as good and bad, angels and prostitutes, a division that was a staple of Victorian culture. They adopted many of the manners associated in the public's mind with prostitution—wearing makeup, smoking cigarettes, going out at night alone, and engaging in sex outside of marriage—yet they clearly distinguished themselves from prostitutes. The young women had not accepted money for sexual favors, and several expressed their clear disapproval of that type of exchange. Yet they acknowledged women's sexual agency and condoned sexual relations in certain circumstances.

Numerous young women had taken an active role in their romantic encounters. Out on the streets, in movie theaters and in dance halls, they encouraged and sometimes initiated contact with young men. When asked how she met her sexual partner, one teenage girl explained to court officials: "A flirtation . . . I turned the corner and looked back and he was standing outside smoking, then I went down a little ways and I looked around again and he was standing on the corner, then he followed me." Another teenager who appeared in court had apparently invited her boyfriend on several occasions to visit her in her bedroom at night without her parents' knowledge. Her family had learned of the relationship when they discovered the following note she wrote to the defendant: "Dear Joseph, I am sleeping in that little room and I felt rather lonesome and cold. I wonder if you couldn't come over to see me tonight about 11:00 . . . From the one that loves you."

Eighteen-year-old Margaret Emerson explained in court how she and her girl-friends met the defendant, George Cheney, and his friends when they went to the "moving picture show" in downtown Oakland one Sunday afternoon. Wearing stylish dresses for the occasion, the girls attracted the attention of the young men, gave out their addresses in East Oakland, and made a date to go to Lincoln Park the following weekend. Margaret explained to the court that "Mama would never let me talk to any fellows unless she saw them." Nevertheless, she went out with George twice before introducing him to her mother. After dating for several months, the couple decided to move in together and made plans to marry once George secured a divorce from his wife. To get Mrs. Emerson's approval for this arrangement, they told her they had already married and did not mention George's previous venture into marriage.

Like Margaret Emerson, many young women formed intimate relationships with their "steadies," men they had been dating and planned to marry. Yet the expectation of marriage was not always a precondition for engaging in sex. One teenage girl of Mexican descent, Edna Morales, fell in love and became intimately involved with a nineteen-year-old man whom she met at the store where she worked in Los Angeles. When questioned by court officials, Edna plainly stated that she had engaged in sex not because of a promise of marriage, but because of the affection she felt for her partner. The probation officer assigned to the case reported that when she asked the young woman about her sexual relations, "she very boldly said, yes . . . She did not seem to think there was anything wrong about it but refused to give me the young man's name."

For other young women, sex was not necessarily linked to marriage or even to love, but was simply a form of pleasure, part of an evening's entertainment and adventure. Julia Townsend, who lived with her parents in southern California, made occasional weekend trips to Los Angeles with her two girlfriends to visit dance halls and cafes. On one of these trips, she and her friends arrived in Los Angeles on a Saturday evening, registered at a downtown hotel, and headed for Solomon's Dance Hall. Julia, who was employed as a stenographer, used her own money to pay for the trip and her share of the room. The young women met several young men at the dance hall and invited them to their hotel room. That night the police raided the hotel and arrested the three couples. Julia was charged with "visit[ing] hotels with men to whom she is not married, sleeping and staying in the same room and apartment with these men." Another young woman expressed a liberal sexual standard similar to Julia Townsend's. According to the probation officer who handled her case, "She told me in talking with her that she did not believe there was any wrong in having sexual intercourse with boys, if she would not take money and if she did not become pregnant."

Other young working-class women had exchanged their sexuality for an evening's entertainment, a ticket to the amusement park, a meal, or a place to stay for the night. In a society that severely restricted women's access to economic independence and self-support, it is not surprising that many young women chose to barter with sex. Even though employment opportunities had expanded for women during this period, they earned only approximately 60 percent of the standard men's wages, and women workers typically earned less than the "living wage," estimated to be $9 or $10 a week in 1910. Young women discovered early on that their sexuality was a valued commodity which they could trade for things they wanted or needed. Because of their low wages, working girls often depended on men to "treat" them if they wanted to take part in urban recreations or enjoy a night on the town. In return, men expected sexual favors, which could range from affectionate companionship to sexual intercourse.

When sixteen-year-old Annie Wilson was asked in court how she became sexually involved with the defendant, she explained that she and her sister had skipped Sunday School to go to the skating rink at Idora Park in Oakland. There they met Andrew Singer, who treated them to refreshments and rides in the park. Later that night Annie returned with the young man to his hotel room and stayed the night. In the meantime her family notified the police, who located her the next morning. When asked by the court why Annie behaved this way, her sister responded, "She didn't like to turn him down, he had given us lunch and paid our way into the rink and she didn't like to turn him down."

Fifteen-year-old Agnes Farrell and her friend Amelia made a similar exchange with sailors they met at the train station in downtown Los Angeles or at the navy dock in San Pedro. They accompanied the sailors to dance halls and the amusement park at Long Beach and on several occasions spent the night with them in hotels along the beach. Agnes explained to court officials that they did not expect to receive money from the sailors but were merely interested in being taken out and shown a good time.

A number of girls used their sexuality as a strategy for survival after running away from home. Runaways often relied on boyfriends or men they met along the way to pay for meals and hotel rooms. In return for such support, the young women engaged in sexual intercourse with their male companions, following an arrangement that was often unspoken. A teenage runaway with no viable means of economic support often had only her sexuality to trade. One teenage girl left home to escape the heavy domestic duties her family demanded of her. She had no money with which to rent a room, but she met a young man in downtown Los Angeles who found and paid for a hotel room and later helped her to find a job at a nearby cafeteria. In return, she had sexual relations with him. A fifteen-year-old African American girl found herself in a similar situation when she left her aunt's home in a small town in northern California, where she had been living ever since her mother died. She ended up stranded in Oakland with no means of support until she ran into a young black man she knew. He offered to pay for her room and board and the two lived together for several days until they were arrested by the police.

Other young women had exchanged their sexuality, not for entertainment or shelter for the night, but for a promise of marriage. Some hoped marriage would offer a way out of tedious employment or an unhappy or overly strict home. Such was the situation of Louise Howard, who met her boyfriend, Robert Camarillo, at an Oakland dance hall. After they had dated for several weeks, Louise suggested that they get married. She desperately wanted to leave home because of the constant fights she had with her stepfather. Robert promised to marry her once he received the approval of his father. In the meantime, he wanted her to prove her love by having sex with him. Louise agreed to his request, but whenever she brought up the question of marriage, Robert claimed he was still waiting for his father's approval. Eventually Louise's mother learned of the couple's relationship, reported her daughter to juvenile authorities, and had the young man arrested. In another case a fifteen-year-old Portuguese girl, who worked in a telephone office, agreed to spend the night with a young man she had been dating after he promised to marry her. She was eager to leave her own home because she did not get along with her parents and was particularly distressed by their plan for her to marry a Portuguese man they had selected for her.

Sexuality was a means of rebellion for young women, but it was also clearly an area in which they were exploited. Engaging in sex outside of marriage involved serious risks for them—pregnancy, disease, abandonment, social ostracism. Although they were far from the helpless victims of reformers' accounts, young women nevertheless entered the sexual relationship from a greatly disadvantaged position compared to their male partners. They had far more restricted access to economic independence and faced greater condemnation for their sexual transgressions. Despite the purity reformers' campaign against the double standard, families and society still punished women more harshly than men for illicit sexual activity. Young women also encountered a popular male culture that viewed them as sexual bait, yet ostracized those who acquiesced as "loose," not fit to be wives and mothers. One young man refused to marry the pregnant teenage girl he had been dating, because, as he told court officials in Los Angeles, she was "a girl of easy morals."

One of the greatest risks of sexual experimentation for working-class daughters was out-of-wedlock pregnancy. Margaret Emerson found herself unmarried and pregnant after she agreed to have sex with her boyfriend, George Cheney. George had persuaded her to move in with him and promised they would marry as soon as he secured a divorce from his wife. After continually delaying the marriage, George finally moved out when Margaret became pregnant a year and a half later. Alone and with few resources, Margaret filed a rape complaint against him and told the court she thought he should marry her and help support the baby.

The social and economic costs of out-of-wedlock pregnancy led some young women to resort to illegal abortion, a dangerous and sometimes deadly procedure. One young woman in Los Angeles nearly died from blood poisoning after a botched abortion she received from a local doctor. Another pregnant teenage girl died from an "operation" shortly after her unsuccessful attempt to make her boyfriend marry her by taking him to court in Alameda County.

Young women's increased social autonomy could also make them vulnerable to forcible assault. At times, the boundaries and limits of the system of sexual exchange were not entirely clear. In some cases girls who were reluctant to comply with the expectation of sexual favors were forcibly raped. This was the case with Ruby Haynes, a teenage girl who accepted a date with a young man she met at the movie theater in Oakland. The night they met, Jason Strand took her to the beach, walked her home that night, and made a date to go to the nickelodeon a few days later. As they were walking home after the show, Jason took Ruby into a vacant lot and urged her to have sex with him. When she refused, he threw her to the ground and raped her.

The cases discussed in this chapter demonstrate the complex meanings that sexuality had for working-class teenage girls. As they explored romantic relations and heterosexual pleasures in new urban environments, teenage girls rebelled against traditional family expectations of daughters. Some were seeking intimacy with boyfriends; others were looking for adventure and excitement; a number sought escape from unhappy or overly strict homes; and still others used sex as a strategy for survival in the face of economic hardship and family abuse. As a result of gender and class discrimination, sexual experimentation involved serious risks for teenage girls. They encountered both pleasure and danger as they navigated the complicated sexual terrain of early-twentieth-century cities.

F U R T H E R   R E A D I N G

Alexander, Ruth M. *The "Girl Problem": Female Sexual Delinquency in New York, 1900–1930* (1995).

Ashby, LeRoy. *Saving the Waifs: Reformers and Dependent Children, 1890–1917* (1984).

Austin, Joe, and Michael Nevin Willard, eds. *Generations of Youth: Youth Cultures and History in Twentieth-Century America* (1998).

Bailey, Beth. *From Front Porch to Back Seat: Courtship in Twentieth-Century America* (1988).

Bremner, Robert H. *Children and Youth in America: A Documentary History* (1971).

Brenzel, Barbara. *Daughters of the State: A Social Portrait of the First Reform School for Girls in North America, 1856–1905* (1983).

Fass, Paula S. *The Damned and the Beautiful: American Youth in the 1920s* (1977).

Felt, Jeremy P. *Hostages of Fortune: Child Labor Reform in New York State* (1965).

Gordon, Linda. *Heroes of Their Own Lives: The Politics and History of Family Violence: Boston, 1880–1960* (1988).

Graff, Harvey J. *Conflicting Paths: Growing Up in America* (1995).

———, ed. *Growing Up in America: Historical Experiences* (1987).

Hawes, Joseph M. *Children in Urban Society: Juvenile Delinquency in Nineteenth-Century America* (1971).

Holloran, Peter C. *Boston's Wayward Children: Social Services for Homeless Children, 1830–1930* (1989).

Kett, Joseph F. *Rites of Passage: Adolescence in America, 1790 to the Present* (1977).

Kunzel, Regina G. *Fallen Women, Problem Girls: Unmarried Mothers and the Professionalization of Social Work, 1890–1945* (1993).

MacLeod, David. *The Age of the Child: Children in America, 1890–1920* (1998).

Meckel, Richard A. *Save the Babies: American Public Health Reform and the Prevention of Infant Mortality, 1850–1929* (1998).

Modell, John. *Into One's Own: From Youth to Adulthood in the United States, 1920–1975* (1989).

Nasaw, David. *Children of the City* (1985).

Odem, Mary E. *Delinquent Daughters: Protecting and Policing Adolescent Female Sexuality in the United States, 1885–1920* (1995).

Peiss, Kathy. *Cheap Amusements: Working Women and Leisure in Turn-of-the-Century New York* (1986).

Platt, Anthony. *The Child Savers: The Invention of Delinquency* (1969).

Riis, Jacob A. *The Children of the Poor* (1892).

Ryerson, Ellen. *The Best-Laid Plans: America's Juvenile Court Experiment* (1978).

Schlossman, Steven L. *Love and the American Delinquent: The Theory and Practice of "Progressive" Juvenile Justice, 1825–1920* (1977).

Schlossman, Steven, and Stephanie Wallach. "The Crime of Precocious Sexuality: Female Juvenile Delinquency in the Progressive Era." *Harvard Educational Review* 48 (February 1978): 65–94.

Stansell, Christine. "Women, Children, and the Uses of the Streets: Class and Gender Conflict in New York City, 1850–1860." *Feminist Studies* 8 (Summer 1982): 309–335.

Tiffin, Susan. *In Whose Best Interest? Child Welfare Reform in the Progressive Era* (1982).

Zelizer, Viviana A. *Pricing the Priceless Child: The Changing Social Value of Children* (1985).

The Family and the State: Origins of the Modern Welfare System in the Early Twentieth Century

In 1995, responding to then-President William Jefferson Clinton's promise to "end welfare as we know it," Congress enacted "welfare reform." That step ended the federal program Aid to Families with Dependent Children (AFDC), the successor to Aid to Dependent Children (ADC), which had been adopted during the Great Depression as part of the comprehensive Social Security Act of 1935 and had been modeled on private and public programs known as "mothers' pensions" that had been pioneered earlier in the twentieth century. But how well did the American public really "know" welfare?

Research on the origins of the modern welfare state has proliferated in the past decade. Using the copious literature produced by advocates for and opponents of government programs, historians of public policy have examined the state programs, federal agencies, and constitutional amendments of the early twentieth century that provided financial support for single mothers, investigated maternal and infant health, and banned child labor. Studies of early programs designed to enhance family stability and ensure child health reveal the contentious nature of "welfare" from the beginning; internally divided by differences of opinion over the best way to aid families, advocates of government assistance were also subject to outsiders' claims that they were dangerous communists. Analysis of early welfare policy also exposes the classism, racism, and sexism that undermined the government's best efforts to support families and protect children. Finally, scholarship on *the forerunners of the modern welfare system sheds light on the creation of a "two-tier" welfare state that treats some forms of government support (for soldiers, farmers, and workers) as "entitlements" and others (for women, children, and minorities) as "handouts."*

But this research, based as it is on the records of private charities and public agencies, is less successful at letting the recipients of aid speak for themselves. In historical literature as in past practice, poor families appear as the objects of concern and anxiety, rather than as active agents in their own families and communities.

Studies of the relationship between the family and the state from the Progressive Era through the New Deal not only provide an understanding of the creation of a national system for child welfare—the now-defunct AFDC—but also reveal the philosophical disagreements and political divisions that accompanied this process. In doing so, such studies raise important questions that shed light on the contemporary welfare debate: What is the proper relationship between the family and the state? Who is responsible for the well-being of children? How did "welfare" become a dirty word?

 ## D O C U M E N T S

Whereas nineteenth-century advocates for children favored removing them from their families and caring for them in institutions, twentieth-century reformers argued that children's interests would be better served by providing services to poor families. Document 1, an excerpt from a report of the Sixth Biennial Session of the National Conference of Jewish Charities in the United States, held in 1910, indicates this shift in public opinion.

As the existence of a national group of Jewish charities indicates, philanthropists assumed the bulk of the burden of supporting the poor in the nineteenth century. In the twentieth century, however, growing numbers of social activists argued that the responsibility for caring for children belonged to the government. A 1914 report from the Commission on Relief for Widowed Mothers in New York State, included as Document 2, illustrates this philosophy.

The establishment of the U.S. Children's Bureau in 1912 indicated increasing support for state-supported programs for children. The federal agency, like its predecessors in both the public and the private sectors, recommended keeping families together whenever possible. This preference is evident in Document 3, a report from the conference on children's welfare that the Children's Bureau held at the White House in 1919.

In 1930, a conference on child health and protection was held at the White House. An address by the chairman of the conference, Secretary of the Interior Ray Lyman Wilbur, makes up Document 4. Secretary Wilbur's speech indicates that child welfare would be one of the priorities of the federal government in the twentieth century. Wilbur also addresses the thorny issue of the proper relationship between the family and the state.

The twentieth century also witnessed a broadening of the definition of "dependent" children who needed and deserved government support. Document 5, a resolution adopted unanimously at the Tenth Annual Convention of the International Society for Crippled Children in 1931, reflects growing public interest in preventing birth defects and caring for disabled children.

1. Jewish Charitable Organizations Recommend Supporting Mothers and Children at Home, 1910

Given a good mother there is no reason, as has been stated frequently on the platform of this Conference, why she should be compelled to add the distress of breaking up her home to the grief occasioned by the loss of her husband, but, if the community has wisely decided to assist her to do this, it must, at the same time, determine that its support shall be adequate. It must give generously and not with niggardly hand. The mother ought not to be compelled to engage in work that will call her away from her own home, nor be forced, in her own home, to perform so large a quantity of work as to cause her to neglect her children, nor should her work be of such character as to impair her own health or that of her offspring. Above all, the keeping of lodgers, other than those related by blood ties to the family, should be prohibited absolutely. The family should not be allowed to remain in the poorer overcrowded neighborhoods of the city, but inasmuch as, in most cases, the majority of the children are below the legal working age, they should be required to move out into suburban or less closely settled neighborhoods, where the opportunities for fresh air and healthful play are unrestricted. The relief granted should be sufficient to enable the child, in addition to remaining at home, to have at least a fair share of the recreative opportunities that are afforded to his fellow in the institution. But, for the proper working out of this class of cases, a much greater degree of supervision must be provided than is furnished by any of the existing New York agencies. This is not work for the salaried employe[e]. It is pre-eminently the task of the friendly visitor . . . Too often the mother is not competent to spend wisely the amount of money that may be necessary to give her adequate relief. The friendly visitor, sympathetic, tactful, with a knowledge of good housekeeping, can be of invaluable service to her. In addition to assisting in the expenditure of funds and the management of the family budget, she may find work to do in advice concerning the preparation of foods and the foods to be used; the cleanliness of the children, their schooling and amusement. With proper supervision, I believe this kind of work can become extremely valuable; without it, I am convinced that it can result only in failure. . . .

Miss Minnie F. Low, Chicago . . .

We have all heard of the unsatisfactory effects of insufficient relief-giving. We give our widows and deserted women a small pension, never enough; a little clothing now and then, never enough; we make of the 365 days of a year a continuous struggle for existence, and yet we expect these women to bring up their children properly, and we expect the children to grow up into the best type of citizenship.

I believe in the home for a child every time, but it must be the right sort of home, and in the right neighborhood. In Chicago we insist that the widows whom

Lowenstein, "A Study of the Problem of Boarding Out Jewish Children and of Pensioning Widowed Mothers," *Proceedings* of the Sixth Biennial Session of the National Conference of Jewish Charities in the United States (1910), 218–219, 229–234. This document can also be found in Robert Bremner, ed., *Children and Youth in America: A Documentary History* (Cambridge, Mass.: Harvard University Press, 1971), 2: pp. 355–357.

we compensate move into the better neighborhoods. We do not give them $15.00 per month, as the relief agencies now give them, but we give them as much as $50.00 per month, the amount depending upon the size of the family. In one case we are allowing a widow with four children $50.00. We saw her last week, and she expressed herself as being "the happiest mother in Chicago." The principal of the school, which the children attend, wrote us a letter, unsolicited, speaking of the splendid condition in which the children are kept, and saying that the Home Finding Society was doing for this family what all the institutions in the world could not do—giving the mother the benefit of her children's love and society, and giving the children a mother's devotion and care.

We do not permit our compensated mothers to go out to work. They can supplement their incomes by doing some work in their homes, especially while the children are at school, but further than this it is a condition imposed upon them that they do not leave the home nor the children to add to their incomes.

We find it is after all not the best plan to separate a mother from her children even temporarily. The mother, being relieved of the care of a home and children grows timid about reassuming the burden and responsibility. One woman, whose children had been in the institution for nearly two years, when told she must remove them and establish a home with compensation of $35.00 per month, said: "I can't take care of my children; I am afraid to try it. If you had offered me this amount when my husband first died, when for days I walked about the building in which my children were put, just to see the place that held them, I would have been a very happy mother, but now my courage is gone." It took weeks of coaxing before this mother made up her mind to take her children.

2. The New York Commission on Relief for Widowed Mothers Demands Government Aid for Poor Women and Children, 1914

Basic Principles

The Commission believes it to be fundamentally true that:

1. The mother is the best guardian of her children.
2. Poverty is too big a problem for private philanthropy.
3. No woman, save in exceptional circumstances, can be both the home-maker and the bread-winner of her family.
4. Preventive work to be successful must concern itself with the child and the home.
5. Normal family life is the foundation of the State, and its conservation an inherent duty of government.

New York State, *Report of the Commission on Relief for Widowed Mothers* (Albany, 1914), pp. 7–10. This document can also be found in Robert Bremner, ed., *Children and Youth in America: A Documentary History* (Cambridge, Mass.: Harvard University Press, 1971), 2: pp. 379–381.

The General Situation

The Commission finds that:

1. Widowhood is the second greatest cause of dependency, the first being the incapacity of the bread-winner.
2. The widowed mother is in peculiar need of adequate assistance, and is uniquely open to constructive educational endeavors.
3. Public aid to dependent fatherless children is quite different in theory and effect from "charity" or "outdoor relief."
4. The experience of twenty-one other states in the Union, and of the larger countries of Europe, proves that it is feasible to administer such aid wisely and efficiently by public officials.
5. The experience elsewhere has shown that such aid is the most economical as well as the most socially advanced method of caring for dependent children.

The Situation in New York State

This Commission finds that:

1. Commitment of Children
   Two thousand seven hundred and sixteen children of 1,483 widowed mothers are at present in institutions at public expense, who were committed for destitution only; 933 children of 489 widows are at present in institutions because of illness of the mother, resulting often from overwork and overworry that might easily have been prevented.
2. Self-Support Impossible
   a. The unskilled widowed mother is unable to support herself and her family at a reasonable standard of living by taking work into the home or going out into the broader fields of industry.
   b. The work available to such women outside of the home inevitably breaks down the physical, mental and moral strength of the family and disrupts the home life through an inadequate standard of living and parental neglect, due to the enforced absence of the mother at the time the children most need her care.
   c. The work available in the home results, equally inevitably, in the prevention of normal family life, by causing overwork, congestion, child-labor, contagion, and a dangerously low standard of living.
3. Normal Childlife Impossible
   This disruption of the home contributes largely and directly to the backwardness and delinquency of children.
4. Present Sources of Assistance Inadequate
   Neither the public outdoor relief system extant in the State, nor the private charities in our larger cities, have sufficient funds to relieve adequately all widows of the grim burden of support so that they might remain at home to take personal care of their dependent children.
5. Present Assistance Wrong in Principle
   That neither public outdoor relief nor private charity constitutes the proper method of carrying on the conservation of the good home.

First Recommendation

With these principles as a basis, and these facts as a reason, the Commission respectfully recommends the immediate enactment into law of the principle of State aid to the dependent children of widowed mothers.

Government Aid the Only Solution

Other solutions that have been suggested to and rejected by the Commission are:

1. That all such relief be left in the hands of private charity.

By a review of the work done in individual families, and through the testimony presented by many charity experts, the Commission finds that private charity has not the funds, and cannot, in the future, raise the funds to give adequate relief in the home, nor to administer such funds in the efficient, wise and sympathetic manner which it has itself set up as the ideal.

2. That the State grant aid through the volunteer relief societies or the private child-caring institutions.

The Commission finds that experience in other states demonstrates clearly that public officials can be found who can administer such assistance as wisely and as sympathetically as can private social workers.

3. That this question be left until a complete system of social insurance be adopted in this State.

The Commission finds that no comprehensive system of social insurance, covering all the possible causes of the death of the bread-winner of the family is apt to be adopted in New York State for a great many years to come, and that the social insurance system of Europe, though in certain instances it has been in operation for more than a generation, has not even yet succeeded in making adequate provision for the homecare of widowed mothers. Further, and as a lesson to be drawn from European experience, the Commission believes that a system of direct governmental aid to the widowed mother with children should be considered not as an alternative to, but as a necessary and integral part of social insurance. . . .

3. The U.S. Children's Bureau Praises "Home Life," 1919

Minimum Standards for the Protection of Children in Need of Special Care

1. General statement

Every child should have normal home life, an opportunity for education, recreation, vocational preparation for life, and for moral and spiritual development in harmony with American ideals and the educational and spiritual agencies by which these

---

United States Children's Bureau, *Standards of Child Welfare: A Report of the Children's Bureau Conference, 1919,* Pub. no. 60 (Washington, D.C., 1919), pp. 440–442. This document can also be found in Robert Bremner, ed., *Children and Youth in America: A Documentary History* (Cambridge, Mass.: Harvard University Press, 1971), 2: pp. 410–412.

rights of the child are normally safeguarded. The Conference recognizes the fundamental rôle of home, religion, and education in the development of childhood.

Aside from the general fundamental duty of the State toward children in normal social conditions, ultimate responsibility for children who, on account of improper home conditions, physical handicap, or delinquency, are in need of special care devolves upon the State. Particular legislation is required for children in need of such care, the aim of which should be the nearest approach to normal development. Laws enacted by the several States for these purposes should be coordinated as far as practicable in view of conditions in the several States, and in line with national ideals.

2. Home care

The aim of all provision for children in need of special care necessitating removals from their own homes, should be to secure for each child home life as nearly normal as possible, to safeguard his health, and provide opportunities for education, recreation, vocational preparation, and moral and spiritual development. To a much larger degree than at present, family homes may be used to advantage in the care of special classes of children.

3. Adequate income

Home life, which is, in the words of the Conclusions of the White House Conference, "the highest and finest product of civilization," cannot be provided except upon the basis of an adequate income for each family, and hence private and governmental agencies charged with the responsibility for the welfare of children in need of special care should be urged to supplement the resources of the family wherever the income is insufficient, in such measure that the family budget conforms to the average standard of the community.

4. Incorporation, licensing, and supervision

A State board of charities, or a similar supervisory body, should be held responsible for the regular inspection and licensing of every institution, agency, or association, public or private, incorporated or otherwise, that receives or cares for children who suffer from physical handicaps, or who are delinquent, dependent, or without suitable parental care.

This supervision should be conceived and exercised in harmony with democratic ideals which invite and encourage the service of efficient, altruistic forces of society in the common welfare. The incorporation of such institutions, agencies, and associations should be required, and should be subject to the approval of the State board of charities or similar body.

5. Removal of children from their homes

Unless unusual conditions exist, the child's welfare is best promoted by keeping him in his own home. No child should be removed from his home unless it is impossible so to reconstruct family conditions or build and supplement family resources as to make the home safe for the child, or so to supervise the child as to make his continued presence safe for the community.

6. Principles governing child placing

This Conference reaffirms in all essentials the resolutions of the White House Conference of 1909 on the Care of Dependent Children. We believe they have been guides for communities and States that have sought to reshape their plans for children in need of special care. We commend them for consideration to all communities whose standards do not as yet conform to them, so that such standards may be translated into practice in the various States.

Before a child is placed in other than a temporary foster home adequate consideration should be given to his health, mentality, character, and family history and circumstances. Remediable physical defects should be corrected.

Complete records of every child under care are necessary to a proper understanding of the child's heredity, development, and progress while under the care of the agency.

Careful and wise investigation of foster homes is prerequisite to the placing of children. Adequate standards should be required of the foster families as to character, intelligence, experience, training, ability, income, and environment.

A complete record should be kept of each foster home, giving the information on which approval was based. The records should also show the agency's contacts with the family from time to time for the purpose of indicating the care it gave to the child entrusted to it. In this way special abilities in the families will be developed and conserved for children.

Supervision of children placed in foster homes should include adequate visits by properly qualified and well-trained visitors and constant watchfulness over the child's health, education, and moral and spiritual development. Supervision of children in boarding homes should also involve the careful training of the foster parents in their task. Supervision is not a substitute for the responsibilities which properly rest with the foster family.

4. The White House Conference on Child Health and Protection Defines Child Welfare as a Community Responsibility, 1930

We all have a common aim, which is to prepare the American child physically, mentally, and morally more fully to meet the responsibility of tomorrow than we have been able to meet that of today. We want to see our children develop into adult citizens with wholesome bodies and prepared minds, both under the control of the developed will operating in the atmosphere of what we call character.

We are conscious in the work of the Conference and in our observations that the emotional element in mankind must be harnessed by the intellect, or individual and mass decisions will be too variable for either individual happiness or mass safety. We want our future men and women to be self-starters operating under their

---

"Address by Ray Lyman Wilbur," White House Conference on Child Health and Protection, 1930, *Addresses and Abstracts of Committee Reports* (New York, 1931), pp. 15–23. This document can also be found in Robert Bremner, ed., *Children and Youth in America: A Documentary History* (Cambridge, Mass.: Harvard University Press, 1971), 2: pp. 1077–1080.

own personal control, not people who follow the herd or develop an emotional storm when confronted by difficulties.

The development of seven pounds of cells and fluids, encased in the helpless frame of a baby, into a Mozart, a Newton, or a Lincoln, is the one great marvel of human experience. But to each mother the development of her baby into a good, useful citizen is the one absorbing and vital experience of life. That development is taking place constantly about us in millions of homes and in tens of millions of individuals. Our studies have shown us that there are perils on every hand for human beings from the very first inception of life. We stand in awe as we watch this current of human life stream by us. Life is our only real possession. It is because of this that its preservation is constantly before us.

Within the past few decades there has been a growing consciousness of the significance of childhood. In so far as organized forces were concerned, aside from those of the church, such responsibility as was assumed for children outside of the home was in the beginning largely based on what we call charity. We have seen what was once charity change its nature under the broader term welfare and now those activities looked upon as welfare are coming to be viewed merely as good community housekeeping. In a word, parental responsibility is moving outward to include community responsibility. Every child is now *our* child. We have injected so many artificial conditions into our industrial civilization that the old normal relationships of mother and child, child and family, family and neighborhood, have been changed. There is now a much less direct struggle with nature and her immediate forces than has ever been the situation before in our country. We have softened this struggle for man by all forms of protection—better houses, better clothing, more and better food supplies, and by preventive medicine and better medicine and sanitation in general. All of this has called for a delegation of functions, once performed by the individual in the home, to all sorts of outside dependencies.

The increased skills which we have acquired due to the applications of science and discovery have given us exuberant results in agriculture and industry. These with the vast resources of an attractive continent have led to a marked increase in our population. As our mechanism has become more intricate the need for education and training of all of our units, and also that of the special training of the expert for the different fields of activity, becomes more and more evident. If we compare the mother of the past who nursed her own child to the one who now must rely on prepared foods, we find that between the mother and the child we have a whole series of persons and forces upon which the safety of the child depends—the inspectors of dairy herds, the inspectors of milk, the promptness of delivery systems, refrigeration, medical advice as to the mixing of formulæ, the chlorination of water, the preparation of sugars and grains, etc. Each one of these new factors must operate well and must be in the hands of those who know the reasons for what they do. The indicators of failure to do any part of this task well are the little headstones in the cemetery.

Beyond babyhood we have substituted another whole series of organized services between the mother and her child and have replaced much of the home training of the child with these activities. We have brought in kindergartens, playgrounds, and schools under government or private auspices, where the time of the child is spent and where proper training is essential. We face the absolute necessity of making good in all of this through expert service. It is probably true that it is beyond the capacity of the individual parent to train her child to fit into the intricate, interwoven, and interdependent social and economic system we have developed. Since we as an organized people have definitely taken on the responsibility, we can only make good in it by the use of those specially trained men and women requisite for the work and we must have them always in touch with the very best that experts can discover.

The parent *plus* the community must be stronger than either the parent *or* the community alone. Sympathetic mutual understanding of the division between them of the responsibility for the child must be the order of the day. We have come a long way from the days when boys in our country were "bound out" to neighbors for apprenticeship. We have deliberately prolonged the period of training of a large proportion of our citizens. We have compelled all elements of our population to attend our schools. We throw each year an increasingly heavy burden upon these schools. Our problems and the future of our country are in the schoolrooms of America today. In them are the future Presidents of our country, as well as the racketeers. Every one of the elements of our future population is to be found there right now—the gamblers, the insane, the criminals, the prostitutes, as well as the business men and women, the lawyers, the physicians, the statesmen, the ministers, the laborers of the future, and more significant than all, the mothers and the fathers of the days ahead.

We can now say that we have the problem surrounded. It is there in our schoolrooms. It is within the joint responsibility of the home and the community, operating in immediate contact with the child. How are we to meet the pressing difficulties before us in dealing with this great mass of forty-odd million children, sixteen million of whom are under the age of six? They are wholly ours to protect and fortify, because they are not yet old enough to have developed satisfactory resistance to disease, nor any degree of self-dependence.

In general, I think that we will agree that we must assist children in their own development, not "bring them up" as has been so often done in the past. We are, I think, convinced, too, that children should not be used as test-tubes for opinionated programs, with no worked-out basis of science or of fact, and that those who have developed methods without scientific preparation are often of the greatest harm in the handling of our childhood. I think we are all more or less suspicious of those whose hearts impel them to "do good" to children when their minds are untrained or guided by fixed fantasies of the crank type.

Just as we have wisely applied the findings of science in other fields, so must we apply them for the benefit of our children. I think we will agree that the health of our children is worth any price, and that in so far as the community can do so, it should see to the environment of the child so that the water and food will be pure and there will be no unnecessary exposures to the micro-organisms causing disease. Our present knowledge of nutrition is complete enough and our food supply is sufficient so that ill-nourished children are a community responsibility.

My sympathy goes out to the child who is facing the years ahead of us. It is not easy to get along with an active, restless mind receiving new impressions every hour. It is not easy to develop sound habits and sound attitudes in the presence of many diverse influences and varied associates. I imagine, too, that the modern parent with his or her ideas regarding vitamins, cod-liver oil, and conduct, is at times an undesirable associate in the view of many of our children. Children, like the sick, respond to what they understand. More time in explanation often leads to less in correction for disobedience. My sympathy, too, goes out to the children whom we classify as handicapped—those who in some way are different from their fellows and yet hope to win out in the game of life. It has been shown that these can be a great social asset to us and that there is much that can be done to make them more effective and happier.

My sympathy goes out even more to those children whose normal motivation, unguided, has brought them into the domain of what we call the court. If there is any field in which the word prevention should outweigh any other one, it is in this field, even though this prevention goes back to the very basic structure of our physical civilization. We can ill afford to save expense along this line.

With all this that is now open before us, we have the challenge of the future. We find it not only here in the United States, but also in Porto Rico, where the conditions for children are deplorable, and also in the Philippines.

What are we going to do to take advantage of the great opportunities offered by the findings of this Conference? I realize that this is a zone in which the art as well as the science of government must be considered. We have the information, we have a large program. How shall it be put into effect? In the first place, it seems to me that we must force the problem back to the spot where the child is. This primarily means, and should mean, the home. Our function should be to help parents, not replace them. The accessories which our civilization has brought for the care, protection, and development of the child, should be accessories to the home and not supplant it. The success of our civilization has come through the relationship of the home to children and consequently to citizenship. In other words, there must be a decentralization into the local field of the great mass of the problems which we have been studying. There must likewise be decentralization of the information which we have gathered so that it will reach every mother and father, every school board, every health officer, and every legislator in the country.

The great need for us to deal with in this Conference is that of getting the gist of our discussions back into action in the lives of children in this country—white and black, yellow and red, rich and poor, and all that lies between. Your deliberations, therefore, have two aspects: to make your facts and findings a true harvest of science and experience, and to develop the means of putting all we have brought together to work for the good of children.

5. The International Society of Crippled Children Issues a "Bill of Rights" for Disabled Children, 1931

I—Every child has the right to be well born; that is to say, the right to a sound body, complete in its members physically whole. In the securing of this right we pledge ourselves to use our influence that proper pre-natal, intra-natal and post-natal care be provided to the end that congenital deformity, insofar as it is humanly and scientifically possible, be prevented.

"The Crippled Child's Bill of Rights," *The Crippled Child* 9 (June 1931): 25. This document can also be found in Robert Bremner, ed., *Children and Youth in America: A Documentary History* (Cambridge, Mass.: Harvard University Press, 1971), 2: pp. 1031–1032.

II—Every child has the right to develop under clean, wholesome, healthful conditions. In declaring this right, this Society undertakes to use its influence to the end that children everywhere, through proper legislation, both local and general, and through proper supervision and protection, may grow to manhood and womanhood free from crippling conditions caused by insufficient nourishment, improper food, or unsanitary environment, and free, so far as possible, from danger of accident, wounding or maiming.

III—Notwithstanding the rights of children to be well born and to be protected throughout childhood, it is recognized that in spite of all human precautions there will be, unfortunately, some crippled children. These we declare to have the right to the earliest possible examination, diagnosis and treatment, recognizing, as we do, the fact that many thousand cases of permanent crippling may be eliminated by early and effective care.

IV—Every crippled child has a right, not only to the earliest possible treatment, but to the most effective continuing care, treatment and nursing, including the use of such appliances as are best calculated to assist in remedying or ameliorating its condition.

V—Every crippled child has the right to an education. Without this, all other provisions, unless for the relief of actual suffering, are vain.

VI—Every crippled child has the right not only to care, treatment and education, but to such treatment as will fit him or her for self-support, either wholly or partially, as the conditions may dictate. Without such practical application education is likewise purposeless.

VII—Every crippled child has the right to vocational placement, for unless the child,—boy or girl—after having been given physical care and treatment, and after being educated and trained, is actually placed in a proper position in the life of the World, all that has gone before is of no avail.

VIII—Every crippled child has the right to considerate treatment, not only from those responsible for its being and for its care, treatment, education, training and placement, but from those with whom it is thrown into daily contact, and every possible influence should be exerted by this and affiliated organizations to secure this right, in order that, so far as possible, the crippled child may be spared the stinging jibe or the bitter taunt, or, worse still, the demoralizing pity of its associates.

IX—Every crippled child has the right to spiritual, as well as bodily development, and, without regard to particular religious or denominational belief, is entitled to have nourishment for soul-growth.

X—In brief, not only for its own sake, but for the benefit of Society as a whole, every crippled child has the right to the best body which modern science can help it to secure; the best mind which modern education can provide; the best training which modern vocational guidance can give; the best position in life which his physical condition, perfected as best it may be, will permit, and the best opportunity for spiritual development which its environment affords.

 E S S A Y S

In the first essay, Joanne L. Goodwin of the University of Nevada at Las Vegas, author of the 1997 book, *Gender and the Politics of Welfare Reform*, examines the country's first "mothers' pension" program, adopted by Illinois in 1911. Goodwin reveals that, despite welfare reformers' "maternalist" rhetoric of permitting poor mothers to stay at home with their children, economic necessity forced many mothers to combine public support with wage work. Moreover, her discussion of the differential treatment of African American and never-married women reveals the ways in which cultural biases dictated that some mothers were less "deserving" of aid than others.

The second essay, an extract from Tennessee Technological University historian Kriste Lindenmeyer's 1997 study of the Children's Bureau, *"A Right to Childhood,"* examines the work of the bureau during the New Deal years. She shows the process by which bureau agents encouraged the federal government to take increased responsibility for child welfare and attempted to convince government officials to adopt their "whole child" philosophy.

Mothers' Pensions in Chicago, 1911–1931

JOANNE L. GOODWIN

Public policy issues for women in the early twentieth century were shaped by debates over the best way to resolve gender inequalities. Should policymakers view all women as potential mothers, industrial partners, or individuals with rights comparable to men? A wide range of politicized and organized women brought the specific problems of women and children to the public's attention as they sought the aid of government to redress the inequitable treatment of women in the family and the workplace. Within this context, a specific policy for impoverished mothers developed. Progressive social workers and women's organizations linked the problems of poverty in mother-only families to the dual role of homemaker and wage-earner which these women adopted out of necessity. Supporters advocated a policy which became known as mothers' pensions or mothers' aid and justified the new public expenditures with arguments as varied as "paid motherhood," cost-effective family rehabilitation, or a new program for social justice. In brief, the policy proposed to supplement the family income of mother-only families so that women might raise their children at home rather than disrupt the family by placing the children in state institutions. Illinois passed the first state-wide legislation in 1911, but within ten years forty states had approved similar laws.

Despite the homage paid to family and motherhood in the debates over mothers' pensions, the proposal fell short of its stated goals once it became law. The shortcomings of this policy and its successor, Aid to Dependent Children, have been the subject of debate for scholars and policy analysts. What explains the selective criteria that gave advantage to some women over others? What factors determined the variable levels of assistance? How did this form of social provision develop as a relief policy rather than a measure of social insurance? In contrast to the discussion on these topics, little attention has been directed toward the central contradiction of the policy: the value of a mother's work at home, primarily as a child caretaker, and the value of self-support, that is, her ability to make her family economically self-sufficient.

Joanne L. Goodwin, "An American Experiment in Paid Motherhood: The Implementation of Mothers' Pensions in Early Twentieth-Century Chicago," *Gender and History 4,* 3 (Autumn 1992): 323–338. Reprinted by permission of Blackwell Publishing.

This article examines these two divergent goals of the policy by exploring the experiences of single mothers who applied for public aid in Chicago in the first decades of this century. It discusses the differences in treatment accorded women who applied for public aid relative to work expectations, family status, and race. This article argues that rather than a policy to "keep mothers at home to raise their children," mothers' pensions actually incorporated public aid with wage-earning not only for mothers, but also for older children. The high rate of wage-earning for women in pensioned families has not received sufficient attention in the literature and yet it serves to explain the vehicle through which exclusions were implemented and the caretaker grant for women was omitted. Although this article cannot explore the full political context of implementation, it focuses on the differences among two groups of gender-conscious advocates. Maternalists and progressive social workers agreed that the state should assist impoverished families, but disagreed on the basis of that claim. Within the contentious political environment of Chicago, the result was a compromised and contradictory policy of social provision which limited aid to needy women. . . .

The plight of poor women raising young children with meager resources cut across the central issues examined by organized women of the time; that is, women's relationship to the family, the economy, and the public sector. Despite a uniform rhetorical commitment to "protect motherhood," women differed on the best method to accomplish this. Two different gender-conscious definitions of the problem and arguments for government involvement evolved from organized women. Traditionalist women's organizations, represented here by the National Congress of Mothers, emphasized the role of mothers within families and the importance of stable family life to the security of the nation. They viewed the problem of "dependent motherhood" as one of a "failed contract" between husband and wife. The National Congress of Mothers believed that the state had a responsibility to support such women so that they might raise their children into healthy citizens. A second gender-conscious perspective on "dependent motherhood" saw the problem as both legal and economic. Sophonisba Breckinridge and Edith Abbott, residents of Chicago's Hull House settlement and members of that reform community, used social survey data to gain support for distributive policies for women. They believed that the state must enlarge its capacity for social provision to include the widows of poor workers and abandoned families on the basis of social justice and individual rights. The efforts of these two groups are important for the public attention they focused on the issues of female-headed families and for the policy measures they developed despite the fact that their agendas differed and led to a weakened political position during the process of implementation.

The National Congress of Mothers attempted to revitalize the ideal of women's traditional role in the home and affirm the value of "mother-work" in contemporary society by emphasizing childrearing and child development. Alice McLellan Birney guided the organization of predominantly white, middle-class mothers in their initial efforts "to raise the standards of home life." The membership believed in the critical link between family life and social stability, but they interjected a specifically maternalist component into this relationship. A mother's power to affect the direction of her children's lives held significant potential for resolving social ills. Their formulation of maternalism endowed women with the authority to shape social forces beyond the walls of the nursery. . . .

In its fullest manifestation, maternalism fostered the idea of "universal mothering," that is, the skills used to shape the development of one's own children could be applied to the children of others. Hannah Schoff, President of the National Congress of Mothers, told her constituency:

> There is a broader motherhood than the motherhood that mothers one's own; there is the spirit of the Lord that is in the mother that mothers all children, and it is because the world has lacked that, that the conditions of the children of this country have not been better. . . .

Maternalist discourse reached a high point at the 1909 White House Conference on the Care of Dependent Children. Representatives of child welfare organizations, public and private relief agencies, and women's organizations met for two days in Washington, D.C. to discuss social policy for impoverished children. The reification of the home and of motherhood created an ideological context for the conference recommendation to shift child welfare policy from institutional care to home care. In the final report, conference participants recognized that, "Home life is the highest and finest product of civilization," and endorsed the idea that the quality of home life and childrearing depended upon the mother's ability to perform her caretaking responsibilities. The conference supported the idea of a privately funded pension for "dependent mothers."

Initially, leaders of the National Congress of Mothers argued that the pension was simply payment for a mother's service to the state. Just as a soldier received a pension for protecting citizens, a mother should receive compensation for raising citizens. No woman who had "divided her body by creating other lives for the good of the state, one who has contributed to citizenship," should be classified as a pauper under any conditions, one member stated emphatically. The claim for public benefits on the basis of motherhood recognized the value of women's labor in childrearing to the entire society. Like many of its proposals, the National Congress of Mothers' vision of mothers' pensions sought to expand women's traditional role without challenging familial or social relations.

A second gender-conscious perspective on "dependent motherhood" that did not rely on the idealization of maternity arose from settlement workers involved in social survey research. Sophonisba Breckinridge and Edith Abbott studied children in the Chicago Juvenile Court system, and produced one of the earliest research-based endorsements for aid to families of single mothers. They defined the problems of impoverished women as part of larger structural phenomena, including the inequality of social relations between the sexes. Low wages, occupational segregation, and women's childcare role in the family shaped and limited women's opportunities to support their families, they argued. It was the dual burden of wage-earning and childcare that needed to be addressed in social policy. Their claims for mothers' pensions, though sometimes expressed in maternalist language, were rooted in the expansion of state services to individuals and workers. . . .

While traditionalist and progressive women agreed on some aspects of aid to "dependent mothers," their ideas differed about the extent of reform. Both groups recognized the value of women's labor in the family, specifically in childrearing, and used this point as a central aspect of their arguments. Each saw the need for action by the government to direct resources toward this segment of the population. However, maternalists stressed the idea that mothers could not only shape their children's future, but could also solve social problems and influence national security. This perspective enhanced the position and authority of some mothers, but reduced the process of social change to individual actions. They resisted reforms which might alter economic or social relations. Alternatively, Breckinridge and Abbott used survey research to promote new policies for expanded state resources on behalf of working women and their families. Their proposals contained inconsistencies on issues of protection or equality, but they raised the issues of structural inequalities between men and women in the workforce and the dual role faced by working-class women. They criticized the "well-meaning persons of other classes, who, accepting the 'sphere of woman' doctrine, would limit the activities of women of all classes to the bearing and rearing of children" and insisted upon the "right of women" to a place in industry. The problem of female-headed families in poverty was best resolved with opportunities for education, training, employment, and a minimum wage for women. Until those policy objectives could be met, mother-only families needed a subsidy.

In 1911, Illinois became the first state in the nation to pass a mothers' pension law. . . . Chicago and Cook County had the largest and most active program in the state. . . . The Chicago case provides an example of enormous political contests for control over expanding state services, in this case mothers' pensions. Opposition from local politicians and restrictive pressures from the city's charity elite also contributed to the policy's outcome. The demand to address the problems of "dependent mothers" from organized women succeeded in drawing attention to the issue, but their conflicting perspectives contributed to a compromised policy which maintained the contradictions of the double day for impoverished women.

Effusive public acclaim greeted the passage of the mothers' pension bill in 1911. Local ministers proclaimed it "one of the most humane measures ever enacted by the Illinois legislature." The *Chicago Tribune* marked the disbursement of the first pensions by noting that the policy lifted "poverty from several score of children." Juvenile Court Judge Merritt Pinckney, who administered the program, called mothers' pensions "the grandest law on the statute books." Pinckney defended the new program against critics by saying "society and the state should encourage, cherish and not destroy this most sacred thing in human life—a mother's love—and should guard, protect and foster the grandest institution of our social and political life—the home." These articles emphasized that pensioned mothers would be able to stay home and raise their children. In doing so they obscured the legal and extralegal enforcement of wage-earning for the majority of mothers.

When Marya Kruszka's husband was shot and killed during a family fight, she became the sole support of four children and a potential beneficiary of the new legislation. Her children ranged in age from eighteen months to eleven years old. The family's insurance paid for the funeral and covered household expenses for several months, but five months later, Marya Kruszka's sister and aunt appealed to a local agency for assistance on her behalf. The caseworker suggested that she apply for day work such as domestic service or dishwashing, homework, or factory work. At first she worked in a box factory for ten hours a day while her sister looked after her children. Then she tried making brushes at home. After six days she had made six brushes for a total wage of 75 cents and decided this would not work, but hated "the thought of going back to the box factory and begging a new person each day to keep her baby." Despite the fact that she did not want to seek charity, within the month Marya Kruszka had accepted a Thanksgiving basket, coal from the county relief agent, and a coupon for milk for one month. The caseworker helped her apply for a mothers' pension but the case was rejected because of a forthcoming benefit from a relative's will. One year after her husband's death, Marya Kruszka found "satisfactory work" in a restaurant. The caseworker noted, "Mrs. Kruszka feels very badly about leaving her children all day long. . . . she deplores the fact that during the next five or six years when supervision will mean so much to the children, she will be unable to oversee them." Marya Kruszka's situation was common among impoverished women. She appeared to be an ideal candidate for a pension, but was denied on the basis of potential income and her ability to earn. In implementation, the new policy encouraged her to continue to work for wages rather than rely on subsidies that would allow her to care for her own children at home.

Mother-only families constituted a significant portion of all families receiving relief by the early twentieth century. Although they accounted for only 5 percent of all Chicago families in 1910, they represented 42 percent of all relief families. Over three-quarters of these families had school-age children under fourteen years old. In 1920, mother-only families increased to 6.7 percent of all Chicago families but their reliance on relief, although slightly decreased, remained high at 40 percent of all families, a proportion which remained constant over the next decade. Private agencies also carried a substantial case-load of mother-only families. One-third of all those cases handled by the United Charities of Chicago in 1921–1922 were headed by women.

Yet, impoverished women, particularly heads of families, also had high rates of wage-earning when compared to the general population. Among married women in 1920, 6.3 percent of native white women, 7.2 percent of foreign-born white women, and 32.5 percent of African American women worked. Widowed and divorced women had higher rates of employment in every category. A study of unpublished Chicago census data found that among two-parent white families, married women had high rates of labor-force participation in families where men were unemployed or unskilled workers, 16.2 and 12 percent respectively. That same study found that in mother-only families, 40 percent of the women worked. A second study of 1920 Chicago census data found that 44 percent of married, African American women worked, but among mother-only families, the rate jumped to 72 percent. Clearly, high rates of employment for single mothers represented an attempt to replace the loss of adult male wages—attempts that were generally futile among unskilled workers whose employment in low-wage jobs could not supply the needs of the family. Thus, many women who headed families and who earned nonetheless appealed to private and public relief agencies for aid.

Receipt of public or private relief did not eliminate the mother's need to work. Chicago agencies agreed that women, when able, should work to provide partial support for their families. "Whether or not relief shall be given so that the mother can stay in her home depends in part upon the physical condition of the mother," stated a Children's Bureau report on Chicago. It was suggested that a medical examination be performed so that the degree of wage-earning to be undertaken by the mother could be determined. The workforce participation of women on welfare changed little with the implementation of mothers' pensions.

One of the conditions for granting aid specifically addressed women's wage-earning in conjunction with [their] home responsibilities. The 1913 revised Illinois law established that a single mother "may be absent [from the home] for work a definite number of days each week to be specified in the court's order, when such work can be done by her without the sacrifice of health or the neglect of home and children." The judge of the Juvenile Court determined the eligibility of a family based on the "potential earnings" of able-bodied family members of working age, as well as savings, property, and relatives' contributions. These family resources were then compared to a standard budget estimate for a minimum standard of living, and a pension stipend was determined. Pensions supplied anywhere from 25 to 75 percent of the family budget. To make up the deficit, women found employment. Two-thirds of the women receiving pensions between 1913 and 1915 worked for wages to support the family. Approximately 70 percent had more than one job. . . .

The wage-earning mothers on pensions in Cook County were concentrated heavily in domestic service jobs. The most common type of job, taken by 61 percent of the women, was washing outside the home. This was followed by cleaning, home laundry, home sewing, and keeping boarders. The higher paid factory and restaurant jobs accounted for only 5 percent of their employment. Only one-third of the 360 jobs listed by the pensioned women were located inside the home. While there is no indication of the amount of time devoted to each job, such proportions suggest that only a minority of women who received pensions were able to care for their children at home while earning. . . .

The ability of women and children to earn wages was given serious consideration in distinguishing which families could get by without public aid in Chicago. Between the years 1911 and 1927, nearly one-half of the dismissed applications and the majority of cancelled pensions were denied for economic reasons. If a woman was believed to be potentially "self-supporting," her case could be dismissed. This section of the policy held tremendous discriminatory potential. For example, one African American woman had received a pension for her five children until the 1913 revisions made her ineligible. She gave her fifteen-year-old daughter the home responsibilities while she went out to earn. Two years later the law was made more inclusive and she reapplied for a pension, but was denied on the basis that she was "a good wage-earner."

Families that were rejected from mothers' pensions in Chicago frequently received referrals to other branches of county government, such as the poor relief office or the division of non-support. This had the most significant impact on deserted women and African American women who headed families. Public resources most readily available to them were those which relied heavily on the woman's ability to earn and the financial support of relatives.

Mothers' pensions did not offer equal provision to all poor women, but differentiated women by marital status. Single mothers who were deserted, separated, or unmarried faced exclusion from the mothers' pensions program. Pension legislation contained specific restrictions relating to family status and when not outlined in the law, Chicago administrators placed additional limits on applicants. . . .

In Chicago, as across the nation, widows were the largest sector of pensioned families. They accounted for 84 percent of all the cases throughout the years of this study. These women lost their husbands at an early age—the average age of death for an applicant's husband was 39 years of age—usually due to illness. The consequences for these families were twofold. Not only did the family lose their primary wage-earner during his peak earning years, but also at a time when small children were most likely to be present.

In addition to widows, deserted women initially drew benefits from mothers' pensions, receiving 10 percent of the pensions in the first year of the program. In 1913, a revision to the initial law revoked their eligibility due to the public's fears that the policy would encourage husbands to desert their families. . . . In 1923, the law once again included these families.

A few other types of mother-only families received aid. Originally, women who had a child outside of marriage were excluded from eligibility on the basis that they were "morally unfit." A Children's Bureau study of the policy's implementation between 1913–1915 challenged the wisdom of this policy, however, arguing that it created an unwarranted hardship for the children. In 1917, the Juvenile Court developed a compromise and allowed the mother to receive aid for the "legitimate" children in the family. Two-parent families in which the father was either institutionalized or disabled were also eligible for aid. . . .

Family size also influenced the availability of mothers' pensions in several cases. The Chicago Juvenile Court followed a standard established by the city's private charities that a mother with only one child over the age of two years should be able to work to support herself, and therefore usually denied her aid. . . .

The treatment of deserted women offers an illustrative example of the variant policy approaches which encouraged wage-earning for some mother-only families. Desertion became identified as an issue when relief agents recognized that a growing portion of families who relied on private and public aid had deserting husbands. In 1904, the poor relief agent in Chicago noted that the majority (63 percent) of deserted families were headed by women between thirty and thirty-five years old, and nearly half of these families (48 percent) had either three or four children. This family configuration meant long-term assistance, and the agent expressed concern about the drain on county finances. His analysis of the problem proved limited, however. Searching for an explanation for the rise in desertion cases, the county agent "advanced the theory that bad cooking, etc., on the part of the woman is the cause, and that the proper training of girls in domestic science, etc., will do away with it to a considerable extent." . . .

Excluded from the mothers' pension provision in Illinois from 1913 until 1923, deserted families and other non-supported women received separate assistance from a new division of the municipal court. A few months before the mothers' pension legislation passed the state legislature, Cook County implemented a new, non-support division of the Court of Domestic Relations for deserted and non-supported families. Mothers who were separated, unmarried, or deserted could apply for assistance from this branch of the court if they were willing to press charges against their children's father. One relief administrator described the dilemma in cases of non-support.

> The desertion of wife and children by the male breadwinner is a continuing and baffling problem. The ineffective legislation under which desertion is a misdemeanor only, the lack of uniform federal law, the difficulty of enforcement of such legislation as exists, results in an unjust burden upon the deserted mothers and a shifting of parental responsibility upon the public.

The primary objective of the court was to secure support payments from the absent husband or to find relatives who were able to assist in the support of the dependent family. Until the absent father could be located, the court coordinated benefits from relatives, and public and private agencies. . . .

. . . In Chicago . . . mothers' pensions had never received the full support of the public. Locally, it had raised fears of unlimited public expense. Nationally, the Chicago "experiment" came under the intense scrutiny of organized charities. The Chicago Juvenile Court opted for a conservative policy—one which selected families most likely to become self-sufficient and least likely to raise the public ire. Rather than assume the expense of supporting such families, administrators of relief promoted separate policies for these mother-only families. This process had a negative impact on African American women. . . . The definition of "dependent motherhood" varied for these women, as it did for deserted or unmarried women, and forced them to rely more heavily on wage-earning.

The Great Migration of southern blacks to Chicago preceding World War I rapidly expanded the African American population and brought increased tensions to race relations. . . . Occupational opportunities for most African Americans were located largely in low-wage sectors. Sixty percent of all African Americans employed in Chicago in 1910 worked in domestic or personal service jobs, and only 15 percent found jobs in manufacturing. Wartime production increased the demand for industrial workers, and more African Americans took those jobs after 1914, yet over one-half of all African American men worked as unskilled laborers. The decline in industrial production and the massive layoffs that accompanied the recession of 1919–1920 hit the African American community hard. During this period, nearly one-third of married, African American women contributed to their family's earnings compared to 6 percent of native-born white, married women. The rates of employment for black female-heads of households rose even higher, estimated at 72 percent by one study of 1920 data.

In addition, the black community had a higher proportion of families headed by women in their child-bearing years. For example in 1910, one-half of all female-headed African American families were headed by women between 15 and 44 years of age, compared to 18 percent of all foreign-born, female-headed families. This points to the greater portion of women responsible for both childcare and wage-earning in the African American community relative to other racial or ethnic groups.

The presence of both low-wages and children generally predicts a higher degree of economic need, but Chicago's African American community found its access to welfare services limited, particularly for dependent children. Publicly funded but privately operated institutions for the care of dependent children refused to take African American youth. This left the children in what county administrators called "very low standard" foster homes organized within the black community, or it resulted in their being kept for extended periods in the Juvenile Detention Home awaiting foster care. Eventually two private homes, the Amanda Smith Home and the Louise Manual Training School, were established for the care of African American dependent children. The lack of constructive social policy for dependent black children was noted by both white and black social workers. In 1921 and again in 1928, informed commentators noted the "very serious problem of a permanent social policy" for Chicago's dependent black children who had suffered from "inadequacy of provision for care" for several decades.

Poor relief offered another form of public aid which allowed families to stay together. A dramatic shift in the constituencies receiving public assistance took place after World War I as African American families utilized public relief in increasingly greater numbers. By 1920, African Americans constituted 4 percent of the population in Chicago, but 8 percent of the public relief families. Ten years later they had increased to 7 percent of the population but were one-third of relief cases. Private agencies also reported major increases in the number of African American families who applied for aid, doubling from 10 percent to 20 percent by the mid-1920s.

Aggregate statistics make it impossible to determine the proportion of African American single mothers within this public relief trend; however individual studies point to a high proportion of female-headed families. A 1904 report found that widows and deserted women totaled 65 percent of the African American families who received assistance from public relief that year. In the 1920s, [sociologist E. Franklin] Frazier noted that 20 percent of the low-income African American families he studied were headed by women, and one-half of the families that received relief were headed by women.

In contrast to their utilization of poor relief, African American women were underrepresented on mothers' pensions. . . . In 1911, the first year of the Chicago pension program, ten African American women applied for pensions. Only 51 women received aid for their children that first year and none of them were African American. By 1916, a few African American families received pensions, 2.7 percent of the new pension cases granted that year. After World War I, African American women received pensions, but they continued to be underrepresented in proportion to their numbers in the population. In 1920, for example, when African Americans accounted for 4 percent of the population and 8 percent of the families on relief, they received only 3 percent of the pensions. In comparison, German, Italian, Irish, and Polish families received pensions in numbers greater than their representation during the 1920s. When one considers the higher rate of mother-only families among African Americans, their low participation rate on mothers' pensions is highlighted further.

A 1931 Children's Bureau report of mothers' pensions programs in thirty-eight states found the provisions for African American families extremely limited when their ratio in the population and their need were taken into account. Some areas excluded African American families entirely despite the fact that they represented a significant portion, 20 to 45 percent, of a county's population.

As the public sector expanded its services for impoverished mothers, African American women were directed to the services of the poor relief office and the Court of Domestic Relations. In contrast to their minimal participation in mothers' pensions, African American women constituted a large group of families that received poor relief and appeared before the court. These programs relied most heavily on self-support through wage-earning and the contributions of relatives. They also offered the least in provision of services, providing in-kind benefits of food and coal rather than a cash stipend.

The definition of women as mothers, workers, or individuals shaped public policy in the early twentieth century. Members of traditionalist women's groups such as the National Congress of Mothers utilized the language of "universal mothering" to promote child welfare policies which included mothers' pensions. They focused on a woman's ability to perform "a mother's work" and minimized the structural causes of poverty. This organization was not alone in using maternalist discourse. Many child welfare workers and juvenile court judges shared the perspective which placed the home at the center of society and a mother's role centrally within it.

However, this belief in the universal experience of mothers obscured real differences between women. In sharp contrast to the vision of mothers' pensions provided by maternalist rhetoric, women who received pensions and other forms of relief were frequently wage-earners. . . .

Previous historical discussions of this policy have underestimated the extent to which women were expected to contribute to the family income. Consequently, they have overlooked the interaction between wage-earning and welfare receipt. Illinois set specific conditions on a woman's wage-earning in its legislation. In Chicago, as in other urban areas, the major criteri[on] used in the means-tested program was the family's potential income. The pension supplied a fraction of the amount necessary for the family's minimum needs; thus women and their older children worked to make up the difference. Furthermore, certain groups of women were held to higher expectations of wage-earning than others. Deserted women, unmarried mothers, women with one child, and African American women were either ineligible by law or underrepresented on the mothers' pension program. These women were directed to entirely separate structures of the local government.

What became of the vision to provide support to "dependent mothers"? How did traditionalist women's organizations and progressive social welfare workers fall short of their goals? The mothers' pension policy represents a case study in the conflict between those who wanted an expanded state and those who feared the result of such expansion. . . . Rather than a policy that universalized the status of motherhood and paid mothers to raise their children at home, the first public policy for single mothers required able-bodied women to earn and reinforced exclusionary practices based on race and family status.

The Children's Bureau and Child Welfare During the Great Depression

KRISTE LINDENMEYER

[Children's Bureau director] Grace Abbott utilized the health care, child labor reform, and social welfare efforts initiated during the Children's Bureau's first two decades of existence as the blueprint for new programs started during the next ten years. As Abbott acknowledged, the bureau had shown that even its limited efforts had helped some children and their families. But throughout the Great Depression the agency's self-defined role as the nation's chief advocate for "the whole child" was aggressively challenged. . . . In addition, the Great Depression highlighted the

Kriste Lindenmeyer, "*A Right to Childhood*": *The U.S. Children's Bureau and Child Welfare, 1912–46* (Champaign: University of Illinois Press, 1997), pp. 163, 176–195. Copyright © 1997. Used with permission of the University of Illinois Press.

uneven application of recommended reforms as well as the inadequacy of the Children's Bureau's programs constructed on the middle-class family ideal. . . .

Initially it looked as though the election of Franklin D. Roosevelt would do little to help gain "security" for children. The Children's Bureau, like other agencies, expected a 25 percent budget cut ($100,000) under the Roosevelt administration's 1933 Economy Act. However, during the first "100 Days" the Roosevelt administration ignored the proposed cut and the Children's Bureau's Social Statistics Project expanded. In fact, the Social Statistics Project provided data utilized to support many New Deal programs. . . . In May 1933, Congress established the Federal Emergency Relief Administration (FERA), the first federal unemployment aid program. The Children's Bureau collected data for the FERA, thereby helping to administer its $500 million annual appropriation. . . .

Following Roosevelt's election, Abbott began to push aggressively for federal programs designed specifically to assist needy children. Two *New York Times* articles illustrate the chief's new strategy of moving the Children's Bureau's role beyond investigation, education, and advocacy. Addressing the question of the depression's effect on children, Abbott maintained that there had been 6,000,000 undernourished children in the United States at the time of Hoover's 1930 White House conference. She estimated that the "number undoubtedly was very much larger" in 1932 and argued that "one-fifth of . . . preschool and school children were showing the effects of poor nutrition, of inadequate housing, and of the lack of medical care." To lessen this problem Abbott called for a federally funded program to aid children in both health and welfare matters. Children were "showing the effects of the anxiety and the sense of insecurity that prevails when the father is unemployed for long periods." She worried that "the strain of living in a state of uncertainty week after week, month after month, and year after year deepens and intensifies the serious effects on the children in the family group." Using evidence gathered for the Children's Bureau's 1932 report presented in the Senate by Robert La Follette, Abbott cited deep economic cuts in existing state and local programs for children. The effect of greater need and diminished funds, according to the Children's Bureau chief, "has discouraged some communities and individuals from doing what they could in the emergency." The Children's Bureau could no longer rely on parents or the states and local communities to serve as the primary providers for children's needs.

. . . [T]he Children's Bureau's first New Deal efforts emphasized nutrition and health care. With Grace Abbott's urging, the newly appointed secretary of labor, Frances Perkins, called for a Child Health Recovery Conference to be held in Washington on October 6, 1933. . . . Perkins's "informal" 1933 Child Health Recovery Conference was attended by representatives from a wide variety of federal agencies along with one hundred and forty individuals from state departments of health, private health organizations, medical societies, and relief agencies. Eleanor Roosevelt also participated at Perkins's request. The conference's purpose was "to stimulate a movement for the recovery of ground lost, during the Depression, in conditions affecting the health and vitality of children." Proposals focused attention on the effects of malnutrition and inadequate health care. As a result of the meeting's discussions, conference participants advocated that the FERA, headed by Harry L. Hopkins, should be responsible for "encouraging" emergency plans within the states to feed the hungry children. Further, conference members resolved that Grace Abbott and the Children's Bureau should "promote" complementary state health care projects, especially in the country's depressed rural areas. School lunch programs, reimbursement plans for private physicians, and nurses' salaries paid through the proposed Civil Works Administration were also to be part of this combined effort to "take care" of the more than 6,000,000 children of families on federal and state relief.

Following this meeting, the FERA and the Children's Bureau instituted the Child Health Recovery Program (CHRP), which concentrated on providing emergency food and medical care to the country's neediest children. Funds came from existing FERA, Civil Works Administration (after its establishment in November 1933), and Children's Bureau appropriations. . . . [L]imited funding necessitated the extensive cooperation of public and private health care and relief organizations. With its funds the Children's Bureau made available five physicians for consultation, and the Civil Works Administration employed as many as two hundred full- and part-time public health nurses per state. In addition, private physicians, nutritionists, and home economics teachers, in cooperation with manufacturers and retailers, contributed expertise, supplies, and food. Schools played an important role in identifying and distributing help to the children in greatest need. CHRP was the New Deal's first and only federal "relief" program for young children until implementation of the 1935 Social Security Act.

Ultimately, despite some success, CHRP did not live up to expectations. Its major handicap was a lack of funds for full-time medical and nursing personnel. Despite the decided need, states under great economic stress had little money to pay for an additional health care and nutrition program. As noted by Abbott, the effort's most successful result was to "show the urgent need of a more extensive and permanent program for maternal and child health," as well as other aspects of child welfare.

In December 1933, Perkins authorized the Children's Bureau to call state relief officials to Washington to discuss other important relief issues. This conference, "Present Emergencies in the Care of Dependent and Neglected Children," found that considerable ground had been lost in the area of mothers' pensions. Thirty-three counties in Michigan, ten in Illinois, six in Wisconsin, four in Pennsylvania, and two in New York had discontinued mothers' aid payments due to a shortage of revenue. These families were either left helpless, dependent on private charity, or placed on local or federal-state relief rolls. Such practices ran contrary to the Children's Bureau's philosophy that mothers' pensions were not "charity" relief but a preventive entitlement. In a March 1934 *Survey* article, Abbott noted that there were "some 300,00 children, most of them fatherless and all of them dependent, . . . supported by mothers' pensions." She argued that the needs of these children should not be answered with emergency relief, but with "the same kind of security . . . as is now being sought for the aged in old age pensions." Abbott warned that "in the long future, our democracy will have to pay in perhaps arithmetical or even geometrical progression for our failure to bring security and stability to the care of these especially disadvantaged children." The chief and her supporters asserted that the nation's dependent children needed more than emergency relief.

President Roosevelt responded to growing pleas for an "economic security" plan by establishing the Committee on Economic Security (CES) on June 29, 1934 (Executive Order #6757). The president instructed executive committee members

(Frances Perkins, chair; Harry L. Hopkins, FERA head; Henry Morgenthau, Jr., secretary of the treasury; Homer S. Cummings, attorney general; and Henry A. Wallace, secretary of agriculture) to "formulate . . . sound legislation [with] these three great objectives—the security of the home, the security of livelihood, and the security of social insurance." . . . The July 1934 announcement concerning the CES's creation cites the major issues to be addressed by the group: unemployment compensation, old age insurance, workmen's compensation, mothers' pensions, maternity benefits, health care, and public relief. . . .

By 1934, it appeared that the welfare of children should be a recognized part of New Deal concerns. Some child welfare issues had been established two years before Roosevelt's election during the Hoover administration's 1930 White House conference, and later during the two Children's Bureau–sponsored meetings held in 1933. An article in *Parents Magazine* outlined the "hopes" Roosevelt administration officials had for children under the New Deal. "Security" for families was at the center of their efforts. However, children's welfare was not initially addressed by the CES. Homer Folks, longtime Children's Bureau ally and chair of the CES Public Health Advisory Committee, noted this circumstance at the National Conference on Economic Security held in Washington, D.C., on November 14, 1934. He complained that the specific subject of children's welfare did not enter into general discussions about economic security "until the announcement of a subcommittee" on children five months after the president's executive order establishing the CES. In fact, no formal announcement confirming the formation of the Advisory Committee on Child Welfare was made until November 19, 1934. . . .

. . . It is fair to speculate that most policy makers in the Roosevelt administration failed to understand the Children's Bureau's "whole child" philosophy, and instead planned to integrate child welfare efforts into its general security program. Further underscoring this possibility, in 1933 the Children's Bureau had to fight another federal reorganization attempt that threatened its principle of serving the "whole child." Responding to rumors of such a move, Mary F. "Molly" Dewson, director of the Democratic National Committee's Women's Division, wired Roosevelt that "nothing would upset women more all over the country than to take health work away from the Children's Bureau. This is a cause celebre. Hoover attempted to do this and was defeated. . . . such an idea is fundamentally unwise and impractical. I have my finger on this pulse." Roosevelt took Dewson's advice and quickly dropped the issue. Whatever the reason for the delay, a child welfare committee was finally organized in November and Secretary Perkins enthusiastically praised its existence. "There can be no economic security for a nation . . . while its children are economically or socially insecure. There are about seven million children under the age of 16 years in families on relief. Many of these children are mal-nourished, crippled, blind; children suffering from tuberculosis and heart disturbances; children living under conditions of physical and moral neglect. For these children there should be more adequate protection."

As Perkins's words suggest, it looked by December 1934 as if the Children's Bureau could fully recover from its loss of "power" during the Hoover years. This was a great relief to bureau supporters since Grace Abbott, ill with tuberculosis, had sent a letter of resignation to President Roosevelt on June 13, 1934, effective July 1. . . .

In her letter of resignation, Abbott, who although ill was only fifty-six years old, explained that she was leaving the Children's Bureau to accept a position as professor of public welfare at the School of Social Service, University of Chicago. She felt that "year by year evidence has accumulated of the [Children's Bureau's] importance in our national life." She argued "that a final test of our recovery program may well be what it does to remove the injustices from which children have suffered in the past." "But," she warned, "as children are not merely pocket editions of adults, special health and protective services for children are essential for their optimum growth and development as well as measures which will bring security to the wage earner and the farmer." Abbott said that she left "in the belief that the Bureau will be developed and expanded during this administration."

Upon accepting Abbott's resignation, President Roosevelt praised her service and noted that while he regretted losing her, "it is with satisfaction that I learn you and your long-time friend, the Secretary of Labor, have worked out a plan whereby you will maintain an advisory relationship to the Children's Bureau." This circumstance, the president felt, "gives us assurance of carrying on the Bureau with the same practical and effective policies." Indeed, it again appeared that the Children's Bureau's overall program started under Julia Lathrop would continue without missing a beat. In addition, Roosevelt's response shows that he believed Abbott would continue to serve as an important influence in the Children's Bureau. . . .

As demonstrated by her coauthorship of "Special Measures for Economic Security of Children," Grace Abbott was able to contribute to the development of the most comprehensive program for children the federal government had ever implemented, despite the fact that she had resigned as chief of the Children's Bureau. Thomas H. Eliot . . . , the man responsible for the legal drafting of the Social Security bill, says that he asked his "colleague" Katharine Lenroot [the new chief of the Children's Bureau] to write the child welfare sections. Lenroot quickly formed a committee composed of herself, Martha Eliot, and Grace Abbott. These women quickly designed the New Deal programs intended to assure "security" for "whole child."

As a first step they established a subcommittee composed of both public health and social workers. . . . Lenroot, Eliot, Abbott, and their subcommittee used the data collected and the experience obtained during the bureau's twenty-two years of work to devise their recommendations for a New Deal program for children. They assumed that the programs they designed would be administered by the Children's Bureau when the economic security bill became law.

According to Lenroot, the president and his advisors used the following criteria to decide which issues would be included in the CES program: "It was felt that it would be most logical and most reasonable to select . . . those parts of the child welfare or child health problems which were closely related to the problem of unemployment; in the second place, measures which would attempt to meet the basic needs of children throughout the country, such as the need for economic security when the father is absent from the home, and the need for a measure of health protection." With these criteria in mind, the three women devised a three-part plan providing "security" for children.

First, they designed a federally aided mothers' pension plan called aid to dependent children. After federal and state relief became available in 1933 through the FERA, many families eligible for mothers' aid were instead on FERA emergency relief rolls. This was largely due to the fact that mothers' aid funds in most states had already been reduced or depleted. By 1934, although mothers' pensions were "authorized by the laws of 45 States . . . [such funds were] actually granted by less than half the local units empowered to provide this form of care." This circumstance was contrary to the Children's Bureau principle that mothers' aid and public relief were not interchangeable. The Children's Bureau argued that these families were entitled to "long time care." Mothers' aid, Grace Abbott maintained "should not be administered in connection with or as part of general relief and must have a different standard of adequacy than emergency relief." The Children's Bureau held that "experience shows that this security and the assistance given to the mother in meeting the problems of family life and child-rearing are important influences in preventing juvenile delinquency and other social difficulties." As has been shown, the Children's Bureau contended that mothers' aid was a form of preventive social welfare, not poor relief. Security for these children and their mothers included federal and state aid to dependent children.

In 1934 the bureau estimated that there were three times more families eligible for mothers' aid than the number actually receiving it. State relief officers found it economically expedient to place families on emergency relief, subsidized by FERA funds, rather than on mothers' aid payrolls funded exclusively by the states. . . . [T]he federal government provided $45 million and state and local governments added another $15 million in emergency relief payments to families that should have been eligible for mothers' aid. State and local governments also spent $37.5 million on mothers' aid funds. The Children's Bureau argued that this appropriation should be much higher and that the federal government should help fund this social insurance effort. The situation was especially critical because by 1934 state and local governments had largely run out of revenue for mothers' aid programs.

After examining the data collected by the Children's Bureau, Lenroot, Eliot, and Abbott submitted their recommendations concerning aid to dependent children to the CES. They proposed that local and state governments increase their contribution to mothers' aid programs (which should then be renamed aid to dependent children) to $40 million. To ease the burden, the federal government should provide $40 million in matching grants. In a further attempt to distinguish aid to dependent children from unemployment relief, Lenroot, Eliot, and Abbott recommended that the "shift from emergency relief to aid to dependent children must be somewhat gradual." This was because trained staffs needed to be hired to distribute the funds. Mothers' aid involved social welfare casework as well as long-term financial assistance. It was not simply temporary "charity" relief. Like old age pensions, aid to dependent children was an entitlement. The CES proposal urged a federal appropriation of $25 million for the first two years with an increase of not more than $50 million per year thereafter. According to this plan, all families eligible for aid to dependent children would then be "properly" included in a program separate from emergency relief. Furthermore, it would be a program "equalized" by the federal government's contributions, but one which maintained state and local control of funds. . . .

The discussions within the CES cabinet committee concerning the proposed plan did not focus on the program's cost or suitability. Instead, conflict arose between the Children's Bureau and the FERA over the bureaucratic administration of the program. . . . [A]rguments over administration were more than simply "turf" disputes or fears that women would lose control of child welfare. The two agencies had contrasting notions about the purpose of the aid to dependent children program. Hopkins argued that all relief efforts, whether temporary or long term, should be administered through the FERA. He and many of his supporters thought that in the future a permanent federal department of public welfare might be established to administer all federal relief programs. In addition, the FERA believed that the aid to dependent children program had a much broader scope than did the Children's Bureau. For the FERA, the term "dependent children" meant "children under sixteen in their own homes, in which there is not an adult person, other than one needed to care for the child or children, who is able to work and provide the family with a reasonable subsistence compatible with decent health." This definition was not as specific as the Children's Bureau's, which required that male breadwinners in families eligible for aid to dependent children be absent through death, separation, or desertion. The FERA's broader interpretation ran contrary to the Children's Bureau's concept of a program designed specifically for "worthy fatherless" families that needed long-term care. According to the bureau, such children, through their mothers, were entitled to a "pension" or benefit. Furthermore, the Children's Bureau's viewpoint maintained that the rearing of children by worthy widowed, divorced, or abandoned mothers was a service just as vital to the national security as military service. Economic security for mothers and children was as much an entitlement as old age or veterans' pensions and should not be confused with relief. They argued that the very phrases "mothers' aid" and "mothers' pensions" misconstrued the intention of such laws. These were "not primarily aids to mothers but defense measures for children." According to Lenroot, Eliot, and Abbott, aid to dependent children was "designed to release from the wage-earning role the person whose natural function is to give her children the physical and affectionate guardianship necessary not alone to keep them from falling into social misfortune, but more affirmatively to rear them into citizens capable of contributing to society."

[CES Chief Edwin] Witte, Perkins, Hopkins, Wallace, Altmeyer, and Treasury Department Assistant Secretary Josephine Roche held an "informal" meeting at Secretary of Labor Perkins's home on December 22 or 23, 1934, to work out a final draft of the CES proposal. There are apparently no minutes of the meeting, but it is clear that during this session the group decided to include the Children's Bureau's interpretation of the aid to dependent children proposal in the CES's final report. However, the committee also recommended that the FERA administer the new program. . . .

The second program devised by Lenroot, Eliot, and Abbott for the CES also had its roots in the Children's Bureau's first two decades of work. This proposal centered on children with "special needs" not necessarily related to unemployment or an absent parent. The 1934 definition of this group included a much broader range of dependent children than the agency's earlier meaning: "situations of neglect in homes, feeblemindedness in parents or children, cruel and abusive parents, illegitimate children without competent guardians, children who are delinquent, truant, or wayward, or who suffer from mental disturbances or handicaps." The Children's Bureau estimated that there were approximately 300,000 dependent and neglected children in the United States, approximately 1 percent of all Americans nineteen and under. Of these three-fifths lived in institutions, and the rest in foster homes. In addition, 200,000 more children fell under juvenile court supervision and another

75,000 children were born to unmarried parents each year. Local services, although modest, were generally available for children living in cities of 100,000 or more. But in smaller localities "services of this kind [were] extremely limited, or non-existent." Only one-fourth of the states had statewide county welfare boards.

At first, Abbott proposed requesting $1 million for a program designed to address children with special needs. However, Lenroot and Eliot increased the recommended appropriation by 50 percent. Abbott was somewhat taken aback by the suggestion fearing that this asked for too much. But the new chief and her assistant dismissed Abbott's objections and asked for $1.5 million; $1 million to be distributed in automatic grants-in-aid to the states ($10,000 to each state with the rest proportional according to population) and $500,000 to states with the greatest need, especially those with large rural populations. . . . [T]he women recommended that the Children's Bureau be made responsible for this new program. There apparently was no disagreement, and the CES submitted the proposal in its final draft exactly as presented by Lenroot, Eliot, and Abbott.

The third program recommended by Lenroot's committee also related to the Children's Bureau's previous experience, this time focusing on maternal and child health care. The loss of Sheppard-Towner [a Children's Bureau–sponsored program that provided prenatal and infant care in the 1920s] combined with the economic depression to cause an extreme drop in the expenditure of public health funds. This was particularly true of programs intended to reduce infant and maternal mortality rates. During 1928 the states used approximately $2,158,000 in combined state and federal funds (of which $1,018,000 was federal money) for use in maternity and infancy work under Sheppard-Towner. By 1934, funds for the promotion of good infant and maternal care had been reduced to $1,157,000 and nine states reported no special appropriations for such work. Twenty-two states funded less than 50 percent of the total amount spent in 1928. Lenroot, Eliot, and Abbott developed a plan to reverse this trend. Modeled on Sheppard-Towner, the program would utilize diagnostic clinics and educational work, but go further by permitting the distribution of actual medical care for needy children and their mothers. In addition, the plan also covered older children. In an interview conducted years later, Eliot explained that it was her idea to expand the proposal to include "children" up to twenty-one years of age. She felt that the CES needed to "think in broader terms—what do children need all through their school years until they are adults." This concept was "a little overwhelming to Grace Abbott; but I being very young and naive, thought 'Why not?' and [Abbott] agreed that we would then title our proposal 'Maternal and Child Health'" instead of maternal and *infant* health care. . . . But at the same time that this proposal broadened Sheppard-Towner, the addition of means testing made it a program accessible to a much smaller constituency. As might be expected, some felt that the PHS [Public Health Service] should be given responsibility for the proposal. However, the CES's final recommendation designated that the Children's Bureau act as the program's administrator.

Lenroot, Eliot and Abbott recognized "crippled" children as another group needing uniform health care. . . . A program for handicapped children was not a revolutionary idea. Thirty-five states already had some provision for such children in 1934, "although in several of these states the appropriations were so small that only a few . . . could be cared for." States and counties spent approximately $5,500,000 annually on the care of handicapped children. However, this only touched a small percentage of the estimated 300,000 to 500,000 physically handicapped youngsters living in the United States. Many were difficult to locate and it was hard to offer follow-up health care for those living in rural areas, especially those residing two hundred miles or more from the closest hospital. Initially Abbott planned to include services for handicapped children within the maternal and child health proposal. But pressure from advocacy groups such as the National Society for Crippled Children influenced the women to make this program a separate section of their plan. They asked for $3 million in federal grant-in-aid funds which would be matched dollar for dollar by the states. The CES's proposal slightly reduced this request to $2,850,000 and recommended that the Children's Bureau be responsible for administering the program.

Ironically, a controversy [over whether to establish a national health care program—a proposal opposed by medical professionals] that materialized even before the child health and "crippled" children proposals were submitted to the CES cabinet committee helped the bureau to retain control of such programs. . . .

. . . For a time a few members of the Roosevelt administration attempted to include a national health care program as part of the New Deal. The [CES's Medical Advisory] committee's statement suggested making "good health services and medical care [available] to all of the population" including those who "cannot otherwise secure them." Providing such benefits, the committee's members argued, is an "obligation of society." . . . The group concluded that in order to successfully uphold these principles a compulsory health insurance plan should be part of the CES's final proposal. The plan also included cash maternity benefits to encourage women "to abstain from employment for some time before or after birth . . . [and] to receive competent prenatal and postnatal, as well as delivery care." . . .

But keeping the power over medical care in the hands of physicians did not quiet objections from the AMA [American Medical Association]. Two AMA members of the committee objected to the majority report and countered with ten principles of their own, proclaiming that "medical service must have no connection with any cash benefits." Furthermore, "no third party must be permitted to come between the patient and the physician. . . . all responsibility for the character of medical service must be borne by the profession" (meaning the AMA). By February 1935, Medical Advisory Committee chair and AMA president Walter Bierring seemingly rejected his committee's recommendation and wrote Witte that he was as "firmly convinced as ever that the delivery of medical service under Federal or State control is not advisable or adaptable for this country."

Ultimately, Perkins, Witte, Hopkins, and Altmeyer removed compulsory health insurance from the CES's final draft because they believed it too controversial and feared that retaining it in the proposal might jeopardize the entire program. The attention focused on compulsory health insurance benefited the Children's Bureau and its constituents by drawing attention away from the child health proposals. The AMA and its supporters worried much more about the implementation of national health insurance than the skimpy maternal and child health proposals given to the Children's Bureau. In addition, the CES's final child health plan emphasized the "close cooperation" of the Children's Bureau with "medical and public welfare agencies." . . .

But, on December 24, 1934, before the proposal reached Congress, Perkins and Hopkins briefed Roosevelt on the CES's recommendations. After a conference lasting several hours, Roosevelt accepted the CES program as submitted. The final signed report, along with a draft of the Economic Security bill, was filed with the president on January 15, 1935. Two days later, Roosevelt sent a special message to Congress recommending that the program be enacted "with a minimum of delay." The Wagner-Lewis bill (S. 1130, H.R. 4120) was introduced on January 18, 1935, and sent to the House Ways and Means Committee and the Senate Finance Committee for hearings three days later. During congressional hearings the bill was renamed the Social Security bill and its organization and content changed.

Public and political attention focused generally on the old age pension and public relief sections of the bill. But during House committee hearings, the aid to dependent children proposal also drew some objections. The first concern focused on the FERA's role as administrator. Some members had previously objected to the FERA, a temporary agency, administering the old age assistance section of the bill. These critics argued that permanent "security" programs should not be given to an emergency agency. Giving the Children's Bureau, a permanent agency, the administrative responsibility for the aid to dependent children program would have muted such criticisms against the children's section, but no one offered such an amendment. Instead, the House committee amended the bill by calling for the establishment of the Social Security Board, a permanent agency that would be responsible for both the old age and aid to dependent children programs. Interestingly, this time objections to a child welfare program focused on the bureaucratic technicalities of the plan and not on the need for or constitutional aspects of federal assistance for mothers and their children. But this change in strategy signaled a rejection of the Children's Bureau's notion that aid to dependent children was a form of social insurance similar to old age pensions, or payments for service (an earned benefit) like veterans' pensions. In addition, the change showed a rejection of the agency's "whole child" philosophy. According to Thomas Eliot, members of the House Ways and Means Committee did not believe that grants-in-aid programs designed to help the needy were insurance or an earned benefit. Instead they viewed programs such as aid to dependent children as noncontributory and therefore a form of "charity" relief. This has become the foundation of the two-tiered U.S. social insurance system. In other words, popular belief holds that the Social Security old age benefit program is a form of savings account in which individuals get back what they paid in. But all FICA (Federal Insurance Corporation of America) taxes are part of a general revenue fund and payments are only partially related to how much an individual has contributed (most people get much more than they paid in). Furthermore, veterans' pensions, funded solely through the federal government, are generally viewed as a benefit for service, while aid to dependent children payments granted to single mothers are stigmatized as relief. Consequently, despite the Children's Bureau's apparent victory over the FERA's interpretation in CES debates, even in 1935 aid to dependent children was viewed as "welfare."

A second concern expressed by House committee members posed a more practical problem for mothers and children who would benefit from the program. In the final CES proposal there had been no limitation on the maximum grant per child appropriated by the federal government if matched by the required amount of state funds. However, the House committee established the maximum grants at $18 per month for the first child and $12 per month for each additional child. They used this standard because it was the same amount allowable under the veterans' pension acts paying benefits to children of servicemen killed during World War I. But committee members ignored the fact that under the veterans' pension acts widows were granted a $30 per month allowance in addition to children's benefits. The aid to dependent children program did not include an allowance to mothers or other caretakers, but it was still written with the intention of keeping women at home to care for "dependent" children. . . . Noting the lack of financial support for mothers, Witte reported that the members of the House committee "acknowledged [the discrepancy] to be a justifiable criticism . . . [but said that] there was so little interest on the part of any of the members in aid to dependent children that no one thereafter made a motion to strike out the section." Grace Abbott noted that "dependent children did not have a large voting lobby." This objection, coupled with the apparent lack of controversy surrounding the children's proposals in the Social Security bill, provides evidence that these sections were largely ignored by most legislators. Even the bill's major designer, Thomas Eliot, admits that the child welfare sections of the bill received little of his attention and were "edited far too hastily." In addition, Edwin Witte maintained that "there was little interest in Congress in . . . aid to dependent children." It was his belief that "nothing would have been done on this subject if it had not been included in the report of the Committee on Economic Security."

On August 14, 1935, President Roosevelt signed the Social Security Act into law (49 *Stat.* 620). The program is often cited as a watershed in American social welfare history, but, like Congress, the press, the public, and the program's designers, most scholars have focused on the old age and unemployment insurance aspects of the law and generally ignored the programs for children included in the act under titles IV, V, and VII. But the children's programs developed under the Social Security Act would touch the lives of more young people in the United States than all the Children's Bureau's investigative and educational efforts during its previous twenty-two years. In addition, under the law, the Children's Bureau changed from an agency responsible for the distribution of $337,371 in 1930 to one dispensing $8,644,500 in 1938 and $10,892,797 by the end of the decade. Its staff grew from 143 to 438. Perhaps most significantly, although believed to be a minor concern at the time, the aid to dependent children program has become one of the most controversial legacies of the New Deal. . . .

. . . For two decades the Children's Bureau had limited its role to investigation, education, and advocacy. The New Deal brought the federal government and the Children's Bureau more aggressively into the effort to protect "a right to childhood." Ironically, activists at the time paid little attention to this dramatic change for children. . . . [D]uring the 1930s maternal and infant health care for poor women and their children became a joint federal-state responsibility. . . . The Social Security Act's aid to dependent children program, a decided improvement over mothers' pensions, for the first time instituted a permanent federal program advancing money to fill the needs of poor children. Between 1934 and 1939, the average mothers' pension–style benefits (now ADC) increased from $22.31 per month to $32.12 and the number of recipients rose from 300,000 to 700,000 (approximately 3 percent of American children). In the original version ADC benefits extended only to children up to sixteen. Amendments in 1939 expanded the program to those eighteen and under. But the program continued to address only the needs of children living in "deserving" families. Mothers who had never married and their children need not apply. Divorced mothers or those hindered by racial or ethnic prejudice could also be excluded. In addition, changes in administrative responsibility for the bill influenced the law's effectiveness for children. Although the designer of the New Deal's child welfare program, the Children's Bureau was not its sole administrator. Instead, the Social Security Board, a federal agency more interested in old age insurance than children's aid, implemented and directed the future of the important aid to dependent children program. The Children's Bureau had won the battle but lost the war. The loss of administrative responsibility for the aid to dependent children program showed that the agency had not successfully convinced policy makers of its "whole child" strategy. In the post–World War II era, the aid to dependent children program (later renamed Aid to Families with Dependent Children [AFDC] became the cornerstone of child welfare efforts and the most controversial aspect of the New Deal's Social Security Act. . . .

 ## F U R T H E R   R E A D I N G

Abramovitz, Mimi. *Regulating the Lives of Women: Social Welfare Policy from Colonial Times to the Present* (1988).
———. *Under Attack, Fighting Back: Women and Welfare in the United States* (2000).
Goodwin, Joanne L. *Gender and the Politics of Welfare Reform: Mothers' Pensions in Chicago, 1911–1929* (1997).
Gordon, Linda. *Pitied but Not Entitled: Single Mothers and the History of Welfare, 1890–1935* (1995).
———, ed. *Women, the State, and Welfare* (1990).
Hagood, Margaret Jarman. *Mothers of the South* (1939).
Hawes, Joseph M. *Children Between the Wars: American Childhood, 1920–1940* (1997).
Koven, Seth, and Sonya Michel, eds. *Mothers of a New World: Maternalist Politics and the Origins of Welfare States* (1993).
Ladd-Taylor, Molly. *Mother-Work: Women, Child Welfare, and the State, 1890–1930* (1994).
———. *Raising a Baby the Government Way: Mothers' Letters to the Children's Bureau, 1915–1932* (1986).
Leff, Mark H. "Consensus for Reform: The Mothers'-Pension Movement in the Progressive Era." *Social Service Review* 47 (September 1973): 297–417.
Lindenmeyer, Kriste. *"A Right to Childhood": The U.S. Children's Bureau and Child Welfare, 1912–46* (1997).
Mink, Gwendolyn. *The Wages of Motherhood: Inequality in the Welfare State, 1917–1942* (1995).
Skocpol, Theda. *Protecting Soldiers and Mothers: The Politics of Social Provision in the United States, 1870s–1920s* (1992).
Vandepol, Ann. "Dependent Children, Child Custody, and the Mothers' Pensions: The Transformation of State-Family Relations in the Early 20th Century." *Social Problems* 29 (February 1982): 221–235.

C H A P T E R
10

The Homefront:
American Families
During World War II

Like the Civil War, World War II has only recently gained the attention of family historians. While the separation of husbands and wives and parents and children in the war years produced countless letters—some of which have been salvaged from dusty attics and musty basements and been published—historians of the family have been slow to exploit these resources. Women's historians, eager to explore the short-term and long-term significance of changes in women's employment patterns during the war, have explored the experiences of women defense workers, known at the time by the catch-phrase "Rosie the Riveter," but changes in the American family as a result of men's absence overseas and women's work on the homefront have received less attention. Still, it is clear that family life was profoundly affected by World War II.

The effects are most evident for a group that was the subject of intense scrutiny in the war years: Japanese Americans. In early 1942 approximately 100,000 legal Japanese immigrants (Issei) and their American-born children (Nisei) were evacuated from their homes on the West Coast, temporarily housed in makeshift "relocation centers," and then detained in "internment camps" in inland western states, such as Wyoming and Utah, for the duration of the war. While this violation of basic civil rights drew little attention or protest during the war years, in the decades that followed as the movement for reparations for Japanese Americans gained strength, the American-born children of the interned Japanese began to publish memoirs of their families' experiences, and sociologists and historians began to take notice of the profound changes in Japanese American family life that resulted from enforced migration and camp life.

While protected from the severe treatment that Japanese Americans experienced, white American families also found their lives disrupted by World War II. Men went to war, women went to work, and children went to daycare. One scholar has estimated that 4 million husbands served in the armed forces between 1941 and 1945; of these, approximately one-tenth, or 400,000, never returned. Called on to fill important positions in war production plants to support the war effort (and their

*families), approximately 6 million women joined the work force for the first time,
bringing the total of employed women in the United States to 18 million. At the
height of the war, 37 percent of adult women worked outside the home. Although
the Lanham Act of 1943 authorized local communities to use federal funds to set up
low-cost daycare centers for the children of women war workers, these centers had
room for only about 10 percent of the 2 million children who needed care. The others
were cared for—as the children of the working poor always had been—by other
family members, by each other, or not at all; during the war reported cases of child
neglect in one community tripled.*

*While the postwar years have received more attention from scholars, World
War II offers ample scope for historians of family life to explore themes such as
migration and separation, the effects of these forces on families (and on different
members of families), and the ways in which family members adapt—or fail to
adapt—to the challenges of rapid social change. Although the experiences of
Japanese Americans and white Americans in the World War II era in many respects offer dramatic contrasts, in other respects there are striking parallels. Both
groups confronted separation from family members during the war as a result
either of military service or forced migration. Both also faced new challenges to
parental—especially paternal—authority, as Issei fathers lost control over their
children in the camps and GI fathers lost contact with their children entirely. Both
groups also assigned women greater responsibilities for maintaining family life;
Japanese mothers took on the task of preserving ethnic identity and kin ties, and
white mothers shouldered the dual burden of parenting and wage earning.*

*These shared experiences raise questions about the long-term consequences of
war for family life: How would white wives' and Nisei children's increased independence affect their expectations about marriage and family in the postwar years?
Would wartime patterns of prolonged separation and frequent migration end with
the coming of peace? And what would children raised in an environment of uncertainty seek from adulthood?*

 # DOCUMENTS

The first three documents detail the experiences of Japanese American families in
internment camps. In Document 1 Yoshiko Uchida, who was attending school at the
University of California at Berkeley at the time of World War II, recalls the process by
which she, her mother, and her older sister, also a college student, were removed from
their home. Yoshiko's father, who had already been removed from the family and sent
to a camp in Montana, was reunited with the rest of the family in their California racetrack relocation center, Tanforan. The family was later moved to Topaz, Utah, which
Yoshiko described as a "city of dust." After a year in the camps, Yoshiko and her sister
were allowed to go east to continue their educations.

In Document 2 Monica Sone recalls her family's relocation, under the watchful
eyes of armed guards, from their home in Seattle, Washington, to a temporary relocation
center in Puyallup. Sone's reminiscences show that, despite her mother's attempt to
maintain the family's ethnic identity by insisting on bringing along *shoyu* (soy sauce),
the crowded communal meals in the camp's mess hall undermined family unity and
encouraged generational divisions between the Issei and Nisei.

Similar themes appear in Document 3, in which Jeanne Wakatsuki writes about
the living conditions at another relocation camp, Manzanar. In addition to describing

the inadequate food, shelter, and sanitation provided in the camp, she details the disruptive effects of internment on her family.

The next three documents, all letters exchanged by husbands overseas and their wives on the homefront, shift the focus to white, middle-class Americans. In the first set of letters, written between 1943 and 1945, Georgia newlyweds Barbara and Charles E. Taylor exchange tender assurances of their mutual love and rejoice in the birth and development of their first child, a daughter they christened Sandra Lee and nicknamed Priss. The Taylors' letters, included as Document 4, also reveal their desire to ensure that young Sandra Lee be acquainted with and fond of her absent father, whose stations ranged from New Jersey to France.

While Barbara Taylor cared for Sandra Lee and kept house for her widowed father during the war, many wives and mothers took war jobs. Letters written by twenty-seven-year-old Polly Crow to her husband William ("Darlin'") in 1944 describe her work as a "Ship-Yard Babe" at the Jefferson Boat and Machine Company. Like Barbara Taylor, Polly lived with relatives during her husband's absence; in 1944 she moved from Pensacola, Florida (where William's parents lived), to Louisville, Kentucky (where her mother lived). Although Polly was fortunate enough to have family members to help her care for her infant son, Bill, her letters, included as Document 5, indicate the strain of being both "a career woman" and an involved mother—particularly since, like other war mothers, she considered it imperative to teach her young son to think of his father often.

Women fortunate enough to live near one of the more than three thousand federally sponsored daycare centers established by the Lanham Act had another option. Edith Speert's letters to her husband, Victor, reprinted as Document 6, describe her work at one of these nurseries, the True Sisters Day Care Center in Cleveland, from 1944 to 1946. Speert's letters also discuss the loss of support for government funding for child care in the postwar era, which would deprive her of the job she had come to love and rob many working women of affordable care for their children.

1. A Nisei Daughter Describes Family Life in a Detention Camp, 1942

. . .

The first mass removal of the Japanese began in Terminal Island, a fishing community near San Pedro, and because these people were close to a naval base, their treatment was harsh. With most of their men already interned as my father was, the remaining families had to cope with a three-day deadline to get out of their homes. In frantic haste they were forced to sell their houses, businesses, and property. Many were exploited cruelly and suffered great financial losses.

We knew it was simply a matter of time before we would be notified to evacuate Berkeley as well. A five-mile travel limit and an 8:00 P.M. curfew had already been imposed on all Japanese Americans since March, and enemy aliens were required to register and obtain identification cards. Radios with short wave, cameras, binoculars, and firearms were designated as "contraband' and had to be turned in to the police.

Yoshiko Uchida, *Desert Exile: The Uprooting of a Japanese American Family* (Seattle: University of Washington Press, 1982), pp. 57–60, 62–63, 67–68. Courtesy of the Bancroft Library, University of California, Berkeley.

Obediently adhering to all regulations, we even brought our box cameras to the Berkeley police station where they remained for the duration of the war. . . .

Each day we watched the papers for the evacuation orders covering the Berkeley area. On April 21, the headlines read: "Japs Given Evacuation Orders Here." I felt numb as I read the front page story. "Moving swiftly, without any advance notice, the Western Defense Command today ordered Berkeley's estimated 1,319 Japanese, aliens and citizens alike, evacuated to the Tanforan Assembly Center by noon, May 1." (This gave us exactly ten days' notice.) "Evacuees will report at the Civil Control Station being set up in Pilgrim Hall of the First Congregational Church . . . between the hours of 8:00 A.M. and 5:00 P.M. next Saturday and Sunday."

This was Exclusion Order Number Nineteen, which was to uproot us from our homes and send us into the Tanforan Assembly Center in San Bruno, a hastily converted racetrack.

All Japanese were required to register before the departure date, and my sister, as head of the family, went to register for us. She came home with baggage and name tags that were to bear our family number and be attached to all our belongings. From that day on we became Family Number 13453.

Although we had been preparing for the evacuation orders, still when they were actually issued, it was a sickening shock.

"Ten days! We have only ten days to get ready!" my sister said frantically. Each day she rushed about, not only taking care of our business affairs, but, as our only driver, searching for old crates and cartons for packing, and taking my mother on various errands as well.

Mama still couldn't seem to believe that we would have to leave. "How can we clear out in ten days a house we've lived in for fifteen years?" she asked sadly.

But my sister and I had no answers for her.

Mama had always been a saver, and she had a tremendous accumulation of possessions. Her frugal upbringing had caused her to save string, wrapping paper, bags, jars, boxes, even bits of silk thread left over from sewing, which were tied end to end and rolled up into a silk ball. Tucked away in the corners of her desk and bureau drawers were such things as small stuffed animals, wooden toys, *kokeshi* dolls, marbles, and even a half-finished pair of socks she was knitting for a teddy bear's paw. Many of these were "found objects" that the child in her couldn't bear to discard, but they often proved useful in providing diversion for some fidgety visiting child. These were the simple things to dispose of.

More difficult were the boxes that contained old letters from her family and friends, our old report cards from the first grade on, dozens of albums of family photographs, notebooks and sketch pads full of our childish drawings, valentines and Christmas cards we had made for our parents, innumerable guest books filled with the signatures and friendly words of those who had once been entertained. These were the things my mother couldn't bear to throw away. Because we didn't own our house, we could leave nothing behind. We had to clear the house completely, and everything in it had either to be packed for storage or thrown out.

We surveyed with desperation the vast array of dishes, lacquerware, silverware, pots and pans, books, paintings, porcelain and pottery, furniture, linens, rugs, records, curtains, garden tools, cleaning equipment, and clothing that filled our house. We put up a sign in our window reading, "Living room sofa and chair for sale." We sold things we should have kept and packed away foolish trifles we should have discarded. We sold our refrigerator, our dining room set, two sofas, an easy chair, and a brand new vacuum cleaner with attachments. Without a sensible scheme in our heads, and lacking the practical judgment of my father, the three of us packed frantically and sold recklessly. Although the young people of our church did what they could to help us, we felt desperate as the deadline approached. Our only thought was to get the house emptied in time, for we knew the Army would not wait. . . .

As our packing progressed, our house grew increasingly barren and our garden took on a shabby look that would have saddened my father. My mother couldn't bear to leave her favorite plants to strangers and dug up her special rose, London Smoke carnations, and yellow calla lilies to take to a friend for safekeeping.

One day a neighboring woman rang our bell and asked for one of Papa's prize gladiolas that she had fancied as she passed by. It seemed a heartless, avaricious gesture, and I was indignant, just as I was when people told me the evacuation was for our own protection. My mother, however, simply handed the woman a shovel and told her to help herself. "Let her have it," she said, "if it will make her happy."

Gradually ugly gaps appeared in the garden that had once been my parents' delight and, like our house, it began to take on an empty abandoned look.

Toward the end, my mother sat Japanese fashion, her legs folded beneath her, in the middle of her vacant bedroom sorting out the contents of many dusty boxes that had been stored on her closet shelves.

She was trying to discard some of the poems she had scribbled on scraps of paper, clippings she had saved, notebooks of her writings, and bundles of old letters from her family and friends. Only now have I come to realize what a heartbreaking task this must have been for her as her native land confronted in war the land of her children. She knew she would be cut off from her mother, brothers, and sister until that war ended. She knew she could neither hear from them nor write to tell them of her concern and love. The letters she had kept for so long were her last link with them for the time being and she couldn't bear to throw them out. . . .

It wasn't until I saw the armed guards standing at each doorway, [of the First Congregational Church, designated as the Civil Control Station where we had been told to report], their bayonets mounted and ready, that I realized the full horror of the situation. Then my knees sagged, my stomach began to churn, and I very nearly lost my breakfast.

Hundreds of Japanese Americans were crowded into the great hall of the church and the sound of their voices pressed close around me. Old people sat quietly, waiting with patience and resignation for whatever was to come. Mothers tried to comfort crying infants, young children ran about the room, and some teenagers tried to put up a brave front by making a social opportunity of the occasion. . . .

Before long, we were told to board the buses that lined the street outside, and the people living nearby came out of their houses to watch the beginning of our strange migration. . . .

Mama, Kay, and I climbed onto one of the buses and it began its one-way journey down familiar streets we had traveled so often in our own car. We crossed the Bay Bridge, went on beyond San Francisco, and sped down the Bayshore Highway. Some of the people on the bus talked nervously, one or two wept, but most sat quietly, keeping their thoughts to themselves and their eyes on the window, as familiar landmarks slipped away one by one.

As we rode down the highway, the grandstand of the Tanforan racetrack gradually came into view, and I could see a high barbed wire fence surrounding the entire area, pierced at regular intervals by tall guard towers. This was to be our temporary home until the government could construct inland camps far removed from the West Coast.

The bus made a sharp turn and swung slowly into the racetrack grounds. As I looked out the window for a better view, I saw armed guards close and bar the barbed wire gates behind us. We were in the Tanforan Assembly Center now and there was no turning back.

2. A Japanese American Student Recalls the Relocation Order, 1942

General DeWitt kept reminding us that E Day, evacuation day, was drawing near. "E day will be announced in the very near future. If you have not wound up your affairs by now, it will soon be too late."

Father negotiated with Bentley Agent and Company to hire someone to manage his business. Years ago Father had signed a long-term lease with the owner of the building and the agent had no other alternative than to let Father keep control of his business until his time ran out. He was one of the fortunate few who would keep their businesses intact for the duration.

And Mother collected crates and cartons. She stayed up night after night, sorting, and re-sorting a lifetime's accumulation of garments, toys and household goods. Those were pleasant evenings when we rummaged around in old trunks and suitcases, reminiscing about the good old days, and almost forgetting why we were knee-deep in them. . . .

On the twenty-first of April, a Tuesday, the general gave us the shattering news. "All the Seattle Japanese will be moved to Puyallup by May 1. Everyone must be registered Saturday and Sunday between 8 A.M. and 5 P.M. They will leave next week in three groups, on Tuesday, Thursday and Friday."

Up to that moment, we had hoped against hope that something or someone would intervene for us. Now there was no time for moaning. A thousand and one details must be attended to in this one week of grace. Those seven days sputtered out like matches struck in the wind, as we rushed wildly about. Mother distributed sheets, pillowcases and blankets, which we stuffed into seabags. Into the two suitcases, we packed heavy winter overcoats, plenty of sweaters, woolen slacks and skirts, flannel pajamas and scarves. Personal toilet articles, one tin plate, tin cup and silverware completed our luggage. The one seabag and two suitcases apiece were going to be the backbone of our future home, and we planned it carefully.

Henry went to the Control Station to register the family. He came home with twenty tags, all numbered "10710," tags to be attached to each piece of baggage, and one to hang from our coat lapels. From then on, we were known as Family #10710. . . .

Monica Sone, *Nisei Daughter* (Seattle: University of Washington Press, 1979; originally published 1953), pp. 165–166, 168–178. Copyright © 1953 by Monica Sone; copyright © renewed 1981 by Monica Sone. By permission of Little, Brown and Company (Inc.).

The front doorbell rang. It was Dunks Oshima, who had offered to take us down to Eighth and Lane in a borrowed pickup truck. Hurriedly the menfolk loaded the truck with the last few boxes of household goods which Dunks was going to take down to the hotel. He held up a gallon can of soy sauce, puzzled, "Where does this go, to the hotel, too?"

Nobody seemed to know where it had come from or where it was going, until Mother finally spoke up guiltily, "Er, it's going with me. I didn't think we'd have shoyu where we're going."

Henry looked as if he were going to explode. "But Mama, you're not supposed to have more than one seabag and two suitcases. And of all things, you want to take with you—shoyu!" . . .

Mother personally saw to it that the can of shoyu remained with her baggage. She turned back once more to look at our brown and yellow frame house and said almost gayly, "Good-by, house."

Old Asthma [the family's pet cat] came bounding out to the front yard, her tail swaying in the air. "And good-by, Asthma, take good care of our home. . . ."

A swallow swooped down from the eaves. "Oh, soh, soh, good-by to you, too, Mrs. Swallow. I hope you have a nice little family."

Mother explained that she had discovered the swallow's little nest under the eaves just outside Sumi's bedroom window, filled with four beautiful blue-speckled eggs like precious-colored stones. The swallow darted low and buzzed over Asthma like a miniature fighter plane. We watched amazed as it returned time and time again in a diving attack on Asthma. Mother said, "She's fighting to protect her family." Asthma leaped into the air, pawed at the bird halfheartedly, then rubbed herself against Mother's woolen slacks.

"Quarter to eight," Dunks gently reminded us. We took turns ruffling Asthma's fur and saying good-by to her. The new tenants had promised us that they would keep her as their pet.

We climbed into the truck, chattering about the plucky little swallow. As we coasted down Beacon Hill bridge for the last time, we fell silent, and stared out at the delicately flushed morning sky of Puget Sound. We drove through bustling China-town, and in a few minutes arrived on the corner of Eighth and Lane. This area was ordinarily lonely and deserted but now it was gradually filling up with silent, labeled Japanese, standing self-consciously among their seabags and suitcases.

Everyone was dressed casually, each according to his idea of where he would be going. One Issei was wearing a thick mackinaw jacket and cleated, high-topped hiking boots. I stared admiringly at one handsome couple, standing slim and poised in their ski clothes. They looked newly wed. They stood holding hands beside their streamlined luggage that matched smartly with the new Mr. and Mrs. look. With an air of resigned sacrifice, some Issei women wore dark-colored slacks with deep-hemmed cuffs. One gnarled old grandmother wore an ankle-length black crepe dress with a plastic initial "S" pinned to its high neckline. It was old-fashioned, but digni-fied and womanly.

Automobiles rolled up to the curb, one after another, discharging more Japanese and more baggage. Finally at ten o'clock, a vanguard of Greyhound busses purred in and parked themselves neatly along the curb. The crowd stirred and murmured. The bus doors opened and from each, a soldier with rifle in hand stepped out and stood stiffly at attention by the door. The murmuring died. It was the first time I had seen a rifle at such close range and I felt uncomfortable. This rifle was presumably to quell riots, but contrarily, I felt riotous emotion mounting in my breast. . . .

Newspaper photographers with flash-bulb cameras pushed busily through the crowd. One of them rushed up to our bus, and asked a young couple and their little boy to step out and stand by the door for a shot. They were reluctant, but the photographers were persistent and at length they got out of the bus and posed, grinning widely to cover their embarrassment. We saw the picture in the newspaper shortly after and the caption underneath it read, "Japs good-natured about evacuation."

Our bus quickly filled to capacity. All eyes were fixed up front, waiting. The guard stepped inside, sat by the door, and nodded curtly to the gray-uniformed bus driver. The door closed with a low hiss. We were now the Wartime Civil Control Administration's babies. . . .

We sped out of the city southward along beautiful stretches of farmland, with dark, newly turned soil. In the beginning we devoured every bit of scenery which flashed past our window and admired the massive-muscled work horses plodding along the edge of the highway, the rich burnished copper color of a browsing herd of cattle, the vivid spring green of the pastures, but eventually the sameness of the country landscape palled on us. We tried to sleep to escape from the restless anxiety which kept bobbing up to the surface of our minds. I awoke with a start when the bus filled with excited buzzing. A small group of straw-hatted Japanese farmers stood by the highway, waving at us. I felt a sudden warmth toward them, then a twinge of pity. They would be joining us soon.

About noon we crept into a small town. Someone said, "Looks like Puyallup, all right." Parents of small children babbled excitedly, "Stand up quickly and look over there. See all the chick-chick and fat little piggies?" One little city boy stared hard at the hogs and said tersely, "They're *bachi*—dirty!"

Our bus idled a moment at the traffic signal and we noticed at the left of us an entire block filled with neat rows of low shacks, resembling chicken houses. Someone commented on it with awe, "Just look at those chicken houses. They sure go in for poultry in a big way here." Slowly the bus made a left turn, drove through a wire-fenced gate, and to our dismay, we were inside the oversized chicken farm. The bus driver opened the door, the guard stepped out and stationed himself at the door again. Jim, the young man who had shepherded us into the busses, popped his head inside and sang out, "Okay, folks, all off at Yokohama, Puyallup." . . .

We were assigned to apartment 2-1-A, right across from the bachelor quarters. The apartments resembled elongated, low stables about two blocks long. Our home was one room, about 18 by 20 feet, the size of a living room. There was one small window in the wall opposite the one door. It was bare except for a small, tinny wood-burning stove crouching in the center. The flooring consisted of two by fours laid directly on the earth, and dandelions were already pushing their way up through the cracks. Mother was delighted when she saw their shaggy yellow heads. "Don't anyone pick them. I'm going to cultivate them."

Father snorted, "Cultivate them! If we don't watch out, those things will be growing out of our hair."

Just then Henry stomped inside, bringing the rest of our baggage. "What's all the excitement about?"

Sumi replied laconically, "Dandelions."

Henry tore off a fistful. Mother scolded, "*Arra! Arra!* Stop that. They're the only beautiful things around here." . . .

Mother and Father wandered out to see what the other folks were doing and they found people wandering in the mud, wondering what other folks were doing. Mother returned shortly, her face lit up in an ecstatic smile, "We're in luck. The latrine is right nearby. We won't have to walk blocks."

We laughed, marveling at Mother who could be so poetic and yet so practical. Father came back, bent double like a woodcutter in a fairy tale, with stacks of scrap lumber over his shoulder. His coat and trouser pockets bulged with nails. Father dumped his loot in a corner and explained, "There was a pile of wood left by the carpenters and hundreds of nails scattered loose. Everybody was picking them up, and I hustled right in with them. Now maybe we can live in style with tables and chairs."

The block leader knocked at our door and announced lunchtime. He instructed us to take our meal at the nearest mess hall. As I untied my seabag to get out my pie plate, tin cup, spoon and fork, I realized I was hungry. At the mess hall we found a long line of people. Children darted in and out of the line, skiing in the slithery mud. The young stood impatiently on one foot, then the other, and scowled, "The food had better be good after all this wait." But the Issei stood quietly, arms folded, saying very little. A light drizzle began to fall, coating bare black heads with tiny sparkling raindrops. The chow line inched forward.

Lunch consisted of two canned sausages, one lob of boiled potato, and a slab of bread. Our family had to split up, for the hall was too crowded for us to sit together. I wandered up and down the aisles, back and forth along the crowded tables and benches, looking for a few inches to squeeze into. . . .

The block monitor, an impressive Nisei who looked like a star tackle with his crouching walk, came around the first night to tell us that we must all be inside our room by nine o'clock every night. At ten o'clock, he rapped at the door again, yelling, "Lights out!" and Mother rushed to turn the light off not a second later.

Throughout the barracks, there were a medley of creaking cots, whimpering infants and explosive night coughs. Our attention was riveted on the intense little wood stove which glowed so violently I feared it would melt right down to the floor. We soon learned that this condition lasted for only a short time, after which it suddenly turned into a deep freeze. Henry and Father took turns at the stove to produce the harrowing blast which all but singed our army blankets, but did not penetrate through them. As it grew quieter in the barracks, I could hear the light patter of rain. Soon I felt the "splat! splat!" of raindrops digging holes into my face. The dampness on my pillow spread like a mortal bleeding, and I finally had to get out and haul my cot toward the center of the room. In a short while Henry was up. "I've got multiple leaks, too. Have to complain to the landlord first thing in the morning."

All through the night I heard people getting up, dragging cots around. I stared at our little window, unable to sleep. I was glad Mother had put up a makeshift curtain on the window for I noticed a powerful beam of light sweeping across it every few seconds. The lights came from high towers placed around the camp where guards with Tommy guns kept a twenty-four hour vigil. I remembered the wire fence encircling us, and a knot of anger tightened in my breast. What was I doing behind a fence like a criminal? If there were accusations to be made, why hadn't I been given a fair trial? Maybe I wasn't considered an American anymore. My citizenship wasn't real, after all. Then what was I? I was certainly not a citizen of Japan as my parents were. On second thought, even Father and Mother were more alien residents of the United States than Japanese nationals for they had little ties with their mother country. In their twenty-five years in America, they had worked and paid their taxes to their adopted government as any other citizen.

Of one thing I was sure. The wire fence was real. I no longer had the right to walk out of it. It was because I had Japanese ancestors. It was also because some people had little faith in the ideas and ideals of democracy. They said that after all these were but words and could not possibly insure loyalty. New laws and camps were surer devices. I finally buried my face in my pillow to wipe out burning thoughts and snatch what sleep I could. . . .

3. A Resident of Manzanar Internment Camp Looks Back on Her Wartime and Postwar Experiences, 1940s

I don't remember what we ate that first morning. I know we stood for half an hour in cutting wind waiting to get our food. Then we took it back to the cubicle and ate huddled around the stove. Inside, it was warmer than when we left, because Woody was already making good his promise to Mama, tacking up some ends of lath he'd found, stuffing rolled paper around the door frame.

Trouble was, he had almost nothing to work with. Beyond this temporary weather stripping, there was little else he could do. Months went by, in fact, before our "home" changed much at all from what it was the day we moved in—bare floors, blanket partitions, one bulb in each compartment dangling from a roof beam, and open ceilings overhead so that mischievous boys like Ray and Kiyo could climb up into the rafters and peek into anyone's life.

The simple truth is the camp was no more ready for us when we got there than we were ready for it. We had only the dimmest ideas of what to expect. Most of the families, like us, had moved out from southern California with as much luggage as each person could carry. Some old men left Los Angeles wearing Hawaiian shirts and Panama hats and stepped off the bus at an altitude of 4000 feet, with nothing available but sagebrush and tarpaper to stop the April winds pouring down off the back side of the Sierras.

The War Department was in charge of all the camps at this point. They began to issue military surplus from the First World War—olive-drab knit caps, earmuffs, peacoats, canvas leggings. Later on, sewing machines were shipped in, and one barracks was turned into a clothing factory. An old seamstress took a peacoat of mine, tore the lining out, opened and flattened the sleeves, added a collar, put arm holes in and handed me back a beautiful cape. By fall dozens of seamstresses were

Jeanne Wakatsuki Houston and James D. Houston, *Farewell to Manzanar: A True Story of Japanese American Experience During and After the World War II Internment* (New York: Bantam Books, 1973), pp. 20–27. Copyright © 1973 by James D. Houston. Reprinted by permission of Houghton Mifflin Company. All rights reserved.

working full-time transforming thousands of these old army clothes into capes, slacks and stylish coats. But until that factory got going and packages from friends outside began to fill out our wardrobes, warmth was more important than style. I couldn't help laughing at Mama walking around in army earmuffs and a pair of wide-cuffed, khaki-colored wool trousers several sizes too big for her. Japanese are generally smaller than Caucasians, and almost all these clothes were oversize. They flopped, they dangled, they hung.

It seems comical, looking back; we were a band of Charlie Chaplins marooned in the California desert. But at the time, it was pure chaos. That's the only way to describe it. The evacuation had been so hurriedly planned, the camps so hastily thrown together, nothing was completed when we got there, and almost nothing worked.

I was sick continually, with stomach cramps and diarrhea. At first it was from the shots they gave us for typhoid, in very heavy doses and in assembly-line fashion; swab, jab, swab, *Move along now,* swab, jab, swab, *Keep it moving.* That knocked all of us younger kids down at once, with fevers and vomiting. Later, it was the food that made us sick, young and old alike. The kitchens were too small and badly ventilated. Food would spoil from being left out too long. That summer, when the heat got fierce, it would spoil faster. The refrigeration kept breaking down. The cooks, in many cases, had never cooked before. Each block had to provide its own volunteers. Some were lucky and had a professional or two in their midst. But the first chef in our block had been a gardener all his life and suddenly found himself preparing three meals a day for 250 people.

"The Manzanar runs" became a condition of life, and you only hoped that when you rushed to the latrine, one would be in working order.

That first morning, on our way to the chow line, Mama and I tried to use the women's latrine in our block. The smell of it spoiled what little appetite we had. Outside, men were working in an open trench, up to their knees in muck—a common sight in the months to come. Inside, the floor was covered with excrement, and all twelve bowls were erupting like a row of tiny volcanoes.

Mama stopped a kimono-wrapped woman stepping past us with her sleeve pushed up against her nose and asked, "What do you do?"

"Try Block Twelve," the woman said, grimacing. "They have just finished repairing the pipes."

It was about two city blocks away. We followed her over there and found a line of women waiting in the wind outside the latrine. We had no choice but to join the line and wait with them.

Inside it was like all the other latrines. Each block was built to the same design, just as each of ten camps, from California to Arkansas, was built to a common master plan. It was an open room, over a concrete slab. The sink was a long metal trough against one wall, with a row of spigots for hot and cold water. Down the center of the room twelve toilet bowls were arranged in six pairs, back to back, with no partitions. My mother was a very modest person, and this was going to be agony for her, sitting down in public, among strangers.

One old woman had already solved the problem for herself by dragging in a large cardboard carton. She set it up around one of the bowls, like a three-sided screen. OXYDOL was printed in large black letters down the front. I remember this well, because that was the soap we were issued for laundry; later on, the smell of it would permeate these rooms. The upended carton was about four feet high. The old woman behind it wasn't much taller. When she stood, only her head showed over the top.

She was about Granny's age. With great effort she was trying to fold the sides of the screen together. Mama happened to be at the head of the line now. As she approached the vacant bowl, she and the old woman bowed to each other from the waist. Mama then moved to help her with the carton, and the old woman said very graciously, in Japanese, "Would you like to use it?"

Happily, gratefully, Mama bowed again and said, *"Arigato"* (Thank you). *"Arigato gozaimas"* (Thank you very much). "I will return it to your barracks."

"Oh, no. It is not necessary. I will be glad to wait."

The old woman unfolded one side of the cardboard, while Mama opened the other; then she bowed again and scurried out the door.

Those big cartons were a common sight in the spring of 1942. Eventually sturdier partitions appeared, one or two at a time. The first were built of scrap lumber. Word would get around that Block such and such had partitions now, and Mama and my older sisters would walk halfway across the camp to use them. Even after every latrine in camp was screened, this quest for privacy continued. Many would wait until late at night. Ironically, because of this, midnight was often the most crowded time of all.

Like so many of the women there, Mama never did get used to the latrines. It was a humiliation she just learned to endure: *shikata ga nai,* this cannot be helped. She would quickly subordinate her own desires to those of the family or the community, because she knew cooperation was the only way to survive. At the same time she placed a high premium on personal privacy, respected it in others and insisted upon it for herself. Almost everyone at Manzanar had inherited this pair of traits from the generations before them who had learned to live in a small, crowded country like Japan. Because of the first they were able to take a desolate stretch of wasteland and gradually make it livable. But the entire situation there, especially in the beginning—the packed sleeping quarters, the communal mess halls, the open toilets—all this was an open insult to that other, private self, a slap in the face you were powerless to challenge.

At seven I was too young to be insulted. The camp worked on me in a much different way. I wasn't aware of this at the time, of course. No one was, except maybe Mama, and there was little she could have done to change what happened.

It began in the mess hall. Before Manzanar, mealtime had always been the center of our family scene. In camp, and afterward, I would often recall with deep yearning the old round wooden table in our dining room in Ocean Park, the biggest piece of furniture we owned, large enough to seat twelve or thirteen of us at once. A tall row of elegant, lathe-turned spindles separated this table from the kitchen, allowing talk to pass from one room to other. Dinners were always noisy, and they were always abundant with great pots of boiled rice, platters of home-grown vegetables, fish Papa caught.

He would sit at the head of this table, with Mama next to him serving and the rest of us arranged around the edges according to age, down to where Kiyo and I sat, so far away from our parents, it seemed at the time, we had our own enclosed nook inside this world. The grownups would be talking down at their end, while we two played our secret games, making eyes at each other when Papa gave the order to begin to eat, racing with chopsticks to scrape the last grain from our rice bowls, eyeing Papa to see if he had noticed who won.

Now, in the mess halls, after a few weeks had passed, we stopped eating as a family. Mama tried to hold us together for a while, but it was hopeless. Granny was too feeble to walk across the block three times a day, especially during heavy weather, so May brought food to her in the barracks. My older brothers and sisters, meanwhile, began eating with their friends, or eating somewhere blocks away, in the hope of finding better food. The word would get around that the cook over in Block 22, say, really knew his stuff, and they would eat a few meals over there, to test the rumor. Camp authorities frowned on mess hall hopping and tried to stop it, but the good cooks liked it. They liked to see long lines outside their kitchens and would work overtime to attract a crowd.

Younger boys, like Ray, would make a game of seeing how many mess halls they could hit in one meal period—be the first in line at Block 16, gobble down your food, run to 17 by the middle of the dinner hour, gulp another helping, and hurry to 18 to make the end of the chow line and stuff in the third meal of the evening. They didn't *need* to do that. No matter how bad the food might be, you could always eat till you were full.

Kiyo and I were too young to run around, but often we would eat in gangs with other kids, while the grownups sat at another table. I confess I enjoyed this part of it at the time. We all did. A couple of years after the camps opened, sociologists studying the life noticed what had happened to the families. They made some recommendations, and edicts went out that families *must* start eating together again. Most people resented this; they griped and grumbled. They were in the habit of eating with their friends. And until the mess hall system itself could be changed, not much could really be done. It was too late.

My own family, after three years of mess hall living, collapsed as an integrated unit. Whatever dignity or feeling of filial strength we may have known before December 1941 was lost, and we did not recover it until many years after the war, not until after Papa died and we began to come together, trying to fill the vacuum his passing left in all our lives.

The closing of the camps, in the fall of 1945, only aggravated what had begun inside. Papa had no money then and could not get work. Half of our family had already moved to the east coast, where jobs had opened up for them. The rest of us were relocated into a former defense workers' housing project in Long Beach. In that small apartment there never was enough room for all of us to sit down for a meal. We ate in shifts, and I yearned all the more for our huge round table in Ocean Park.

Soon after we were released I wrote a paper for a seventh-grade journalism class, describing how we used to hunt grunion before the war. The whole family would go down to Ocean Park Beach after dark, when the grunion were running, and build a big fire on the sand. I would watch Papa and my older brothers splash through the moonlit surf to scoop out the fish, then we'd rush back to the house where Mama would fry them up and set the sizzling pan on the table, with soy sauce and horseradish, for a midnight meal. I ended the paper with this sentence: "The reason I want to remember this is because I know we'll never be able to do it again." . . .

4. Wartime Newlyweds Exchange
Love Letters, 1943–1945

Fort Dix, New Jersey, 18 July 1943

My Dearest Barbie:

Darling, please don't ever get blue for really everything is going to turn out all right. In fact, everything is o.k., now, so please don't worry, will you? You are home under the best of care and near Fort McPherson in case anything happens and that relieves my mind of quite a bit. Still in all, I know it meant a lot to you and I both to be together all along, but it will not be but a short while before we shall be together again. By that time, we will have a baby and really something to build on. Barbie, did you ever stop to think how wonderful it is to bring someone into this wonderful life of reality and being. Besides being responsible for their being here, to have the job of being their teacher of all of the many things of life. Darling, can you see how that seals a marriage to a concrete stage of endurance?? How could anything break up our world after the baby gets here to really make us realize what this thing called marriage is. . . .

Your loving husband, Charlie

Fairburn, Georgia, July 22, 1943

My dearest sweetheart,

Well, this time next month, you will be a "papa," we hope, eh? Won't that be simply grand! Honestly, I can't even imagine what it's going to be like to have a little ole baby, of our very own! I see Annie Sara (you know, Robert's wife), over there with Robertine now—she has the best time with her. I just can't wait—really if something should happen—but we won't allow ourselves to even think about that, will we?

Charlie, I went to the doctor today and . . . he said I was in perfect condition! . . .

We went on into town and I got practically everything I'll need for the baby. Didn't spend so much money, either. Will make a list (complete) and send you just as soon as I can. Right now, however, I'm "worn out" and my legs hurt and I certainly intend to have them rubbed down good tonight. . . .

Please continue writing the same sweet letters. Remember me to the fellers and darling, above all, do something for that cold.

I love you,

Always, Just Your Barbie

Judy Barrett Litoff and David C. Smith, eds., *Miss You: The World War II Letters of Barbara Wooddall Taylor and Charles E. Taylor* (Athens: University of Georgia Press, 1990), pp. 98–101, 104–106, 157–159, 285–287, 300–301. Reprinted by permission of The University of Georgia Press.

Fairburn Georgia, August 22, 1943

My dearest sweetheart,

I really was a happy woman today when I received your letter. No, I didn't think you had forgotten me—just didn't let myself look too hard for a letter until it actually came. . . .

Now for Sandra Lee—oh, Charlie, she is a zillion times cuter than she was a week ago. She's gained 3-½ oz. (now weighs 6 lbs 9-½ oz) and almost seems to know people now. I wonder how I ever got along without her. I'm proud of her because she's "us" all wrapped up in one. If something should happen to me or you, the one left would always have Sandra Lee. I'm so glad we had her while we're young—it'll be nice for her as well as for us. And everytime I look at her I see you and love you more and more. She has "oodles" of hair now. Today she sat in water for the first time and does she like it?!?!?! Won't it be fun when the three of us can be together forever and ever!! . . .

Mother loves Sandra Lee more than she ever loved me, so you see, she isn't worrying her a bit. And Daddy got up three times the other night to see about her because she *wasn't* crying. She really has been a good baby at night. Just almost impossible to wake her for two o'clock feeding. Am going to cut that out pretty soon.

I just enjoyed your being here so very much. Really couldn't have had the baby without you. You do so much for me, darling, and I love you for everything. Please be good—take good care of Charlie—and love me always!!

Sandra Lee has lots more gifts and cards and *visitors!!* . . .

Surely do wish you'd call me today. Started once to put in a call to you, but don't know if I should or not. If I were there could I be with you today?? You know how much I miss you and I'm living for the day "we three" can be together!!

Write me when you have time and remember that I love you.

Lovingly, Your Barbie

Fairburn, Georgia, October 10, 1944

My dearest sweetheart,

Sandra Lee and Grandmother went to the Post Office this afternoon and came home with two wonderful letters from you—written Sept. 25 & 26—14 days ago. Good mail service, don't you think? . . .

While I was reading your letters Sandra Lee came up and kissed them. No one told her to, understand, she just did it. She's finally catching on to what a letter means and she gets so excited over it. Now when asked where her Daddy is—she'll say, "Gone, gone." She never fails to kiss you "good-morning" and "good-night," so you may as well expect that from now on. . . .

Remember that I'm praying for you and I love you.

Always, Your Barbie

Fairburn, Georgia, October 24, 1944

My dearest sweetheart,

. . . Emily came by and the three of us went to the P.O. Mother and Daddy received a letter from you written October 13 and so did I. I was more than relieved. But, somehow, I felt kinda bad, for there I had ten pages from you and sometimes I only write two. I certainly have more time and news to write, and I'm certainly in a better condition both mentally and physically to write. I've told you all along, my dear, that I didn't deserve you—I'm not half as good as the girl you should have married; but I'm awfully glad that you did marry me and I'm so proud of our little girl. Oh, Charlie, I pray that I might learn to be the wife I should be to you. I love you so very much, Charlie baby. . . .

You know, I was just thinking how grand it is that we are Americans. Sandra Lee looks at airplanes in the sky and claps her hands and says "Purty" (pretty). She'll never have to realize the terror of an enemy plane that might drop a bomb on her. She gets a thrill out of soldiers and she'll never see the ragged, bloody, dirty soldier who is tired and hungry but has to keep on the go, and that soldier might be her own Daddy. Oh, she'll hear all the terrible stories and read books on them and see movies of them; but it won't hit her as if she were a French or English or some other girl in the War Zones. It'll all be just a little exciting and romantic with enough sadness to make it good. I thank God for the fact that she is here in the United States. . . .

My dear Charlie, help me pray for God to see us through this War and for Him to let you come home again. I love you, truly I do.

Always, Your Barbie

P.S. Sandra Lee sends her love too.

Fairburn, Georgia, August 17, 1945

My dearest sweetheart,

Your birthday letter to Sandra Lee was beautiful. She understood almost every part of it. . . . Daddy always hands her the mail—and she in turn hands it to me. She's learned to 'feel' for chewing gum—and gets so excited when she actually finds some. I hit the jackpot today too—two August 7th letters and one August 10th. I'm not even thinking about your coming home—really, this time I'm just gonna wait 'til I hear that you are on the way. . . .

You should hear your daughter sing "When Charlie Comes Marching Home Again." She says and does everything. Says 11- and 12-word sentences now—and it makes sense, too. Her memory is a mile long—so she'll do o.k., always. Really you do have something to be proud of—and you won't really know how much until you are with her. I just can't wait for the three of us to be together. Oh, what a happy day that will be!

Remember that I love you, I love you, I love you!

Always, Just Your Barbie

Reims, France, 17 August 1945

My Dearest Darling:

Well, Barbie, I go to see the Swiss—I leave by jeep to Chalons at nine—catch the train at midnight—and go to Mulhouse—then on to Switzerland. I can't believe it is me that's getting to really go any place, you know, sorta on a vacation in a way, it is a vacation for it (7 days) counts against my leave time. Well, I know it will do me good to go to a country that has seen no war at all. I'll probably get a chance to get a big glass of milk, eh? Captain Flannigan is sending his jeep by for me at nine and it's seven-thirty now. I have yet to clean up and shave. I have all of my junk packed and everything. You, I hope, will enjoy my letters from there. I bought a little note-book to take notes down in as I go on my tour, so I shan't forget any of the names of the places etc. Will do my best to get some souvenirs for you and Sandra Lee too. Of course I'd rather be coming home, but maybe I'll be home in two months, who knows? . . .

   Barbie, are your eyes really as pretty and expressive as they look in this picture you sent me. This picture looks just as I remember you, and it renews my spirit, for I feel that all of the memories and thoughts of the past that I have are not dreams but are really the truth. God, I love you, honey, so please be mine forever, can you? . . . Please tell Sandra Lee all about her Pop. Oh, he is a hell of a Dad for a little girl, but after we are home again, I am certain he can learn all of the tricks of being a Dad and a good husband that he does not know.

Lovingly, Your Charlie

Fairburn, Georgia, October 8, 1945

My dearest sweetheart,

Sure hope you don't get this letter. What I mean is—I hope (unless you get your mail in seven days) that you'll be leaving dear ole France before you have time to get this. I really think you will sail on the 15th and I'll be a lost li'l gal if you don't! Every one of us are 'cited over your coming home. Even Priss tells everyone (of her own accord) that "my Daddy's coming home." . . .

   Charlie baby, you don't know how my heart skips a beat whenever I think of you. Judy Canova (on the radio) is singing, "I'm gonna love that guy like he's never been loved before"—and *"them's my sentiments."* I just can't wait, Charlie, oh, I'm so happy.

   Be real good, and real careful, and remember that I love you very, very much.

Always, Your Barbie

5. A Woman War Worker Describes
Work and Family Life, 1944

Pensacola, June 6, 1944

Darlin':

. . . All that's on the radio and in the papers this day is the Invasion. I can take so much of it then I feel like I'd like to crawl in a hole somewhere. Suppose I won't hear from you for quite a while but have gotten so I can take just about anything, come what may—'twill be H—, but I've no choice in such things but just hope and pray you'll be o.k., darlin'. Don't know if you'll get my letters or not but certainly hope so. I'm glad the fire works have started so this thing will be over with, but the way they broadcast it reminds me of a horse race or ball game. I may be a sissy but I can't take too much of it. Radios blare from every direction so you can't get away from it for even a minute. I love you terribly, Darlin' and can hardly wait to see you again.

Good night, precious,

I love you, Polly

Pensacola, June 8, 1944

Darlin':

. . . After I get settled in Louisville I'm thinking seriously of going to work in some defense plant there on the swing shift so I can be at home during the day with Bill as he needs me—would like to know what you think of the idea, if you can write. Of course, I'd much rather have an office job but I couldn't be with Bill whereas I could if I worked at nite which I have decided is the best plan as I cain't save any thing by not working and I want to have something for us when you get home so you can enjoy life for awhile before going back to work and Bill and I want all of your time too for awhile so's we can all three make up for lost time.

Gotta scoot as I have several more chores to do.

I love you, Darlin', Polly

Louisville, June 12, 1944

Darlin':

You are now the husband of a career woman—just call me your little Ship Yard Babe! Yeh! I made up my mind that I wanted to work from 4:00 p.m. 'till midnight so's I could have my cake and eat it too. I wanted to work but didn't want to leave Bill all day—in the first place it would be too much for Mother altho' she was perfectly

Judy Barrett Litoff and David C. Smith, eds., *Since You Went Away: World War II Letters from American Women on the Home Front* (New York: Oxford University Press, 1991), pp. 146–150. Copyright © 1991 by Judy Barrett Litoff and David C. Smith. Used by permission of Oxford University Press, Inc.

willing and then Bill needs me. This way Mother will just have to feed him once and tuck him in which is no trouble at all any more as I just put him in bed and let him play quietly until he's ready to go to sleep and he drops right off. . . . I finally ended up with just what I wanted. Comptometer [calculator] job—4:00 'till midnite—70 cents an hour to start which amounts to $36.40 a week, $145.60 per month, increase in two months if I'm any good and I know I will be. Oh yeh! At Jeffersonville Boat and Machine Co. I'll have to go over to Jeffersonville, Ind. which will take about 45 minutes each way. Hope I can get a ride home each nite as that's the only feature I dislike but I'm not gonna be a sissy. If I can't get a ride, I'll get tags for our buggy and probably use it. . . . If I don't need it for work I may not get them but will just have to see how things work out. Want to take Bill out swimming a lot this summer so I may need it for that. . . .

Opened my little checking account too and it's a grand and a glorious feeling to write a check all your own and not have to ask for one. Any hoo, I don't want it said I charged things to 'em and didn't pay it so we don't owe anybody anything and I'm gonna start sockin' it in the savings and checking too so's we'll have something when our sweet little Daddy comes home.

Good nite, Darlin'

I love you, Polly

Louisville, June 13, 1944

Darlin':

Just got home from work at 12:30 a.m. Got a ride both ways with one of the girls in the office who lives about ten blocks from here—certainly am glad 'cause I didn't go for the idea of coming home alone. Like my job fine and it was great fun to get going on a comptometer again. I'm figuring the pay checks as everyone with Jefferson Boat is paid by the hour so that makes plenty of work. I haven't sat in one position and an erect one at that for so long that it was rather hard to do so I made several trips to the water fountain mainly for the exercise. We have 30 minutes for lunch at 7:15 and go across the park to a little cafe which slings out pretty good hash. At about 9:30 we all give the boss, Mr. Toby, a nickel and he goes and gets all a good old ice cold coke which is most refreshing. Haven't counted the office force, but there must be about 20 of us in the nite shift. They seemed very generous with my work last nite and couldn't get over the most legible figures I made. They must be used to sloppy jobs or something. I turned over as much work as the other girls and didn't make one single error which they couldn't get over. . . . Will write you before I go to work each day so's I can tuck me in just as soon as I get home so I get plenty of good old shut eye.

I dreamed this morning that you'd come home on furlough but had to return shortly 'n you were in civilian clothes and had received 4 of ten boxes we'd sent you. I was so glad to see you I almost popped, then I woke up. Shucks.

Good nite, Darlin'

I love you terribly, Polly

Louisville, Nov. 9, 1944

Darlin':

. . . The union came in to-nite. Join or else! The gals have all been in a stew since the maids and porters got their raises as they now make more than we do. A fine thing, uh! yeah! We were ready to take up the scrub jobs around in place of ours. They all, of course, belong to the union, soooo, all the office employees all over the yards joined and we had to too. I always said I'd never join one but I sat right here and did. We, of course, are all supposed to get a raise out of it so I figured I wouldn't be losing any thing if we did, so if we don't then I can always get a job elsewhere. I like it here and like the hours so I don't want to quit and am out for every penny I can get while the gettings good, right? We now have about $780.00 in the bank and 5 bonds which sho looks good to me and as soon as I get the buggie in good shape and all the Xmas extras over then I can really pile it away. . . .

   Good nite, Darlin'

I love you, Polly

Louisville, Dec. 5, 1944

Darlin':

There's rumors out that by March 1st there will be no more nite shift in any part of Jefferson Boat as work will be completed by then and they're letting men go over in the yards at the rate of 50 a week and expect to have 5,000 gone by March 1. If it's true then I suppose my greatly enjoyed working career will come to an end, as you know we build L.S.T.s [Landing Ship Tanks, used primarily for invasion purposes] for the Navy and I cain't understand how they can cut down like that with the war still going on. One of the boys in New Caledonia wrote his wife that they heard on the radio that the war with Germany will be over in two months and the war with Japan over by the 1st of June. She wrote him tonite asking from what source the announcement came and if it was just a prophecy. Have you all heard any such sentiments? 'Twould be wonderful if it is really true but I certainly won't count on it. They would probably find a place for me on the day shift, if I wanted it but I couldn't do that as Bill needs me too much and it would be too hard on Mother to care for him all day. I have enough savings piled up to last me several months and I know if I don't get it done before you return I never will. However by the time I get all finished and you aren't home by then, or at least have hopes of returning soon thereafter, I'll start pounding the pavements again as I gotta save all the money I can now while the getting is good, but I'll just hope and pray each nite that you will be home by next summer at the latest. . . .

   I love you,

Darlin', Polly

Louisville, Jan. 30, 1945

Darlin':

Thought for a while this a.m. I would have to take Bill to work with me, or stay at home. He was evidently dreaming a bad dream and awakened just as I was getting up. He wanted me and no one else would do and while I ate breakfast, he clung onto me like he'd never let me go. We finally convinced him that I was just going to work until 10:00. Going out into the snow at 7:00 a.m. and catching buses wasn't half bad and I really enjoyed it. I was the only one out on our street, and lots of the houses had lights on which looked very welcoming. I liked the feeling of not depending on some one else to get me to and from work. However if I get a regular ride, I'll take it too sometime for it seems like I don't have any time with Bill at all. Got home at 6:00 this afternoon as I had to stop and get the groceries for tomorrow. By the time we ate, did the dishes, I washed out a few things, mended the fur coat again and bathed us both, it was time to go to bed. Bill and I are sitting in bed writing you but he is having a horrible time getting enough stationery, as he has already had three sheets and is yelling for more. Yet, he even scribbled on this [V-Mail] as you can see. He gets a bigger kick out of writing Daddy than anything else he does. I'm going to teach him to say his little prayers for you each nite. Good nite, Darlin'.

I love you forever, Polly

Mailed your package.

6. A Child Care Worker Discusses Her Trials and Triumphs, 1944–1946

Cleveland, Oct. 4, 1944

Dearest beloved,

Today seemed to roll very fast at our observation nursery! However, today was the first day I found a "bed wetter" or any kind of wetter, so today marks the first day I have changed a child's clothes since April. Oh me! . . .

Today I spoke to a head teacher who had little or no training in the field except eight months of actual experience. She said that they tell you there is no chance of becoming a head teacher, but that teachers come and go so fast that if you just "hold tight" you're there! Well, I'll "hold tight" until you get back. . . .

All my love always, Edith

Cleveland, Dec. 4, 1944

Dearly beloved,

Now that I've kind of calmed down I can tell you the news of the day! . . .

When they offered me a head teacher's job at this nursery they're opening on 2916 Mayfield Rd. I nearly fainted! Of course, I remembered to accept the job. Here's the set up: Mrs. Lang, City Supervisor, is turning me over to Mrs. Yost, County Supervisor. However, the county is also run by the Cleveland Board of Education. The federal government put this private nursery at the same address out of

Judy Barrett Litoff and David C. Smith, eds., *Since You Went Away: World War II Letters from American Women on the Home Front* (New York: Oxford University Press, 1991), pp. 153–159. Copyright © 1991 by Judy Barrett Litoff and David C. Smith. Used by permission of Oxford University Press, Inc.

business because the owners didn't have a license. Then the federal government bought it and will run it under the Lanham Act. However, True Sisters #30 had a $7,000 surplus and wanted to invest it in a welfare project. They gave it to the Lanham Fund for this nursery plus every month contributing $100. When the war is over, the federal government will step out and True Sisters will be in full charge; which means I'll probably have a postwar job, too.

At present I work only with the Cleveland Board of Education and my check comes from them. I still make my $130 as my contract calls for, but I get $20 more for assuming the head teacher's job. So, plus that $10 cost of living increase wage, I'll make $160 every four weeks. It means $40 weekly. However, the responsibility will be tremendous, as I'm responsible for the health care, children, kitchen, food and buying. I shall have a cook and a janitor and two assistant teachers. . . .

I love you and always will. You are part of me. Edith

Cleveland, Dec. 9, 1944

My darling,

. . . . Since I've taken on this new job, it seems I haven't got a minute to myself. Well, guess this is as good a time as any to give you the full details. . . .

I took the job knowing I was getting into a tremendous project, but not quite realizing how tremendous. The house was absolutely, positively the dirtiest, filthiest place I have ever been in. The people living there moved out a day after we took over. They used to live on the second floor and run a disgusting, ill-equipped nursery on the first floor. You can imagine how dirty it is if the place had to be fumigated, and then, there was so damn much trash in the attic the federal government didn't even think it could be cleaned, so the attic was merely bolted! The basement . . . we finally got cleaned out!

I had to wash and sterilize all the toys and equipment, supervise the going over of the lights, gas, furnace, telephone, plumbing, etc. Had to order food, and equipment, and had to supervise all the housecleaning and keep track of all the bills and the time sheet. Well, honey, I've been working 9 and 10 hours a day. You can see, it is really a job!

Monday morning we opened up with merely 4 children. We will have not more than 10 children for the next 2 or 3 weeks since there is a lot of work to be done. They are scraping and sanding the floors so that linoleum can be put from corner to corner on the first floor. . . .

The quota of children for this nursery is 35. Although it is considered a large house, it is not a large nursery school except for the yard. . . .

Today, I was supposed to get a half day off, but couldn't do it. I merely ran down and got my hair set, and took some books back to the library. Then, I went right back to the nursery. When I got home at 6:30, I had planned to eat, wrap a package to mail to you, and write letters, but I had so much bookkeeping to do that I only wrapped a package for you, did my bookkeeping and now, I'm writing this letter to you. Honey, I'm really worn out! . . .

I'm thinking of you every hour, every minute, every second of the day and night!

Edith

Cleveland, Aug. 14, 1945

Oh darling,

The great news finally came over the radio. I want to write to you and I want to listen to the radio.

I decided to turn off the radio and write you a super-duper letter cause I'm so utterly happy—anyhow, as happy as I can be without you!

At 6:45 p.m. I came upstairs and got in bed to write you a letter. I turned on the radio—and boom—I heard the news and immediately, horns started to blow—there were shouts, etc. Mother had heard the news downstairs and we began to yell wildly to each other. . . .

It seems like a new era has started for me. You see, as far back as I can remember, there has always been a war—Oh darling—if only you could come home now—right now! I love you so very much. Do you think that this may speed up your homecoming?

Honey, before I forget, there is a Maternal and Child Health Bill #1318 before the Senate, and if public pressure would help, perhaps we could get it passed. Please drop a V-Mail to Senator Burton or Senator Taft asking him to vote for the bill. This bill would continue federal day care centers when Lanham Funds stop. Get some of the boys to write to their senators—please. I've bought 25 cards and passed them around and mailed them already! I'm getting more too!

Dearest—I'm so "hepped up" I can hardly write! We have been waiting so long for this news! . . .

I love you very much. Edith

Cleveland, Aug. 21, 1945

My darling,

. . . Well, honey, this morning's papers came out with the announcement that Lanham Funds have ceased and all the day care centers all over the country will be closed by October 30, 1945. Everyone knew that Lanham Funds cease 30 days after the emergency but they were hoping for an amendment to the bill or something. Anyhow, Senator Lanham is only out for the business interests and therefore doesn't care what happens to all these mothers and children. All that he originated the bill for was to get women in industry—after the war—the hell with them! Anyhow, the nation as a whole is excited (I hope). It really is a lousy deal for servicemen's wives with children who are using these centers in order for them to work and supplement their husbands' allotment!

Mrs. Yost called me to tell me that our center would be one of the last to close—and officially it would close October 15th—only, at that time, True Sisters would step in and take over at our place.

You can't imagine the excitement around the center all day! Mothers kept calling in—people and staff kept asking me—as if I knew it all. I'm really going around in circles!

Anyhow, everyone thinks that some other agency will cover the operation of these centers in Cleveland. In the meanwhile, all my mothers have written to

Senator Burton and Senator Taft to hurry up and pass Bill No. 1318—Maternal and Child Health. Many of the women have written to their husbands to write in too! Please darling, cooperate with me, and get all the boys you know and yourself to write to their respective senators to vote for Bill 1318. I just called your folks and told them to all send in cards! . . .

Sweetest boy—I adore you madly—I'm tired of being brave and good and honorable—I want you home!

I love you, Edith

By the way—this "galls me": The city of Cleveland is raising thousands of dollars to build a fountain in Public Square as a memorial to soldiers of World War II. Wouldn't it be a really swell thing if they donated this money to housing for veterans or for day care centers for servicemen's children—but no—why bother—everyone will go look at a fountain—ha! ha!

Cleveland, Oct. 21, 1945

Darling,

Lately I just haven't had the time to sit down and write you all of what I think and feel, but I think I've given you a smattering of my moods in all my letters. . . .

In a way I'm disgusted with everybody and everything—all I want is for you to come home so that I can really live! . . .

Last night Mel and I were talking about some of the adjustments we'll have to make to our husbands' return. I must admit I'm not exactly the same girl you left— I'm twice as independent as I used to be and to top it off, I sometimes think I've become "hard as nails"—hardly anyone can evoke any sympathy from me. No one wants to hear my troubles and I don't want to hear theirs. Also—more and more I've been living exactly as *I* want to and I don't see people I don't care about—I do as I damn please. As a whole, I don't think my changes will effect our relationship, but I do think you'll have to remember that there are some slight alterations in me. I'm pretty sure that holds true for you too—am I correct? . . .

I love you. Edith

Cleveland, Nov. 9, 1945

Darling,

At last a bunch of your letters came through—airmail 10/28 through 10/31 and V-Mails 10/28 and 10/29. Believe me I was "tickled" with the "haul" I made! . . .

Sweetie, I want to make sure I make myself clear about how I've changed. I want you to know *now* that you are not married to a girl that's interested solely in a home—I shall definitely have to work all my life—I get emotional satisfaction out of working; and I don't doubt that many a night you will cook the supper while I'm at a meeting. Also, dearest—I shall never wash and iron—there are laundries for that! Do you think you'll be able to bear living with me?

I love you, Edith

Cleveland, Nov. 18, 1945

My darling sweetheart,

. . . This "waiting for you" seems so endless! Sometimes, when I'm working, or when I'm plain not thinking about my troubles, it doesn't bother me too much, and I think that I can patiently wait until you get home; but sometimes, like this morning when I was ready to get up and thought that this is only November, I thought my heart would burst out of it's shell—I just didn't think I'd live through another day without you! And sometimes, like when I'm driving to work in the morning sunlight I don't think I can go on much longer without you—I feel as though I don't care whether I live or die—all I want is you! I buy clothes to keep up my morale, but each garment only keeps up my morale for the space of buying it! I miss you horribly—nothing can substitute for you, although I've tried very hard to make some things do the trick! No go!

When you come back, there are so many things I want to do together. Although I want to settle down, and although there's a whole future together to plan, I still want to do the little ordinary things I've missed doing with you in the past 14 months! I want to smile at you across the table at the Statler's; I want to hold your hand at the Playhouse and the Hanna; I want to walk proudly down the aisle with you to the dress circle at the Music Hall; I want you to watch me try on dresses at Halle's; I want to stroll down Euclid Ave. with you; I want to love you madly each night; I want you to meet every child in the school; I want to ride with you in the morning sunlight past Shaker Lakes; I want to take a shower with you; I want you to kiss me good-morning and good-night; I want to watch you shave. Oh darling—I want you so very much! I love you more than I can ever put into words—I wish my heart could spill love on you, like my mouth can water yours with kisses! . . .

All my love ever and ever, Edith

Cleveland, Jan. 7, 1946

My dearest darling,

. . . Altho' I spend quite a bit of time writing to you, I hope you never receive these letters because you are on your way home.

Boy—I really love my job! I felt 100% better today after I got to work and got busy. Nothing like work to keep your mind off your troubles. . . .

If you do get this letter before you leave (hope not) call me, if you can, when you dock. Call me at work or at home. However, and God forbid, if you come in later than the end of February call me at home, since the entire program *may* "fold up" the end of February. If you can get a hotel accommodation, fine, or, would you like me to get it? We can decide when you phone me. Would love to meet you at the Terminal—please plan on that! I *definitely* don't want our folks to know. If you call me from N.Y.—and even if you call at home—no one needs to know *when* I'll meet you or *where,* because, you see, I have a suitcase at work for just such a "happening." I can just call home and say I'm staying at Gallaghers or some such thing. I want just *one*—just *one complete* day and night absolutely alone with you!

Darling—I, too, have gotten to the point where I don't care about writing letters to friends or anyone. All I want is for the days to just fly by—For my part this could be the 27th of January instead of the 7th—I'm still hoping you'll be home around the first of February. . . .

Dearest—it can't be much longer before we'll be talking instead of this silly writing.

I love you, Edith

 ## E S S A Y S

In the first essay, historian Valerie Matsumoto of the University of California at Los Angeles uses oral histories and other sources to examine the lives of Japanese Americans before, during, and after World War II. Focusing on the experiences of American-born (Nisei) girls, she shows how communal living, paid work, and higher education strained family ties and hastened the deterioration of parental authority that was already underway in Japanese American families.

The second essay, an excerpt from University of Kansas historian William M. Tuttle Jr.'s 1993 study of children during World War II, *"Daddy's Gone to War,"* takes the experiences of white, middle-class children of soldiers as its focus. Combining wartime correspondence with later reminiscences, Tuttle argues that the absence of fathers affected children in profound—and largely negative—ways. At the same time, he pays close attention to the role of other family members—mothers and grandparents—in children's lives.

Japanese Families and Japanese American Daughters in World War II Detention Camps

VALERIE MATSUMOTO

Thirty years after her relocation camp internment, . . . [a] Nisei woman, the artist Miné Okubo, observed, "The impact of the evacuation is not on the material and the physical. It is something far deeper. It is the effect on the spirit." Describing the lives of Japanese American women during World War II and assessing the effects of the camp experience on the spirit are complex tasks: factors such as age, generation, personality, and family background interweave and preclude simple generalizations. In these relocation camps Japanese American women faced severe racism and traumatic family strain, but the experience also fostered changes in their lives: more leisure for older women, equal pay with men for working women, disintegration of traditional patterns of arranged marriages, and, ultimately, new opportunities for travel, work, and education for the younger women.

I will examine the lives of Japanese American women during the trying war years, focusing on the second generation—the Nisei—whose work and education

Valerie Matsumoto, "Japanese American Women During World War II," *Frontiers* 8 (1984): pp. 6–14. This document can also be found in Vicki L. Ruiz and Ellen Carol DuBois, eds., *Unequal Sisters: A Multi-Cultural Reader in U.S. Women's History* (New York: Routledge, 1994), pp. 436–477. Reprinted by permission of the University of Nebraska Press. © 1984 Frontiers Editorial Collective.

were most affected. The Nisei women entered college and ventured into new areas of work in unfamiliar regions of the country, sustained by fortitude, family ties, discipline, and humor. My understanding of their history derives from several collections of internees' letters, assembly center and relocation camp newspapers, census records, and taped oral history interviews that I conduc[t]ed with eighty-four Nisei (second generation) and eleven Issei (first generation). Two-thirds of these interviews were with women.

The personal letters, which comprise a major portion of my research, were written in English by Nisei women in their late teens and twenties. Their writing reflects the experience and concerns of their age group. It is important, however, to remember that they wrote these letters to Caucasian friends and sponsors during a time of great insecurity and psychological and economic hardship. In their struggle to be accepted as American citizens, the interned Japanese Americans were likely to minimize their suffering in the camps and to try to project a positive image of their adjustment to the traumatic conditions.

Prewar Background

A century ago, male Japanese workers began to arrive on American shores, dreaming of making fortunes that would enable them to return to their homeland in triumph. For many, the fortune did not materialize and the shape of the dream changed: they developed stakes in small farms and businesses and, together with wives brought from Japan, established families and communities.

The majority of Japanese women—over 33,000 immigrants—entered the United States between 1908 and 1924. The "Gentlemen's Agreement" of 1908 restricted the entry of male Japanese laborers into the country but sanctioned the immigration of parents, wives, and children of laborers already residing in the United States. The Immigration Act of 1924 excluded Japanese immigration altogether.

Some Japanese women traveled to reunite with husbands; others journeyed to America as newlyweds with men who had returned to Japan to find wives. Still others came alone as picture brides to join Issei men who sought to avoid army conscription or excessive travel expenses; their family-arranged marriages deviated from social convention only by the absence of the groom from the *miai* (preliminary meeting of prospective spouses) and wedding ceremony. Once settled, these women confronted unfamiliar clothing, food, language, and customs as well as life with husbands who were, in many cases, strangers and often ten to fifteen years their seniors.

Most Issei women migrated to rural areas of the West. Some lived with their husbands in labor camps, which provided workers for the railroad industry, the lumber mills of the Pacific Northwest, and the Alaskan salmon canneries. They also farmed with their husbands as cash or share tenants, particularly in California where Japanese immigrant agriculture began to flourish. In urban areas, women worked as domestics or helped their husbands run small businesses such as laundries, bath houses, restaurants, pool halls, boarding houses, grocery stores, curio shops, bakeries, and plant nurseries. Except for the few who married well-to-do professionals or merchants, the majority of Issei women unceasingly toiled both inside and outside the home. They were always the first to rise in the morning and the last to go to bed at night.

The majority of the Issei's children, the Nisei, were born between 1910 and 1940. Both girls and boys were incorporated into the family economy early, especially those living on farms. They took care of their younger siblings, fed the farm animals, heated water for the *furo* (Japanese bath), and worked in the fields before and after school—hoeing weeds, irrigating, and driving tractors. Daughters helped with cooking and cleaning. In addition, all were expected to devote time to their studies: the Issei instilled in their children a deep respect for education and authority. They repeatedly admonished the Nisei not to bring disgrace upon the family or community and exhorted them to do their best in everything.

The Nisei grew up integrating both the Japanese ways of their parents and the mainstream customs of their non-Japanese friends and classmates—not always an easy process given the deeply rooted prejudice and discrimination they faced as a tiny, easily identified minority. Because of the wide age range among them and the diversity of their early experiences in various urban and rural areas, it is difficult to generalize about the Nisei. Most grew up speaking Japanese with their parents and English with their siblings, friends, and teachers. Regardless of whether they were Buddhist or Christian, they celebrated the New Year with traditional foods and visiting, as well as Christmas and Thanksgiving. Girls learned to knit, sew, and embroider, and some took lessons in *odori* (folk dancing). The Nisei, many of whom were adolescents during the 1940's, also listened to the *Hit Parade*, Jack Benny, and *Gangbusters* on the radio, learned the jitterbug, played kick-the-can and baseball, and read the same popular books and magazines as their non-Japanese peers.

The Issei were strict and not inclined to open displays of affection towards their children, but the Nisei were conscious of their parents' concern for them and for the family. This sense of family strength and responsibility helped to sustain the Issei and Nisei through years of economic hardship and discrimination: the West Coast anti-Japanese movement of the early 1920s, the Depression of the 1930s, and the most drastic ordeal—the chaotic uprooting of the World War II evacuation, internment, and resettlement.

Evacuation and Camp Experience

The bombing of Pearl Harbor on December 7, 1941, unleashed war between the United States and Japan and triggered a wave of hostility against Japanese Americans. On December 8, the financial resources of the Issei were frozen, and the Federal Bureau of Investigation began to seize Issei community leaders thought to be strongly pro-Japanese. Rumors spread that the Japanese in Hawaii had aided the attack on Pearl Harbor, fueling fears of "fifth column" activity on the West Coast. Politicians and the press clamored for restrictions against the Japanese Americans, and their economic competitors saw the chance to gain control of Japanese American farms and businesses.

. . . On February 19, 1942, President Franklin Delano Roosevelt signed Executive Order 9066, arbitrarily suspending the civil rights of American citizens by authorizing the removal of 110,000 Japanese and their American-born children from the western half of the Pacific Coastal States and the southern third of Arizona.

During the bewildering months before evacuation, the Japanese Americans were subject to curfews and to unannounced searches at all hours for "contraband" weapons, radios, and cameras; in desperation and fear, many people destroyed their belongings from Japan, including treasured heirlooms, books, and photographs. Some families moved voluntarily from the Western Defense zone, but many stayed, believing that all areas would eventually be restricted or fearing hostility in neighboring states.

Involuntary evacuation began in the spring of 1942. Families received a scant week's notice in which to "wind up their affairs, store or sell their possessions, close up their businesses and homes, and show up at an assembly point for transportation to an assembly center." Each person was allowed to bring only as many clothes and personal items as he or she could carry to the temporary assembly centers that had been hastily constructed at fairgrounds, race tracks, and Civilian Conservation Corps camps: twelve in California, one in Oregon, and one in Washington.

The rapidity of evacuation left many Japanese Americans numb; one Nisei noted that "a queer lump came to my throat. Nothing else came to my mind, it was just blank. Everything happened too soon, I guess." As the realization of leaving home, friends, and neighborhood sank in, the numbness gave way to bewilderment. A teenager at the Santa Anita Assembly Center wrote, "I felt lost after I left Mountain View [California]. I thought that we could go back but instead look where we are." Upon arrival at the assembly centers, even the Nisei from large urban communities found themselves surrounded by more Japanese than they had ever before seen. For Mary Okumura, the whole experience seemed overwhelming at first:

> Just about every night, there is something going on but I rather stay home because I am just new here & don't know very much around. As for the people I met so many all ready, I don't remember any. I am not even going to try to remember names because its just impossible here.

A Nisei from a community where there were few Japanese felt differently about her arrival at the Merced Assembly Center: "I guess at that age it was sort of fun for me really [rather] than tragic, because for the first time I got to see young [Japanese] people. . . . We signed up to work in the mess hall—we got to meet everybody that way."

Overlying the mixed feelings of anxiety, anger, shame, and confusion was resignation. As a relatively small minority caught in a storm of turbulent events that destroyed their individual and community security, there was little the Japanese Americans could do but shrug and say, *"Shikata ga nai,"* or, "It can't be helped," the implication being that the situation must be endured. The phrase lingered on many lips when the Issei, Nisei, and the young Sansei (third generation) children prepared for the move—which was completed by November 1942—to the ten permanent relocation camps organized by the War Relocation Authority: Topaz, Utah; Poston and Gila River, Arizona; Amache, Colorado; Manzanar and Tule Lake, California; Heart Mountain, Wyoming; Minidoka, Idaho; Denson and Rohwer, Arkansas. Denson and Rohwer were located in the swampy lowlands of Arkansas; the other camps were in desolate desert or semi-desert areas subject to dust storms and extreme temperatures reflected in the nicknames given to the three sections of the Poston Camp: Toaston, Roaston, and Duston.

The conditions of camp life profoundly altered family relations and affected women of all ages and backgrounds. Family unity deteriorated in the crude communal facilities and cramped barracks. The unceasing battle with the elements, the poor food, the shortages of toilet tissue and milk, coupled with wartime profiteering and mismanagement, and the sense of injustice and frustration took their toll on a people uprooted, far from home.

The standard housing in the camps was a spartan barracks, about twenty feet by one hundred feet, divided into four to six rooms furnished with steel army cots. Initially each single room or "apartment" housed an average of eight persons; individuals without kin nearby were often moved in with smaller families. Because the partitions between apartments did not reach the ceiling, even the smallest noises traveled freely from one end of the building to the other. There were usually fourteen barracks in each block, and each block had its own mess hall, laundry, latrine, shower facilities, and recreation room.

Because of the discomfort, noise, and lack of privacy, which "made a single symphony of yours and your neighbors' loves, hates, and joys," the barracks often became merely a place to "hang your hat" and sleep. As Jeanne Wakatsuki Houston records in her autobiography, *Farewell to Manzanar,* many family members began to spend less time together in the crowded barracks. . . .

The large communal mess halls also encouraged family disunity as family members gradually began to eat separately: mothers with small children, fathers with other men, and older children with their peers. "Table manners were forgotten," observed Miné Okubo. "Guzzle, guzzle, guzzle; hurry, hurry, hurry. Family life was lacking. Everyone ate wherever he or she pleased." Some strategies were developed for preserving family unity. The Amache Camp responded in part by assigning each family a particular table in the mess hall. Some families took the food back to their barracks so that they might eat together. But these measures were not always feasible in the face of varying work schedules; the odd hours of those assigned to shifts in the mess halls and infirmaries often made it impossible for the family to sit down together for meals. . . .

After the first numbness of disorientation, the evacuees set about making their situation bearable, creating as much order in their lives as possible. With blankets they partitioned their apartments into tiny rooms and created benches, tables, and shelves as piles of scrap lumber left over from barracks construction vanished; victory gardens and flower patches appeared. . . .

Despite the best efforts of the evacuees to restore order to their disrupted world, camp conditions prevented replication of their prewar lives. Women's work experiences, for example, changed in complex ways during the years of internment. Each camp offered a wide range of jobs, resulting from the organization of the camps as model cities administered through a series of departments headed by Caucasian administrators. The departments handled everything from accounting, agriculture, education, and medical care to mess hall service and the weekly newspaper. The scramble for jobs began early in the assembly centers and camps, and all able-bodied persons were expected to work.

Even before the war many family members had worked, but now children and parents, men and women all received the same low wages. In the relocation camps, doctors, teachers, and other professionals were at the top of the pay scale, earning $19 per month. The majority of workers received $16, and apprentices earned $12. The new equity in pay and the variety of available jobs gave many women unprecedented opportunities for experimentation, as illustrated by one woman's account of her family's work in Poston:

First I wanted to find art work, but I didn't last too long because it wasn't very interesting . . . so I worked in the mess hall, but that wasn't for me, so I went to the accounting department—time-keeping—and I enjoyed that, so I stayed there. . . . My dad . . . went to a shoe shop . . . and then he was block gardener. . . . He got $16. . . . [My sister] was secretary for the block manager; then she went to the optometry department. She was assistant optometrist; she fixed all the glasses and fitted them. . . . That was $16.

As early as 1942, the War Relocation Authority began to release evacuees temporarily from the centers and camps to do voluntary seasonal farm work in neighboring areas hard hit by the wartime labor shortage. The work was arduous, as one young woman discovered when she left Topaz to take a job plucking turkeys:

> The smell is terrific until you get used to it. . . . We all wore gunny sacks around our waist, had a small knife and plucked off the fine feathers.
> This is about the hardest work that many of us have done—but without a murmur of complaint we worked 8 hours through the first day without a pause.
> We were all so tired that we didn't even feel like eating. . . . Our fingers and wrists were just aching, and I just dreamt of turkeys and more turkeys.

Work conditions varied from situation to situation, and some exploitative farmers refused to pay the Japanese Americans after they had finished beet topping or fruit picking. One worker noted that the degree of friendliness on the employer's part decreased as the harvest neared completion. Nonetheless, many workers, like the turkey plucker, concluded that "even if the work is hard, it is worth the freedom we are allowed."

Camp life increased the leisure of many evacuees. A good number of Issei women, accustomed to long days of work inside and outside the home, found that the communally prepared meals and limited living quarters provided them with spare time. Many availed themselves of the opportunity to attend adult classes taught by both evacuees and non-Japanese. Courses involving handcrafts and traditional Japanese arts such as flower arrangement, sewing, painting, calligraphy, and wood carving became immensely popular as an overwhelming number of people turned to art for recreation and self-expression. Some of these subjects were viewed as hobbies and leisure activities by those who taught them, but to the Issei women they represented access to new skills and a means to contribute to the material comfort of the family.

The evacuees also filled their time with Buddhist and Christian church meetings, theatrical productions, cultural programs, athletic events, and visits with friends. All family members spent more time than ever before in the company of their peers. Nisei from isolated rural areas were exposed to the ideas, styles, and pastimes of the more sophisticated urban youth; in camp they had the time and opportunity to socialize—at work, school, dances, sports events, and parties—in an almost entirely Japanese American environment. Gone were the restrictions of distance, lack of transportation, interracial uneasiness, and the dawn-to-dusk exigencies of field work.

Like their noninterned contemporaries, most young Nisei women envisioned a future of marriage and children. They—and their parents—anticipated that they would marry other Japanese Americans, but these young women also expected to choose their own husbands and to marry "for love." This mainstream American ideal of marriage differed greatly from the Issei's view of love as a bond that might evolve over the course of an arranged marriage that was firmly rooted in less romantic notions of compatibility and responsibility. The discrepancy between Issei and

Nisei conceptions of love and marriage had sturdy prewar roots; internment fostered further divergence from the old customs of arranged marriage.

In the artificial hothouse of camp, Nisei romances often bloomed quickly. As Nisei men left to prove their loyalty to the United States in the 442nd Combat Team and the 100th Battalion, young Japanese Americans strove to grasp what happiness and security they could, given the uncertainties of the future. Lily Shoji, in her "Fem-a-lites" newspaper column, commented upon the "changing world" and advised Nisei women:

> This is the day of sudden dates, of blind dates on the up-and-up, so let the flash of a uniform be a signal to you to be ready for any emergency. . . . Romance is blossoming with the emotion and urgency of war.

In keeping with this atmosphere, camp newspaper columns like Shoji's in *The Mercedian, The Daily Tulean Dispatch*'s "Strictly Feminine," and the *Poston Chronicle*'s "Fashionotes" gave their Nisei readers countless suggestions on how to impress boys, care for their complexions, and choose the latest fashions. These evacuee-authored columns thus mirrored the mainstream girls' periodicals of the time. Such fashion news may seem incongruous in the context of an internment camp whose inmates had little choice in clothing beyond what they could find in the Montgomery Ward or Sears and Roebuck mail-order catalogues. These columns, however, reflect women's efforts to remain in touch with the world outside the barbed wire fence; they reflect as well women's attempt to maintain morale in a drab, depressing environment. "There's something about color in clothes," speculated Tule Lake columnist "Yuri"; "Singing colors have a heart-building effect. . . . Color is a stimulant we need—both for its effect on ourselves and on others."

The evacuees' fashion columns addressed practical as well as aesthetic concerns, reflecting the dusty realities of camp life. In this vein, Mitzi Sugita of the Poston Sewing Department praised the "Latest Fashion for Women Today—Slacks," drawing special attention to overalls; she assured her readers that these "digging duds" were not only winsome and workable but also possessed the virtues of being inexpensive and requiring little ironing.

The columnists' concern with the practical aspects of fashion extended beyond the confines of the camps, as women began to leave for life on the outside—an opportunity increasingly available after 1943. Sugita told prospective operatives, "If you are one of the many thousands of women now entering in commercial and industrial work, your required uniform is based on slacks, safe and streamlined. It is very important that they be durable, trim and attractive." Women heading for clerical positions or college were more likely to heed Marii Kyogoku's admonitions to invest in "really nice things," with an eye to "simple lines which are good practically forever."

Resettlement: College and Work

Relocation began slowly in 1942. Among the first to venture out of the camps were college students, assisted by the National Japanese American Student Relocation Council, a nongovernmental agency that provided invaluable placement aid to 4,084 Nisei in the years 1942–46. Founded in 1942 by concerned educators, this organization persuaded institutions outside the restricted Western Defense zone to accept Nisei students and facilitated their admissions and leave clearances. A study of the first 400 students to leave camp showed that a third of them were women. Because of the cumbersome screening process, few other evacuees departed on indefinite leave before 1943. In that year, the War Relocation Authority tried to expedite the clearance procedure by broadening an army registration program aimed at Nisei males to include all adults. With this policy change, the migration from the camps steadily increased.

Many Nisei, among them a large number of women, were anxious to leave the limbo of camp and return "to normal life again." With all its work, social events, and cultural activities, camp was still an artificial, limited environment. It was stifling "to see nothing but the same barracks, mess halls, and other houses, row after row, day in and day out, it gives us the feeling that we're missing all the freedom and liberty." An aspiring teacher wrote: "Mother and father do not want me to go out. However, I want to go so very much that sometimes I feel that I'd go even if they disowned me. What shall I do? I realize the hard living conditions outside but I think I can take it." Women's developing sense of independence in the camp environment and their growing awareness of their abilities as workers contributed to their self-confidence and hence their desire to leave. Significantly, Issei parents, despite initial reluctance, were gradually beginning to sanction their daughters' departures for education and employment in the Midwest and East. One Nisei noted:

> [Father] became more broad-minded in the relocation center. He was more mellow in his ways. . . . At first he didn't want me to relocate, but he gave in. . . . I said I wanted to go [to Chicago] with my friend, so he helped me pack. He didn't say I could go . . . but he helped me pack, so I thought, "Well, he didn't say no."

The decision to relocate was a difficult one. It was compounded for some women because they felt obligated to stay and care for elderly or infirm parents, like the Heart Mountain Nisei who observed wistfully, "It's getting so more and more of the girls and boys are leaving camp, and I sure wish I could but mother's getting on and I just can't leave her." Many internees worried about their acceptance in the outside world. The Nisei considered themselves American citizens, and they had an allegiance to the land of their birth: "The teaching and love of one's own birth place, one's own country was . . . strongly impressed upon my mind as a child. So even though California may deny our rights of birth, I shall ever love her soil." But evacuation had taught the Japanese Americans that in the eyes of many of their fellow Americans, theirs was the face of the enemy. Many Nisei were torn by mixed feelings of shame, frustration, and bitterness at the denial of their civil rights. These factors created an atmosphere of anxiety that surrounded those who contemplated resettlement: "A feeling of uncertainty hung over the camp; we were worried about the future. Plans were made and remade, as we tried to decide what to do. Some were ready to risk anything to get away. Others feared to leave the protection of the camp."

Thus, those first college students were the scouts whose letters back to camp marked pathways for others to follow. May Yoshino sent a favorable report to her family in Topaz from the nearby University of Utah, indicating that there were "plenty of schoolgirl jobs for those who want to study at the University." Correspondence from other Nisei students shows that although they succeeded at making the dual transition from high school to college and from camp to the outside world, they were not without anxieties as to whether they could handle the study load and the reactions of the Caucasians around them. One student at Drake University in

Iowa wrote to her interned sister about a professor's reaction to her autobiographical essay, "Evacuation":

> Today Mr.—, the English teacher that scares me, told me that the theme that I wrote the other day was very interesting. . . . You could just imagine how wonderful and happy *I* was to know that he liked it a little bit. . . . I've been awfully busy trying to catch up on work and the work is *so* different from high school. I think that little by little I'm beginning to adjust myself to college life.

Several incidents of hostility did occur, but the reception of the Nisei students at colleges and universities was generally warm. Topaz readers of *Trek* magazine could draw encouragement from Lillian Ota's "Campus Report." Ota, a Wellesley student, reassured them: "During the first few days you'll be invited by the college to teas and receptions. Before long you'll lose the awkwardness you might feel at such doings after the months of abnormal life at evacuation centers." Although Ota had not noticed "that my being a 'Jap' has made much difference on the campus itself," she offered cautionary and pragmatic advice to the Nisei, suggesting the burden of responsibility these relocated students felt, as well as the problem of communicating their experiences and emotions to Caucasians.

> It is scarcely necessary to point out that those who have probably never seen a nisei before will get their impression of the nisei as a whole from the relocated students. It won't do you or your family and friends much good to dwell on what you consider injustices when you are questioned about evacuation. Rather, stress the contributions of [our] people to the nation's war effort.

Given the tenor of the times and the situation of their families, the pioneers in resettlement had little choice but to repress their anger and minimize the amount of racist hostility they encountered.

In her article "a la mode," Marii Kyogoku also offered survival tips to the departing Nisei, ever conscious that they were on trial not only as individuals but as representatives of their families and their generation. She suggested criteria for choosing clothes and provided hints on adjustment to food rationing. Kyogoku especially urged the evacuees to improve their table manners, which had been adversely affected by the "unnatural food and atmosphere" of mess hall dining:

> You should start rehearsing for the great outside by bringing your own utensils to the dining hall. It's an aid to normality to be able to eat your jello with a spoon and well worth the dishwashing which it involves. All of us eat much too fast. Eat more slowly. All this practicing should be done so that proper manners will seem natural to you. If you do this, you won't get stagefright and spill your water glass, or make bread pills and hardly dare to eat when you have your first meal away from the centers and in the midst of scrutinizing caucasian eyes.

Armed with advice and drawn by encouraging reports, increasing numbers of women students left camp. A postwar study of a group of 1,000 relocated students showed that 40 percent were women. The field of nursing was particularly attractive to Nisei women; after the first few students disproved the hospital administration's fears of their patients' hostility, acceptance of Nisei into nursing schools grew. By July 1944, there were more than 300 Nisei women in over 100 nursing programs in twenty-four states. One such student wrote from the Asbury Hospital in Minneapolis: "Work here isn't too hard and I enjoy it very much. The patients are very nice people and I haven't had any trouble as yet. They do give us a funny stare at the beginning but after a day or so we receive the best compliments."

The trickle of migration from the camps grew into a steady stream by 1943, as the War Relocation Authority developed its resettlement program to aid evacuees in finding housing and employment in the East and Midwest. A resettlement bulletin published by the Advisory Committee for Evacuees described "who is relocating":

> Mostly younger men and women, in their 20s or 30s; mostly single persons or couples with one or two children, or men with larger families who come out alone first to scout opportunities and to secure a foothold, planning to call wife and children later. Most relocated evacuees have parents or relatives whom they hope and plan to bring out "when we get re-established."

In early 1945, the War Department ended the exclusion of the Japanese Americans from the West Coast, and the War Relocation Authority announced that the camps would be closed within the year. By this time, 37 percent of the evacuees of sixteen years or older had already relocated, including 63 percent of the Nisei women in that age group.

For Nisei women, like their non-Japanese sisters, the wartime labor shortage opened the door into industrial, clerical, and managerial occupations. Prior to the war, racism had excluded the Japanese Americans from most white-collar clerical and sales positions, and, according to sociologist Evelyn Nakano Glenn, "the most common form of nonagricultural employment for the immigrant women (issei) and their American-born daughters (nisei) was domestic service." The highest percentage of job offers for both men and women continued to be requests for domestic workers. In July 1943, the Kansas City branch of the War Relocation Authority noted that 45 percent of requests for workers were for domestics, and the Milwaukee office cited 61 percent. However, Nisei women also found jobs as secretaries, typists, file clerks, beauticians, and factory workers. By 1950, 47 percent of employed Japanese American women were clerical and sales workers and operatives; only 10 percent were in domestic service. The World War II decade, then, marked a turning point for Japanese American women in the labor force.

Whether they were students or workers, and regardless of where they went or how prepared they were to meet the outside world, Nisei women found that leaving camp meant enormous change in their lives. Even someone as confident as Marii Kyogoku, the author of much relocation advice, found that reentry into the Caucasian-dominated world beyond the barbed wire fence was not a simple matter of stepping back into old shoes. Leaving the camps—like entering them—meant major changes in psychological perspective and self-image. . . .

. . . [M]any Nisei women discovered that relocation meant adjustment to "a life different from our former as well as present way of living" and, as such, posed a challenge. Their experiences in meeting this challenge were as diverse as their jobs and living situations.

"I live at the Eleanor Club No. 5 which is located on the west side," wrote Mary Sonoda, working with the American Friends Service Committee in Chicago:

> I pay $1 per day for room and two meals a day. I also have maid service. I do not think that one can manage all this for $1 unless one lives in a place like this which houses

thousands of working girls in the city. . . . I am the only Japanese here at present. . . . The residents and the staff are wonderful to me. . . . I am constantly being entertained by one person or another.

The people in Chicago are extremely friendly. Even with the Tribune screaming awful headlines concerning the recent execution of American soldiers in Japan, people kept their heads. On street cars, at stores, everywhere, one finds innumerable evidence of good will.

Chicago, the location of the first War Relocation Authority field office for supervision of resettlement in the Midwest, attracted the largest number of evacuees. Not all found their working environment as congenial as Mary Sonoda did. Smoot Katow, a Nisei man in Chicago, painted "another side of the picture":

I met one of the Edgewater Beach girls. . . . From what she said it was my impression that the girls are not very happy. The hotel work is too hard, according to this girl. In fact, they are losing weight and one girl became sick with overwork. They have to clean about fifteen suites a day, scrubbing the floors on their hands and knees. . . . It seems the management is out to use labor as labor only. . . . The outside world is just as tough as it ever was.

These variations in living and work conditions and wages encouraged—and sometimes necessitated—a certain amount of job experimentation among the Nisei.

Many relocating Japanese Americans received moral and material assistance from a number of service organizations and religious groups, particularly the Presbyterians, the Methodists, the Society of Friends, and the Young Women's Christian Association. . . .

The Nisei also derived support and strength from networks—formed before and during the internment—of friends and relatives. The homes of those who relocated first became way stations for others as they made the transition into new communities and jobs. In 1944, soon after she obtained a place to stay in New York City, Miné Okubo found that "many of the other evacuees relocating in New York came ringing my doorbell. They were sleeping all over the floor!" Single women often accompanied or joined sisters, brothers, and friends as many interconnecting grapevines carried news of likely jobs, housing, and friendly communities. Ayako Kanemura, for instance, found a job painting Hummel figurines in Chicago; a letter of recommendation from a friend enabled her "to get my foot into the door and then all my friends followed and joined me." Although they were farther from their families than ever before, Nisei women maintained warm ties of affection and concern, and those who had the means to do so continued to play a role in the family economy, remitting a portion of their earnings to their families in or out of camp, and to siblings in school.

Elizabeth Ogata's family exemplifies several patterns of resettlement and the maintenance of family ties within them. In October 1944, her parents were living with her brother Harry who had begun to farm in Springville, Utah; another brother and sister were attending Union College in Lincoln, Nebraska. Elizabeth herself had moved to Minneapolis to join a brother in the army, and she was working as an operative making pajamas. "Minn. is a beautiful place," she wrote, "and the people are so nice. . . . I thought I'd never find anywhere I would feel at home as I did in Mt. View [California], but I have changed my mind." Like Elizabeth, a good number of the 35,000 relocated Japanese Americans were favorably impressed by their new homes and decided to stay.

The war years had complex and profound effects upon Japanese Americans, uprooting their communities and causing severe psychological and emotional damage. The vast majority returned to the West Coast at the end of the war in 1945—a move that, like the initial evacuation, was a grueling test of flexibility and fortitude. Even with the assistance of old friends and service organizations, the transition was taxing and painful; the end of the war meant not only long-awaited freedom but more battles to be fought in social, academic, and economic arenas. The Japanese Americans faced hostility, crude living conditions, and a struggle for jobs. Few evacuees received any compensation for their financial losses, estimated conservatively at $400 million, because Congress decided to appropriate only $38 million for the settlement of claims. It is even harder to place a figure on the toll taken in emotional shock, self-blame, broken dreams, and insecurity. One Japanese American woman still sees in her nightmares the watchtower searchlights that troubled her sleep forty years ago.

The war altered Japanese American women's lives in complicated ways. In general, evacuation and relocation accelerated earlier trends that differentiated the Nisei from their parents. Although most young women, like their mothers and non-Japanese peers, anticipated a future centered on a husband and children, they had already felt the influence of mainstream middle-class values of love and marriage and quickly moved away from the pattern of arranged marriage in the camps There, increased peer group activities and the relaxation of parental authority gave them more independence. The Nisei women's expectations of marriage became more akin to the companionate ideals of their peers than to those of the Issei.

As before the war, many Nisei women worked in camp, but the new parity in wages they received altered family dynamics. And though they expected to contribute to the family economy, a large number did so in settings far from the family, availing themselves of opportunities provided by the student and worker relocation programs. In meeting the challenges facing them, Nisei women drew not only upon the disciplined strength inculcated by their Issei parents but also upon firmly rooted support networks and the greater measure of self-reliance and independence that they developed during the crucible of the war years.

Children and Families During World War II

WILLIAM M. TUTTLE JR.

"Being born in 1937," wrote Ruby Angela in 1990, "and my father serving in World War II, I thought I could be of some help to you in gathering information for your book. But the strangest thing happened shortly after I began to write down my memories—I couldn't. I was recalling my father being separated from us, then my mother leaving to join him in a stateside camp, my living with my grandparents—and suddenly as if I was paralyzed I could go no further." Ruby was not alone. To these homefront girls and boys, nothing was more unsettling than the father's departure for military service. . . .

William M. Tuttle Jr., *"Daddy's Gone to War": The Second World War in the Lives of America's Children* (New York: Oxford University Press, 1993), pp.30–38, 40–45, 47–48. Copyright © 1993 by William M. Tuttle Jr. Used by permission of Oxford University Press, Inc.

Seven-year-old Kay Branstone recalled lying in bed at night "crying myself to sleep, because I was so scared my Daddy would go to war. I didn't ever mention this to anyone," being "too scared to talk about it." She fervently hoped there would be "something wrong with him" so that he would be IV-F, physically disqualified. While Kay's father was not drafted, her two uncles were, and Kay, who often stayed with her grandparents during the war, lived with their anxieties.

When Maureen Dwyer's father returned from his draft physical, he told her that he had been certified I-A: "I can still feel my stomach drop when he said that." . . .

Statistics do not exist to tell precisely how many wives and children suffered from the absence of a husband and father during the war, but it is possible to estimate their numbers. In June 1945 a total of 2,818,000 Army wives (and about 1,825,000 children) received family allowances from the Office of Dependency Benefits; in line with this, the Bureau of Labor Statistics estimated that there were 3,000,000 Army wives. At that time there also were 3,855,497 persons in the Navy and Marines, an estimated 35 percent of whom, or about 1,350,000, were married; so the total of armed forces wives exceeded four million. Finally, there is a most helpful statistic that places the subject of male wartime absence—whether of fathers, sons, or brothers—in a broader context. During the war, nearly one family of every five— 18.1 percent—contributed one or more family members to the armed forces.

While some fathers were drafted, others volunteered. . . . Whether draftee or volunteer, father's departure was usually traumatic. Many of these farewells took place in crowded railroad stations. Carol Helfond's family escorted her father to the station. "My mother held up well until the train carrying my father pulled away. Then she ran into a phone booth and sobbed her heart out." Ruth Ann Grinstead was eight when her father joined the Navy, leaving her mother with the sole responsibility for ten children. Seeing the human interest angle in this sailor's departure, a newsreel company staged the event and filmed it. "We were all lined up on the sidewalk in front of our home, with mom holding the baby and my Dad walking away from us, and we all waved goodbye." Her father actually left the next day, and, later, the family went to the local theater "to see the newsreel of us waving my Dad goodby, and we all cried. . . ."

Some children resented their fathers' decision to leave home; they felt abandoned. The infants, however, were more confused than anything else. Sandy Newton's father, a fighter pilot, was shipped overseas in 1943, when she was only three weeks old. To keep Sandy's father's memory alive, her family would point to the sky every time an airplane flew over and say, "See, Sandy, airplane. Your Daddy flies an airplane." In time, she came to think that her father *was* an airplane, "a fantastic flying machine." A little girl born in 1944 had a different problem; she thought every man in a sailor suit was her father.

Children missed their fathers deeply. "How I miss you Daddy," wrote a seven-year-old girl in 1943. "Gee when in the dickens are you ever going to get to come home. I'm not putting the Blame up to you but I do wish you would get a furlough . . . Please won't you tell me if you . . . get word from the Major? Will you call up when you get orders[?] . . ."

Some children were taunted about their absent fathers. Ruth Larson was born the week after Pearl Harbor; when her father was shipped overseas, she and her mother returned to the family farm near Arapahoe, Nebraska. One day an older cousin told the little girl that she had no father. "I do," she protested, but she remembered this episode of cruelty. Ethel Geary, a second-grader, was the daughter of a sailor. She too was taunted, in this case by a boy at school. "'You don't have a father,' he began to chant for all to hear." Ethel waited for him after school; she handed her eyeglasses to another child and then "proceeded to beat the kid up with my lunch pail."

What the children and their mothers feared most, of course, was that Dad would not return. A homefront girl in Newark, Ohio, wrote that she cried herself "to sleep many nights thinking about my father being killed by the Japs." . . .

America's girls and boys who were separated from their fathers or other important relatives probably endured more heartache than any other children on the homefront. Clearly, the war's consequences were great for those boys and girls who experienced the sudden departure of loved ones for faraway battlefields. In line with these observations, this book assumes that the most important institution in the lives of children, especially young children, is the family. When the family's circumstances change, so the child's life invariably changes as well. The wartime absence of the father was a prime example; other examples were the new and expanded roles for women, with mothers filling voids both at home and in the factories; the mass migration of more than 30,000,000 men, women, and children to Army posts and war-boom communities; and booms in both marriages and births. . . .

Still, it is difficult to generalize about the effects of a father's absence on his family and children. "Reactions to their absence," wrote one therapist during the war, "are as varied and numerous as were the reactions to their presence." Families adapted in different ways, depending upon the family's prior history and the ages of the family's members. Reuben Hill, sociologist and author of a book about "war separation and reunion" on the homefront, observed that men who went to war had "played widely different roles in their respective families"—from companion, handy man, lover, and disciplinarian to bread winner—and, Hill concluded, "each family missed its man in terms of his special role in the home."

Long before the outbreak of the war, for example, many of America's fathers had relinquished their paternal responsibilities to other family members, such as older sons. There were absent fathers during the 1930s too, but those who left did so either to search for jobs or to escape the shame of being unemployed. Suffering from joblessness during the Great Depression, many demoralized fathers also turned to heavy drinking. These fathers became less important to a family's functioning than older brothers who had assumed the duty of directing younger siblings' lives. . . .

Although psychologists have assessed the impact of a father's absence on a child's identity, there is a void in the literature—and this void is particularly galling because the issue of identity is central to human development. In the father-absence research done on America's homefront children, there is precious little on girls. During the war years the published cases focused almost exclusively on how boys dealt with father absence. These articles were entitled "A Boy Needs a Man," "What Shall I Tell Him?," and "Sons of Victory." No article on father absence asked, "What Shall I Tell Her?" Likewise, postwar research on the life-span results of father absence has generally examined only boys. Thus, to locate the evidence and assess its importance, the historian needs to look not only at what is there but also for what is not there.

There is a retrospective solution, however—the recollections of the homefront girls as well as the boys, as expressed in letters. Even if not put down on paper until years later, these letters provide valuable information, including deep personal insights into tightly held feelings.

To begin, one must recognize that father absence is more complicated than it might appear. As one psychologist has written:

> Children growing up in a single-parent home headed by the mother may be affected by any of the following: the altered family structure and consequent differences in maternal role behavior; . . . the presence of surrogate care-givers associated with the mother's employment; or qualitatively different maternal behavior vis-a-vis the child because of the emotional meaning the father's absence has to her. There are many other factors which also may operate either singly or in concert with each other, allowing absolutely no possibility for delineating the "true" causal agents in the child's development.

The children's first-person testimony about the war years, gathered from their letters, validates the contention that for numerous families the operative issue was not really the absence of a father, but rather the manner in which the mother responded to that absence. And here, as one might expect, the variety was wide. Eleven percent of the wives in a wartime study of Iowa farm families, for example, "welcomed the separation as a release from an intolerable marital situation or as an opportunity to think through an unsatisfactory relationship." Indeed, for some families the most traumatic wartime event—though ostensibly the happiest one—was the return home of the soldier or sailor father.

Other mothers, however, were devastated by the separation and absence. Leona Gustafson, who was four when her father reported for induction, recalled that "beginning on the first night Dad left . . . my mother had awakened me with her crying. I can remember going into her room and stroking her forehead while telling her every thing would be all right, that Daddy would be home as soon as he could. I became what I was to remain for the rest of my mother's life—her daughter, her best friend and, in a sense, her mother."

The memories of Lois B. Heyde, born in 1937, are the opposite. She pictured her mother not as a woman needing comfort and support, but as an heroic part of the war effort. Her mother, who worked on the flight line at an aircraft factory, had skin that was "burned deep tan from the reflection of the summer sun and the aluminum." When Lois's father joined the Army in 1942, her mother took a job at the Boeing plant near Atlanta. Eventually Lois and her younger brother went to live with their grandparents on a farm north of Nashville. Every few weeks, their mother would ride the bus to visit. Since the bus stopped at a nearby town, her mother would have to walk five or six miles to the farm, sometimes at night. And since she was quite pretty, she carried a revolver "to discourage persistent types who wanted to give her a ride."

Because of absent fathers, numerous children lived in families of women. "While my Father was overseas," stated Rachel Love, born in 1938, "my Mother and I lived with Grandmother in her house." Two aunts with husbands in the service and another girl, a cousin, also resided there. "It was a house made up entirely of women. The sisters all worked and my grandmother looked after the children." Anita

McCune, whose father was a Marine fighting in the South Pacific, lived with her mother Eva, her Aunt Goldie, her thirteen-year-old sister Lahoma, and Aunt Goldie's daughter Margaret Ann, who, like Anita, was seven. "Most of the time it was just us five women," she remembered, and they not only survived, they prospered. Her mother and aunt raised chickens and slaughtered them in the backyard, and they painted and fixed up their old house.

When Jane Coad's father was killed in Germany in November 1944, she was living with her mother and two sisters in Omaha. Asked about her father's death, she replied that "the long-term effects on my sisters and myself were that we grew up in a family of women. Strong women, not brought up to show affection." Her mother idealized her eight-year marriage, "so we really had no idea how a marriage truly worked. We didn't realize that couples argued and yet still loved one another. We laugh now, but for years we were really terrified by a male voice raised in anger."

Wartime separations resulted in the rearrangement of family roles and thus wrought great changes in the lives of American families. But one thing was clear: It was the mother whose response to wartime change most affected the homefront children. Secondarily, it was grandparents who filled the voids caused by changing family circumstances. In order to understand the effects of father absence, it is necessary to inquire into the contributions, as well as the tribulations, of mothers and grandparents.

Mothers suffered no shortage of advice during the war. During a father's absence, they learned, one of their primary tasks was to keep "the memory of Daddy crystal clear through long periods of separation." As a step in this direction, boasted one mother, "We even celebrated Daddy's birthday in absentia with a party, cake, candles and all." A letter from Daddy, wrote a child-guidance expert, could become "a piece of happiness to share" with the child. After reading it aloud, the mother and child could work together to prepare a reply and then walk to the corner for the child to place it in the mail box. Similarly, mothers read that they could use photographs, gifts, foods, and sports to tell children about their father. For example, a mother could show the child pictures of Daddy from the time he was a little boy until he donned a military uniform. As for food, explain that this "is the way Daddy likes [his oatmeal] best." If Daddy is a good tennis player, tell the child that "when Daddy comes home, he will play tennis" with you. "I was amazed," wrote the mother of a two-year-old, "at how many opportunities present themselves for talking about Daddy, for making him a part of their lives."

Mothers were told to give frank answers to their children's questions. "'No, we don't know how long Daddy will be gone. . . . Yes, of course we hope Daddy will come back safe, and we believe he will. Yes, some men will be killed on our side too, but that is what war means. . . . No, you will not be alone. If Daddy doesn't come back I will still take care of you.'"

Dorothy Humphrey took such advice seriously. She and her doctor husband had two children, ages three and one, when he joined the Army in 1942. During her husband's long absence overseas, she wrote him daily, and from reading her loving, detailed letters, it is evident that family conversations revolved around "Daddy." Likewise, she filled her letters to him with stories about the children's accomplishments, their "quaint sayings," and compliments they had received, not to mention their physical ailments and emotional struggles. Dorothy wrote about "her unsatisfied physical longing" for her husband, and she told him that "the terms of single-parenting are demanding." Yet she persevered; Dorothy Humphrey and other mothers of father-absent children were homefront heroes.

Homefront mothers served as powerful examples to sons as well as daughters. Clearly, these wartime "Moms" were inspirations to their own children. Jean Beydler, who at age seven had moved with her family from Ashland, Kansas, to southern California, recalled that her mother "knew that history was in the making and had an adventurous spirit. She hauled us kids—on the streetcars and on foot—everywhere." Mother and children frequented the Los Angeles Coliseum for bond drives and patriotic rallies featuring Generals Jimmy Doolittle and George Patton. They took in the Hollywood Christmas Parade, visited museums, and got tickets to such radio shows as Fibber McGee and Molly, Spike Jones, and Al Jolson. They also went to dances at the Venice Pier Amusement Park, seeing Bob Wills and the Texas Playboys so many times that Wills knew the children by name. "We were a busy little troop," Jean remembered. "We saw everything . . . that was happening in Los Angeles during those war years." As Jean happily recalled this period, she said, "My mother was the real hero in our lives." . . .

The homefront children recalled their mothers' strength, but embedded in their wartime memories were also images of great sadness. Wives and mothers were anxious about their husbands' safety and welfare. Many were extremely lonely. A wide variety of events could trigger tears. Some children had never seen their mothers cry until the day their fathers left for the service. Another occasion for mothers' tears was the arrival of V-mail. Lucretia Spence's mother had been only twenty when Lucretia was born in 1940; her father but eighteen. He enlisted in the Army Air Corps soon after the Pearl Harbor attack, and while he served overseas, she worked at the shipyard in South Portland, Maine. She was pregnant when her husband left, but stayed on the job. She returned to work shortly after giving birth to a second child; her sister and parents cared for the children during the working day. Lucretia's mother also had a brother fighting in the infantry in North Africa; she worried about him too. Worry and stress consumed her life. She spent her days working and "her evenings writing letters to my dad and," Lucretia remembered, "reading letters from him. I recall her crying often because of loneliness. Her praying and tears are much a part of my early memories. . . ."

. . . Sally Applebury was five in 1942 when her father, a small-town doctor in Missouri, left for the service. He was gone until she was nine. Sally recalled the "incredible sadness at holidays. I can still see my mother standing on the back porch crying on Thanksgiving and Christmas. I think the war changed their relationship," she continued, "because once having been submissive . . . she had to be the one in charge for 4 years all alone; she was not the same person when he returned. Needless to say, neither was he." . . .

Clearly, one of the most unheralded homefront stories was that of the grandparents who took in daughters, daughters-in-law, and a multitude of grandchildren. Some children moved in with their grandparents for periods of a few months or a year, while others became part of the household for the war's duration. One grandmother offered the proposition that "If anyone should ask for a name for this war, it's 'Grandmother's War.'" For their part, the homefront children who lived with grandparents generally remembered these as happy years—years of affection, if not adoration. When Ruth Larson's mother was working, her grandmother cared for her, from the time she was a baby until she was almost four. "I really think I was bonded to Grandma!" Ruth remembered. "I'm sure she instilled a lot of moral values & genuine love in me."

Perhaps it is not surprising that, in the absence of father, it was grandfather whose love and care were remembered by many of the homefront children. When Carol Strachan's father left for sea duty, she and her mother moved in with her maternal grandparents. Looking back, she wrote, "I realize that my Grandaddy took over for my Daddy in many ways. He read the funny papers to me, . . . took me to the park and movies, and bought me a cherry smash . . . after church. . . . [And] he would sing me to sleep at night with 'You Are My Sunshine.'" Tutti Cantrell, born in September 1942, boasted that she was her "Grandpa's" darling. Her father had been inducted into the Army when she was just ten days old, but Grandpa had promised his son-in-law that "he would take care of his baby while he was gone. And that he did!"— becoming not only her protector, but also her buddy, bundling her up on Saturday afternoons and, she recalled, taking "me to town . . . to show me off and buy me ice cream." When Tutti's father returned two and a half years later, "he was sure that I was spoiled and that I needed him to straighten me out."

Grandparents lavished affection on their homefront grandchildren. "My grandparents loved and spoiled me," recalled a homefront girl, Kathy Lynn Betti. Kathy's father was home on leave when she was born on Christmas 1942, but she did not see him again until the war was over. Meanwhile, "my mother and I lived with my Italian maternal grandparents, and I was pampered to the hilt. When my father did come home I wanted nothing to do with him. I remember hiding. . . ."

Grandparents were also protective of these children. Phil Wright, who was born in 1938, moved to his mother's hometown of Protection, Kansas, when his father was shipped overseas. Phil noted that while "I loved my father very much . . . I believe that my mother and grandmother must have been very skillful at shielding my younger brother and me. I cannot remember . . . ever contemplating that he would not return."

Surrogate fathers were also important, giving needed attention to the homefront children. "If you want to do something worth-while try this," advised *Parents' Magazine,* "let your child invite Jimmy or Jane whose father is overseas to dinner one night. . . . Competent as any mother may be to direct her child's energies and activities, there is simply no escaping the fact that when a man takes a hand in the youngsters' games a sort of rough and ready masculinity adds to the fun." It was the "'strong man stuff,'" noted Dr. Milton I. Levine, a pediatrician with New York City's Bureau of Child Hygiene, "that little boys need and that mothers can't supply. . . ." One beneficiary of such advice was Phil Wright, who explained that in addition to loving relatives, a neighboring rancher "'took up the slack' and acted as a surrogate father." Many mornings before dawn, the man drove over in his pickup truck and took Phil to his ranch for fishing. For an urban boy, Billy Whortle in Detroit, there were two men who filled in for his father. One was the father of Billy's best friend, whose family included him on trips to their cottage in northern Michigan. The other was a middle-aged man who had two grown daughters, but no son, and who took Billy to Detroit Tigers baseball games.

But neither grandparents nor surrogates could entirely fill the void caused by absent fathers and mothers. Barbara J. Carter's parents took two of their children and relocated in San Francisco, but left six-year-old Barbara to be reared by her grandmother and aunt. "I did not get to see my parents from the time I was 6 until I was 11 years old. By then they were complete strangers to me," as were her brother and sister, who were four and seven when they left, but nine and twelve the next time she saw them.

Some homefront children bear scars of abandonment; they were expendable. David Childers's father "disappeared into the Army Air Corps" in 1942; at the same time, his mother and aunt began to talk about job opportunities in the defense plants. "Little did I know that at 8 years of age I too was about to be affected by the war. The plan was this: Mother and her sister will go to New York, get jobs, and split the expenses. Son, me, gets to live with my maternal Grandmother, a widow who ran a Boarding House. So that's the way it was." David's parents divorced at the end of the war. . . .

Most of the men who served in the war were either fathers, brothers, uncles, or all three. Their lives were at risk, and tens of millions of relatives worried about them. And it was their letters home that maintained the essential connections, no matter how imperfectly, between the soldiers and sailors overseas and their homefront families. When war separated a family, wrote [wartime family sociologist] James H.S. Bossard, "a face-to-face relationship gives way to a letter-to-letter relationship." Letters told war stories, and they offered advice to the boys and girls. In May 1943, a Marine lieutenant stationed in the Solomon Islands advised his infant daughter to "set a goal and strive . . . to attain it." More than that, he wrote, "Your Mother and my Wife is a wonderful woman. Be like her." Letters often concerned family responsibilities. It "looks like it might be a while before your daddy sees you again," Will Whortle, an Army surgeon, wrote his eight-year-old daughter Susan. "You must in the meantime be a good girl. Be a help to your Mother and always do the things she tells you to because she knows best and is older and wiser. Study hard in school. Then when the war is over we will have a lot of fun together. Your part . . . is to be good & work hard & help Mother with the boys."

Children got these messages whether they could read or not, since families congregated in living rooms and read the letters aloud. Letters home even became neighborhood events. When Gayle Kramer's father shipped out to Okinawa, she and her mother moved into her grandmother's house in New Orleans, which was bulging with aunts, uncles, and other relatives. Mail was supremely important to this household. Their postman would "shout through the screendoor, 'Carrie, you got a letter from Malcolm.'" He also would tell people up and down the block, so that later in the day, "neighbors would walk by and say, 'I heard you got a letter from Malcolm. How is he?'" . . .

Letters certainly buoyed the spirits of wives and mothers, and their happiness, however momentary, heartened the children. Years later, one of the homefront children expressed the pleasure and surprise she felt when she read the letters that had passed between her parents. "It seemed so strange," she wrote, "that these romantic letters were to and from my parents. They became . . . real people with real feelings."

"I do love you so much and always will," Will Whortle wrote his wife Geneva on August 2, 1943. "You are the whole world to me and I will only be happy when it is all over and I am back with you and our babies forever." Stationed at Camp Carson, Colorado, Major Whortle expected to receive orders soon, and his letters became increasingly affectionate and philosophical. On August 6, he told her: "You are so wonderful and my darling I love you more each day. The years past have been short and those when I come back cannot be long enough." At Camp Carson, rumors were rife that Whortle's unit was due to be shipped out. On August 11, he wrote his last stateside letter to his wife, telling her that "when all is over & you come to meet me, we will have a hell of a time and it will be a great day." Then he was gone. His next letter bore an APO address in care of the postmaster in New York City; Whortle was in North Africa. "Keep everything together by hook or crook," he implored. She did.

Fathers corresponded with their families not only by letter, but also through photographs, recordings, and drawings. "Daddy sent us a record that he had made in a recording booth in Hawaii . . . ," recalled a homefront girl. "He spoke with a very clear, slow voice. . . . He sounded so far away and so alone. It was a mixed blessing." Not all the recordings evoked sadness, however. One uncle, an accordion player, took his instrument with him when he was inducted into the Army. He sent his family a small yellow disk on which he had recorded "The Sheik of Araby." Families not only played such recordings "over and over," they also responded in kind. Ten-year-old Nancy Hart and her younger sister Barbara made a recording for their father, singing "Coming in on a Wing and a Prayer" and telling him about recent events in their lives.

Men overseas also drew pictures for the children. Barbara Hooper's father was drafted in 1943, when she was seven. While on a ship in the South Pacific, another serviceman taught him to draw a dog in profile. "We looked forward to his sending us a drawing of that dog. We copied it so much I believe I can still draw it." More ambitious were the cartoon drawings done by Joe Wally, a talented artist, for his daughter Diane, whom he adored. Joe dedicated his 1945 war diary to "my daughter and first born child Diane. Like my life it is dedicated to her. . . ." Stationed on Guam, Joe created a cartoon character named "lil Lulu," who became Diane's friend and role model. Lulu, who wore long braids like Diane, practiced the Golden Rule, went to Sunday school, said her prayers nightly, shared her toys with the little girl next door, held "Mommie's hand" when she crossed the street, took "a nap each day without complaining," and was "always kind and never selfish." Joe Wally mailed several dozen Lulu drawings, often to the dismay of censors. In the corner of one cartoon, he explained: *"Censor:* To My 3 Year-Old Daughter." Joe even gave Diane drawing lessons, showing her in one letter how to draw a stick figure in motion and add clothes to it. Diane, who would become a commercial artist, stated that Joe was "the predecessor artist in my genetic make up, I know." More than that, however, it was the "lil Lulu" drawings that made Diane feel very loved and important and taught her many worthwhile lessons.

Naturally, the most wonderful letters for children were those written to them only, especially by their fathers. "Hello Putsie," wrote Maureen Dwyer's father, a gunner on a PT boat in the South Pacific. "Don't feel bad about me at Christmas because we will have everything but home out here . . . so you just be a good girl."

In their loneliness, fathers told their children how much they missed them and loved them. Terms of endearment abounded. "Such a . . . lovely picture," wrote Cheryl Kolb's father from England. "I wonder who the little girl is on the swing? Do you suppose that could be my Cherry-Pie—my little wrinkle nose—my little button nose or my little blond bomber?" While on duty in England and France, Cheryl's father wrote her every few weeks. "And how is Daddy's little angel? . . . You're my little bunch of sweetstuff with the great big grin." He composed poems for her on her sixth and seventh birthdays, and she in turn sent him her drawings and told him, "I love you soooooooooooo much!"

Major Charles R. Kolb did return from the war. Other fathers . . . did not, however. These absences became permanent, and the homefront girls and boys struggled with their grief.

Blue and gold star service flags hung in the front windows of homes across the United States. Hanging from a gold cord with a field of white bordered in red, the flag had a star in the middle. A blue star designated that a family member was in the service; a gold star signified that a father, husband, brother, or son had been killed in the war. The American death toll from the Second World War was 405,399. In addition, 670,846 Americans were wounded. But how many "war orphans" were there? During the Second World War, about 183,000 homefront children lost their fathers.

The children were very aware of these flags and what they meant. Mary Maloney, a grammar-school girl in Davenport, Iowa, walked sixteen blocks to school. One morning, she decided to count all of the flags and stars on her side of the street. She counted 86 flags and 183 stars, showing that many of these families had two or more members serving. Four of the stars were gold, which her father explained meant making "the supreme sacrifice." After that, Mary began watching for new gold stars, "and sadly they increased in number." One day, she saw a woman sitting on the front porch of a house with a gold star hanging in the window. "I stopped and looked up at her. I wanted to say I was sorry. . . . I stood there for what seemed like a long time and finally gave a little wave. . . ." Because of her sadness, Mary stopped counting the gold stars after that. The enormity of what was transpiring did not escape the children. . . .

In assessing the impact of the Second World War on America's homefront children, it is clear that the most devastating event was the death of a loved one. Without exception, homefront girls and boys who experienced such losses have stated that the war fundamentally altered their lives. The war "totally changed my life," wrote Kay Britto, "—it took away two brothers I never got to know, brought *great* grief to my parents and changed our whole family structure." Bill Moore was twelve years older than his sister Erlyn, but she adored and idolized him. Bill was her mother's favorite too. In 1941 he joined the Army Air Corps and became a bomber pilot. When he was shipped overseas, his young wife and baby girl moved in with the Moores. On September 27, 1944, his bomber was lost over Germany, and the life went out of his family. "As the years went by Bill stood higher and higher on the pedestal mom had put him on. He was the last one in her thoughts when she died at 81 in 1980." As for Erlyn, she named her first son after Bill. She often talked with her children about him. "I want them to know him. . . . Not a day goes by that I don't think of him."

During the war Henrietta Bingham lived in a small town in western Montana; she was nine at the time of the Pearl Harbor attack. "The war changed my childhood & ultimately my life. In Dec. 1941 all the war meant to me . . . was excitement. . . . By 1945 that excitement had turned our family to tragedy & sorrow. . . ." In 1942, Gerald, her sixteen-year-old brother, falsified his age, enlisted in the Army Air Corps, and became a top turret gunner on a B-25. He was killed the next year on a mission in the Pacific. Henrietta's parents asked their next son, Gene, not to enlist until he had graduated from high school. The day after graduation, in May 1943, he joined the Air Corps and became a nose gunner on a B-24; the next year, he was killed on a training mission. Gene's body, which was shipped to Montana, was escorted by his best friend, Corporal Marvel Best. Marvel became part of the family. That fall he was killed in Italy. "My parents felt they had lost another son." In 1945, when Gerald's class was graduated from high school, "they left an empty chair for him. . . . I was then 13." Her parents had aged greatly during this period; her "young pretty mother had turned almost white," her father "appeared as an old man." "I remember sitting at that graduation ceremony," Henrietta wrote, "& remembering how excited I was at age 9 when the war began in 1941 & how I now felt just a few short years later. I had lost my childhood."

. . . Because of the war, many homefront girls and boys suffered a premature loss of invulnerability. All else paled beside this fact.

FURTHER READING

Dratch, Howard. "The Politics of Child Care in the 1940s." *Science and Society* 38 (Summer 1974): 167–204.

Fiset, Louis. *Imprisoned Apart: The World War II Correspondence of an Issei Couple* (1997).

Glenn, Evelyn Nakano. *Issei, Nisei, War Bride: Three Generations of Japanese American Women in Domestic Service* (1986).

Gluck, Sherna. *Rosie the Riveter Revisited* (1983).

Hosokawa, Bill. *Nisei: The Quiet Americans* (1969).

Houston, Jeanne Wakatsuki, and James D. Houston. *Farewell to Manzanar* (1973).

Kikuchi, Charles. *The Kikuchi Diary: Chronicle from an American Concentration Camp* (1973).

Kitagawa, Daisuke. *Issei and Nisei: The Internment Years* (1967).

Kitsuse, John I., and Leonard Broom. *The Managed Casualty: The Japanese American Family in World War II* (1956).

Litoff, Judy Barrett, and David C. Smith, eds. *Miss You: The World War II Letters of Barbara Wooddall Taylor and Charles E. Taylor* (1990).

———. *Since You Went Away: World War II Letters from American Women on the Home Front* (1991).

May, Elaine Tyler. *Homeward Bound: American Families in the Cold War Era* (1988).

Meyer, Dillon S. *Uprooted Americans: The Japanese Americans and the War Relocation Authority During World War II* (1972).

Sone, Monica. *Nisei Daughter* (1979).

Tuttle, William M. Jr. *"Daddy's Gone to War": The Second World War in the Lives of America's Children* (1993).

Uchida, Yoshiko. *Desert Exile: The Uprooting of a Japanese American Family* (1982).

Yanagisako, Sylvia Junko. *Transforming the Past: Tradition and Kinship Among Japanese Americans* (1985).

The 1950s: Family Life
in Modern America

Clean-cut, well-mannered boys; sweetly sexy, yet shyly modest girls; good-natured,
affectionate parents—thanks to the situation comedies so popular at the time and
still shown on late-night television today, these images of family life, 1950s-style,
are familiar to most Americans. Indeed, many Americans today regard the 1950s
as a time when children were respectful and well behaved, parents stayed together
through thick and thin, and family "togetherness" was the norm. Just as television
shows such as Happy Days, Leave It to Beaver, *and* Father Knows Best *promoted*
these images of family life in the post–World War II decades, in more recent years
shows such as The Wonder Years, *"classic rock" nostalgia festivals, and popular*
memory have commemorated the 1950s as a "golden age" for American families.
In an ironic historical twist, Americans living in the "postmodern" era, much like
Americans living in the postwar years, look to the family as a source of stability
and security in a rapidly changing and often dangerous world. Yet as historians of
the 1950s—or, more accurately, of the two decades following World War II—have
pointed out, the so-called traditional family of the 1950s was itself a new invention, a
product of the "modern" era ushered in on the heels of massive economic deprivation
and the detonation of the atomic bomb.

Scholars of the modern family interested in exploring such hallmarks of the
era as the "baby boom," the flight to suburbia, and the enthusiasm for consumer
goods have ample source material, ranging from popular media—television, film,
magazines, and novels—to the advice books so beloved by a generation fascinated
with the authority of self-proclaimed "experts." Statistical information helps to give
substance to the ideals promoted in these sources—and, sometimes, to give the lie to
them as well. And finally, the firsthand accounts of those who grew up, got married,
and raised families in the 1950s—whether captured at the time in surveys and
questionnaires or collected later through interviews and memoirs—add depth
and richness to the picture presented in idealized images and hard numbers.

Research on family life in the modern era both reaffirms and challenges the
common view of the 1950s as a golden age for American families. Certainly, family
life was celebrated, honored, even revered in the mid-twentieth-century United
States, yet a narrow definition of the family also functioned as a way to register

social disapproval of those who failed—or refused—to conform to the postwar
ideal: unwed mothers, African Americans, and gays and lesbians. A close look at
the numbers reveals that the decade of the 1950s, far from being a return to "traditional" values, was a statistical anomaly characterized by unusually high rates of
marriage and childbearing. And despite early marriages and infrequent divorces,
a record number of children were born to teen parents (the highest rate of teenage
childbearing in the twentieth century occurred in 1957), and a remarkable number
of couples concealed their alienation and discontent beneath a veneer of alcoholism
and drug abuse. As scholars explode the myths of the 1950s, they must begin to ask
themselves not simply what the modern family was really like, but also why Americans so stubbornly cling to their misconceptions of the era.

Because many Americans continue to regard the 1950s as the standard by which
to measure contemporary family life, examining this formative period in modern
American life can offer insight into several pressing questions: Which families are
defined as legitimate? Who measures the value of children? And how and why did
the statistically anomalous 1950s become symbolic of the American family?

D O C U M E N T S

Document 1, an excerpt from Dr. Benjamin Spock's best-selling guide, *The Common
Sense Book of Baby and Child Care*, first published in 1946, offers an example of the
convergence of the baby boom with the era of the expert. Although Spock urges parents,
especially mothers, to "trust yourself," both his repeated reassurances and the fact that
many mothers owned (and still own) well-thumbed pages of this how-to book suggest
that parents increasingly sought expert opinions rather than relying on their own instincts or on their extended family's advice.

The Common Sense Book of Baby and Child Care also demonstrates the centrality
of children to family life in the post–World War II era, a theme that is repeated in a 1960
study performed by the Joint Commission on Mental Illness and Health. Based on interviews conducted nationwide, the study revealed that Americans regarded marriage,
children, and money as necessary to happiness. An excerpt from the introduction to
this lengthy volume is included as Document 2.

The assumption that marriage and family life were bulwarks against personal
unhappiness and social disorder is evident in the Moynihan Report, selections of
which are included as Document 3. Published in 1965 under the direction of liberal
Democratic senator Daniel Patrick Moynihan, the report decries the alleged decline
of the black family and points to increasing numbers of illegitimate births as both
the cause of African Americans' socioeconomic difficulties and a drain on national
resources.

As the Moynihan Report's disparaging comments on illegitimacy indicate, the
value of childbearing depended on race. It also depended on marital status. The next
two documents highlight dramatically different responses to pregnancy. In Document 4,
an excerpt from feminist poet Adrienne Rich's 1976 reflection on motherhood, *Of
Woman Born*, Rich recalls the approval that her first pregnancy evoked and the disapproval she faced when she determined, after giving birth to three children, to curtail
her childbearing. In Document 5, an excerpt from novelist Marge Piercy's 1982 book,
Braided Lives, the protagonist, an unmarried college student, describes her desperation,
her mother's shame, and her father's studied ignorance when the young woman discovered that she was pregnant.

1. Dr. Benjamin Spock Offers
Advice to New Parents, 1946

Trust Yourself

You know more than you think you do. Soon you're going to have a baby. Maybe you have him already. You're happy and excited, but, if you haven't had much experience, you wonder whether you are going to know how to do a good job. Lately you have been listening more carefully to your friends and relatives when they talked about bringing up a child. You've begun to read articles by experts in the magazines and newspapers. After the baby is born, the doctor and nurses will begin to give you instructions, too. Sometimes it sounds like a very complicated business. You find out all the vitamins a baby needs and all the inoculations. One mother tells you you must use the black kind of nipples, another says the yellow. You hear that a baby must be handled as little as possible, and that a baby must be cuddled plenty; that spinach is the most valuable vegetable, that spinach is a worthless vegetable; that fairy tales make children nervous, and that fairy tales are a wholesome outlet.

Don't take too seriously all that the neighbors say. Don't be overawed by what the experts say. Don't be afraid to trust your own common sense. Bringing up your child won't be a complicated job if you take it easy, trust your own instincts, and follow the directions that your doctor gives you. We know for a fact that the natural loving care that kindly parents give to their children is a hundred times more valuable than their knowing how to pin a diaper on just right, or making a formula expertly. Every time you pick your baby up, even if you do it a little awkwardly at first, every time you change him, bathe him, feed him, smile at him, he's getting a feeling that he belongs to you and that you belong to him. Nobody else in the world, no matter how skillful, can give that to him.

It may surprise you to hear that the more people have studied different methods of bringing up children the more they have come to the conclusion that what good mothers and fathers instinctively feel like doing for their babies is usually best after all. Furthermore, all parents do their best job when they have a natural, easy confidence in themselves. Better to make a few mistakes from being natural than to do everything letter-perfect out of a feeling of worry. . . .

The father's part. Some fathers have been brought up to think that the care of babies and children is the mother's job entirely. This is the wrong idea. You can be a warm father and a real man at the same time.

We know that the father's closeness and friendliness to his children will have a vital effect on their spirits and characters for the rest of their lives. So the time for him to begin being a real father is right at the start. That's the easiest time. The father and mother can learn together. In some cities, classes in baby care are given for fathers too. If a father leaves it all to his wife for the first two years, she gets to be the expert and the boss, as far as the children are concerned. He'll feel more bashful about pushing his way into the picture later.

Benjamin Spock, *The Common Sense Book of Baby and Child Care* (New York: Duell, Sloan and Pearce, 1946), pp. 3–4, 15–17. Reprinted from *Fully Revised and Expanded Dr. Spock's Baby and Child Care* by Benjamin Spock, M.D., and Steven J. Parker, M.D., with the permission of Pocket Books, an imprint of Simon & Schuster Adult Publishing Group. Copyright © 1945, 1946, 1957, 1968, 1976.

Of course, I don't mean that the father has to give just as many bottles or change just as many diapers as the mother. But it's fine for him to do these things occasionally. He might make the formula on Sunday. If the baby is on a 2 A.M. bottle in the early weeks, when the mother is still pretty tired, this is a good feeding for him to take over. It's nice for him, if he can, to go along to the doctor's office for the baby's regular visits. It gives him a chance to bring up those questions which are bothering him and of which he doesn't think his wife understands the importance. It pleases the doctor, too. Of course, there are some fathers who would get goose flesh at the very idea of helping to take care of a baby, and there's no good to be gained by trying to force them. Most of them come around to enjoying their children later "when they're more like real people." But many fathers are only a little bashful. They just need encouragement.

The blue feeling. It's possible that you will find yourself feeling discouraged for a while when you first begin taking care of your baby. It's a fairly common feeling, especially with the first. You may not be able to put your finger on anything that is definitely wrong. You just weep easily. Or you may feel very badly about certain things. One woman whose baby cries quite a bit feels sure that he has a real disease; another that her husband has become strange and distant; another that she has lost all her looks.

A feeling of depression may come on a few days after the baby is born or not till several weeks later. The commonest time is when a mother comes home from the hospital, where she has been waited on hand and foot, and abruptly takes over the full care of baby and household. It isn't just the work that gets her down. She may even have someone to do all the work, for the time being. It's the feeling of being responsible for the whole household again, plus the entirely new responsibility of the baby's care and safety. Then there are all the physical and glandular changes at the time of the birth, which probably upset the spirits to some degree.

The majority of mothers don't get enough discouraged in this period to ever call it depression. You may think it is a mistake to bring up unpleasant things that may never happen. The reason I mention it is that several mothers have told me afterwards, "I'm sure I wouldn't have been so depressed or discouraged if I had known how common this feeling is. Why, I thought that my whole outlook on life had changed for good and all." You can face a thing much better if you know that a lot of other people have gone through it too, and if you know that it's just temporary.

If you begin to feel at all depressed, try to get some relief from the constant care of the baby in the first month or two, especially if he cries a great deal. Go to a movie, or to the beauty parlor, or to get yourself a new hat or dress. Visit a good friend occasionally. Take the baby along if you can't find anyone to stay with him. Or get your old friends to come and see you. All of these are tonics. If you are depressed, you may not feel like doing these things. But if you make yourself, you will feel a lot better. And that's important for the baby and your husband as well as yourself. (The rare mother who becomes deeply depressed should have the help of a psychiatrist without delay.)

As for a mother's feeling, when she's blue, that her husband seems different, far away, there are two sides to it. On the one hand, anyone who is depressed feels that other people are less friendly and affectionate. But on the other hand, it's natural for a father, being human, to feel "put out" when his wife and the rest of the household are completely wrapped up in the baby. So it's a sort of vicious circle. The mother (as if she didn't have enough to do already!) has to remember to pay some attention to her husband. And she should give him every chance to share the care of the baby. . . .

2. Americans Describe Marriage and Family as Necessary to Happiness, 1960

. . .

The kinds of questions asked by the survey [conducted by the Joint Commission on Mental Health and Illness] fall into two general categories. The first deals with the way people feel they have adjusted to life—whether they think they are happy or unhappy, worried or unworried, the picture they have of themselves, and their attitudes toward the three most important areas of their lives—marriage, parenthood, and work.

The second group of questions follows from the first. How do people cope with problems? What motivates them to seek help and where do they turn for it? How effective do they think help has been? Why do some people fail to look for help, and how do they get along without it? The authors were particularly interested to discover if there is any connection between the attitudes that different kinds of people adopt toward themselves and the extent to which they seek help for their problems. The answer to this question has considerable significance in planning the most effective use of mental health resources, as we shall see later. Now what of the findings? What does this monograph tell us about the concerns of the American people?

Money and other material and economic considerations (or the lack of them) are one of the major sources of happiness and unhappiness, according to the study. Three out of ten say it is central to their happiness—or unhappiness. They see money, however, in the light of the material comforts, adequacy of living, and the security it can buy, rather than in terms of luxury.

On the other hand, roughly the same proportion of people regard their children as one of their primary sources of happiness. In addition, one out of five sees marriage as the wellspring of happiness, and approximately the same percentage look to their family in general.

One other interesting point can be made. Unlike the distress accompanying lack of material considerations, most people do not spontaneously mention family relationships as a source of distress.

All in all, it is clear that well over half the population finds its greatest happiness in the home, a state that is conditioned strongly by feelings of economic security.

It may come as a surprise to persons heavily involved in public affairs that international tensions, fear of atomic extinction, and the anxious atmosphere of a troubled world do not figure importantly among the things the American people say trouble them. Fewer than one in ten expressed an outstanding concern for community,

Gerald Gurin, Joseph Veroff, and Sheila Feld, *Americans View Their Mental Health* (New York: Basic Books, 1960), pp. xii–xiii. Copyright 1960 by Perseus Books Group. Reproduced with permission of Perseus Books Group in the format textbook via Copyright Clearance Center.

national, or world problems. The reason for this finding is unclear. This indifference may be due partly to the fact that most of us are concerned with the realities of our immediate environments, and that the extent to which sources of worry and tension affect us decreases in proportion to their remoteness. It may also reflect a retreat from the realities of a larger world, a sense of helplessness in the face of events that the individual feels are beyond his ability to control. Or it could be a symptom of political immaturity combined with a persistent undercurrent of isolationism, resulting in a renunciation of social responsibility. . . .

3. Senator Daniel Patrick Moynihan Bemoans the Breakdown of the Black Family, 1965

At the heart of the deterioration of the fabric of Negro society is the deterioration of the Negro family.

It is the fundamental source of the weakness of the Negro community at the present time.

There is probably no single fact of Negro American life so little understood by whites. The Negro situation is commonly perceived by whites in terms of the visible manifestations of discrimination and poverty, in part because Negro protest is directed against such obstacles, and in part, no doubt, because these are facts which involve the actions and attitudes of the white community as well. It is more difficult, however, for whites to perceive the effect that three centuries of exploitation have had on the fabric of Negro society itself. Here the consequences of the historic injustices done to Negro Americans are silent and hidden from view. But here is where the true injury has occurred: unless this damage is repaired, all the effort to end discrimination and poverty and injustice will come to little.

The role of the family in shaping character and ability is so pervasive as to be easily overlooked. The family is the basic social unit of American life; it is the basic socializing unit. By and large, adult conduct in society is learned as a child.

A fundamental insight of psychoanalytic theory, for example, is that the child learns a way of looking at life in his early years through which all later experience is viewed and which profoundly shapes his adult conduct.

It may be hazarded that the reason family structure does not loom larger in public discussion of social issues is that people tend to assume that the nature of family life is about the same throughout American society. The mass media and the development of suburbia have created an image of the American family as a highly standardized phenomenon. It is therefore easy to assume that whatever it is that makes for differences among individuals or groups of individuals, it is not a different family structure.

There is much truth to this; as with any other nation, Americans are producing a recognizable family system. But that process is not completed by any means. There are still, for example, important differences in family patterns surviving from

Office of Policy Planning and Research, *The Negro Family: The Case for National Action* (Washington, D.C.: U.S. Department of Labor, 1965), pp. 5–6, 8–9, 12, 14.

the age of the great European migration to the United States, and these variations account for notable differences in the progress and assimilation of various ethnic and religious groups. A number of immigrant groups were characterized by unusually strong family bonds; these groups have characteristically progressed more rapidly than others.

But there is one truly great discontinuity in family structure in the United States at the present time: that between the white world in general and that of the Negro American.

The white family has achieved a high degree of stability and is maintaining that stability.

By contrast, the family structure of lower class Negroes is highly unstable, and in many urban centers is approaching complete breakdown.

N.b. There is considerable evidence that the Negro community is in fact dividing between a stable middle-class group that is steadily growing stronger and more successful, and an increasingly disorganized and disadvantaged lower-class group. There are indications, for example, that the middle-class Negro family puts a higher premium on family stability and the conserving of family resources than does the white middle-class family. The discussion of this paper is not, obviously, directed to the first group excepting as it is affected by the experiences of the second—an important exception. (See Chapter IV, The Tangle of Pathology.)

There are two points to be noted in this context.

First, the emergence and increasing visibility of a Negro middle-class may beguile the nation into supposing that the circumstances of the remainder of the Negro community are equally prosperous, whereas just the opposite is true at present, and is likely to continue so.

Second, the lumping of all Negroes together in one statistical measurement very probably conceals the extent of the disorganization among the lower-class group. If conditions are improving for one and deteriorating for the other, the resultant statistical averages might show no change. Further, the statistics on the Negro family and most other subjects treated in this paper refer only to a specific point in time. They are a vertical measure of this situation at a given moment. They do not measure the experience of individuals over time. Thus the average monthly unemployment rate for Negro males for 1964 is recorded as 9 percent. But *during* 1964, some 29 percent of Negro males were unemployed at one time or another. Similarly, for example, if 36 percent of Negro children are living in broken homes *at any specific moment,* it is likely that a far higher proportion of Negro children find themselves in that situation *at one time or another* in their lives.

Nearly a Quarter of Urban Negro Marriages Are Dissolved

Nearly a quarter of Negro women living in cities who have ever married are divorced, separated, or are living apart from their husbands. . . .

The rates are highest in the urban Northeast where 26 percent of Negro women ever married are either divorced, separated, or have their husbands absent.

On the urban frontier, the proportion of husbands absent is even higher. In New York City in 1960, it was 30.2 percent, *not* including divorces.

Among ever-married nonwhite women in the nation, the proportion with husbands present *declined* in *every* age group over the decade 1950–60. . . . Although similar declines occurred among white females, the proportion of white husbands present never dropped below 90 except for the first and last age group [i.e., fifteen to nineteen and forty to forty-nine].

Nearly One-Quarter of Negro Births Are Now Illegitimate

Both white and Negro illegitimacy rates have been increasing, although from dramatically different bases. The white rate was 2 percent in 1940; it was 3.07 percent in 1963. In that period, the Negro rate went from 16.8 percent to 23.6 percent.

The number of illegitimate children per 1,000 live births increased by 11 among whites in the period 1940–63, but by 68 among nonwhites. There are, of course, limits to the dependability of these statistics. There are almost certainly a considerable number of Negro children who, although technically illegitimate, are in fact the offspring of stable unions. On the other hand, it may be assumed that many births that are in fact illegitimate are recorded otherwise. Probably the two opposite effects cancel each other out.

On the urban frontier, the nonwhite illegitimacy rates are usually higher than the national average, and the increase of late has been drastic.

In the District of Columbia, the illegitimacy rate for nonwhites grew from 21.8 percent in 1950, to 29.5 percent in 1964.

A similar picture of disintegrating Negro marriages emerges from the divorce statistics. Divorces have increased of late for both whites and nonwhites, but at a much greater rate for the latter. In 1940 both groups had a divorce rate of 2.2 percent. By 1964 the white rate had risen to 3.6 percent, but the nonwhite rate had reached 5.1 percent—40 percent greater than the formerly equal white rate.

Almost One-Fourth of Negro Families Are Headed by Females

As a direct result of this high rate of divorce, separation, and desertion, a very large percent of Negro families are headed by females. While the percentage of such families among whites has been dropping since 1940, it has been rising among Negroes.

The percent of nonwhite families headed by a female is more than double the percent for whites. Fatherless nonwhite families increased by a sixth between 1950 and 1960, but held constant for white families.

It has been estimated that only a minority of Negro children reach the age of 18 having lived all their lives with both their parents.

Once again, this measure of family disorganization is found to be diminishing among white families and increasing among Negro families.

The Breakdown of the Negro Family Has Led to a Startling Increase in Welfare Dependency

The majority of Negro children receive public assistance under the AFDC [Aid to Families with Dependent Children] program at one point or another in their childhood.

At present, 14 percent of Negro children are receiving AFDC assistance, as against 2 percent of white children. Eight percent of white children receive such assistance at some time, as against 56 percent of nonwhites, according to an extrapolation based on HEW [Department of Health, Education, and Welfare] data. (Let it be noted, however, that out of a total of 1.8 million nonwhite illegitimate children in the nation in 1961, 1.3 million were *not* receiving aid under the AFDC program, although a substantial number have, or will, receive aid at some time in their lives.)

Again, the situation may be said to be worsening. The AFDC program, deriving from the long established Mothers' Aid programs, was established in 1935 principally to care for widows and orphans, although the legislation covered all children in homes deprived of parental support because one or both of their parents are absent or incapacitated.

In the beginning, the number of AFDC families in which the father was absent because of desertion was less than a third of the total. Today it is two-thirds. HEW estimates "that between two-thirds and three-fourths of the 50 percent increase from 1948 to 1955 in the number of absent-father families receiving ADC may be explained by an increase in broken homes in the population."

A 1960 study of Aid to Dependent Children in Cook County, Ill. stated:

> The "typical" ADC mother in Cook County was married and had children by her husband, who deserted; his whereabouts are unknown, and he does not contribute to the support of his children. She is not free to remarry and has had an illegitimate child since her husband left. (Almost 90 percent of the ADC [Aid to Dependent Children] families are Negro.)

The steady expansion of this welfare program, as of public assistance programs in general, can be taken as a measure of the steady disintegration of the Negro family structure over the past generation in the United States.

4. Adrienne Rich Recalls the Cultural Promotion of Motherhood in Cold War Era-America, 1976

. . . I became a mother in the family-centered, consumer-oriented, Freudian-American world of the 1950s. My husband spoke eagerly of the children we would have; my parents-in-law awaited the birth of their grandchild. I had no idea of what *I* wanted, what *I* could or could not choose. I only knew that to have a child was to assume adult womanhood to the full, to prove myself, to be "like other women." . . .

As soon as I was visibly and clearly pregnant, I felt, for the first time in my adolescent and adult life, not-guilty. The atmosphere of approval in which I was bathed—even by strangers on the street, it seemed—was like an aura I carried with me, in which doubts, fears, misgivings, met with absolute denial. *This is what women have always done.*

Two days before my first son was born, I broke out in a rash which was tentatively diagnosed as measles, and was admitted to a hospital for contagious diseases to await the onset of labor. I felt for the first time a great deal of conscious fear, and

Adrienne Rich, *Of Woman Born: Motherhood as Experience and Institution* (New York: Norton, 1986), pp. 25–26, 29–30. Copyright © 1986, 1976 by W. W. Norton & Company, Inc. Used by permission of the author and W. W. Norton & Company, Inc.

guilt toward my unborn child, for having "failed" him with my body in this way. In rooms near mine were patients with polio; on one was allowed to enter my room except in a hospital gown and mask. If during pregnancy I had felt in any vague command of my situation, I felt now totally dependent on my obstetrician, a huge, vigorous, paternal man, abounding with optimism and assurance, and given to pinching my cheek. I had gone through a healthy pregnancy, but as if tranquilized or sleep-walking. I had taken a sewing class in which I produced an unsightly and ill-cut maternity jacket which I never wore; I had made curtains for the baby's room, collected baby clothes, blotted out as much as possible the woman I had been a few months earlier. My second book of poems was in press, but I had stopped writing poetry, and read little except household magazines and books on child-care. I felt myself perceived by the world simply as a pregnant woman, and it seemed easier, less disturbing, to perceive myself so. After my child was born the "measles" were diagnosed as an allergic reaction to pregnancy.

Within two years, I was pregnant again. . . .

Before my third child was born I decided to have no more children, to be steril-ized. (Nothing is removed from a woman's body during this operation; ovulation and menstruation continue. Yet the language suggests a cutting- or burning-away of her essential womanhood, just as the old word "barren" suggests a woman eternally empty and lacking.) My husband, although he supported my decision, asked whether I was sure it would not leave me feeling "less feminine." In order to have the oper-ation at all, I had to present a letter, counter-signed by my husband, assuring the com-mittee of physicians who approved such operations that I had already produced three children, and stating my reasons for having no more. Since I had had rheumatoid arthritis for some years, I could give a reason acceptable to the male panel who sat on my case; my own judgment would not have been acceptable. When I awoke from the operation, twenty-four hours after my child's birth, a young nurse looked at my chart and remarked coldly: "Had yourself spayed, did you?"

5. Marge Piercy Describes a Woman's Response to an Unplanned Pregnancy Before *Roe* v. *Wade*, 1982

I have sworn I would not check again until two and I have held out, but the other promise I forced on myself—that I would not hope—I cannot keep. As I bolt the stall door, I whimper to myself, of course I have not started, not yet. When I look at my panties and see nothing, a cold nausea slides through me. I was sure this time. I felt the blood. Donna was fourteen days late and I am only eleven. Given the mute embroiled misery in which I stew, no wonder my period is off. Yet I am afraid.

As I pass her desk the older secretary Mrs. Papich looks up with her stubby fingers poised on the keys. "Do you have the runs?"

I nod, looking meek.

"That's the third day you've spent dashing to the powder room. Better see a doctor, doll, before the boss gets annoyed." . . .

Marge Piercy, *Braided Lives* (New York: Summit Books, 1982), pp. 202, 208–211, 214–216, 218–220. Copyright © 1982 by Marge Piercy and Middlemarsh, Inc. Used by permission of the Wallace Literary Agency, Inc.

I walk toward the bathroom to be sick. Twenty-nine days and no period. Twenty-nine mornings with that razor edge cutting me from sleep, twenty-nine days of seizing hope from every cramp and twinge, looking always for the blood that does not come. Red is the invisible color of hope.

Saturday morning I wake to see Mother standing by my dresser holding my calendar. Her face is hard. "Jill, are you with child?"

I swing out of bed, clutching my old pajama bottoms with one hand. "I don't know."

"How late are you?"

She can count it too. "Thirty-two days."

"Why didn't you tell me?"

I heist up my pajamas. "Are you kidding?"

"Do you have other symptoms?"

"Nausea. I've been throwing up."

"Do your breasts itch?"

They begin at once, O psychosomatic me. "I'm late because of the turmoil."

She shakes her head briskly. "A month late? Never. You're regular, like all the rest of my family."

Outside a mad robin chirrups in the tree. "You think I'm pregnant?"

"I knew it! You disobeyed me, going behind my back. Now you've brought this down on yourself."

"If you try to make me marry him now I'll leave this house." I step closer to her clenching my free hand.

"Does he know?"

"No! And he won't either. I'll walk out and you'll never see me again. You won't know whether I'm alive or dead, but I'll never marry him."

We stand with our faces a handsbreadth apart while her black eyes try to force mine to flinch. I will not be put down.

"We have to talk fast. Your father's in the yard gabbing with old man Wilensky. You don't want to be saddled with a fatherless child!"

"I don't want it. I want an abortion."

"No! They're dirty men, Jill. They charge a fortune and they blackmail you."

"We needn't give our right names."

"It's against the law. You can go to jail. Your father would kill me!"

"People go to them all the time and don't get caught."

"Half the time they don't do it right. No!" Her hands seek each other in her apron, her gaze darts about the room. "They butcher you so you can't have babies after."

"Mother! I'll take my chances. I've got to."

"No. You've made your bed and you'll lie in it." She shifts from foot to foot, her face twitching. "All right, I'll tell you what to do."

"Mother, a doctor knows what to do. I don't want to kill myself."

"Then have the bastard if you won't listen to me." She turns and pushes past me. I grab her arm. "Mother, don't!"

"Will you listen, then? I'll tell you what to do." She rakes me with her gaze. "You've always been a weakling and a coward. Sickly since you were seven. You'll have to do this for yourself. You'll do what I say or I'll wash my hands of you. If you go running around to doctors, and you can't trust a one of them, only in it for the money, I'll tell your father and he'll make you have it."

"All right." I sit on the bedside clutching my stomach. Fish cold.

"Don't think it's easy. It's hard, hard."

"You'll see that I'm strong enough." The bile wells in my throat and I swallow it down. "Tell me what to do."

Steam clouds the mirror, coalescing on the yellow wall and running down in rivulets. While the tub fills I sit on the toilet seat staring at my belly smooth and flat from harsh laxatives. Under the cushion of fat lurks the womb, spongy fist that will not open while in it cells divide and divide. The steam swirling hot from the tub smothers me as this body goes its animal way. I seldom felt feminine: I felt neuter. An angel of words. I could imagine myself a Hamlet, a Trotsky, a Donne. I thought I was projects, accomplishments, tastes: I am only an envelope of guts. This is what it is to be female, to be trapped. This sac of busy cells has its own private rhythms of creation and decay, its viruses and cancers, its twenty-eight-day reminders of birth and death. My body can be taken over and used against my will as if I were a hall to be rented out. Hot baths with Epsom salts, hot baths with pennyroyal; I am parboiled and still pregnant. . . .

Mother sits on the couch, her thighs spread wearily. "You aren't trying hard enough."

All the furniture is shoved back to back. I let the rust chair stay blocking the passage to the dining room and drop in it in humid collapse. "How can I try harder?"

"If you want this baby, say so. But don't fool around."

"Mother, damn it, I've lost twelve pounds with laxatives and taking those vile herbs and throwing up and jumping off porches."

She snorts. "You can't diet a baby away."

"I've lifted and heaved and jumped and pocked and twisted and boiled myself."

She looks at her plump hands red with washing. "I don't know . . ."

"Mother, maybe it isn't going to work. Let's go to a doctor. Please."

"And end up in jail? Never. You do it yourself, they can't prove it on you. They can't take you to court."

"I'm sick as a dog. I can't stand without dizziness. I almost passed out climbing the stairs at work yesterday. But nothing happens!"

"Keep your voice down." She taps her foot. Her thighs quiver nervously under the washdress. "There's another way. But it's bad for the heart."

"Anything."

She turns her head away. "We'll get you quinine and you take that and then the next day a mustard bath. If that fails you have to open the womb yourself. There's no more time."

I am watched all the time at home but at work since I have given up lunch I have time to get my rolls of quarters at the bank and shut myself up in a pay phone on a corner. I am calling New York.

"Is Lennie there?" I ask the woman who answers. "I'm a friend from school."

"What friend?"

"My name is Jill."

"I thought maybe you were that Donna. Lennie's been expecting her to call. Just a minute."

I thought he might be home because he works as a waiter six nights a week from four to twelve.

"Jill!" he roars. "What's up? Anything wrong with Donna?"

"No, I haven't seen her. Listen, Lennie what was the name and phone number of that doctor who does abortions?"

"What's wrong, you in trouble?"

He's a friend of Mike's rather than mine. "No, it's a friend of mine from the neighborhood. I told her I knew somebody."

"Just a minute. I got it written down somewhere." He disappears off the line while the operator coos, "Please signal when through." Meaning I have run past three minutes. Lennie, hurry up!

Finally he comes back. "Yeah, well he's Dr. Lytton Manning in Dexter. You call and say you need to have a growth removed. That's the phrase."

"He's got some sense of humor, that man."

"Yeah, well you bring one hundred dollars in cash in an envelope and you give it to the receptionist. Then she gives you a date. You pay the other two hundred when you go in. You give it to the receptionist the same way."

"Three hundred dollars?"

"That's it. So how are you otherwise? How's Mike? I wrote him but the bugger never answered me."

"He's fine," I say limply. "Listen I'm on my lunch hour."

"Well, have a ball. See you at school."

Maybe. I walk very slowly back to work. Three hundred: that's what I've earned for six weeks' work. It would eat up my fall payment for the goddamned dormitory where we are forced to live. Plus I would have to manage to get to Dexter, Michigan, twice. Hopeless.

On my next two lunch hours I see a doctor a day. Each gynecologist examines me, painfully, and tells me I am pregnant. I try out my routine, including telling each of them I will kill myself. They tell me they can call the police; they tell me I must have the baby; they charge me one ten dollars and one fifteen; they lecture me on morality. I am late back to work both days. . . .

Thursday night. I am half dead and nausea is a constant state, my heart is beating erratically, and yet I am still pregnant. Upstairs in the hot and airless attic, I prepare to follow Mother's last instructions. Through the floorboards the hoofbeats and gun-shots of a Western arise. "Don't cry out," my mother warned me. "Keep your mouth shut." Squatting in the ruins of my old sanctuary, by force I open my womb. . . .

Friday I do not go to work because finally hard pain wakes me and my fingers on the pillow show wet and red. Now in my belly giant hands twist. Contractions. Wryly I realize what I did not understand: that I am going into labor. My ears ring, the room hangs speckled as I gape at it. Five minutes, five hours? I swell and split until I cannot lie on my back or my right side or my left side but writhe like a landed fish on the dock gasping for oxygen. The lowered shades and the blue-and-white curtains rise and fall, rise and fall languidly. The air lies like a warm damp towel on my sweating face. I knead my body trying to squeeze the pain out. Occa-sionally Mother comes in, speaks.

"What?" My ears buzz.

"How is it?"

"Bad."

She unwinds the sheets from my legs and tucks them in far away at the foot. Biting her lips she stands over me, then hurries away.

The pains deepen. Pain is bigger than I am; I drown in it. The contractions sharpen and ease in regular quickening waves but under the crests continuing is a substantial mass of pain always deepening. When I cry out, Mother comes at once and glares at me, drawing back her hand as if she will slap me. I know I must be silent and so I am. I twist my hands, trash in bed, writhe. . . .

In my mouth, a bitter ragged taste. Black fungus on the tongue, the taste of dying. All the blood is rushing from me, I feel it flowing. Forever, pain wrings me and the blood bubbles out. "Mother!" Why doesn't she come? Has she run away? "Mother?"

She trots in. "Shhhh! Don't make noise."

"I was calling. Not noise. Help me up." I am being squashed. The press closes on me. Got to move. Leaning on her I drag into the bathroom. "Go away. Wait outside."

She backs from me hesitantly. Fear rises from her like the smell of sweat.

"Shut door!" Vomit hot and acid charges up my throat. Back uphill to bed, leaning. Blood runs down my legs, red footsteps across the throw rug. I sink into bed. Pain sings in my ears like a choir of giant and hungry mosquitoes. My hands knead my body as if they could pinch out sensation. I ring like a cracked bell, bong, bong, pulling my guts out with it, all, out and down and down.

I open my eyes as if tearing open a package. . . . How much blood boils out, bright, beautiful on the sheets, huge rose that blooms from me. Mother peers down, hands plucking at her apron, lips moving. "You're so pale, chickie, your lips are white. What to do. . . . Oh God, dear God, don't let her die. She's punished enough now. Listen to me!"

Punished. I want to laugh. We are always in different stories.

"Push, Jill!" She squeezes my arm. "Push it out of you. Bear down. You have to push it out!"

I hear myself moan far away. Her hand covers my mouth and nose. I stop making the sound and she lets me breathe. She paces biting her thumb, tugging at her hair. Through the whine of pain I cannot hear, but her lips mutter ceaselessly. Sweat hisses through my pores. Blood scalds my thighs. I thrash. My belly ripples spasmodically. The bed buckles, kicks under me. Must go. Something is forcing me. I heave over the side and crumple. "Bathroom. Must."

She pulls me up screaming, "Stand up! I can't carry you!" The mirror dandles me dead white, a grey face. My vision burns out speckled. The room swings into black. "Jill, don't fall. I can't hold you!"

I hang my head till the light seeps back. Must sit, must. Stumbling I trip on rubbery tissue, dark and clotted. Long hell corridor swinging, closing like a press. Must.

The bathroom floor is cold against me as I squat. A nail drives in blow after blow. Push on it. Must.

Slowly the room slides back. the contractions ebb, rise serrated, ebb. Gradually my body quiets like a pond long after a rock. I pull myself up.

"Did you pass it, Jill?"

"Yes." Back to bed. "Blood's pouring out."

"Raise your legs."

"Can't."

She props a mound of rags under me.

"I'm cold."

"It's hot in here." She fans herself.

The air across the sill freezes me. "I'm cold."

She shuts the window. "Is that better?"

My teeth are chattering. "I'm cold."

"I don't want to spoil the blanket. Everything's soaked." She hovers, then sighs and pulls it up. . . .

 E S S A Y S

The first essay, an excerpt from University of Minnesota historian Elaine Tyler May's 1988 book on family life in the post–World War II era, *Homeward Bound*, connects family history with world events—in this case, the cold war. May uses popular media, the writings of the era's respected experts, and the results from the Kelly Longitudinal Study (one of several long-term studies conducted by said experts from the 1950s through the 1980s) to illustrate that in the uncertain atmosphere that followed the Great Depression and World War II, Americans looked to the home and family for peace and security. In the process, she illuminates the origins of and the tradeoffs involved in what many Americans continue to regard as a golden age for the American family.

In the second essay, independent scholar Rickie Solinger, author of *Wake Up Little Susie* (1992), examines one aspect of the postwar enthusiasm for family life—the baby boom—from the perspective of black and white teenage mothers. The reproductive consensus of the 1950s was shattered when the mothers-to-be were unmarried. Both black and white women who became pregnant out of wedlock faced severe criticism as social deviants. But the consequences of single pregnancy, as Solinger demonstrates, were not consistent; rather, they varied by race. While white mothers were encouraged to give up their children for adoption and reintegrate themselves into respectable domestic life, black mothers were criticized for relying on public assistance in order to raise their children themselves. The stereotypes of black and white single mothers that were promulgated in the decades after World War II continue to shape contemporary understandings of teen pregnancy and "welfare moms."

Visions of Family Life in Postwar America

ELAINE TYLER MAY

In 1959, when the baby boom and the cold war were both at their peak, Vice President Richard M. Nixon traveled to the Soviet Union to engage in what would become one of the most noted verbal sparring matches of the century. In a lengthy and often heated debate with Soviet Premier Nikita Khrushchev at the opening of the American National Exhibition in Moscow, Nixon extolled the virtues of the

Elaine Tyler May, *Homeward Bound: American Families in the Cold War Era* (New York: Basic Books, 1988), pp. 16–20, 22–36. Copyright 1988 by Perseus Books Group. Reproduced with permission of Perseus Books Group in the format textbook via Copyright Clearance Center.

American way of life, while his opponent promoted the Communist system. What was remarkable about this exchange was its focus. The two leaders did not discuss missiles, bombs, or even modes of government. Rather, they argued over the relative merits of American and Soviet washing machines, televisions, and electric ranges—in what came to be known as the "kitchen debate."

For Nixon, American superiority rested on the ideal of the suburban home, complete with modern appliances and distinct gender roles for family members. He proclaimed that the "model" home, with a male breadwinner and a full-time female homemaker, adorned with a wide array of consumer goods, represented the essence of American freedom:

> To us, diversity, the right to choose, . . . is the most important thing. We don't have one decision made at the top by one government official. . . . We have many different manufacturers and many different kinds of washing machines so that the housewives have a choice. . . . Would it not be better to compete in the relative merits of washing machines than in the strength of rockets?

Nixon's focus on household appliances was not accidental. After all, arguments over the strength of rockets would only point out the vulnerability of the United States in the event of a nuclear war between the superpowers; debates over consumer goods would provide a reassuring vision of the good life available in the atomic age. So Nixon insisted that American superiority in the cold war rested not on weapons, but on the secure, abundant family life of modern suburban homes. In these structures, adorned and worshiped by their inhabitants, women would achieve their glory and men would display their success. Consumerism was not an end in itself; it was the means for achieving individuality, leisure, and upward mobility.

The American National Exhibition was a showcase of American consumer goods and leisure-time equipment. But the main attraction, which the two leaders toured, was the full-scale "model" six-room ranch-style house. This model home, filled with labor-saving devices and presumably available to Americans of all classes, was tangible proof, Nixon believed, of the superiority of free enterprise over communism. . . .

Nixon's visit was hailed as a major political triumph. Popular journals extolled his diplomatic skills in the face-to-face confrontation with Khrushchev. Many observers credit this trip with establishing Nixon's political future. Clearly, Americans did not find the kitchen debate trivial. The appliance-laden ranch-style home epitomized the expansive, secure lifestyle that postwar Americans wanted. Within the protective walls of the modern home, worrisome developments like sexual liberalism, women's emancipation, and affluence would lead not to decadence but to a wholesome family life. Sex would enhance marriage, emancipated women would professionalize homemaking, and affluence would put an end to material deprivation. Suburbia would serve as a bulwark against communism and class conflict, for according to the widely shared belief articulated by Nixon, it offered a piece of the American dream for everyone. Although Nixon vastly exaggerated the availability of the suburban home, he described a type of domestic life that had become a reality for many Americans—and a viable aspiration for many more.

The momentum began to build toward this ideal long before it became widely available. Those who came of age during and after World War II were the most marrying generation on record: 96.4 percent of the women and 94.1 percent of the men. These aggregate statistics hide another significant fact: Americans behaved in striking conformity to each other during these years. In other words, not only did the average age at marriage drop, almost everyone was married by his or her mid-twenties. And not only did the average family size increase, most couples had two to four children, born sooner after marriage and spaced closer together than in previous years. At a time when the availability of contraceptive devices enabled couples to delay, space, and limit the arrival of offspring to suit their particular needs, this rising birthrate resulted from deliberate choices. Nixon could, therefore, speak with some conviction when he placed the home at the center of postwar ideals.

What gave rise to the widespread endorsement of this familial consensus in the cold war era? The depression of the 1930s and World War II laid the foundation for a commitment to a stable home life. . . . Economic hardship had torn families asunder, and war had scattered men far from home and drawn women into the public world of work. The postwar years did little to alleviate fears that similar disruptions might occur again. In spite of widespread affluence, many believed that the reconversion to a peacetime economy would lead to another depression. Even peace was problematic, since international tensions were palpable. The explosion of the first atomic bombs over Hiroshima and Nagasaki marked not only the end of World War II but the beginning of the cold war. At any moment, the cold war could turn hot. The policy of containment abroad faced its first major challenge in 1949, with the Chinese revolution. In the same year, the USSR exploded its first atomic bomb. The nation was again jolted out of its sense of fragile security when the Korean War broke out in 1950. Many shared President Truman's belief that World War III was at hand. . . .

Americans were well poised to embrace domesticity in the midst of the terrors of the atomic age. A home filled with children would create a feeling of warmth and security against the cold forces of disruption and alienation. Children would also be a connection to the future and a means of replenishing a world depleted by war deaths. Although baby-boom parents were not likely to express conscious desires to repopulate the country, the devastation of thousands of deaths could not have been far below the surface of the postwar consciousness. . . .

In secure postwar homes with plenty of children, American women and men might be able to ward off their nightmares and live out their dreams. The family seemed to be the one place where people could control their destinies and perhaps even shape the future. Of course, nobody actually argued that stable family life could prevent nuclear annihilation. But the home represented a source of meaning and security in a world run amok. Marrying young and having lots of babies were ways for Americans to thumb their noses at doomsday predictions. Commenting on the trend toward young marriages, one observer noted, "Youngsters want to grasp what little security they can in a world gone frighteningly insecure. The youngsters feel they will cultivate the one security that's possible—their own gardens, their own . . . home and families."

Thoughts of the family rooted in time-honored traditions may have allayed fears of vulnerability. Nevertheless, much of what had provided family security in the past became unhinged. For many Americans, the postwar years brought rootlessness. Those who moved from farms to cities lost a familiar way of life that was rooted in the land. Children of immigrants moved from ethnic neighborhoods with extended kin and community ties to homogeneous suburbs, where they formed nuclear families and invested them with high hopes. Suburban homes offered freedom from kinship obligations, along with material comforts that had not been available on the farm or in the ethnic urban ghetto. As [sociologist William] Whyte noted about the promoters of the Illinois suburb he studied, "At first they had advertised Park Forest as housing. Now they began advertising happiness." But consumer goods would not replace community, and young mobile nuclear families could easily find themselves adrift. Newcomers devoted themselves to creating communities out of neighborhoods composed largely of transients. As Whyte noted, "In suburbia, organization man is trying, quite consciously, to develop a new kind of roots to replace what he left behind."

Young adults aged 25 to 35 were among the most mobile members of the society, constituting 12.4 percent of all migrants but only 7.5 percent of the population. Higher education also prompted mobility; fully 45.5 percent of those who had one year of college or more lived outside their home states, compared to 27.3 percent of high school graduates. Overwhelmingly, these young educated migrants worked for large organizations: three-fourths of all clients of long-distance movers worked for corporations, the government, or the armed services, with corporate employees the most numerous. In their new communities, they immediately endeavored to forge ties with other young transients that would be as rewarding and secure as the ones they left behind, but free of the restraints of the old neighborhood.

Postwar Americans struggled with this transition. The popular culture was filled with stories about young adults who shifted their allegiances from the old ethnic ties to the new nuclear family ideal. When situation comedies shifted from radio to television, working-class ethnic kin networks and multigenerational households faded as the stories increasingly revolved around the middle-class nuclear family. . . .

Whyte called the suburbs the "new melting pot," where migrants from ethnic working-class neighborhoods in the cities moved into the middle class. Kin and ethnic ties were often forsaken as suburban residents formed new communities grounded in shared experiences of homeownership and childrearing, and conformity to the modern consumer-oriented way of life. Young suburbanites were great joiners, forging new ties and creating new institutions to replace the old. One such suburban community, Park Forest, Illinois, had sixty-six adult organizations, making it a "hotbed" of participation. Churches and synagogues, whose membership reached new heights in the postwar years, expanded their functions from prayer and charity to recreation, youth programs, and social events. Church membership rose from 64.5 million in 1940 to 114.5 million in 1960—from 50 percent to 63 percent of the population (100 years earlier only 20 percent of all Americans belonged to churches). Religious affiliation became associated with the "American way of life." Although many observers have commented on the superficiality and lack of spiritual depth in much of this religious activity, there is no question that churches and synagogues provided social arenas for suburbanites, replacing, to some extent, the communal life previously supplied by kin or neighborhood.

Still, these were tenuous alliances among uprooted people. With so much mobility and with success associated with moving on to something better, middle-class nuclear families could not depend on the stability of their communities. As much as they tried to form ties with their neighbors and conform to each other's lifestyles, they were still largely on their own. The new vision of home life, therefore, depended heavily on the staunch commitment of individual family members. Neither the world nor the newly forged suburban community could be trusted to provide security. What mattered was that family members remained bound to each other—and to the modern, emancipated home they intended to create.

The wisdom of earlier generations would be of little help to postwar Americans who were looking toward a radically new vision of family life and trying self-consciously to avoid the paths of their parents. Thus, young people embraced the advice of experts in the rapidly expanding fields of social science, medicine, and psychology. After all, science was changing the world. Was it not reasonable to expect it to change the home as well?

Postwar America was the era of the expert. Armed with scientific techniques and presumably inhabiting a world that was beyond popular passions, the experts had brought us into the atomic age. Physicists developed the bomb, strategists created the cold war, and scientific managers built the military-industrial complex. It was now up to the experts to make the unmanageable manageable. As the readers of *Look* magazine were assured, there was no reason to worry about radioactivity, for if ever the time arrived when you would need to understand its dangers, "the experts will be ready to tell you." Science and technology seemed to have invaded virtually every aspect of life, from the most public to the most private. Americans were looking to professionals to tell them how to manage their lives. The tremendous popularity of Benjamin Spock's *Baby and Child Care* reflects a reluctance to trust the shared wisdom of kin and community. Norman Vincent Peale's *The Power of Positive Thinking* provided readers with religiously inspired scientific formulas for success. Both these best-selling books stressed the centrality of the family in their prescriptions for a better future.

The popularity of these kinds of books attests to the faith in expertise that prevailed at the time. One retrospective study of the attitudes and habits of over 4,000 Americans in 1957 found that the reliance on expertise was one of the most striking developments of the postwar years. Long-term individual therapy, for example, reached unprecedented popularity in the mid-1950s. The authors concluded:

> Experts took over the role of psychic healer, but they also assumed a much broader and more important role in directing the behavior, goals, and ideals of normal people. They became the teachers and norm setters who would tell people how to approach and live life. . . . They would provide advice and counsel about raising and responding to children, how to behave in marriage, and what to see in that relationship. . . . Science moved in because people needed and wanted guidance.

The Kelly Longitudinal Study (KLS) confirmed these findings. By the mid-fifties, one out of six respondents had consulted a professional for marital or emotional problems; yet fewer than one-third that number considered their personal problems to be severe. It seems evident, then, that people were quick to seek professional help. When the experts spoke, postwar Americans listened.

Despite the public's perceptions of scientific mastery and objectivity, professionals groped for appropriate ways to conceptualize and resolve the uncertainties of the times. Like other Americans, they feared the possibility of social disintegration during this period. As participants in the cold war consensus, they offered solutions to the difficulties of the age that would not disrupt the status quo. In the process, they helped focus and formulate the domestic ideology. For these experts, public dangers merged with private ones, and the family appeared besieged as never before. The noted anthropologist Margaret Mead articulated this problem in a 1949 article addressed to social workers. The methods of the past, she wrote, offered "an inadequate model on which to build procedures in the atomic age." Children were now born into a world unfamiliar even to their parents, "a world suddenly shrunk into one unit, in which radio and television and comics and the threat of the atomic bomb are everyday realities." The task for helping professionals—psychologists, psychiatrists, family counselors, and social workers—would be especially complicated because conditions had changed so drastically. Each adult faced "the task of trying to keep a world he [*sic*] never knew and never dreamed steady until we can rear a generation at home in it."

According to the experts, political activism was not likely to keep the world steady. They advocated adaptation rather than resistance as a means of feeling "at home." The modern home would make the inherited values of the past relevant for the uncertain present and future, but it had to be fortified largely from within. Married couples were determined to strengthen the nuclear family through "togetherness." With the help of experts to guide them, successful breadwinners would provide economic support for professionalized homemakers, and together they would create the home of their dreams.

The respondents to the 1955 KLS survey articulated that fervent commitment. These white middle-class Americans were among the first to establish families according to the new domestic ideology. Relatively affluent, more highly educated than the average, they were among those Americans who were best able to take advantage of the postwar prosperity. They looked toward the home, rather than the public world, for personal fulfillment. No wonder that when they were asked what they thought they had sacrificed by marrying and raising a family, an overwhelming majority of them replied, "Nothing."

One of the striking characteristics of the KLS respondents was their apparent willingness to give up autonomy and independence for the sake of marriage and a family. Although the 1950s marked the beginning of the glamorization of bachelorhood, most of the men expressed a remarkable lack of nostalgia for the unencumbered freedom of a single life. Typical responses to the question, "What did you have to sacrifice or give up because of your marriage?" were "nothing but bad habits" and "the empty, aimless, lonely life of a bachelor." One who gave up only "a few fishing and hunting trips" claimed that "the time was better . . . spent at home." Many of these men had been married for over a decade and had their share of troubles. The comment of one man was especially poignant. Although he described his wife as addicted to alcohol and "sexually frigid," he claimed that "aside from the natural adjustment, I have given up only some of my personal independence. But I have gained so much more: children, home, etc. that I ought to answer . . . 'nothing at all.'"

Women were equally quick to dismiss any sacrifices they may have made when they married. Few expressed regrets for devoting themselves to the homemaker role—a choice that effectively ruled out other life-long occupational avenues. Although 13 percent mentioned a "career" as something sacrificed, most claimed that they gained rather than lost in the bargain. One wife indicated how her early marriage affected the development of her adult identity: "Marriage has opened up far more avenues of interest than I ever would have had without it. . . . I was at a very young and formative age when we were married and I think I have changed greatly over the years. . . . I cannot conceive of life without him."

Many wives who said they abandoned a career were quick to minimize its importance and to state that they "preferred marriage," which suggests that the pursuit of both was not viable. Many defined their domestic role as a career in itself. One woman defended her decision to give up her career: "I think I have probably contributed more to the world in the life I have lived." Another mentioned her sacrifices of "financial independence [and] freedom to choose a career. However, these have been replaced by the experience of being a mother and a help to other parents and children. Therefore the new career is equally as good or better than the old." Both men and women mentioned the responsibilities of married life as sources of personal fulfillment rather than sacrifice.

Further evidence of the enormous commitment to family life appears in response to the question, "What has marriage brought you that you could not have gained without your marriage?" Although the most common answers of men and women included family, children, love, and companionship, other typical answers were a sense of purpose, success, and security. It is interesting to note that respondents claimed that these elements of life would not have been possible without marriage. Women indicated that marriage gave them "a sense of responsibility I wouldn't have had had I remained single" or a feeling of "usefulness . . . for others dear to me." One said marriage gave her a "happy, full, complete life; children; a feeling of serving some purpose in life other than making money." Another remarked, "I'm not the 'career girl' type. I like being home and having a family. . . . Working with my husband for our home and family brings a satisfaction that working alone could not."

Men were equally emphatic about the satisfactions brought about by family responsibility. Nearly one-fourth claimed that marriage gave them a sense of purpose in life and a reason for striving. Aside from love and children, no other single reward of marriage was mentioned by so many of the husbands. Included in the gains they listed were "the incentive to succeed and save for the future of my family," "a purpose in the scheme of life," and "a motivation for intensive effort that would otherwise have been lacking." One man confessed, "Being somewhat lazy to begin with, the family and my wife's ambition have made me more eager to succeed businesswise and financially." A contented husband wrote of the "million treasures" contained in his family; another said that marriage offered "freedom from the boredom and futility of bachelorhood."

Others linked family life to civic virtues by claiming that marriage strengthened their patriotism and morals, instilling them with "responsibility, community sprit, respect for children and family life, reverence for a Supreme Being, humility, love of country." Summing up the feelings of many in his generation, one husband said that marriage

> . . . increased my horizons, defined my goals and purposes in life, strengthened my convictions, raised my intellectual standards and stimulated my incentive to provide moral, spiritual, and material support; it has rewarded me with a realistic sense of family and security I never experienced during the first 24 years of my life.

The respondents expressed a strong commitment to a new and expanded vision of family life, focused inwardly on parents and children and bolstered by affluence and sex. They claimed to have found their personal identities and achieved their individual goals largely through their families. Yet, the superlatives ring hollow, as if these women and men were trying to convince themselves that the families they had created fulfilled all their deepest wishes. For as their extensive responses to other questions in the survey will show, they experienced disappointments, dashed hopes, and lowered expectations. Many who gave their marriages high ratings had actually resigned themselves to a great deal of misery. As postwar Americans endeavored to live in tune with the prevailing domestic ideology, they found that the dividends required a heavy investment of self. For some, the costs were well worth the benefits; for others, the costs were too high.

Ida and George Butler were among those who felt the costs of marriage were worth the benefits. After more than a decade together, they both claimed that they were satisfied with the life they had built. When they first embarked on married life, they brought high hopes to their union. Ida wrote that George "very nearly measures up to my ideal Prince Charming." George, in turn, noted Ida's attractiveness, common sense, and similar ideas on home life and sex. He was glad she was not the "high stepping" type, but had "experience in cooking and housekeeping." For this down-to-earth couple, the home contained their sexuality, her career ambitions, his drive for success, and their desires for material and emotional comforts.

Yet, like all things worth a struggle, it did not come easy. Ida's choices reflect the constraints that faced postwar women. She sacrificed her plans for "a professional career—I would [have] liked to have been a doctor—but we both agreed that I should finish college, which I did." Following her marriage, there were "obstacles" to her continuing to pursue a career in medicine. It was difficult to combine a professional life with a family. For one thing, the children were primarily her responsibility. She explained:

> My husband works very hard in his business and has many hobbies and friends. The care and problems of children seem to overwhelm him and he admits being an "only" child ill prepared him for the pull and tug of family life. We work closely together on discipline and policies, but he is serious minded and great joy and fun with the children [are] lacking.

If Prince Charming's shining armor tarnished a bit with the years, Ida was not one to complain. She had reasons for feeling contented with the family she helped build:

> I think a *stability* which runs through my life is important. I cannot recall any divorce or separation in my immediate family. We are a rural close-to-the-soil group and I was brought up to take the "bitter with the sweet"—"you made your own bed, now lie in it" philosophy, so it would not occur to me to "run home to mother."

Although marriage was not Ida's first career choice, it eventually became her central occupation: "Marriage is my career. I chose it and now it is up to me to see that I do the job successfully in spite of the stresses and strains of life." She felt that the sacrifices she made were outweighed by the gains—"children, a nice home, companionship, sex, many friends." George also claimed to be "completely satisfied" with the marriage. He wrote that it brought him an "understanding of other people's problems, 'give and take,' love and devotion." He felt that he sacrificed "nothing but so-called personal freedom." Her medical career and his so-called personal freedom seemed to be small prices to pay for the stable family life they created together.

For couples like the Butlers, the gains were worth the sacrifices. But their claims of satisfaction carried a note of resignation. Combining a profession with a family seemed an unrealistic goal for Ida; combining personal freedom with the role of provider seemed equally out of reach for George. They both thought they faced an either/or situation and they opted for their family roles. At first glance, this case appears unremarkable: two people who made a commitment to marriage and made the best of it. But the Butlers' choices and priorities take on a larger significance because they were typical of their generation, which was unique in its commitment to family life. The costs and benefits articulated by the Butlers—and their willingness to settle for less than they bargained for—were conditions they shared with their middle-class peers.

Unlike the Butlers, Joseph and Emily Burns emphasized the costs of family life. Haunted by the legacy of the Great Depression and World War II, Joseph expected marriage to yield the "model home" described by Nixon, where affluence, intimacy, and security would prevail. But the worrisome state of the world was inescapable for him, even in the family. Nevertheless, he articulated the way in which the world situation contributed to the intense familism of the postwar years.

At the time of his engagement, Joseph Burns had high expectations for his future marriage. He had chosen his fiancee because he could trust and respect her, her "past life has been admirable," she did not drink or smoke, and "she is pleasing to the eye." If anything made him uneasy about their prospects for future happiness, it was the fear of another depression: "If the stock market takes another drop . . . business will be all shot." The depression had already made him wary, but his disillusionment would be complete by the end of World War II.

Looking back over his life from the vantage point of the 1950s, Joseph Burns reflected:

> As I review the thoughts that were mine at the time of my marriage and as they are now, I would like to give an explanation that should be considered. . . . A young couple, much in love, are looking forward to a happy life in a world that has been held up to them by elders as a beautiful world. Children are brought up by their parents to love God and other children, honesty is a must, obedience to the Ten Commandments and to the golden rule is necessary.
>
> With such training, I started out my life only to find out the whole thing is a farce. Blundering politicians lusting for power and self-glory have defiled what is clean and right, honesty is just a word in the dictionary, love of God—who really believes in God? Love of neighbor . . . get him before he gets you.
>
> I agree it does sound cynical, but let us face the facts. Mankind has been slowly degenerating, especially since 1914, and today, what do we have to look forward to? Civil defense tests, compulsory military training, cold wars, fear of the atomic bomb, the diseases that plague man, the mental case outlook? . . . I submit these things to show how a marriage can be vitally affected as was ours and, therefore, many of my ideals, desires, and, most of all, my goal.

Joseph's cynicism toward the wider world made him place even higher hopes on the family to be a buffer. When world events intruded into that private world, he was devastated: "On December 7, 1941, the question burned in my mind, How can so-called Christian nations tear each other apart again?" Joseph resolved his personal anguish in a unique manner: he became a Jehovah's Witness. But he continued to cling to the family as security in a chaotic world. Although he claimed that the world situation had dashed his ideals, he still rated his marriage happier than average and said it gave him "the opportunity to think and reason." As far as what he sacrificed for his marriage, he wrote, "Whatever [I gave] up, which probably would have been material possessions, has been offset by the things [I] gained." Joseph's rage at the world was tempered by the benefits of having a family. He believed that the family provided him with security and satisfaction, and fulfilled at least some of the hopes he originally brought to it.

Emily Burns had a different view of their marriage, and found little comfort in her life with Joseph. Although his religious conversion was at the center of her dissatisfaction, her responses raise other issues as well. Emily complained about her husband's pessimism, coldness, aloofness, and lack of a love of beauty. She emphasized that her husband's change of religion had affected his whole life— "[his] attitude toward wife, children, home, friends, and world. Unless I become absorbed in [his religion], we [will come] to a parting of the ways, since I'm an outsider in my own home."

In addition to the major rift over her husband's conversion, Emily enumerated her sacrifices as follows:

1. A way of life (an easy one).
2. All friends of long duration; close relationships.
3. Independence and personal freedom.
4. What seemed to contribute to my personality.
5. Financial independence.
6. Goals in this life.
7. Idea as to size of family.
8. Personal achievements—type changed.
9. Close relationship with brother and mother and grandmother.

Her complaints add up to much more than religious incompatibility. They suggest some of the costs of adhering to the domestic ideology of the postwar era: an emphasis on the nuclear family at the expense of other relatives and friends, loss of personal freedom, financial independence, "goals" and "personal achievements." For Emily, like Ida Butler and others of their generation, marriage and family life led to a narrowing of options and activities. But it was a bargain she accepted because it appeared to be the best route toward achieving other goals in life. Although she would not have married the same person if she had to do it over again, she never considered divorce. The benefits she gained in marriage offset her discontent with her spouse. Her list of benefits reveals why she chose the domestic path:

1. The desire to give up all for the love of one.
2. The placing of self last.
3. A harmonious relationship until religion . . . changed this.
4. Two ideal children even though the boy is cold and indifferent like his father. (They have strong religious ties in common.)

5. A comfortable home independent of others.

6. Personal satisfaction if all turns out well.

7. Personal satisfaction in establishing a home.

In this list, Emily mentioned practically all the major subjective compensations that made marriage such an important commitment for so many women at the time. Yet, it was a qualified list. Her dissatisfaction was obvious even in her enumeration of her gains. So she struggled to improve her situation as best she could. While her husband used the last space in the questionnaire to brood over the world situation and explain his turn toward religion, Emily used it to reaffirm her faith in the potential for happiness in marriage. She wrote to Kelly and his research team: "Honestly wish this survey will help future generations to maintain happiness throughout marriage and that your book will become more than cold facts and figures. We have enough such now!"

Emily revealed a submerged feminist impulse that also surfaced in numerous testimonies of her peers. To help her formulate these ideas and influence her husband, she turned to experts:

> Have tried to arouse interest in the woman's point of view by reading parts of Dr. Marie Carmichael Stopes' works pertaining to marriage, to my husband. He says, "Oh, she is just a woman, what does she know about it?" and "How can such things (marriage relationship) be learned from a book?" I have ideas on marriage and when I see the same ideas expressed in print by a person of authority, at least I can see that I am not the only woman or person who thinks "such and such."

Recognizing that her husband was not sympathetic to her rebellion against female subordination, she predicted, "Because of a developing hard, slightly independent attitude on my part, I believe my husband's report on me will be anything but favorable."

Joseph and Emily Burns, in spite of their numerous complaints, stayed together. Through all their disillusionment and anger, they never waivered in their commitment to their imperfect relationship and insisted that their marriage was worth the struggle. Emily chafed against the limits to her freedom and turned to experts to bolster her status within the family. Joseph turned to the home to provide solace from the miseries that surrounded him in the public world. Both had invested a great deal of their personal identities in their domestic roles and were not willing to abandon them. Even if the home did not fulfill their dreams of an emancipated, fulfilling life, it still provided more satisfaction and security than they were likely to find elsewhere. For all their struggles and strains, Joseph and Emily Burns had created something together that met their needs. In 1980, they were still married to each other.

Like the Butlers, the Burnses demonstrate the powerful determination and the considerable sacrifice that went into the creation of the postwar family. Even if the result did not fully live up to their expectations, these husbands and wives never seriously considered bailing out. It is important to consider the limited options and alternatives that these men and women faced. It was not a perfect life, but it was secure and predictable. Forging an independent life outside marriage carried enormous risks of emotional and economic bankruptcy, along with social ostracism. As these couples sealed the psychological boundaries around the family, they also sealed their fates within it.

Illegitimacy and Adoption:
Black and White Teen Mothers, 1945–1965

RICKIE SOLINGER

Sally Brown and Brenda Johnson both became pregnant in 1957. Both girls waited desperately for periods that never came. Both worried about angry parents, disloyal boyfriends, and the knowing looks of classmates. Within the year, Sally and Brenda both became unwed mothers. There were limits, however, to what Sally and Brenda shared. In fact, the two girls were separated by race most effectively and more enduringly than by the private burdens of their unwed pregnancies.

Short case histories of Sally and Brenda's pregnancies show the profound commonalities and extreme differences in the experiences of black and white single pregnant females in the United States in the decades after World War II. Sally's story, so familiar to readers of women's magazines in the 1950s, goes like this:

> In 1957, Sally Brown was 16. Just before Thanksgiving, she missed her period for the second month in a row. She concluded, in terror, that she was pregnant. Sally was a white girl, the elder daughter of the owners of a small drycleaning establishment in a medium-sized city in western Pennsylvania. The Friday after Thanksgiving, she told her mother. Mrs. Brown told Mr. Brown. Both parents were horrified—furious at Sally and particularly at her boyfriend, Tim, a local "hood" they thought they had forbidden Sally to date. In October, Sally told Tim about the first missed period and in November, the second. It was obvious to Sally that Tim's interest in her was dwindling rapidly. She felt heartsick and scared.

> Mr. Brown, a businessman for twenty years with deep roots in his community, was bitterly obsessed with what the neighbors, the community and their friends at church would say if they knew about Sally. He proposed a sensible solution: to send Sally away and tell the townspeople that she was dead. The Monday following Thanksgiving, however, Mrs. Brown put her own plan into action. She contacted the high school and informed the principal that Sally would not be returning for the second half of her junior year because she'd been offered the wonderful opportunity to spend the Spring semester with relatives in San Diego. She then called up the Florence Crittenton Home in Philadelphia and arranged for Sally to move in after Christmas vacation.

> Before Sally began to "show," she left home, having spent six weeks with parents who alternately berated her and refused to speak to her. They also forbid her to leave the house.

> At the maternity home, Sally took classes in good grooming, sewing, cooking and charm. In her meetings with the Home's social worker, Sally insisted over and over that she wanted to keep her baby. The social worker diagnosed Sally as borderline schizophrenic with homosexual and masochistic tendencies. She continued to see Sally on a weekly basis.

> In mid-June, after the birth of a 7 pound 14 ounce boy, Sally told her social worker that she wanted to put the baby up for adoption because, "I don't think any unmarried girl has the right to keep her baby. I don't think it's fair to the child. I know I don't have the right."

Rickie Solinger, *Wake Up Little Susie: Single Pregnancy and Race Before* Roe v. Wade (New York: Routledge, 1992), pp. 1–9, 12–13, 15–18. Copyright © 1992. Reproduced by permission of Routledge/Taylor & Francis Books, Inc., and the author.

On June 21, Sally's baby was claimed and later adopted by a Philadelphia lawyer and his infertile wife. Before Sally's 17th birthday in July, she was back home, anticipating her senior year in high school. She had been severely warned by the social worker and her parents never, ever, to tell anyone of this episode and to resume her life as if it had never happened.

Brenda Johnson had quite a different experience in 1957, and, undoubtedly, in the decades that followed.

In February, 1957, Brenda Johnson was 16 and expecting a baby. Brenda was black. She lived near Morningside Park in upper Manhattan with her mother, an older sister, and two younger brothers. Brenda hadn't had to tell anyone about her pregnancy. Her mother had picked up on it in September when Brenda was beginning her third month. Mrs. Johnson had been concerned and upset about the situation, sorry Brenda would have to leave school and disgusted that her daughter was thinking about marrying Robert, her 19-year-old boyfriend. On the day she discovered the pregnancy, she said to Brenda, "It's better to be an unwed mother than an unhappy bride. You'll never be able to point your finger at me and say, 'If it hadn't been for her.'"

In October, Brenda had been called into the Dean of Girls office at school, expelled and told not to plan on coming back.

At first, Robert stayed around the neighborhood. He continued to be friendly, and he and Brenda spent time together during the first half of Brenda's pregnancy. As she got bigger, though, she felt sure that Robert was spending time with other girls too.

During the winter, Brenda hung around her family's apartment, ran errands and helped her mother who worked as a domestic for a middle-class family downtown. She went for her first pre-natal examination at seven months.

As Brenda got close to her due date, she worried how she would take care of a baby. There was no extra space in the apartment and no extra money in the family budget for a baby. Brenda asked her mother and her older sister about giving the baby up, maybe to her mother's relatives in South Carolina, but her mother told her firmly, "You put your child away, you might as well kill him. He'll think no one wants him."

In early March, Brenda had a girl she named Jean in the maternity ward of the local public hospital. Brenda told the nurse, "I love the baby as much as if I was married." Having no money of her own, and having been offered little help from Robert who she heard had left for Florida to find work, Brenda went to the Welfare Office. There she received a long, sharp lecture about young girls having sex that taxpayers have to bear the costs of. She was told she would have to find Robert if she wanted to get on welfare and that the welfare people would be watching her apartment building for him. The welfare worker asked Brenda if she knew what happened in some places to girls in her situation who got a second baby. The worker told her that in some states, a girl with a second illegitimate child would lose her welfare grant. She also said that some people liked the idea of putting a repeater in jail or making it impossible for her to have any more bastards.

The stories of Sally and Brenda suggest that single, pregnant girls and women were a particularly vulnerable class of females in the post–World War II era. Regardless of race, they were defined and treated as deviants threatening to the social order. Single, pregnant girls and women of whatever race shared the debased status of illegitimate mother: a mother with no rights, or a female who had, according to the dominant culture, no right to be a mother. For Sally and Brenda and the several hundred thousand girls and women in their situations each year between 1945 and 1965, illegitimate motherhood was a grim status.

The stories of Brenda and Sally also suggest that the scenarios prepared for white and black unmarried mothers diverged dramatically. This was, in part, because in the immediate pre–*Roe v. Wade* period, politicians, service providers, the media, and communities constructed the experiences of unwed mothers, black and white, in new ways. By considering the nature of these constructions, we can understand why and how racially specific prescriptions for unwed mothers emerged in the postwar era, took the particular forms that they did, and were institutionalized. In addition, we can explore the major, though still race-based, changes in the ways that black and white single pregnancy were constructed by substantial and influential segments of the public in the United States between 1945 and 1965. . . . [T]his study of unwed motherhood in the postwar era argues that many politicians and academicians, the popular media, social service professionals, and sizable segments of the public-at-large incorporated unwed mothers into the political arena and assigned them political value by race. In this way, the reproductive capacity and activity of single girls and women in this period were used to explain and present solutions for a number of social problems. . . .

In *The Feminine Mystique,* Betty Friedan identified the socially sanctioned (and presumably racially neutral) career ladder for women in the post–World War II years: Having a baby is the only way to become a heroine. But consider the response to black and white unwed mothers to see what was really demanded of women in the era of family togetherness. An unwed mother was not part of a legal, domestic, and subordinate relation to a man, and so she could be scorned and punished, shamed, and blamed. She gave birth to the baby, but she was nobody's heroine.

Many unmarried girls and women got pregnant and for one of a number of possible reasons did not get an illegal or "therapeutic" abortion. So many spent most of their months of pregnancy in some or all of the following ways: futilely appealing to a hospital abortion committee; being diagnosed as neurotic, even psychotic by a mental health professional; expelled from school (by law until 1972); unemployed; in a Salvation Army or some other maternity home; poor, alone, ashamed, threatened by the law. If a girl were so reckless as to get herself pregnant outside of a legally subordinate relation to a man in the postwar era, all of society had the right to subordinate her human dignity to her shame.

By taking a closer look at a few of the slim alternatives open to a single, pregnant woman in the two decades after World War II, we can evoke the desperate character of her predicament. We can also see how her capacity to bear children was used against her.

Consider the possibility in the mid-1950s of getting a safe, legal, hospital abortion. If a girl or woman knew about this possibility, she might appeal to a hospital abortion committee, a (male) panel of the director of obstetrics/gynecology, and the chiefs of medicine, surgery, neuropsychiatry, and pediatrics. In hospitals, including Mt. Sinai in New York, which set up an abortion committee in 1952, the panel of doctors met once a week and considered cases of women who could bring letters from two specialists diagnosing them as psychologically impaired and unfit to be mothers.

By the early 1950s, procedures and medications had eliminated the need for almost all medically indicated abortions. That left only psychiatric grounds, which might have seemed promising for girls and women desperate not to have a child.

After all, psychiatric explanations were in vogue, and white unwed mothers were categorically diagnosed as deeply neurotic, or worse. There was, however, a catch. These abortion committees had been set up to begin with because their very existence was meant to reduce requests for "therapeutic" abortions,which they did. It was, in fact, a matter of pride and competition among hospitals to have the highest ratio of births to abortions on record. But even though psychiatric illness was the only remaining acceptable basis for request, many doctors did not believe in these grounds. A professor of obstetrics in a large university hospital said, "We haven't done a therapeutic abortion for psychiatric reasons in ten years. . . . We don't recognize psychiatric indications." So an unwed pregnant girl or woman could be diagnosed and certified as disturbed, probably at considerable cost, but she couldn't convince the panel that she was sick enough. The committee may have, in fact, agreed with the outside specialists that the abortion petitioner was psychotic, but the panel often claimed the problem was temporary, with sanity recoverable upon delivery.

The doctors were apparently not concerned with questions about when life begins. They were very concerned with what they took to be their responsibility to protect and preserve the links between femininity, maternity, and marriage. . . . The mere request, in fact, was taken, according to another doctor, "as proof [of the petitioner's] inability and failure to live through the destiny of being a woman." If such permission were granted, one claimed, the woman "will become an unpleasant person to live with and possibly lose her glamour as a wife. She will gradually lose conviction in playing a female role." . . . The bottom line was that if you were single and pregnant (and without rich or influential parents who might, for example, make a significant philanthropic gesture to the hospital), your chances with the abortion committee were pretty bleak.

If a girl were white and broadly middle class, and failed to obtain a therapeutic abortion, or never sought one, there was a pretty fair chance her parents would pack her off to a maternity home just before she began to "show." Her destination was terrifying and likely out of town, but the silent interval before the departure was equally chilling. A woman, in her late fifties, remembers the freezing day in 1952 when she stood alone, outside, at the top of the majestic stairs of the law school where she was a student. Certain that she was pregnant, she considered throwing herself down the icy steps because, "You just couldn't have a baby." A Radcliffe student in the same era needed to tell someone about her pregnancy. Jean chose a close male friend who'd been her pal for years, a "regular guy." But hearing the news, he became so aroused that he attacked her sexually. Horrified, Jean rebuffed the attack and faced the young man's petulant anger: "You're pregnant, aren't you? So what's the worry, let's have some fun." Jean felt that she had "gotten herself pregnant." She thought, "I wanted to die, but he was right. I got what I deserved."

It is important to understand why it was so easy for young white women to blame themselves. Many aspects of the culture supported such feelings, but two were explicitly and immediately to the point. A single, pregnant woman was expected to take responsibility for violating norms against premarital sex and conception. Plus, she was expected to acknowledge, as a condition of changing herself, that her pregnancy was a "neurotic symptom." The experts—social workers, psychologists, psychiatrists, clergy, and others—insisted that unmarried girls and women got pregnant willfully and spitefully, if unconsciously. Professionals particularly stressed that the young woman was determined, through her pregnancy, to get back at her domineering mother. The blame was out there, authoritative and easily internalized.

Once a girl or woman entered a maternity home, there was safety and protection of a sort. Many residents appreciated the protection but felt they paid a very high price. Among some young women, it appeared to be a toss-up whether the loneliness or the lie were worse. Karen, at a Salvation Army home in California in the early 1960s said, "I think the worst part of it has been the damned loneliness. I've adjusted pretty well to the hiding and the lying to the outside world, but I've just never gotten used to being all alone inside." A recent arrival in the same Salvation Army home, angered by a moment of good-spirited camaraderie among the girls, expressed her frustration. "We're all in here to have babies we don't want. We're hiding it from the world and we'll leave here pretending it didn't happen. I hate those lies—and you just laugh."

One experience that the overwhelming majority of maternity-home residents, and many white unwed mothers who did not make it to these homes, did share was the experience of giving their babies up for adoption. In the years before *Roe v. Wade,* the experts were, again, pretty unanimously agreed that only the most profoundly disturbed unwed mothers kept their babies, instead of turning them over to a nice, middle-class man and woman who could provide the baby with a proper family. Leontine Young, the prominent authority on social casework theory in the area of unwed mothers, cautioned in 1954, "The caseworker has to clarify for herself the differences between the feelings of the normal [married] woman for her baby and the fantasy use of the child by the neurotic unmarried mother."

For complex cultural, historical, and economic reasons, black, single, pregnant women were not, in general, spurned by their families or shunted out of their communities into maternity homes, which usually had "white only" policies in any case. For the most part, black families accepted the pregnancy and made a place for the new mother and child. As one Chicago mother of a single black pregnant teenager said at the time, "It would be immoral to place the baby [for adoption]. That would be throwing away your own flesh and blood." In contrast to the very large percentage of white girls and women who gave up their babies for adoption, about nine out of ten blacks kept theirs. In a postwar New York study, 96 percent of blacks keeping their babies reported deep satisfaction with this decision eighteen months later. Yet welfare and social caseworkers persisted for years in their claims that the only reason why blacks kept their babies was that no one would adopt them.

Social workers and other human service professionals claimed repeatedly that black single pregnancy was the product of family and community disorganization. Yet in comparing the family and community responses among blacks and whites to out-of-wedlock pregnancy and childbearing, it is striking how the black community organized itself to accommodate mother and child while the white community was totally unwilling and unable to do so. The white community simply organized itself to expel them. Still, black girls and women who became pregnant while single faced a forceful array of prejudices and policies threatening to the well-being of poor, minority, single mothers and their children.

Most women in this situation felt that lack of money and adequate housing were their biggest problems, but many got hassles and worse from the agencies meant to help them. . . . A black woman in her twenties summed up the public treatment she and others faced: "I don't know. I feel that wherever you go or whatever you do, if they find out you are an unwed mother, you've had it! Like when you go to Welfare, I know they would treat you like you were nothing. I bet if I went to look for another place right now and they know I wasn't married and I had a kid, they'd refuse to even talk to me. It's just in little ways that you're looked down upon and that's what really begins to work on you." . . .

The issue of unwed motherhood was a growing concern of various professional and academic communities, government agencies and foundations, and the community-at-large during the period of this study. As these various constituencies worked to account for the rising rate of illegitimate pregnancy and to address the need and costs for services to unwed mothers, members of these groups relied on race- and class-defined stereotypes of single pregnant girls and women as they structured their particular missions. The representative white unwed mother—the one described by academic studies, government officials, agency personnel, and the media as typical, was, in general, broadly middle class, in the sense that she was perceived as having resources of value to her credit. That is, she was perceived as having parents who could and would, in her behalf, negotiate with helping institutions and underwrite their daughter's care. She had, despite her unfortunate sexual misstep, the likely potential to become a wife and mother in the postcrisis phase of her life. And most important, she was in the process of producing a white baby of value on the postwar adoption market.

The representative black unwed mother, according to the same influential groups, was a poor, Aid to Dependent Children [ADC] grant recipient who kept her illegitimate child or children. This unwed mother was most often perceived as bereft of resources. She was, rather, perceived as burdened by her illegitimate child, by her financial dependency, and by the social and cultural pathology allegedly infecting the black population in the United States.

In the postwar era, the site of the problem afflicting the typical white unwed mother was relocated from her body to her mind. The white unwed mother was no longer a genetically flawed female, as she would have been in the Progressive and prewar eras. She became, instead, a treatable neurotic. While there had been no solvent for the biological stain of illegitimacy, psychologists and social workers believed that the neuroses of illegitimacy responded to treatment. The biological stain, however, remained affixed to black unwed mothers, who were often portrayed by politicians, sociologists, and others in the postwar period as unrestrained, wanton breeders, on the one hand, or as calculating breeders for profit on the other.

These stereotypes of unwed mothers occurred so often, so predictably, and uncontestedly in postwar studies and commentaries on single pregnancy that they came to stand for *naturally occurring,* racially specific subjects. In addition, the stereotypes were so pervasive, inclusive, and powerful that the public discussion of unwed mothers at this time routinely conflated race and class, despite the fact that some white single pregnant girls and women had no resources in the sense that policy makers and social service professionals defined these, or came from communities that did not disparage or eject single pregnant girls and women and their babies. Likewise, the stereotypes were not undermined by the fact that some black single pregnant girls and women were neither poor nor ADC recipients, and some did not want to keep their illegitimate children.

In fact, it must be emphasized at this point that politicians, social workers, and others who addressed or responded to illegitimate pregnancy in the postwar years distinguished between blacks and whites, but not between rich, poor, and middle class. Thus the difficulties and options before, for example, an upper-middle-class pregnant high-school senior in Scarsdale, New York, and a pregnant, white working-class girl from Mobile, Alabama, were not publicly distinguished from each other by government officials, social workers, psychiatrists, educators, or clergy. This was the case, in part, because anybody's white baby had become valuable in the post-war era. With the rise of the psychological explanation of white single pregnancy and the decline in the belief in the genetically flawed illegitimate mother and child, white babies were born out of wedlock not only untainted but *unclassed* as well. Thus, the salient demographic fact about white unwed mothers was that they were white. The salient demographic fact about black unwed mothers, then, was that they were not white. . . .

The "case histories" of Sally Brown and Brenda Johnson obscure several aspects of the sources on postwar unmarried mothers. For the most part, quantitative and qualitative data on whites were captured *during* the pregnancy by maternity home staff, national organizations, and the governmental agencies that gave financial, re-search, and ideological support to shelters and treatment programs for white, single, pregnant girls and women. Since the black community adjusted itself to accommo-date single pregnancy and since most maternity homes discouraged or refused ad-mittance to blacks, the circumstances of these unmarried mothers were most often documented *after* the pregnancy, when the black girl or woman was a recipient of some form of public assistance.

In the sources, therefore, a white unwed mother was almost always in a state of potential motherhood. She was described and evaluated in psychological terms as she prepared for the institutional abortion of her maternity via the adoption process. The black unmarried mother, on the other hand, was institutionally de-fined as a sociological and economic disaster, and evaluated as a supplicant-dyad; a mother-and-child. . . .

In 1957, for the first time, the official number of illegitimate births in the United States broke 200,000. As high as this number was, most people who found it mean-ingful considered it a serious undercount. It was common knowledge that many white unwed mothers had the resources to conceal their pregnancies, often by travel-ing far from home to have their babies, to states that didn't record illegitimacy on birth certificates. Whatever the precise number of babies born out of wedlock, statis-ticians, policy makers, and service providers acknowledged that the illegitimacy rate (the percent of women of childbearing age who had babies out of wedlock) had tripled between 1940 and 1957, and the number of illegitimate births had increased by 125 percent since World War II began. Experts further acknowledged that while black women, far more often than white, had babies without being married, the ille-gitimacy rate for white girls and women was rising faster than for blacks. In this con-text of the rapidly increasing incidence of nonmarital childbearing, new distinctions between black and white single pregnant women emerged. Government policies and the agencies charged with carrying them out supported different meanings of black and white sexuality, pregnancy, and motherhood, meanings that justified, even demanded, different treatment of black and white single, pregnant females. The study of single pregnancy in the pre–*Roe v. Wade* era demonstrates quite clearly the reciprocal relationship between ideology and public policy—how the former infuses the latter, and how, in turn, public policies create outcomes that strengthen the bases of ideology. . . .

. . . .[I]n three major ways, all interrelated, the context in which white single pregnancy occurred and was handled had changed by the end of World War II. First, annual rates of white unwed motherhood began a steady increase in the mid-1940s and continued to climb throughout the period of this study. The demographic facts of single pregnancy were changing. As nonmarital sex and pregnancy became more common (and then very common during the later postwar period), it became increasingly difficult to sequester, punish, and insist on the permanent ruination of ever-larger numbers of girls and women, as later it became difficult to label rapidly growing numbers neurotic. In addition, in the postwar period, a growing proportion of the population in the United States assumed an affiliation with the "middle class." Many unwed mothers were also the daughters of this engrossing segment. Again, it became increasingly difficult for parents and the new service professionals, with middle-class affiliations themselves, to sanction treating "our daughters" as permanently ruined.

Secondly, the Florence Crittenton or Salvation Army maternity home may have looked the same in 1950 as in 1935, but in many ways the institutional setting for handling unwed pregnancy had altered significantly. Its postwar program was largely secular; its staff dominated by professional social workers; its funding drawn partly from community sources. Postwar maternity homes sustained the rescue homes' innovation of serving the private and individual needs of their clientele, but were, at the same time, increasingly beholden and responsive to the interests of the community. Many communities began to expect maternity homes to offer an attractive option to white unwed mothers who might otherwise turn to alternatives that parents, government officials, clergy, doctors, psychiatrists, and other service professionals did not sanction: illegal abortion, black market adoptions, or motherhood.

Finally, the ideological context in which illegitimacy occurred changed radically after the war. During the Progressive Era and throughout the 1930s, social science commentators and social service professionals explained female sexual deviance, which included illegitimate pregnancy, as the result of poisonous interaction between environmental conditions and moral degeneracy. . . .

By the mid-1940s, medical and social work professionals disdained this explanation. They accused its proponents of depending on the pessimistic view that the individual unwed mother, or potential unwed mother, was at the mercy of harmful environmental and other "forces" that had the power to determine her fate. The postwar, modern alternative claimed that illegitimacy reflected a mental not environmental or biological disorder and was, in general, a symptom of individual, treatable neuroses. An episode of illegitimacy was contingent upon the mutable mind, rather than upon fixed, physical entities—the city or the girl's body. The girl could undergo psychological treatment; she could change. She could escape being permanently defined by her error. With professional help, in a triumph of individualism, she could prevail over her past, her mistakes, her neuroses. This more positive and forward-looking postwar explanation suggested that the American environment was not culpable, nor was the female *innately* flawed. Reliance on the psychological explanation redeemed them both.

The psychological model also offered, of course, an alternate view of sexuality. Early-twentieth-century commentators believed an unwed mother had indulged in intercourse and become pregnant because she was "subnormal," suggesting an identity between mental degeneracy and the degeneracy of sex. The postwar analysts, however, accepted the neo-Freudian view that sex "expressed one's deepest sense of self." Thus, even though an unmarried girl who had coitus and became pregnant was, perforce, maladjusted, it was not her relationship to sex that was the basis of the diagnosis; it was her psychological inability to form a sanctioned relationship to a man that proved her anormative. Under these conditions a girl or woman could transcend her maladjustment simply by marriage, or by preparing herself for a marriageable future.

These more optimistic views of society, the individual, and sexuality included a paradoxically more expansive and restrictive view of the family with significant implications for the unwed mother. On the one hand, the typical middle-class white family was depicted as no longer beleaguered or threatened by economic depression or war. Families with access to postwar resources defined children as a desirable asset; in fact, culturally, "family" now required two parents and at least that many offspring. On the other hand, this postwar definition of family strongly suggested a new definition of motherhood—that it could not be achieved without a husband, outside of a properly constructed family—as postwar "womanhood" could not be achieved without a man. Both constructs insisted on the centrality of the male to female adult roles, an idea that offset the postwar concern that women were aggressively undermining male prerogatives in the United States. At the same time, then, in an environment where white illegitimate babies could be a resource for childless couples who wanted to achieve a proper family, unwed mothers became not-mothers. Further, the experts insisted that by accepting themselves as not-mothers, unwed mothers were contributing to their own rehabilitation. This prescription, again, suggested a triumph of individualism, and a triumph of American society in which even the lowly unwed mother was generously offered the option of the second chance.

The postwar recasting of white illegitimate mothers offered these girls and women a remarkable trade-off. In exchange for their babies, they could reenter normative life. A very high percentage accepted the neo-Faustian deal, suggesting that the postwar female and family ideals were powerful constructs, indeed. It also suggested that a white unwed mother in the middle decades of the twentieth century understood that not-mothers who tried to be mothers anyway stood to suffer too much. Perhaps having internalized this, or perhaps in a self-protective act of obedience, she could relinquish her baby.

An unmarried black pregnant girl looking for help in the early decades of the twentieth century could probably have found assistance only within her own family and community. Most maternity homes excluded blacks; most of the few government assistance programs that existed excluded unmarried mothers. In any case, black families and communities did not typically require each other to expel their unmarried pregnant daughters, as white families and communities did.

The combination of this and several other factors ensured that the experience of the black unwed mother was not the concern of white policy makers, taxpayers, or social service professionals before World War II. Single pregnant black women did not look beyond the boundaries of family and community for help. Thus, black single pregnancy and childbearing cost white America little, and few whites felt they had a vested interest in the subject, which, until the late 1940s, mainly stimulated the commentary of anthropologists and sociologists. Moreover, high rates of black illegitimate pregnancy supported century-old and older white beliefs about the uncontrollable sexuality and promiscuous childbearing of blacks and the source of these alleged behaviors in biologically determined inferiority. . . .

The 1940s marked a turning point in public attitudes about black single pregnancy because during this decade, for the first time, public money became available to substantial numbers of unmarried mothers and their children through the Aid to Dependent Children program; many potential recipients were black. The white public's commitment to expenditures of this type was at best ambivalent, and during succeeding decades, with the emergence of the civil rights movement, some politicians, taxpayers, and social commentators in every section of the country mounted campaigns of resistance against black unmarried childbearing women. These campaigns were implicitly or explicitly tied to the larger, related campaigns of resistance against tax-supported welfare programs for blacks and against civil rights for blacks. Some policy makers and segments of the public drew on an interpretation of culture of poverty theory that constructed black unwed mothers as a key symbol in the middle decades of endemic black pathology. They became bearers of syndromes for which white society could not be blamed and for which it should not be forced to assume responsibility. While the plight of black males, some conceded, could be tied to hiring and firing policies in industry, for example, the behavior of black women was often defined as simply and completely biologically determined and thus beyond remedy. By the mid-1960s, many politicians, taxpayers, and social analysts had become willing to locate the genesis of problems in the black community—and many problems that threatened the white community—in the wombs of black unwed mothers. . . .

 F U R T H E R   R E A D I N G

Billingsley, Andrew. *Black Families in White America* (1968).
———. *Children of the Storm: Black Children and American Child Welfare* (1972).
———. *Climbing Jacob's Ladder: The Enduring Legacy of African-American Families* (1992).
Breines, Wini. *Young, White, and Miserable: Growing Up Female in the Fifties* (1992).
Carp, E. Wayne. *Family Matters: Secrecy and Disclosure in the History of Adoption* (1998).
Cowan, Ruth Schwartz. *More Work for Mother: The Ironies of Household Technology from the Open Hearth to the Microwave* (1983).
Eisler, Benita. *Private Lives: Men and Women of the Fifties* (1986).
Graebner, William. *Coming of Age in Buffalo: Youth and Authority in the Post-War Era* (1986).

Faderman, Lillian. *Odd Girls and Twilight Lovers: A History of Lesbian Life in Twentieth-Century America* (1991).

Gilbert, James B. *A Cycle of Outrage: America's Reaction to the Juvenile Delinquent of the 1950s* (1986).

Harvey, Brett. *The Fifties: A Women's Oral History* (1993).

Kaledin, Eugenia. *Mothers and More: American Women in the 1950s* (1984).

Kennedy, Elizabeth Lapovsky, and Madeline D. Davis. *Boots of Leather, Slippers of Gold: The History of a Lesbian Community* (1993).

Luker, Kristin. *Dubious Conceptions: The Politics of Teenage Pregnancy* (1996).

Marsh, Margaret. *Suburban Lives* (1990).

May, Elaine Tyler. *Homeward Bound: American Families in the Cold War Era* (1988).

Meyerowitz, Joanne. *Not June Cleaver: Women and Gender in Postwar America, 1945–1960* (1994).

Penn, Donna. "The Meanings of Lesbianism in Post-War America." *Gender and History* 3 (Summer 1991): 190–203.

Solinger, Rickie. *Wake Up Little Susie: Single Pregnancy and Race Before* Roe v. Wade (1992).

Weiss, Jessica. *To Have and to Hold: Marriage, the Baby Boom, and Social Change* (2000).

Weiss, Nancy Pottisham. "The Invention of Necessity: Dr. Benjamin Spock's 'Baby and Child Care.'" *American Quarterly* 29 (Winter 1977): 519–546.

CHAPTER
12

The New Immigrant Family,
1965 to the Present

Prior to 1965 a quota system restricted immigration to maintain the primarily European background of immigrants to the United States. The 1965 amendments to the Immigration and Naturalization Act of 1952 replaced "national origins" quotas with preference for family members and workers and thus dramatically changed patterns of worldwide migration and the definition of an "American" family. Before 1965 approximately 80 percent of legal immigrants came from European countries; after 1965 this percentage declined to 20 percent. Since 1965 immigration from Mexico, Central America, South America, Asia, the West Indies, and Africa has increased dramatically. This influx of newcomers has profound implications for the family as immigrants simultaneously experiment with family life in their new homes and maintain ties with kin in their homelands.

With a few exceptions, historians have not yet turned their attention to the study of the "new" immigrants, perhaps because the sources for such studies—statistics collected by the U.S. government and other agencies and interviews with the immigrants themselves—are not standard fare for historians. Instead, it has so far been up to the social sciences—sociology, psychology, and anthropology—to explore the dynamics of family life among the newest Americans. Because many such studies originate in the "helping professions"—social work, for example—they tend to focus on problems of adjustment within immigrant families, such as acculturation and economic status. Due to the nature of the sources, many of these studies are also laden with statistics. But some scholars, by combining statistical information with careful fieldwork in particular immigrant communities, have produced insightful studies of the families of the new immigrants—particularly the so-called Asian model minorities, who have obtained education and succeeded economically, and the apparently more problematic Latin American immigrants, who experience more difficulties in adjusting to life in the United States at the same time that they maintain what some scholars have labeled a "transnational" orientation. The best work on recent immigrant families emphasizes the twin themes of changing gender roles and widening generation gaps,

*calling attention to the ways in which Americanization alters the power dynamics
of immigrant families.*

*Studying the families of recent immigrants is important for a number of reasons.
Most obviously, as scholars have recognized for some time, it is critical to study the
members of a "minority" population that is quickly becoming the majority. But in
addition, as some scholars have pointed out, studying the changes in new immigrant
families offers insights into changes in all American families. Indeed, many of the
changes in "the American family" over the past three decades—innovative or
frightening, depending on one's perspective—were first experienced within the
families of American immigrants.*

*Examining the history of immigrant families, then, can offer clues to several
important questions: How do different family members experience change? Who
promotes change, and who resists it? Where does power reside in the family?*

 D O C U M E N T S

The massive influx of Latin American immigrants after 1965 was foreshadowed by
the immigration of Puerto Ricans. Although more than fifty thousand Puerto Ricans
had relocated to the United States by the 1930s, immigration dramatically increased
in the 1950s as a result of Operation Bootstrap, a U.S.-sponsored effort to indus-
trialize the still largely agricultural island. Document 1 presents a daughter's interpretation of her mother's stories about one aspect of Operation Bootstrap: female
sterilization as a form of population control. The Spanish phrase *no nascas* translates
as "Do not be born."

Likewise, Document 2 features a daughter's interview with her mother. In this
oral history Ana Juarbe presents her mother's recollections about her migration to the
United States in 1951. Anastasia Juarbe's account highlights both the family nature of
the migration process and her own individual agency in the decision to migrate.

In the spring of 1975 in the wake of the communist takeover of Vietnam, Laos,
and Cambodia, nearly 1 million natives of Indochina fled their homelands for the
United States. The experience of these refugees seeking political asylum in America
represents a distinct aspect of the immigrant experience, but it also sheds light on the
generational conflict common among immigrant families.

The remaining documents present the reflections of aging Vietnamese immigrants
on the discipline of children and relationships between the generations in the United
States. In Document 3 the narrator, who came to the United States in 1975, attributes
the decline in children's respect for their elders to American ways—in particular, the
prohibition of physical punishment. Yet he also reveals that his own problems with
authority began even before migration. Ultimately, however, he blames immigration
for the widening distance between the generations, which he predicts will doom him
to loneliness in his old age.

Document 4, the comments of Ba That, echoes these concerns. Although this informant, an elderly woman who migrated to Santa Clara County, California, in 1975,
maintains close ties with her children, she suggests that in the United States the power
balance between parents and children has shifted in fundamental ways. She also indicates that while the younger generation easily adopts American ways, older people
persist in adhering to Vietnamese traditions.

1. An Immigrant Daughter Describes Population Control in Puerto Rico in the 1950s

In the countryside, women in white uniforms administer the experimental pills, test out the intrauterine devices [IUDs], encourage the operation. They are the fingertips of an immense hand reaching out to close around the wombs of Puerto Rican women and stop the children from coming. The colony does not need more workers now. It needs fewer mouths to feed, fewer voices clamoring, fewer ideas, fewer Puerto Ricans. The fist of empire clamps around the fallopian tubes of women and says to the tiny sparks of potential life in their ovaries: No nascas.

She has six children living, the oldest only nine. She has two more in the cemetery. She has piles of laundry to scrub by hand, half a dozen small mouths always hungry for more than she has in her rice pot. His touch is sweet fire in the night, but she turns away. She will have no more swelling in her belly, no more little ones crying for what she doesn't have, no more anguish than she already carries in her heart. She can feel his frustration, his hunger for her edging toward a sullen anger, and weeps dry tears, her own desire imprisoned in fear as she counts the days since last she bled, whispering into the dark: No nascas.

One in five women over twenty have had the operation, have had the tiny passageways of life severed and clamped. After a decade of propaganda it will be one in three. They are still testing other methods. The pill sometimes kills the women in these trials. They tinker with the recipe and keep handing them out. The IUDs cause intolerable cramping, especially in the young. No one tells the women that there are such things as diaphragms. An option that fits in the palm of a woman's hand. The population-planners do not trust women to make the right decisions. They will follow primitive instincts, have unscheduled children, forget their own best interests. Surgery is the method of choice. Surgery is permanent. The policymakers promote surgery. They misinform, bribe, and coerce. It is not imperial greed that causes hunger, according to their reports. It is that the colonized are too numerous. They say to the unborn generations of us: No nascas.

She is eager for the little knife that will free her from the annual babies her mother and sister bore. She enters the white room happily. Two will have to be enough. She is young still, and maybe in a few years she would have had another, but the nurse says it's the only method that is sure. This little incision will change the shape of her life, open doors, relieve her from ever having to worry again. The nurse hands her a paper to sign and she signs as if it were the deed to a house: her womb. No one has told her she could have kept her options open, used other ways to prevent babies, until she was sure. The staff of the clinic are sure. They say to the last kid she might have had when she got out of school, her newfound power of choice: No nascas.

I am the body of this story. I have tried almost every method. Spent ten days a month in an agony of cramping from the IUD, burned from the chemical gels and foams, felt my cervix turn raw and bleeding from the sponge, struggled with the

Aurora Levins Morales, *Remedios: Stories of Earth and Iron from the History of Puertorriqueñas* (Boston: Beacon Press, 1998), pp. 198–200. Copyright © 1998 by Aurora Levins Morales. Reprinted by permission of Beacon Press, Boston.

slippery caps and diaphragms, battled over condoms, charted temperatures and mucous endlessly. Raged at the thought that anyone could invent so sadistic a shape as the Dalkon shield. One day I, too, walk into the clinic. I hold the exterminating grip of empire in one hand, centuries of women counting days in the other. I can hardly bear the cheerful woman behind the desk, how unambiguous it is for her. How she can see nothing in this choice but freedom.

There is no provision in this world for the choice to be easy. Either way, we fight to live. I say to the second child I will never have, I would build a joyous entry, make a home here for you if I could. They have made you unaffordable, pressed us to the wall. I listen to all the echoes, clamoring, cascading, changing the sound of my voice when I say to my unborn child, to the children we cannot bear to bear: No nascas.

2. A Puerto Rican Remembers the Move to New York City, 1951

. . .

I wanted to come to this country, since by then [my husband] Israel's veterans benefits had run out. One hundred dollars a month to study, which we used to live on. There wasn't any work and Israel had set up a little radio repair shop (that's what he studied) but it wasn't enough to live on. I worked on a sewing machine making blouses by the dozen and I sewed to sell on my own. I set up a little business while Israel was still there [in Puerto Rico].

Then, *Comadre* Miguelina came to this country and I wanted to come even more than before and she would write about how good it was here and that you could make money . . . making dresses. Then, Israel started farming in Puerto Rico but it didn't pay. He would bundle tobacco to sell, going half and half with *Compadre* Berto.

At that point, I jumped on Israel telling him I wanted to come to this country. By then, Reynaldo [Israel's brother] had already gone to Miami and Ani [his wife] was there too. Then, Israel left for Miami. Well, he had already been there four months and he wasn't sending me a penny. He would write, but he didn't send me a single penny. But since I had rented out my house and gone to live with *Comadre* Miguelina's (for $15 a month), he figured I was making $25 a month on the house and never sent us a cent. I had gone to this guy ('cause, you know, I'm a woman who's always been a fighter), I told this guy who was a soldier, "Look, I'll rent you my house on the condition that you pay me five month's rent in advance." And he said yes right away and I made the deal.

So, Israel was already in this country but he didn't want me to come. He wanted me to stay over there in Puerto Rico. I rented out the house anyway (you see, I've done things on my own a lot, I've always been independent).

Then, I wrote Israel a letter [saying] that I'd be able to come over later on. I wrote him a letter: "Israel, I'm coming on such and such a date." I didn't pay any attention to what he said. "Israel, I arrive on such and such a date. Pick me up." So, in Isabela I bought the ticket to come here. I don't remember how much it cost me

Ana Juarbe, "Anastasia's Story: A Window into the Past, a Bridge to the Future," *Oral History Review* 16, 2 (Fall 1988): 19–20. Reprinted by permission of the Estate of Ana Juarbe.

but they were cheap in those days, $50 or $45. Well, I got here I think in September. Come to think of it, I came here at a time when about two or three weeks later a bit of snow fell. I think I got here at the end of 1951. . . .

3. An Elderly Vietnamese Man Despairs of Parent-Child Relations in the United States, 1989

. . .

The behavior of Vietnamese children in America is just beginning to change to the American direction. In Vietnam, children must listen to their parents and must not argue against them. They see the freedom of teenagers here, so they tend to imitate them. One of my good friends from Vietnam is really disturbed by the behavior of his five children here. One day, they did something wrong, I don't know what, but he got so mad! He threatened them with a kitchen knife. His wife called the police. Later, the man complained to me and other friends, "In Vietnam, my children listened to me, but over here they are not afraid of me anymore. They call the police." He was depressed.

With my family, too, my children, and their children, do not obey strictly. One of my sons has children who disobey and argue against him. He is afraid that they have too much freedom going to school; they associate too freely with girls, and they might run away together. So my son prohibited his sons from using the telephone, and as a result there is much disappointment in that family.

These things are very difficult, and I don't know what to do because of the loss of traditional custom. Other people also complain that their children living in the United States imitate the new life and distort our old Vietnamese ways. They have freedom to be promiscuous. I know that in Vietnam some girls are not good, too. But because of the strict control of the parents, that really helped the children. Both boys and girls need to be controlled. If boys have lots of freedom, if they are let loose, that is not good. They will do anything they want, pay no respect to their parents, lie to them, and fool around while pretending to take money for school. . . .

Girls here have parents who cannot control them. They will grow up and marry anyone they want. Our old way was good in Vietnam, but it won't work here. My eldest son has two daughters about 15 and 20 years of age who told their father that he is too strict. They wanted to move out and live with their friends. My son consulted a counselor, saying, "My daughters are really stubborn ones. What shall I do?"

The counselor, an American female teacher, said, "You cannot beat your children in America; that is against the law. Since the eldest daughter wants to move out, let her go; you cannot do anything about it. The other one is too young and cannot go. Try to control her, but not the older one."

I agree that if the eldest child is out of control, we have to let him or her go, but often I do not think it is good. Such a child is inexperienced and will make many

James M. Freeman, *Hearts of Sorrow: Vietnamese-American Lives* (Stanford, Calif.: Stanford University Press, 1989) pp. 362–368. Copyright © 1989 by the Board of Trustees of the Leland Stanford, Junior University. Used with the permission of Stanford University Press, www.sup.org.

mistakes. With regard to the Confucian rule, a girl should never escape the control of her parents until she gets married. Over here, females are as free as males. . . .

Many people say that the difficulties with the Vietnamese family are a result of living in America, but that is not entirely true. Even in Vietnam, our children did not always follow our wishes.

In Vietnam we try to select a wife for our son who relates well to the family, so the selection should be done very carefully. In America, it is not the same way. Here children are very free; they marry whomever they choose, and they don't pay attention to what their parents say.

That happened to me in Vietnam. I had a friend who wanted to marry one of his daughters with one of my older sons. On the eve of the lunar New Year, that man and his wife brought gifts to us, so I had to do the same in turn. But my son kept silent. He took a girl in Saigon city, married her, and had two children by her. He misled me. Although he had been married for a long time, he never told me. He just kept quiet and avoided our attempts to arrange his wedding. Finally in 1968 my wife told him, "If you will not have a wedding, I will delay the wedding of your younger sister because the elder must marry first."

His mother was absent when he told me the truth. "I already have a wife. Not only that, but we already have two girls." It was a real embarrassment. The wife we had selected for him was well educated; the woman he took for a wife had a very low education. My wife and I were very upset, for our son had made us lose face. On the eve of the New Year, I had to go for the last time to my friend's house and offer him the last gift and confess that my son had already become married behind my back. I got so mad that I said to my son, "From now on, I never want to see you again! Please leave the family forever!" For about four years I did not see him.

In 1975, like us, my son and his family escaped by boat to the United States. He now lives in another part of the country, where he has a successful professional career. He and his family have visited us only once, when we lived in another state.

The behavior of this son affected our next two sons and several of our other children. His behavior was the key, because he set a bad example for the others. In Vietnam, when I mentioned how displeased my wife and I were about his choosing a girl whom we had never known, my next two sons would reply, "We are now adults. Why are you worried about who our wives might be? Let us be free about that matter." From that time, my wife and I connived to choose the right girls for them.

One day the second son roared up to our house in his Honda motorcycle accompanied by a girl sitting in back. "This is my friend," he said to his mother. He said nothing to me. My wife was silent. The woman came to the sitting room and stayed there alone. No one chatted with her. After an hour my son left with her. We never saw her again.

The third son also refused to listen to his mother. He knew many girls. And he refused the offer of a marriage set up for him by one of our relatives. One day in 1973 he came to us and said he wanted to marry a girl he had met in Saigon. We did not know that girl, but he insisted many times. He said he loved her and she loved him; no matter what, they would be married. So I consulted a fortune-teller who lived in my hamlet.

After reading the fortune-telling book, that man said, "The couple are not well matched. Their ages are against each other. Their future life will not be good."

I told my son what the fortune-teller had told me, and he in turn told his prospective father-in-law. That man, however, was a Christian who did not believe in fortune-telling. He said, "It's okay; I agree to marry my girl to you." He didn't care about bad fortune; he didn't care that the parents had not arranged the wedding, as long as his daughter had a husband. So I could not do anything else. We did not organize a big wedding; we just went through the formality.

The fortune-teller was right; it has not worked out well. In America, they live in the same city as we do, but we have no contact with them at all. We do not even know their telephone number or address.

A fourth son also does not obey us. He was for a while involved with a girl-friend of his own choice of whom the family was a troublemaker. We fear that he will follow the direction of his eldest brother.

Our eldest daughter married a man whom we did not think was a good match. Her husband has now left her.

Still another son, who lives at home with us and has seen all this, says, "You, Father and Mother, are always serious. After my wedding we will live apart."

Another of our daughters is married happily and has a small child. We gave her complete freedom to choose her husband here in America. I do not know much about her husband's behavior, but I gave permission, first, because she wanted him; second, because her brothers and sisters accepted him; and finally, because we also liked him when he came to visit us. We also write frequently to his parents in Viet-nam. That marriage has worked out well. Even so, when I think back on it, I do not have any happy memories of our children.

In Vietnam, if a son refused to obey his parents, they might throw him out and say that he should never see them again. When they died, he would not be allowed to come back for the ceremonies, nor would he be allowed to wear symbols of mourn-ing. In any family, most children are obedient, but I know many people who have been disowned. Sometimes parents relent when it is a son they have dismissed; for girls, disobedience is unforgivable.

These rules were strictly enforced in Vietnam. In America, the problem is that we emphasize control of children, while Americans emphasize their freedom. One of my wife's sisters-in-law in Saigon had a son who brought home a girl whom he said he wanted to marry. It is very peculiar for a bride to visit the groom's house before the groom visits the bride's house. The groom should do some sort of service of help to her family; we call it "groom's work." [This was found in the past in the country-side, where the economy was agricultural.]

Even after the engagement, the future bride is not allowed to visit the future groom's house. In fact, in embarrassment, she often avoids him when he visits her house. My wife's sister-in-law was quite offended, and so she replied with a big in-sult, "What an ill-bred girl she is! The boy is not yet a groom, but already she makes herself like a bride." Perhaps had her son not brought that girl to the house in violation of the custom, his mother might have relented, but she was so angry she refused to hold a wedding for him.

Parents will not be able to hold back the changes that are happening. In America, girls will select their own husbands. Among my friends, the majority now do that, including my own youngest daughter. . . .

Many times I go to the gatherings of the Vietnamese elderly people. Most of the time, I hear them talking about the good behavior of the Vietnamese children.

They talk of the piety of their children and the good behavior of their married children. Sometimes I felt bad; my family has had a rough time, while these people bragged that everything was going well.

Then I took a trip to Hawaii with other Vietnamese people, most of them women. When they discussed their sons, daughters, and daughters-in-law, it was very different: bad behavior, how wives cheated on their husbands, how children disobeyed and showed no respect, how they told their parents not to interfere in their lives because it's none of their business, how they said that they had a higher regard for their spouse than their parents. When I heard all that, I did not feel so bad.

In America, there is nothing to hold our family together. In this city alone, my family numbers some 16 people spanning three generations: we live in several different locations in the city. We also have others of our family living elsewhere in America. Even so, we have nothing to look forward to. If I returned to Vietnam, the Communists would put me in a reeducation camp, which would kill me. But here in America, my wife and I will die a lonely death, abandoned by our children.

4. Ba That Explains Changing Power Dynamics in the Vietnamese American Family, 1989

. . .

I regret that we moved. I wanted to stay there. My children insisted that we move. Now I would like to go back, but my children are here, so I cannot. I prefer to live in the countryside, as we first did when we came to America, and not in a city as we do now. It is like Vietnam. I didn't want to leave Vietnam, but all of my children were gone; I'm old, and they have to take care of me. So I had to follow them. That's what I did again in America. . . .

My children take care of me like usual. I have a hot temper; I always yell at them if they do something wrong. I see that children do not obey me as much as when they were in Vietnam. It's sad sometimes; it creates anger. When I lived in Vietnam, it was different. My children were young at that time. We took care of them so they obeyed us more. They were afraid of us and respected us more.

Here we need them more; they don't need us.

In Vietnam, if I wanted to go to the market, I just picked up a basket and went. I didn't need anybody to take us. Over here, I have to wait until the [children] take us. If they don't go, we don't go. This makes me feel sad, yes.

Here in America, I just remain. I don't change my traditional ways; I still keep them. My children have adapted to American customs in hair styles and dress. While I was on the island of Guam, I heard women say, "Now most Vietnamese women in the U.S.A. will become men [dress like men]." And that is true; they dress according to what the people here do, except older women like me, who keep our old ways. The older women don't change much, and most of the older men don't change either.

We see big differences in food given to babies. In Vietnam, we did not have baby food. Mothers nursed their babies or gave them condensed milk or powdered

James M. Freeman, *Hearts of Sorrow: Vietnamese-American Lives* (Stanford, Calif.: Stanford University Press, 1989), pp. 371–375. Copyright © 1989 by the Board of Trustees of the Leland Stanford, Junior University. Used with the permission of Stanford University Press, www. sup.org.

milk or cow milk. Children here get used to American food. Our granddaughter eats hamburgers and canned food, but she will not touch Vietnamese food. She is unable to eat. She tastes only a teaspoonful; then she sits there and looks. So her mother buys her hamburgers. For breakfast she eats cereals, bread, milk, and noodles. When she was young, she ate Vietnamese food, but only a little. She likes bread. Once in a while I cook rice chicken soup; she will eat only the rice, nothing more. Now she can eat imperial rolls and fried rice, but will not touch regular rice. Once in a while we just force her to eat it. Her mother still feeds her rice, even though she's now 11 years old. I hear that other Vietnamese children are the same.

Me, I cannot eat American food. No hamburgers. I cannot eat butter or cheese, not even beef, ham, or milk. I can eat some American cake, but no cookies; they are too sweet. But my husband, he can eat anything. As for me, I eat lots of chicken with lots of salt and lemon crust, and I barbecue them. I eat roast pork, eggs, chicken curry, chicken rice soup, duck rice soup, boiled vegetables such as squash, fried vegetables, fried fish, and potato. I eat a lot of the American vegetables because we have the same kinds in Vietnam; fruits too.

If it were peaceful, I would live in Vietnam. I would live in the countryside because I have property and fields near the river, also a big garden with lots of fruits such as jackfruit and banana. I'd go back and live there. I'd make my living selling rice paper or chicken and pigs. It's more of a comfortable life.

Over here, for older people, we receive money from the government; if not, we would die of starvation because we are older and don't know what to do. In Vietnam, we have less fear of survival, but over here, I'm afraid that when I get older I'll have to go into a nursing home to stay there, because all of my children are working. My husband and I have to stay home ourselves, all alone. Now I am fine and can stay home, but later what will happen? Old age here is scary.

Children over here don't take care of their parents. In Vietnam, if poor, a person lived with his children; if rich, with only one child, possibly the youngest. Life was much more comfortable if rich because children and grandchildren would take care of you.

In America, every time we want to go somewhere, we have to wait for our children to take us. If we want to visit relatives, we don't know what to do. In Vietnam, we could travel around much more easily.

In Vietnam, a person would build a house. Children would want to remain in that house. Even if they went away for some reason, they would want to be close by at the time of the death of the parent, and they themselves would want to be buried near their ancestors. Rich people preserve a piece of property on which to bury the family members; it's a grave property. From the twenty-third to the thirtieth day of the new year, children must visit the graves of their ancestors.

In Vietnam we had a house. Once in a while our children came back to visit. Our youngest remained in the family, while those who lived close by would see us often. Here in America, that's not so. Two of my sons I never see. I don't even know my grandchildren, how tall they are.

The difference is that over here children do not obey their parents; in Vietnam, they obeyed us more. Over here, whenever we say something, they like to argue about it. My husband and I dislike this. If our children want something and we don't like it, they will not listen to us. Things we consider to be right they consider wrong.

Like a wife they select whom we don't like. They argue with us, against it, saying that it's right for them and that they will take the responsibility for it. They claim it's their *right* and that we don't have the right to tell them what to do. It is just like we are strangers; they won't let us interfere. One of my sons has a girlfriend. She came to visit him several times. Each time she ignored my family, just walked in and did not say hello, sat down on the sofa and faced the window. I assume she came from Central Vietnam because she didn't talk to us. I assume that every time she came here she must have called my son first because I see that my son always waits at the door to greet her at the first ring. After conversation with her, they take off.

Sometimes I get really upset. I talk to him. He argues with me. It's his selection, his way; it depends on him; parents don't have the right; nobody has the right; this is his right. Not only does he tell us this, but he wrote me a letter like that.

Once I talked to my younger son. I told him that when a son marries, the family must like the marriage to have happiness. If the family does not like your wife, it's very complicated, less happy. So when getting married, let your parents choose for you the right one so that when your wife bears children, they will look very nice. But if she's ugly, she'll give birth to ugly children.

My son replied, "You're too old-fashioned. Parents-in-law must be equal to your own parents to satisfy you. The wife's parents must be suitable or equal to your own family. My wife will stay with me; she won't stay with you parents. Therefore there is no need to select to suit you."

This sort of behavior is found among the educated younger children, who consider themselves to be higher in evolution, less old-fashioned. Even in Vietnam, this began, and they have continued this trend here in America. In Vietnam, I had lots of granddaughters-in-law. They dared not behave like this girlfriend of my youngest son. In Vietnam, they respected us a lot; not here. What has happened to me has also happened to others. My niece found that her daughters-in-law behave like that, with disrespect. So her children are like my children.

What makes me most upset is when I talk to my children and they argue. Then I am very sad. I told my children that I do not say anything now, but that they should not disturb me. I told them, whoever they marry, whenever they come to my house, they should not disturb me. If I am disturbed, I will curse them, and they will have to carry bad things forever. "I don't want to see your faces. Do not disturb me." So they know and they don't come. Our children do not keep the old traditions. They live apart from one another. . . .

 E S S A Y S

In the first essay, Maura I. Toro-Morn, a professor of sociology and anthropology at Illinois State University, uses in-depth interviews with Puerto Rican women living in Chicago to explore the gendered dynamics of migration to the United States. Toro-Morn highlights women's productive and reproductive work as both *mujeres de la casa* (housewives) and wage workers, calling attention to the ways that socioeconomic status and education affect these women's attitudes toward work and family.

The second essay, an excerpt from Boston University sociologist Nazli Kibria's 1993 study of Vietnamese Americans in Philadelphia, *Family Tightrope*, examines relationships among older and younger Asian Americans. Using oral histories, popular folklore, and proverbs, Kibria explores both the attitudes of Vietnamese elders toward Vietnamese American youth and the values and behavior of Vietnamese American children, adolescents, and young adults. Rather than emphasizing either generational conflicts or intergenerational continuity, she concludes that both patterns characterize the Vietnamese American community she studies.

Puerto Rican Women and Their Families in Chicago

MAURA I. TORO-MORN

. . .

This article examines how working-class and better-educated middle-class Puerto Rican women enter the migration process, how gender relations shape their move, and how women adapt to their new homes in the United States. Specifically, I focus on the experiences of married working-class and middle-class women. My interviews suggest that while both groups migrated to the United States as part of what sociologists have called a "family stage migration," there are important differences between them that challenge our understanding of women's migration.

In the first part of this article, I explore how working-class and middle-class Puerto Rican women moved to the United States. I pay particular attention to the language women used to describe this process. While middle-class women talked about their migration as motivated by professional goals, working-class Puerto Rican women talked about how they came to take care of their children, husbands, and families. When confronted with these answers, I found that the experiences of married working-class women did not fit the traditional explanations found in the migration literature. Here, I draw on the feminist construct of productive and re-productive work, to argue that our current definition of "labor migration" is too narrow. Not all labor migrations need to relate to productive activities (i.e., the entrance of immigrant women in the labor market). One very important aspect of labor migrations should include the work of women who migrate and do not necessarily join the labor force, but stay and do the reproductive work that supports families and immigrant communities. Within this category, there are women who migrate as wives, as grandmothers, or as relatives, and whose major responsibility is to help with the reproductive tasks—be they housework or child care—of their own families and/or their extended families.

The second part of this article explores how, once in the United States, both working-class and middle-class Puerto Rican women had to confront the duality of being responsible for the reproductive work that takes place at home and the productive work outside the home. The interviews indicate that both working-class and middle-class Puerto Rican women tried to provide as much continuity in the process of forming and re-creating family life. Again, important class differences emerged when comparing married working-class and middle-class migrants. The interviews suggest that working-class husbands may have accommodated to their

Maura I. Toro-Morn, "Gender, Class, Family, and Migration: Puerto Rican Women in Chicago," *Gender and Society* 9, 6 (December 1995): 713–725. Copyright © 1995 by Sage Publications, Inc. Reprinted by permission of Sage Publications, Inc.

wives' temporary employment, but that did not change the traditional division of labor within the household. Instead, working-class women had to develop strategies to accommodate their roles as working wives. Middle-class women developed strategies both as family members and as individuals in the process of adjusting to life in Chicago. The strategies they devised, however, reflected their class position. When juggling family and work responsibilities, educated and professional women gave career goals equal standing alongside family obligations.

Methodology

From March 1989 to July 1990, I interviewed women in the Puerto Rican community of Chicago, which covers the areas of West Town, Humboldt Park, and Logan Square. . . . The sample of married women consisted of 17 informants. Eleven were mostly working class, with little education, who came to Chicago in the early 1950s and 1960s. Generally, at the time of migration, they were married—or were soon to be married—and most had children. The six professional and educated women in the sample had all migrated in the late 1960s and had over 14 years of education at the time of their move. Most educated informants described themselves as predominantly middle class and from urban backgrounds in Puerto Rico. At the time of the interview, two informants had earned doctorate degrees. Ten respondents were in their sixties; seven were in their forties and fifties. Different respondents will be identified by pseudonyms. . . .

Gender, Class, and Migration

The most significant movement of Puerto Ricans to the United States took place at the end of World War II. . . . In the late 1940s, the impact of U.S. investment and modernization of the economy transformed Puerto Rico from a predominantly agricultural to an industrial economy. Operation Bootstrap, as the development model became popularly known in Puerto Rico, attracted labor intensive light manufacturing industries such as textiles and apparel to Puerto Rico by offering tax incentives, cheap labor, and easy access to U.S. markets. . . . These changes in Puerto Rico's economy had profound consequences for Puerto Rican families. The development model was unable to create enough jobs, and working-class Puerto Ricans began to leave the island, heading for familiar places like New York City and new places like Chicago. News about jobs spread quickly throughout the island, as informal networks of family members, friends, and relatives told people of opportunities and helped families migrate.

My interviews suggest that working-class women and their families used migration as a strategy for dealing with economic problems. Married working-class women, in particular, talked about migration as a family project. For them, migration took place in stages. Husbands moved first, secured employment and housing arrangements, and then sent for the rest of the family. Even single men frequently left their future brides in Puerto Rico, returning to the island to get married as their employment and economic resources permitted. Some women came as brides-to-be, as they joined their future husbands in Chicago. For example, Rosie's mother came to Indiana in order to join her husband working in the steel mills. He had been recruited earlier, along with other workers in Puerto Rico. Once at the mills in Indiana, these men often found better jobs and moved on. They went back to Puerto Rico, got married, and returned to Indiana. Others arranged for the future brides to join them in Chicago. Alicia's explanation indicates how these decisions took place within the family context.

> My husband and I were neighbors in San Lorenzo. Before he left to come to Chicago, he had demonstrated an interest in me. Initially, I did not accept him, because I did not want to get married so young. We started corresponding and I agreed to the relationship. . . . In one letter, he asked me to marry him and come to live with him in Chicago. I told him that he needed to ask my father's permission. . . . He wrote to my father but my father did not agree . . . it took some convincing by my cousins who were coming to Chicago so that he would let me come and get married. My cousin took it upon himself to be responsible for me and that's how I came. Within two weeks of getting here, we got married.

Alicia's experience suggests that even within the constraints of a patriarchal society, single women were active in negotiating their moves to Chicago.

Married working-class women left the island to be with their husbands and families, even though some reported to have been working before leaving. Lucy and Luz were working in apparel factories in Puerto Rico when their unemployed husbands decided to move. Economic opportunities seemed better for their husbands in the United States and they both quit their jobs to move. For others, like Teresa and Agnes, both husband and wife were looking for work, when news about job opportunities came via relatives visiting the island. Similarly, Agnes also came with her husband in the 1970s after a cousin who was visiting from Chicago convinced them that there were better job opportunities for both of them.

Working-class women also talked about the struggles over the decision to move. Fear of the unknown bothered Lucy. In addition, with a baby in her arms and pregnant with a second child, Lucy did not have anyone to help her in Chicago, but accompanied by her sister and her youngest child, Lucy followed her husband. Shortly after her migration, Lucy's mother and her sister-in-law arrived to care for the children while Lucy worked. Asuncion's husband could not find work in Puerto Rico either, so he migrated to Chicago with his relatives. Asuncion took a vacation from work and came to visit. Her family

> started talking about how they were recruiting case workers in the welfare office that could speak Spanish. They all had connections there and could very easily help me get a job. In fact, I went just to try it.

Asuncion gave in to the pressure and started working while still holding her job in Puerto Rico:

> I worked for six months, but I had so many problems, I wanted to go back. Life here [in Chicago] is really different when compared to the Island's. I was really confused. I cried a lot. I had left my children behind and I missed them a lot.

In fact, Asuncion went back to Puerto Rico because she missed her daughters; she was uncertain about what would happen to her marriage. She remembered how she felt when her husband took her to the airport:

> I really did not know whether I was going to see him again. He wanted to stay here and start a new life. I really did not care about what would happen to us and our relationship;

I thought about my daughters. I owe it to my mother that my marriage was saved. After I returned to Puerto Rico, she sat me down and told me that my place was to be with my husband. That he was a good man and that my place was next to him. That I had to think about my children growing up without a father, so I returned again.

As Asuncion's case illustrates, she struggled between her husband's needs in Chicago and those of her children on the Island. Ultimately, moving to Chicago meant maintaining the family and saving her marriage.

Victoria's story is somewhat similar. She was living in her hometown of Ponce when she fell in love with the son of a family visiting from Chicago. She became pregnant and, in keeping with Puerto Rican culture, she was forced to marry him. Without consulting with Victoria, the young man's parents sent him a ticket so that he could return to Illinois. Once in Chicago, he expected she would follow.

I did not want to come. . . . One day he sent me a ticket for me and my baby girl. I sent it back because I did not want to come. But he send it back again. So I had to come. . . . I had no idea where I was going, I had lived all my life in Ponce and had never left Ponce. I was so scared. . . . In 1966, she followed her husband to Chicago against her will.

The emotional and cultural shock was very strong:

I cried my eyes out. In Puerto Rico, you are always outside and carefree. Here, we lived in small apartments, we could not go outside. We could not open the windows. We did not know the language.

When her second child was to be born, Victoria was so intimidated with the city that she asked her mother to send a plane ticket so that she might give birth in Puerto Rico. Within less than a year, she had returned to Puerto Rico. Eventually her husband joined her also, but he was not happy. Soon he began to disappear and neglect his responsibilities as a father. In one of his escapades, he went back to Chicago. Once again, he sent for her. This time, however, Victoria began to analyze the situation in different ways.

In Puerto Rico, I did not have any money to pay rent, electricity, and other bills or even feed my babies. I recognized it was a difficult situation, but I thought to myself that if I stayed I had less opportunities to do something with my life. So, I thought that if I returned and brought my other brother with me they could help me and eventually even my mother could come and I could get myself a job. I had noticed that there were factories close to where we lived and my sister-in-law had offered to help me as well. My brother who had moved with me the first time had gotten married and brought his wife with him.

Victoria had changed; as a married woman who followed her husband to Chicago, she began to develop her own agenda and use migration as a way for its realization.

Of the women who followed their husbands to Chicago, only two (Luz and Rita) complained that their husbands failed to fulfill their end of the bargain, forcing them to use migration as a way to assert their claims as wives. Lucy's husband had just returned from the military when he began talking about migrating to Chicago. Initially he went to Indiana where some relatives helped him find a job. When he was laid off, he learned through other friends that there were job opportunities in Illinois. He then moved to Chicago, promising to send for the family once he secured employment. But, according to Luz, he had been working for quite a while and had not sent for her and the children. Also, he was not sending any money to support the family. Instead, her husband kept putting off sending for her, and she was forced to confront him. Finally, Lucy left Arecibo in 1951 to join her husband and save her marriage. Rita was also forced to confront her husband by letter, reminding him of his promise to bring the rest of the family to Chicago. Even though it was over 20 years ago, Rita stated with emotion that she

> had to write him a letter. Because it had been over a year and he didn't send for me. I had three babies and I was alone. When he left, he said that he was going to send for me shortly and it had been a year and I was still waiting.

He replied that he did not want her to come, because living in Chicago was hard and she and the children would not be able to get used to the weather. She replied, "either you send the ticket or send me the divorce papers." Apparently, this was a typical problem for Puerto Rican women when their husbands preceded them in migration. . . .

Middle-Class Migrants

. . .

In contrast to working-class migrants, moving was a joint family project for married middle-class women. In addition, the language this group used to describe the move differs from that of the working-class married woman. Middle-class women came with their husbands and had an agenda of their own. Aurea met her husband while attending the University of Puerto Rico. Initially, the couple moved from San Juan to Boston to enable her husband to take a university position. In 1971, a new job opportunity brought them to Chicago. In fact, Aurea talked about moving as a mutual arrangement between her and her husband. She saw the move to Chicago as an opportunity to join community and political struggles. Shortly after arriving in the city, they bought a house—something that took years for working-class families to accomplish.

Brunilda had just completed her bachelor's degree and was working as a field researcher for the University of Puerto Rico when she was asked to work with a group of American scholars who came to Puerto Rico to conduct research in the 1970s. The researchers were very pleased with her work and offered her a position if she would relocate to Chicago. They promised they would help her to make the transition. She had just been married when the job offer came, and she felt that was a big problem:

> My husband did not want to come, he said that he did not know English. He just did not want to come. I told him that there were no doubts in my mind as to what that job meant for me. It was a great opportunity, and I was not going to let it go. If he did not want to come, then I guess that was it, I knew I was coming with him or without him.

In this case the roles changed. It was the husband who was asked to follow his wife; initially he resisted, but the job meant so much to Brunilda that she was willing to sacrifice her marriage. Brunilda, therefore, moved within a professional rather than a family network. In addition, she did not live close to other Puerto Ricans in Chicago because the research team found her a place to stay closer to the university. After completing her work with the university researchers, Brunilda started graduate studies at a local university. She went to school full time for a year and in 1971 started working as a community organizer in the south side of Chicago.

Vilma had moved from San Juan to Wisconsin to go to graduate school. While in Madison, she met her future husband and they moved in together. They had completed their degrees when he was offered a job in Chicago. In 1986, they both relocated to Chicago. Vilma described her move

> as very traditional in terms that I had just finished my masters and was looking for a job when my "compañero" (living in boyfriend) got a job offer in Chicago. I followed him to Chicago, but I came not only for him, but also knowing that in Madison there was no professional future for me.

Comparing the migration of married working-class and middle-class Puerto Rican women offers some insights into how gender and class shapes the migration process. As my interviews suggest, both working-class and middle-class Puerto Rican women found themselves migrating as part of a family migration. Married working-class women came to support their husbands and be with their families. In other words, their roles as mothers and wives compelled them to migrate. The narratives suggest that some women struggled over the decision to move. In contrast, educated married middle-class women were less encumbered by such relations of authority. They shared in the decision making and were less dependent on other family members to make the move. As Vilma's and Brunilda's stories indicate, these middle-class migrants clearly had professional agendas of their own. How does each confront the problem of balancing family and work responsibilities?

Gender, Family, and Work

In Puerto Rican culture, there is a gender-specific division of labor consisting of men's work (*trabajo de hombre*) as the providers and women's work (*trabajo de mujer*) as the caretakers of the home and children. Underlying this gender division of labor is a patriarchal ideology, machismo, emphasizing men's sexual freedom, virility, and aggressiveness, and women's sexual repression and submission. Machismo represents the male ideal and plays an important role in maintaining sexual restrictions and the subordination of women. This ideology rationalizes a double standard where a woman can be seen as *una mujer buena o una mujer de la casa* (a good woman or a good homemaker) or as *una mujer mala o una mujer de la calle* (a bad woman or a woman of the streets). A man has to show that *él lleva los pantalones en las casa* (he is the one who wears the pants in the family) and that he is free to *echar una canita al aire* (literally meaning, blow a gray hair to the wind; culturally, it means to have an affair).

The counterpart of machismo is *marianismo* in which the Virgin Mary is seen as the role model for women. Within this context, a woman's sexual purity and virginity is a cultural imperative. Motherhood, in Puerto Rican culture, lies at the center of such ideology. A woman is viewed in light of her relationship to her children and, as Carmen, one of my informants, put it, in her ability "dar buenos ejemplos" (to provide a good role model).

Among working-class Puerto Ricans, gender roles are very rigid. Although industrialization and the entrance of women in the labor force completely contradicts this ideal of *la mujer es de la casa* (women belong to the home), in Puerto Rico the domestic role of working class remains intact. Working mothers are primarily responsible for the care of the home and the children.

In Chicago, in keeping with this ideology surrounding family values, some working-class husbands resisted their wives working. The men would take a double shift so that wives could stay home, take care of the children, and do housework. Carmen stayed home to care for her children and was very proud of her accomplishments as a mother, but economic necessity obliged other husbands to conform to women's work outside the home. Like Lucy said, "I did not come here to work, but I had to." Alicia elaborates, "in those days one paycheck was like nothing. We put together both paychecks and there were times that he had very little next to nothing left. By that time there were other relatives living with us and there were lots of mouths to feed."

The same network of family and friends that helped in the process of migration helped working wives find employment in Chicago factories. Josefa, Lucy, Luz, Rita, and Teresa all reported working in factories. Chicago's political economy in the 1950s allowed these women to find factory jobs with relative ease; however, most working-class married women viewed employment as a temporary necessity. The way women talked about their work experiences reflected this attitude. Josefa and her husband worked not only to meet the family needs but also to take care of the medical expenses of their child. When her daughter started going to school, she stopped working. Alicia worked in a factory prior to getting pregnant; after having the baby, she stopped working. When the family wanted to buy a house, Alicia went back to work for two years. After her second child, she stopped working altogether. Brunilda started working in a factory immediately upon arriving from Puerto Rico, but when she became pregnant, she stopped. Lucy was the only married respondent who stayed in the factory for a prolonged period of time. Eventually, she stopped working when she got sick.

Although most working-class married women gave in to their husbands' wishes for them to stay home, Rita illustrates how a woman resisted those traditional roles and even sought to change them. Rita's husband did not want her to work. According to Rita:

> After I got to Chicago, my husband didn't want me to work. But I wanted to work. I wanted to work because you can meet people, learn new things, and one can also leave the house for a while. I saw all the women in the family, his sisters and cousins, working and earning some money, and I wanted to work too. They used to tell me that I should be working. But I had four children, and who was going to take care of them?

Rita succumbed to the pressure and started working secretly for about three months. When asked how she managed to work without her husband knowing about it, Rita replied that

> since he left to work very early, I found someone to take care of my smallest child, and the others went to school. My work hours were from 9:00 to 3:30, so by the time my husband got home, I had everything done. I had the house clean, the children were cleaned and had eaten, and I was all put together. My husband did not like when I was not put together.

Rita eventually told her husband about her work escapades because she did not like doing things *a la escondida* (in hiding); however, her husband's traditionalism prevailed, and Rita was forced to give up working. To relent was a blow, because the money she had earned had gone to clothe the children and to purchase a sewing machine. Note the tone of pride:

> With the money I earned I was able to buy my sewing machine and I felt so proud of myself that I was able to buy it with my own money. We saved a lot of money afterwards. I sew for the family; I felt so proud.

Although she gave in to her husband's traditionalism, Rita found a source of pride and accomplishment even within the confines of the house. She may have stopped working, but her contributions to the household continued as she was able to sew her children's clothing and other items for the house and the family.

Others reported that they stopped working for wages, but continued to contribute to the family's income by working in their husbands' neighborhood stores. They used the word "helped," but, in reality, they actually ran the stores while their husbands worked elsewhere.

Puerto Rican men may have accommodated to the wife's employment, but the traditional division of labor within the family did not change. Lucy best articulated the working woman's problem:

> It was very hard work because I had to take care of the house, the children, and the store. Since my husband never learned how to drive, I had to learn to drive. I had to go to the warehouse, do the bookkeeping, everything. In the store, I used to do everything. My husband helped, but I was practically in charge of everything.

Puerto Rican working mothers, regardless of whether they worked outside the home or with their husbands in the family business, were still responsible for the care of the children and housework. Child care first became a problem at the time of migration since families could not afford to travel all at once. A strategy women used to deal with this problem was to leave the children in Puerto Rico in the care of grandparents. This arrangement was a widespread practice in the Island for many years.

Once the family was in Chicago, women developed short-term arrangements to deal with the daily problems of child care. Shift work represented one strategy that couples used to allow these women to stay home with the children. The husband could work the day shift, and the wife worked at night. Haydee's father worked the day shift in a factory, while her mother worked the evening shift as a cook in a hotel. Josefa worked the night shift in a candy store; her husband worked the day shift. I asked Josefa if they ever switched, where he worked nights and she worked days. She replied that working at night allowed her to take care of her daughter during the day.

When children were school age, both husband and wife might be able to work during the day. For wives, however, there was always the added responsibility of returning home to care for the children and do the household chores. Here, girls were introduced to the household responsibilities very early and were left to care for younger brothers and sisters. When Claudia reached nine years, she acquired household responsibilities. She was given keys to the apartment, and after school she was expected to clean the kitchen, pick up around the house, and start dinner. This was also a way mothers trained their daughters in the traditional gender roles.

Given the ease of migration, other working-class women brought over relatives with them to help care for the children, suggesting that women can get involved in the migration process to do the reproductive work, allowing other women to do work outside the home. Lucy and Daniela brought their mothers, and Teresa brought a younger sister to Chicago to help take care of the children. Teresa's sister stayed home and took care of her children until she met a fellow and got married. That was when Teresa then turned to a woman in her building who took care of them for a small fee. Teresa gave her $12.00 weekly for the two girls and provided their food. . . .

When Teresa stopped working, she became a child care provider for the women in her building. Now, she no longer cares for other people's children, but instead cares for her own grandchildren. Teresa's history represents an example of the cycle of care that women provided. Such a cycle may begin when a woman places her children with a neighbor while she works. Then she may care for other neighbor's children while they work and, finally, care for her own children's children.

Middle-Class Migrants

Middle-class women placed their career goals equally alongside their family responsibilities. Rosa talked about how she had managed to work full time in Puerto Rico and go to school to acquire an associate's degree because her extended family helped take care of the children and the household chores. In Chicago, since they did not have their extended family, they had to adjust differently. Shortly after arriving in the city, Rosa, who had given birth to her youngest child, opted to stay home with her children until they were of school age. Rosa recognized that she wanted to be with her children, but she also wanted to stay active.

> When I arrived, I saw a lot of possibilities, but I chose to stay home with my baby because I wanted to be with my children. When the baby was three years old, I started thinking what can I do to keep myself busy? In Puerto Rico, I had always worked, and I was not used to be a full-time mom. I was very independent. I was very active. So I started helping the church. I started just because I wanted to get out of the house.

Eventually it became a full-time job. Then, when she started working full time, her husband took on more household responsibilities:

> Here he has learned all kinds of domestic chores. At times I get home from work and he has everything ready, I don't have to do a thing in the house. Other times, we decide to go out for dinner.

Brunilda could not have made it without her husband, who helped her take care of the children as she pursued both her educational goals and, later, her political activism:

> My husband was very understanding of my goals and political interest. We shared many of the household responsibilities. . . . I have to admit that I spent a lot of time outside of the house during my children's childhood; for that I am a little bit sorry.

Later on she elaborated on her struggles and how she resolved them:

> When you are a professional, you face what Americans call "conflicting priorities." It's like I want to be everywhere at the same time. For me, community work has always interested me, whereas being a housewife has always been secondary. I feel more gratification in my role as a professional.

At the time of the interview, Brunilda worked as a professor in a local university. Aurea too placed her community activism (which was her professional orientation) alongside her family responsibilities:

For me, both are part of the same process. I define my family network beyond the nuclear family, or better yet, beyond the traditional American concept of the nuclear family. My family is part of my social activism.

I asked whether this brought about any conflicts. She replied:

Without doubt, my husband is part of this sexist society and obviously expects privileges that this society accords men, but we have worked and negotiated these roles quite successfully; moreover, we both made a political pact. It worked rather well because he shares the same vision of the world and social change as I do.

Conclusion

Evidence from this research has only begun to show how, in the context of a changing political economy, migration emerged as a strategy for families across class backgrounds. Initially, migration was a strategy working-class families used to deal with shrinking economic opportunities for the men in the family, but eventually middle-class better-educated men and women joined working-class Puerto Ricans in the migration process.

The political economy that rendered working-class husbands unemployable forced women to migrate to Chicago as part of a family strategy. Gender relations within the family were a major factor shaping the migration of married working-class women to Chicago. Some married women went willingly, thinking that the move would improve their families' financial situation. Others resisted, but ultimately their roles as mothers and wives compelled them to follow their husbands to Chicago.

Whether working class or middle class Puerto Rican women, like other immigrant women, confronted a basic duality in family and work. Families provided economic and emotional support. They see the family as the only area where people are free to be themselves, and where people come for affection and love, but the family is also an institution that has historically oppressed women. When individuals and families confront economic deprivation, legal discrimination, and other threats to their survival, conflict within the context of the family is muted by the pressure of the family to unite against assaults from the outside. The focus on the family as a site of resistance often underestimates how certain family arrangements can be oppressive to women. Often misunderstood by scholars is the reproductive work of women on behalf of the family and the benefits such work brings to the men.

Working-class women saw themselves in keeping with Puerto Rican culture as primarily *mujeres de la casa*, but many found themselves working, albeit temporarily, given the family's economic situation. Here, families accommodated to the wives' temporary employment, but in ways that did not challenge the traditional patriarchal structure in the family. Wives were still responsible for cooking, cleaning, and child care. Given this situation, working-class married women developed strategies to accommodate their roles as working wives.

The area of child care best reflects the resourcefulness of working-class Puerto Rican women migrants in developing accommodating strategies. Some women left their children behind in Puerto Rico, others brought relatives from Puerto Rico to help them. Still others turned to older daughters as helpers. Some became involved in a cycle of child care. . . .

Married working-class Puerto Rican women adapted to life in Chicago in ways that did not disturb traditional family arrangements. They also developed strategies to resist some arrangements. Some sought to change their husbands' view about work outside the home and created networks to help accomplish their goals. Others stopped working for wages, but continued contributing as mothers, giving them influence and power within the family. In addition, some women remained active in income-generating activities, such as working in the family business. When husbands neglected their responsibilities as fathers, women took charge of the household, providing for their children and family.

Although middle-class women felt differently about work and family obligations, they also struggled over their roles as mothers and wives. They rejected traditional ideologies about women's roles and saw no conflict in doing both. Some husbands supported them, but when husbands resisted, they also negotiated the work and family responsibilities. Their class position afforded them options, such as staying home until they were ready to return to work, hiring help, postponing having children, and organizing their schedule around their children's schooling. This study has only begun to explore a very small slice of the Puerto Rican experience in Chicago, namely that of married working-class and middle-class women. Much empirical work needs to be done to fully understand how gender shapes the migration process for other groups of Puerto Rican women in different family arrangements and across class backgrounds.

Vietnamese Parents and Children in Philadelphia

NAZLI KIBRIA

On the morning of April 4, 1991, three brothers—Loi, Pham, and Long—told their parents they were going fishing. After leaving the house, they were joined by another young Vietnamese American male, Cuong Tran, aged seventeen. But instead of making their way to the Sacramento River, the four proceeded to a nearby Good Guys electronics store, armed with two nine-millimeter pistols. What followed was a eight-and-a-half-hour siege in which they held forty people hostage at the store. Although the exact motives of the young men were unclear to observers, it was later reported that the gunmen had talked to their hostages about the difficulty of finding jobs in the United States and about their desire to go back to Southeast Asia to fight the Viet Cong. The siege ended with a shootout in which six persons were killed—three of the hostages and three of the gunmen.

According to news reports, the four gunmen were members of a gang called the "Oriental Boys." Despite their gang affiliation, many of those who had known the young men were shocked and puzzled by the incident. Although none of the youths had been successful in school, their teachers recalled them as obedient and pleasant, as did the priest of the Vietnamese Catholic Church they attended. Particularly stunned were the parents of the three brothers, who could offer no explanation for

Nazli Kibria, *Family Tightrope: The Changing Lives of Vietnamese Americans* (Princeton, N.J.: Princeton University Press, 1993), pp. 144–166. Copyright © 1993 by Princeton University Press. Reprinted by permission of Princeton University Press.

their sons' actions. A Vietnamese American acquaintance of the parents, however, suggested the following: "In this country, there is too much freedom. We cannot tell the kids what to do. They were nice guys, but they grew up in this country. They watched the TV. They learned a lot of bad things."

The incident, which received wide coverage in the mainstream media, countervailed the image of young Vietnamese refugees as highly studious and obedient to their family elders—an image that has been perpetuated by many media reports of Vietnamese Americans. The incident in Sacramento instead suggested a picture of deeply troubled youth, unsuccessful at school and distant from their families. It is clear that both these extreme images seriously distort the experiences of Vietnamese American youth, most of whom would certainly not conform to either of them. Nonetheless, I suggest that when meshed together these images do contain, albeit in simplified fashion, elements central to the familial experiences of Vietnamese American youth. The process of migration to the United States had generated distance and conflicts between the young and their families. At the same time, young Vietnamese Americans upheld and affirmed the importance of family ties in their lives and expressed support for preserving the traditional Vietnamese family system in the United States.

Intergenerational Battles

Vietnamese Americans, both young and old, felt that migration had enhanced intergenerational tensions among them. At the root of these tensions were growing cultural schisms between the generations as well as a decline in the power and authority of family elders. As both young and old conceded, younger Vietnamese Americans were becoming more "American" in many ways, ranging from dating practices and modes of dress and speech to their increasingly individualistic orientation toward life. Further exacerbating the depth and significance of these cultural changes was the growing inability of family elders to control the young—to halt or slow down the pace of cultural assimilation.

. . . Vietnamese American kin elders viewed the central culprit in the battle between the generations to be the social environment of the United States—in particular, such powerful cultural agents as U.S. television, popular music, and schools. The tendency to pinpoint blame for generational conflicts on the cultural environment of the United States was perhaps facilitated by traditional Vietnamese beliefs about the importance of social environment, rather than inherent personality characteristics, in molding personal character. These beliefs are expressed by such traditional proverbs as "If you live in a round thing you become round; if you live in a long thing you become long" and "If the straw is set near the fire, sooner or later it will catch fire." Given the ubiquity of U.S. social and cultural institutions, many elders felt that they were involved in an uphill battle in their efforts to socialize the young properly. This was suggested by Toan, a father of three children, who was in his early forties: "I have children and I can't educate them. The films and TV show bad things, things which are not suited for an Asian culture. On TV, they show love couples doing things, and I think that way it directly teaches the children bad behavior. Books and magazines show naked pictures of women, and the children who don't know, they see it and try to find out about it. If one plays with the ink, one will get black."

Besides the popular media, schools were another important cultural culprit. The school environment led to the adoption of popular cultural fads by Vietnamese American children who sought to emulate their school peers: "A lot of Vietnamese kids behave like American children; they compare themselves to the American children. The question the children here usually ask their parents is, why can those children do things and why can't I? They want to do things like go out late at night and spend their parents' money."

One problem often discussed by parents was the increasing demands made by children for toys, clothes, and other items that were in vogue among their peers at school. Some elders also spoke disapprovingly of the lax discipline in the schools, which failed to inculcate respect for elders and teachers into their students. After looking over the report card of her son and finding a complaint from his teacher that he was too disruptive and talkative in class, one woman made the following comment: "I don't understand the schools here. If he talks too much, they should punish him. One day I went to the school and I saw a class in which the children were laughing and talking. And the teacher didn't do anything. In Vietnam they would hit you if you did that." . . .

For family elders, U.S. society not only offered a cultural environment that countered their efforts to educate and socialize the young in ways that they chose; migration to the United States had also, in a variety of ways, weakened the strength of their efforts to enforce appropriate values and norms on the young. For one thing, as so many family elders told me, U.S. society did not support the right of parents to discipline their children as they chose. This absence of support for parental rights was dramatically highlighted for my informants by situations in which school or police officials directly intervened in conflicts between children and their family elders, often in response to complaints of physical abuse made by children. . . .

I heard of several cases of Vietnamese American children turning to school authorities or to the police for protection from physical assaults by older family members. For older informants, these cases symbolized the impotence of the old in relation to the young in the context of U.S. society. One such case involved a sixteen-year-old named Tin, who had been in the United States since the age of eleven. Tin's father had held an administrative position in a military hospital in South Vietnam before 1975, but since his arrival in the United States in 1979, he had been chronically unemployed. Conflicts between Tin and his father had become increasingly frequent since Tin's alleged involvement with a Vietnamese American youth gang in the city during the past year. Tin frequently skipped school and sometimes stayed out all night. During one confrontation with his father, Tin called the police. About two weeks after this occurred, his mother described the incident:

> When Tin came home that night, his father was angry. I don't know about him [Tin] anymore; I just hope he finds a job and doesn't steal money from other people. His father was so mad he hit him with a stick. And Tin hit him back. We were surprised because in Vietnam the son can never hit his father. Tin went into that room [an adjoining room], he locked the door, and called the police. Then he came out and his father hit him again. The police then came to the apartment. Everyone from the building came to see what happened. The police told my husband to stop it or they would arrest him. Then they told Tin not to be so bad. My husband was sad that Tin called the police, and he didn't understand why the police thought he was doing a bad thing, hitting his son.

The intervention of the police not only helped to undermine the legitimacy of the father's authority but also represented a profound loss of face for the father. Shortly after this incident, Tin dropped out of school and moved into an apartment with friends. Embittered by the situation, Tin's father grew increasingly despondent and was eventually hospitalized for acute depression.

. . . [E]pisodes such as this were widely recounted in the neighborhoods of study, serving as a focal point for discussions about the conflicting nature of family life in Vietnamese and U.S. cultures, particularly with regard to parental rights and authority. The importance of parental guidance and discipline of children was frequently mentioned to me by adult men and women in the community. Several proverbs were reiterated to lend support to the idea that parental discipline was crucial to molding the character of children. One of the most popular of these was "The fish that is not preserved in salt will be rotten; the children who disobey their parents will be corrupted." Others included "Bamboo trees, when they are still young, are easy to bend" and "If one has children and does not educate them, it's better to spend one's time rearing pigs for their tripes." . . .

Not only had the authority of parents and other kin elders diminished because of the legal and cultural context of life in the United States; the social and economic resources that had previously supported the authority of elders had also waned. . . . Some parents, especially those with teenage or adult children, spoke pointedly of how the greater economic opportunities available to the young in the United States had weakened the control of parents over their children. Binh, in his early fifties and the father of two sons in the United States, spoke of this at some length:

> In Vietnam, parents raised children and paid for their schooling. When they come to America it's different, they can get help from the government, the government will pay for their schooling. For instance, my older son is supported by the government in college and even in high school. So he can study, and if the government doesn't give him enough he can work in the summer for money. Slowly, he lives like Americans. The children don't listen to the parents because they are not supported by them.

In the extremely competitive and closed educational system of pre-1975 South Vietnam, children had depended on financial support from their families to make it through the system. Family elders, for example, had paid for the young to attend private schools, a necessity for the large numbers of students who were unable to qualify for entrance to the public schools. As Binh's words suggest, with migration to the United States there had emerged greater opportunities for the young to pursue their educational goals independently from family resources. Besides financial support for education, in Vietnam the economic dependence of the young on their families had also been fostered in many cases by the expectation that the young would inherit the family business in the future. With migration to the United States, these familial economic resources were no longer as substantial or as crucial for children as before. This is by no means to suggest that familial economic support had become inconsequential to the educational and occupational achievements of young Vietnamese Americans. . . . Nonetheless, in comparison to the situation in Vietnam, the young generally had more financial independence from their families. This condition, coupled with a decline in the economic resources that families were actually able to offer to the young, had eroded the economic basis of parental authority.

For kin elders, the move to the United States had not only reduced the economic resources that they were able to offer to the young; it had also resulted in a decline in their social resources in comparison to the young, as exemplified by the greater difficulties experienced by many elders in effectively communicating and dealing with people and institutions of the "host" society. In many households, the English-language fluency of the children had clearly surpassed that of their parents. Thus some children had assumed an important role in dealing with institutions outside the ethnic community on behalf of the household—a situation that could result in an unprecedented degree of power for children. For example, in one household, twelve-year-old Danny interpreted and paid bills for his parents. Sometimes, he kept some of the money allocated to paying bills for himself. His mother was aware of his deception but seemed reconciled to it:

> I have difficulty reading English, so Danny reads all the letters that come to the house. He tells me how much to pay for the electric, the telephone. I give him the money and he takes it to the post office. I know Danny keeps money because he buys some things like this [points to a black leather jacket], and he doesn't work. I know it's not good. I asked him, why do you do like that? He doesn't say anything. If it was in Vietnam his father would beat him, but here it's different. We can't hit him because the police will come.

Rarely was the disregard of parental authority as blatant and extreme as in this situation. However, in many other households, too, the young's greater English-language fluency and familiarity with the procedures of bureaucracies in the United States had resulted in enhanced power and freedom for them. A fourteen-year-old girl, living with her older brother and his family, spoke at some length about the benefits she derived from being the most fluent in English and adept at dealing with persons outside the ethnic community:

> I learned English fast because when we first came here we lived in a place where there were no other Vietnamese people. Now I help my brother and sister with the landlord, and when my brother tried to get a loan from the bank, I helped him with that. It's weird, to be so important, because at home I was the baby in the family. I think I can get away with a lot more now, and my mother isn't here to tell me what to do. Before we came to Philadelphia, our school had a camp for a week out in the countryside. All my friends were going and I really wanted to go. But my brother and sister didn't understand. So I told them it was required, that my teacher said I had to go. It wasn't true, but they believed me because they didn't understand the letter about it from the school. I don't like to lie, but my brother and sister are old; they don't understand about living in America, so when I want to do something I have to do that.

This loss of parental social and economic resources, coupled with a deepening cultural gap between the young and the old, was ripe ground for intergenerational conflict. I recorded many instances of overt discord between the young and the old in household settings. Not surprisingly, among teenagers, conflicts with family elders often revolved around dating and the freedom to "go out" when one chose. A seventeen-year-old girl spoke somewhat glumly about her parents' strictness:

> I think my parents are more strict now than they were in Vietnam, because they see that the environment and the living conditions here are very different. Sometimes I feel that my parents are too strict; they don't give me enough independence. My parents won't let me associate with boys or have boyfriends. I just work, study, sometimes I go out

with friends on the weekend. My parents don't want us to do something disgraceful so they don't have to disown us.

Some teenagers, particularly boys, were far less acquiescent of the rules set by parents than the girl quoted in the preceding. Khanh, who had been living in the United States with his father and brother for about five years, increasingly refused to accept his father's authority:

I'm eighteen years old, right? And he always looks after me like I'm a little boy. Every time I go out the door I have to ask him. That's not fair for an eighteen-year-old. Sometimes my girlfriends call me, and he just doesn't like it. He doesn't like me to have a girlfriend. Once here in America, he hit me with a stick. I didn't touch him but I said, "don't do that again or I'll call the police." He never hit me again.

One fourteen-year-old boy stunned household members when he began to deviate in his speech from Vietnamese norms regarding the proper forms of address and reference for older persons. The boy told me that he had stopped using the traditional forms because he felt that "everyone should be equal"—a sentiment that was not shared by his mother and uncle. While such explicit calls for greater equality among the young were rare, I did find many younger informants who wished for "more open communication" with older family members. This desire for more democratic communication patterns was coupled with complaints among the young about the absence of open expressions of affection among Vietnamese family members, such as hugging and kissing, in contrast to the behaviors that they had observed in "American families."

Such complaints suggested a growing generational divergence in conceptions of ideal family life among Vietnamese Americans. For parents and other family elders, this cultural divergence had many implications, not the least of which was a loss in their ability to exercise influence and authority over the young. But beyond this, the growing generation gaps also raised the prospect of the defection of the young from the collectivist household economy—a prospect that threatened the economic aspirations of family elders. Many family elders that I met pinned their hopes for acceptance and prosperity in their adopted society on the future occupational attainments of the young. For example, when I asked Suong, a woman in her late fifties, about her hopes for the future, she replied that so far as she and her adult children were concerned, her only hope was that they would have enough to eat and a warm place to sleep at night until her grandchildren had completed their education. She hoped and indeed expected that her grandchildren would do well at school and eventually become doctors, teachers, and engineers and support their parents in their old age. These hopes and expectations led her, like other family elders, to invest resources into the education of the young. However, not all young Vietnamese Americans were able to respond to this investment by doing well at school.

Academic success was widely viewed by Vietnamese Americans as the central route by which the young could achieve acceptance and prosperity for their families in the future. Besides the frequently cited influence of Confucian tradition, which assigned high status and privilege to scholars, a number of other historical and structural circumstances had also contributed to the development of the emphasis on academic success. The ideology of education among Vietnamese Americans was one that emphasized the efficacy of education as an approach toward or vehicle for realizing life goals. Although in pre-1975 Vietnam academic achievement had been difficult because of the extremely competitive nature of the schooling system, for those who were able to succeed, the academic credentials they procured had been likely to secure them a middle- or high-ranking place in the government bureaucracy or military or in the professions. Thus, while schooling was seen as a difficult process, it was also understood to be an effective route for socioeconomic achievement. Formal education was valued not simply as an end in itself but as a process that carried specific, concrete rewards. The vigor with which Vietnamese immigrants stressed education for the young in the United States reflected their view of education as an effective approach for realizing goals, as well as the difficulty that they had experienced in obtaining education in the past. . . . In fact, providing education for the young was widely identified as a central goal of the migration process; many parents remarked to me that the only reason they were living in the United States was for the sake of providing education for their children. Similarly, school-aged Vietnamese refugees who had come to the United States alone talked of how the greater opportunities for education abroad had motivated their parents to grant them permission to leave Vietnam.

The value placed on the education of the young by family elders was coupled with the expectation that the kin group as a whole would reap certain rewards from the young's academic achievements. In the short run, the academic achievements of the young were a source of status and prestige for kin in the ethnic community. In the informal social gatherings that I attended, it was not unusual for parents or other family elders to pass around and compare the report cards of school-aged children. In the long run, family members expected to gain not only status privileges but also material rewards. In accordance with the prescriptions of the ideology of family collectivism, the young were expected to pay back their families after completing their education. In fact, many parents explicitly identified the education of the young as an investment that they made for their future and for the collective future of the kin group. These expectations of payback were also shared, although not without ambivalence, by young Vietnamese Americans, who often focused their areas of study in high school or college in fields that would enable them to honor their financial obligations to their families more effectively. Thus a young Vietnamese American who was studying for a degree in pharmacy (although he would have preferred to study art) told me that he planned to buy a house for his sister and brother-in-law, with whom he was living, as soon as he completed college, in order to fulfill his obligations to them. . . .

The manner in which Vietnamese immigrants understood and approached education had important consequences for the academic experiences of the young. Perhaps most important, it created a context in which the stakes for doing well at school were extremely high. For the young, it was not only their own future that hinged on their ability to do well at school but also that of other family members. While some young Vietnamese Americans were able to meet these pressures successfully and perform well at school, others slipped into a pattern of academic failure. For the latter group, the general sense of failure that stemmed from their inability to do well at school was overwhelming; they felt that they had let their families down. One twelve-year-old Vietnamese American boy who was not doing well at school told me that his academic failure threatened his family's fundamental rationale or purpose for migrating to the United States. He, like many other children, felt that the burden of the migration process rested on his shoulders—and specifically on his ability to do well at school.

Such pressures were especially difficult given that young Vietnamese Americans faced many difficulties in the schooling process. In other words, whereas young Vietnamese refugees faced tremendous pressure to succeed, they also faced many barriers to academic success. The first of these was language difficulties, a problem that was easier to overcome for those arriving in the United States at a young age. There was also the problem of prior educational skills, since many had been out of school for years before arriving in the United States. These difficulties could be further aggravated by such school policies as age-grade matching (matching the ages and grades of the students as closely as possible) and mainstreaming (rapidly integrating students into regular classes regardless of their English-language skills). Some young Vietnamese Americans also felt the school environment to be a significant barrier to academic success in that it was so threatening as to make them less inclined to attend classes regularly. A male high school student to whom I talked compared school to a "war-zone" in which he and his peers were continually harassed by other students and called a variety of names such as "Yang," "Nip," "Chink," and "Jap." . . .

Those who were unable to do well at school sometimes joined the ranks of the *bụi đời,* a term used by Vietnamese Americans to refer to those youth who belonged to gangs or engaged in criminal activities. Literally meaning the "dust of life," *bụi đời* refers more generally to a person who is alone, without family, or to someone in a lowly position—"no better than dust." While *bụi đời* included those who had become disenchanted with the pressures and demands posed by schools and families, it also included those youth who had arrived in the United States alone or under the guardianship of relatives such as brothers and cousins. Those who arrived alone, called "unaccompanied minors" by the social service bureaucracy, were usually placed in non-Vietnamese foster homes. . . .

Among the Vietnamese American teenagers who had abandoned their homes were those who had been sent to the United States with family members other than parents, such as siblings, cousins, and uncles. In some such households, relations between the teenager and appointed guardian(s) were harmonious. But in others, conflicts abounded and sometimes resulted in the teenager's moving out or running away from the home. In some cases, the high level of disharmony in such households stemmed from the fact that the young person perceived the authority of the guardian as less legitimate than that of his or her parents. In addition, it was not uncommon for relatives neither to expect nor to welcome the guardianship that had been assigned to them. A sixteen-year-old male teenager, who had left Vietnam with his married female cousin and her family, eventually left their home because of conflicts with the cousin's husband:

> I don't get along with my cousin's husband. When I arrived here with my cousin and her two little kids, he was already here, and he wasn't pleased to see me. He yells at me all the time, calls me stupid, and watches me to see if I make any mistake, so he can yell some more. In Vietnam, my parents yelled at me too, but that was different, and they never yelled at me like that. I got tired of that, so I left and now I live with some friends. I don't feel good here; I feel like a fish out of water.

Another case again illustrates the sometimes fragile and troubled quality of the relations between the young and their appointed guardians. Lien had arrived in the United States alone at the age of thirteen. She had been sent by her parents to join her brother, who had been resettled in Philadelphia for a few years. Lien had never closely known her brother, who had been away from home since she was a small child. Soon after her arrival, as Lien put it, her brother began "beating me up every day, for no reason." Eventually, she moved into the home of a friend whose mother and siblings informally adopted her into their family.

As these cases suggest, young Vietnamese Americans responded to the changes wrought by the migration process on their family lives in a variety of ways. Although joining a gang was simply one in a whole range of responses I encountered, it was one that attracted much attention and was widely discussed by my informants. For older Vietnamese Americans, the highly visible presence of *bụi đời* in the United States was of tremendous concern. . . .

In the eyes of many older Vietnamese Americans, there was another subgroup of young Vietnamese refugees who also threatened Vietnamese identity in the United States. This subgroup was composed of the large numbers of young, single male adults with few or no family ties in the United States. Some of these young single men, living and socializing primarily among themselves, had developed lifestyles that were viewed as unconventional or deviant by older Vietnamese Americans. There was some indication that many of these young unattached men were, on average, more Westernized than other Vietnamese Americans even prior to their arrival in the United States, because of the higher social class status of their fathers in Vietnam. Older Vietnamese Americans saw their apparent lack of attachment to family ties and their adoption of "American" ways of dress, speech, and public behavior as contributing to the erosion of Vietnamese familial values and cultural identity in the United States, in part by providing a dangerous and negative example for children.

Notwithstanding such concerns, I found much evidence to suggest that as a group, these young adults remained in many ways deeply tied to the traditional family system. This attachment undoubtedly had much to do with the age at which they had migrated—late teens or early twenties—well after core socialization processes had taken place. . . .

There is little doubt that for young adult Vietnamese refugees, particularly those who had migrated alone, the move to the United States had been accompanied by many, often basic, changes in their experience of family life. . . . For these young Vietnamese Americans, the physical separation from the force of familial authority and control that had been created by migration was one of the most important changes in their lives. Many of the young men with whom I spoke valued the freedom they had gained to adopt new behaviors and life-styles. For twenty-four-year-old Tang, the son of a former middle-ranking army officer in the South Vietnamese government, the distance from his father created by the move to the United States was especially welcomed:

> My old man was very, very strict when I was in Vietnam. He was a military man, a very difficult person. I didn't get along with him; I had a lot of arguments. At that time I was

young, also. We argued about everything, and he didn't like that I disagreed with him. He also beat me up many times because I didn't do well at school or something else. After the Communists came in 1975 I started to spend more and more time at school, in the activities organized by the Communists. I always wanted to get away from my father. That's why when he went to the reeducation camp in 1975, I only went to visit him there once. Here I smoke and drink; if I was in Vietnam maybe I wouldn't do that because of my family.

Others expressed a sense of apprehension about the increased freedoms:

If I was in Vietnam I would have a very different kind of life. Here I work where I want to, and if I want to go out with a girl, that's my business. In Vietnam my parents would decide many of these things. Maybe not decide, but they would influence my decision. Of course it's good to have freedom, but sometimes I worry about if I'm doing the right thing in my life, then I wish my family was here so they could give me advice.

Regardless of whether the changes were welcomed or shunned, for these young men, migration had fundamentally transformed their experience of family life by removing them from the immediate influence of familial authority. Greater independence from familial authority was also experienced by those young adults who had arrived in the United States with parents or other family elders. According to my informants, the shifts in generational power caused by the migration process had deeply affected relationships between adult children and their family elders. In the following, Thanh, a widow in her late fifties and the mother of five, bemoaned her growing lack of control over her adult children:

In Vietnam I had a lot of power. The children listened to me; that's the Vietnamese custom. They didn't do anything unless I said it was okay. Here, my sons have girlfriends and they don't ask me about them. Even my daughter, she goes out without my permission. Here my children, when they go out, they just call to report to me that they're going to be late, not to ask my permission. My son has an American girlfriend, and I don't like that. Still, I think that my children are better than others; they work hard and they work together. My family has good discipline.

While there is little doubt that migration had transformed the relationship of young adults to parents and other family elders, there was also an abundance of evidence to indicate the continued importance of familial ties for young adults. The continued importance of family ties found expression in the struggle of many young adults to send money to family members in Vietnam, often at considerable sacrifice to themselves. Some young adults informed me that sending money was a way for them to alleviate their guilt about leaving family members behind in Vietnam. Others reiterated to me the importance of obligations to the kin group over fulfillment of their own personal needs. In one case, a twenty-five-year-old man had recently begun a program in computer science at a local college. By working for a few years, he had saved enough money to pay for most of his tuition and living expenses. But shortly after beginning his studies, he received a letter from his mother requesting money to help with a family emergency—his sister had fallen deeply into debt and was being threatened by creditors. In response to his sister's emergency, the man sent her his savings and postponed his educational plans. He felt that this was the only reasonable course of action.

As this example suggests, for young adults, even those who were in the United States without kin, the connection to family, both moral and emotional, remained strong and powerful. As a result, despite the geographical distance, parental authority continued to exert influence in subtle but important ways. Man, who was in his midtwenties, had recently received a letter from his mother in Vietnam asking him to move from Philadelphia to Oklahoma, where his older brother lived. His mother wrote that she would feel better and worry less about her two sons in the United States if she knew that they were living together. The arrival of the letter sent Man into a state of panic because he did not want to leave Philadelphia, where he had lived for four years and had built up a large social circle. Man also did not get along with his older brother, who, after converting to Roman Catholicism in the refugee camp, had developed strong moral and religious convictions that Man found distasteful. Despite these misgivings, Man departed for Oklahoma six months after receiving his mother's letter. He felt obliged to honor the wishes of his mother. . . .

In another situation in which a mother sent instructions from Vietnam, Lien received letters from her mother and sister in Vietnam shortly before the birth of her first child. The letters instructed her to observe the traditional Vietnamese postbirth restrictions: she was not to go out of the house for a month, not to eat seafood and certain vegetables, and not to wash her hair. Lien was extremely troubled by these restrictions, especially when she was unable to attend the wedding of a friend that was taking place that month. She told me that she did not believe in the taboos that aimed to ward off malevolent spirits and restore the health of the mother. But she obeyed the restrictions, out of respect for her mother and also out of fear of reprimands from her sister-in-law, who called her every hour to make sure that she had not left the apartment.

The continued importance of parental wishes for the young, unattached adults was also reflected in the significance attached to parental acknowledgment and approval of marriage decisions made in the United States. In the absence of older kin in the United States, couples first wrote to their parents or other family members in Vietnam, informing them of their desire to marry. In some cases, the parents of the couple met in Vietnam to discuss the marriage and assess the character of their children's future in-laws. Following this, they wrote back with their impressions and approval. In other cases, particularly when families lived in different areas of Vietnam, the meeting of the families occurred after the marriage had taken place in the United States. When they met, the families performed ancestral worship rites together, acknowledging their newly acquired kinship ties. Except in the case of proposed marriage to non-Vietnamese persons, I heard of no case in which parents forbade a child in the United States to marry, either before or after the meeting with the prospective in-laws. This was in contrast to Vietnam, where parental disapproval of proposed marriages was apparently a common predicament. In this sense, the involvement of the family in the marriage decisions of the young adults was far more superficial and symbolic in quality than it had been in Vietnam.

But the anticipation of family disapproval of marriage to non-Vietnamese persons strengthened the antipathy that existed among my young adult informants toward marrying across ethnic boundaries. The antipathy was somewhat surprising given the high sex ratio, which made the potential for intermarriage seem high.

While conducting research, I heard of five intermarriages in the community. In three of these, Vietnamese American men had married women of Asian (Chinese, Cambodian) origin. The other two involved marriages to whites—in one case a man, and in the other a woman. In general, ethnic intermarriages seemed to be somewhat less common among Vietnamese American women than men. This was no doubt related to the high sex ratio, which had enlarged rather than shrunk the pool of Vietnamese American male partners for women. Young Vietnamese American women who went out with whites tended to be seen as more promiscuous and more liberated in their relations with men, as these words of a female informant in her early twenties suggests: "Some Vietnamese boys in the high school go out with American girls because they're easy. But just a few girls go out with Americans. The ones who do are more Americanized, and they don't worry about having sex with their boyfriends. Those girls who go out with Americans say they have more freedom, to get a divorce, to decide things."

However, most young, adult Vietnamese Americans, both male and female, did not favor marrying a non-Vietnamese person, because of cultural differences between them. This attitude was present even among those young men who were dating non-Vietnamese women. As one young man told me, women of other ethnic backgrounds were "okay to go out with, but not to marry." For the men, perceived differences in attitudes about gender relations between themselves and non–Vietnamese American women were an important consideration: "Vietnamese women want to be good wives and mothers. I think that's not so important for American women. I want my wife to stay at home with the children, so I don't think I'll marry an American woman." . . .

In general, my young adult informants voiced aspirations for family life that were rather traditional in character. For example, in talking about how they would raise their future children, young adults, both men and women, spoke of how they would inculcate respect for the elderly and for parental authority in their children. A twenty-five-year-old Vietnamese man who had arrived in the United States alone at the age of twenty-one spoke with conviction about how he would work to instill such traditional familial values in his children. But what also emerges in his words is a recognition of the need to adopt a less rigid approach toward these values in light of the different social environment of the United States:

> I want to get married soon and have children. I hope my first child is a son; that's important to us because the son will remember the family and not the daughter. I will teach my children to obey and respect their parents, but I think I will be considerate of them. I understand that America is a very different place from Vietnam and my children will understand America more. But I don't want my children to live alone until they get married, and if I have a daughter I will be very careful that she doesn't have many boyfriends. We're in a new place and we have to change, but we also have to keep our customs.

The importance of preserving but also softening the traditional normative hierarchies of Vietnamese family life was also affirmed by another young informant, a female: "We're living in a different country that has very different customs. So I think Vietnamese people here should keep some of the traditions and should learn something new. I think children should listen to their parents, but the parents should know that they're living in a different country, so they should be considerate."

But there were other aspects of traditional Vietnamese family life, besides its age and gender hierarchies, that young Vietnamese Americans spoke of when I questioned them about their reasons for wanting to marry only others of Vietnamese origin. Families in the United States were invariably described in negative terms, as entities that were marked by selfish, distant, and uncaring relations among members. My young adult informants spoke of how Vietnamese families, in contrast, were cooperative and caring groups in which members were willing to sacrifice for one another. The desire to marry within ethnic boundaries arose in part from a sense that intermarriage threatened the possibility of maintaining such cooperative and caring family relations in the United States. The distinctive character of Vietnamese family life was also viewed with great pride, not only by young adults but also by Vietnamese Americans of all ages. Repeatedly I was told that what set Vietnamese apart from "Americans" was the more close-knit character of their family life:

> We're different from Americans because our families are much closer. I think that's the biggest difference between Americans and Vietnamese. For Vietnamese people their family is the most important thing in their lives; for an American it's not that important. I think that's why Americans have a lot of problems. [What kinds of problems?] A lot of Americans feel lonely, they live alone and they don't know their families, they don't care about them. I think that's why they feel sad and depressed a lot.

Migration to the United States had introduced more conflict and distance in the relations of young and old family members. However, both the extent and the character of the generation gap among Vietnamese Americans varied enormously, depending on the age and family circumstances of those involved. For family elders, besides signifying a loss of power and authority over the young, these generational schisms portended the defection of the young from their families, a prospect that in turn threatened their hopes of eventually attaining middle-class status via their children. But in addition to these concerns, older Vietnamese Americans also saw cultural rifts between the generations as a threat to the continued survival and integrity of Vietnamese culture and identity in the United States. Thus in speaking to me about the implications of cultural changes among the young for the cultural identity of Vietnamese in the United States, a local Vietnamese American community leader remarked that "the bamboo is dying but there are no shoots."

But the relationship of the young to their families and to the traditional Vietnamese family system was far more complex than kin elders often made it out to be. There is little doubt that many young Vietnamese Americans, particularly those who had arrived in the United States before their teen years, viewed the traditional family system as an outdated relic of the past. They chafed at the obligations and pressures imposed on them by this system and looked with favor and longing on the greater individual autonomy and egalitarianism of U.S. families. But this rebellious stance was rarely accompanied by a desire to reject Vietnamese family traditions completely. Even among the most rebellious Vietnamese American children and teenagers that I met, what I encountered was a struggle to come to terms with the traditional family system in ways that did not involve a complete rejection but a reworking, a "compromising" of these traditions.

This struggle to come to terms with the traditional Vietnamese family system in a manner that could be sustained in the context of life in the United States was particularly apparent among my young, single adult informants who were at a stage in their lives at which they expected to marry soon and have children. These informants voiced concerns about how to achieve a balance between the past and present, a family life that melded together the old and the new. In part, their attempts to create this ideological balance stemmed from the fact that they, like other young Vietnamese Americans, saw the distinctive features of Vietnamese family life as what set them apart as a group in the United States, what gave meaning to their ethnic identity as Vietnamese in the United States. Along with the traditional age and gender hierarchies of Vietnamese family life, they identified cooperative and caring relations between kin as distinctive core features of Vietnamese family life.

 F U R T H E R   R E A D I N G

Benmayor, Rita, Ana Juarbe, Blance Vazquez Erazo, and Celia Alvarez. "Stories to Live by: Continuity and Change in Three Generations of Puerto Rican Women." *Oral History Review* 16, 2 (Fall 1998): 1–46.

Blank, Susan, and Ramon S. Torrecilha. "Understanding the Living Arrangements of Latino Immigrants: A Life Course Approach." *International Migration Review* 32, 1 (Spring 1998): 3–20.

Booth, Alan, Ann C. Crouter, and Nancy Lansdale, eds. *Immigration and the Family: Research and Policy on U.S. Immigrants* (1997).

Foner, Nancy. "The Immigrant Family: Cultural Legacies and Cultural Changes." *International Migration Review* 31, 4 (Winter 1997): 961–975.

Freeman, James M. *Hearts of Sorrow: Vietnamese-American Lives* (1989).

Fuligni, Andrew D., Tiffany Yip, and Vivian Tseng. "The Impact of Family Obligation on the Daily Activities and Psychological Well-Being of Chinese American Adolescents." *Child Development* 73, 1 (January-February 2002): 302–315.

Glick, Jennifer E. "Economic Support from and to Extended Kin: A Comparison of Mexican Americans and Mexican Immigrants." *International Migration Review* 33, 3 (Fall 1999): 745–765.

Hickey, M. Gail. " 'Go to College, Get a Job, and Don't Leave the House Without Your Brother': Oral Histories with Immigrant Women and Their Daughters." *Oral History Review* 23, 2 (Winter 1996): 63–93.

Hondagneu-Sotelo, Pierrette. *Gendered Transitions: Mexican Experiences of Immigration* (1994).

Kibria, Nazli. *Family Tightrope: The Changing Lives of Vietnamese Americans* (1993).

———. "Power, Patriarchy, and Gender Conflict in the Vietnamese Immigrant Community." *Gender and Society* 4 (March 1990): 9–24.

Lewis, Oscar. *La Vida: A Puerto Rican Family in the Culture of Poverty* (1966).

Min, P. G. *Traditions and Changes: Korean Immigrant Families in New York* (1998).

Morales, Aurora Levins. *Remedios: Stories of Earth and Iron from the History of Puertorriqueñas* (1998).

Pettys, Gregory L., and Pallassana R. Balgopal. "Multigenerational Conflicts and New Immigrants: An Indo-American Experience." *Families in Society: The Journal of Contemporary Human Services* 79, 4 (1998): 410–424.

Rumbaut, Ruben G., and Wayne A. Cornelius, eds. *California's Immigrant Children* (1995).

Rumbaut, Ruben G., and K. Ima. *The Adaptation of Southeast Asian Refugee Youth: A Comparative Study* (1988).

Safa, Helen. "Female Employment and the Social Reproduction of the Puerto Rican Working Class." *International Migration Review* 18, 4 (Winter 1984): 1168–1187.

Simon, Rita, and Caroline Brettell, eds. *International Migration: The Female Experience* (1986).

Suárez-Orozco, Carola, and Marcelo Suárez-Orozco. *Transformations: Immigration, Family Life, and Achievement Motivation Among Latino Adolescents* (1995).

Takaki, Ronald. *Strangers at the Gates Again: Asian American Immigration After 1965* (1995).

Taylor, Ronald L. ed. *Minority Families in the United States: A Multicultural Perspective* (1994).

Wolf, Diane L. "Family Secrets: Transnational Struggles Among Children of Filipino Immigrants." *Sociological Perspectives* 40, 3 (Fall 1997): 457–483.

Zhou, M. "Growing Up American: The Challenge Confronting Immigrant Children and Children of Immigrants." *Annual Review of Sociology* 23 (1997): 63–95.

Zhou, M. and C. L. Bankston. *Growing Up American: How Vietnamese Children Adapt to Life in the United States* (1998).

CHAPTER
13

Family Politics in Late-Twentieth-Century America

While immigrants from Asia and Latin America quietly reshaped their families, often in ways that African American and working-class Americans would have found familiar, white, middle-class Americans also experienced change. As the domestic consensus of the 1950s was supplanted by the turbulent rebelliousness of the 1960s, familiar indicators of family stability—marriage, divorce, and birth rates—reversed the trends of the previous decade. Although Americans' later marriages, more frequent divorces, and smaller families in the late twentieth century actually represented a continuation of long-term trends in American family history, many Americans perceived these changes as dramatic disruptions. Contrasting the current situation to a supposedly more stable past, many observers worried that "the family" was in decline, reflecting widespread social, cultural, and moral decay. Adding to this anxiety were a number of factors, among them women's increasing participation in the paid work force; teenagers' attraction to rock 'n' roll, "beat" and "hippie" culture, and protest movements; feminists' demands for increased rights for women; and gays' and lesbians' refusal to remain "in the closet."

By the 1970s an increasing number of social commentators called attention to what cultural conservative and intellectual historian Christopher Lasch labeled a "culture of narcissism" in which Americans, preoccupied with their own selfish desires, abandoned the traditional moral values—including a commitment to strong families—that were vital to the nation's well-being. The debate over "family values" soon penetrated all aspects of American society, receiving airtime on popular talk shows, serious consideration by psychologists and sociologists, and attention from politicians such as President Ronald Reagan, who praised the strong father figure featured in The Cosby Show and called for a return to traditional values. The debate reached its high point in 1992 when Vice President Dan Quayle, during an electoral campaign speech, denounced the title character of another television show, Murphy Brown, for giving birth out of wedlock.

In addition to providing fodder for front-page stories in such magazines as
Time *and* Newsweek *and fueling vigorous political debate, the family values debate
prompted many scholars, historians among them, to take a closer look at family dynamics, past and present. Pointing to the persistence of change in families ever since
American settlement, some scholars commented that rather than being a culture of
narcissism, the prevailing mood in the 1970s and 1980s was a "culture of nostalgia"
in which Americans wistfully recalled a mythical past. But the late twentieth century
was more than an era of anxieties about the present and fantasies about the past;
it was also a critical period during which Americans—in grass-roots organizations,
popular media, and the courts—debated the meaning (or meanings) of the family.*

*Studying American families—and the debate over family values—in the late
twentieth century offers scholars the opportunity to address several important, and
as yet unresolved, questions: What is happening to the family? Who benefits—and
who loses—from changing patterns of family life? How can individuals, scholars,
and policymakers transcend debates over the future of the American family and lay
the groundwork for the success of American families?*

 D O C U M E N T S

In the landmark *Roe* v. *Wade* case in 1973, the United States Supreme Court affirmed a
woman's constitutional right to choose to terminate a pregnancy by means of abortion.
Both supporters and opponents of the decision have tended to overstate the extent of the
Court's support for this right, however. Document 1, taken from Justice Harry Blackmun's majority statement, clarifies the parameters within which a woman (in consultation with her physician) has the legal option of abortion.

In response to the "pro-choice" decision in *Roe*, a "pro-life" movement opposed to
abortion developed. With support from the Catholic Church and conservative politicians,
the pro-life movement helped spawn a number of proposed constitutional amendments
barring women's access to abortion, including the Human Life Amendment, debated in
Congress in 1974, which sought to bestow legal rights of personhood on "all human
beings, including their unborn offspring at every stage of their biological development,
irrespective of age, health, function or condition of dependency." In Document 2
Dr. Mildred F. Jefferson, an assistant clinical professor of surgery at the Boston University School of Medicine and president of the National Right to Life Committee, presents
her testimony to Congress on behalf of the Human Life Amendment.

Legal, safe abortions were both cause and consequence, according to some
social commentators, of a decline in family values in late-twentieth-century America.
In Document 3, originally published in 1983 in *The Futurist*, family sociologists
Andrew Cherlin and Frank F. Fursternberg Jr. contest these dire predictions, forecasting
instead that the family will survive in the twenty-first century, in part because of its
flexibility and diversity.

Some social critics saw the alleged decline of the American family as the result
of men's loss of status within the family. In the late 1980s poet-guru Robert Bly inau-
gurated a "men's movement" in which men sought to reclaim the "wild man" within.
Document 4 is an excerpt from Bly's 1990 book on the wild man concept, *Iron John*.

Others, however, disputed that the American family was in decline or, indeed, that
there ever was such a thing as the American family. Document 5, authored by sociologist
Judith Stacey, a founding member of the Council on Contemporary Families and author
of a 1990 book, *Brave New Families*, satirizes Americans' anxieties about changes in the
American family and proposes measures to support actual American families.

1. The U.S. Supreme Court Defines Women's Right to Choose Abortion, 1973

Mr. Justice Harry A. Blackmun delivered the opinion of the Court:

We forthwith acknowledge our awareness of the sensitive and emotional nature of the abortion controversy, of the vigorous opposing views, even among physicians, and of the deep and seemingly absolute convictions that the subject inspires. One's philosophy, one's experiences, one's exposure to the raw edges of human existence, one's religious training, one's attitudes toward life and family and their values, and the moral standards one establishes and seeks to observe, are all likely to influence and to color one's thinking and conclusions about abortion.

In addition, population growth, pollution, poverty, and racial overtones tend to complicate and not to simplify the problem.

Our task, of course, is to resolve the issue by constitutional measurement, free of emotion and of predilection. We seek earnestly to do this. . . .

The principal thrust of the appellant's attack on the Texas statutes is that they improperly invade a right, said to be possessed by the pregnant woman, to choose to terminate her pregnancy. Appellant would discover this right in the concept of personal "liberty" embodied in the Fourteenth Amendment's Due Process Clause; or in personal, marital, familial and sexual privacy said to be protected by the Bill of Rights . . . or among those rights reserved to the people by the Ninth Amendment. . . .

It perhaps is not generally appreciated that the restrictive criminal abortion laws in effect in a majority of States today are of relatively recent vintage. Those laws, generally proscribing abortion or its attempt at any time during pregnancy except when necessary to preserve the pregnant woman's life, are not of ancient or even of common-law origin. Instead, they derive from statutory changes effected, for the most part, in the latter half of the nineteenth century. . . . At common law, at the time of the adoption of our Constitution, and throughout the major portion of the nineteenth century . . . a woman enjoyed a substantially broader right to terminate a pregnancy than she does in most states today. . . .

When most criminal abortion laws were first enacted, the procedure was a hazardous one for the woman. This was particularly true prior to the development of antisepsis. . . . Abortion mortality was high. . . . Modern medical techniques have altered this situation. Appellants . . . refer to medical data indicating that abortion in early pregnancy, that is, prior to the end of the first trimester, although not without its risk, is now relatively safe. Mortality rates for women undergoing early abortions, where the procedure is legal, appear to be as low as or lower than the rates for normal childbirth. Consequently, any interest of the State in protecting the woman from an inherently hazardous procedure . . . has largely disappeared. . . . The State has a legitimate interest in seeing to it that abortion, like any other medical procedure, is performed under circumstances that insure maximum safety for the patient. . . .

The Constitution does not explicitly mention any right of privacy. In a line of decisions, however . . . the Court has recognized that a right of personal privacy, or

Linda K. Kerber and Jane Sherron De Hart, eds. *Women's America: Refocusing the Past,* 3d ed. (New York: Oxford University Press, 1991), pp. 550–552.

a guarantee of certain areas or zones of privacy, does exist under the Constitution. . . . This right . . . whether it be founded in the Fourteenth Amendment's concept of personal liberty . . . or . . . in the Ninth Amendment's reservation of rights to the people, is broad enough to encompass a woman's decision whether or not to terminate her pregnancy. . . . We . . . conclude that the right of personal privacy includes the abortion decision, but that this right is not unqualified and must be considered against important state interests in regulation. . . .

. . . the State does have an important and legitimate interest in preserving and protecting the health of the pregnant woman . . . and . . . it has still *another* important and legitimate interest in protecting the potentiality of human life. These interests are separate and distinct. Each grows in substantiality as the woman approaches term, and, at a point during pregnancy, each becomes "compelling."

With respect to the State's important and legitimate interest in the health of the mother, the "compelling" point, in the light of present medical knowledge, is at approximately the end of the first trimester. This is so because of the now-established medical fact . . . that until the end of the first trimester mortality in abortion may be less than mortality in normal childbirth. It follows that . . . for the period of pregnancy prior to this "compelling" point, the attending physician, in consultation with his patient, is free to determine, without regulation by the State, that in his medical judgment, the patient's pregnancy should be terminated.

. . . For the state subsequent to approximately the end of the first trimester, the State, in promoting its interest in the health of the mother, may, if it chooses, regulate the abortion procedure in ways that are reasonably related to maternal health.

For the state subsequent to viability, the State in promoting its interest in the potentiality of human life may, if it chooses, regulate, and even proscribe, abortion except where it is necessary, in appropriate medical judgment, for the preservation of the life or health of the mother. . . .

2. The National Right to Life Committee Opposes Abortion, 1974

The surpassing value of the Hippocratic tradition in medicine is that it represents an ethical system where killing and curing functions of the doctor are separated and the society is obliged not to ask the doctor to kill. The assignment of killing functions to the doctor even with the permission of the highest court in the land jeopardizes the entire foundation of an organized society.

A society must indulge in considerable subterfuge to avoid realizing the consequences of such an action. One way of avoiding such realization is to assume a notion that pregnancy is a condition that somehow only affects a woman. This notion disregards the fact that a woman cannot be pregnant without the young of her own kind growing within her body.

Statement of Mildred F. Jefferson, M.D., U.S. Congress, House Subcommittee on Civil and Constitutional Rights of the Committee on the Judiciary, *Hearings on Proposed Constitutional Amendment on Abortion,* 94th Cong., 2d sess. (Washington, D.C.: GPO, 1976), pp. 452–454. This document can also be found in Andrea Tone, ed., *Controlling Reproduction: An American History* (Wilmington, Del.: Scholarly Resources, 1997), pp. 202–204.

It ignores the biological reality that no matter how she may claim to control her own fertility, she cannot reliably become pregnant without the help of the male of her own species even though it may be without consent by artificial means. As long as the human family has only woman naturally equipped to bring forth its own kind, it must not grant her the privilege of throwing the offspring away.

Why is there an unwillingness to see the consequences of asking the doctor to kill for social and economic reasons? Why are there no Ob-Gyn specialists with the experience of a Dr. Jasper F. Williams, now president of the National Medical Association, to show the women with complications that do not go back to the abortionists? Where are the women who have started the organizations WHA—Women Who Have Had Abortions—and WE—Women Exploited—who would tell from their personal experiences the aftermath of this perversion of surgical practice?

Where are the parents who have had their rights to protect the lives and health of their pregnant minor daughters canceled on order of Federal courts? Where are the fathers who now have no defined rights to protect the lives of their children before birth? Where are the representatives of hospitals which have been forced under court orders to provide abortion on their premises against the voted will of their staffs?

Where are the attorneys for the women who have been irreparably damaged or who have lost their lives after the abortion sold as "clean, safe and legal"? Where are the members of the State legislatures that are defending against passive and active euthanasia bills in at least 20 States across the land?

Leaving the final decision on abortion up to a doctor's medical judgment has been too great a burden for some doctors who are suspending all medical judgment and are using the Supreme Court's decisions as an excuse for doing abortion. Others have thought the abortion permission dissolved the network of moral, civil, and criminal laws that border a doctor's every action in treating a patient. Some who have so willingly accepted the direction from outside the experience of their own profession and historical tradition are considered social technicians by their colleagues who no longer consider them worthy of the designation "professionals."

The most cruel effect of the abortion decisions is to legitimatize the requirement of "viability" in evaluating an immature, premature infant. The ability to survive outside the mother, albeit with artificial means, does not depend solely on the child. Aside from the child's biological capability, there is the sophistication and availability of necessary support equipment, the skill of the staff and their willingness to use it in saving the life of a particular premature child. Enforcing the viability concept requires that the struggling child prove that it can survive before being provided with the equipment that would help it survive.

There are some very good pro-abortion emotional appeals and they work on a very wide range of people.

First, of course, is the appeal to the kind gullibility of men who generally have been closed away from the mysterious reproductive business conducted by women. Because they are kind, they are easily intimidated and will believe anything about pregnancy and will do almost anything to spare their pregnant wives or girlfriends any discomfort that they can be blamed for. They never understand that they are only half responsible for the pregnancy.

Second, proposing to defend a "right to choose" without finishing the sentence, which regarding pregnancy means demanding the private right to choose to kill an unborn child.

Three, restoring the protection of the law would drive women back to the "backroom abortionist." In the first 12 weeks now, the "backroom abortionist," if a licensed doctor, may be in the front room and advertising in the local papers under protection of the U.S. Supreme Court's decisions.

Four, "Every child should be a wanted child." "Wantedness" is a changing thing and has never been proved as necessary to success, fame or fortune. The attitude makes the poor child responsible for the social crime against it and demands that it pay the capital penalty of its life. As one of a group of people that has been variously unwanted in various times and places, I do not care very much for the philosophy.

Five, attempting to relate the defense of the traditional respect for life against abortion as a "Catholic position." The great religions based on the Judaeo-Christian tradition have had a shared heritage of the sanctity-of-life ethic.

. . . Our objective is to reestablish the protection of life as the principle that we assumed under the Constitution until the U.S. Supreme Court canceled the right to life of the unborn child.

. . . The human life amendment establishes human life as a priority of this society. We will not compromise. We will not accept anything less.

3. Sociologists Make Predictions About Family Life in the Next Millennium, 1988

"Diversity" is the word for the future of the American family. There will be more divorces, single-parent families, and mixed families from remarriages, but the ideal of marrying and having children is still very much a part of the American experience.

• At current rates, half of all American marriages begun in the early 1980s will end in divorce.

• The number of unmarried couples living together has more than tripled since 1970.

• One out of four children is not living with both parents.

The list could go on and on. Teenage pregnancies: up. Adolescent suicides: up. The birthrate: down. Over the past decade, popular and scholarly commentators have cited a seemingly endless wave of grim statistics about the shape of the American family. The trends have caused a number of concerned Americans to wonder if the family, as we know it, will survive the twentieth century.

And yet, other observers ask us to consider more positive developments:

• Seventy-eight percent of all adults in a recent national survey said they get "a great deal" of satisfaction from their family lives; only 3% said "a little" or "none."

• Two-thirds of the married adults in the same survey said they were "very happy" with their marriages; only 3% said "not too happy."

• In another recent survey of parents of children in their middle years, 88% said that if they had to do it over, they would choose to have children again.

• The vast majority of the children (71%) characterized their family life as "close and intimate."

Andrew Cherlin and Frank F. Furstenberg Jr., "The American Family in the Year 2000," *The Futurist* (June 1983): 7–14. Used with permission from the World Future Society, 7910 Woodmont Avenue, Suite 450, Bethesda, Maryland, 20814. Telephone: 301/656-8274; Fax: 301/951-0394; http://www.wfs.org

Family ties are still important and strong, the optimists argue, and the predictions of the demise of the family are greatly exaggerated.

Neither the dire pessimists who believe that the family is falling apart nor the unbridled optimists who claim that the family has never been in better shape provide an accurate picture of family life in the near future. But these trends indicate that what we have come to view as the "traditional" family will no longer predominate.

Diverse Family Forms

In the future, we should expect to see a growing amount of diversity in family forms, with fewer Americans spending most of their life in a simple "nuclear" family consisting of husband, wife, and children. By the year 2000, three kinds of families will dominate the personal lives of most Americans: families of first marriages, single-parent families, and families of remarriages.

In first-marriage families, both spouses will be in a first marriage frequently begun after living alone for a time or following a period of cohabitation. Most of these couples will have one, two, or, less frequently, three children.

A sizable minority, however, will remain childless. Demographer Charles F. Westoff predicts that about one-fourth of all women currently in their childbearing years will never bear children, a greater number of childless women than at any time in U.S. history.

One other important shift: in a large majority of these families, both the husband and the wife will be employed outside the home. In 1940, only about one out of seven married women worked outside the home; today the proportion is one out of two. We expect this proportion to continue to rise, although not as fast as it did in the past decade or two.

Single-Parent Families

The second major type of family can be formed in two ways. Most are formed by a marital separation, and the rest by births to unmarried women. About half of all marriages will end in divorce at current rates, and we doubt that the rates will fall substantially in the near future.

When the couple is childless, the formerly married partners are likely to set up independent households and resume life as singles. The high rate of divorce is one of the reasons why more men and women are living in single-person households than ever before.

But three-fifths of all divorces involve couples with children living at home. In at least nine out of ten cases, the wife retains custody of the children after a separation.

Although joint custody has received a lot of attention in the press and in legal circles, national data show that it is still uncommon. Moreover, it is likely to remain the exception rather than the rule because most ex-spouses can't get along well enough to manage raising their children together. In fact, a national survey of children aged 11 to 16 conducted by one of the authors demonstrated that fathers have little contact with their children after a divorce. About half of the children whose parents had divorced hadn't seen their father in the last year; only one out of six had managed to see their father an average of once a week. If the current rate of divorce persists, about half of all children will spend some time in a single-parent family before they reach 18.

Much has been written about the psychological effects on children of living with one parent, but the literature has not yet proven that any lasting negative effects occur. One effect, however, does occur with regularity: women who head single-parent families typically experience a sharp decline in their income relative to before their divorce. Husbands usually do not experience a decline. Many divorced women have difficulty reentering the job market after a long absence; others find that their low-paying clerical or service-worker jobs aren't adequate to support a family.

Of course, absent fathers are supposed to make child-support payments, but only a minority do. In a 1979 U.S. Bureau of the Census survey, 43% of all divorced and separated women with children present reported receiving child-support payments during the previous year, and the average annual payment was about $1,900. Thus, the most detrimental effect for children living in a single-parent family is not the lack of a male presence but the lack of a male income.

Families of Remarriages

The experience of living as a single parent is temporary for many divorced women, especially in the middle class. Three out of four divorced people remarry, and about half of these marriages occur within three years of the divorce.

Remarriage does much to solve the economic problems that many single-parent families face because it typically adds a male income. Remarriage also relieves a single parent of the multiple burdens of running and supporting a household by herself.

But remarriage also frequently involves blending together two families into one, a difficult process that is complicated by the absence of clear-cut ground rules for how to accomplish the merger. Families formed by remarriages can become quite complex, with children from either spouse's previous marriage or from the new marriage and with numerous sets of grandparents, stepgrandparents, and other kin and quasi-kin.

The divorce rate for remarriages is modestly higher than for first marriages, but many couples and their children adjust successfully to their remarriage and, when asked, consider their new marriage to be a big improvement over their previous one.

The Life Course: A Scenario for the Next Two Decades

Because of the recent sharp changes in marriage and family life, the life course of children and young adults today is likely to be far different from what a person growing up earlier in this century experienced. It will not be uncommon, for instance, for children born in the 1980s to follow this sequence of living arrangements: live with both parents for several years, live with their mothers after their parents divorce, live with their mothers and stepfathers, live alone for a time when in their early twenties, live with someone of the opposite sex without marrying, get married, get divorced, live alone again, get remarried, and end up living alone once more following the death of their spouses.

Not everyone will have a family history this complex, but it is likely that a substantial minority of the population will. And many more will have family histories only slightly less complex.

Overall, we estimate that about half of the young children alive today will spend some time in a single-parent family before they reach 18; about nine out of ten will eventually marry; about one out of two will marry and then divorce; and about one out of three will marry, divorce, and then remarry. In contrast, only about one out of six women born in the period 1910 to 1914 married and divorced and only about one in eight married, divorced, and remarried.

Without doubt, Americans today are living in a much larger number of family settings during their lives than was the case a few generations ago.

The life-course changes have been even greater for women than for men because of the far greater likelihood of employment during the childbearing years for middle-class women today compared with their mothers and grandmothers. Moreover, the increase in life expectancy has increased the difference between men's and women's family lives. Women now tend to outlive men by a wide margin, a development that is new in this century. Consequently, many more women face a long period of living without a spouse at the end of their lives, either as a widow or as a divorced person who never remarried.

Long-lived men, in contrast, often find that their position in the marriage market is excellent, and they are much more likely to remain married (or remarried) until they die.

Convergence and Divergence

The family lives of Americans vary according to such factors as class, ethnicity, religion, and region. But recent evidence suggests a convergence among these groups in many features of family life. The clearest example is in childbearing, where the differences between Catholics and non-Catholics or between Southerners and Northerners are much smaller than they were 20 years ago. We expect this process of convergence to continue, although it will fall far short of eliminating all social class and subcultural differences.

The experiences of blacks and whites also have converged in many respects, such as in fertility and in patterns of premarital sexual behavior, over the past few decades. But with respect to marriage, blacks and whites have diverged markedly since about 1960.

Black families in the United States always have had strong ties to a large network of extended kin. But in addition, blacks, like whites, relied on a relatively stable bond between husbands and wives. But over the past several decades—and especially since 1960—the proportion of black families maintained by a woman has increased sharply; currently, the proportion exceeds four in ten. In addition, more young black women are having children out of wedlock; in the late 1970s, about two out of three black women who gave birth to a first child were unmarried.

These trends mean that we must qualify our previously stated conclusion that marriage will remain central to family life. This conclusion holds for Americans in general. For many low-income blacks, however, marriage is likely to be less important than the continuing ties to a larger network of kin.

Marriage is simply less attractive to a young black woman from a low-income family because of the poor prospects many young black men have for steady employment and because of the availability of alternative sources of support from public-assistance payments and kin. Even though most black women eventually marry, their marriages have a very high probability of ending in separation or divorce. Moreover, they have a lower likelihood of remarrying.

Black single-parent families sometimes have been criticized as being "disorganized" or even "pathological." What the critics fail to note is that black single mothers usually are embedded in stable, functioning kin networks. These networks tend to center around female kin—mothers, grandmothers, aunts—but brothers, fathers, and other male kin also may be active. The members of these networks share and exchange goods and services, thus helping to share the burdens of poverty. The lower-class black extended family, then, is characterized by strong ties among a network of kin but fragile ties between husband and wife. The negative aspects of this family system have been exaggerated greatly; yet it need not be romanticized, either. It can be difficult and risky for individuals to leave the network in order to try to make it on their own; thus, it may be hard for individuals to raise themselves out of poverty until the whole network is raised.

The Disintegrating Family?

By now, predictions of the demise of the family are familiar to everyone. Yet the family is a resilient institution that still retains more strength than its harshest critics maintain. There is, for example, no evidence of a large-scale rejection of marriage among Americans. To be sure, many young adults are living together outside of marriage, but the evidence we have about cohabitation suggests that it is not a lifelong alternative to marriage; rather, it appears to be either another stage in the process of courtship and marriage or a transition between first and second marriages.

The so-called "alternative lifestyles" that received so much attention in the late 1960s, such as communes and lifelong singlehood, are still very uncommon when we look at the nation as a whole.

Young adults today do marry at a somewhat older age, on average, than their parents did. But the average age at marriage today is very similar to what it was throughout the period from 1890 to 1940.

To be sure, many of these marriages will end in divorce, but three out of four people who divorce eventually remarry. Americans still seem to desire the intimacy and security that a marital relationship provides.

Much of the alarm about the family comes from reactions to the sheer speed at which the institution changed in the last two decades. Between the early 1960s and the mid-1970s, the divorce rate doubled, the marriage rate plunged, the birthrate dropped from a twentieth-century high to an all-time low, premarital sex became accepted, and married women poured into the labor force. But since the mid-1970s, the pace of change has slowed. The divorce rate has risen modestly and the birthrate even has increased a bit. We may have entered a period in which American families can adjust to the sharp changes that occurred in the 1960s and early 1970s. We think that, by and large, accommodations will be made as expectations change and institutions are redesigned to take account of changing family practices.

Despite the recent difficulties, family ties remain a central part of American life. Many of the changes in family life in the 1960s and 1970s were simply a continuation of long-term trends that have been with us for generations.

The birthrate has been declining since the 1820s, the divorce rate has been climbing since at least the Civil War, and over the last half century a growing number of married women have taken paying jobs. Employment outside the home has been gradually eroding the patriarchal system of values that was a part of our early history, replacing it with a more egalitarian set of values.

The only exception occurred during the late 1940s and the 1950s. After World War II, Americans raised during the austerity of depression and war entered adulthood at a time of sustained prosperity. The sudden turnabout in their fortunes led them to marry earlier and have more children than any generation before or since in this century. Because many of us were either parents or children in the baby-boom years following the war, we tend to think that the 1950s typify the way twentieth-century families used to be. But the patterns of marriage and childbearing in the 1950s were an aberration resulting from special historical circumstances; the patterns of the 1960s and 1970s better fit the long-term trends. Barring unforeseen major disruptions, small families, working wives, and impermanent marital ties are likely to remain with us indefinitely.

A range of possible developments could throw our forecasts off the mark. We do not know, for example, how the economy will behave over the next 20 years, or how the family will be affected by technological innovations still at the conception stage. But, we do not envision any dramatic changes in family life resulting solely from technological innovations in the next two decades.

Having sketched our view of the most probable future, we will consider three of the most important implications of the kind of future we see.

Growing Up in Changing Families

Children growing up in the past two decades have faced a maelstrom of social change. As we have pointed out, family life is likely to become even more complex, diverse, unpredictable, and uncertain in the next two decades.

Even children who grow up in stable family environments will probably have to get along with a lot less care from parents (mothers in particular) than children received early in this century. Ever since the 1950s, there has been a marked and continuous increase in the proportion of working mothers whose preschool children are cared for outside the home, rising from 31% in 1958 to 62% in 1977. The upward trend is likely to continue until it becomes standard practice for very young children to receive care either in someone else's home or in a group setting. There has been a distinct drop in the care of children by relatives, as fewer aunts, grandmothers, or adult children are available to supplement the care provided by parents. Increasingly, the government at all levels will be pressured to provide more support for out-of-home daycare.

How are children responding to the shifting circumstances of family life today? Are we raising a generation of young people who, by virtue of their own family experiences, lack the desire and skill to raise the next generation? As we indicated earlier, existing evidence has not demonstrated that marital disruption creates lasting personality damage or instills a distinctly different set of values about family life.

Similarly, a recent review on children of working mothers conducted by the National Research Council of the National Academy of Sciences concludes:

> If there is only one message that emerges from this study, it is that parental employment in and of itself—mothers' employment or fathers' or both parents'—is not necessarily good or bad for children.

The fact that both parents work *per se* does not adversely affect the well-being of children.

Currently, most fathers whose wives are employed do little childcare. Today, most working mothers have two jobs: they work for pay and then come home to do most of the childcare and housework. Pressure from a growing number of harried working wives could prod fathers to watch less television and change more diapers. But this change in fathers' roles is proceeding much more slowly than the recent spate of articles about the "new father" would lead one to expect. The strain that working while raising a family places on working couples, and especially on working mothers, will likely make childcare and a more equitable sharing of housework prominent issues in the 1980s and 1990s.

Family Obligations

Many of the one out of three Americans who, we estimate, will enter a second marriage will do so after having children in a first marriage. Others may enter into a first marriage with a partner who has a family from a previous marriage. It is not clear in these families what obligations remain after divorce or are created after remarriage. For one thing, no clear set of norms exists specifying how people in remarriages are supposed to act toward each other. Stepfathers don't know how much to discipline their stepchildren; second wives don't know what they're supposed to say when they meet their husbands' first wives; stepchildren don't know what to call their absent father's new wife.

The ambiguity about family relations after divorce and remarriage also extends to economic support. There are no clear-cut guidelines to tell adults how to balance the claims of children from previous marriages versus children from their current marriages. Suppose a divorced man who has been making regular payments to support his two small children from a pervious marriage marries a woman with children from her previous marriage. Suppose her husband isn't paying any child support. Suppose further that the remarried couple have a child of their own. Which children should have first claim on the husband's income? Legally, he is obligated to pay child support to his ex-wife, but in practice he is likely to feel that his primary obligation is to his stepchildren, whose father isn't helping, and to his own children from his remarriage.

Our guess, supported by some preliminary evidence from national studies, is that remarriage will tend to further reduce the amount of child support that a man pays, particularly if the man's new family includes children from his new wife's previous marriage or from the current marriage. What appears to be occurring in many cases is a form of "childswapping," with men exchanging an old set of children from a prior marriage for a new set from their new wife's prior marriage and from the remarriage.

Sociologist Lenore J. Weitzman provides a related example in her book *The Marriage Contract.* Suppose, she writes, a 58-year-old corporate vice president with two grown children divorces his wife to marry his young secretary. He agrees to adopt the secretary's two young children. If he dies of a heart attack the following year:

> In most states, a third to half of his estate would go to his new wife, with the remainder divided among the four children (two from his last marriage, and his new wife's two children). His first wife will receive nothing—neither survivors' insurance nor a survivors' pension nor a share of the estate—and both she and his natural children are likely to feel that they have been treated unjustly.

Since the rate of mid-life divorce has been increasing nearly as rapidly as that of divorce at younger ages, this type of financial problem will become increasingly common. It would seem likely that there will be substantial pressure for changes in family law and in income security systems to provide more to the ex-wife and natural children in such circumstances.

Intergenerational Relations

A similar lack of clarity about who should support whom may affect an increasing number of elderly persons. Let us consider the case of an elderly man who long ago divorced his first wife and, as is fairly typical, retained only sporadic contact with his children. If his health deteriorates in old age and he needs help, will his children provide it? In many cases, the relationship would seem so distant that the children would not be willing to provide major assistance. To be sure, in most instances the elderly man would have remarried, possibly acquiring stepchildren, and it may be these stepchildren who feel the responsibility to provide assistance. Possibly the two sets of children may be called upon to cooperate in lending support, even when they have had little or no contact while growing up. Currently, there are no clear guidelines for assigning kinship responsibilities in this new type of extended family.

Even without considering divorce, the issue of support to the elderly is likely to bring problems that are new and widespread. As is well known, the low fertility in the United States, which we think will continue to be low, means that the population is becoming older. The difficulties that this change in age structure poses for the Social Security system are so well known that we need not discuss them here. Let us merely note that any substantial weakening of the Social Security system would put the elderly at a great disadvantage with regard to their families, for older Americans increasingly rely on Social Security and other pensions and insurance plans to provide support. A collapse of Social Security would result in a large decrease in the standard of living among older Americans and a return to the situation prevailing a few decades ago in which the elderly were disproportionately poor.

The relations between older people and their children and grandchildren are typically close, intimate, and warm. Most people live apart from their children, but they generally live close by one or more of them. Both generations prefer the autonomy that the increased affluence of the older generation has recently made possible. Older people see family members quite often, and they report that family members are their major source of support. A survey by Louis Harris of older Americans revealed that more than half of those with children had seen them in the past day, and close to half had seen a grandchild. We expect close family ties between the elderly and their kin to continue to be widespread. If, however, the economic autonomy of the elderly is weakened, say, by a drop in Social Security, the kind of friendly equality that now characterizes intergenerational relations could be threatened.

One additional comment about the elderly: Almost everyone is aware that the declining birthrate means that the elderly will have fewer children in the future on whom they can rely for support. But although this is true in the long run, it will not be true in the next few decades. In fact, beginning soon, the elderly will have more children, on average, than they do today. The reason is the postwar baby boom of the late 1940s and 1950s. As the parents of these large families begin to reach retirement age near the end of this century, more children will be available to help their elderly parents. Once the next generation—the baby-boom children—begins to reach retirement age after about 2010, the long-term trend toward fewer available children will sharply reassert itself.

Were we to be transported suddenly to the year 2000, the families we would see would look very recognizable. There would be few unfamiliar forms—not many communes or group marriages; and probably not a large proportion of lifelong singles. Instead, families by and large would continue to center around the bonds between husbands and wives and between parents and children. One could say the same about today's families relative to the 1960s: the forms are not new. What is quite different, comparing the 1960s with the 1980s, or the 1980s with a hypothetical 2000, is the distribution of these forms.

In the early 1960s, there were far fewer single-parent families and families formed by remarriages after divorce than is the case today; and in the year 2000 there are likely to be far more single-parent families and families of remarriage than we see now. Moreover, in the early 1960s both spouses were employed in a much smaller percentage of two-parent families; in the year 2000, the percentage with two earners will be greater still. Cohabitation before marriage existed in the 1960s, but it was a frowned-upon, bohemian style of life. Today, it has become widely accepted; it will likely become more common in the future. Yet we have argued that cohabitation is less an alternative to marriage than a precursor to marriage, though we expect to see a modest rise in the number of people who never marry.

4. Robert Bly Proposes a Cure for Modern Men's "Softness," 1990

We talk a great deal about "the American man," as if there were some constant quality that remained stable over decades, or even within a single decade.

The men who live today have veered far away from the Saturnian, old-man-minded farmer, proud of his introversion, who arrived in New England in 1630, willing to sit through three services in an unheated church. In the South, an expansive, motherbound cavalier developed, and neither of these two "American men" resembled the greedy railroad entrepreneur that later developed in the Northeast, nor the reckless I-will-do-without culture settlers of the West.

Robert Bly, *Iron John: A Book About Men* (Boston: Addison-Wesley, 1990), pp. 1–6. Copyright © 1990 by Perseus Books Group. Reproduced with permission of Perseus Books Group in the format textbook via Copyright Clearance Center.

Even in our own era the agreed-on model has changed dramatically. During the fifties, for example, an American character appeared with some consistency that became a model of manhood adopted by many men: the Fifties male.

He got to work early, labored responsibly, supported his wife and children, and admired discipline. Reagan is a sort of mummified version of this dogged type. This sort of man didn't see women's souls well, but he appreciated their bodies, and his view of culture and America's part in it was boyish and optimistic. Many of his qualities were strong and positive, but underneath the charm and bluff there was, and there remains, much isolation, deprivation, and passivity. Unless he has an enemy, he isn't sure that he is alive.

The Fifties man was supposed to like football, be aggressive, stick up for the United States, never cry, and always provide. But receptive space or intimate space was missing in this image of a man. The personality lacked some sense of flow. The psyche lacked compassion in a way that encouraged the unbalanced pursuit of the Vietnam war, just as, later, the lack of what we might call "garden" space inside Reagan's head led to his callousness and brutality toward the powerless in El Salvador, toward old people here, the unemployed, schoolchildren, and poor people in general.

The Fifties male had a clear vision of what a man was, and what male responsibilities were, but the isolation and one-sided-ness of his vision were dangerous.

During the sixties, another sort of man appeared. The waste and violence of the Vietnam war made men question whether they knew what an adult male really was. If manhood meant Vietnam, did they want any part of it? Meanwhile, the feminist movement encouraged men to actually look at women, forcing them to become conscious of concerns and sufferings that the Fifties male labored to avoid. As men began to examine women's history and women's sensibility, some men began to notice what was called their *feminine* side and pay attention to it. This process continues to this day, and I would say that most contemporary men are involved in it in some way.

There's something wonderful about this development—I mean the practice of men welcoming their own "feminine" consciousness and nurturing it—this is important—and yet I have the sense that there is something wrong. The male in the past twenty years has become more thoughtful, more gentle. But by this process he has not become more free. He's a nice boy who pleases not only his mother but also the young woman he is living with.

In the seventies I began to see all over the country a phenomenon that we might call the "soft male." Sometimes even today when I look out at an audience, perhaps half the young males are what I'd call soft. They're lovely, valuable people—I like them—they're not interested in harming the earth or starting wars. There's a gentle attitude toward life in their whole being and style of living.

But many of these men are not happy. You quickly notice the lack of energy in them. They are life-preserving but not exactly life-giving. Ironically, you often see these men with strong women who positively radiate energy.

Here we have a finely tuned young man, ecologically superior to his father, sympathetic to the whole harmony of the universe, yet he himself has little vitality to offer.

The strong or life-giving women who graduated from the sixties, so to speak, or who have inherited an older spirit, played an important part in producing this life-preserving, but not life-giving, man.

I remember a bumper sticker during the sixties that read "WOMEN SAY YES TO MEN WHO SAY NO." We recognize that it took a lot of courage to resist the draft, go to jail, or move to Canada, just as it took courage to accept the draft and go to Vietnam. But the women of twenty years ago were definitely saying that they preferred the softer receptive male.

So the development of men was affected a little in this preference. Nonreceptive maleness was equated with violence, and receptive maleness was rewarded.

Some energetic women, at that time and now in the nineties, chose and still choose soft men to be their lovers and, in a way, perhaps, to be their sons. The new distribution of "yang" energy among couples didn't happen by accident. Young men for various reasons wanted their harder women, and women began to desire softer men. It seemed like a nice arrangement for a while, but we've lived with it long enough now to see that it isn't working out.

I first learned about the anguish of "soft" men when they told their stories in early men's gatherings. In 1980, the Lama Community in New Mexico asked me to teach a conference for men only, their first, in which about forty men participated. Each day we concentrated on one Greek god and one old story, and then late in the afternoons we gathered to talk. When the younger men spoke it was not uncommon for them to be weeping within five minutes. The amount of grief and anguish in these younger men was astounding to me.

Part of their grief rose out of remoteness from their fathers, which they felt keenly, but partly, too, grief flowed from trouble in their marriages or relationships. They had learned to be receptive, but receptivity wasn't enough to carry their marriages through troubled times. In every relationship something *fierce* is needed once in a while: both the man and the woman need to have it. But at the point when it was needed, often the young man came up short. He was nurturing, but something else was required—for his relationship, and for his life.

The "soft" male was able to say, "I can feel your pain, and I consider your life as important as mine, and I will take care of you and comfort you." But he could not say what he wanted, and stick by it. *Resolve* of that kind was a different matter.

In *The Odyssey*, Hermes instructs Odysseus that when he approaches Circe, who stands for a certain kind of matriarchal energy, he is to lift or show his sword. In these early sessions it was difficult for many of the younger men to distinguish between showing the sword and hurting someone. One man, a kind of incarnation of certain spiritual attitudes of the sixties, a man who had actually lived in a tree for a year outside Santa Cruz, found himself unable to extend his arm when it held a sword. He had learned so well not to hurt anyone that he couldn't lift the steel, even to catch the light of the sun on it. But showing a sword doesn't necessarily mean fighting. It can also suggest a joyful decisiveness.

The journey many American men have taken into softness, or receptivity, or "development of the feminine side," has been an immensely valuable journey, but more travel lies ahead. No stage is the final stop.

One of the fairy tales that speak of a third possibility for men, a third mode, is a story called "Iron John" or "Iron Hans." Though it was first set down by the Grimm brothers around 1820, this story could be ten or twenty thousand years old.

As the story starts, we find out that something strange has been happening in a remote area of the forest near the king's castle. When hunters go into this area, they disappear and never come back. Twenty others go after the first group and do not come back. In time, people begin to get the feeling that there's something weird in that part of the forest, and they "don't go there anymore."

One day an unknown hunter shows up at the castle and says, "What can I do? Anything dangerous to do around here?"

The King says: "Well, I could mention the forest, but there's a problem. The people who go out there don't come back. The return rate is not good."

"That's just the sort of thing I like," the young man says. So he goes into the forest and, interestingly, he goes there *alone,* taking only his dog. The young man and his dog wander about in the forest and they go past a pond. Suddenly a hand reaches up from the water, grabs the dog, and pulls it down.

The young man doesn't respond by becoming hysterical. He merely says, "This must be the place."

Fond as he is of his dog and reluctant as he is to abandon him, the hunter goes back to the castle, rounds up three more men with buckets, and then comes back to the pond to bucket out the water. Anyone who's ever tried it will quickly note that such bucketing is very slow work.

In time, what they find, lying on the bottom of the pond, is a large man covered with hair from head to foot. The hair is reddish—it looks a little like rusty iron.They take the man back to the castle, and imprison him. The King puts him in an iron cage in the courtyard, calls him "Iron John," and gives the key into the keeping of the Queen.

Let's stop the story here for a second.

When a contemporary man looks down into his psyche, he may, if conditions are right, find under the water of his soul, lying in an area no one has visited for a long time, an ancient hairy man.

The mythological systems associate hair with the instinctive and the sexual and the primitive. What I'm suggesting, then, is that every modern male has, lying at the bottom of his psyche, a large, primitive being covered with hair down to his feet. Making contact with this Wild Man is the step the Eighties male or the Nineties male has yet to take. That bucketing-out process has yet to begin in our contemporary culture. . . .

5. Judith Stacey Relates "The Family Values Fable," 1999

Once upon a fabulized time, half a century ago, there was a lucky land where families with names such as Truman and Eisenhower presided over a world of Nelsons, Cleavers, and Rileys. Men and women married, made love, and produced gurgling Gerber babies (in that proper order). It was a land where, as God and Nature had ordained, men were men and women were ladies. Fathers worked outside the house for pay to support their wives and children, and mothers worked inside the home

Judith Stacey, "The Family Values Fable: A Bedtime Story for the American Century," *National Forum: The Phi Kappa Phi Journal 75,* 3 (Summer 1995). Copyright by Judith Stacey. By permission of the publishers. This document can also be found in Stephanie Coontz, ed., *American Families: A Multicultural Reader* (New York: Routledge, 1999), pp. 487–490.

without pay to support their husbands and to cultivate healthy, industrious, above-average children. Streets and neighborhoods were safe and tidy. This land was the strongest, wealthiest, freest, and fairest in the world. Its virtuous leaders, heroic soldiers, and dazzling technology defended all the freedom-loving people on the planet from an evil empire that had no respect for freedom or families. A source of envy, inspiration, and protection to people everywhere, the leaders and citizens of this blessed land had good reason to feel confident and proud.

And then, as so often happens in fairy tales, evil came to this magical land. Sometime during the mid-1960s, a toxic serpent wriggled its way close to the pretty picket fences guarding those Edenic gardens. One prescient Jeremiah, named Daniel Patrick Moynihan, detected the canny snake and tried to alert his placid country*men* to the dangers of family decline. Making a pilgrimage from Harvard to the White House, he chanted about the ominous signs and consequences of "a tangle of pathology" festering in cities that suburban commuters and their ladies-in-waiting had abandoned for the crabgrass frontier. Promiscuity, unwed mother-hood, and fatherless families, he warned, would undermine domestic tranquility and wreak social havoc. Keening only to the tune of black keys, however, this Pied Piper's song fell flat, inciting displeasure and rebuke.

It seemed that overnight those spoiled Gerber babies had turned into rebellious, disrespectful youth who spurned authority, tradition, and conformity, and scorned the national wealth, power, and imperial status in which their elders exulted. Rejecting their parents' gray flannel suits and Miss America ideals, as well as their monogamous, nuclear families, they generated a counter-culture and a sexual revolution, and they built unruly social movements demanding student rights, free speech, racial justice, peace, and liberation for women and homosexuals. Long-haired, unisex-clad youth smoked dope and marched in demonstrations shouting slogans like "Question Authority," "Girls Say Yes to Boys Who Say No," "Smash Monogamy," "Black is Beautiful," "Power to the People," "Make Love, Not War," "Sisterhood is Powerful," and "Liberation Now." Far from heeding Moynihan's warning, or joining in his condemnation of "black matriarchs," many young women drew inspiration from such mothers and condemned Moynihan instead for "blaming the victims."

Disrupting families and campuses, the young people confused and divided their parents and teachers, even seducing some foolish elders into emulating their sexual and social experiments. But the thankless arrogance of these privileged youth, their unkempt appearance, provocative antics, and amorality also enraged many, inciting a right-wing, wishful, "moral majority" to form its own backlash social movement to restore family and moral order.

And so it happened that harmony, prosperity, security, and confidence disappeared from this once most fortunate land. After decimating African American communities, the serpent of family decline slithered under the picket fences, where it spewed its venom on white, middle-class victims as well. Men no longer knew what it meant to be men, and women had neither the time nor the inclination to be ladies. Ozzie had trouble finding secure work. He was accused of neglecting, abusing, and oppressing his wife and children. Harriet no longer stayed home with the children. She too worked outside the home for pay, albeit less pay. Ozzie and Harriet sued for divorce. Harriet decided she could choose to have children with or without a marriage certificate, with or without an Ozzie, or perhaps even with a Rozzie. After all, as front-page stories in her morning newspaper informed her, almost daily, "Traditional Family Nearly the Exception, Census Finds."

As the last decade of the century dawned, only half the children in the land were living with two married parents who had jointly conceived or adopted them. Twice as many children were living in single-parent families as in male-breadwinner, female-homemaker families. Little wonder few citizens could agree over what would count as a proper family. Little wonder court chroniclers charted the devolution of the modern family system in books with anxious titles such as: *The War Over the Family, Embattled Paradise, Disturbing the Nest, Brave New Families, The Way We Never Were, Fatherless America,* and *Families on the Faultline.*

The clairvoyant Daniel Patrick Moynihan found himself vindicated at last, as political candidates from both ruling parties joined his hymns of praise to Ozzie and Harriet and rebuked the selfish family practices of that rebellious stepchild of the Nelsons, Murphy Brown.

The era of the modern family system had come to an end, and few could feel sanguine about the postmodern family condition that had succeeded it. Unaccustomed to a state of normative instability and definitional crisis, the populace split its behavior from its beliefs. Many who contributed actively to such postmodern family statistics as divorce, remarriage, blended families, single parenthood, joint custody, abortion, domestic partnership, two-career households, and the like still yearned nostalgically for the *Father Knows Best* world they had lost.

"Today," in the United States, as Rutger's historian John Gillis so aptly puts it, "the anticipation and memory of family means more to people than its immediate reality. It is through the families we live *by* that we achieve the transcendence that compensates for the tensions and frustrations of the families we live *with*." Not only have the fabled families of midcentury we live *by* become more compelling than the messy, improvisational, patchwork bonds of postmodern family life, but as my bedtime story hints, because they function as pivotal elements in our distinctive national imagination, these symbolic families are also far more stable than any in which past generations ever dwelled.

In the context of our contemporary social, economic, and political malaise, it is not difficult to understand the public's palpable longing for the world of innocence, safety, confidence, and affluence that Ozzie and Harriet have come to signify. Unfortunately, this nostalgia does little to improve conditions for the beleaguered families we live *with,* and a great deal to make them even worse. The family-values campaign helped to fuel the passage of budget-cutting and anti-welfare "reform" measures that will plunge the growing ranks of our least fortunate families, and especially the children whose interests the campaign claims to serve, into ever-greater misery and decay. For apart from exhorting or coercing adults to enter or remain in possibly hostile, even destructive marriages, family-decline critics offer few social proposals to address children's pressing needs. Further stigmatizing the increasing numbers who live in "nontraditional" families will only add to their duress.

We can watch *Ozzie and Harriet* reruns as long as we like, but we cannot return to the world it evokes, even if we wish to. What we can do, and what I sorely believe we must do instead, is to direct public attention and resources to measures that could mitigate the unnecessarily injurious effects of divorce and single parenthood on the fourth of our nation's children who now suffer these effects. Having surmised that one must fight fables with fables, I offer my personal utopian wish list of such genuinely "pro-family" measures:

- restructure work hours and benefits to suit working parents;
- redistribute work to reduce under- and overemployment;
- enact comparable-worth standards of pay equity so that women as well as men can earn a family wage;
- provide universal health, prenatal and child care, sex education, and reproductive rights to make it possible to choose to parent responsibly;
- legalize gay marriage;
- revitalize public education;
- pass and enforce strict gun control laws;
- end the economic inequities of property and income dispositions in divorce;
- house the homeless;
- institute a universal national-service obligation;
- fund libraries, parks, public broadcasting, and the arts;
- read a fable of democratic family values to the children of the next millennium.

 E S S A Y S

In the first essay, an excerpt from University of California at Berkeley sociologist Kristin Luker's 1984 book, *Abortion and the Politics of Motherhood*, Luker discusses the heated abortion debate in late-twentieth-century America. Using in-depth interviews with pro- and anti-choice activists, Luker contends that the abortion debate is about more than the definition of a "viable" life; it is a public discussion of the definition and importance of motherhood in American society.

In the second essay, taken from Robert L. Griswold's 1993 book, *Fatherhood in America*, Griswold, a historian at Oklahoma University, shifts the focus to fatherhood. Pointing to women's increased levels of participation in the work force, feminist demands for shared responsibilities, and pop psychology's and popular culture's support for "involved" fathers, Griswold describes the closing decades of the twentieth century as a major watershed for definitions of fatherhood. At the same time, however, he warns that the "men's movement" at times seeks to reinvigorate, rather than obliterate, patriarchy.

Abortion and the Politics of Motherhood

KRISTIN LUKER

According to interested observers at the time, abortion in America was as frequent in the last century as it is in our own. And the last century . . . had its own "right-to-life" movement, composed primarily of physicians who pursued the issue in the service of their own professional goals. . . . From a quiet, restricted technical debate

Kristin Luker, *Abortion and the Politics of Motherhood* (Berkeley and Los Angeles: University of California Press, 1984), pp. 192–210, 213–215. Copyright © 1984 The Regents of the University of California. Reprinted by permission of the University of California Press.

among concerned professionals, abortion has become a debate that seems at times capable of tearing the fabric of American life apart. How did this happen? What accounts for the remarkable transformation of the abortion debate? . . .

. . . [T]he abortion debate has been transformed because it has "gone public" and in so doing has called into question individuals' most sacrosanct beliefs.

But this is only part of the story. . . . [A]ll the previous rounds of the abortion debate in America were merely echoes of the issue as the nineteenth century defined it: a debate about the medical profession's right to make life-and-death decisions. In contrast, the most recent round of the debate is about something new. By bringing the issue of the moral status of the embryo to the fore, the new round focuses on the relative rights of women and embryos. Consequently, the abortion debate has become a debate about women's contrasting obligations to themselves and others. New technologies and the changing nature of work have opened up possibilities for women outside of the home undreamed of in the nineteenth century; together, these changes give women—for the first time in history—the option of deciding exactly how and when their family roles will fit into the larger context of their lives. In essence, therefore, this round of the abortion debate is so passionate and hard-fought *because it is a referendum on the place and meaning of motherhood.*

Motherhood is at issue because two opposing visions of motherhood are at war. Championed by "feminists" and "housewives," these two different views of motherhood represent in turn two very different kinds of social worlds. The abortion debate has become a debate among women, women with different values in the social world, different experiences of it, and different resources with which to cope with it. How the issue is framed, how people think about it, and, most importantly, where the passions come from are all related to the fact that the battlelines are increasingly drawn (and defended) by women. While on the surface it is the embryo's fate that seems to be at stake, the abortion debate is actually about the meanings of *women's* lives. . . .

Who Are the Activists?

On almost every social background variable we examined, pro-life and pro-choice women differed dramatically. For example, in terms of income, almost half of all pro-life women (44 percent) in this study reported an income of less than $20,000 a year, but only one-fourth of the pro-choice women reported an income that low, and a considerable portion of those were young women just starting their careers. On the upper end of the income scale, one-third of the pro-choice women reported an income of $50,000 a year or more compared with only one pro-life woman in every seven.

These simple figures on income, however, conceal a very complex social reality, and that social reality is in turn tied to feelings about abortion. The higher incomes of pro-choice women, for example, result from a number of intersecting factors. Almost without exception pro-choice women work in the paid labor force, they earn good salaries when they work, and if they are married, they are likely to be married to men who also have good incomes. An astounding 94 percent of all pro-choice women work, and over half of them have incomes in the top 10 percent of all working women in this country. Moreover, one pro-choice woman in ten has an annual *personal* income (as opposed to a family income) of $30,000 or more, thus putting her in the rarified ranks of the top 2 percent of all employed women in America. Pro-life women, by contrast, are far less likely to work: 63 percent of them do not work in the paid labor force, and almost all of those who do are unmarried. Among pro-life married women, for example, only 14 percent report any personal income at all, and for most of them, this is earned not in a formal job but through activities such as selling cosmetics to groups of friends. Not surprisingly, the personal income of pro-life women who work outside the home, whether in a formal job or in one of these less-structured activities, is low. Half of all pro-life women who do work earn less than $5,000 a year, and half earn between $5,000 and $10,000. Only two pro-life women we contacted reported a personal income of more than $20,000. Thus pro-life women are less likely to work in the first place, they earn less money when they do work, and they are more likely to be married to a skilled worker or small businessman who earns only a moderate income.

These differences in income are in turn related to the different educational and occupational choices these women have made along the way. Among pro-choice women, almost four out of ten (37 percent) had undertaken some graduate work beyond the B.A. degree, and 18 percent had an M.D., a law degree, a Ph.D., or a similar postgraduate degree. Pro-life women, by comparison, had far less education: 10 percent of them had only a high school education or less; and another 30 percent never finished college (in contrast with only 8 percent of the pro-choice women). Only 6 percent of all pro-life women had a law degree, a Ph.D., or a medical degree.

These educational differences were in turn related to occupational differences among the women in this study. Because of their higher levels of education, pro-choice women tended to be employed in the major professions, as administrators, owners of small businesses, or executives in large businesses. The pro-life women tended to be housewives or, of the few who worked, to be in the traditional female jobs of teaching, social work, and nursing. (The choice of home life over public life held true for even the 6 percent of pro-life women with an advanced degree: of the married women who had such degrees, at the time of our interviews only one of them had not retired from her profession after marriage.)

These economic and social differences were also tied to choices that women on each side had made about marriage and family life. For example, 23 percent of pro-choice women had never married, compared with only16 percent of pro-life women; 14 percent of pro-choice women had been divorced, compared with 5 percent of pro-life women. The size of the families these women had was also different. The average pro-choice family had between one and two children and was more likely to have one; pro-life families averaged between two and three children and were more likely to have three. (Among the pro-life women, 23 percent had five or more children; 16 percent had seven or more children.) Pro-life women also tended to marry at a slightly younger age and to have had their first child earlier.

Finally, the women on each side differed dramatically in their religious affiliation and in the role that religion played in their lives. Almost 80 percent of the women active in the pro-life movement at the present time are Catholics. The remainder are Protestants (9 percent), persons who claim no religion (5 percent), and Jews (1 percent). In sharp contrast, 63 percent of pro-choice women say that they have no religion, 22 percent think of themselves as vaguely Protestant, 3 percent are Jewish, and 9 percent have what they call a "personal" religion. We found no one in our sample of pro-choice activists who claimed to be a Catholic at the time of the interviews.

When we asked activists what religion they were raised in as a child, however, a different picture emerged. For example, 20 percent of the pro-choice activists were raised as Catholics, 42 percent were raised as Protestants, and 15 percent were raised in the Jewish faith. In this group that describes itself as predominantly without religious affiliation, therefore, only 14 percent say they were not brought up in any formal religious faith. By the same token, although almost 80 percent of present pro-life activists are Catholic, only 58 percent were raised in that religion (15 percent were raised as Protestants and 3 percent as Jews). Thus, almost 20 percent of the pro-life activists in this study are converts to Catholicism, people who have actively chosen to follow a given religious faith, in striking contrast to pro-choice people, who have actively chosen not to follow any.

Perhaps the single most dramatic difference between the two groups, however, is in the role that religion plays in their lives. Almost three-quarters of the pro-choice people interviewed said that formal religion was either unimportant or completely irrelevant to them, and their attitudes are correlated with behavior: only 25 percent of the pro-choice women said they *ever* attend church, and most of these said they do so only occasionally. Among pro-life people, by contrast, 69 percent said religion was important in their lives, and an additional 22 percent said that it was very important. For pro-life women, too, these attitudes are correlated with behavior: half of those pro-life women interviewed said they attend church regularly once a week, and another 13 percent said they do so even more often. Whereas 80 percent of pro-choice people never attend church, only 2 percent of pro-life advocates never do so.

Keeping in mind that the statistical use of averages has inherent difficulties, we ask, who are the "average" pro-choice and pro-life advocates? When the social background data are looked at carefully, two profiles emerge. The average pro-choice activist is a forty-four-year-old married women who grew up in a large metropolitan area and whose father was a college graduate. She was married at age twenty-two, has one or two children, and has had some graduate and professional training beyond the B.A. degree. She is married to a professional man, is herself employed in a regular job, and her family income is more than $50,000 a year. She is not religiously active, feels that religion is not important to her, and attends church very rarely if at all.

The average pro-life woman is also a forty-four-old married woman who grew up in a large metropolitan area. She married at age seventeen and has three children or more. Her father was a high school graduate, and she has some college education or may have a B.A. degree. She is not employed in the paid labor force and is married to a small businessman or a lower-level white-collar worker; her family income is $30,000 a year. She is Catholic (and may have converted), and her religion is one of the most important aspects of her life: she attends church at least once a week and occasionally more often.

Interests and Passions

To the social scientist (and perhaps to most of us) these social background characteristics connote lifestyles as well. We intuitively clothe these bare statistics with assumptions about beliefs and values. When we do so, the pro-choice women emerge as educated, affluent, liberal professionals, whose lack of religious affiliation suggests a secular, "modern," or (as pro-life people would have it) "utilitarian" outlook on life. Similarly, the income, education, marital patterns, and religious devotion of pro-life women suggest that they are traditional, hard-working people ("polyester types" to their opponents), who hold conservative views on life. We may be entitled to assume that individuals' social backgrounds act to shape and mold their social attitudes, but it is important to realize that the relationship between social worlds and social values is a very complex one.

Perhaps one example will serve to illustrate the point. A number of pro-life women in this study emphatically rejected an expression that pro-choice women tend to use almost unthinkingly—the expression *unwanted pregnancy*. Pro-life women argued forcefully that a better term would be a *surprise* pregnancy, asserting that although a pregnancy may be momentarily unwanted, the child that results from the pregnancy almost never is. Even such a simple thing—what to call an unanticipated pregnancy—calls into play an individual's values and resources. Keeping in mind our profile of the average pro-life person, it is obvious that a woman who does not work in the paid labor force, who does not have a college degree, whose religion is important to her, and who has already committed herself wholeheartedly to marriage and a large family is well equipped to believe that an unanticipated pregnancy usually becomes a beloved child. Her life is arranged so that for her, this belief is true. This view is consistent not only with her values, which she has held from earliest childhood, but with her social resources as well. It should not be surprising, therefore, that her world view leads her to believe that everyone else can "make room for one more" as easily as she can and that therefore it supports her in her conviction that abortion is cruel, wicked, and self-indulgent.

It is almost certainly the case that an unplanned pregnancy is never an easy thing for anyone. Keeping in mind the profile of the average pro-choice woman, however, it is evident that a woman who is employed full time, who has an affluent lifestyle that depends in part on her contribution to the family income, and who expects to give a child as good a life as she herself has had with respect to educational, social, and economic advantages will draw on a different reality when she finds herself being skeptical about the ability of the average person to transform unwanted pregnancies into well-loved (and well-cared-for) children.

The relationship between passions and interests is thus more dynamic than it might appear at first. It is true that at one level, pro-choice and pro-life attitudes on abortion are self-serving: activists on each side have different views of the morality of abortion because their chosen lifestyles leave them with different needs for abortion; and both sides have values that provide a moral basis for their abortion needs in particular and their lifestyles in general. But this is only half the story. The values that lead pro-life and pro-choice women into different attitudes toward abortion are the same values that led them at an earlier time to adopt different lifestyles that supported a given view of abortion.

For example, pro-life women have *always* valued family roles very highly and have arranged their lives accordingly. They did not acquire high-level educational and occupational skills, for example, because they married, and they married because their values suggested that this would be the most satisfying life open to them.

Similarly, pro-choice women postponed (or avoided) marriage and family roles because they chose to acquire the skills they needed to be successful in the larger world, having concluded that the role of wife and mother was too limited for them. Thus, activists on both sides of the issue are women who have a given set of values about what are the most satisfying and appropriate roles for women, and they have made *life commitments that now limit their ability to change their minds.* Women who have many children and little education, for example, are seriously handicapped in attempting to become doctors or lawyers; women who have reached their late forties with few children or none are limited in their ability to build (or rebuild) a family. For most of these activists, therefore, their position on abortion is the "tip of the iceberg," a shorthand way of supporting and proclaiming not only a complex set of values but a given set of social resources as well.

To put the matter differently, we might say that for pro-life women the traditional division of life into separate male roles and female roles still works, but for pro-choice women it does not. Having made a commitment to the traditional female roles of wife, mother, and homemaker, pro-life women are limited in those kinds of resources—education, class status, recent occupational experiences—they would need to compete in what has traditionally been the male sphere, namely, the paid labor force. The average pro-choice woman, in contrast, is comparatively well endowed with exactly those resources: she is highly educated, she already has a job, and she has recent (and continuous) experience in the job market.

In consequence, anything that supports a traditional division of labor into male and female worlds is, broadly speaking, in the interest of pro-life women because that is where their resources lie. Conversely, such a traditional division of labor, when strictly enforced, is against the interests of pro-choice women because it limits their ability to use the valuable "male" resources that they have in relative abundance. It is therefore apparent that attitudes toward abortion, even though rooted in childhood experiences, are also intimately related to present-day interests. Women who oppose abortion and seek to make it officially unavailable are declaring, both practically and symbolically, that women's reproductive roles should be given social primacy. Once an embryo is defined as a child and an abortion as the death of a person, almost everything else in a woman's life must "go on hold" during the course of her pregnancy: any attempt to gain "male" resources such as a job, an education, or other skills must be subordinated to her uniquely female responsibility of serving the needs of this newly conceived person. Thus, when personhood is bestowed on the embryo, women's nonreproductive roles are made secondary to their reproductive roles. The act of conception therefore creates a pregnant woman rather than a woman who is pregnant; it creates a woman whose life, in cases where roles or values clash, is defined by the fact that she is—or may become—pregnant.

It is obvious that this view is supportive of women who have already decided that their familial and reproductive roles are the major ones in their lives. By the same token, the costs of defining women's reproductive roles as primary do not seem high to them because they have already chosen to make those roles primary anyway. For example, employers might choose to discriminate against women because they might require maternity leave and thus be unavailable at critical times, but women who have chosen not to work in the paid labor force in the first place can see such discrimination as irrelevant to them.

It is equally obvious that supporting abortion (and believing that the embryo is not a person) is in the vested interests of pro-choice women. Being so well equipped to compete in the male sphere, they perceive any situation that both practically and symbolically affirms the primacy of women's reproductive roles as a real loss to them. Practically, it devalues their social resources. If women are only secondarily in the labor market and must subordinate working to pregnancy, should it occur, then their education, occupation, income, and work become potentially temporary and hence discounted. Working becomes, as it traditionally was perceived to be, a pastime or hobby pursued for "pin money" rather than a central part of their lives. Similarly, if the embryo is defined as a person and the ability to become pregnant is the central one for women, a woman must be prepared to sacrifice some of her own interests to the interests of this newly conceived person.

In short, in a world where men and women have traditionally had different roles to play and where male roles have traditionally been the more socially prestigious and financially rewarded, abortion has become a symbolic marker between those who wish to maintain this division of labor and those who wish to challenge it. . . .

Thus, the sides are fundamentally opposed to each other not only on the issue of abortion but also on what abortion *means.* Women who have many "human capital" resources of the traditionally male variety want to see motherhood recognized as a private, discretionary choice. Women who have few of these resources and limited opportunities in the job market want to see motherhood recognized as the most important thing a woman can do. In order for pro-choice women to achieve their goals, therefore, they *must* argue that motherhood is not a primary, inevitable, or "natural" role for all women; for pro-life women to achieve their goals, they *must* argue that it is. In short, the debate rests on the question of whether women's fertility is to be socially recognized as a resource or as a handicap. . . .

Because of their commitment to their own view of motherhood as a primary social role, pro-life women believe that other women are "casual" about abortions and have them "for convenience." There are no reliable data to confirm whether or not women are "casual" about abortions, but many pro-life people believe this to be the case and relate their activism to their perception of other people's casualness. . . .

The assertion that women are "casual" about abortion, one could argue, expresses in a short-hand way a set of beliefs about women and their roles. First, the more people value the personhood of the embryo, the more important must be the reasons for taking its life. Some pro-life people, for example, would accept an abortion when continuation of the pregnancy would cause the death of the mother; they believe that when two lives are in direct conflict, the embryo's life can be considered the more expendable. But not all pro-life people agree, and many say they would not accept abortion even to save the mother's life. (Still others say they accept the idea in principle but would not make that choice in their own lives if faced with it.) For people who accept the personhood of the embryo, any reason besides trading a "life for a life" (and sometimes even that) seems trivial, merely a matter of "convenience."

Second, people who accept the personhood of the embryo see the reasons that pro-abortion people give for ending a pregnancy as simultaneously downgrading the value of the embryo and upgrading everything else but pregnancy. The argument that women need abortion to "control" their fertility means that they intend to subordinate pregnancy, with its inherent unpredictability, to something else . . . participation in the paid labor force. Abortion permits women to engage in paid work on an equal basis with men. With abortion, they may schedule pregnancy in order to take advantage of the kinds of benefits that come with a paid position in the labor force: a paycheck, a title, and a social identity. The pro-life women in this study were often careful to point out that they did not object to "career women." But what they meant by "career women" were women whose *only* responsibilities were in the labor force. Once a woman became a wife and a mother, in their view her primary responsibility was to her home and family.

Third, the pro-life activists we interviewed, the overwhelming majority of whom are full-time homemakers, also felt that women who worked *and* had families could often do so only because women like themselves picked up the slack. Given their place in the social structure, it is not surprising that many of the pro-life women thought that married women who worked outside the home were "selfish"—that they got all the benefits while the homemakers carried the load for them in Boy and Girl Scouts, PTA, and after school, for which their reward was to be treated by the workers as less competent and less interesting persons.

Abortion therefore strips the veil of sanctity from motherhood. When pregnancy is discretionary—when people are allowed to put anything else they value in front of it—then motherhood has been demoted from a sacred calling to a job. In effect, the legalization of abortion serves to make men and women more "unisex" by deemphasizing what makes them different—the ability of women to visibly and directly carry the next generation. Thus, pro-choice women are emphatic about their right to compete equally with men without the burden of an unplanned pregnancy, and pro-life women are equally emphatic about their belief that men and women have different roles in life and that pregnancy is a gift instead of a burden. . . .

It is stating the obvious to point out that the more limited the educational credentials a woman has, the more limited the job opportunities are for her, and the more limited the job opportunities, the more attractive motherhood is as a full-time occupation. In motherhood, one can control the content and pace of one's own work, and the job is *intrinsically meaningful.* Compared with a job clerking in a supermarket (a realistic alternative for women with limited educational credentials) where the work is poorly compensated and often demeaning, motherhood can have compensations that far transcend the monetary ones. . . .

All the circumstances of her existence will therefore encourage a pro-life woman to highlight the kinds of values and experiences that support childbearing and childrearing and to discount the attraction (such as it is) of paid employment. Her circumstances encourage her to resent the pro-choice view that women's most meaningful and prestigious activities are in the "man's world."

Abortion also has a symbolic dimension that separates the needs and interests of homemakers and workers in the paid labor force. Insofar as abortion allows a woman to get a job, to get training for a job, or to advance in a job, it does more than provide social support for working women over homemakers; it also seems to support the value of economic considerations over moral ones. Many pro-life people interviewed said that although their commitment to traditional family roles meant very real material deprivations to themselves and their families, the moral benefits of such a choice more than made up for it. . . .

For pro-life people, a world view that puts the economic before the noneconomic hopelessly confuses two different kinds of worlds. For them, the private world of family as traditionally experienced is the one place in human society where none of us has a price tag. Home, as Robert Frost pointed out, is where they have to take you in, whatever your social worth. Whether one is a surgeon or a rag picker, the family is, at least ideally, the place where love is unconditional.

Pro-life people and pro-life women in particular have very real reasons to fear such a state of affairs. Not only do they see an achievement-based world as harsh, superficial, and ultimately ruthless; they are relatively less well-equipped to operate in that world. . . . Pro-life people have relatively fewer official achievements in part because they have been doing what they see as a moral task, namely, raising children and making a home; and they see themselves as becoming handicapped in a world that discounts not only their social contributions but their personal lives as well.

It is relevant in this context to recall the grounds on which pro-life people argue that the embryo is a baby: that it is genetically human. To insist that the embryo is a baby because it is genetically human is to make a claim that it is both wrong and impossible to make distinctions between humans at all. Protecting the life of the embryo, which is by definition an entity whose social worth is all yet to come, means protecting others who feel that they may be defined as having low social worth; more broadly, it means protecting a legal view of personhood that emphatically rejects social worth criteria.

For the majority of pro-life people we interviewed, the abortions they found most offensive were those of "damaged" embryos. This is because this category so clearly highlights the aforementioned concerns about social worth. To defend a genetically or congenitally damaged embryo from abortion is, in their minds, defending the weakest of the weak, and most pro-life people we interviewed were least prepared to compromise on this category of abortion.

The genetic basis of the embryo's claim to personhood has another, more subtle implication for those on the pro-life side. If genetic humanness equals personhood, then biological facts of life must take precedence over social facts of life. One's destiny is therefore inborn and hence immutable. To give any ground on the embryo's biologically determined babyness, therefore, would be extension call into question the "innate," "natural," and biological basis of women's traditional roles as well.

Pro-choice people, of course, hold a very different view of the matter. For them, social considerations outweigh biological ones: the embryo becomes a baby when it is "viable," that is, capable of achieving a certain degree of social integration with others. This is a world view premised on achievement, but not in the way pro-life people experience the word. Pro-choice people, believing as they do in choice, planning, and human efficacy, believe that biology is simply a minor given to be transcended by human experience. Sex, like race and age, is not an appropriate criterion for sorting people into different rights and responsibilities. Pro-choice people downplay these "natural" ascriptive characteristics, believing that true equality means achievement based on talent, not being restricted to a "women's world," a "black world," or an "old people's world." Such a view, as the profile of pro-choice people has made clear, is entirely consistent with their own lives and achievements.

These differences in social circumstances that separate pro-life from pro-choice women on the core issue of abortion also lead them to have different values on topics that surround abortion, such as sexuality and the use of contraception. With respect to sexuality, for example, the two sides have diametrically opposed values; these values arise from a fundamentally different premise, which is, in turn, tied to the different realities of their social worlds. If pro-choice women have a vested interest in subordinating their reproductive capacities, and pro-life women have a vested interest in highlighting them, we should not be surprised to find that pro-life women believe that the purpose of sex is reproduction whereas pro-choice women believe that its purpose is to promote intimacy and mutual pleasure.

These two views about sex express the same value differences that lead the two sides to have such different views on abortion. If women plan to find their primary role in marriage and the family, then they face a need to create a "moral cartel" when it comes to sex. If sex is freely available outside of marriage, then why should men, as the old saw puts it, buy the cow when the milk is free? If many women are willing to sleep with men outside of marriage, then the regular sexual activity that comes with marriage is much less valuable an incentive to marry. And because pro-life women are traditional women, their primary resource for marriage is the promise of a stable home, with everything it implies: children, regular sex, a "haven in a heartless world."

But pro-life women, like all women, are facing a devaluation of these resources. As American society increasingly becomes a service economy, men can buy the services that a wife traditionally offers. Cooking, cleaning, decorating, and the like can easily be purchased on the open market in a cash transaction. And as sex becomes more open, more casual, and more "amative," it removes one more resource that could previously be obtained only through marriage.

Pro-life women, as we have seen, have both value orientations and social characteristics that make marriage very important. Their alternatives in the public world of work are, on the whole, less attractive. Furthermore, women who stay home full-time and keep house are becoming a financial luxury. Only very wealthy families *or families whose values allow them to place the nontangible benefits of a full-time wife over the tangible benefits of a working wife* can afford to keep one of its earners off the labor market. To pro-life people, the nontangible benefit of having children—and therefore the value of procreative sex—is very important. Thus, a social ethic that promotes more freely available sex undercuts pro-life women two ways: it limits their abilities to get into a marriage in the first place, and it undermines the social value placed on their presence once within a marriage.

For pro-choice women, the situation is reversed. Because they have access to "male" resources such as education and income, they have far less reason to believe that the basic reason for sexuality is to produce children. They plan to have small families anyway, and they and their husbands come from and have married into a social class in which small families are the norm. For a number of overlapping reasons, therefore, pro-choice women believe that the value of sex is not primarily procreative: pro-choice women value the ability of sex to promote human intimacy more (or at least more frequently) than they value the ability of sex to produce babies. But they hold this view because they can afford to. When they bargain for marriage, they use the same resources that they use in the labor market: upper-class status, an education very similar to a man's, side-by-side participation in the man's world, and, not least, a salary that substantially increases a family's standard of living.

It is true, therefore, that pro-life people are "anti-sex." They value sex, of course, but they value it for its traditional benefits (babies) rather than for the benefits that pro-choice people associate with it (intimacy). Pro-life people really do want to see "less" sexuality—or at least less open and socially unregulated sexuality—because they think it is morally wrong, they think it distorts the meaning of sex, and they feel that it *threatens the basis on which their own marital bargains are built.* . . .

Pro-choice women, therefore, value (and can afford) an approach to sexuality that, by sidelining reproduction, diminishes the differences between men and women; they can do this *because they have other resources on which to build a marriage.* Since their value is intimacy and since the daily lives of men and women on the pro-choice side are substantially similar, intimacy in the bedroom is merely an extension of the intimacy of their larger world.

Pro-life women and men, by contrast, tend to live in "separate spheres." Because their lives are based on a social and emotional division of labor where each sex has its appropriate work, to accept contraception or abortion would devalue the one secure resource left to these women: the private world of home and hearth. This would be disastrous not only in terms of status but also in terms of meaning: if values about fertility and family are not essential to a marriage, what supports does a traditional marriage have in times of stress? To accept highly effective contraception, which actually and symbolically subordinates the role of children in the family to other needs and goals, would be to cut the ground of meaning out from under at least one (and perhaps both) partners' lives. Therefore, contraception, which sidelines the reproductive capacities of men and women, is both useless and threatening to pro-life people.

The Core of the Debate

In summary, women come to be pro-life and pro-choice activists as the end result of lives that center around different definitions of motherhood. They grow up with a belief about the nature of the embryo, so events in their lives lead them to believe that the embryo is a unique person, or a fetus; that people are intimately tied to their biological roles, or that these roles are but a minor part of life; that motherhood is the most important and satisfying role open to a woman, or that motherhood is only one of several roles, a burden when defined as the only role. These beliefs and values are rooted in the concrete circumstances of women's lives—their educations, incomes, occupations, and the different marital and family choices they have made along the way—and they work simultaneously to shape those circumstances in turn. Values about the relative place of reason and faith, about the role of actively planning for life versus learning to accept gracefully life's unknowns, of the relative satisfactions inherent in work and family—all of these factors place activists in a specific relationship to the larger world and give them a specific set of resources with which to confront that world.

The simultaneous and on-going modification of both their lives and their values by each other finds these activists located in a specific place in the social world. They are financially successful, or they are not. They become highly educated, or they do not. They become married and have a large family, or they have a small one. And at each step of the way, both their values and their lives have undergone either ratification or revision.

Pro-choice and pro-life activists live in different worlds, and the scope of their lives, as both adults and children, fortifies them in their belief that their own views on abortion are the more correct, more moral, and more reasonable. When added to this is the fact that should "the other side" win, one group of women will see the very real devaluation of their lives and life resources, it is not surprising that the abortion debate has generated so much heat and so little light.

Patriarchy and the Politics of Fatherhood

ROBERT L. GRISWOLD

In a room full of "smoke and anger," some sixty men gathered in Portland in 1986 at the fifth annual meeting of the National Convention for Men. Denouncing "father bashing" and "female chauvinism," some went so far as to compare "the law's treatment of divorcing men to the Holocaust and Salem witchhunts." At issue were custody laws that allegedly favored mothers and discriminated against fathers. In the same year, the *New York Times Magazine* reported that millions of working fathers were now experiencing a conflict between family commitments and work obligations, a problem that Los Angeles lawyer and father John Kronstadt attributed to changing expectations of fatherhood: "Society hasn't lowered its level of job performance, but it has raised its expectations of our roles in our children's lives." Clearly, many men tried to fulfill these new expectations. A Pasadena father, for example, compared his experience with that of his own father: "My father has proudly stated that he never changed a diaper; I am similarly proud that I have changed hundreds." Meanwhile, future fathers rushed to childbirth classes or signed up for classes in "baby massage." More sedentary sorts cheered Dustin Hoffman's Ted Kramer as he struggled with the pitfalls and triumphs of single fatherhood in the movie *Kramer vs. Kramer.* For Kramer, as for millions of other American men, fatherhood had become part of the therapeutic culture, a "growth experience" that enriched one's life, enlarged one's sense of self, and destroyed outmoded conceptions of masculinity.

Against these voices from the new fatherhood, critics complained of "deadbeat dads" who refused to provide child support, lazy fathers who condemned their wives to the "second shift," and dangerous fathers who treated incest as a patriarchal prerogative. Memoirs and psychological studies of grown children added to the dissent as "wounded children" bemoaned their fathers' absence from home and called them to task for their neglect, silence, and insensitivity. Criticism came from the other end of the political spectrum as well, as New Right thinkers and evangelical Christians joined in decrying the decline of paternal authority and in calling for a reinvigoration of traditional family values.

Dangerous or nurturing, ever-present or always absent, the patriarch of old or the pal of the new, fatherhood in recent decades has become a kaleidoscope of images and trends, a sure sign that it has lost cultural coherence. As a result, the identity that men once gained from fatherhood and breadwinning no longer prevails. Buffeted by powerful demographic, economic, and political changes, fatherhood in American culture is now fraught with ambiguity and confusion. Not surprisingly, so, too, are fathers themselves. Fred Farina can speak for a generation of men. As

Robert L. Griswold, *Fatherhood in America: A History* (New York: Basic Books, 1993), pp. 243–248, 250–265. Reprinted with permission of the author, Robert L. Griswold, Professor of History, University of Oklahoma.

he and his wife contemplated divorce, he could not fathom being uninvolved in his children's upbringing: "I wanna be more than just the father image. I wanna be involved in the raising of those kids. I wanna see them, day after day, I wanna see them mature, I wanna see the cutting of their hair, the whole thing." Yet, his allegiance to traditional beliefs was not far below the surface: "I thought that as a man you couldn't raise children. It never came to my mind that children could be raised by their father and live with their father. I always thought it was a natural thing for kids to be raised by their mother."

Farina's confusion is not difficult to understand. The "natural thing" for at least a century had been for mothers to rear children, fathers to support them. Fatherhood and manhood were inextricably linked in American culture: men organized their lives and their identity around fatherly breadwinning. Much of this changed, however, in the last twenty-five years under the influence of two profoundly important developments. . . . [T]he tremendous increase in the number of married women and mothers in the work force fundamentally challenged ideas about manhood, masculinity, and attendant breadwinning and fatherly responsibilities. Second, the effects of this change were augmented by the reemergence of feminism in the mid-1960s, which made all gender assumptions, including those about fatherhood, problematic. Together they prompted a far-reaching cultural debate about fatherhood never before known in American history. . . .

Both women and men have shaped the second coming of the new fatherhood and provided its political meaning. Over the last twenty years, liberal women feminists have called repeatedly for reconceptualizing parental responsibilities and for restructuring the work environment to transform parenting. In a 1970 press release, the National Organization for Women (NOW) decried the assumption that child care was primarily a maternal responsibility: "[We believe] that the care and welfare of children is incumbent on society and parents. We reject the idea that mothers have a special child care role that is not to be shared equally by fathers." In the same year NOW adopted a resolution stating that "marriage should be an equal partnership with shared economic and household responsibility and shared care of the children" and asked that institutions "acknowledge that parenthood is a necessary social service by granting maternal and paternal leaves of absence without prejudice and without loss of job security or seniority." . . .

Male feminists elaborated these ideas, especially as they related to fatherhood. Inspired by feminist theory, critical of the increasing bureaucratization and routinization of work, and cognizant of changing gender relationships in general, men in the early 1970s began formulating a critique of traditional masculinity and made some of the earliest calls for a new, politically informed fatherhood. In the view of these men, the breadwinning role was anachronistic, dysfunctional, and a symbol of outmoded patriarchal prerogatives. Women's liberation, went their argument, encompassed male liberation from stereotypical assumptions about traditional male roles, including hoary notions of fatherly responsibilities. Fathers with working wives must assume 50 percent of the child care; otherwise, the promise of gender equality at the core of feminism would be unfulfilled. The feminist perspective on the "politics of housework" necessarily included the "politics of childcare," and for some men the "new fatherhood" of the 1970s, 1980s, and 1990s represented a genuine effort to fulfill the promises of the liberal feminist vision.

This liberal, ostensibly feminist perspective averred that traditional manhood and fatherhood were a kind of prison, a set of "roles" with unrealistic expectations that led men to do bad things and put them out of touch with their "real," more nurturing selves. . . . The problem lay, then, not in the structure of relationships but in the tyranny of roles and ultimately in the heads of men. The problem was one of character and misguided socialization, not power. Masculinity, and fatherhood with it, had to be modernized if men were to escape the oppression of sex-role confinement.

The new fatherhood thus became part of "male liberation," a movement defined not as struggling against the powerful but as breaking free of conventions. As critics have pointed out, this perspective could lead to the mystification of patriarchal relations, to the view that men and women alike were victims of patriarchy, women for obvious reasons, men because patriarchal assumptions prevented them from "getting in touch with their feelings." Men could thus applaud feminists as fellow travelers on the road to human liberation and personal fulfillment, assumptions that ultimately eased into a therapeutic rather than a political perspective on fatherhood. While seemingly harmless, the implications of this development for feminism could be dire indeed. By deflecting attention from the political realm of social change to the private realm of the enhanced self, therapeutic visions of fatherhood could potentially hamper efforts to reconstruct gender relations.

And the vision was everywhere. In books, newspaper articles, newsletters, and radio and television programs, in classes for expectant fathers, new fathers, and fathers of children of every age, in university courses on fathering and in support groups of fathers in every conceivable situation, the message was more or less the same: the new, liberated father was a nurturing man. . . .

Liberal feminists drew support from the psychological community. Spurred on by changes in family structure, feminism, the reality of the new fatherhood, and changing assumptions about parent-child relations in general, scholars began researching the father-child bond from every conceivable angle. What followed was a geometric increase in the number of articles about fatherhood that reflected a host of different major perspectives and signaled a shift of important dimensions. Parenthood was no longer synonymous with motherhood. Although debates of every kind raged within this literature, one clear result was to legitimate fatherhood as a field of study and to recognize its growing cultural importance. . . .

Evidence seemed to suggest that children simply needed the presence of a father. Research on children reared in homes without fathers reported that boys tended to be less masculine or, ironically, hypermasculine compared with boys reared in homes with fathers. Father absence prompted poorer moral development, more juvenile delinquency, and a deterioration in boys' school performance, whereas paternal presence was associated with ease in establishing solid peer friendships and, later, successful heterosexual relationships. After an exhaustive survey of the research literature on sex-role development, Henry Biller affirmed the importance of fatherly nurture to children's lives: "The optimal situation for the child is to have both an involved mother and involved father. The child is then exposed to a wider degree of adaptive characteristics." Summarizing twenty years of her research on father-child relationships, Norma Radin told Congress that nurturing fathers promoted more favorable attitudes toward women's work, higher levels of intellectual functioning among sons (the evidence for daughters was more ambiguous), better social functioning and peer relationships, and a greater ability to empathize with others.

Psychologists and child development specialists have thus added their support for the new fatherhood in the context of an approving culture. The flood of articles about fatherhood and the "daddy track," the birth classes and workshops on fathering, and the interest in reorganizing the workplace all suggest that the new fatherhood has gained an important measure of cultural legitimacy. It is good politics and good therapy. It is also good psychology. In a nation perplexed about family values, it is comforting to learn that nurturant, involved fathers will produce happier, smarter, better-adjusted children.

The new fatherhood has also gained cultural legitimacy because it has become an important marker of class. In a world in which even middle-class men cannot adequately support their families without their wives' wages, older styles of fatherhood no longer make sense. Men can neither claim the solitary status of breadwinning nor the prerogatives that come with that status. This being the case, fathers have made a virtue of necessity. They embrace an expanded role for themselves that is publicly commended and yet largely free of the onerous aspects of child rearing that still fall to women. . . .

The new fatherhood as a marker of social class becomes clearer in light of the general experience of the middle class in the 1970s and 1980s. Beset by anxieties ranging from the youth revolt of the late 1960s to the stagflation of the 1970s, the economically hard-pressed middle class suffered what Barbara Ehrenreich has called a "fear of falling." Faced with soaring housing costs, rising tuition, and insufficient male paychecks, the middle class looked for ways to set itself off from the working class. This effort took a variety of forms, most notably the creation of a blue-collar stereotype perhaps best symbolized by television character Archie Bunker. In sociology texts, Hollywood productions, television shows, and magazine articles, blue-collar workers (inevitably male) appeared as ethnocentric, authoritarian, intolerant, and bigoted buffoons or as menaces to society. By implication, of course, the middle-class male was all those things the working-class male was not, including more nurturing, tolerant, flexible, and knowledgeable in his approach to fatherhood. Thus, although social class is actually a poor predictor of fathers' involvement in child care, it is not surprising that the popular image of the new father was, and is, relentlessly middle class. . . .

The new fatherhood, then, can become a badge of class, a sign that one has the knowledge, time, and inclination to embrace more progressive visions of parenting. On one side of the abyss, Archie Bunker screams nonsense at his son-in-law; on the other, yuppie Ted Kramer learns the exquisite joys of rearing children. The new fatherhood thus becomes part of a middle-class strategy of survival in which men accommodate to the realities of their wives' careers and the decline of their breadwinning capabilities. . . .

Pram-pushing fathers may be staking out class boundaries, enhancing their own sense of good feeling, or actually doing a stint on the "second shift." Regardless of how we interpret their motivations, we generally applaud their behavior. But feminists have alerted us to a darker side of fatherhood as well. While most fathers do not harbor violent or incestuous intent toward their children, some do, and one of the achievements of feminism has been the rediscovery of family violence, particularly the role of husbands and fathers in perpetrating such violence. . . . From the feminist perspective, the victimization of women and children by husbands and fathers is rooted in patriarchy and will not disappear until male supremacy ends. . . .

. . . In fact, over 90 percent of incest assailants are males, and a similarly high percentage of their victims are female. And although brother-sister incest is far more common than father-daughter, experts estimate that the latter occurs in over 1 percent of families, a figure that translates into hundreds of thousands of victims. Recent evidence suggests that the figure may be considerably higher. In a study of 930 women in San Francisco, 4.5 percent had been sexually abused by their fathers before the age of eighteen. If this figure holds for the population at large, 45,000 out of every one million women are victimized by their fathers before their eighteenth birthday.

These victims were largely ignored until feminists brought attention to the sexual crimes of fathers. . . . Above all, incest remained hidden from view because it was simply a particularly brutal expression of unequal power relations within families. In other words, it was embedded within patriarchy.

As feminists began to decode family relationships, the tradition of blaming the victims of incest for the crimes of fathers came under withering attack. In both scholarly works and more popular offerings, writers insisted that father-daughter incest represented patriarchy at its rawest. . . .

Clinical evidence and first-person testimonials expose the complexity and the tragedy of father-daughter incest. Reading victims' accounts is an excursion into a world of denial, pain, confusion, and loss. It is a world of daughters who may feel enraged and yet stubbornly maintain affection for their abusive fathers, of young girls consumed by guilt and fear, of mothers paralyzed by shame and powerlessness, and, worst of all, of fathers who feel no remorse. . . .

Against the sadness of such daughters falls the callousness of the fathers. Incestuous fathers seldom seek treatment or stop their assaults. In a study of forty incestuous families, Judith Herman found that not one father voluntarily stopped the abuse. Once charged with incest, many fathers use all the power at their disposal, including efforts to turn other family members against the victim, to fight the charges. And they are often successful. Evidence suggests that incest offenders are notoriously difficult to prosecute. Rather than remorse, many of these men display an appalling insensitivity and a tendency to blame everyone but themselves for the breakdown in sexual order. And why should they not? If incest is an extreme expression of patriarchy, then one would expect its perpetrators to defend themselves in its terms.

For feminists, father-daughter incest is a manifestation of patriarchy at its worst and will cease only when male supremacy gives way to egalitarian relations. To that end, feminists and advocates for the men's movement hope that the new fatherhood will be a progressive step in redefining American manhood, a step in line with building more equality between husbands and wives and more nurturing, meaningful relationships between fathers and children. To critics from the right, however, such changes merely signify the erosion of traditional relationships on which the good of society depends. What society desperately needs, they argue, is not the new fatherhood but the reassertion of traditional paternal authority: "The family is an organization," writes conservative psychiatrist Harold Voth, "and it is consistent with all known patterns of animal behavior, including that of man, that the male should be the head of the family." Although fathers should be "loving, compassionate, understanding, capable of gentleness and the like . . . all should know he is the protector, the one who is ultimately responsible for the integrity and survival of the family." Such knowledge, Voth assured his readers, is a prerequisite of success: "It is known that the most successful families are those where all members, including the wife, look up to the father-husband."

Worried that Americans families were in deep trouble, convinced that the welfare system sapped the strength of fathers, galvanized by the battle against feminism and the Equal Rights Amendment (ERA), conservatives like Voth fought back in the 1970s and 1980s, hoping to forestall the corrosive effects of social and political change by reasserting paternal authority within families and reemphasizing men's obligation to support their dependents. Families needed clear lines of authority that only a father could provide: "There must be no role confusion between the mother and father," asserts Voth, "and though . . . distributions of responsibility and authority exist, everyone in the family must also know, appreciate and respect the fact that the father has the overall responsibility for the family; he is its chief executive, but like all good executives he should listen to all within his organization." With this authority came responsibility. Men had the time-honored obligation to support their wives and children, an obligation firmly established by law but now under siege by misguided proponents of feminism. In the view of conservatives, traditional laws insured "the right of a woman to be a full-time wife and mother, and to have this right recognized by laws that obligate her husband to provide the primary financial support and a home for her and their children, both during their marriage and when she is a widow." These laws originated in biology and religion: "Since God ordained that women have babies," writes antifeminist leader Phyllis Schlafly, "our laws properly and realistically establish that men must provide financial support for their wives and children."

But feminism put all this at risk. What was at stake for conservative women in the battle for the ERA, for example, was the legitimacy of women's and children's claims on men's income. The stakes were high: "The Equal Rights Amendment," warned Schlafly, "would invalidate all the state laws that require the husband to support his wife and family and provide them with a home, because the Constitution would then prohibit any law that imposes an obligation on one sex that it does not impose equally on the other." Such a turn of events would leave women doubly burdened: "ERA would impose a constitutionally mandated legal equality in all matters, including family support. This would be grossly unfair to a woman because it would impose on her the double burden of financial obligation plus motherhood and homemaking." Schlafly was certainly right on the last point. As she put it, "The law cannot address itself to who has the baby, changes the diapers, or washes the dishes."

And men were more than willing to let women assume the burden of the "double shift." Underlying much of the conservative defense of patriarchy, as Barbara Ehrenreich has pointed out, was the deep suspicion that men, free of traditional obligations, would simply refuse to support their families. The fear persisted that men supported dependents only so long as it was convenient, a situation that would only become worse by passage of the ERA, which would destroy the legal foundations of male obligation. Schlafly spoke for millions of anti-ERA homemakers in denouncing the proposed amendment: "The moral, social, and legal evil of ERA is that it proclaims as a constitutional mandate that the husband no longer has the primary duty to support his wife and children." Hence the deep hostility to feminism on the part of Phyllis Schlafly and her supporters: it was a force that meant to help women but in reality helped legitimate male irresponsibility. In a culture eviscerated by the collapse of traditional family values, men acted responsibly only if their wives (and the obligations they felt toward their children) compelled it: "Man's role as family provider," Schlafly writes, "gives him the incentive to curb his primitive nature. Everyone needs to be needed. The male satisfies his sense of need through his role as provider for the family." If this need were subverted by feminist impulses, warned Schlafly, a man "tends to drop out of the family and revert to the primitive masculine role of hunter and fighter."

This grim view was most fully developed by best-selling author George Gilder, who, in *Sexual Suicide* and *Wealth and Poverty,* argued that men were fundamentally brutes who became good citizens and productive workers only because women made them so. Sex—irresponsible, insatiable, and unrelenting—drove men, and this primal, destructive, and uncivilizing force could be checked only by women and children: "A married man . . . is spurred by the claims of family to channel his otherwise disruptive male aggressions into his performance as a provider for a wife and children." By extending men's horizons beyond the fulfillment of their sexual impulses, fatherhood gives men a vision of the future: "The woman gives him access to his children, otherwise forever denied him; and he gives her the product of his labor, otherwise dissipated on temporary pleasures. The woman gives him a unique link to the future and a vision of it; he gives her faithfulness and a commitment to a lifetime of hard work."

Traditional breadwinning cooled male ardor and deflected it into worthwhile channels, but woe to the society that allowed women to intrude into this male domain: "A society of relatively wealthy and independent women will be a society of sexually and economically predatory males. . . . If they cannot be providers, they have to resort to muscle and phallus." And muscle and phallus do not for good social order make; what does is men and women bound "to identities as fathers and mothers within the 'traditional' family." Children encourage respectability, the work ethic, and economic productivity among fathers, commitments that restrain men's sexuality and counteract antisocial behavior. In the view of the New Right, writes the sociologist Allen Hunter, "anarchic male energy is disciplined not by civic virtue in the society at large but by sexual responsibility toward one woman and economic responsibility to her and their offspring." In short, fatherhood disciplines men to accept their responsibilities and obligations in the face of a variety of forces—feminism, humanism, godlessness, the welfare state—working to destroy conservatives' visions of social order.

In the view of the New Right, the contemporary liberal state has relentlessly encroached on parental authority and responsibilities and has sapped the initiative of breadwinners. To conservatives, as Allen Hunter has explained, "judicial activism and liberal, humanist social legislation have threatened the traditional family by penetrating it with instrumental, individualistic values, and by creating a paternalistic state which takes over child-rearing from parents and subverts the market." The image is one of the family under siege by the so-called "new class," the welfare bureaucrats and social planners so despised by New Right thinkers. These architects of liberalism subvert male authority by eroding female dependence on male breadwinning. Worse, they create unemployment and poverty by causing family breakdown. Dusting off the assumptions put forth in the Moynihan Report, conservatives argue that it is family breakdown that causes poverty, not poverty that causes family breakdown. And family breakdown, as George Gilder explains in his inimitable fashion, came when the welfare state usurped paternal responsibilities to wives and children: "The man has the gradually sinking feeling that his role as provider, the definitive male activity from the primal days of the hunt through the industrial revolution and on into modern life, has been largely seized from him; he has been cuckolded by the compassionate state." With male breadwinning made optional, a father "feels dispensable, his wife knows he is dispensable, his children sense it." Men respond by leaving their wives and children and reverting to a less civilized state, exhibiting "that very combination of resignation and rage, escapism and violence, short horizons and promiscuous sexuality that characterizes everywhere the life of the poor."

Gilder's apocalyptic vision of fathers stems from a peculiar mix of Victorian biology and political conservatism, but his position has received support from other quarters as well. . . . The fathers' rights movement began as part of "men's liberation" in the 1970s. This large movement initially reflected the desire of men on the left to align with feminism and to stake out and legitimate new modes of masculinity. The goal, in essence, was to reconstruct masculinity in order to free men's softer, more sensitive selves from the prison of machismo. One way to do so was to emphasize men's ability to nurture, and thus men's movement writers embraced the new fatherhood as a way to transcend the flinty reserve allegedly characteristic of an earlier generation of breadwinning drones. As we have already seen, this vision of manhood had within it as much therapy as politics, and by the mid to late 1970s the liberal feminism of some of these men ironically legitimated efforts to rectify the iniquities of child custody awards in divorce suits. For how could divorced men remain loving, committed new fathers and how could they gain the deep personal satisfactions that came with parenthood if courts routinely marginalized them in divorce settlements?

What these men shared was a feeling of intense, palpable anger at a system they deemed stacked against them. In meetings all over America, aggrieved fathers gathered to voice their frustration and hostility toward the courts, social workers, and most of all their ex-wives for cutting them off from their children. Part therapy group, part reform movement, the fathers' rights organizations combined feminism's language of equal rights with the vocabulary of male nurturance to fight for change. Their goal was to overcome the decades-old assumption that mothers were the more capable parent and to insist that fathers be assured continued involvement in the lives of their children. By the mid-1980s, over two hundred fathers' rights organizations with names such as Fathers for Justice (Mobile, Alabama), Fathers United for Equal Justice (Eliot, Maine), and Fathers Are Capable Too (Lubbock, Texas) had sprung up in virtually every state and were lobbying successfully for the reform of custody laws. In fact, by the end of the 1980s men's groups had played key roles in passing joint custody bills in more than thirty states.

One cannot read these fathers' accounts without sympathizing with their loss, frustration, and anger. Their stories reverberate with tales of vindictive ex-wives, uncooperative, obstructionist social workers, and inattentive, insensitive judges. They tell, too, of children turned against them by maniacal former spouses, of specious sexual abuse allegations that destroyed peace of mind, of their dawning sense that they would be forever alienated from their children. At a meeting of the Equal Rights for Fathers organization in New York City, one father's anger could stand for that of thousands of others:

> I see my kid every weekend but it's become a nightmare. Lately, my six-year-old son acts terrified. My ex-wife has accused me, in front of him, of physically abusing him when I'm alone with him. Last time he threw up as soon as he got into the car. I know my wife is angry with me, but does she have a right to destroy my relationship with my child in order to revenge herself?

Deeply moved by this man's testimony, another participant said simply, "Fathers love their children," and then repeated the statement as if to underscore the point and reaffirm his own pain.

The most frequent complaint is that ex-wives make visitation impossible and that courts do little or nothing to enforce fathers' visitation rights. (Fathers' rights activists, it deserves note, reject the term *visitation* and argue that it should be called *parenting time.* Said one activist, "Fathers are not cousins once removed or casual friends of the family; they don't *visit* their own children.") Their concerns are not without foundation. One study found that 40 percent of custodial wives admitted that they had refused, at least once and for punitive reasons, to allow their ex-husbands to see their children in the first two years after divorce. Another investigation found that 20 percent of divorced wives saw no benefit to fathers' continued involvement with their children and worked actively to sabotage their efforts to do so.

Clearly these fathers' grievances must be taken seriously and their frustrations deserve sympathy. One cannot read accounts of men denied access to their children for months on end without feeling their sadness and loss, nor can one read of men falsely accused of sexually abusing their children without sharing their bitterness. But another dimension to this debate deserves attention. In the judgment of critics, the fathers' rights movement has taken the language of shared parenting and the new fatherhood and used it to increase men's control over women. As part of a wider backlash against women's gains, the fathers' rights movement increases men's legal control over their children outside marriage while effective day-to-day care of children remains where it always has been—with mothers.

Thus, critics argue that joint custody, the principal demand of the fathers' rights movement, empowers men but has nothing positive to offer women. Mandatory joint custody legislation misses the point that mothers almost always provide primary care both before and after divorce. Despite this imbalance, fathers in joint custody arrangements gain equal legal control over their children's lives without, in essence, having to assume equal responsibility for their care: "Joint legal custody," writes Carol Smart, "would not involve men in the daily care of children, but it would enhance their access rights and would mean that they had to be consulted over major issues concerning the child." Moreover, as Smart notes, because joint custody presupposes equality in decision making about the children, when conflicts arise the custodial parent (in most cases, women) would be open to increased surveillance by the courts. Thus, under joint custody arrangements women remain as the primary care givers but are subject to the enhanced power of their ex-husbands backed by the power of the state. How, they ask, can such a development benefit them?

Critics also worry that the fathers' rights movement poses even greater dangers. Although most fathers do not request custody, when they do they increasingly gain it. In a California study from the late 1970s, 63 percent of fathers who requested custody received it, up from 35 percent in 1968 and 37 percent in 1972. Of contested cases settled by trial, fully one-third of the awards went to fathers. Other studies reveal success rates of fathers in contested cases ranging from 40 to 50 percent, evidence that belies the claim of fathers' rights activists that men suffer terrible discrimination in divorce court. That women receive custody in about 90 percent of divorce cases obscures the fact that most men do not request custody. When they do, they have a good chance of receiving it even though in most instances women have been the primary care givers.

In many, perhaps most instances, the good intentions of these men should not be questioned. Single fathers are a rapidly growing segment of the population—in 1991 almost 15 percent of single parents were fathers, up from 10 percent in 1980—and their triumphs and struggles have begun to attract both popular and scholarly attention. In an article "It's Not Like Mr. Mom," *Newsweek* offered profiles of several such men and chronicled how single fatherhood had changed their lives, changes that were novel, it is worth noting, only because they happened to men, not women. Their stories were heartwarming, even inspiring, but they should not obscure an important point made by feminist critics of the politics of custody. Although fathers' rights activists use the rhetoric of equality to their advantage, critics point out that caretaking is not an equal proposition in most American homes. The choice in custody suits is not between two parents who provide care equally but between one parent who does most of the care giving and another who does far less. That courts and legislatures have increasingly couched the matter in abstract terms of equality devalues care giving and conceals women's real work in rearing children. Worse, by seeking to avoid an automatic preference for mothers and holding instead to a sex-neutral standard in settling custody disputes, courts weigh equally fathers' financial support against mothers' nurturance. A feminist critic of the fathers' rights movement, Nancy Polikoff, rejects the logic of this equation:

> But the only appropriate purpose of a sex-neutral standard is to require evaluation of who is providing primary nurturance without automatically assuming it to be the mother; its purpose should not be to eliminate the importance of nurturance from the custody determination and equate the provision of financial support with the provision of psychological and physical needs.

The obvious point is to extend equality to nurturing fathers, not to equate paternal financial support with maternal nurture.

Feminists have pointed out other difficulties women encounter in courts attracted to the assumptions of the fathers' rights movement. Mothers who do less than everything may draw the negative attention of judges, whereas fathers who do a bit more than nothing attract positive comment. Other judges tend to see mothers who work outside the home in the same light as fathers who do so, ignoring that working mothers also tend to do most of the child care during the "second shift."

Thus, a Missouri appellate court could state that "if the mother goes and returns as a wage earner like the father, she has no more part in the responsibility [of child care] than he." Courts have gone even further and criticized working mothers' ability to care for their children, a prejudice working fathers seldom encounter. So, too, divorcing mothers new to the labor market who must take time out for training and education appear less settled and stable to judges than ex-husbands who have a long employment history. Finally, if courts use financial support as a criterion for custody—and they have—mothers clearly find themselves in a difficult spot: "At a time when the myth that men are unfairly denied custody has pervaded public consciousness," writes Polikoff, "judges can latch on to the father's economic superiority as a reason to support paternal custody."

Feminists argue not that the principle of equality should be ignored, not that a sex-neutral standard in custody awards is wrong, but that in practice judges have devalued mothers' work and have hopelessly confused the real nature of family life and child care by adhering to abstractions that work against women's interests. Polikoff puts the feminist case forcefully: "The concern lies with mothers who lose custody although they have performed the primary nurturing role throughout the marriage. A system that produces such a result is one that penalizes women and children, denigrates the mothering role, and shifts yet another form of social control to men." The fathers' rights movement, the emergence of joint custody statutes, and the evolution of case law custody decisions over the last decade are, in the judgment of feminists, perfect examples of patriarchy at work. Only a system that give custody preference to the primary caretaker—in most cases mothers, but in some fathers—is truly fair and congruent with the reality of child care in America.

 F U R T H E R   R E A D I N G

Bane, Mary Jo. *Here to Stay: American Families in the Twentieth Century* (1976).
Bullough, Vern L. "Why There Is No 'Crisis of Families': They're Different, but Better."
    Free Inquiry 19 (1998): 19–21.
Carlson, Allan. "The Family: Where Do We Go from Here?" *Society* 32 (1995): 63–72.
Crittenden, Ann. *The Price of Motherhood: Why the Most Important Job in the World Is
    Still the Least Valued* (2001).
Ehrenreich, Barbara. *The Hearts of Men: American Dreams and the Flight from Commitment*
    (1983).
Faludi, Susan. *Backlash: The Undeclared War Against American Women* (1987).
———. *Stiffed: The Betrayal of the American Man* (1999).
Farrell, Betty G. *Family: The Making of an Idea, an Institution, and a Controversy in
    American Culture* (1993).
Gallagher, Maggie, and David Blankenhorn. "Family Feud." *American Prospect* 33 (1997):
    12–17.
Garbarino, James. "A Vision of Family Policy for the 21st Century." *Journal of Social Issues*
    52 (1996): 197–214.
Gerson, Kathleen. *No Man's Land: Men's Changing Commitments to Family and Work*
    (1993).
Griswold, Robert L. *Fatherhood in America: A History* (1993).
Hochschild, Arlie. *The Second Shift: Working Parents and the Revolution at Home* (1989).
Lasch, Christopher. *The Culture of Narcissism* (1979).
———. "What's Wrong with the Right?" *Tikkun* 1 (1987): 23–29.

————. "Why the Left Has No Future." *Tikkun* 1 (1987): 92–97.

Luker, Kristin. *Abortion and the Politics of Motherhood* (1984).

O'Brien, Margaret. *Who's Minding the Children?* (1974).

Popenoe, David. *Life Without Father: Compelling New Evidence That Fatherhood and Marriage Are Indispensable for the Good of Children and Society* (1996).

Popenoe, David, Jean Bethke Elshtain, and David Blankenhorn, eds. *Promises to Keep: Decline and Renewal of Marriage in America* (1996).

Rubin, Lillian B. "A Feminist Response to Lasch." *Tikkun* 1 (1987): 89–91.

————. *Worlds of Pain: Life in the Working-Class Family* (1976).

Sere, Adriene. "Reality Check: Inequality and the American Family." *Humanist* 56 (1996): 30–32.

Skolnick, Arlene. *Embattled Paradise: The American Family in an Age of Uncertainty* (1991).

————. "Family Values: The Sequel." *American Prospect* 32 (1997): 86–95.

Stacey, Judith. *Brave New Families: Stories of Domestic Upheaveal in Late-Twentieth-Century America* (1990).

Tucker, Scott. "Lesbian Witches, Socialist Sodomites, and Cultural War." *Humanist* 53 (1993): 42–44.

Weitzman, Lenore J. *The Divorce Revolution: The Unexpected Social and Economic Consequences for Women and Children in America* (1985).

Whitehead, Barbara Dafoe. *The Divorce Culture* (1997).

CHAPTER
14

Families and Children
in Contemporary
America

At the same time that historians responding to the anxieties of the late twentieth century exploded the myth that the family had ever been free from change and struggle, they also explored the ways in which American families were, indeed, undergoing wrenching—and perhaps permanent—changes. Calling attention to the multiplicity of families in what some scholars now label "postmodern" America, scholars of contemporary family life remind us that childless couples, single parents, blended families, empty nesters, and domestic partners now constitute the majority of American families. Despite this recognition, most historians of the family conclude that, as sociologist Mary Jo Bane expresses it, the family is "here to stay": Americans continue to regard the family as a central institution in their lives, and even as increasing numbers of men and women are postponing or forgoing marriage and childbearing, gays and lesbians are flocking to the altar and creating their own "gay-by boom."

While concern in the 1970s and 1980s focused on the family, anxiety in the 1990s and in the first decade of the twenty-first century has centered on children. Pick up any newspaper, turn on any television show, or simply eavesdrop on any conversation, and you are likely to hear some variant on the question "What is wrong with kids these days?" In recent years images of "children having children," girls starving themselves to approximate the fashion models and rock stars they admire, and boys seeking revenge for social ostracism through school shootings have come to dominate our conversations about childhood in contemporary America.

The best work on families and children in contemporary America examines the current situation in light of long-term trends. Such scholarship avoids overstatement by placing changes in historical (and often global) perspective. By examining the present without forgetting (or mythologizing) the past, scholars of the history of family and childhood can offer speculative, but informed, answers to some of our most troubling—and exciting—questions: What is the future of marriage in American society? Where can parents turn when their influence over their children seems diminished or overshadowed by other forces? How can understanding the past enable us to shape the future?

 D O C U M E N T S

The first two documents consist of interviews conducted in 1989 with two homosexual couples: Tede Matthews and Chuck Barragan, an unmarried, "mostly monogamous" couple who had been together for five years at the time of the interview, and Nina Kaiser and Nora Klimist, who celebrated their commitment with a wedding ceremony in 1987. Both couples, who reside in San Francisco, reflect on the personal, social, and legal ramifications of marriage and of domestic partnership registration, an option for homosexual couples in California.

In Document 1 Tede, commenting on the legal standing of same-sex relationships, refers to a situation in which Karen Thompson was refused permission to visit her lover, Sharon Kowalski, in the hospital after Kowalski was badly injured and permanently disabled in a car accident in Minnesota in 1983. After a lengthy legal battle, Thompson won guardianship in 1992. In Document 2 Nina and Nora are joined in the interview by their daughter, Kellen Kaiser-Klimist. Kellen, Nina's biological daughter, refers to both Nina and Nora as "mom"; she also recognizes Nina's long-term housemate, Helen, and Nina's former lover, MK, as her co-parents.

Document 3 is an official report from the U.S. Census Bureau on families and living arrangements in America. Based on the 2000 census returns, the report details the current situation and suggests long-term trends. Of these trends, the authors, Jason Fields and Lynne M. Casper, take particular note of a decline in the proportion of households consisting of a married couple and their own children; in 2000 such families made up only one-third of all American households. The report also suggests a rise in other types of households: single-parent families, single people living alone, and unmarried, cohabiting couples with or without children.

Document 4 is an essay by sociologist Michael Kimmel written in the aftermath of the notorious school shootings in Columbine, Colorado, in April 1999, in which two disaffected teenagers, Eric Harris and Dylan Klebold, opened fire on their classmates and teachers, killing fifteen people (including themselves) and wounding another twenty-eight. Kimmel argues that the shooting is best understood not as the act of two social deviants, but rather as the natural consequence of a culture that teaches boys that violence equals manliness and a society that regards gun ownership as an inalienable right.

Document 5, which appeared in the *Atlantic Monthly* in November 2001, explores the impetus behind the burgeoning home-schooling movement. Surveying writings on home schooling from the 1960s to the present, including Mitchell L. Stevens's recent study, *Kingdom of Children*, author Margaret Talbot points out that the home-schooling movement reflects both conservative and radical impulses. Whether Christian or countercultural, however, the home-schooling movement illustrates modern parents' desire to maintain (or reassert) control over their children's education and socialization.

Document 6, written by Tammy Whitlock, the mother of a two-year-old boy, criticizes "toymania" in the twenty-first century. The author suggests that parents' toy purchases reflect broader patterns of overconsumption in American society—what John De Graaf labeled "affluenza" in a 2002 book by that title. She also suggests a link between consumerism and competition in today's ambitious atmosphere.

1. Two Gay Men Describe Their Relationship, 1989

Chuck: We've been together since the day we met. We didn't live together until December of that year, but we were basically hooked on each other from the start. That's the anniversary we celebrate, the day we met in March. We give little gifts to each other, go out to dinner, talk about it. On our fifth anniversary we actually had a public celebration.

Tede: We had a big party at El Rio, the bar where we met.

Chuck: I wanted to throw a little party for Tede, but then he decided why not have a real party, and it started growing. We agreed to have it at our bar, El Rio, and have it catered, just make it a fun affair and celebrate our five years together, which I saw as being a real milestone considering how different we are from each other.

Tede: Our friends came together to celebrate our relationship. It was a real mixed crowd—from Chuck's very straight coworkers to my wild Latina lesbian artist friends. That was all the validation I wanted. In our everyday life I feel that we get a lot of respect for our relationship.

I call our relationship "being married," but to me, it means being committed to somebody. I'd never been five years with another person. I think it's strange that people celebrate a wedding like that's a big accomplishment when the real accomplishment is staying with somebody and having your lives weave together. So many people spend thousands of dollars on a wedding and then divorce in a few years. I think people should celebrate longevity.

Chuck: Our commitment has never been anything really spoken. We just understand that we're in this for the long haul. We're crazy about each other and we don't expect things to change. It's a given that it's Chuck and Tede, we've been together, and we're going to stay together. Nothing's going to come between us.

Tede: It's the first time I've felt that if bad things do happen, I don't have to worry about the relationship breaking up. Occasionally we look at each other and find it hard to believe we've been with somebody for over seven years. We think about growing old together. We've already got our rocking chairs.

Chuck: We don't have written agreements about what goes on, or financial agreements, it just works without our having to spell it out. We have separate bank accounts but everything is shared pretty much fifty-fifty. I pay a little bit more for rent, because I earn a bit more than Tede, and I feel it's only fair for me to do that. But it's right down the middle for utilities.

Tede: We write down the groceries on a little list. When we go out to eat or to a movie, we trade off on treating each other. It's never really verbalized much because it just works out.

Chuck: I went to law school and I believe in having wills and powers of attorney. I've already filled out a will naming Tede. I've also had a power of attorney drafted for health care. My sister knows about both of these and has copies, so parts of my family know that I have a relationship with this man and if anything should happen, there are steps outlined that should hopefully give him the authority to take care of me.

Suzanne Sherman, ed., *Lesbian and Gay Marriage: Private Commitments, Public Ceremonies* (Philadelphia: Temple University Press, 1992), pp. 49, 51–57. Reprinted by Temple University Press. © 1992 by Suzanne Sherman. All Rights Reserved.

Tede: I didn't go to law school, I'm an anarchist, and I hate the state having anything to do with my life. So I've put it off. But I do intend to do it. I really should because my mother, who is cool and hip, is very old, and my father died, which leaves my sister, who is a right-wing Fundamentalist homophobe, and I would not want her to step into my life and do anything. So I know I have to do something, especially in light of the Sharon Kowalski case.

My father and mother have known since the early 1970s that I'm gay. They pretty much accept Chuck as a son-in-law. My mother sends a little check for Christmas, and she says, This is for you and Chuck. Last August, after my father died, my mother came out and stayed with us. It was the first time she'd met Chuck. We got to hang out in the kitchen and be with Mom. My mother's a wonderful person. My sister—I don't throw it in her face, or anything—but I always talk about Chuck, and maybe she'll mention his name after I've said it six times in a row.

Chuck: My parents and two sisters and all my relatives live in Los Angeles. One sister and her husband moved up to San Jose recently. I told her about me and Tede a couple years ago. She accepts us totally. In fact, we got joint Christmas presents and we get joint cards and letters. We're into bears (teddy bears, of course!), and she sends us appropriate bear things. She's the only person I've told in my family. Another sister sort of guessed it, and my San Jose sister confirmed it.

When my parents come up to visit, Tede and I take them out. They basically know, but it's unspoken. It's sort of traditional in Latin families—they understand what the relationship is, but they don't want to discuss it. When they stay with us, we sleep together and they sleep in my room. Last year, Tede and I went down for a wedding, and I just introduced him by name. I'm sure people speculate and know it, but I'm not going to go out and tell them.

Tede: I was at all the wedding rehearsals, I took pictures for the family, I was at all the parties at the house. A Latino family is used to being an extended family, and I think anyone's welcome in the family as long as you don't talk about stuff. On one hand, it's better than Anglo families that want to send you to a shrink, or convert you, or whatever, but on the other hand you're invisible as a couple, you're not validated as a couple. But I'm there as a member of the family. Last time his parents were here, his mother insisted that we have our picture taken and that I be in it for the family album. . . .

Chuck: I consider our relationship fairly monogamous. There have been times when one of us has been away on travel. Tede's a writer, and he goes away to Central America. The first time he left me for three months, it was very hard for me to stay monogamous. We didn't have an agreement on monogamy, and we fooled around without having one. I think we came to the realization that we were kidding ourselves that we could be totally monogamous when we were away from each other. We came to an understanding that when we're away from each other for an extended period, it's okay to be intimate as long as we're safe and we realize that it's just an experience, and it's kept out of the house. We are life partners and we let the other people know it. The few times we've had an "extended" relationship, it's for pleasure and that's it. . . .

Chuck: I would say that "mostly monogamous" describes us.

Tede: There's a swinging gate on the cage. It works for me. I don't think 100 percent sexual monogamy is that healthy. I haven't felt that way since my first relationship, which was heavily battering. I almost got killed by my lover over jealousy.

After that, I really combated being a jealous person. I feel that it's a very harmful emotion. . . . Monogamy among men . . . there isn't much place for it in the gay community, even though there are probably thousands of gay male couples in the city here that are committed to each other. But I think gay men have trouble recognizing relationships and giving validity and place in the gay community to other men having long-term relationships, though it's more a premium now with AIDS.

Chuck: I think marriage is a relic from the past. It's basically slavery to another person. I just don't like the whole idea of marriage; I think it's totally wrong. It's unrealistic to say to people we're going to be together the rest of our lives, we're going to be legally bound by this, and all these rights and obligations flow from this ceremony. If you look at the divorce rate, people cannot realistically expect to plan their life around one person. Everybody is so different, not everybody can meet those standards.

Tede: Marriage puts a concept as more important and more central to the structure of this patriarchal society than the actual happiness and growth of the people within it. The old vows were for the woman to love and obey the man—a marriage of man and wife. This thing called "marriage" becomes almost like a third person in the relationship, and that's not the kind of relationship I want. I want our relationship to be a refuge for us and a place for growth and commitment.

I call Chuck my lover. I think that "life partner" sounds like you're in business, and "significant other" is not an endearing term. To me, "lover" means commitment. If I was just going out with somebody, I'd call them "boyfriend."

Chuck: I say "lover," or "significant other," since people know what that means.

We don't wear relationship rings. Tede wants to exchange rings, but I refuse to. I've offered to give him one if he wants it, but I'm not going to wear one. It's like a symbolic ring through the nose. It's like you're trying to say to the world, You should know what that means, and watch out. If people want to know if you're single or not, they should ask you.

Tede: I don't see it as something I'd be doing for anyone else. I see it as something between us.

Chuck: I know you feel that way, but I don't need that kind of symbolism in my life.

I would only get married if I was going to get something very substantial out of it. I don't have quite the same attitude as Tede about the state, though I respect his opinion. To be honest, since I've got the power of attorney and his name on all these insurance forms, the state already knows about his being my partner, or someone will, if they get access to this information. Our relationship is already a matter of legal record.

As far as the domestic-partnership registration goes, I don't plan to do it. I've done my share of enforcing our relationship based on the will and the power of attorney and the fact that everybody I deal with at work regarding my finances and insurance knows about Tede because his name is on my beneficiary cards. I think I've done all I can at this point to preserve any rights.

Tede: I don't believe in registering just to be part of the numbers. If there was a practical reason—if it would give us lower taxes, or as far as insurance goes—then maybe I could see more reason to do it. The way this world is going, I really don't want the government to have any more information on me than it already has. I don't trust that this country has the ability to take care of gay people's lives. Passing the domestic-partners bill in San Francisco didn't stop this city from being the main capital of hate crimes against gays in the nation in 1990. . . .

I don't think couples should have privileges single people don't have, whether you're heterosexual, gay, or lesbian. I resent the fact that married people get lower taxes. But as long as there is this institution of marriage and heterosexuals are getting that privilege, then gay people should be able to do it too. . . .

2. Kellen Kaiser-Klimist and Her Two Moms Discuss Marriage and Family, 1989, 1991

Nora: I'm monogamous, so I wasn't giving up something for this relationship. This is the first monogamous relationship Nina has had in eight years, so this was a big step for her. I had to put a lot of faith in her commitment, and that's a scary thing to do. The fact that she was willing to get up in front of people and make the commitment reassured me a lot.

Nina: One of the things we talked about at six months into the relationship is how to stabilize a family. We already had Kellen, and we want another child. Nora was sure she wanted to have a child and didn't want to do it as a single parent if she didn't have to. She wants to carry the next pregnancy.

So, that brought up the discussion of whether or not we have the same goals. For Nora, it needed to be a monogamous relationship, and that was fine with me. It wasn't an issue of monogamy versus nonmonogamy, it was an issue of whether we have the same goals as a couple and as a family.

Our marriage helped Kellen feel more secure. In the eight years that I was nonmonogamous, Kellen saw a lot of women coming and going—well, not a lot, but too many, for her. I had two ongoing primary relationships for over two years before I was with Nora, and both those women played a sort of motherly role in Kellen's life, then took off. She didn't take too kindly to having to adjust, having to get used to new people, their rules, their way of relating to her. It was very clear that she was not going to do it with Nora unless Nora was sticking around.

Kellen: Before they got married, I was like, Don't let this person into my house. This is where I live, don't let her in. And then when they got married, I really settled down. I said, You can come in our house, you're part of the family now. When my mom was switching off, I got used to the people, and then they went away. And Nora hasn't gone away yet. The marriage meant a lot to me because I know that they're going to stay together.

Nora: There was a big difference in my relationship with Kellen after Nina and I were married. I think we got along better. We still have our battles, because I came in when she was five and here's this little person already with her own way of doing things. I'm very different in some ways from Nina in my way of parenting. Kellen's had to make adjustments. The first year was hard; she put me through the wringer.

Suzanne Sherman, ed., *Lesbian and Gay Marriage: Private Commitments, Public Ceremonies* (Philadelphia: Temple University Press, 1992), pp. 109, 111–119. Reprinted by Temple University Press. © 1992 by Suzanne Sherman. All Rights Reserved.

Kellen calls Nina "Mom" or "Mommy." I don't get called "Mommy," she's made that clear, but I get called "Mom" all the time, or "Nora."

Nina: I took care of my baby needs with Kellen. Helen, who lives with us here, has lived with me since Kellen was six months old. She has never been my lover. Helen and I have been friends for years, prior to my conceiving Kellen (which I did on a vacation, when I saw my opportunity). We would probably live together even if I hadn't had Kellen. Helen has a commitment to coparenting, to being involved in Kellen's life.

The woman I was involved with when I got pregnant, MK, was also one of her moms. The three of us haven't lived together at any time. MK also has kept her commitment and is still involved in Kellen's life. MK takes her for some time during the summer. She sees Kellen once a week, financially supports her.

Kellen celebrates the holidays with MK's family. In fact, Nora, Kellen, Helen, and I all go to MK's mother's house for Christmas. They come to her birthdays and celebrate Jewish holidays with us. It's very different from the traditional couple; it's a nucleus, and then we have this extended version. When Kellen started kindergarten she had four, five, six moms.

When I first had Kellen, both MK and Helen said they saw me as the primary mom. I had unilateral decision-making power. Now, we all are involved in decision making. First, I discuss the issue with MK, then we discuss it with Helen, then we all talk about what we think about it. In the beginning, I planned that MK, Helen, and I would raise her and be together; we all made that commitment when I was pregnant. It's been a little trickier maintaining that.

It was tough to make sure that Helen and MK didn't feel replaced by Nora, seeing that Nora was now my permanent partner and new mom in a relationship to Kellen. They needed to know they weren't going to become insignificant. I don't think it's true in other families, either, that when somebody remarries or becomes involved with somebody new other relationships just fall off the face of the earth. It's been somewhat hard for Helen and Nora to adjust to each other.

Nora: They'd been living together since Kellen was six months old. When I moved in, I got the whole family!

Nina: We had a bunch of different responses to our wedding announcement. Some were positive, some people wouldn't come if you paid them, some couldn't come but sent a gift to show they supported us. My family didn't respond at all. My sister wrote and said, "This is my last chance to try to talk you out of being a lesbian." I'd been a lesbian for fifteen years before this relationship, and she'd known all my lovers, but to her this meant the final commitment to lesbianism rather than to a particular person.

Nora's father couldn't understand why we would want to do something "so traditional and oppressive." He said he thought she was a feminist. It was wild. He wouldn't come to our wedding. But then he wanted us to come to her brother's wedding the following year. Three of Kellen's friends came to the wedding, even one whose mother is Fundamentalist Christian.

Kellen: And she came anyway.

Nina: She's a good friend. The mother doesn't support the idea of any validation of our relationship because she sees us as a threat to the family, which is interesting, because the reason we did this is for family support, for structure.

Nora: The friend who was my witness had definite problems with it. This was very patriarchal to her, not an okay thing to do. But she agreed to be a witness because she loves us both. . . .

Nora: I'm a romantic. I always knew I was going to get married, but I didn't know it would be to a woman. For me this was a very political thing to do. You can't be more "out" about who you are and about wanting your relationship considered valid in society than to get married.

The marriage hasn't changed how out I am. I'm out to anyone bold enough to ask if I'm a lesbian. If people notice my ring and refer to my husband, I correct them by simply saying "my partner." Nina's and Kellen's pictures are on my desk at work.

Nina: We've made a few changes since we've been married as far as handling legal issues. For custody issues in the event of my death, an attorney suggested that we establish in as many ways as we can that we are a couple. So, we joined our checking accounts, we buy things in common, we plan to buy a house, we have arranged power of attorney for serious health matters. We did that probably a year after we were married. Nora's on Medi-Cal because she can't get on my insurance from work. They wouldn't even let me pay for it. Now the state ends up paying for it.

Since we've married, I take our relationship and the consequences of my behavior more seriously. Before we got married, people asked whether we thought this would keep us together, and I said I don't think an agreement keeps you together, I think it sets a tone for what kinds of agreements you're willing to make. It was very scary for me to make that kind of solid commitment to somebody. Was I ready to say in front of fifty people that I am going to try very, very hard to stay with this woman? In front of my friends, who are not of this tradition, that I am going to be monogamous? It's much easier to just live with someone and say, Okay, we're together as long as we're together, as long as it feels good. There's a lot more room to get out of it.

Nora: Whenever you make a big commitment like this you always wonder if you're going to be able to do it, if you're setting yourself up to fail. All your doubts come up —is this the right person? Nina had a fever that day—I mean, we were stressed out! But it felt good, too. Having done it, I feel more relaxed. I don't worry as much as I did the first year and a half of our relationship about whether we'll stay together or whether she would be tempted by someone else. Whatever anyone says, you get up in front of fifty people and it's real hard to back down. You break up and there are all these people who knew what this relationship meant to you— it's real different.

Financially and emotionally, it's gotten more complicated, which is as it should be if you're a family. Straight married couples set up a financial being together; if they break up they have a lot to deal with, and so will we if that should ever happen—let's hope it doesn't. You have to push past your fear. It's easier to do knowing that someone is committed to the relationship and isn't going to turn around and leave when it gets hard, and it does get hard. Long-term monogamous relationships are a lot of work. And there's a lot of joy in it, too.

Nina: I think that we carry a certain sense of hope for our friends and for people who want to see that there is such a thing as long-term relationships in the lesbian community, that relationships can stand up under all the social pressure. Our friends want us to make it. Maybe that's because they were part of that beginning ritual.

When we're unhappy, we can go to our friends and tell them we're having a hard time and they say, "Let's work this out. Don't quit." They want us to get through hard times.

Nora: Before we got married, friends asked why we wanted people to be there. To me, you have as many people as possible join a ritual to add their energy and affirm what the ritual is about. The rabbi talked about how part of what we were doing was making a statement of hope, optimism, self-affirmation, and affirmation of ourselves as a couple. We asked people there to bring that affirmation to life.

Two Years Later

Nora: A year before the first interview, I'd miscarried a child at six months. The following year, I got pregnant and miscarried a few days after I found out I was pregnant. This year, we've managed to stay pregnant! The baby is due in two months.

We put an ad for a donor in a gay/lesbian paper, basically asking for somebody who was willing to do this but who didn't want to be a parent. We found someone who fit that bill really well, a gay man who's seen a lot of death, who's lost a lot of friends. It was very altruistic; it was about wanting to do something about life. So, we'd drive over there, pick it up and inseminate. It took me five times over six months. It was scary, because of my history. This last trimester psychologically has been better because I've gotten past twenty-three weeks and it's a great relief.

The first year, I'm going to be more responsible for the child, but things will even out. It won't be like "This is Nora's kid," that kind of thing. Things will even out as Nina becomes more available and I'm less available, because I'm going to go back to work part-time in six months. And I'll be breast-feeding. It used to be that I'd take Kellen to school in the morning and Nina would pick her up. Now I take her to school, pick her up, take her home. I spend more time with her because I'm not working.

I had to go back on Medi-Cal in the middle of my pregnancy because I lost my job. To make life simple, I had to get off Nina's accounts. It's a rigmarole you have to go through over and over again. It's a real drag.

Nina: We registered as domestic partners the day it started, on Valentine's Day. One of our reasons for doing that is that I'm a veteran, and there was a rumor that vets and health-care professionals were at risk of being called up if they decided to reinstate the draft [during the Persian Gulf War]. When they sign people up they ask if you've ever had homosexual tendencies. If you say yes, they'll ignore it if they need people. We figured they couldn't ignore it if we registered as domestic partners because it would be a legal document that could serve as evidence. I know the military, and I had no doubt they would take a lesbian during a war and then, after the war, kick her out. So we went down and did it. It's the only form of legal recognition of any sort we have; it's the first in-road into legal rights.

Nora: Registering was a political statement for us, whatever we can do to keep the issue in the foreground.

Nina: It's amazing how little has changed in the last two years. In a family-therapy session recently, Kellen said exactly what she said two years ago—that it was originally really hard for her to accept Nora because other people had come and gone before, and after we'd gotten married she realized Nora wasn't going to leave and she was going to have to work out her issues with accepting Nora. Kids change their opinions, but nothing has changed there.

Nora: My parents live in Israel and had never met Nina or Kellen until a couple of years ago, when they visited. Since then, they've been much warmer. They had basically ignored Nina's and Kellen's existence before they met them, and, after that, they've changed a lot, at least my mother has. She treats Kellen as a grandchild, sends her presents and talks to her on the phone occasionally, signs postcards "Grandma." They sent Nina a birthday present last year.

Nina: Helen plans to retire in a few years, when she's around seventy, and go live on her ranch up north.

Nora: Helen recognizes that this second child will be Kellen's sibling and she'll need to treat this child equally. The attachment will occur naturally the way attachments do, but she doesn't see herself making a lifetime commitment to this child because she knows she's going to be leaving eventually. When she moves away, Kellen will be fifteen. She sees them as being able to continue their relationship living separately; she doesn't see that happening with a five-year-old. We'll go up and visit, and Helen will come down occasionally; it's not like she'll just completely drop out of this baby's life.

Nina: Both MK and Helen see Kellen and this baby as inseparable. If anything ever happened to me and Nora, both kids would go to whoever was going to be the guardian mother.

Nora: There will be provisions in the will for Nina having custody if something were to happen to me. If anybody were to contest the will that would cut them out of it automatically.

Nina: . . . We celebrate two anniversaries, from when we got together and when we got married. We haven't really decided which is more important. This year was our fifth anniversary. I took her some flowers and chocolate and a card. We celebrate our wedding anniversary alone, often with a weekend away, but we usually celebrate the anniversary of our meeting together with Kellen, since that was a new and important time for all of us.

Editor's Note: In August 1991, Nora gave birth to a healthy boy, Ethan Andrew.

3. The U.S. Census Reveals Change and Continuity in Family Life, 2000

Introduction

Since 1970, the composition of households and families and the marital status and living arrangements of adults in the United States both experienced marked changes. For example, the proportion of the population made up by married couples with children decreased, and the proportion of single mothers increased, while the median age at first marriage grew over time. Much of this variety has been regularly

Jason Fields and Lynne M. Casper, *America's Families and Living Arrangements: March 2000,* Current Population Reports, P20-537 (Washington, D.C.: U.S. Census Bureau, 2001), pp 1–14.

reported in two separate Census Bureau reports—*Household and Family Charac-teristics* and *Marital Status and Living Arrangements.* Beginning with the March 2000 Current Population Survey, these two reports are being replaced by this new publication, *America's Families and Living Arrangements.*

In addition to discussing basic trends about households, families, and living arrangements, this new report highlights characteristics of single-parent families, differences in the living arrangements of younger and older adults, and new data on unmarried-couple households.

Households

Changes in the number and types of households depend on population growth, shifts in the age composition of the population, and the decisions individuals make about their living arrangements.

Demographic trends in marriage, cohabitation, divorce, fertility, and mortality also influence family and household composition. Additionally, changes in norms, values, laws, the economy, and improvements in the health of the elderly over time can influence people's decisions about how they organize their lives. The effects of these trends and individual decisions produce aggregate societal changes in house-hold and family composition.

Growth in the number of households slowed dramatically in the 1990s.

In 2000, the number of U.S. households reached 105 million, up from 63 million in 1970. The growth rate in the number of households has been slowing since the 1970s, from 1.7 million per year between 1970 and 1980, to 1.3 million per year during the 1980s and to 1.1 million per year in the 1990s, the same as it had been during the 1960s.

Nonfamily households were more common and family households less common in 2000 than in 1970.

Traditionally, family households have accounted for a large majority of all house-holds—81 percent of households in 1970 were family households, but by 2000, family households made up only 69 percent of all households.

. . . The most noticeable trend is the decline in the proportion of married-couple households with own children, from 40 percent of all households in 1970 to 24 per-cent in 2000.

In contrast, the proportion of households that were made up of married couples without children remained relatively stable over the period—29 percent in 2000 and 30 percent in 1970. The third family household component—families whose householder has no spouse present, but with other relatives, including children—increased from 11 percent of all households in 1970 to 16 percent in 2000.

The . . . majority of the increase in nonfamily households was due to the growth in one-person households, people living alone. For example, the proportion of house-holds containing one person increased by 9 percentage points between 1970 and 2000 (from 17 percent to 26 percent) compared with other nonfamily households, which increased by 4 percentage points (from 2 percent to 6 percent) during the same period. Women living alone represented 67 percent of one-person households in 1970. By 2000, men were closing this gap, but women living alone still represented more than half (58 percent) of one-person households.

Householders who lived only with nonrelatives comprised the other nonfamily household type, and grew substantially since the 1970s (although they account for a much smaller component of the growth in nonfamily households overall). "Co-habiting" households, or households with unmarried partners, are included in this category. These households will be discussed later in this report.

Households and families have become smaller over time.

Households have decreased in size, with the most profound differences occurring at the extremes, the largest and smallest households. Between 1970 and 2000, households with five or more people decreased from 21 percent to 10 percent of all households. During the same period, the share of households with only one or two people increased from 46 percent to 59 percent. In addition, between 1970 and 2000 the average number of people per household declined from 3.14 to 2.62 percent.

Households with own children made up only a third of all households in 2000.

The decline in the proportion of households with own children under age 18 is an important component in the overall decline in household and family size over the last 30 years. Households with own children dropped from 45 percent of all house-holds in 1970 to 35 percent in 1990 and to 33 percent in 2000.

Changes in fertility, marriage, divorce, and mortality have all contributed to declines in the size of American households. Between 1970 and 1990, the births among unmarried women increased, raising the proportion of children living with a single parent. Over this period. the proportion of women remaining childless also rose. The cumulative effect of these trends was to reduce the average size of house-holds. Increases in divorce also reduced the size of households; divorce generally separates one household into two smaller ones, although the divorce rate's rapid rise through the 1970s and 1980s leveled off during the 1990s. Delays in marriage and improvements in the life expectancy and health of the elderly may have mixed effects on the average household size. Delays in marriage may increase the number of one-person households or may increase the size of households when children continue living with their parents into young adulthood. Better health status of the elderly could either increase the number of married couples, if both men and women live longer, but if health improves for only one gender, then one-person households would become more common.

Families and Family Groups

The family is a vital institution in American society. Families are often the first and frequently the last source of support for individuals. To measure the demographic changes and characteristics of families, the Census Bureau developed two different conceptual universes. Family households are identified when there are members of the household related to the householder. The count of family units, regardless of whether the householder is in that "family," is a count of "family groups." In 2000, there were 72 million family households and 76 million family groups. The additional family groups were largely related subfamilies (3 million), with 571,000 additional unrelated subfamilies.

Married couples made up a smaller portion of family households in 2000 than in 1970.

There were 55 million married-couple family households in 2000, representing 77 percent of family households. Although the number of married-couple family households has increased since 1970 when they numbered 45 million, they increased at a far slower rate than other family households did—by an average of 0.7 percent per year compared with 3 percent per year in other types of family households.

Householders in married-couple family households were older than householders in other family households. Thirty-two percent of married-couple family householders were at least 55 years old, while only about 21 percent of unmarried male and female family householders were this age. Less than one-half (48 percent) of Black family households in 2000 were married-couple households. A higher percentage of Hispanic (68 percent) than of Black households were married-couple households, but not as high as for Asian and Pacific Islander and for White non-Hispanic households (80 percent and 83 percent, respectively).

Families are smaller today.

In 2000, only half of the 76 million family groups in the United States included own children—46 percent of married-couple family groups included an own child under age 18 compared with 61 percent of unmarried-couple family groups. As was the case with households, much of the change in the composition of family groups occurred among larger families. For example, the percentage of family groups with children that have four or more children decreased from 17 percent in 1970 to 8 percent in 1980 and to about 6 percent in 1990 and 2000. Similar proportions of married-couple family groups and family groups with a male reference person included own children under 12 (about 34 percent each) in 2000, while 50 percent of family groups with a female reference person included own children under 12.

Married couple family groups are more likely to live in the suburbs and have college graduates than other family groups.

The majority (55 percent) of married-couple family groups lived in suburban areas (in metropolitan areas outside of central cities) compared with 48 percent of family groups with a male reference person, and 44 percent of family groups with a female reference person. Most married-couple family groups (82 percent) lived in households that were owned or being bought by the householder. Much smaller proportions of family groups with male or female reference people lived in households that were owned or being bought (58 percent and 49 percent, respectively).

Reference people in married-couple family groups also had higher levels of completed education than in family groups with either male or female reference people.

In 2000, 29 percent of the former had graduated from college, and 55 percent had attended college, compared with 13 percent and 40 percent, respectively, of the latter. Reference people in married-couple family groups were also less likely to be unemployed or out of the labor force (29 percent) than those in family groups maintained by women (35 percent). About 34 percent of reference people in male- and female-maintained family groups were divorced; another 41 percent in male-maintained, and 35 percent in female-maintained family groups were never married.

One-parent families numbered 12 million in 2000.

Another way of looking at family change is by examining the marital status of the parents with whom children reside. In 2000, 37 million family groups included children in the United States, up from 30 million in 1970. Single-mother families increased from 3 million in 1970 to 10 million in 2000, while the number of single-father families grew from 393,000 to 2 million.

Because the number of two-parent families remained relatively stable at about 26 million over the same period, the proportion of all families that were married-couple families with children declined from 87 percent in 1970 to 69 percent in 2000. Meanwhile, the proportion of single-mother families grew to 26 percent and single-father families grew to 5 percent by 2000 (from 12 percent and 1 percent, respectively, in 1970).

Several demographic trends have affected the shift from two-parent to one-parent families. A larger proportion of births occurred to unmarried women in the 1990s compared with the 1960s and 1970s, increasing the proportion of never-married parents. A partial explanation is that the delay of marriage also increased the likelihood of a nonmarital birth, because adults were single for more years. Another factor was the growth in divorce among couples with children. These trends have important implications for the well-being of children, and the programs and policies that relate to welfare, family leave, and other areas of work and family life. Further, the family's resources are strongly influenced by the number of parents in the household. Of the 12 million one-parent families, the 10 million maintained by women were more likely to include more than one child than the 2 million families maintained by men (46 percent compared with 36 percent). One-parent families maintained by women were also more likely than those maintained by men to have family incomes below the poverty level (34 percent compared with 16 percent). Women maintaining one-parent families are also more likely than men in similar situations to have never married (43 percent and 34 percent, respectively).

Whether the single parent is divorced or never married may be an important indicator of the quality of life for children in these family groups. Children living with divorced single mothers typically have an economic advantage over children living with those who never married. Divorced parents are, on average, older; have more education; and have higher incomes than parents who never married. White non-Hispanic single-mother families are more likely to be the result of a marital disruption (50 percent were divorced) than an out-of-wedlock birth (30 percent were never married). Black single mothers are the least likely to be divorced (17 percent), and the most likely to be never married (65 percent). Black and Hispanic single mothers are also more likely than White non-Hispanic single mothers to be in a related subfamily (18 percent and 22 percent, respectively, compared with 14 percent).

Marital Status of Individuals

The median age at first marriage is rising for both men and women.

One reason that nonfamily households increased over this period is the postponement in marriage as characterized by the rise in the age of first marriage that has occurred since 1970. In 1970, the median age at first marriage was 20.8 years for women and 23.2 years for men. By 2000, these ages had risen to 25.1 years and 26.8 years, respectively. The gap between men and women has narrowed over the years, but on average, men are still 1.7 years older than women the first time they marry. Changes in marriage patterns also can be observed in the proportion of the population that has married. In 2000, 31 percent of men and 25 percent of women 15-years-old and over had never married, up from 28 and 22 percent for men and women respectively in 1970.

More young adults have not been married.

The delaying of marriage since 1970 by both men and women has led to a substantial increase in the percentage of young, never-married adults. The proportion of women 20 to 24 years old who had never married doubled between 1970 and 2000—from 36 percent to 73 percent. This increase was relatively greater for women 30 to 34 years old; the proportion of never married women more than tripled over this time period from 6 percent to 22 percent. Changes were similarly dramatic for men— the proportion of men 20 to 24 years old who had never married increased from 55 percent in 1970 to 84 percent in 2000. Men 30 to 34 years old experienced an increase from 9 percent to 30 percent. However, the vast majority of men and women in 2000 had been married by their 35th birthday (74 percent), and by age 65, about 95 percent of men and women had been married, indicating that marriage is still very much a part of American life.

Since the 1970s, as the median age of first marriage was increasing, divorce was also on the rise, though leveling off during the 1990s. Both of these demographic shifts have altered the marital composition of the population. Overall, never married and divorced men and women now make up a larger share of the population than they did in 1970 while the proportion currently married has declined. For example, 25 percent of women 15 years old and over were never married and 13 percent were divorced or separated in 2000 compared with 22 percent and 6 percent, respectively in 1970. In contrast, 52 percent of women 15 and over were currently married in 2000, down from 60 percent in 1970. The same trend occurred for men, but . . . men were more likely than women to have been currently married. They were also more likely to have been never married. Women, on the other hand, were more likely than men to have been widowed or divorced.

Living Arrangements of Adults

Over one-half of young men lived with their parents in 2000.

Differences in marriage and divorce patterns by age and sex translate into very different living arrangements for young adults. In 2000, 56 percent (7.5 million) of men 18 to 24 years old lived at home with one or both of their parents. Although women typically marry at younger ages, a sizable proportion (43 percent) lived at home with at least one of their parents. Among people 18 to 24 years old, 10 percent of men and 18 percent of women were married and living with their spouses. In 2000, living alone was not very common among these younger adults—only 4 percent did so. Both men and women in this age group were more likely to cohabit, with roommates or people other than spouses, or live with their parents than to live alone or with a spouse. Thirty percent of men and 35 percent of women in this age group lived with others who were neither their spouses nor parents.

For 25- to 34-year olds, married life becomes the modal type of living arrangement. In 2000, 50 percent of men and 57 percent of women in this age group were married and living with their spouse. Living alone also becomes more common for both men and women: 12 percent and 8 percent, respectively lived by themselves in 2000. Many 25- to 34-year olds still lived with at least one of their parents: 12 percent of men and 5 percent of women.

Men 75 and over are more likely to live with their spouse—women of that age are more likely to live alone.

Among the population 75 years and over, 67 percent of men were living with spouses in 2000 compared with only 29 percent of women the same age. For women, 49 percent were living alone while another 22 percent were not currently married but living with either relatives or nonrelatives. Only 21 percent of men lived alone at this age.

Among the population 65 to 74 years old, the likelihood of living with a spouse is higher for both men and women than among people 75 years and over: 77 percent of men in the younger age group live with their spouses compared to 53 percent of women. Living alone is also less common for people 65 to 74 years old than for people 75 years and over for both men and women. These differences in living arrangements between men and women reflect higher male mortality. With increasing age, however, both men and women experience a greater likelihood of living alone.

In 2000, more than 3 million unmarried couples cohabited.

In addition to couples identifying themselves as married in the CPS [Current Population Survey], a householder may identify the person he or she is cohabiting with as an unmarried partner. In 2000, there were 3.8 million households that were classified as unmarried-partner households, representing 3.7 percent of all households in the United States. These numbers may underrepresent the true number of cohabiting couples because only householders and their partners are tabulated (not all unmarried couples present in a household), and respondents may be reluctant to classify themselves as such in a personal interview situation and may describe themselves as roommates, housemates, or friends not related to each other. Taking these qualifications into consideration, the characteristics of these partners are examined in the following sections.

Married couples are older than unmarried partners.

In 2000, 7.6 million men and women were cohabiting, representing 3.8 million unmarried-partner households. Women tended to be younger than men—25 percent of women were under 25 compared with 16 percent of men. In contrast, only 2 percent of married men and 4 percent of married women were under 25 years old. The proportion of unmarried partners 25 to 34 years old, while considerable (37 percent of men and 33 percent of women), was slightly smaller than the proportion 35 years and over (47 percent of men and 42 percent of women). Among married couples, the vast majority of husbands and wives were 35 years old and over (81 and 76 percent respectively).

Two-fifths of unmarried-partner households included children under 18 years in 2000.

Forty-one percent of unmarried-partner households included children under 18, just slightly less than the proportion of married-couple households with children under 18 (46 percent). About 44 percent of men and 49 percent of women had at least some college education. In 2000, 83 percent of men and 76 percent of women in unmarried-partner households were employed. Married men and women were employed somewhat less, 76 and 60 percent, respectively. This difference is affected by both the older men and women who are retired and by lower labor force participation among married women than among single women.

Twenty-eight percent of women had more education than their partners in unmarried-partner households in 2000.

. . . Twenty-eight percent of women in unmarried-partner households had higher levels of education than their partners, compared with 21 percent of wives in married-couple households. Unmarried partners were more egalitarian in terms of their labor force status. Sixty-five percent of unmarried partners had both partners working in 2000, compared with only 54 percent of married couples.

Women in unmarried-partner households were less likely to be in a traditional homemaking role than were their married counterparts. For example, in 18 percent of unmarried-partner households only the male was employed, compared with 22 percent of married couples. Women in unmarried-partner households were more likely to earn more than their partners when compared with married women—22 percent of women in unmarried-partner households earned at least $5,000 more than their partners compared with only 15 percent of married women. In addition, only 14 percent of unmarried partners included men who earned at least $30,000 more than their partners. For married couples, men earned at least $30,000 more than their spouses 30 percent of the time.

Four percent of unmarried partners were of different races and 6 percent were of different ethnicities in 2000.

In 2000, unmarried partners were less similar in other demographic characteristics than spouses. For instance, 21 percent of female unmarried partners were 2 or more years older than their male partners: by contrast 12 percent of wives were 2 or more years older than their husbands. Most partners and spouses are of the same race, and either both are Hispanic or both are not Hispanic. However, unmarried partners were about twice as likely to be of different races than married couples (4 percent compared with 2 percent). They were also more likely to consist of one Hispanic and one non-Hispanic person (6 percent compared with 3 percent). Cohabitation, because of a more informal structure and perceived impermanence, may often be viewed as a trial relationship, a proving ground for relationships prior to marriage, or in some cases a substitute for a more traditional marriage. . . .

4. Sociologist Michael Kimmel Comments on School Shootings, 2000

For the past few days, the nation has stared at the pictures of Eric Harris and Dylan Klebold, trying to understand the unfathomable—how these two young boys could arm themselves to the teeth, and open fire on their classmates and teachers. We'll stare at those pictures as the explanations begin to pour in from the experts and the pundits alike.

We'll hear from psychologists who'll draw elaborate profiles of misfits and loners, of adolescent depression and acting out. Cultural critics on the right will throw some blame on Goth music, Marilyn Manson, violent video games, the Internet. More liberal critics will tell us it's guns. President Clinton chimed in about violence in the media. Perhaps we'll soon hear about fatherlessness or the disappearance of modesty. The Denver School Board has already banned the wearing of black trench coats.

All the while we will continue to miss the point—even though it is staring right back at us: the killers were middle-class white boys who live in gun states.

Skeptical? Try a little thought experiment: imagine that the killers in Littleton—and in Pearl, Mississippi; Paducah, Kentucky; Springfield, Oregon; and Jonesboro, Arkansas—were all black girls from poor families who lived in New Haven, Connecticut; Newark, New Jersey; or Providence, Rhode Island.

I believe we'd now be having a national debate about inner-city poor black girls. The entire focus would be on race, class, and gender. The media would invent a new term for their behavior, as they did with "wilding" a decade ago after the attack on the Central Park jogger. We'd hear about the culture of poverty, about how living in the city breeds crime and violence, about some putative natural tendency among blacks towards violence. Someone would even blame feminism for causing girls to become violent in vain imitation of boys.

Yet the obvious fact that these school killers were all middle-class white boys seems to have escaped everyone's notice.

In these cases, actually, it's unclear that class or race played any part in the shootings, although the killers in Colorado did target some black students. But that's the point: imagine the national reaction if black boys had targeted whites in school shootings. We would assume that race alone explained the tragedy. (Some

© 2001. Reprinted by permission of the author. All rights reserved.

would, of course, blame rap music and violent movies.) Or if poor boys had targeted those with the fancy cars, we'd assume that class-based resentment caused the boys' rage. (That Dylan Klebold drove a BMW has not prompted the Denver School Board to consider banning those cars, has it?)

That all these murders were committed [by] young boys with guns raises not a ripple. We continue to call them "teens," "youth," or "children" rather than what they really are: boys. Yet gender is the single most obvious and intractable difference when it comes to violence in America. Men and boys are responsible for 95% of all violent crimes in this country. Every day twelve boys and young men commit suicide—seven times the number of girls. Every day eighteen boys and young men die from homicide—ten times the number of girls.

From an early age, boys learn that violence is not only an acceptable form of conflict resolution, but one that is admired. Four times more teenage boys than teenage girls think fighting is appropriate when someone cuts into the front of a line. Half of all teenage boys get into a physical fight each year.

The belief that violence is manly is not a trait carried on any chromosome, not soldered into the wiring of the right or left hemisphere, not juiced by testosterone. (It is still the case that half the boys don't fight, most don't carry weapons, and almost all don't kill: are they not boys?) Boys learn it.

They learn it from their fathers, nearly half of whom own a gun. They learn it from a media that glorifies it, from sports heroes who commit felonies and get big contracts, from a culture saturated in images of heroic and redemptive violence. They learn it from each other.

And this parallel education is made more lethal in states where gun control laws are most lax, where gun-lobbyists are most powerful. Because all available evidence suggests that all the increases in the deadliness of school violence is attributable to guns. Boys have resorted to violence for a long time, but sticks and fists and even the occasional switchblade do not create the bloodbaths of the past few years. Nearly 90% of all homicides among boys aged 15 to 19 are firearm related, and 80% of the victims are boys. If the rumble in *West Side Story* were to take place today, the death toll would not be just Riff and Bernardo, but all the Sharks and all the Jets—and probably several dozen bystanders.

Some will throw up their hands and sigh that "boys will be boys." In the face of these tragic killings, such resignation is unacceptable. And it doesn't answer the policy question; it begs the question: if boys have a natural propensity towards violence and aggression, do we organize society to maximize that tendency, or to minimize it?

Perhaps the most sensible reform that could come from these tragedies is stricter gun control laws, at least on assault weapons and handguns. Far more sweeping—and necessary—is a national meditation on how our ideals of manhood became so entangled with violence.

Make no mistake: Eric Harris and Dylan Klebold were real boys. In a sense, they weren't deviants, but over-conformists to norms of masculinity that prescribe violence as a solution. Like real men, they didn't just get mad, they got even. Until we transform that definition of manhood, this terrible equation of masculinity and violence will add up to an increasing death toll at our nation's schools.

5. Christian Parents Turn to Home-Schooling, 2001

In the 1980s, when newspapers and magazines first started reporting on parents who had rejected school in favor of teaching their children at home, it seemed that the movement would never last—or if it lasted, would never grow. More and more mothers were working outside the home. More and more parents, especially in the upper middle class, were fretting about their children's pursuit of academic excellence and healthy socialization, while simultaneously outsourcing the management of both to recognized experts and paid caregivers. It did not seem an auspicious time for a movement that demanded the intensive labor of mothers willing to forgo careers and income; that set little store by certification, licensing, degrees, and other signifiers of professional expertise; that took pride in a kind of rustic do-it-yourselfism; and that, even in its large, conservative Christian wing, held fast to the progressive-educational notion of not rushing kids into academics too early. Like so many other self-conscious reversions to the way of our forebears, the home-schooling movement seemed destined to sputter out.

Instead it has developed over the past decade or so into a surprisingly vigorous counterculture. In 1985 about 50,000 children nationwide were learning at home. Current estimates range from 1.5 to 1.9 million. (The former is probably the more reliable number, though precision is hard to come by because neither the census nor any other national survey distinguishes between home-schooled children and others.) By comparison, charter schools—the most celebrated alternative in public schooling—enroll only about 350,000 students. Patricia Lines, a former Department of Education researcher who has studied home schooling since the mid-1980s, points to evidence, such as Florida's annual survey of home schoolers, suggesting that the population of kids learning at home is growing by 15 to 20 percent a year. Moreover, home schoolers as a group are extraordinarily committed—not only to educating their children as they see fit but also to building and sustaining organizations. They have founded thousands of local support groups across the country, along with an influential lobbying and legal-defense organization, dozens of publishers and curriculum suppliers, and six nationally circulated magazines. By now it seems reasonable to agree with Lines that "the rise of homeschooling is one of the most significant social trends of the past half century."

To understand why this should be so, it helps first of all to give up on the idea of home schooling as a throwback. It's true that mandatory school attendance is a relatively new phenomenon in the broad sweep of history, and that during the eighteenth and much of the nineteenth centuries most American children acquired what learning they got—precious little if they came from laboring or farming families—at home. The first common schools in the United States were established in the 1840s, but it was not until the early twentieth century, in the first flush of Progressivism, that most states legislated compulsory education, and even then many of the laws covered only a few months of the year. It is true, as the Web site of the Home

Margaret Talbot, "The New Counterculture," *Atlantic Monthly* (November 2001): 136–143. Reprinted by permission of the author.

School Legal Defense Association reminds us, that "American history is full of men and women who were taught at home, from colonial patriot Patrick Henry to President John Quincy Adams to inventor Thomas Edison"—although many of them were taught not by parents but by tutors, which is rather a different thing.

Yet for all the claims that it is resurrecting a hallowed American tradition, for all its old-timey affections (the home-schooling activist Michael Farris once felt compelled to warn home schoolers against un-Christian bragging about baking their own bread), home schooling is a distinctly modern, even forward-looking movement. It is modern in some superficial ways, such as in its use of the Internet to pass along curricula and teaching tips and to create instant support networks. And it is modern in some deeper ways—for example, in its capacity to fulfill needs that could have arisen only in our present social circumstances. Those include the need many parents feel to shield their families from a commercial culture they regard as soulless, acquisitive, overly sexualized, and corrosive of family ties. And, as Mitchell Stevens shows in *Kingdom of Children,* his readable sociological survey of the movement, they include the needs of many American women, mostly conservative Christians, whose beliefs do not permit them to work outside the home but whose aspirations have nonetheless been shaped by feminism and its discontents.

But that's to get ahead of the story. Though they tend to dominate it now, conservative Christians were not home schooling's pioneers. Its first inspiration came from 1960s leftists such as Ivan Illich, Paul Goodman, and A.S. Neill, the founder of the British free school at Summerhill. Many of these innovators started out as critics of subpar schools for the urban poor and became critics of formal education itself—tests, grades, curricula, the very idea that a specific body of knowledge ought to be transmitted from adults to children. Among them was a childless patrician writer named John Holt, who became the first home-schooling activist. Holt was born in New York City in 1923, and, although he later refused to say what schools he had attended, on the grounds that they had taught him nothing, his obituaries revealed that he had enrolled at Phillips Exeter Academy and graduated from Yale with a degree in industrial engineering. After a stint teaching fifth-graders at two private schools in Cambridge, Massachusetts, Holt emerged as an impassioned, slightly moony school reformer, the author of the best-selling diary-style books *How Children Fail* (1964) and *How Children Learn* (1967). "What is essential is to realize that children learn independently, not in bunches," he wrote, "that they learn out of interest and curiosity, not to please or appease the adults in power, and that they ought to be in control of their own learning; deciding for themselves what they want to learn and how they want to learn it." Holt had a Salingeresque softness for kids, whom he regarded as superior in every way to adults. Children "are better at [learning] than we are," he said; left to their own devices, they would learn their little hearts out.

By the late 1970s Holt had abandoned any hope that schools themselves would allow children to learn what they wanted to at their own pace and in their own admirably childish spirit, and had begun urging parents to "unschool" at home. His timing was just right, because many former sixties radicals were by then turning to hearth and home. As the founder of a magazine called *Growing Without Schooling,* Holt went on to guide a loose congregation of hippie parents across the country as they took their children's education into their own experimental, studiously nonauthoritarian hands. These first home educators were suspicious of institutions, Rousseauvian in their pedagogy, and big on learning by doing, whether it was milking goats or weaving a wall hanging or digging a well. They were the kinds of people who thought of themselves as "alternative," who met one another at the food co-op or at La Leche League meetings or at folk-dance fundraisers for Guatemalan refugees. Their world, as Stevens puts it, was "a small world now, short on cash, physical plants, and new blood, but still a hotly idealistic and quietly optimistic place," and Holt's child-centered, liberationist teachings resonated there.

At the same time, two other critics of conventional schooling, Raymond and Dorothy Moore, were launching a campaign against sending children to school in the early grades. The Moores were educational researchers and Seventh-Day Adventists. As young parents living in Tokyo in the 1940s, they had kept their children out of school and had never regretted the decision. Schools, they argued, were factory-like places, from which the "instinctual" knowledge and casual intimacy of family was coldly, and disastrously, excluded. "The tendency for most schools and similar institutions is to make the child's program rigid," they wrote. "This is a necessary feature of mass production. The youngster's activity for much of the day is focused in a few square feet area around his desk, and timed out to the minute." The Moores believed that children were developmentally unable to conform to such routines or to benefit from formal academic instruction until they had reached the "integrated maturity level," which differed from child to child but might be as late as age ten or twelve. If children were hustled into school nonetheless, and then overlooked by busy teachers, the likely results were learning disabilities, nearsightedness, and behavior problems such as hyperactivity. In this the Moores sounded like Holt and other critics who regarded schools as engines of conformity, too big and impersonal to meet the needs of the individual child.

But the Moores were also harbingers of home schooling's quite different future. Unlike Holt and his followers, they were religious conservatives who worried that schools undercut the authority of parents and forced children to face peer pressure before they were able to withstand it. The Moores first gained a national reputation with a 1972 article in *Harper's* magazine. But their great breakthrough occurred in the early 1980s, when James Dobson started inviting the Moores to speak on his nationally syndicated radio program, *Focus on the Family*. With Dobson's immense reach, the Moores' message found an eager audience among the evangelicals and fundamentalists of the new Christian right. For these converts home schooling offered the possibility of editing out evolutionary theory, secular humanism, and other knowledge they abhorred, while reviving or reinventing a model of learning that encouraged children to cleave to their families and keep the blandishments of consumerism at arm's length. Conservative Christians understood that it was easier to strengthen the influence of families against that of pop culture if families had something explicit and comprehensive to *do,* and education was the obvious function.

Christian home schoolers brought new energy and much-improved organizational skills to the movement. It was thanks to them, and particularly to the Home School Legal Defense Association, that home schooling earned the legal status it enjoys today. The Constitution offers broad guarantees of parents' right to direct their children's education, and the Supreme Court has repeatedly upheld those guarantees in cases involving, for example, the rights of the Old Order Amish and other religious minorities to keep their children out of public school. Still, in 1983 only four states had laws explicitly permitting home education. In the early days many of the Holtian "unschoolers" fashioned themselves as a kind of underground. (Holt himself, in one of his more distasteful analogies, championed the notion of a "new Underground Railroad to help children escape from schools.") Some unschoolers courted prosecution under truancy laws. Christian home schoolers, however, tended to want legal recognition for their interpretation of parents' rights, and they got it. By 1993 home education was legal in all fifty states, subject to varying degrees of regulation.

For a while the two wings of the movement cooperated, bound together by their mutual skepticism toward mainstream education. But by the early 1990s the unschoolers were complaining in their publications that conservative white Christians had become the face of the movement. This was true—for the simple reason that white Christians had become the overwhelming majority among home schoolers. In a 1995 study of home educators the sociologist Maralee Mayberry found that 84 percent believed the Bible was literally true, 78 percent said they went to church at least once a week, and 98 percent were white. Later studies have confirmed, as Stevens puts it, that home schooling is "statistically associated with white, religious, two-parent households." Home-schooling parents are not, as a rule, any wealthier than the American norm, but they do tend to have more years of education. (A sizable minority have teaching degrees.) And their families are larger than average: the majority have three or more children. Conservative Christians have become the new counterculture, far more vital than what remains of the 1960s version, and home schooling is their most successful alternative institution.

Despite its precipitate growth, however, comparatively little has been written about home schooling, and what there is tends to focus on more or less measurable outcomes for the kids. Do they make friends? Go to college? Feel like weirdoes? Learn what they're supposed to learn? Score well on standardized tests? On this last point, as it happens, the evidence is fairly strong, and coverage of it has helped to win a grudging social acceptance for teaching outside of school. The news that home-schooled kids had been dominating national spelling and geography bees, and that several surveys showed them scoring higher than the national average on standardized tests, including the SAT, got plenty of press.

In contrast, almost nothing has been written about home schooling as a social movement with its own utility for adults. Stevens, a professor of sociology at Hamilton College, spent ten years interviewing home-schooling families, watching them teach, pitching tents at their summer camps, hanging out at their conferences, and reading their publications. He has written a careful, intelligent book that fills that gap, seeking to explain "what homeschooling means to the people who do it." The book suffers, unfortunately, from the constraints of Stevens's discipline, at least as he interprets them. To protect the privacy of his subjects, he says, he resorts to pseudonyms and alters biographical details. At any rate, vivid descriptions of people and places don't seem to be his forte.

But his analysis is often fascinating, especially when it comes to what women who home school get out of it. Most of the women Stevens interviewed never seriously considered working outside the home after they had children. Full-time motherhood had in some cases been their goal and ideal since childhood, and was often inseparable from their conservative Protestant religious beliefs. To be a godly woman meant to put child-rearing above ambition and acquisition, and sound child-rearing required the devotion of steady, unfragmented attention. "Love is spelled T-I-M-E," as one home-schooling family's Web site puts it. "We give ourselves to our children while they are young and need our instruction . . . By the time they complete the high school years they are firmly anchored in GOD'S WORD, and have learned to stand against the world."

Deeply immersed in these values as they were, however, the women Stevens interviewed were hardly immune to the more mainstream ideals of womanhood shaped in part by liberal feminism. Like their contemporaries who had chosen to combine outside careers with the raising of children, they felt the attractions of using their minds and education in systematic, diligent ways; of possessing a sense of purpose independent from their husbands'; and of avoiding the tedium of house-cleaning. The daily life of, say, the stereotypical 1950s housewife, trussed up in an apron and a short strand of pearls, seemed pallid and irrelevant to them, too. They wanted, as several women told Stevens, to be recognized as more than "just moms." Home schooling was in some ways the perfect solution—a souped-up domesticity with higher stakes and more respect. Though it did not afford economic autonomy, it did offer an intellectual outlet. And it provided social, political, and even entrepreneurial opportunities—through the home-schooling movement's local associations; its frequent conferences, retreats, and multi-family field trips; and its expanding market for new teaching materials, guidebooks, and the like, many of which home-schooling mothers write.

It's true that the work is formidable—the basic care and feeding of young children is labor-intensive enough even when one is not solely responsible for educating them. And mother-teachers do seem to get more respect within the home-schooling world than teachers and child-care workers get in the larger world. This is particularly true in the Christian wing of the movement, where women's teaching role is seen as sanctified by God. "Women are admonished to be committed full-time to their children," Stevens observes, "but their submission to God's plan is also explicitly recognized and celebrated from pulpits and on the pages of [the movement's own] glossy magazines." Moreover, fathers are actively encouraged to help their wives in whatever way the wives find useful, since the job of training young minds is regarded as both singularly important and singularly demanding. Christian home schoolers are "refreshingly explicit about the human costs of raising children," Stevens found. "They devote considerable energy to explaining why children 'need' full-time mothers, and they also are careful to celebrate the doing of that work." (The unschoolers, in contrast, tended to celebrate the creativity of the child over the labors of the mother.)

In the end, *Kingdom of Children* suggests that the benefits of home schooling may be greater for women than for children or for society in general. To be fair, Stevens doesn't even pose the comparison. But it is surely worth some tentative evaluation—especially if the movement continues to grow. Home-schooled kids, I think it's fair to say, are all right. They do well on tests, and they go on to fancy colleges when they want to; admissions officers and professors like them because they are self-motivated and have good study habits. Home-schooled kids watch less television than their peers and—though this has not been measured—are, I suspect, less likely to be medicated with Ritalin and other drugs whose function has at least something to do with classroom management.

I don't think we need worry much about their socialization in the narrow sense, either. With the exception of a few wackos in the Idaho panhandle, home-schooling parents are not bent on isolating their children, and most home-schooled kids make friends through the Scouts or church groups or volunteering. Indeed, in a study conducted a few years ago the sociologists Christian Smith and David Sikkink found that home-schooling families are actually more enmeshed in their communities than public school families. They are more likely, for example, to have voted in the previous five years, participated in an ongoing community-service activity, or gone to the public library. And the few psychological studies that have looked at categories such as "self-concept" and sociability have detected no problems and some advantages for home-schooled kids. It would be ill-advised to set much store by such studies, given the difficulty of measuring something like self-concept, but at least they don't raise any alarms.

More difficult, I think, is the question of whether home schooling poses any sort of a problem for society—a threat to social cohesion, for example, or a brain drain from the public schools. Smith and Sikkink's study suggests that there is little reason to worry that home schooling diverts people from civic life. What may be more worrisome is the prospect that home schooling will attract new recruits motivated mainly by disenchantment with the quality of their public schools. There is some evidence that recent converts to home schooling fit this profile. In a Florida state survey conducted from 1995 to 1996, for example, "dissatisfaction with public school" edged out "religious" motivations for the first time as the leading reason for home schooling.

For ideologically or religiously motivated home schoolers, keeping their kids out of school is not a consumer's whim; it's the exercise of a constitutionally sanctioned right to guide their children's education in accordance with their most deeply held beliefs. And in a democratic society only considerations as profound as those are significant enough to outweigh the potential harm of sectarianism. The decision to home school also represents a complicated but reasonable compromise with the rest of us. Rather than agitate to get Darwinism out of the public schools, for example, conservative Christian home schoolers may opt to withdraw from them while continuing (for the most part) to pay taxes that support those schools and to participate in civic and political life. Moreover, as Stevens shows, home schooling offers some conservative Christian women, whose values prevent them from working outside the home, a measure of fulfillment and autonomy that they might not otherwise enjoy—a social good in itself. If the rest of us (people nursing vague beefs with the public schools, people without a powerful religious or ideological justification) started pulling our kids out of the schools, I doubt it would serve any social good at all.

Secular liberals may not much care for the particular forms of social capital that evangelicals and fundamentalists build, but build them they do. And if one shares the worry that the American citizenry is growing more selfish and monadic, the home schoolers' brand of civic participation is no small thing. Of course, one might argue that the home schoolers' activism is too narrow and self-interested to count as social capital. But that may be too narrow a way of thinking. As Smith and Sikkink argue,

> American democracy thrives on the widespread participation of its citizens in a host of *different kinds* of associations that mediate between the individual and the state, often even when those associations are not manifestly political or liberal . . . [T]he experience of association and participation itself tends to socialize, empower, and incorporate citizens in ways that stimulate democratic self-government, even if they involve some particularity and conflict in the process.

Besides, Christian home schoolers embody a coherent, living critique of mainstream education and child-rearing that can be bracing, a model of carefully negotiated, mildly irritating separateness, of being in but not of modern consumer society. For the rest of us, the tensions that creates may be the most useful thing about them.

6. A Toddler's Mother Criticizes "Toymania," 2003

My son hates toys with batteries. They count. They whistle. They beep. . . . [S]ome even make fake crashing noises. He hates them. Usually he simply stomps on them or throws them to make them stop. Sometimes this works. However, lately, he has added a new phrase to his two-year-old vocabulary: "Mommy, turn it off!" At this point, my son either picks up the toy with renewed interest and sees what he can make it do on its own, or he turns away and plays with his "kid-powered" wooden train or snaps blocks together. He may even play out an adventure with his pirate ship—complete with cannons and a shipboard parrot. His mounds of "learning" toys mechanically and LOUDLY reciting numbers and letters lay unloved and unused in the bottom of his toy box.

Now, as a modern parent, I should be horrified. A child who has reached his second birthday without mastering his toddler-sized toy laptop computer and refuses to interact with a toy that enthusiastically and once again LOUDLY tries to teach letters and numbers to the pre-preschool set is obviously doomed for failure. Based on the barrage of advertisements directed at me and my little Einstein, I know that my son will never go to Harvard, because he is not learning with his "teaching toad" toys. I can only watch wistfully, as the little girl on television dazzles her father with her mastery of the alphabet that she has conquered all seemingly before school with only the help of a repetitive learning toy that taught her the alphabet, which she proudly posts all over her parents' refrigerator.

Alas, my refrigerator is barren. I don't even have an ice dispenser like the one in the ad. I guess college is out for my dear boy. Instead, he will have to be a pirate. He's really good at that.

But before I start planning our move to the Caribbean, it might be worth a moment to reconsider. Why do parents feel guilt if their children do not own $500 worth of "learning" and other toys by the age of 12 months? . . . My son actually owns a

---

T. C. Whitlock, "'Turn It Off, Mommy!' Conspicuous Toy Consumption and the Modern Child circa 2003." Reprinted by permission of the author.

battery-powered car that could probably get him at least to the corner drugstore if he was not scared to get in it. It leaps and lurches with the power of a toddler SUV, which is what it actually is. But with our children, it is more than merely having more stuff (always an important American occupation). We believe that more stuff = better child. After all, if my son can learn how to operate a car at the age of twelve months—by sixteen years it should be a piece of cake. However, more important than the concept of "my child will have more than I did" is the concept of modern learning toys. It is not simply consumption for consumption's sake, but buying those key learning toys gives our sons and daughters that required edge they will need in an ever more competitive and information-centered world.

We, the parents, are suckers on two fronts. Suffering ourselves from [what John De Graaf calls] "affluenza," we extend and pass on the need for consumption of goods to our children. But the more insidious form of toymania is the illusion that talking and "interactive" toys can either replace adults or . . . give our children an unfair edge in the learning process. We simply have to buy our way to our children's future. As an added bonus, as little Suzie beeps and whistles her way to academic success, Mom is free to work on a report for work or watch her favorite cooking show. It is a tempting scenario. And lest I seem too judgemental here, check out OUR toy closet, box, shelves, and various other stowing places.

Although I often feel like some Lorax-ian throwback failing to recognize progress, I frequently find other mothers share similar worries. For example, my friend, an artist, is scandalized by Fisher-Price toys. Yes, I said Fisher-Price . . . [t]hose past champions of imaginative play. It seems that in a competitive market they have abandoned those peg-shaped plastic people of the past for more realistic "Little People" with arms and legs. It wouldn't be so bad if that were all. But the new "Little People" come with battery-powered houses and vehicles that SPEAK for them. My son owns one, a cute fire truck, with an against-stereotype female firefighter. Bravo, I say, until I realize that—when placed in the appropriate seat in her truck—she spouts messages and even tells us her name, Cheryl. What if my son wants to call his firefighter Wanda? When toys speak . . . , there is very little left for a kid to do—except as my son so often does, simply walk away. For parents, walking away is much harder when we feel the pressures of providing our children with the best and brightest of everything.

Perhaps overly technical toys that beep, bleat, and flash are only the worst offenders. Toy consumption also has its designer aspects. For those of us parents whose guilt (and pocketbooks) know no bounds, there is the Pottery Barn Kids Catalog. . . . My favorite item [in the latest edition] is the "Tumble 'n' Set." . . . Here I can buy a colorful foam mat for $299 (on sale) and a foam block the size of a large couch cushion for $89. Or I could just do what I did yesterday and let my toddler build forts out of our own couch cushions for free. . . .

Don't get me wrong. I'm not one of these people who wants to bring back some idealized past of toy consumption. . . . I do not yearn for the days of wind-up metal cars, cast-iron play stoves able [to] smash a toddler hand and various other sharp, metal, and glass toys. I shiver when I watch the toy collectors show off their bounty on Antiques Roadshow with their razor-sharp edges and total disregard for safety. Leave the "old-fashioned" toys to the adults, I say. Nor do I want, like some depression-era grandparent, to advocate that completely less is more. For example,

"Yes, when I was growing up, I just had a stick named 'Jimmy.' I loved that stick. It is all a kid really needs to be happy. . . ."

There must be a happy medium between playing with a stick . . . and overconsuming on the scale of hundreds of dollars a year (thousands if you shop regularly at Pottery Barn). . . . As parents, we have to recognize and treasure our sons' and daughters' childhood without succumbing to the enormous pressure to overprovide for them. Meanwhile, I have a new strategy to cut down on at least toys given as gifts to my son. I'm telling all the grandparents that he ONLY likes toys from Pottery Barn Kids. Who knows how this will affect his future? Just in case, if, twenty years from now, you find yourself on a pleasure cruise in the South Seas and a cute redheaded pirate with blue eyes stops and asks for your money, give it to him. His mother didn't buy him enough toys.

E S S A Y S

In the first essay, Yale University historian Nancy F. Cott, author of *Public Vows* (2000), examines marriage in contemporary America. Cott employs the metaphor of disestablishment to describe marriage in the twenty-first century. Just as the disestablishment of an official state church in early America led not to irreligiosity, but to a proliferation of religious denominations, she argues, so, too, the disestablishment of state-sanctioned heterosexual marriage in recent times has led not to unregulated pairings, but to an array of committed living arrangements. Moreover, she argues, legal marriage retains a special status both as a romantic ideal and as a public institution.

In the second essay, Gary Cross of Pennsylvania State University, the author of *Kids' Stuff* (1997), reflects on the changes in children's playthings in recent America. Although Cross takes a long view, pointing out that toys are not now, and never have been, timeless, he regards changes in the toy industry since the 1960s as particularly dramatic and disruptive. While toys once were selected by parents and prepared children for adult roles and responsibilities, he argues, toys now are marketed directly to children and bear little relationship to adulthood.

The Meaning(s) of Marriage in Postmodern America

NANCY F. COTT

A phenomenon such as President William Jefferson Clinton—a leader who remained popular and in office despite public knowledge of his sexual strayings outside marriage—had never been seen in American politics before the 1990s. . . . Clinton attracted frequent condemnation for his moral failings and embarrassing lack of self-restraint. He escaped rejection, however, because the majority generously (or cynically) tolerated a wide range of behavior in couples, seeing husbands and wives as accountable principally to each other for their marital performance. . . .

The public forgiveness of Clinton's sexual misadventures can only be understood against the background of a generation's seismic shift in marriage practices.

Nancy F. Cott, *Public Vows: A History of Marriage and the Nation* (Cambridge, Mass.: Harvard University Press, 2000), pp. 200–206, 209–225. Excerpted and abridged by permission of the publisher. Copyright © 2000 by Nancy F. Cott.

Drastic eruptions and reorientations began in the 1960s, with a sexual revolution that deserved that name. As much as 1950s tremors had given some hints, emancipatory claims based on sex burst out from the nourishment given by 1960s political movements. The New Left, the antiwar movement, black power, women's liberation, and gay liberation—along with the hippies and flower children who constituted themselves the counterculture—all fused dissident politics with purposeful cultural disobedience and devil-may-care hijinks centering on defiance of sexual norms. . . .

The sexual revolution was not unique to the United States. Extraordinary shifts in sexual and marital practices and in the shape of households were taking place all over the industrialized world. A French demographer named Louis Roussel, looking at trends across North America, Europe, Japan, Australia, and the Soviet Union in the late 1980s, identified 1965 as a rare axis of change. In the subsequent fifteen years, a whole set of demographic indicators was reshuffled. Among the billion people encompassed in these nations, rates of formal marriages and of births tumbled; divorces and the proportion of births outside formal wedlock both shot up. The increases and decreases were substantial and even spectacular, often 50 percent or more. . . .

In the United States, the number of unmarried-couple households recorded by the Census Bureau multiplied almost ten times from 1960 to 1998. It grew more than five times as fast as the number of households overall. The General Social Survey, conducted every year since 1972 by sociologists of the National Opinion Research Center at the University of Chicago, reported in 1999 that cohabitation had become the "norm" for men and women as their first form of heterosexual living (as well as for post-divorce unions). Almost two thirds of those born between 1963 and 1974 first cohabited, without marrying.

At the twentieth century's close, marriage could no longer be considered the predictable venture it once had been. People living alone composed a quarter of all households in 1998. This reflected growth in the elderly population who were widows and widowers, but it also showed marriage itself losing ground. The proportion of adults who declined to marry at all rose substantially between 1972 and 1998, from 15 percent to 23 percent. The divorce rate rose more furiously, to equal more than half the marriage rate, portending that at least one in two marriages would end in divorce. . . . Only 56 percent of all adults were currently married in the late 1990s, down from three quarters in the early 1970s. . . .

Along with the decline in marriage overall, the birth rate dropped, from more than 3.5 births per woman in 1960 to about 2 births per woman in the mid-1990s. The household without children, rather than with children, was the norm (62 percent) in the United States. What had been typical adult status in the long past—married, with minor children—described barely more than one quarter of adults in 1999, the General Social Survey found. Children's parents were unmarried far more often than in the past; unmarried mothers accounted for almost one third of births in 1998, compared to about 5 percent in 1960. White women's rate of unmarried childbearing more than doubled after 1980. Black women's rate moved up only 2 percent during the same years, so that where their rate had been 4 or 5 times that of whites in 1960, in the late 1990s it was only about twice as high. As a result of both nonmarriage and divorce among women with children, one fifth of family-based households of whites were female-headed in the 1990s, as were almost three fifths of black families and almost one third of Hispanic families. . . .

State legislatures . . . contributed to the moral and legal reframing of marriage, by reforming divorce law. In less than two decades, beginning in the mid-1960s, the adversary principle in divorce was virtually eliminated. California first adopted "no-fault" divorce in 1969 and within four years at least thirty-six states had made it an option. By 1985 every state had fallen into step, not always under the rubric of "no-fault" but offering essentially the same thing, that a couple who had proven incompatible could end their marriage. . . . [T]he innovation of no-fault divorce, or divorce on the ground of "irretrievable breakdown" of the marriage as defined by the spouses, indicated a major shift. Earlier, the petitioner for divorce had to show that the other spouse failed to uphold state-defined obligations by committing adultery or desertion or another legislatively set deviation from marriage. No-fault divorce implied instead that the state should refrain from passing judgment on performance in an ongoing marriage and allow the partners to decide whether their behavior matched their own expectations; if it did not, the marriage could be legally dissolved.

Feminist activists did not speak for the no-fault principle but did press for subsequent reforms treating post-divorce arrangements such as child custody, child support, alimony, and the division of marital assets. Custom if not legal doctrine for the preceding century had typically awarded custody of children of "tender years" to the mother, and expected child support from the father. Divorce reforms intended to see the roles of both husband and wife more gender-neutrally, with both able to be earners and caring parents. Most states revised their law and practice to make joint custody and child support from both parents the standard, to be tailored to each situation. Alimony was made gender-neutral as a result of a U.S. Supreme Court decision of 1979. In corollary, virtually every state took up the principle that the material assets belonging to either spouse should be seen as belonging to both when a marriage ended. Dividing marital property "equitably" between husband and wife upon divorce was meant to credit the unpaid work that the typical non-employed homemaker put into the partnership, and it also benefited ex-husbands who had been supported by their wives' earnings or assets. . . .

A contractual emphasis in marriage appealed to feminists as the main hope for restructuring the institution to shed its history of inequality. Some feminists recommended that couples devise their own private contracts to substitute for the state's prescription of marital obligations. Unlike earlier centuries' prenuptial contracts, which were intended to stabilize the descent of rich couples' assets, feminist contracts in the 1970s set out the obligations and rewards of the ongoing marriage—what husband and wife would owe each other in financial support, housework, childcare, sex, and so on. The content of "model" contracts testified to concern that the heavy weight of marital convention would drag any marriage down the old path, regardless of the couple's initial good intentions. This contractual approach reaccentuated the element of consent in monogamy, which had always been central to its prominence as a public institution. Like the Supreme Court's finding (in *Griswold v. Connecticut*) that constitutional protection of "liberty" freed birth control from state interference, this reinvention of marriage employed a longstanding principle to new effect.

The courts responded by taking couples' prenuptial contracts seriously, and also those composed once the couple was married. The principle that courts would assess spousal contracts dealing with post-divorce arrangements for fairness, and would enforce them, was well established by the 1990s—but there were limits. A court would not allow a wife to contract away her marital obligation to serve her husband's needs, nor a husband his obligation to support the wife. In 1993 a California appeals court refused to support a wife's claim to collect assets from her husband's estate as compensation for taking care of him at home as he had begged, after he suffered a stroke, rather than placing him in a nursing home (as she preferred to do). He had agreed to increase his bequest to her if she cared for him at home, but his will did not follow through. The court, finding "sickbed bargaining" offensive and "antithetical to the institution of marriage as the Legislature has defined it," would not award the wife the compensation she sought. Citing precedents from 1937 and 1941, the majority opinion emphasized that the wife's care for her husband was simply part of her "marital duty of support"—even in the face of a dissenting colleague's objection that this "smack[ed] of the common law doctrine of coverture." Thus the traditional marriage bargain survived in skeleton form to the end of the twentieth century.

The contractual emphasis moved understandings of marriage toward the private side, and there was another strong reason for feminists to see intimate relationships as private. The legal argument for women to exercise freedom of choice over childbearing, or "reproductive rights," rested on privacy. The decisions in *Griswold* and *Eisenstadt* had used reasoning about privacy to remove state constraints on birth control, but abortion remained criminal. Feminist efforts to change that led to *Roe v. Wade,* the U.S. Supreme Court decision of 1973 that freed abortion (for the first trimester of pregnancy) from state restrictions. The opinion rested on a woman's right to consider privately, with her doctor, whether she would bear a child.

Feminist legal strategies had to work both sides of the private/public divide that marriage inhabited, however. To defend reproductive choice, as in *Roe,* or to try to secure equalitarian marriages, it was necessary to see intimate decisions taking place in a sheltered private realm. But in order to protect wives and daughters from being overpowered physically by the men in their households, feminists wanted to bring public authority into the private domestic sanctum. The doctrine of domestic privacy, allowing the home to be curtained off from public scrutiny, could work just like the old assumption of marital unity to maintain superior power in the hands of an abusive husband. If domestic violence was going to be prosecuted and if a husband's exemption from rape charges for coercing his wife into sex was going to be eliminated, then the zone of domestic privacy had to be opened up and the notion that "a man's home is his castle" unseated.

Both of those intentions have been substantially accomplished in the law since the 1970s. Almost everywhere, legislation and police directives allow public authorities to breach the "sacred precincts" in order to arrest violent men. . . .

The downfall of the marital rape exemption has to be seen as a very significant emblem of change. Of all the legal features of coverture, this right of the husband to his wife's body was the longest lasting. Through the 1970s sweep of legal sex discriminations from the law, it was not moved. Not until 1984, after at least a decade of feminist arguments, did a New York appellate court overturn that state's marital rape exemption—then other states followed. . . .

Dissolving the husband's privilege, this decision eliminated a historically central feature of marriage in the law, and subsequent developments showed that states were putting their public force behind the denial of marital unity. The law of marriage no longer gave bodily possession of the wife to her husband. This change announced a new norm of the wife's self-possession, with the potential to reframe the roles of both marriage partners. Marital rape was not altogether blended in to the category of rape, however. While all states criminalized it, at least a third of them distinguished marital rape from other forms. The police, lawyers, judges, and juries involved in prosecuting marital rape tend to make assumptions that exonerate the husband. Still, no state of the United States any longer puts a husband's right to coerce his wife into sex in the definition of marriage.

It could be contended, then, that by the 1980s the states and the nation had let go their grip on the institution of marriage along with their previous understanding of it. States' willingness to prosecute marital rape and wife abuse formed the most recent items in a trail of evidence, including the unchaining of morality from formal monogamy, the demise of the fiction of marital unity, and the institution of no-fault divorce. States legislatures and courts had moderated their former definitional role and resuscitated their much earlier willingness to treat couples "living together" as if they were married, at least in economic terms. The families of unmarried couples are treated as families in court. Parents' rights over children do not diminish—nor do their enforceable responsibilities for support—just because of birth out of wedlock. This public willingness to see marriage-like relationships *as* marriage is driven by the aim of guaranteeing economic support by family members, thereby minimizing demands on public assistance, but it also diversifies social views of family relationships.

This alteration in the relation between marriage and the state might be called "disestablishment," if the term can be borrowed from the history of religion. A national church supported by church taxes or tithes in the past was called the "established" religion or religious "establishment," and the ending of that special status for one religion was called disestablishment. Disestablishment did not mean that piety or religious institutions disappeared. On the contrary, the consequence more often was that religious sects proliferated, while no single model was, any longer, supported and enforced by the state. By analogy one could argue that the particular model of marriage which was for so long the officially supported one has been disestablished. Continuing the analogy to religious disestablishment, one could say that with the weight of the one supported faith lifted, plural acceptable sexual behaviors and marriage types have bloomed. . . .

These remarkable and probably irrevocable transformations in the marital landscape have not been uncontested. Political and ideological backlash has been in the mix since the mid-1970s. The emergence in American politics of a New Right, strongly allied with Protestant fundamentalism and centered simultaneously on "family values" and embrace of the free market, responded in part to the apparent disestablishment of traditional marriage. . . . This vocal minority, effective beyond its numbers in electoral politics in the 1980s and 1990s, still made a vivid connection between the stability of conventional Christian-model monogamy and the health of the nation-state. Alarms about the degradation of family life in the United States have sounded from many political angles, but only partisans of the New Right (and not all of them) openly voice the desire to reinstate a patriarchal model of marriage with the husband/father as the provider *and* and the primary authority figure. . . .

Despite the extensive gains made by the New Right both culturally and politically, it seems dubious that conventional legal marriage can recover the primacy it once had. Economic reasons for two-earner families and feminist transformations of self-understanding make that unlikely. Houses hold unrelated groups, cohabiting couples, multigenerational rather than couple-based households, single-person households, and single adults raising children. . . . The boundaries of acceptable heterosexual behavior generally follow lines of consent rather than marriage—with adultery a partial exception. Though acknowledged to occur, and even shrugged at, marital infidelity was pronounced to be always wrong by about 80 percent of adults at the end of the century, a figure rising back from a low of about 70 percent in the combative 1970s.

Bring same-sex marriage into view, however, and the suitability of the disestablishment parallel fails. If disestablishment of formal and legal Christian-model monogamy were real, public authorities would grant the same imprimatur to every kind of couple's marriage. That has not happened. Opponents of same-sex marriage have drawn a line in the moving sand of disestablishment. Marriages between two women or two men can be validated *only* by like-minded communities, not by formal public authorities. (Clergy members, including Unitarian-Universalists, reform Jews, and various Protestants, have stepped increasingly into the breach to perform religious ceremonies of marriage—without legal standing—for same-sex couples.) The morality that the law has dropped or soft-pedaled with respect to consensual heterosexual acts still lives in the law's prosecution of homosexual behavior. As late as 1986, the U.S. Supreme Court upheld a Georgia law under which two consenting male homosexuals were arrested for what they did in private and at home. In 1996, Supreme Court Justice Antonin Scalia grouped murder, polygamy, and homosexuality together as kinds of inherently reprehensible conduct against which he assumed laws could constitutionally "exhibit 'animus.'" Both prosecution of homosexual behavior and resistance to same-sex marriage show that the profound transformation of disestablishment has *not* taken place. . . .

By the spring of 2000, a total of thirty-five of the fifty states had legislated their unwillingness to recognize same-sex marriage. Despite the Golden State's reputation for sexual liberalism, more than three fifths of voters there endorsed the resolution that "only marriage between a man and a woman is valid and recognized in California." Yet simultaneously Vermont created a legal status called "civil union" for same-sex couples. The state high court, using reasoning about equal protection of the laws, declared in December 1999 that same-sex couples deserved access to the benefits that heterosexual couples gain from marrying. Even though Catholic, Mormon, and conservative groups mobilized in opposition, in April 2000 Vermont enacted a historic law, reserving "marriage" to one man and one woman but allowing a same-sex couple in the state to identical rights and protections in "civil union."

Conservative advocacy groups, intending to preempt validation of same-sex marriage by state referenda and constitutional amendments, were fashioning symbolic statements as much as pragmatic instruments. So were the large majorities in both houses of Congress who had ushered through a "defense of marriage act" with very unusual speed in 1996. The Defense of Marriage Act was not a complex piece of legislation. It was a "modest proposal" based on "common sense," according to one Senate sponsor. The act did two things. First, it explicitly defined the words "marriage" and "spouse" in federal law as involving one man and one woman. Second—and far more questionable constitutionally—it provided that no state would be required to give effect to a same-sex marriage contracted in another state, despite the constitutional rule that each state should give "full faith and credit" to the public acts of others. . . .

Congressional rhetoric on behalf of the Defense of Marriage Act, relying more on pronouncement than on reasoning, undercut the idea that disestablishment of the traditional institution of marriage was well under way. The bill's supporters announced that traditional heterosexual marriage was "the fundamental building block of our society"; that nature and the Judeo-Christian moral tradition commanded or comported with it; that it was the basis of "civilization." One or two said homosexuality was immoral, a perversion, based on lust; more often the fear was expressed that licensing same-sex marriage would start the descent down a slippery slope to licensing polygamy, incest, even marriage to animals. The most fervent urged that the disparity between homosexual and heterosexual relationships could not become a matter of moral indifference. To treat the two as moral equivalents was to "completely erase whatever boundaries that currently exist on the definition of marriage and say it is a free-for-all, anything goes."

. . . Congressman James M. Talent of Missouri summed up a predominant viewpoint among the bill's supporters when he declared, "it is an act of hubris to believe that marriage can be infinitely malleable, that it can be pushed and pulled around like silly-putty without destroying its essential stability and what it means to our society, and if marriage goes, then the family goes, and if the family goes, we have none of the decency or ordered liberty which Americans have been brought up to enjoy and to appreciate." . . .

In the 1996 debate as in the past, observance of Christian-model monogamy was made to stand for customary boundaries in society, morality, and civilization; the nation's public backing of conventional marriage became a synecdoche for everything valued in the American way of life. . . . Those who opposed the Defense of Marriage Act also had American values to marshal on their side, however. They reasoned that marriage was a basic right that should not discriminate on the basis of gender, that the American values of liberty and the pursuit of happiness should apply to couples of the same sex. They invoked the social value of love between partners who chose each other and contended that Congress should not step into the making of private relationships. . . .

. . . The bill passed the House by a vote of 342 to 67 (with 22 not voting and 2 "present") and the Senate by 85 to 14. As had often been the case in previous legislative contentions over marriage forms, the debate on the Defense of Marriage Act revealed a cultural contest being waged between the majority and a nonconforming minority. Senator Jesse Helms's speech epitomized the strongly ideological stance of the bill's supporters, condemning "homosexual extremists" for eviscerating the nation's "moral stamina." Calling marriage "sacred," Helms proclaimed that "the moral and spiritual survival of this Nation" was at stake in the measure and that the vote would decide "whither goeth America."

Putting the nation's imprimatur on one man and one woman in sacred union, Congress signified its concern for more than heterosexuality alone. Further assumptions wrapped in the word "marriage" reverberated loudly in the contemporaneous welfare reform law. The federal act that fulfilled President Clinton's promise to "end welfare as we know it" was called the Personal Responsibility and Work Opportunity Reconciliation Act of 1996 (formally a set of revisions in public assistance under the Social Security Act). It answered years of polemics against welfare clients for purportedly taking unfair advantage of an overgenerous system. The act replaced "welfare" with "workfare," by putting federal public assistance to needy mothers and fathers in the form of block grants to states, contingent on the states' providing the recipients (in the words of the act) "with job preparation, work and support services to enable them to leave the program and become self-sufficient." . . .

The Personal Responsibility and Work Opportunity Act (PRWO) zeroed in on marriage as a solution to the ballooning welfare caseload. While the main lineaments of the bill mandated work requirements and the means to chase down deadbeat dads, the bill opened with the normative claims "(1) Marriage is the foundation of a successful society. (2) Marriage is an essential institution of a successful society which promotes the interests of children." According to the social science analysis incorporated in the act, the availability of public assistance for poor and unemployed single mothers had allowed the men who fathered children to forget about marrying the women they made pregnant, and to shirk financial responsibility for their children. In this view, "welfare" encouraged shiftless women to get pregnant in order to be supported by the public purse in female-headed households. Their children, lacking responsible employed fathers as worthwhile role models, were doomed to making this cycle of nonmarriage and illegitimacy and consequent poverty and dependence on public assistance repeat itself.

. . . Female-headed households with children are far poorer, on average, than married-couple households, but proponents of the Personal Responsibility act spoke as though the marriage ceremony itself magically solved the problem of poverty. Proponents assumed rather than probed what were the reasons behind the correlation between marriage and greater economic stability. They did not give equal attention to highly relevant and complex issues of sex segregation and racial stratification in the labor market; they did not question how far the rise in illegitimacy and female-headed households, and the decline in marriage, were larger phenomena not caused by welfare. They said "get a job!" and "get married!" The Personal Responsibility and Work Opportunity Act offered substantial incentives to states to reduce out-of-wedlock pregnancies (especially among teenagers) while lowering abortion rates—as if wedded parents would always be adequate parents, and would not split up or fall into poverty.

. . . In pursuit of its aim to reduce welfare caseloads through private support, the Personal Responsibility and Work Opportunity Act echoed centuries of enforcement of the husband's obligation to provide. Like the Defense of Marriage Act, it sought to impose majority norms of marriage on a minority, for the ostensible benefit of the nation. Yet there was a catch. The methods of implementing the Personal Responsibility and Work Opportunity Act . . . brought public oversight into the personal lives of the poor. The national value placed on marital and familial privacy did not extend to families in need of help. Welfare mothers and fathers could not enjoy a "private realm of family life where the state cannot enter."

These two major acts of Congress in the late 1990s, along with the myriad marital obligations and benefits in the federal legal apparatus, illustrated the national government's continuing investment in traditional marriage. . . .

Despite sweeping reformulations in intimate relationships in the past quarter century, one can doubt whether most Americans' "common sense" about marriage has vastly changed. So flayed and scorned in the 1960s and 1970s, conventional and legal marriage like the phoenix has arisen from its ashes, even alongside innovations and deviations. It is the main theme around which the variations take place. Even with no-fault divorce common, marriage commands greater respect from popular opinion and implies a greater commitment than "living together." The position of legal marriage above comparable relationships resists toppling. Contestation over same-sex marriage has, ironically, clothed the formal institution with renewed honor. . . .

The resiliency of belief in legal marriage as the destination of a love match and as a safe haven begs for explanation, even when hyperbole about love seems to demand none. Love is exalted in our society—it is the food and drink of our imaginations. Sexual love has even more of a halo, because we assume that an individual's full subjectivity blossoms in the circle of its intimacy. But where does marriage stand, when there is widespread awareness that half of all marriages end in divorce? Alarmists declare certainly that marriage is withering, but its firm grip is more of an enigma. Even with failed marriages staring them in the face, individuals still hope to beat the odds. The belief persists that a couple have achieved the ultimate reward, the happy ending, by adding the imprimatur of public authority and making their relationship formal and legal. Dating services certainly advertise it this way, promising to introduce "Mr. Right" and "Ms. Right" to each other. Splendid, elaborately detailed weddings have swelled in popularity, as though the money spent on a wedding is ballast destined to keep the marriage afloat.

The preeminent stature of marriage in public opinion is not unwarranted because it still *is* a public institution, building in material rewards along with obligations. History and tradition cement the hold of marriage on individual desires and social ideals. Marriage also continues to appeal subjectively, despite the alternatives visible, because of the relief it seems to offer from the ineffable coercions and insistent publicity of the postmodern world. . . .

Conspicuous Toy Consumption and Modern Childhood

GARY CROSS

Most of us find ourselves at one time or another in a toy shop, looking for a gift for a child. Those of us who have not been in such stores since our youth can easily be bewildered, especially if we were born before the 1960s. Our favorite toys or games—fire engines, Tinkertoys, or baby dolls—have disappeared or are hidden in row after row of heroic fighters, fashion dolls, and exotic stuffed animals.

The more practical of us enter the store with a list of items desired by the child—this season's action figure, the newest Barbie, or the latest video game. Veteran toy

Gary Cross, *Kids' Stuff: Toys and the Changing World of American Childhood* (Cambridge, Mass.: Harvard University Press, 1997), pp. 1–10. Reprinted by permission of the publisher. Copyright © 1997 by the President and Fellows of Harvard College.

shoppers may enjoy the inevitable transformations as Teenage Mutant Ninja Turtles give way to Mighty Morphin Power Rangers and Locket Surprise Barbie to Tropic Splash Barbie. But equally we may be appalled to think about the dozens of Ninja Turtles that an older boy just had to have a year earlier but that were then shunned by a younger brother who just had to have Power Rangers. Why don't kids pass down their toys as we remember giving our building blocks and dollhouses to our younger brothers and sisters? It is easy to wonder whether each year's must-have toys are really for children's play or whether their ever-changing forms represent other forces at work.

We often lament a loss of innocence in the young. We recall playing ball in the street, holding "secret" meetings in treehouses, or pushing baby dolls in miniature wicker carriages, We assume that this is the way children "traditionally" played, that childhood "used to be" unchanging. We remember a less commercialized youth. Some of our wagons were handmade from scraps of lumber and discarded wheels, and grandmas sewed dolls' clothes, Even if most of our playthings were, in fact, manufactured, we had far fewer of them. Toys came at birthdays, Christmas, and Hanukkah. And, on those rare occasions when we bought them for ourselves, we did so with money saved from jobs and allowances, and at neighborhood toy stores or five-and-dimes. We window shopped for weeks before we had saved enough to make the plunge and buy. We knew the storekeepers and they knew us. Our parents understood when we should have a gun-and-holster set or a dress-up doll. Dolls and tea sets, electric trains and erector sets had been part of the rites of passage for generations of Americans. Parents understood the toys of children because they had been *their* toys once and were still so in memory.

These images contrast sharply with today's cornucopia of playthings. The toy store today is no longer a special place where customary gifts can be found but a well-organized warehouse for the experienced consumer. Only the merchandise excites. The sheer quantity from which to choose may well dull the imagination but encourages the filling of shopping carts. Gone are the "Mr. Hoopers" once nostalgically portrayed on *Sesame Street,* shopkeepers who patiently displayed each toy so that parents and kids could make a wise choice. Instead there are endless aisles with boxes piled high and clerks who look beyond the child for those price-code strips to be passed over their computer scanners. The desire for a toy comes not so much from reaching the age when children "naturally" got a bicycle or a dress-up doll as from advertising campaigns aimed to whet the child's appetite for more. Shopping for toys has become saddening, irritating, or bewildering to many adults.

Toymakers seem to be pied pipers leading our children away from us. They manufacture and endlessly promote fantasy war play that appears to teach violence as a way of resolving conflict. Toy manufacturers have made fortunes promoting sexist and unattainable images of women to young girls. Barbie's hourglass figure (at estimated projected measurements of 36"-18"-33") encourages little girls to have distorted expectations of their own bodies. Today's toys do not often convey the values that we wish our children to embrace and that we believe we learned with our toys in childhood.

Occasionally parents protest and form organizations to combat these trends. . . . Articles in *Parents' Magazine* ceaselessly offer obviously good advice: Buy "open-ended toys," not mere novelties. Find playthings depicting real adult work activities and toys that are truly "age-appropriate." But is such advice useful or realistic? By the time children are in kindergarten or even preschool, they want the G.I. Joes and Barbies that they see in TV advertisements and that other kids own. Mothers and fathers give in to their offspring's nagging and their fear of isolating their children from peers. Parents feel impotent to shape their children's play.

Most adults doubt that children should be exposed to incessant change. It used to be that childhood was the dependable repository of our traditions such as Valentine's Day, Halloween, and the Fourth of July. Childhood symbolized the unchanging spirit of free play.

Now, however, the ever-transforming toy store offers novelty at every step of growing up. Being aware of the latest fad has come to define what it means to be a child. We do still give babies and toddlers traditional objects—rattles, teething rings, and push toys in the image of ageless clowns and circus animals. And we still listen to child psychologists and their popularizers in magazines who provide us with lists of time-tested toys. But as soon as our children are old enough to watch television (and advertisements), they want the new playthings they see glittering on the screen. We want to give the young the playthings that we remember, but they are hard to find on the overcrowded shelves of today's toy stores.

There have been disturbing changes in the making of playthings in the last few decades. Since the late 1960s many old toy companies, venerated for manufacturing toys passed from one generation to the next, have disappeared. The death of A.C. Gilbert in 1967 and the sale of his company shortly after ended a tradition of manufacturing boy's construction and science sets since 1913. Gilbert's most famous creation, the erector set, promised parents that their children would be preparing to join the adult world of engineering, industry, and science. Tinkertoys and Lincoln Logs, which appeared about the same time as the erector set, also declined in the 1970s. The old kitchen play sets, dollhouses, and baby dolls that were to teach girls the arts of housekeeping and childcare are also less in evidence today. Toys that seem to prepare children for adult life have become harder to find.

Other old companies, such as Playskool and Fisher-Price, which had built trusted clientele around well-tested toys for small children, succumbed to the control of bigger corporations. Playskool and Fisher-Price specialized in so-called educational playthings. They offered age-appropriate toys, designed and approved by experts in child development. They advertised, if at all, in adult publications like *Parents' Magazine* and stressed that their toys were safe and prepared children for school. Their toys were largely free of novelty. Gradually, however, these companies abandoned this idealism. Finally, Playskool was taken over in 1984 by Hasbro and Fisher-Price in 1993 by Mattel, companies whose success has been in novelty toys. Old-style educational toys survive in the upscale children's and hobby shops where plain blocks and challenging craft sets still can be found. But they are not featured in the discount stores or warehouse toy marts where most toys are purchased.

While many playthings before the 1970s trained children for adult roles or prepared preschoolers for education, others were whimsical novelties. For more than fifty years, Louis Marx manufactured thousands of playsets and mechanical toys that stressed fantasy and novelty. Marx toys were cheap, often recycling old themes. He used cartoon characters to sell his toys, and he mass marketed them through chain and department stores. A windup "crazy car" driven by a "college boy" one year would reappear with Mickey Mouse at the wheel in another year. But despite Marx's changing toy line, he was tradition-bound. Until the 1960s he used practically no advertising and his toys were often based on real life—parking garages and airports, for example. His toys appealed as much to adults as to children. However, his company too was caught in the crush of business buyouts and was sold to Quaker Oats in 1972, disappearing finally in 1979.

The Gilberts, Playskools, and Marxes were toymakers of a different era. Although they offered very different types of toys, they all produced creative playthings that parents could delight in giving their children. This is much less true today. In their place have come a new breed of companies that specialize in novelty and appeal directly to the imaginations of children. By the mid-1980s the dominant toymakers were Mattel and Hasbro. Mattel originated in 1945 in California and made its mark with the Barbie doll. Hasbro, founded in 1923 in Providence, Rhode Island, grew rich with G.I. Joe action figures and through the acquisition of a host of smaller companies. Both these giants helped to transform an industry that had primarily addressed the needs and values of parents into one that appealed directly to the longings and imaginations of children.

Mattel and Hasbro pioneered television advertising in the 1950s on children's programs. Hasbro holds claim to the first (local) TV advertisements for toys (Mr. Potato Head in 1951). Mattel climbed to the top of the industry when it became a major advertiser on the Mickey Mouse Club in 1955. Their well-designed sales pitches presented not only the toys themselves but stories that told children how to play. These advertisements provided the scripts that suggested children's play and made the toys into props for their make-believe dramas. So successful was this form of advertising for sales that, by the early 1980s, these companies and others turned cartoon TV programs into half-hour commercials featuring specific toys as the cartoon characters. "G.I. Joe, A Great American Hero" (Hasbro) and "He-Man and Masters of the Universe" (Mattel) were typical animated stories of the struggle between the forces of good and evil, but their real purpose was to sell G.I. Joe and He-Man action figures. By providing children with a fantasy starring their favorite brand of superhero, Mattel and Hasbro made great inroads into the toy market.

Mattel and Hasbro revolutionized the toy industry by turning toys into a product line that virtually demanded multiple purchases. Mattel spun endless fashion accessories around Barbie, and Hasbro launched its own arms race as G.I. Joe figures fought bad guys with an escalating array of space-age weapons. It was no fun unless a child's Barbie doll had friends like Ken or little sisters like Skipper. And G.I. Joe required both good guys and bad guys in order to play war. Toy companies rode the coattails of popular cartoon and movie characters, turning their images into playthings. Action figures, stuffed dolls, games, and eventually computer-operated video games were increasingly sold under character licenses.

Mattel, Hasbro, and many imitators created toys that no longer reflected adult life as did Gilbert, or taught basic skills like Playskool, or even offered innocent whimsy as Louis Marx often did. Their toys led children into a new world of play, one which simulates activities more familiar in movies and television than at home or office. The popularity of traditional training and educational toys declined while fantasy/novelty playthings became increasingly central to children's lives. The toy lost much of its role as a conveyor of messages between parent and child or even as a source of shared enjoyment between the generations.

While old toy companies folded or were sold, the way consumers bought toys also changed. In the 1980s the discount stores and warehouse outlets beat out the department stores and toy shops in competition for the rising toy dollar. By 1992 Charles Lazarus's Toys "R" Us was dominant, with 126 stores abroad to add to its 497 American stores. These warehouses of playthings beckoned consumers to buy much and to buy often by charging less for each item. Toys "R" Us operated on the premise that toys could be sold all year round, not just at Christmas and Hanukkah, and accordingly marketed them in all seasons.

For millions of children, new toys have become not only a year-round treat but a regular part of mealtime. Increased competition led fast-food chains to offer toy premiums to lure families with young children to their counters. McDonald's Happy Meals regularly include toys featuring characters from children's movies or miniature versions of Barbie, Hot Wheels, or other toy lines. In the late 1980s Wendy's Restaurants found that 84 percent of parents let their children help decide where to eat. Inevitably a major factor in the choice was the toy in the children's packaged meal. The miniature Barbies or Transformers offered in Happy Meals created a demand for the "real" thing at the store. The child's expectation that a plaything would come with every fast-food meal led most franchises to adopt this practice. The toy "prize" became as regular as the fast-food habit.

Is it surprising that children have been inundated with toys and dolls? Retail sales rose from $4.2 billion in 1978 to $17.5 billion in 1993, not including the $3.97 billion for video games. Today's children have rooms filled with toys while many of their parents remember having only a shelf or two. American toymakers issue endless new products—three to six thousand new toys each year. And adults buy them at an increasingly brisk pace. . . .

Many critics assume that toy companies alone are responsible for the quantity and cost of today's playthings. But the new world of toys is by no means simply the product of a profit-mad cabal of toy pushers discovering new ways of exploiting the child market. Playthings have always been subject to evolving and conflicting attitudes toward, and styles of, childrearing. Until the end of the nineteenth century, parents gave children few toys and those they did give reflected the convenience and taste of adults more than the desires and imagination of children. About 1900 a more child-centered approach arose that allowed youth their own material culture of play. The present surfeit of toys can be understood as the culmination of this century-long development. Toymakers certainly collaborated and cashed in on this trend, taking it further than many thoughtful parents wished it to go, but they did not create the overstuffed toybox by themselves.

The electric trains and baby dolls that adults remember as timeless classics were, in fact, products of childrearing ideas that emerged early in the twentieth century. The decline of these toys has more to do with changes in our society than with manipulation by toymakers. The erector set was supposed to teach boys to dream of becoming engineers and scientists at a time in American history when most adults had faith in a world of endless technological progress. The dollhouse and the baby doll taught the girl to be a modern homemaker and mother during the years when those roles were the expected futures of most American girls. But these roles were not timeless, and neither were the toys. Not even the teddy bear is a timeless plaything—even though children in many cultures and times have found soft and cuddly objects to hold and give them comfort. The bear began as a fad, sparked by the fame of Teddy Roosevelt, that amused adults as much as children.

Erector sets, baby dolls, and teddy bears reflected an American (especially middle-class) idea of childhood that dates from the beginning of the twentieth century. At that time, toys were to train children to be adults through imaginative play. Toys reflected parents' desire to give their kids a childhood free from work but still very much controlled by and shared with parents. Toymakers accommodated grown-ups with playthings that appealed to their goals and permitted them to stand between the toy business and their children's toys.

But by the late 1960s traditional cultural values were besieged and in flux. Parents were no longer very sure about what it meant to be a successful grown-up man or woman. As technology changed faster and faster, parents became less confident in their ability to predict the tools their children would need in adult life. Toys could not so easily serve as playful miniatures of those more complex tools. Kids played with computers but did not build toy electronics the way their fathers and grandfathers had once built models of factory machinery. The erector sets and baby dolls that had trained children to assume adult roles made less sense to parents who no longer knew what to train their children to become.

While early-twentieth-century toys had expressed the parents' toleration of the child's freedom in play, the new toys gave vent to a world of children's imagination in which adults had no real place. The modern toys that invite children into a fantasy world free of adults had their origins in playthings that were supposed to allow children to express themselves in ways embraced by adults. The Care Bears of the 1980s, whose story only children know, were the descendants of the teddy bears of the 1900s, whose magic was shared by adults and children. The disappearance of the certainties and shared feelings expressed in those earlier toys causes many parents to mourn the loss and to blame the toymakers of recent decades. This may be understandable but it obscures deeper truths.

The ever-expanding toy industry reflects a general American commitment to unrestrained markets and to constant change, a commitment at least a century old. Americans have long admired the new and have enriched those who produce it. For decades American parents have enjoyed sharing the world of consumption with their offspring. At first they did so knowing that they ultimately mediated between toys and their children. When the floodgates were opened and torrents of toys were presented directly to kids, parents found themselves merely providers of funds to buy toys.

Parents have long sought to protect children from the excesses of the consumer market. The toy industry offered toys intended to alleviate their fears. But the toy industry also discovered how to sell directly to children by tapping their imaginations in playthings inspired by characters in the mass media. The pace of this direct marketing was slow until after midcentury but has accelerated since the 1970s. The long-submerged tension between satisfying the parent, the child, and the need for profit has given way to a system in which the parent is an onlooker rather than an active participant. . . .

FURTHER READING

Austin, Joe, and Michael Nevin Willard, eds. *Generations of Youth: Youth Cultures and History in Twentieth-Century America* (1998).

Brumberg, Joan Jacobs. *The Body Project: An Intimate History of American Girls* (1997).

Charles, Casey. *The Sharon Kowalski Case* (2003).

Coontz, Stephanie. *The Way We Really Are: Coming to Terms with America's Changing Families* (1998).

Cott, Nancy F. *Public Vows: A History of Marriage and the Nation* (2000).

Cross, Gary. *Kids' Stuff: Toys and the Changing World of American Childhood* (1997).

Del Mar, David Peterson. *What Trouble I Have Seen: A History of Violence Against Wives* (1996).

Inness, Sherrie, ed. *Delinquents and Debutantes: Twentieth Century American Girls' Culture* (1998).

Lehmann, Jennifer M., ed. *The Gay and Lesbian Marriage and Family Reader* (2001).

Lehr, Valerie. *Queer Family Values: Debunking the Myth of the Nuclear Family* (1999).

Meyerowitz, Joshua. "The Adultlike Child and the Childlike Adult: Socialization in an Electronic Age." In Harvey J. Graff, ed., *Growing Up in America: Historical Experiences* (1987), pp. 612–631.

Pipher, Mary. *Reviving Ophelia: Saving the Selves of Adolescent Girls* (1994).

Postman, Neil. *The Disappearance of Childhood* (1982).

Rafkin, Louise, ed. *Different Mothers: Sons and Daughters of Lesbians Talk About Their Lives* (1990).

Rothchild, John, and Susan Berns Wolf. *The Children of the Counterculture* (1976).

Sherman, Suzanne, ed. *Lesbian and Gay Marriage: Private Commitments, Public Ceremonies* (1992).

Skolnick, Arlene, and Jerome Skolnick, eds. *The Family in Transition* (2002).

Stacey, Judith. *In the Name of the Family: Rethinking Family Values in the Post-Modern Age* (1996).

Stevens, Mitchell L. *Kingdom of Children: Culture and Controversy in the Homeschooling Movement* (2001).

Thompson, Karen, and Julie Andrzjewski. *Why Can't Sharon Kowalski Come Home?* (1988).

Thompson, Sharon. *Going All the Way: Teenage Girls' Tales of Sex, Romance, and Pregnancy* (1995).

Wolf, Naomi. *The Beauty Myth* (1991).

———. *Promiscuities: The Secret Struggle for Womanhood* (1997).